Multiculturalism in the United States

Current Issues, Contemporary Voices

TITLES OF RELATED INTEREST FROM PINE FORGE PRESS

Race, Ethnicity, Gender, and Class: The Sociology of Group Conflict and Change, 2nd Edition by Joseph F. Healey

Ethnicity and Race: Making Identities in a Changing World by Stephen Cornell and Doug Hartmann

Diversity in America by Vincent Parrillo

Global Inequalities by York W. Bradshaw and Michael Wallace

Illuminating Social Life: Classical and Contemporary Theory Revisited by Peter Kivisto

Key Ideas in Sociology by Peter Kivisto

Sociology: Exploring the Architecture of Everyday Life, Third Edition by David Newman

Sociology: Exploring the Architecture of Everyday Life, (Readings) Third Edition by David Newman

Enchanting a Disenchanted World: Revolutionizing the Means of Consumption by George Ritzer

The McDonaldization of Society, New Century Edition by George Ritzer

Social Statistics for a Diverse Society, Second Edition by Chava Frankfort-Nachmias and Anna Leon-Guerrero

Adventures in Social Research: Data Analysis Using SPSS™ for Windows 95/98® Versions 9.0 and 10.0 with 1998 GSS Data by Earl Babbie, Fred Halley, and Jeanne Zaino

Investigating the Social World: The Process and Practice of Research, Second Edition by Russell K. Schutt

Multiculturalism in the United States

Current Issues, Contemporary Voices

PETER KIVISTO

Augustana College

GEORGANNE RUNDBLAD

Illinois Wesleyan University

Editors

PINE FORGE PRESS

Thousand Oaks, California

For information address:

PINE FORGE PRESS
A Sage Publications Company
2455 Teller Road
Thousand Oaks, California 91320
(805) 499-4224
e-mail: sdr@pfp.sagepub.com

Sage Publications Ltd.
6 Bonhill Street
London EC2A 4PU
United Kingdom

Sage Publications India Pvt. Ltd.
M-32 Market
Greater Kailash I
New Delhi 110 048 India

Acquisition Editor: Stephen Rutter
Editorial Assistant: Ann Makarias
Production Editor: Sanford Robinson
Editorial Assistant: Karen Wiley
Typesetter: Danielle Dillahunt
Indexer: Will Ragsdale
Cover Designer: Candice Harman

Printed in the United States of America

00   01   02   03   04   05   06   7   6   5   4   3   2   1

Library of Congress Cataloging-in-Publication Data

Multiculturalism in the United States: Current issues,
contemporary voices / edited by Peter Kivisto and
Georganne Rundblad.
    p. cm.
Includes bibliographical references and index.
  ISBN 0-7619-8648-0 (pbk.: alk. paper)
  1. Pluralism (Social sciences)—United States. 2.
Multiculturalism—United States. 3. United States-Ethnic
relations. 4. United States—Race relations. 5.
Minorities—United States—Social conditions. I. Kivisto,
Peter, 1948- II. Rundblad, Georganne. E184.A1 M854 2000
  305.8'00973—dc21

00-008016

This book is printed on acid-free paper.

About the Editors

Peter Kivisto (Ph.D., New School for Social Research) is Professor and Chair of Sociology at Augustana College, Rock Island, Illinois. Among his books dealing with race and ethnicity in the United States are *Americans All* (1995), *American Immigrants and Their Generations* (1990), *The Ethnic Enigma* (1989), and *Immigrant Socialists in the United States* (1984). Active in several professional organizations, he is currently a member of the Executive Board of the Immigration and Ethnic History Society.

Georganne Rundblad (Ph.D., University of Illinois at Urbana/Champaign) is an Associate Professor of Sociology and Anthropology at Illinois Wesleyan University. The courses she teaches include Marriage and Family; Medical Sociology; Sex and Gender in Society; Race and Ethnic Relations; Class, Status, and Power; and Work and Occupations. She has published journal articles in *Teaching Sociology, Multicultural Prism: Voices from the Field* (with Thomas J. Gerschick), and *Gender and Society*.

About the Contributors

Amy E. Ansell is Assistant Professor of Sociology at Bard College.

Cheryl L. Cole is Associate Professor of Sociology and Kinesiology and in the Women's Studies Program at the University of Illinois at Urbana-Champaign.

Sharon M. Collins is Associate Professor of Sociology at the University of Illinois at Chicago.

F. James Davis is Professor of Sociology, Emeritus, at Illinois State University.

Sara K. Dorow is a doctoral candidate in sociology at the University of Minnesota.

Mary Patrice Erdmans is Assistant Professor of Sociology at the University of North Carolina at Greensboro.

Thomas Faist is a Research Sociologist at the University of Bremen.

Joe R. Feagin is Professor of Sociology at the University of Florida.

Abby L. Ferber is Professor of Sociology at the University of Colorado at Colorado Springs.

Timothy P. Fong is an Assistant Professor in the Department of Ethnic Studies and Director of the Asian American Studies Program at California State University at Sacramento.

Nathan Glazer is Professor Emeritus in Sociology and Education at Harvard University.

Steven J. Gold is Associate Professor at Michigan State University.

Kevin Fox Gotham is Assistant Professor of Sociology at Tulane University.

Andrew Hacker is Professor of Political Science at Queens College and the City University of New York.

Jennifer L. Hochschild is Professor of Politics at Princeton University.

Gerald David Jaynes is Professor of Economics and in the Program of African and African American Studies at Yale University.

Sut Jhally is Professor of Communication at the University of Massachusetts at Amherst.

C. Richard King is Assistant Professor of Anthropology at Drake University.

Samantha King is a doctoral candidate in the Department of Kinesiology and Women's Studies Program at the University of Illinois at Urbana-Champaign.

Justin Lewis is Professor of Communication at the University of Massachusetts at Amherst.

C. Eric Lincoln is Professor of Religion and Culture at Duke University.

Sarah J. Mahler teaches in the Sociology Department at Florida International University.

Lawrence H. Mamiya is Associate Professor of Religion and African American Studies at Vassar College.

Pyong Gap Min is Professor of Sociology at Queens College and the City University of New York.

Joan Moore is Professor of Sociology, Emerita, at the University of Wisconsin at Milwaukee.

Joane Nagel is Professor of Sociology at the University of Kansas.

Orlando Patterson is Professor of Sociology at Harvard University.

Alejandro Portes is Professor of Sociology at Princeton University.

Joseph T. Rhea is Assistant Professor of Sociology at Arizona State University.

David O. Sears is Professor of Psychology at the University of California at Los Angeles.

Rocky L. Sexton is Assistant Professor of Anthropology at Augustana College.

John David Skrentny is Associate Professor of Sociology at the University of California at San Diego.

Charles Fruehling Springwood is Assistant Professor of Anthropology at Illinois Wesleyan University.

Stephen Steinberg is Professor of Sociology at Queens College and the City University of New York.

Ronald Takaki is Professor of Ethnic Studies at the University of California at Berkeley.

Orlando P. Tizon received his Ph.D. in Sociology at Loyola University in Chicago.

Hernán Vera is Professor of Sociology at the University of Florida.

James Diego Vigil teaches in the Anthropology Department at the University of Southern California.

Roger Waldinger is Professor of Sociology at the University of California at Los Angeles.

Howard Winant is Professor of Sociology at Temple University.

Robin M. Williams, Jr., is Henry Scarborough Professor of Social Science, Emeritus, at Cornell University.

William Julius Wilson is Professor of Sociology at the Kennedy School, Harvard University.

Alan Wolfe is Professor of Sociology at Boston University.

Min Zhou is Associate Professor of Sociology at the University of California at Los Angeles.

About the Publisher

Pine Forge Press is a new educational publisher dedicated to publishing innovative books and software throughout the social sciences. On this and any other of our publications, we welcome your comments and suggestions.

Please call or write us at:

Pine Forge Press
A Sage Publications Company
31 St. James Ave. Suite 510
Boston, MA 02116
615-753-7512
e-mail: sdr@pfp.sagepub.com
Visit our World Wide Web site, your direct link to a multitude of online resources:
www.pineforge.com

Brief Contents

Contents

PART II

Representations of Race and the Politics of Identity

PART IV

New Immigrants and the Dilemmas of Adjustment

PART V

What Is Multicultural America?

Preface

At the dawn of the twenty-first century, it is clear that the United States is a multicultural society. It is, however, not altogether clear what it means to be multicultural.

- Does it mean that the nation inevitably will suffer from a disintegration of a shared sense of national identity as racial groups opt to define themselves primarily in terms of their own particular group identities?
- Or, on the contrary, does multiculturalism suggest openness to diversity and difference and a revived sense of inclusiveness?
- What does it mean to be a member of a particular racial group?
- Are these identities fixed once and for all, or are they capable of changing over time?
- Can people pick and choose their identities?
- Does multiculturalism fuel conflict among groups?
- What does it mean for the future of racism?
- Can newcomers to our shores expect that they, or at least their children, will one day be fully incorporated into the country?
- Do they look forward to or do they fear the prospect of losing their old-world cultures due to assimilation?
- Is it reasonable to talk about the advent of a "rainbow coalition" of people united across racial lines, or will these lines harden and will new forms of conflict mingle with older unresolved conflicts?
- Is multiculturalism as a movement a worthy goal, or is it something to be resisted?

These and a host of related questions must be wrestled with if we are to begin to make sense of the nation's multicultural future. For this reason, in recent years growing numbers of sociologists have increasingly set their sights on these kinds of questions and have begun to offer answers, however provisional, tentative, and subject to debate those answers may be. A rapidly expanding body of sociological research has enriched our understanding of race relations in the United States several decades into the post-civil rights era. At the dawn of the twentieth century, the black intellectual W. E. B. Du Bois argued that central to the tensions and conflicts that the nation could anticipate in the future was what he referred to as "the problem of the color line." In retrospect, his anticipation of the twentieth century was remarkably prescient. But, after dramatic changes in the latter half of the century, we are forced once again to consider exactly where we have come and where we are headed. Implicitly or explicitly, sociologists are now considering the extent to which Du Bois's claim concerning the century we have just left will apply to the century we have entered. Put simply, they ask, to what extent and in what ways will we continue in the decades ahead to confront the problem of the color line?

This book is designed to address this question. In doing so, it has a very simple goal: to assist students as they attempt to come to terms with the complex, contested, and shifting nature of contemporary race relations in the United States. We have compiled a selection of readings that explores from a variety of angles and with a wide range of concrete examples the kinds of questions posed above. That being said, it should be noted what we do not claim the book does. We do not purport that it offers anything resembling definitive answers to those questions. Instead, it offers compelling partial answers that are intended to stimulate the reader to think more deeply about these matters. As such, the readings are ideal vehicles for stimulating critical thinking and writing as well as for providing bases for focused class discussions. Although a few of the articles have a polemical cast to them and several authors make clear that they are arguing for a particular interpretation or assessment, the articles have not been selected to provoke debates that too often look at race relations in stark either/or terms. Instead, the readings contained herein allow—indeed, encourage—students to appreciate the complexities, ambiguities, and ironies of race relations.

The collection includes articles that explore the social structural constraints on racial minorities, the character of intergroup relations in a multicultural context, and the world inside various ethnic communities. We want the book as a whole to reflect an appreciation of the impact of external social structural forces on people, individually and collectively. However, we also want to show that people and groups have a say in how their lives are shaped. While we examine the extent to which racial minorities continue to be the victims of racism and a legacy of second-class citizenship, we also want to indicate the ways in which they are not mere victims but are actively involved in the construction of their own social worlds.

To achieve this multifaceted scope, we sought to offer a representative cross section of current scholarship by people who have produced work that is at the cutting edge. Among the people represented are some of the most distinguished scholars in the field. On the other hand, also well represented are younger scholars who are only beginning to make their mark in this field. In addition, reflecting trends in the discipline at large, many of the contributors are members of the racial groups they are studying and, as such, are in an ideal position to get at issues related to the internal life worlds of various racial and ethnic groups. At the same time, we also see advantages to looking at groups from the outside, and other articles have been written by people who make no claims to membership in the groups they are investigating.

In all cases, articles were selected for inclusion based on their ability to present salient issues in an engaging and thought-provoking way. The 36 selections are divided into five sections that, we believe, articulate the most central issues framing current scholarship.

- Our introductory essay sets the stage for what follows by offering a brief historical overview of changes in race relations since the 1960s, thereby providing the student with a framework that contextualizes the readings.

- The first section, "Racial Fault Lines," examines questions about the salience of racism and the new kinds of racial divisions that have emerged in recent years.

- This leads, in "Representations of Race and the Politics of Identity," to issues related to the social construction of racial identities, examining it from both cultural and political perspectives.

- "African Americans since the 1960s" looks at the largest and most historically consequential racial group in America, taking stock of what was and was not achieved by the civil rights movement and what new dilemmas have arisen in its aftermath.

- The following section, "New Immigrants and the Dilemmas of Adjustment," addresses the impact on the nation of the wave of new immigrants who have come to the United States since 1965 and examines the ways the nation has had an impact on these newcomers.

- The collection is rounded out with a series of essays that offer different answers to the question "What Is Multicultural America?" thus moving to an examination of the big picture and the questions we raised at the outset of the preface.

In putting this collection together, we incurred a number of debts and acknowledge the role played by several people, who either offered concrete advice about the book or in other ways supported us in this endeavor. Among the people Peter Kivisto thanks are John Farley, John Guidry, Melvin Holli, Rick Jurasek, Susan Kivisto, Stanford Lyman, Martin Marger, Ewa Morawska, Rocky Sexton, and Bill Swatos.

Georganne Runblad thanks Curtis and Megan White for their unending support and care. Thomas Gerschick and Bob Broad provided friendship and encouragement, especially when it was needed the most. F. James Davis, many years ago, and more recently David

Schoem, provided invaluable inspiration and direction. Georganne also thanks Janet McNew and the Provost's Office at Illinois Wesleyan University for the opportunity to attend the pivotal American Association of Colleges and Universities 10-day seminar on "American Commitments: Diversity, Democracy and Liberal Learning," which, with the help of David Schoem, transformed how Georganne teaches about race and ethnic relations. Kristin Vogel was like a wizard at gathering impossible, but necessary, information from the library. Georganne also thanks all of the students in her Race and Ethnic Relations class for being willing and able to take hard steps toward social change. They are what makes all this work worthwhile.

Thanks from both editors to Pine Forge's reviewers (in alphabetical order):

JoAnn DeFiore, University of Washington, Bothell
Doug Hartmann, University of Minnesota
Jeremy Hein, University of Wisconsin, Eau Claire
David McBride, Pennsylvania State University
Luis Posas, Mankato State University
Bruce Williams, Mills College.

A special thanks to Jean Sottos, who knows how important a role she played and who also knows that we owe her! Working with the Pine Forge crew has proven to be a delight, and we especially extend our thanks to a few of them. For Ann Makarias, this book surely must have been her baptism by fire; we hope she is pleased with the result. Sherith Pankratz at Pine Forge and Karen Wiley and Sanford Robinson at Sage have been most helpful. And, of course, there is Steve Rutter. He has been a delight to work with, even when the adrenaline was flowing. As anyone who has worked with him knows, Steve stands by his authors and makes all of the hard work somehow a labor of love.

Overview: Multicultural America in the Post-Civil Rights Era

Peter Kivisto and Georganne Rundblad

Diversity has been a hallmark of the American experience. The country's multicultural character has had a profound impact on our sense of national identity and purpose, on our ability to absorb and integrate new arrivals, and on our views of who should be included and who excluded from living among us as equals. One sign of the centrality of this issue in American life is the vigor of the continuing debate about the extent to which we have lived up to the ideals of the "American Creed"—freedom, equality, opportunity for all—and the reasons for the gulf between ideals and reality.

The divisions that have separated us along racial and ethnic lines have produced some of our most enduring and obdurate social problems, and certain minority groups have paid a particularly heavy price as a result of these divisions. We certainly have a legacy of intense prejudice and discrimination. Moreover, persistent attention to race and ethnic differences continues to raise profound questions about what justice and fair play mean.

At the same time, however, we have managed to a large extent to avoid the worst forms of racial and ethnic violence, and people have not fled our borders seeking safe refuge elsewhere (Holli 1999). Rather, just the opposite is the case. The United States continues to be a magnet attracting newcomers from around the world (more than 20 million since World War II)—and they continue to arrive daily, whether landing in a jumbo jet at LAX or passing through a border crossing along the Rio Grande River (Ueda 1994).

The purpose of this book is to try to make sense of these seemingly contradictory facts. Although we consider the history of ethnic and racial relations in this country, our main focus is the recent past, which has seen some noteworthy changes.

The Advent of the Post-Civil Rights Era

The 1960s marked the beginning of a new era in racial and ethnic relations in the United States. Two watershed events contributed to the emergence of the new era (Omi and Winant 1986):

- End of Legalized Segregation and Discrimination. The civil rights movement is generally credited with this achievement, which culminated in the 1954 Brown v. Board of Education Supreme Court decision and the passage of such landmark legislation as the Civil Rights Act of 1964 and the Voting Rights Act of 1965.

- Reinstatement of Mass Immigration. Passage in 1965 of the Hart-Cellar Act reopened the nation's doors to mass immigration after a hiatus of four decades. Since then, we have witnessed a mass influx of newcomers. Unlike the past, when most immigrants came from Europe, today's come chiefly from Latin America, Asia, and the Caribbean.

The consequences of these two events are the topic of extensive debate. For example, there is considerable uncertainty about the extent to which the civil rights movement succeeded in achieving its goals. Bluntly put, did the civil rights movement result in the end of racism? Dinesh D'Souza (1995), a conservative thinker, thinks so, whereas scholars on the political left, such as Joe Feagin and Hernán Vera (1994), contend that racism has far from disappeared. Instead, they argue, although only small groups of militant white supremacists still exhibit overt racism, today racism takes new, subtler forms. The larger issue is how far we have come in remedying the worst features of a segregated American society. But because we can point readily to both gains and losses, most of these discussions take on the form of arguing whether the glass is half full or half empty.

The issue of mass immigration offers similar opportunity for debate. Can the United States comfortably absorb new immigrants by the millions, and, if so, how selective should we be in determining whom to welcome? Critics of our current immigration laws, such as Peter Brimelow (1995), have argued that admitting so many "aliens" to our shores (especially poor ones) threatens our economic, political, and cultural well-being. Given the fact that Brimelow is himself an immigrant—from England—there is a certain irony to his complaint. On the other hand, supporters of a liberal immigration policy, such as Alejandro Portes and Ruben G. Rumbaut (1990), believe that "in the long run the diverse talents and energies of newcomers will reinforce the vitality of American society and the richness of its culture" (p. 246). Beyond the matter of who to allow into the country are questions about what we ought to do to help new arrivals to adjust. Should we offer bilingual language programs, or should we demand the immediate acquisition of English? Should we encourage the maintenance of homeland cultures and traditions, or should we promote an aggressive Americanization campaign? These are not new questions—they were raised at earlier periods of peak migration—but they have acquired a renewed salience today.

To make sense of these competing perspectives, we should locate the consequences of these two events—the civil rights movement and the change in immigration policy—in larger sociohistorical context. Only by knowing something about where we have been can we make sense of where we are headed.

Demographic Shifts

The population of the United States is more heterogeneous than that of any other nation on earth. From the colonial period to the present, the North American continent has exerted a powerful pull on people around the world. Millions of voluntary immigrants—particularly from Europe, Asia, and Latin America—have settled in North America. They came and continue to come for a variety of reasons, but primarily they come because they think the United States will afford them greater economic opportunities than they would have if they remained in their homelands (Kivisto 1995; Martin and Widgren 1996).

The United States has sometimes been referred to as a nation of immigrants (Handlin 1973). The vast majority of Americans are either immigrants or can trace their ancestry to immigrants. However, two important components of the American population— American Indians and African Americans—did not come voluntarily. Between 2 and 5 million American Indians inhabited this continent before the arrival of the first European immigrants (Snipp 1989:9; Thornton 1987). As the indigenous peoples of the North American continent, they were, obviously, not voluntary immigrants. Rather, they were the victims of colonial conquest. Africans arrived in the Americas involuntarily, victims of the slave trade. From the first arrival of about 20 Africans in Virginia in 1619 until the eve of the Civil War, an estimated 480,000 Africans were forcibly transported to the United States (Curtin 1969). The historical experiences of these two groups are unique and must be taken into account when assessing the reasons that they remain the two most disadvantaged racial groups in the country.

These distinctive histories have considerable influence on the current and projected ethnic and racial makeup of the U.S. population. Herein, we briefly examine recent demographic changes that have affected the respective sizes of five major groups in the United States: European Americans, African Americans, American Indians, Hispanic Americans, and Asian Americans.

European American Decline

Since the founding of the republic in 1776, a majority of the nation's occupants have been able to trace their origins to Europe. In

1810, those of European origin composed 73 percent of the population. Due chiefly to the mass migration of Europeans (and laws that favored them at the expense of Asians and other nonwhite groups), this percentage steadily rose until 1930, when it peaked at around 88 percent. However, because Europeans are no longer immigrating in large numbers and because their fertility rates have lowered over time, since 1930 the percentage of European Americans has declined gradually.

Although European Americans still constitute a significant majority of the overall population, by 1990, they composed only about 75 percent of the total. This figure is similar to the percentage in 1810.

Current trends suggest that this percentage will decline further between now and the year 2050. Because it is difficult to predict both what immigration levels will be like in the future and how group fertility rates might change, the extent of the decline is not certain. However, demographer Antonio McDaniel (1995:183–84) speculated that the European American population might slip to less than 55 percent of the total by the middle of the twenty-first century.

African American Trends

African Americans historically have constituted the largest racial minority, but as a percentage of the overall population, they, too, have witnessed decline. In 1810, African Americans accounted for 19 percent of the overall population. However, because of the end of the slave trade and the lack of voluntary immigration from Africa, that figure fell throughout the nineteenth century and into the twentieth, reaching an all-time low of less than 10 percent by 1930. Since then, the relative size of the African American population has grown slightly, accounting for just over 12 percent of the total by 1990 (U.S. Census Bureau 1992).

Some projections suggest that this percentage will increase during the first half of the new century, but this result is far from certain (Parrillo 1996:179). Blacks have a higher fertility rate than whites, but so do Hispanics. And unlike Hispanics, African Americans cannot count on heavy immigration to increase their numbers (Pinkney 2000:61–65).

American Indian Resurgence

Colonization of the Americas produced a demographic and human tragedy for American Indians. From a high figure of several million, the population was reduced to less than a quarter of a million by 1890. From this nadir, the absolute numbers grew gradually through 1950, at which point a veritable explosion in the number of Indians occurred. Reaching more than half a million by 1960, the American Indian population continued to grow dramatically, so that by 1990 more than 1.9 million people identified themselves as of Indian ancestry.

Despite this dramatic growth, Indians remain the smallest of the racial groups, accounting for less than 1 percent of the total population (Kivisto 1995:74–76).

In this case, as Joane Nagel (1996) has shown, the dramatic increase in numbers of American Indians during the past three decades cannot be adequately accounted for on the basis of changes in fertility and death rates. Rather, it must be partially accounted for by the increased tendency for people to self-identify as Indian (especially people of mixed ancestry).

The New Immigrants

The two groups that have experienced the most dramatic increases in size are, not surprisingly, the two that have contributed most heavily to immigration since 1965: Hispanic Americans and Asian Americans. These are panethnic terms that incorporate numerous national-origin groups.

The dramatic growth of Hispanic America. Hispanic Americans come from a wide variety of backgrounds. They include voluntary labor migrants, illegal immigrants, and political refugees. The largest Hispanic groups are, in rank order, Mexicans, Puerto Ricans (not technically an immigrant group, because the island is a territory of the United States), and Cubans, followed by smaller numbers from various nations in Central America, South America, and the Caribbean.

Though for some time Hispanics were the second-largest minority group, following African Americans, their population—particularly the Mexican component—has steadily increased since 1970, with the most dramatic growth occurring recently. The 22 million Hispanic people reported in the 1990 census represent a remarkable 53 percent increase since 1980. Since that time, they grew from 7 percent of the population to 9 percent (Holmes 1995). If immigration and fertility rates among Hispanics continue to remain high in the new century, Hispanics could replace African Americans as the nation's largest minority group as early as 2010.

The impact of Hispanic immigration is pronounced in states where the new arrivals are heavily concentrated: California, Texas, New York, Florida, and Illinois. Not surprisingly, given the fact that Hispanics are also heavily urbanized, their presence is especially felt in major cities in these states and in other states along the Mexican border. The 1990 census found that in 4 of the nation's 10 largest cities—Los Angeles, Houston, Phoenix, and San Antonio—Hispanics already have overtaken African Americans as the largest minority group. This shift also has taken place in a number of other cities. In the largest city in the country, New York, Hispanics constituted 24 percent of the population, only 2 percent less than African Americans (Roberts 1994).

Asians: Immigrants from different shores. Among Asian groups, the largest in rank order are the Chinese, Filipinos, Japanese, and Koreans, followed by immigrants from Southeast Asia and the Indian subcontinent. Overall, Asian numbers have grown significantly during the past three decades—but not nearly to the extent of the Hispanic population. Of the four largest groups, only the Japanese have not increased their numbers appreciably, because, unlike the other groups, they have not been part of the new wave of immigration.

On the other hand, the oldest Asian group in the United States, the Chinese, has witnessed a large new wave of immigration since 1965. These newcomers, who have come primarily from Taiwan and Hong Kong, have swelled Chinatowns in major cities. In New York, for example, the historic boundaries of Chinatown can no longer contain all of the new immigrants, and, as a result, Chinatown has spilled over into adjoining neighborhoods, including parts of Little Italy. At the same time, Chinese enclaves have emerged as a presence in such multi-ethnic neighborhoods of the city as Flushing and Elmhurst (Chen 1992).

Two groups with a very small presence in the United States prior to 1970 have grown dramatically during the past three decades: Filipinos and Koreans. The Filipino population exceeded 1.4 million by 1990, making it the second-largest Asian group, and the Korean population reached a level of more than 800,000 by 1990, making it 12 times larger than it had been a mere two decades earlier (U.S. Census Bureau 1991).

The result of these recent changes is not that the United States has for the first time become a multicultural nation; as noted at the outset, it has always been characterized by its ethnic and racial diversity. What is new is how this diversity is configured. To appreciate this fact, we examine the most significant transformations that have occurred in the nation's five major ethnic groups.

The Social Construction of European Americans

One of the key features characterizing Americans of European ancestry has been their great diversity. Until after the middle of the twentieth century, European-origin Americans spoke a wide array of languages, embraced different religious traditions (Protestants, Roman Catholics, Eastern Orthodox, and Jewish), held divergent political views, and displayed considerably varied cultural practices. These immigrant groups included small numbers of Albanians from the southeastern edges of Europe, Icelandic immigrants from the northwestern periphery of the continent, and people from every European nation between these two countries (Daniels 1990; Takaki 1993).

Nonetheless, certain groups played a more significant role in the peopling of America because of the sheer volume of immigrants they supplied. The largest groups include the English, the Irish, Germans, Poles, Italians, and Jews. These groups have had a greater imprint on the development of American society and culture than have smaller groups.

From Immigrants to White Ethnics

Over time, as the members of all these groups adjusted to their new homeland and became acculturated to it, immigrants and their offspring relied less and less on their ethnic communities to sustain them. Rather, they began to merge into the larger society. Acculturation occurred more quickly for some groups because they were more readily accepted by the host society. It occurred more slowly and less completely for those groups that were the victims of prejudice and discrimination. The victims were primarily groups from southern and eastern Europe, such as Poles and Italians, who differed in significant ways from the dominant white Anglo-Saxon Protestant majority. However, no group confronted greater ethnic animosity than did Jews, who continue to confront the effects of anti-Semitism (Dinnerstein 1994).

Nonetheless, beginning in the 1950s, a major transfiguration redefined ethnic identity for all European-origin groups (though at different rates of speed for different groups). The children and grandchildren of European immigrants progressively abandoned ethnic institutions. They moved out of ethnic neighborhoods, often for the suburbs. They failed to make efforts to preserve their ancestral languages and abandoned many traditional cultural practices.

The ethnic boundaries that earlier had separated these groups became increasingly permeable. Ultimately, with the extensive intermarriage among European Americans, the ethnic factor progressively became less significant in their lives (Alba 1990; Lieberson and Waters 1988). Although among European-origin groups ethnic differences have not disappeared, their significance has declined appreciably (Alba 1990; Waters 1990).

Symbolic Ethnicity

Herbert Gans (1979) suggested that the kind of ethnic identity experienced by most European Americans today can best be referred to as "symbolic ethnicity," by which he means that ethnicity has a low level of intensity and as a result is exhibited by individuals only occasionally. Gans believes that the erosion of ethnic institutions and cultures makes it increasingly impossible for European Americans to exhibit meaningful signs of ethnic identity or affiliation. Ethnicity is a phenomenon driven primarily by nostalgia for the lost world of the immigrant generation. It entails a feeling of being ethnic without "ethnic behavior that requires an arduous or time-consuming commitment" (Gans 1979:203).

Mary Waters (1990) agrees in fundamental ways with Gans's idea of symbolic ethnicity. However, she also contended that ethnicity "is not something that will easily or quickly disappear" (p. 155). She suggested that people who are willing to identify as ethnic have a desire for a sense of community that they see as lacking or threatened in contemporary American society.

At the same time, white ethnics adhere to a sense of individualism that demands the right to make choices. Thus, their ethnicity has a decidedly voluntary quality about it. Taking part in a St. Patrick's Day parade or preparing German cuisine at various holidays are examples of ways to periodically connect with one's ethnic past without great outlays of time and energy. People pick and choose features of the ethnic tradition to embrace and display and ignore or abandon others. For example, the immigrant culture may have defined women's role as limited to the domestic realm, but contemporary European Americans seldom perpetuate this particular gender division of labor (Waters 1990:168).

Simultaneously, because of European Americans' high level of assimilation, their identities and group boundaries are very fluid. For example, in one household the husband might trace his ancestry to England, Germany, and Italy, and the wife's ancestors might have originated in Sweden, Poland, and Belgium. The result is a complex mix of ethnic identities, and how people put them together varies considerably. Richard Alba (1990) observed that extensive intermarriage among European Americans is gradually producing a kind of panethnic identity:

> The transformation of ethnicity among whites does not portend the elimination of ethnicity, but instead the formation of a new ethnic group: one based on ancestry from anywhere on the European continent. The emergence of this new group, which I call the "European Americans," . . . lies behind the ethnic identities of many Americans of European background. (Pp. 292–93)

Today, what Europeans of different nationalities share tends to be far more important than the differences among them.

The Possessive Investment in Whiteness

One of the things European-origin groups share today is an understanding of themselves as "white." In the past, however, that was not the case, as not all Europeans were considered to be white. In the early decades of the twentieth century, for example, Italians, Slavs, Greeks,

Jews, and others often were described as members of distinct—and nonwhite—groups. But the boundaries of inclusion and exclusion have changed in the past few decades (Allen 1994; Lipsitz 1998; Roediger 1991).

Today, in viewing Europeans as a whole as a "we," non-Europeans are viewed as "they." The social construction of "whiteness" historically has implied the racial superiority of whites. What makes the situation different today is that all Europeans are granted this privileged position. All non-Europeans, especially people of color, are relegated to distinctive positions of subordination based on differing perceptions of these groups by the dominant group (Winant 1999, 1994). We turn now to the new racial conditions confronting these groups.

African Americans and the Enduring Dilemma of Race

The history of Africans in America, which is as old as that of Europeans in America, can be divided into three major historical periods:

- Slave era, which extended from the colonial period until the Civil War.
- Jim Crow era, which covered the time from shortly after the Civil War until the 1960s.
- Post-civil rights era, which began in the 1960s and continues to the present.

To appreciate the scope of the changes that propelled us into the third period, we need briefly to look at the system of racial oppression that the civil rights movement sought to challenge.

The End of the Jim Crow Era

Much has been written about slavery and its impact, but perhaps nowhere was its destructive capacity captured so poignantly and succinctly as in the words of novelist Ralph Ellison. In his unfinished novel *Juneteenth* (1999), a revivalist preacher chants variations on the following theme of deprivations endured by African Americans: "Eyeless, tongueless, drumless, danceless, songless, hornless, soundless, sightless, wrongless, rightless, motherless, fatherless, brotherless, sisterless, powerless" (p. 124). Such a legacy, it goes without saying, could not be easily overcome.

Nevertheless, during the Jim Crow period, blacks became intent on undoing the damage caused by centuries of servitude in the slave economy. The African American leader and early sociologist W. E. B. Du Bois ([1903] 1961) wrote, "The problem of the twentieth century is the problem of the color line" (p. 23). Part of the reason he drew this predictive conclusion was his understanding of the ultimate outcome of the post-Civil War years. During the short-lived period of Reconstruction, African Americans voted for the first time, and many were elected to office at the local, state, and national levels. A substantial number entered arenas of the economy from which they previously had been excluded.

However, Reconstruction ended and in its place a new form of racial subjugation and exclusion arose known as Jim Crow. Although the origin of the term is uncertain, it referred to laws in the South that were designed to disenfranchise blacks from politics and segregate them from whites in public facilities, including schools, parks, housing, and public transportation (Woodward 1974). The creation of a segregated caste system was endorsed by the Supreme Court in *Plessy v. Ferguson* (1896), which declared that segregation was constitutionally permitted and thus ratified the doctrine of "separate but equal." This legal basis for racial oppression was backed up by the perpetual threat of violence and terror, seen most vividly in the activities of the Ku Klux Klan and in the pervasiveness of lynching.

This system of oppression and segregation shaped race relations for the better part of a century. Historian Leon Litwack (1998) described the era of Jim Crow from the perspective of blacks: "No matter how hard they labored, no matter how they conducted themselves, no matter how fervently they prayed, the chances of making it were less than encouraging; the basic rules and controls were in place" (p. 149).

The Civil Rights Movement

Beginning in the 1940s, a civil rights movement arose to challenge the color line. It operated on two fronts, one consisting of legislative and judicial challenges and the other consisting of protest activities. Key organizations promoting racial equality and an end to segregation included the National Association for the Advancement of Colored People, the Congress of Racial Equality, and the Southern Christian Leadership Conference (SCLC). The SCLC was led by the person who became the most important figure associated with the civil rights movement, Martin Luther King, Jr. (McAdam 1982; Morris 1984).

Major victories during the 1950s and 1960s ultimately dismantled the Jim Crow system. Landmark events included the 1954 *Brown v. Board of Education* decision, which revisited the *Plessy v. Ferguson* ruling and overturned the doctrine of separate but equal. A consequence of this reversal was school integration, through what proved to be a controversial policy of court-mandated busing. The Civil Rights Act of 1964 prohibited discrimination in the areas of employment and education. The Voting Rights Act of 1965 made possible the reentry of blacks into the political arena in southern states, and the Housing Act of 1968 forbade discrimination in the renting and selling of housing.

These changes did not come about easily. On the one hand, efforts to effect significant social changes met with considerable white resistance. On the other hand, militant blacks associated with the Black Power movement thought the changes were too little too late. Discontent increased among poor blacks, and, during the latter part of the 1960s, urban riots erupted in cities across the country, resulting in hundreds of deaths, thousands of injuries, and millions of dollars of property damage.

The Post-Civil Rights Era

What have been the net effects of the civil rights movement? What did it accomplish, and what did it fail to accomplish? As we see, answering these questions is a complicated matter.

On the positive side, a substantial majority of white Americans have come to endorse the principles of equality and integration (Sniderman and Carmines 1997; Taylor, Sheatsley, and Greeley 1978). Blacks have found greater educational and employment opportunities, and a growing number of blacks have entered the middle class. According to projections by sociologist Bart Landry (1987), 56.4 percent of blacks will have reached the middle class by the year 2000, compared to 63 percent of whites—a dramatic change since 1960, when only 13.4 percent of blacks could be considered members of the middle class. Growing numbers of blacks have been elected to political office. The role of Jesse Jackson in the Democratic Party and the fact that many Republicans would have liked retired Gen. Colin Powell to run for the presidency under their party's banner in 1996 suggest that positive changes have taken place.

However, some contend that the civil rights movement did not accomplish as much as many think it did. Andrew Hacker (1992), for example, believes that we have not moved beyond the conclusion drawn by members of the National Advisory Commission on Civil Disorders in 1968. The commission was created to explain why America's cities were rocked by racial riots in the second half of the 1960s, after the judicial and legal victories of the civil rights movement. The members of the commission concluded pessimistically that the nation was becoming increasingly polarized along racial lines. Hacker believes that "separate, unequal, and hostile" characterizes black/white relations at present, as well. He points out the disparity between blacks and whites in terms of incomes and unemployment rates and suggested that white intransigence is the brake that prevents genuine economic parity. He similarly shows that blacks lag behind whites in educational attainment and that school segregation remains pervasive. Indeed, in many major metropolitan areas, most blacks attend virtually all-black urban schools, and their white counterparts go to school in the predominantly white suburbs (Farley 1984:193–99; Massey and Denton 1993).

Michael Omi and Howard Winant (1986) support the view that whites are impeding black progress. They have pointed to a shift in the nature of race relations beginning around 1970. A conservative white reaction to the civil rights movement has led to attacks on such controversial policies as school busing to achieve integration and affirmative action in employment and education. Nonetheless, Omi and Winant believe that a "great transformation" occurred in response to the civil rights movement that cannot be totally undone. The question remains: How far have we come, and how far do we have to go as a nation to achieve genuine racial equality?

The Black middle class. The economic status of blacks as a whole improved in relation to whites between 1940 and 1970, but, since then, black incomes have leveled off or declined (Jaynes and Williams 1989:16–18). But looking at African Americans in the aggregate obscures the bifurcation within black America between a now sizable middle class and a remaining core of disadvantaged blacks. Some think that middle-class blacks have, in effect, "made it."

Yet, considerable evidence suggests that middle-class blacks are far from achieving parity with their white counterparts. In an important recent study, Melvin L. Oliver and Thomas M. Shapiro (1995) showed that if we look at individual wealth (i.e., total assets) and not income alone, a huge disparity continues to exist between the black and white middle classes. They found that middle-class blacks possess only 15 cents for every dollar of wealth owned by middle-class whites.

Moreover, middle-class blacks are not immune to the persistence of racial discrimination. For example, Joe R. Feagin (1991) showed the subtle and not-so-subtle forms of racism that successful middle-class blacks continue to confront in everyday life, including avoidance, poor service, verbal epithets, and various kinds of harassment and threats. Researchers at the Urban Institute have explored patterns of housing discrimination through the use of "audits" (which entail sending out black and white "auditors" to apply for jobs, loans, homes, apartments, etc.). They found that discrimination in housing and employment continues to be far more pervasive than most whites think is the case (Fix and Struyk 1993).

Finally, although increasing numbers of middle-class blacks have moved out of center cities to the suburbs, they are not necessarily now living in integrated neighborhoods. In fact, the white flight from cities that became so pronounced during the 1960s has a contemporary equivalent in the 1990s: Some suburbs that were once entirely or predominantly white are experiencing white flight with the arrival of blacks. For example, Matteson, Illinois, located 30 miles outside of Chicago, went from 84 percent white in 1980 to only 47 percent white a mere 15 years later (Terry 1996:A6).

Poor Blacks. For poor blacks, especially those at the bottom of the socioeconomic ladder, whom William Julius Wilson (1987) characterizes as the "truly disadvantaged," the world continues to be as segregated—in some instances more segregated—as it was during the Jim Crow era. Inner-city blacks live in segregated neighborhoods, attend segregated schools, worship in segregated churches, shop at segregated stores, and so forth (Massey and Denton 1993). They continue to confront discriminatory practices such as redlining—a tacit practice of denying loans to residents of what are perceived by lenders to be high-risk areas.

The economic situation for this segment of the African American community has become increasingly precarious. Deindustrialization has reduced the number of manufacturing jobs, and new jobs have moved to the suburbs. The result is that large numbers of inner-city blacks end up either unemployed; underemployed; working at dead-end, low-paying jobs; or working in the illicit underground economy (Wilson 1996).

Social problems—including the explosion of drug use, the increase in violent crime, the pervasiveness of gangs, the problems associated with teen pregnancy and low academic achievement, and the AIDS epidemic—have had a devastating impact on poor blacks (Anderson 1990). One need merely note that the leading cause of death for young black men is murder, usually at the hands of another black youth. Not surprisingly, poor blacks—especially younger blacks—have concluded that the American Dream has eluded them, and they see themselves three decades after the civil rights movement as still victims of the "scar of race" (Sniderman and Piazza 1993; see also Fordham 1996; Hochschild 1995;).

American Indians: The First of This Land

American Indian identities are complex and multifaceted. In part, this is because American Indians are defined in three different, and sometimes conflicting, ways:

- Tribal identities, which are determined in various ways by the tribes themselves.
- Pan-Indian affiliations.

- Personal decisions regarding whether to identify as Indian, especially for many of the more than 50 percent of Indians who have intermarried (Nagel 1996; Snipp 1989:157–65).

Indians and the Federal Government

The reservation system was a total institution intended to separate Indians from the larger American society. The first reservation was created in New Jersey in 1758, and others were established early in the nineteenth century. Due to widespread expansion of the reservation system thereafter, a majority of Indians ended up residing on reservations by the end of the 1800s.

Since then, the policies of the federal government, administered through the Department of the Interior's Bureau of Indian Affairs (BIA), have fluctuated between, on the one hand, efforts to end tribal affiliations and to promote assimilation and, on the other hand, efforts to strengthen and preserve tribal cultures, identities, and allegiances. For example, the Indian Reorganization Act of 1934 (IRA)—sometimes referred to as the "Indian New Deal"—promoted cultural preservation and enhancement. The Eisenhower administration in the 1950s sought to undo the IRA, replacing it with a policy that became known as "Termination." Its goal was to abolish the reservation system, withdraw federal support for tribal sovereignty, encourage the migration of Indians to cities, and sever the unique relationship that had existed between the federal government and tribal organizations. In effect, this was a policy of forced assimilation (Fixico 1986).

The vast majority of American Indians concluded that Termination was not in their best interest. They established pan-Indian organizations such as the National Congress of American Indians, which engaged in a political campaign of opposition to the Eisenhower administration's plans. Because of this opposition, when the Kennedy administration came into office, it quickly abandoned Termination. Since then, the federal government has not attempted to implement assimilationist policies (Cornell 1988).

Part of President Johnson's planning for the Great Society (which was seen as a return to and expansion of the policies of the New Deal) was to resuscitate aspects of the IRA. The federal government also attempted to address the endemic poverty that characterized reservation life. The significance of these attempts was that Native Americans were given considerable power to shape and control various aspects of community development and antipoverty, educational, and cultural programs. These efforts were funded through the Office of Economic Opportunity and thus often circumvented the much-criticized BIA and many traditional tribal leaders who were perceived to be pawns of the BIA. The result was considerable conflict within American Indian communities.

The Red Power Movement

These conflicts were linked to the advent of the Red Power movement, the Native American counterpart to the black civil rights movement (Nagel 1996). Militants demanded Indian self-determination and greater economic and political power. The Red Power movement began at the local level with such confrontational tactics as "fish-ins" and hunting out of season. Defying state laws was intended to highlight the fact that the states had violated treaty rights, which guaranteed American Indians special fishing and hunting privileges.

The movement was catapulted into the national spotlight with three dramatic episodes: the 1969 occupation of Alcatraz (the former federal prison in San Francisco Bay); the 1972 Trail of Broken Treaties March, a parallel to the black civil rights movement's historic 1963 March on Washington, only in this case culminating in the occupation of BIA headquarters; and the 1973 takeover of the community of Wounded Knee (the site of the 1890 massacre of 150 unarmed Sioux Indians).

This movement played a singularly important role in encouraging ethnic renewal. It aimed to resist assimilation and acculturation and to stimulate instead a renewed vitality within American Indian culture and society (Cornell 1988:187–201; Nagel 1996).

Although the militancy of the 1960s and 1970s has waned, considerable conflict persists. Recent examples include the ongoing dispute between Chippewa Indians and whites in northern Wisconsin over whether the Chippewa have a right to engage in spearfishing. It can be seen in the conflict between the Blackfeet of Montana and the oil industry over oil exploration in part of the Lewis and Clark National Forest. More generally, it is evident in the numerous court cases initiated by Native Americans in attempts to reclaim or obtain land taken by whites in violation of various laws or treaties. One of the consequences of this assertiveness is an anti-Indian backlash on the part of whites.

Reservation Life Today

Despite the Indian rights movement, life on reservations continues to be characterized by endemic poverty. Housing on reservations is considerably worse than that of most Americans. For example, as late as 1980, more than half the homes on the Hopi reservation did not have indoor plumbing (Snipp 1989:96–126). Unemployment and underemployment levels remain extremely high. As a result, on 15 of the 16 most populous reservations, between one third and one half of the families live below the poverty line (Snipp 1989:259).

Linked to poverty are a variety of health and social problems. Native Americans may be the least healthy racial group in the country. Their infant mortality rate is higher than the national average, and their life expectancy is 10 years shorter than the national average. The suicide rate slightly exceeds the national average, and the homicide rate is nearly twice that of all racial groups. Alcoholism is an extremely prevalent problem, and the alcohol-related death rate is five times that of all other racial groups. Linked to this problem is fetal alcohol syndrome, which only recently has received much media attention.

Reservation political leaders have attempted to combat these problems, but, to date, they have had limited success. Economic development plans tend to revolve around establishing gambling casinos on reservation land (because they are not bound by state laws regarding gambling) or using such land for the disposal of hazardous wastes. Both of these enterprises are highly controversial in the Native American community and reveal the desperation of reservation inhabitants.

Urban Indians

Given the economic plight of reservations, increasing numbers of people have left them for cities—a movement that began during the 1950s but has increased in recent years. Sizable Indian enclaves exist in such major cities as Los Angeles, Chicago, Denver, San Francisco, Phoenix, and Minneapolis-St. Paul. Urban Indians are far more likely to intermarry with other racial and ethnic groups and are generally more stable economically than their counterparts on the reservations (Snipp 1989:165).

Cities have been crucibles for an emerging pan-Indian identity. Tribal organizations, which in metropolitan areas are generally weak, have been replaced by supratribal organizations. However, only a small minority of urban dwellers actually participate in Native American institutions (Weibel-Orlando 1991).

The pull of assimilation is strongest for intermarried Native Americans who have made it into the middle class and are not involved to any significant extent with Native American institutions or cultural practices. Their ethnic identity is largely a matter of personal choice and does not involve communal activities. The future of this segment of the American Indian population likely will be quite different from that of the American Indians remaining on reservations.

New Immigrants in an Advanced Industrial Society

The newest Americans include immigrants from around the globe. They include, in addition to the groups cited previously, Jews from both Israel and the former Soviet Union living in Los Angeles, Hmong refugees residing in Minneapolis, undocumented Irish workers in Boston, Jamaicans who have settled in New York City, Poles in

Chicago, Haitians in Miami, Salvadorans who have fled political turmoil at home, and immigrants from India who call Chicago home. They include highly trained professionals with advanced degrees and people with limited educational backgrounds. Among their ranks are people prepared to enter the world of white-collar professionals, people who expect to work in the service industry or as field hands in American agriculture, and people who will live on the margins and will struggle to survive (Kessner and Caroli 1982; Mahler 1995; Portes and Rumbaut 1990). Collectively, they have had a significant impact on American race and ethnic relations, with the largest groups having the most profound impacts.

Hispanic Americans: Immigrants from the New World

The three largest Hispanic groups—Mexicans, Puerto Ricans, and Cubans—share many things besides a common language, but they also exhibit important differences (Bean and Tienda 1987). The Mexican American community is not only the largest of the three, but it also has the longest history in the United States and contains an extremely diverse population. It includes people who were in regions of what later became the United States long before the arrival of Anglos to the area and also includes the illegal immigrants who cross the border today in search of work. Due to the permeability of the border, Mexicans frequently have headed for El Norte when political or economic conditions at home become difficult. They fled to the United States in the bloody aftermath of the Mexican Revolution in 1910. Between 1942 and 1964, they were encouraged to work in America's agricultural fields as contract laborers under the "bracero program." Since 1965, they have immigrated voluntarily in large numbers (Gutierrez 1995).

A study in contrasts: Puerto Ricans and Cubans. Neither Puerto Rican nor Cuban immigrants have as long a historical experience as do Mexican Americans. Although all Puerto Ricans have been recognized as U.S. citizens since 1917, they did not begin to relocate to the mainland until after World War II and the beginning of inexpensive airfares. Perhaps more than any other group, Puerto Ricans exhibit considerable "circular migration," moving back and forth, depending on where better economic opportunities can be found at the moment (Fitzpatrick 1987).

In the Cuban case, the exodus began when the revolutionary government of Fidel Castro, which gained control of the island nation in 1959, proclaimed itself Marxist and became a client state of the Soviet Union. Cubans came in several distinctive waves, in part of a cat-and-mouse game of international relations between Cuba and the United States: the "Golden Exiles" in the early 1960s, the "Freedom

Flight" immigrants, who arrived between 1965 and 1973, and the "Marielitos" in 1980 (Daniels 1990:372–76; Pedraza 1992). Although immigrants from all these groups have had to struggle to adjust to life in their new homeland and have had to deal with considerable prejudice and discrimination, they have had different levels of success in gaining a foothold in the American economy and in achieving a political voice. At one extreme, Puerto Ricans are the poorest Hispanic group, experiencing high levels of unemployment, underemployment, and welfare dependency. In New York City (where second-generation Puerto Ricans are called "Nuyoricans"), many have found work in low-paying blue-collar jobs, especially in the service industry. Given their limited resources and relative lack of economic success, their ethnic community is more fragile and less institutionally complete than those created by the two other major Hispanic groups. The result has been limited Puerto Rican political influence.

In contrast, Cubans are the most successful of the three groups. Their success should not be surprising, given the fact that the earliest people to emigrate from Cuba came from the upper and middle classes and brought both financial resources and educational credentials that gave them a distinct advantage. Moreover, as perceived victims and opponents of communism during the height of the Cold War, they were welcomed with open arms. However, the final wave of immigrants—the Marielitos—were much poorer than the earlier waves, and among them were what the Cuban government called "social undesirables," including perhaps as many as 5,000 hard-core criminals. Their arrival has been the source of considerable controversy (Boswell and Curtis 1983:51–57).

Cubans in Miami have created an "ethnic enclave" economy, which has provided opportunities for entrepreneurial success. At the same time, it has benefited Cuban workers, many of whom have limited English-language skills. The community has been quite cohesive and has been able to exert considerable political clout, especially in South Florida, where Cubans have tended to align themselves with the Republican Party.

Younger Cuban Americans are moving out of the community and into the mainstream of American society. Among this American-born generation, English is generally their language of choice, they are less likely than most new immigrants to claim to have experienced discrimination, and they have a comparatively high level of educational attainment (Portes and Schauffler 1996; Rumbaut 1996).

Mexican Americans in transition. A well-established Mexican American community has existed for decades. Like African Americans and American Indians, Mexican Americans engaged in civil rights struggles during the 1960s and early 1970s. Chicano politics promoted ethnic pride and entailed an assertive demand for improvements in economic and educational opportunities and greater political power in regions where Mexicans were highly concentrated (Gomez-Quinones 1990; Gutierrez 1995). Mexicans were the most important group in the campaigns of a multi-ethnic coalition that made up the United Farm Workers. Given the prominent role they have played historically as agricultural laborers, their role in this effort to unionize the fields to improve economic conditions is not surprising. The period of militancy ended by the mid-1970s, with mixed results in achieving the movement's goals.

Mexican Americans today have a poverty rate similar to that of blacks and have higher-than-average unemployment and school drop-out rates. As with other disadvantaged groups, residents of the barrio suffer from a variety of social problems. Gangs and drugs have had a particularly destructive impact on the locales where poor Mexican Americans reside (Moore and Pinderhughes 1993).

On the other hand, the middle class has grown. In a fashion somewhat parallel to African Americans, Mexican Americans have a bifurcated community composed of a middle class moving into the mainstream; their poorer counterparts are left behind. This middle class is increasingly likely to reside in suburbs; by 1990, slightly more than 45 percent of Hispanics lived in suburbs. Those with English-language proficiency who have resided for some time in the United States are more likely to be suburban residents than are new arrivals possessing weak English-language skills (Alba et al. 1999:451).

The third generation and beyond are especially more likely than recent immigrants to find work today in white-collar professions and to own their own businesses. In contrast, recent immigrants typically are located in the bottom tier of the dual labor market, working in the garment industry, in service industries such as hotels and restaurants, and as agricultural laborers.

Given their geographic concentration in southwestern border states, Mexicans have become increasingly important politically. Both major political parties have courted their votes, although at the moment their allegiances remain fairly firmly located in the Democratic Party. Efforts to mobilize Mexican American voters have produced some notable successes at the ballot box at the state and local levels.

As this brief overview indicates, these major Hispanic groups have had rather different immigrant experiences and appear to have contrasting future prospects. Cubans appear poised to enter the mainstream, Puerto Ricans remain on the margins, and the Mexican American community reveals a split between those who are upwardly mobile and those who remain caught in impoverished barrios. What is clear is that Hispanics have become a more prominent factor in America's ethnic and racial mix, and, given population projections, they will play an even greater role in shaping American society in the twenty-first century.

Asian Americans: The Model Minority?

The Asian presence in America also has grown dramatically during the past quarter of a century. Collectively, Asian Americans are sometimes referred to as a "model minority" (Takaki 1989) because they have the highest per capita incomes and educational attainment levels of any racial minority. Indeed, in many ways they appear to do better than whites. For example, as Andrew Hacker (1992:143) pointed out, Asian American students have higher average scores than their white counterparts on the Scholastic Aptitude Test.

Some of the most negative stereotypes of Asian groups have declined and along with them previous levels of discrimination. Nonetheless, many Asian immigrants have not gained a foothold in the American economy and do not look like success stories. To appreciate why this is so, we turn to brief examinations of the three largest Asian groups that have contributed significant numbers to the new immigration (thus excluding the most successful Asian group, the Japanese): the Chinese, Filipinos, and Koreans.

The growth of Chinese America. The Chinese presence in North America began in the nineteenth century, when adventurous immigrants responded to the discovery of gold in California by sojourning to "Gold Mountain" in quest of fortune. Confronting intense hostility, they became in 1882 the first targets of anti-immigration legislation. After that time, the number of Chinese gradually declined, reaching its nadir by the middle of the twentieth century.

With the relaxation of immigration restrictions after 1965, the Chinese American community once again began to grow. Today, it has risen to more than 1.5 million, a twentyfold increase in 50 years. By 1980, 63 percent of the Chinese in America were immigrants (Kitano and Daniels 1988; Takaki 1989).

At present, Chinese Americans constitute a diverse group, including middle-class Chinese whose ancestors have been in the United States for several generations and recent arrivals who do not speak English and who are highly dependent on the powerful business interests that control America's Chinatowns. Thus, their circumstances bear a resemblance to those of Mexican Americans. Poorer new arrivals live in crowded Chinatowns, work long hours for low wages, and confront a variety of economic and social problems. On the other hand, much of the middle class has chosen to live in the suburbs, where middle-class Chinese Americans no longer live in isolation from the larger society (Fong 1994).

Filipinos and Koreans. Though both groups have had a presence in America prior to 1965, Filipinos and Koreans are largely recent arrivals. Although people from a wide strata of Philippine society have emigrated to the United States, a significant number are college-educated professionals, with a particularly large number being trained in health professions, particularly doctors, nurses, and pharmacists. As a result, despite the fact that many new arrivals experience a period of downward mobility as they adjust to their new society, many (but by no means all) Filipinos are gaining an economic foothold.

In part because Filipinos are divided along regional and dialect lines, and due to internal conflicts over homeland politics, a powerful and coherent ethnic community has not evolved. The American-born second generation that is growing up tends to be quite Americanized (Pido 1986; Tizon 1999).

As for Korean immigrants, they are not typical of most Koreans, who are Buddhists; a majority of Korean immigrants are Christian. Like Filipinos, many are middle-class professionals. These economic and cultural factors contribute in part to the fact that despite their relatively short time in the United States, Korean Americans are generally doing quite well.

Koreans have a high level of self-employment. Many own small family-run businesses, such as grocery stores, fruit stands, flower shops, repair stores, liquor stores, and clothing stores. Recent arrivals have managed to get into business by relying on savings they brought to the United States and on credit associations in the Korean community known as *Kye*, which provide loans to get business ventures off the ground. Many Korean American businesses are located in black urban ghettos, and considerable tension has developed between blacks and Koreans. In the 1992 Los Angeles riot, Korean stores were targeted by rioters, resulting in destruction of more than 1,000 Korean-owned businesses at a price exceeding $300 million (Abelmann and Lie 1995; Min 1996).

Korean Americans place a premium on education as a means for their children to become economically successful. Thus, it appears that they do not wish for their offspring to continue in family-owned businesses but instead to enter the world of white-collar professionals.

Model minority or competitive threat? Collectively, although Asian Americans are a distinct numerical minority, their presence has become more consequential in recent decades, especially on the West Coast and in such major cities as New York and Chicago (Tizon 1999). Thus, Korean shopkeepers in black neighborhoods, Chinese workers in the garment industry, and many Asians in institutions of higher education are now perceived by some members of other groups as a competitive threat.

On the other hand, Asian Americans have been held up as a model of success. Without downplaying their genuine achievements, we should note that this term is often used to make invidious comparisons between the "Asian American success story" and the failures and presumed personal shortcomings of other racial minorities. The implicit message amounts to a form of blaming the victim: If only these other groups could emulate the work ethic of the model minority, they too would be successful (Takaki 1989:474–84).

Multicultural America

In the preceding pages, we have seen something of the complexity and fluidity of a highly diverse society. Making sense of that complexity and fluidity is not easy. In a multicultural society such as ours, does assimilation or cultural pluralism best characterize the present state of ethnic relations? Are prejudice and discrimination decreasing or remaining constant? Are Americans committed to the notion of racial justice, or have they turned their back on it (Steinberg 1995)? As this overview of the "American kaleidoscope" reveals, there is evidence to support both sides of the argument that each of these questions raises. Some groups—including some recent arrivals—are doing relatively well and are becoming integrated into American society. Others—in particular African Americans and American Indians—continue to experience considerable adversity and are far from overcoming historical legacies of racial oppression. What is clear is that race remains a potent force in the United States, and people's life chances are in no small part defined by their racial identity.

At the same time, no group lives in a vacuum. Each racial and ethnic group interacts in various ways with other groups and with the larger society, shaping and transforming American culture and society in the process. As sociologist Orlando Patterson (1994) has indicated, different geographical regions in the United States acquire distinct "personalities" because of the interplay of differing ethnic and racial traditions. For example, he noted that the Afro-Caribbean influence in the Atlantic region, centered in Miami, is quite different from the Tex-Mex culture of the Southwest—which, in turn, differs "from the Southern California cosmos, with its volatile, unblended mosaic of Latin, Asian, and Afro-European cultures" (Patterson 1994:111).

This description suggests two things. First, diversity will continue to characterize the nation well into the future. Second, because there is nothing fixed about ethnicity and race, the inequality and oppression that have characterized and continue to characterize intergroup relations are not inevitable. Still, at the beginning of the twenty-first century, "the problem of the color line" is far from being solved.

References

Abelmann, Nancy and John Lie. 1995. *Blue Dreams: Korean Americans and the Los Angeles Riots*. Cambridge, MA: Harvard University Press.

Alba, Richard D. 1990. *Ethnic Identity: The Transformation of White America.* New Haven, CT: Yale University Press.

Alba, Richard D., John R. Logan, Brian J. Stults, Gilbert Marzan, and Wenquan Zhang. 1999. "Immigrant Groups in the Suburbs: A Reexamination of Suburbanization and Spatial Assimilation." *American Sociological Review* 64:446–60.

Allen, Theodore. 1994. *The Invention of the White Race.* Vol. 1. London: Verso.

Anderson, Elijah. 1990. *Streetwise. Chicago:* University of Chicago Press.

Bean, Frank D. and Marta Tienda. 1987. *The Hispanic Population of the United States.* New York: Russell Sage Foundation.

Boswell, Thomas D. and James R. Curtis. 1983. *The Cuban-American Experience.* Totowa, NJ: Rowman and Allan.

Brimelow, Peter. 1995. *Alien Nation: Common Sense about America's Immigration Disaster.* New York: Random House.

Brown v. Board of Education. 1954. 347 U.S. 483.

Chen, Hsiang-Shui. 1992. *Chinatown No More: Taiwan Immigrants in Contemporary New York.* Ithaca, NY: Cornell University Press.

Civil Rights Act of 1964. 1965. Pub. L. 88–352.

Cornell, Stephen. 1988. *The Return of the Native: American Indian Political Resurgence.* New York: Oxford University Press.

Curtin, Philip. 1969. *The Atlantic Slave Trade.* Madison: University of Wisconsin Press.

Daniels, Roger. 1990. *Coming to America: A History of Immigration and Ethnicity in American Life.* New York: HarperCollins.

Dinnerstein, Leonard. 1994. *Anti-Semitism in America.* New York: Oxford University Press.

D'Souza, Dinesh. 1995. *The End of Racism.* New York: Free Press.

Du Bois, W. E. B. [1903] 1961. *The Souls of Black Folk.* Reprint, New York: Fawcett World Library.

Ellison, Ralph. 1999. *Juneteenth.* New York: Random House.

Farley, Reynolds. 1984. *Blacks and Whites: Narrowing the Gap?* Cambridge, MA: Harvard University Press.

Feagin, Joe R. 1991. "The Continuing Significance of Race: Antiblack Discrimination in Public Places." *American Sociological Review* 56:101–16.

Feagin, Joe R. and Hernán Vera. 1994. *White Racism.* New York: Routledge.

Fitzpatrick, Joseph. 1987. *Puerto Rican Americans.* Englewood Cliffs, NJ: Prentice Hall.

Fix, Michael and Raymond J. Struyk, eds. 1993. *Clear and Convincing Evidence.* Washington, DC: Urban Institute.

Fixico, Donald L. 1986. *Termination and Relocation.* Albuquerque: University of New Mexico Press.

Fong, Timothy. 1994. *The First Suburban Chinatown.* Philadelphia, PA: Temple University Press.

Fordham, Signithia. 1996. *Blacked Out: Dilemmas of Race, Identity, and Success at Capital High.* Chicago: University of Chicago Press.

Gans, Herbert. 1979. "Symbolic Ethnicity: The Future of Ethnic Groups and Cultures in America." Pp. 193–220 in *On the Making of Americans*, edited by H. Gans, N. Glazer, J. Gusfield, and C. Jencks. Philadelphia, PA: University of Pennsylvania Press.

Gomez-Quinones. 1990. *Chicano Politics.* Albuquerque: University of New Mexico Press.

Gutierrez, David G. 1995. *Walls and Mirrors: Mexican Americans, Mexican Immigrants, and the Politics of Identity.* Berkeley: University of California Press.

Hacker, Andrew. 1992. *Two Nations: Black and White, Separate, Hostile, Unequal.* New York: Scribner.

Handlin, Oscar. 1973. *The Uprooted. Boston,* MA: Little, Brown.

Hochschild, Jennifer L. 1995. *Facing Up to the American Dream.* Princeton, NJ: Princeton University Press.

Holli, Melvin. 1999. "E Pluribus Unum: The Assimilation Paradigm Revisited." *Siirtolaisuus* 2:4–13.

Holmes, Steven A. 1995. "A Surge in Immigration Surprises Experts and Intensifies Debate." *New York Times,* August 30, pp. Al, A10.

Housing and Urban Development Act of 1968. Pub. L. 90–448.

Indian Reorganization Act of 1934. 25 U.S.C. 461.

Jaynes, Gerald David and Robin M. Williams, eds. 1989. *A Common Destiny: Blacks and American Society.* Washington, DC: National Academy Press.

Kessner, Thomas and Betty Boyd Caroli. 1982. *Today's Immigrants: Their Stories.* New York: Oxford University Press.

Kitano, Harry and Roger Daniels. 1988. *Asian Americans: Emerging Minorities.* Englewood Cliffs, NJ: Prentice Hall.

Kivisto, Peter. 1995. *Americans All: Race and Ethnic Relations in Historical, Structural, and Comparative Perspective.* Belmont, CA: Wadsworth.

Landry, Bart. 1987. *The New Black Middle Class.* Berkeley: University of California Press.

Lieberson, Stanley and Mary Waters. 1988. *From Many Strands: Ethnic and Racial Groups in Contemporary America.* New York: Russell Sage Foundation.

Lipsitz, George. 1998. *The Possessive Investment in Whiteness: How White People Profit from Identity Politics.* Philadelphia, PA: Temple University Press.

Litwack, Leon. 1998. *Trouble in Mind: Black Southerners in the Age of Jim Crow.* New York: Knopf.

Mahler, Sarah. 1995. *American Dreaming: Immigrant Life on the Margins.* Princeton, NJ: Princeton University Press.

Martin, Philip and Jonas Widgren. 1996. "International Migration: A Global Challenge." *Population Bulletin* 51(1):1–48.

Massey, Douglas S. and Nancy A. Denton. 1993. *American Apartheid: Segregation and the Making of the Underclass.* Cambridge, MA: Harvard University Press.

McAdam, Doug. 1982. *Political Process and the Development of Black Insurgency, 1930–1970.* Chicago: University of Chicago Press.

McDaniel, Antonio. 1995. "The Dynamic Racial Composition of the United States." *Daedalus* 124:179–98.

Min, Pyong Gap. 1996. *Caught in the Middle: Korean Merchants in America's Multiethnic Cities.* Berkeley: University of California Press.

Moore, Joan and Raquel Pinderhughes, eds. 1993. *In the Barrios: Latinos and the Underclass Debate.* New York: Russell Sage Foundation.

Morris, Aldon D. 1984. *The Origins of the Civil Rights Movement.* New York: Free Press.

Nagel, Joane. 1996. *American Indian Ethnic Renewal: Red Power and the Resurgence of Identity and Culture.* New York: Oxford University Press.

Oliver, Melvin L. and Thomas M. Shapiro. 1995. *Black Wealth/White Wealth: A New Perspective on Racial Inequality.* New York: Routledge.

Omi, Michael and Howard Winant. 1986. *Racial Formation in the United States: From the 1960s to the 1980s.* Boston, MA: Routledge and Kegan Paul.

Parrillo, Vincent N. 1996. *Diversity in America.* Thousand Oaks, CA: Pine Forge Press.

Patterson, Orlando. 1994. "Ecumenical America: Global Culture and the American Cosmos." *World Policy Journal* 11(2):103–17.

Pedraza, Silvia. 1992. "Cubans in Exile, 1959–1989: The State of the Research." Pp. 24–36 in *Cuban Studies since the Revolution,* edited by D. J. Fernandez. Gainesville: University Presses of Florida.

Pido, Antonio. 1986. *The Filipinos in America.* New York: Center for Migration Studies.

Pinkney, Alphonso. 2000. *Black Americans.* 5th ed. Upper Saddle River, NJ: Prentice Hall.

Plessy v. Ferguson. 1896. 163 U.S. 537.

Portes, Alejandro and Ruben Rumbaut. 1990. *Immigrant America: A Portrait.* Berkeley: University of California Press.

Portes, Alejandro and Richard Schauffler. 1996. "Language and the Second Generation: Bilingualism Yesterday and Today." Pp. 8–29 in *The New Second Generation,* edited by A. Portes. New York: Russell Sage Foundation.

Roberts, Sam. 1994. "Census Reveals a Surge in Hispanic Population." *New York Times,* October 9, p. A15.

Roediger, David R. 1991. *The Wages of Whiteness: Race and the Making of the American Working Class.* London: Verso.

Rumbaut, Ruben G. 1996. "The Crucible Within: Ethnic Identity, Self-Esteem, and Segmented Assimilation among Children of Immigrants." Pp. 119–70 in *The New Second Generation,* edited by A. Portes. New York: Russell Sage Foundation.

Sniderman, Paul M. and Edward G. Carmines. 1997. *Reaching beyond Race.* Cambridge, MA: Harvard University Press.

Sniderman, Paul M. and Thomas Piazza. 1993. *The Scar of Race.* Cambridge, MA: Belknap.

Snipp, C. Matthew. 1989. *American Indians: The First of This Land.* New York: Russell Sage Foundation.

Steinberg, Stephen. 1995. *Turning Back: The Retreat from Racial Justice in American Thought and Policy.* Boston, MA: Beacon.

Takaki, Ronald. 1989. *Strangers from a Different Shore: A History of Asian Americans.* Boston, MA: Little, Brown.

———. 1993. *A Different Mirror: A History of Multicultural America.* Boston, MA: Little, Brown.

Taylor, D. Garth, Paul B. Sheatsley, and Andrew M. Greeley. 1978. "Attitudes toward Racial Integration." *Scientific American* 238 (June):42–51.

Terry, Don. 1996. "In White Flight's Wake, a Town Tries to Keep Its Balance." *New York Times,* March 11, p. A6.

Thornton, Russell. 1987. *American Indian Holocaust and Survival: A Population History since 1492.* Norman: University of Oklahoma Press.

Tizon, Orlando. 1999. "Congregation and Family: Changing Filipino Identities." Ph.D. dissertation, Loyola University.

Ueda, Reed. 1994. *Postwar Immigrant America: A Social History.* Boston, MA: Bedford Books.

U.S. Census Bureau. 1991. *Statistical Abstract of the United States.* Washington, DC: U.S. Government Printing Office.

———. 1992. *The Black Population in the United States.* Current Population Reports, Series P-20, No. 462. Washington, DC: U.S. Government Printing Office.

Voting Rights Act of 1965. 1966. Pub. L. 89–110.

Waters, Mary. 1990. *Ethnic Options: Choosing Identities in America.* Berkeley: University of California Press.

Weibel-Orlando, Joan. 1991. *Indian Country, LA.* Urbana: University of Illinois Press.

Wilson, William Julius. 1987. *The Truly Disadvantaged.* Chicago: University of Chicago Press.

———. 1996. *When Work Disappears: The World of the New Urban Poor.* New York: Knopf.

Winant, Howard. 1994. *Racial Conditions.* Minneapolis: University of Minnesota Press.

———. 1999. "Whiteness at Century's End." Pp. 23-45 in *The Making and Unmaking of Whiteness,* edited by M. Wray. Durham, NC: Duke University Press.

Woodward, C. Vann. 1974. *The Strange Career of Jim Crow.* New York: Oxford University Press.

PART I

Racial Fault Lines

During the past half-century, we have witnessed sweeping changes in the landscape of race relations. Yet, in spite of these changes, the past has not disappeared. By all indications, we have made progress in redressing past injustices in some areas of social life, but we have failed to make the same kind of headway in others. We have seen the end of some forms of discrimination (for example, mandatory segregation in public facilities), while new and often more subtle forms of discrimination have arisen. We have experienced an upsurge of job integration and mixed marriages, while patterns of residential and school segregation remain deeply entrenched. We have witnessed the decline of some ethnic neighborhoods and the simultaneous emergence of new immigrant communities. The net result is that we have entered a new stage in the nation's race relations history. There are a number of reasons that this shift to a new stage has occurred. However, none is more significant than the following two factors: (1) the legislative and judicial victories that emerged out of the civil rights movement of the 1950s and 1960s, and (2) changes in the racial mix of the nation brought about by the resumption of mass immigration after 1965.

The essays in Part I focus on what we term "racial fault lines." By speaking of fault lines, we are borrowing from geological language. In geology, a fault line refers to a fissure in the earth's surface where different land masses come into contact with each other. Sometimes those masses move side by side without problem. Sometimes, one slides over the other one. At other times, the movement results in trouble as pressure builds between the two masses, resulting in tremors that shake the earth's surface, in the worst instances leading to devastating earthquakes. In translating this imagery to the social topography of race relations, we are interested in exploring potential trouble: those places where the friction in intergroup relations is the most intense. Just as geologists are keenly interested in what is happening at the fault lines, so sociologists are interested in knowing what is happening at the racial fault lines.

The first selection, by Gerald David Jaynes and Robin M. Williams, Jr., traces the changes in white attitudes toward African Americans from the Jim Crow era through the volatile times of the civil rights years, ending with an assessment of white attitudes 20 years into the post-civil rights era. As such, it is intended to provide a context within which the subsequent essays in Part I can be placed. The authors reveal that white attitudes have improved appreciably over this time period. For example, few whites now see blacks as biologically inferior, though this was a commonplace conviction earlier in the twentieth century. Jaynes and Williams note that whites claim to be advocates of equality of opportunity and that they assert their opposition to prejudice and discrimination. At the same time, however, whites exhibit considerable opposition to policies designed to redress past discrimination and exploitation. Thus, though asserting their belief in the virtue of equal opportunity in principle, whites are opposed to measures such as affirmative action. The picture that emerges is a complicated one.

Public opinion surveys such as those employed by Jaynes and Williams, while useful in tapping into the attitudes of large numbers of people systematically, have their limitations. Perhaps most significantly, what is captured is what people are thinking or feeling at a particular moment, and it does not necessarily address how they behave. In addition, by concentrating on the individual, we fail to appreciate the role played by institutional—not by individual—racism.

This is the thrust of Howard Winant's essay, which explores the ways racism has been transformed since the 1960s. Winant's essay throws cold water on the views of optimists who think racism has ended in the aftermath of the civil rights era. In his view, racism today operates in a more institutional and subtle manner. He suggests that as our definitions of race itself have evolved, so has racism. It has not disappeared but rather taken on new form. To understand contemporary racism, Winant contends, we must pay attention to the ways in which political, economic, and demographic forces have shaped the new racial formation of the United States, the nature of which he sketches.

If we rely too heavily on survey research, we also fail to appreciate the full spectrum of opinions that exist across the entire society, and, in particular, we fail to comprehend the differing shape and form of racism in different sectors of society. Amy E. Ansell's essay is influenced by the conceptual work of Winant. She is especially interested in exploring the racism of the "new right" in American politics. Here, she has in mind not the extremism of white supremacists; instead, what she seeks to reveal is the covert racism of more mainstream political conservatives who adamantly assert that they and their policies are nonracist. What Ansell offers is a concrete instance of the place of the new racism in contemporary American politics.

In contrast, the articles by Joe R. Feagin and Hernán Vera and by Abby L. Ferber examine instances of racism in its more virulent and least subtle forms. On the extreme fringes of the right wing, the ugliest forms of old-fashioned racism persist—updated by relying on modern forms of communication such as public access television and the Internet. In the essay by Feagin and Vera, we are offered a case study of racism in the heartland of the nation, namely in the midwestern city of Dubuque, Iowa. Responding to a city plan—interesting in its own right—that was intended to attract blacks to Dubuque, racists from the area who were affiliated with the Ku Klux Klan commenced a campaign of racial harassment. The controversy received national notoriety when a leader of one of the branches of the KKK decided to use the episode as a forum for presenting white supremacist views to a large audience. Ferber's article does something quite different. She examines in depth the ideology of white supremacists, concentrating on a careful analysis of the movement's literature. In so doing, Ferber is intent on illustrating how this literature seeks to articulate a vision of white superiority combined with a call to action in defense of a race that is presumed to be threatened by the rising tide of people of color.

The concluding two essays in this part reveal a distinctive feature of contemporary racial fault lines, namely, that the old bifurcated view of whites versus blacks, or even the view of whites versus all other racial groups, fails to capture the complicated nature of the current situation. In particular, it fails to recognize the tensions and potential conflict pitting blacks against various other racial minorities. The 1992 riot in Los Angeles, which occurred in the wake of the Rodney King verdict that saw the police officers who beat him found innocent, serves as an instructive flash point. Pyong Gap Min's chapter treats one important instance of new racial tensions, that which characterizes contemporary Korean-African American relationships. Koreans have become major owners of stores in African American inner-city neighborhoods, and, as a consequence, a relationship defined by mutual suspicion and acrimony has developed. Min discusses this situation from the perspective of the new immigrants from Korea, who, as the title of his article suggests, feel that they are caught in the middle, between whites and blacks. David O. Sears examines the riot itself, comparing it to an earlier riot in 1965, which took place in the Watts section of the city. In the earlier event, the riot was clearly one pitting whites against blacks, but in 1992, the riot was what some commentators have referred to as the first multiracial riot in the nation's history. The implications of these new complications in race relations are reflected in the remaining essays in the volume.

1

Changes in White Racial Attitudes

Gerald David Jaynes and Robin M. Williams, Jr.

Change in Racial Attitudes: An Overview

Beginning in the late 1930s, the methodology and institutional base for conducting scientific sample surveys improved (see Rossi et al., 1983). This made it possible to develop an "attitudinal record" over time based on the recorded replies of sample survey respondents to questions concerning black-white relations (Schuman et al., 1985). In some cases, these questions have been asked in identical or near-identical form from the 1940s to the 1980s.

Several clear patterns emerge from these trend studies. Schuman and colleagues (1985) drew several conclusions regarding change in the attitudes of whites. We supplement their list with other conclusions regarding the attitudes of blacks.

- Black Americans have supported racially equalitarian principles as far back as there are data.
- There has been a steady increase in support among white Americans for principles of racial equality, but substantially less support for policies intended to implement principles of racial equality.

- Blacks also exhibit a gap between support for principles and support for policies intended to implement those principles, and blacks show recent decreases in support for policy implementation strategies.
- Whites are more accepting of equal treatment with regard to the public domains of life than private domains of life, and they are especially accepting of relations involving transitory forms of contact.
- Openness to equal treatment also varies by the number or proportion of blacks likely to be involved. Where blacks remain a clear minority, the data indicate growing white acceptance of racial equality. Where blacks approach a majority, change is less frequent and overall levels of pro equal-treatment response are low.
- Whites living in the North have been and remain more pro equal treatment than those living in the South. Patterns of change are usually the same in each region.
- Measures of black alienation from white society suggest an increase in black alienation from the late 1960s into the 1980s.
- The process of change during the 1960s and early 1970s appeared to involve both generational changes (cohort replacement effects) and individual change. For the late

1970s and into the 1980s, what change has occurred is almost entirely a product of cohort replacement.

What factors are responsible for changes in Americans' attitudes toward black-white relations? We identify three basic social forces: alterations in social context (historical change), individual modification of attitudes, and cohort replacement. Change over time in attitudes, whether positive or negative in direction, can be brought about through a process of demographic or cohort replacement, or it can be brought about by modifications in individual attitudes. In the former case, older generations who have one set of attitudes are replaced by younger people who hold a different set of attitudes. In the case of individual change, a person who expressed a particular attitude at one time changes to a different position at a later time.

For example, previous studies of white attitudes (Hyman and Sheatsley, 1964; Schuman et al., 1985; Taylor et al., 1978) found that change during the 1960s and early 1970s involved both cohort replacement and individual change. But Schuman and colleagues (1985) reported that positive change recorded in the late 1970s was mainly a product of cohort replacement. They also found that the difference between the very youngest cohorts and other recent cohorts had narrowed. Thus, recently, even cohort replacement was weakening as a mechanism for producing change in whites' attitudes toward blacks.

White Attitudes

The Scientific American Reports

Until fairly recently the most widely known and best studies of change in racial attitudes were based almost exclusively on data collected in early surveys by the National Opinion Research Center (NORC) and reported in a series of articles published in *Scientific American*. The first of these articles (Hyman and Sheatsley, 1956) focused on issues of desegregation, reporting particularly on change between 1942 and 1956 in attitudes toward desegregation of schools, housing, and public transportation. On each of these issues there was evidence of increasing support for desegregation. Hyman and Sheatsley also reported that there were often large differences between North and South: there was majority sentiment for desegregation by northerners and for continued segregation by southerners. Also, younger people were more likely than older people to favor desegregation, and highly educated people were more open to desegregation than were people with low levels of education. The age differences and the apparent effects of education provided grounds for expecting that further change would occur as younger, better educated individuals "replaced" older, less educated individuals.

Hyman and Sheatsley suggested that attitudes were importantly linked to actual social conditions. Thus, where segregation existed without significant challenge, the attitudes reflected such conditions. They did not find that many Americans sensed a moral dilemma on race issues. They tried to examine Myrdal's (1944) concern with the contradiction between American values and the treatment of blacks by asking a question on whether or not blacks were being treated fairly. As they explained (Hyman and Sheatsley, 1956:39):

Certainly a study of the comments people make in answering the questions reveals little soul-searching, hesitation or feeling of guilt. Many declare: "They're being treated too doggone good." Respondents remark: "Just look around you. They are being given every opportunity for progress that they never had before."

These results notwithstanding, there were two key reasons at that time to think that further change was probable. First, belief in the innate intellectual inferiority of blacks, a fundamental ideological factor in the case for segregation, had greatly declined between 1942 and 1956, falling from roughly 60 percent to just over 20 percent. Second, the survey findings suggested that positive change in attitudes followed the implementation of concrete social change.

The large sample sizes of the surveys allowed the analysts to divide southern communities into areas that had desegregated their schools, those that were moving in the direction of doing so, and those that were adamantly resisting change. They found the more change that had already taken place, the more positive were the attitudes toward school desegregation. Thus, 31 percent of respondents in areas with desegregated schools supported desegregation, compared with 17 percent in areas just beginning to take steps toward desegregation and only 4 percent in areas resisting desegregation. Some areas were probably more receptive to desegregation than others to begin with, but none even approached majority support. Hyman and Sheatsley did not argue that overwhelming opposition to change could be readily converted, but rather that where openness to racial change existed among at least a substantial minority of whites, it was likely that leaders could act to influence majority opinion.

The second article in the series (Hyman and Sheatsley, 1964) stressed many of the same points. In particular, it noted that the growing pace and intensity of the civil rights struggle had not slowed improvement in attitudes toward desegregating the schools, public transportation, and housing. The pace of change in attitudes from 1956 to 1963 was, in fact, faster than the pace of change had been between 1942 and 1956. For example, support among southern whites for school desegregation rose from 2 percent to 14 percent between 1942 and 1956, an increase of 12 points in 14 years; between 1956 and 1963, support for desegregation went from 14 percent to 30 percent, an increase of 16 points in just 7 years. Hyman and Sheatsley reported that change was not simply a function of younger, better educated people replacing older, poorly educated people: many people who had supported segregation at an earlier time had, at least in terms of their verbal replies to survey questions, changed to support for desegregation.

Hyman and Sheatsley again stressed that opinion bore an important connection to prevailing social conditions. Their 1963 data confirmed important differences among southern communities. Support for school desegregation ranged from a high of 54 percent in areas that had implemented desegregation, to 38 percent in areas that had made only token steps in that direction, to 28 percent in those areas where the schools remained segregated. In this case Hyman and Sheatsley were more certain than earlier that action by public officials had probably encouraged attitude change rather than the other way around.

In a subtle manner, the content and tenor of the *Scientific American* reports on racial attitudes changed as key social issues and events in the nation changed. While the first two articles stressed the strength of a positive trend in racial attitudes, the third article in the series (Greeley and Sheatsley, 1971) was also more directly and extensively concerned with the issue of "white backlash." Key questions used in the earlier analyses continued to show positive change, especially in the South. The overall level of support for desegregated public transportation was so high, 88 percent in 1970, that the question could not be used to elicit evidence of much further change. On the basis of these data, Greeley and Sheatsley saw little support for the idea that a white backlash against racial progress had arisen. Only among poorly educated "white ethnics" did they find any indication of a backlash, and even those effects were not large (Bobo, 1987).

The fourth and most recent article in the series (Taylor et al., 1978) found little support for the white backlash hypothesis. Indeed, this article reported just the opposite, a remarkable "liberal leap" forward between 1970 and 1972 followed by steady positive change between 1972 and 1976. The sharp upturn in support for racial desegregation in the early 1970s was matched by similar upturns in positive attitudes on social and civil liberties. Thus, Taylor and colleagues argued that more favorable racial attitudes were part of a general and robust trend in public opinion. Although the replacement of older cohorts by younger cohorts and the increasing average level of education were important factors in the trend, much of the observed change involved individual changes in attitudes, not just cohort replacement.

In sum, from the early 1940s to the late 1970s there were important shifts in white attitudes, from widespread belief that blacks were born less intelligent than whites to the belief that the races were of equal intelligence and from majority support for segregation of public places, schools, and housing to majority support for equal treatment. Even assuming that social pressures for "correct" answers affected responses and that attitudes were only tenuously connected to behavior, the change had been impressive.

One analyst characterized this research as having shown such sweeping progress that questions on some issues, for example, desegregation of public transportation and of schools, had become obsolete; that the survey data provided no support for the white backlash hypothesis; that changes in racial attitudes were closely linked to the liberalization of public opinion on other issues; and that both cohort replacement and individual change in attitudes contributed to the trends documented in the *Scientific American* reports (Seeman, 1981:394).

However, the consistency, unambiguity, and comprehensiveness of the changes documented in these studies were not completely replicated by other studies. Condran's (1979) analysis of the NORC data for five questions asked in 1963, 1972, and 1977 suggested that change from 1972 to 1977 had not been as consistently positive as had the change from 1963 to 1972. He also found that on questions concerning residential integration and on those that asked if blacks should "push" themselves where they were not wanted, younger age cohorts were less positive than older cohorts. He concluded that much of the positive change in racial attitudes may have involved only verbal adherence to newly institutionalized racial norms and that certainly "the liberals of 1977 [had] less reason to be sanguine concerning white American racial attitudes than their counterparts of 1972" (Condran, 1979:475).

In addition, the widespread controversies over school busing, opposition to some affirmative action plans, and the continuing pervasiveness of residential segregation also raised questions about the meaning of the changes reported in the *Scientific American* reports. In an article published separately from the *Scientific American* reports, Greeley and Sheatsley (1974) directly addressed the extent and implications of whites' opposition to school busing. Fewer than one-fifth of whites in 1972 favored "the busing of black and white school children from one school district to another." Yet, Greeley and Sheatsley noted, blacks were far from uniform in their attitudes toward school busing, and whites' support for the principle of school desegregation continued to grow. They concluded that opposition to busing could not be reduced to simple racism. They did note that the crucial race issues had shifted from matters of broad principles to the far more problematic issues "of the practical policies which most effectively will achieve racial justice" (Greeley and Sheatsley, 1974:249).

Social Distance

Social distance preferences further complicate the picture of change. These questions pose hypothetical social settings that vary in racial composition. Respondents are asked to indicate whether they would take part in such settings, withdraw from such settings, or in other ways respond positively or negatively. Three of these questions pertain to willingness to allow one's children to attend schools with different numbers of black students, ranging from a few, to about half, to more than half. The National Opinion Research Center and Gallup have used nearly identical versions of these questions. The Gallup data provide the longer series, the questions having first been asked in a survey in 1958. At that point 75 percent of whites said they would not object to sending their children to a school in which a few of the students were black; 50 percent said they would have no objection to a school in which half of the students were black. Responses to all three questions show positive change over time. But, the increase in openness to desegregated schooling is much lower when the question specifies that most of the children in the school would be black. In addition, the educational and regional differentials are more pronounced for the "few" and "half black" questions than for the "most" question (see Table 1.1; see also Smith, 1981).

The patterns of results are largely similar when the questions pertain to residential areas and housing. Two questions address contact under circumstances in which blacks would be the clear minority ("next door" and "same block"); one implies a more substantial black presence in the neighborhood ("great numbers"). As is true for schools, the number of blacks mentioned in the question has an important effect on white openness to interracial contact.

Thus, when asked in 1958, "If black people came to live next door, would you move," 56 percent of whites said they would not move. But when asked about moving "if black people came to live in great numbers in your neighborhood," 20 percent said they would not move, 29 percent said they might move, and 51 percent said they definitely would move. This difference in levels of openness to

interracial contact is present at the most recent time for these two questions (1978) and is slightly larger than it was in 1958. Although 86 percent in 1978 said they would not move if black people lived next door to them, only 46 percent said they would not move if large numbers of blacks were in the neighborhood.

All three of the social distance questions concerned with residential contact undergo positive change. This result is surprising for the "great numbers" question, which otherwise behaves very much like the question on majority black schools; both show low absolute levels of support and are not strongly related to level of education. For the two questions involving just a few blacks ("same block" and "next door"), people who have more education express greater openness to interracial contact than those with less education. In sum, the social distance questions that pertain to smaller numbers of blacks undergo change and relate to region and education in much the same way as do principle-type questions, such as "same schools." When larger numbers of blacks are mentioned—in particular, if blacks are stated to be a clear majority—the results more closely parallel those for the policy implementation-type questions, such as school busing (see below).

Social Policy, Social Context, and Racial Attitudes

Greeley and Sheatsley (1974) suggested that the shift in emphasis from matters of principle to matters of practical social policy was the decisive change in racial issues in the 1970s. The most recent of the *Scientific American* articles (Taylor et al., 1978) did not emphasize this important shift, however, presumably because the task was to trace change with items included in the early surveys. Thus, sustained attention to attitudes on policies on race issues was largely lacking until recently (Campbell [1971] is an exception). One trend study of black-white attitudes that did move beyond the types of questions relied on in the *Scientific American* reports to include questions on policy changes concluded that the basic patterns of change were indeed more complex.

This study (Schuman et al., 1985) differed from the *Scientific American* reports in three aspects. First, in addition to the NORC data, Schuman and colleagues also relied on data collected by the Institute for Social Research (ISR) at the University of Michigan and data collected by the Gallup organization. Thus, three major sources of trend data on racial attitudes were considered. Second, this more comprehensive coverage of data resources allowed consideration of two additional types of questions that played little or no part in the NORC surveys. Results for these additional questions differ from results obtained for the types of questions in the NORC surveys. Third, Schuman and colleagues also examined change in the racial attitudes of blacks and compared them with results for whites.

Schuman and colleagues examined trends for racial attitude questions that had been asked in national sample surveys in identical (or near[ly] identical) form at 2 or more times and spanned at least a 10-year period over the years from 1942 to 1983. These criteria resulted in a pool of 32 questions. The questions were placed into three groupings: those concerned with racial principles, those concerned with the implementation of principles, and those concerned with social distance preferences.

Racial principle questions addressed attitudes about the general goals of integration and equal treatment of the races; they did not cover what steps or policies should be undertaken to achieve these ends. Implementation questions addressed the steps that might be taken, usually by the federal government, to put the principles regarding black-white relations into concrete practice. The social distance questions—asked only of whites—concerned personal willingness to take part in social settings involving contact with varying numbers of blacks. The conceptual categories not only highlighted differences in the content of the questions, but also showed that different types of questions had different patterns of change over time. Table 1.1 shows the results for the main questions used by Schuman and colleagues for blacks and whites. Each question is given the same descriptive content label used by Schuman and colleagues.

The questions are organized into the three major conceptual categories and a residual miscellaneous category. Dates for the first and most recent times questions were asked are presented along with the percentage of respondents giving the more pro desegregation response at the most recent time questions were asked. Also shown is a difference score as a rough indicator of overall change. In some instances the most recent figures we report, and thus the difference scores, differ from those reported by Schuman and colleagues because more recent data are now available.

Focusing first on the results for whites, all of the racial principle questions show positive change. For example, the question labeled "same schools," which spans the period from 1942 to 1982, has moved 58 points in a pro desegregation direction. This change reflects substantial movement in a pro desegregation direction. This change occurred both in and outside the South. Furthermore, there is considerable narrowing of the gap between those with high and low levels of education.

This question can be treated as the prototypical racial principle item. The principle questions typically involved large positive change over time, regional convergence as the North reached a ceiling and the South continued to change, and a narrowing of educational differences over time. By the end of the series, most of these questions revealed very high absolute levels of support for the pro desegregation response.

The results do vary, however, by subject matter and by wording of the question. Support for school desegregation thus attains a much higher absolute level than does opposition to laws that forbid racial intermarriage. So it is clear that whites do not uniformly give the socially desirable response to racial principle questions. Still, the *Scientific American* reports are based almost exclusively on results for principle-type questions. An examination of trends in response to implementation questions qualifies the portrait of positive change.

Support for the implementation of principles of equalitarian black-white relations has been much less than support for the principles themselves. Moreover, support for implementation policies has seldom shown as much positive change as has support for the principles. Although the implementation questions usually do not span as many years as the principle items, there are several such questions that closely parallel several principle items in wording and that involve considerable overlap in the time points covered by the two types of questions.

The most striking case of divergence in trends between principle and implementation involves the questions of "federal school intervention" and "same schools": the former asks whether or not the federal government should become involved in efforts to desegregate the schools; the latter asks if black and white school children should attend the same schools. Although support for the principle of desegregated schools ("same schools") rose by 22 points from 1964 to 1977–1978 (the period of years for which there are data on both questions), support for federal efforts to implement this principle declined by 17 points. This decline occurred when the real-world context of the question was changing considerably. In 1964, desegregation of schools was primarily focused on the South and involved the dismantling of separate

school systems that had been created and maintained under state laws. By the early 1970s, school desegregation was focused on the North, and federal involvement was symbolized by busing children to and from schools in segregated residential areas. These changes no doubt affected the 17-point decline. And, indeed, Schuman and colleagues reported that the decline was restricted almost entirely to the North, clearly involved change at the individual level, and occurred in the post-1972 period. The decline thus occurred after the introduction of mandatory desegregation and busing in the North. Further analysis showed that the decline in support for the implementation of school desegregation is not attributable to confusion between questions of the goal of school desegregation and of the use of federal authority; trust in the federal government, although it may contribute to the low absolute level of support for implementation, does not affect the trend (Bobo, 1987).

A gap also exists between support for principles and support for implementation with regard to questions on job opportunities ("equal jobs" and "federal job intervention"), residential desegregation ("residential choice" and "open housing"), and access to public accommodations ("same accommodations" and "accommodations intervention"). None of these pairings [shows] the sharp divergence in trends observed for the questions on schools. In particular, support for the implementation of rights for blacks to freely use hotels and restaurants and to live wherever they choose did increase over time. But the trends were not as strong as those for comparable principle items, and a substantial gap in support remained.

The importance of the distinction between principle and implementation is underscored by differences in the responses to these questions by educational level and region. Schuman and colleagues found that education usually had small or no effects on implementation questions (see also Jackman,

Table 1.1
Trends in Racial Attitudes

	Whites					Blacks			
Type of Question	Question	First and Last Year Asked	Percent Change: Last Minus First Year	Percent Positive at Last Time Asked	Type of Question	Question	First and Last Year Asked	Percent Change: Last Minus First Year	Percent Positive at Last Time Asked
Principle	Same schools	1942/1982	+58	90	Principle	Same schools	1972/1982	0	96
	Equal jobs	1944/1972	+52	97		Residential choice (ISR)	1964/1976	+1	99
	Same transportation	1942/1970	+42	88		Black candidate (Gallup)	1958/1983	+4	96
	Residential choice (NORC)[a]	1963/1982	+32	71		Black candidate (NORC)	1974/1982	0	97
	Residential choice (ISR)	1964/1976	+23	88		Intermarriage	1972/1983	+2	78
	Same accommodations	1963/1970	+15	88		General segregation[b]	1964/1978	+8	35
	Black candidate (Gallup)	1958/1983	+44	81					
	Black candidate (NORC)	1972/1983	+12	85					
	Against intermarriage laws	1963/1982	+28	66					
	Intermarriage	1958/1983	+36	40					
	General segregation[b]	1964/1978	+8	35					
Implementation	Federal job intervention	1964/1974	−2	36	Implementation	Federal job intervention	1964/1974	−10	82
	Open housing	1973/1983	+12	46		Federal school intervention	1964/1978	−22	60

Item	Years	Change	%
Federal school intervention	1964/1978	-17	25
Busing (ISR)	1972/1980	0	9
Busing (NORC)	1972/1983	+6	21
Accommodations intervention	1964/1974	+22	66
Spending on blacks	1973/1983	-1	26
Aid to minorities	1970/1982	-4	18
Social distance			
Few (Gallop)	1958/1980	+20	95
Few (NORC)	1972/1983	+2	95
Half (Gallup)	1958/1980	+26	76
Half (NORC)	1972/1983	0	76
Most (Gallup)	1958/1980	+9	42
Most (NORC)	1972/1983	-6	37
Next door	1958/1978	+30	86
Great numbers	1958/1978	+26	46
Same block	1942/1972	+49	85
Black dinner guest	1963/1982	+26	78
Miscellaneous			
Thermometer rating[c] of blacks	1964/1982	+1	61
Ku Klux Klan rating[d]	1965/1979	-13	71
Intelligence	1942/1968	+30	77
Civil rights push	1964/1980	+6	9
Black push	1963/1982	+18	39

Item	Years	Change	%
Busing (ISR)	1972/1980	+3	49
Busing (NORC)	1972/1983	0	56
Accommodations intervention	1964/1974	+2	91
Spending on blacks	1973/1983	-3	80
Aid to minorities	1970/1982	-29	49
Miscellaneous			
Thermometer rating[c] of blacks	1964/1982	-13	76
Ku Klux Klan[d]	1965/1979	-8	80
Civil rights push	1964/1980	+18	45
Civil rights progress	1964/1976	-28	32

Note: NORC, National Opinion Research Center; ISR, Institute for Social Research.
[a] This item uses a Likert scale response format. The percentages reported involve a combination of "disagree slightly" and "disagree strongly" responses.
[b] The trend for this item is probably affected by a contextual linkage to the federal school intervention implementation item.
[c] The feeling thermometer is a standard question used in the National Election Study. It calls for respondents to rank groups or individuals on a 100-point scale, where 0 indicates very cold feelings, 50 indicates neutral feelings, and 100 indicates very warm feelings.
[d] The rating scale runs from -5 to +5. The figures reported indicate the percentage of people giving "highly unfavorable" ratings of the Ku Klux Klan (scores of -4 or -5).
Sources: Data from Schuman et al. (1985) and Bobo (1987).

Table 1.2

Opposition to School Busing, by Race and Year (in percent)

Race	1972	1974	1975	1976	1977	1978	1982	1983	1985	1986	Change, 1986–1972
Black	45	37	53	48	52	48	44	44	43	38	–7
White	87	85	86	87	87	83	84	79	81	75	–12
Difference: black minus white	–42	–48	–33	–39	–35	–35	–40	–35	–38	–37	

Note: The question wording was as follows: "In general, do you favor or oppose the busing of (Negro/black) and white school children from one district to another?"
Sources: Davis and Smith (1987); data from 1972–1987 General Social Surveys.

1978; Jackman and Muha, 1984). Two exceptions were the open housing question and the accommodations intervention question; as noted above, these were the two implementation questions that showed positive change. In addition, regional differences were usually smaller for questions of implementation than for questions of principle.

But as we observed earlier, attitudes may change if the social context changes. This holds for reactions to issues of policy implementation as well as to matters of principle. Recent reports have indicated that the degree of opposition to school busing among whites has declined (Harris, 1987; Schuman and Bobo, 1988). Our analysis confirms that resistance to school busing is less extreme than in the past. Table 1.2 shows the percentage of blacks and whites expressing opposition to school busing in General Social Surveys between 1972 and 1986. Blacks are always more likely to favor busing than whites, but both groups show a slight overall decline in opposition to school busing. This change occurs in the post-1978 period and to a larger degree among whites.

Table 1.3 shows the percentage of whites opposed to school busing by both region of the country and age. These data indicate that the change among whites occurred mainly in the post-1978 period, with the decline

emerging most clearly in 1985 and 1986. The decline in opposition to school busing is somewhat larger among those in the 18- to 27-year-old age range. Among the youngest age group in both the North and South, more than one-third express support for school busing. The change is also larger in the South than in the North for three of the four age categories. A small tendency for greater opposition to school busing in the South has disappeared.

That these positive changes occur in response to a question that asks about "the busing of black and white school children from one district to another" should be underscored. This question poses one of the stronger versions of busing: it implies busing both blacks and whites and potentially crossing district boundaries. The positive trend may suggest considerable underlying attitude change. In general, it is a well-established finding that the exact wording of questions influences responses; that is, people do not respond to an abstract underlying issue or concept but to a question as posed (Schuman and Kalton, 1985; Turner and Martin, 1984). For example, Schuman and Bobo (1988) found in a 1985 national telephone survey that support for school busing among whites was higher than 40 percent when the question referred to busing blacks to predomi-

Table 1.3

Opposition to School Busing Among Whites, by Region, Age, and Year (in percent)

Region and Age (years)	1972	1974	1975	1976	1977	1978	1982	1983	1985	1986	Change, 1986–1972
Non-South											
18–27	76	76	75	76	80	77	74	66	70	63	−13
28–39	85	88	86	89	83	81	85	77	78	71	−14
40–56	88	84	90	88	86	85	87	82	88	71	−17
57 and over	88	87	87	87	89	85	87	84	87	82	−6
South											
18–27	83	76	74	91	92	82	77	78	71	63	−20
28–39	95	90	85	89	96	87	85	84	74	72	−23
40–56	94	91	92	94	93	93	96	86	89	84	−10
57 and over	97	91	88	91	95	85	86	89	83	77	−20

Notes: The question wording was as follows: "In general, do you favor or oppose the busing of (Negro/black) and white school children from one district to another?" The following are classified as southern states: Alabama, Arkansas, Delaware, District of Columbia, Florida, Georgia, Kentucky, Louisiana, Maryland, Mississippi, North Carolina, Oklahoma, South Carolina, Tennessee, Texas, Virginia, West Virginia.

Sources: Davis and Smith (1987); data from 1972–1987 General Social Surveys.

nantly white schools. That the observed change occurs disproportionately among younger and southern whites is consistent with the claim that actual experience with school desegregation and busing is weakening the previously solid wall of white opposition to this method of desegregating schools.

References

Bobo, Lawrence. 1987. Racial Attitudes and the Status of Black Americans: A Social Psychological View of Change Since the 1940's. Paper prepared for the Committee on the Status of Black Americans, National Research Council, Washington, D.C.

Campbell, Angus. 1971. *White Attitudes Towards Black People.* Ann Arbor, Mich.: Institute for Social Research.

Condran, John G. 1979. Changes in white attitudes towards blacks: 1963–1977. *Public Opinion Quarterly* 43 (Winter):463–476.

Greeley, Andrew M., and Paul B. Sheatsley. 1971. Attitudes towards racial integration. *Scientific American* 225:13–19.

Greeley, Andrew M., and Paul B. Sheatsley. 1974. Attitudes towards racial integration. In Lee Rainwater, ed., *Inequality and Justice.* Chicago: Aldine.

Harris, Louis. 1987. *The Harris Survey.* Orlando, Fla.: The Tribune Media Services, Inc.

Hyman, Herbert H., and Paul Sheatsley. 1956. Attitudes towards desegregation. *Scientific American* 195 (December):35–39.

Hyman, Herbert H., and Paul Sheatsley. 1964. Attitudes towards desegregation. *Scientific American* 211(1) (July):16–23.

Jackman, Mary R. 1978. General and applied tolerance: does education increase commitment to racial integration? *American Journal of Political Science* 22:302–324.

Jackman, Mary R., and Michael J. Muha. 1984. Education and intergroup attitudes: Moral enlightenment, superficial democratic commitment or ideological refinement? *American Sociological Review* 49:751–769.

Myrdal, Gunnar. 1944. *An American Dilemma: The Negro Problem and Modern Democracy.* 2 vols. New York: Harper and Brothers.

Rossi, Peter H., James D. Wright, and Andy B. Anderson. 1983. *Handbook of Survey Research.* Orlando, Fla.: Academic Press.

Schuman, Howard, and Lawrence Bobo. 1988. Survey-based experiments on white racial attitudes toward residential integration. *American Journal of Sociology* 94(2)[September]:273–299.

Schuman, Howard, and Graham Kalton. 1985. Survey methods. In Gordon Lindzey and Elliot Aronson, eds., *Handbook of Social Psychology.* 3d ed. New York: Random House.

Schuman, Howard, Charlotte Steeh, and Lawrence Bobo. 1985. *Racial Attitudes in America: Trends and Interpretations.* Cambridge, Mass.: Harvard University Press.

Seeman, Melvin. 1981. Intergroup relations. Pp. 378–410 in Morris Rosenberg and Ralph H. Turner, eds., *Social Psychology: Sociological Perspectives.* New York: Basic Books.

Smith, A. Wade. 1981. Racial tolerance as a function of group position. *American Sociological Review* 46:558–573.

Taylor, D. Garth, Paul B. Sheatsley, and Andrew M. Greeley. 1978. Attitudes toward racial integration. *Scientific American* 238(6)[June]:42–50.

Turner, Charles F., and Elizabeth Martin, eds. 1984. *Surveying Subjective Phenomena.* 2 vols. Panel on Survey Measurement of Subjective Phenomena, Committee on National Statistics, National Research Council. New York: Russell Sage Foundation.

Jaynes and Williams:

1. Discuss each of the factors that complicates the increase in support that whites hold for racial equality in the United States. Discuss what accounts for the differences between "principle" and "social distance" or "policy" issues with regard to white support for racial equality.

2. Discuss why you think whites tend to hold "convenience equality" beliefs—specifically with regard to social distance scales.

2

Racism Today:
Continuity and Change
in the Post-Civil Rights Era

Howard Winant

In the complex crosscurrents of the post-civil rights era, what is racism? Is it the same old thing or has it changed in response to the changing dynamics of race itself in the post-civil rights era? To answer such questions, to understand the meaning of racism today, to take an informed and politically effective stand in such complex crosscurrents, is no easy matter.

Before we even tackle the matter of racism, we must first develop a working understanding of what we mean by race. This is not so easy either. Today we recognize that the concept of race is problematic, that the meaning of race is socially constructed and politically contested. This is a hard-won recognition, one which has obtained fairly generally only since World War II (Omi and Winant 1994).

But obviously problematizing race is not enough. We must steer between the Scylla of thinking that race is a mere illusion, mere ideology (in the sense of false consciousness) on the one hand, and the Charybdis of thinking that race is something objective and fixed. Both of these positions have their temptations, and by no means only for those who would deny the significance of race. The former position ('race as illusion') is upheld to-

day not only by neo-conservatives but also by radical theorists of race such as Anthony Appiah and Barbara Fields. In the work of these scholars, whatever its other merits, there is little recognition of the autonomy and depth of racialization in the United States. The latter view ('race as objective') is accepted not only by biological determinists and scientific racists, but also by many social scientists (some of them quite progressive), for example William Julius Wilson, Milton Gordon, and Michael Banton. In the work of these analysts, whatever its other merits, there is little recognition of the socially constructed, politically contested meaning of racial categories, of racial identity, of racialized experience.

In contrast to these approaches, Michael Omi and I have proposed the theory of racial formation, which looks at race not only as the subject of struggle and contest at the level of social structure, but also as a contested theme at the level of social signification, of the production of meanings. By the former we mean such issues as the racial dimensions of social stratification and distribution, of institutional arrangements, political systems, laws, etc. By the latter we mean the ways in which race is culturally figured and represented, the manner in which race comes to be meaningful as a descriptor of group or individual identity, social issues, and experience.

We have sought to theorize racial formation as a permanent process in which historically situated projects interact: in the clash and conflict, as well as the accommodation and overlap of these projects, human bodies and consciousness as well as social institutions and structures, are represented and organized. We argue that in any given historical context, racial signification and racial structuration are ineluctably linked. To represent, interpret, or signify upon race, then, to assign meaning to it, is at least implicitly and often explicitly to locate it in social structural terms.

The linkage between culture and structure, which is at the core of the racial formation process, gives racial projects their coherence and unity. Thus, once it is argued that the US is inherently a 'white man's country' (as in certain far-right racial discourses), or that race is a spurious anachronism beneath the notice of the state (as in neo-conservative positions), or that racial difference is a matter of 'self-determination' (as in certain radical racial discourses), the appropriate political orientation, economic and social programmes, etc., follow rather quickly.

The reverse is also true: when organizations, institutions, or state agencies advocate or resist a certain racial policy or practice, when they mobilize politically along racial lines, they necessarily engage in racial signification, at least implicitly and usually explicitly. Thus, when the Supreme Court rules that individualism and meritocracy are the only legitimate criteria for employment decisions or university admissions today, it inevitably and simultaneously represents race as illusory and spurious. Let me give some other examples. Consider the implications when spokespersons for the Aryan Nations or the Church of the Creator (two U.S. fascist groups) propose setting aside areas of the country for 'whites only': in this structural initiative they simultaneously represent race as a natural, invariant, biological difference. On the polar opposite end of the political spectrum, consider what happens when radical democratic organizations, such as the Highlander Center or UNITE—the recently merged needle trades union—engage in community or labor organizing that seeks both to build multiracial organizations and to recognize the relevance of distinct racialized experiences among their constituents. Here too, in this effort to mobilize politically, to change the social structure, they necessarily represent race in terms of decenteredness, flexibility, and the relative permanence of difference, embracing the Du Boisian synthesis of full democracy and racial 'conservation' (Du Bois 1995 [1897]).

The theory of racial formation through racial projects, then, is based on the argument that to represent or signify race necessarily assigns to race a certain social structural location, and that to organize (or attempt to organize) the social structure along racial lines necessarily involves representing racial meanings or signifying race. This emphatically does *not* mean that all representations of race are necessarily racist, or that any assignment (or attempted assignment) of racially-defined groups to a given location in the social structure is necessarily racist. Such a view would pitch us back into the 'race as illusion' error that I have already discussed. Rather, racial formation theory seeks to provide the tools which would allow us to distinguish among various racial projects, thereby allowing us to identify which types of signification, and which forms of social organization, can fairly be characterized as racist. As will be argued, only specific combinations of representation and structuration, only certain types of racial projects, can be considered racist.

Keep this idea of racial formation through racial projects on hold while the discussion is refocused on racism; I shall return to the dynamics of racial formation presently. In what follows I shall first discuss the transformations that have affected the concept of racism since the ambiguous triumph of the civil rights 'revolution' in the mid-1960s. Next, I shall offer an account of contemporary racism which I believe more adequately addresses present conditions. Finally, in a brief conclusion, I offer some thoughts about the changing link between racial formation and racism as the millennium approaches.

Our Concept of Racism Has Deteriorated

The understanding we have of racism, an understanding which was forged in the 1960s, is now severely deficient. A quarter century of sociopolitical struggle has rendered it inadequate to the demands of the present. At the same time, I would hardly wish to argue (in the manner of neo-conservatives) that racism itself has been largely eliminated in the post-civil rights era. But although we are pretty sure that racism continues to exist, indeed flourish, we are less than certain about what it means today.

In fact, since the ambiguous triumph of the civil rights movement in the mid-1960s, clarity about what racism means has been slipping away. The concept entered the lexicon of 'common sense' only in the 1960s. Before that, although the term had surfaced occasionally, the problem of racial injustice and inequality was generally understood in a more limited fashion, as a matter of prejudiced attitudes or bigotry on the one hand, and of discriminatory actions on the other.

Solutions, it was believed, would therefore involve two elements: first, the overcoming of prejudiced attitudes through the achievement of tolerance, the acceptance of 'brotherhood' etc.; and second, the passage of laws which prohibited discrimination with respect to access to public accommodations, jobs, education, etc. Social scientific work tended to focus on the origins of prejudiced attitudes (Adorno et al. 1950; Allport 1954), on the interests served by discrimination (Rose 1948; Becker 1957; Thurow 1969), and on the ways in which prejudice and discrimination combined or conflicted with each other (Merton 1949).

The early civil rights movement explicitly reflected such views. In its espousal of integration and its quest for a 'beloved community' it sought to overcome racial prejudice. In its litigation activities and agitation for civil rights legislation it sought to challenge discriminatory practices.

The later 1960s, however, signalled a sharp break with this vision. The emergence of the slogan 'black power' (and soon after, of 'brown power,' 'red power,' and 'yellow power'), the wave of riots that swept the urban ghettoes from 1964 to 1968, and the founding of radical movement organizations of nationalist and Marxist orientation, all coincided with the recognition that racial inequality and injustice had much deeper roots. They were not simply the product of prejudice, nor was discrimination only a matter of intentionally informed action. Rather, prejudice was an almost unavoidable outcome of patterns of socialization that were 'bred in the bone,' affecting not only whites but even minorities themselves. Discrimination, far from manifesting itself only (or even principally) through individual actions or conscious policies, was a structural feature of U.S. society, a product of centuries of systematic exclusion, exploitation, and also cultural assaults of various types upon racially-defined minorities.

It was this combination of relationships—prejudice, discrimination, and structural inequality (aka 'institutional racism')—which defined the concept of racism at the end of the 1960s. Without a doubt, such a synthesis was an advance over previous conceptions. Its very comprehensiveness was better suited to the rising tide of movement activity and critique of white supremacy. Notably, its emphasis on the structural dimensions of racism allowed it to address the intransigence which racial injustice and inequality continued to exhibit, even after discrimination had supposedly been outlawed and bigoted expression stigmatized.

But such an approach also had clear limitations. As Robert Miles has argued (1989), it tended to 'inflate' the concept of racism to a point at which it lost precision. If the 'institutional' component of racism were so pervasive and deeply rooted, it became difficult to recognize what accomplishments the movement had achieved or what progress civil rights reforms represented. How, under these conditions, could one validate the premises of political action aimed at racial justice and greater substantive social equality? If institutional racism were indeed so ubiquitous, it became difficult to affirm the existence of any democracy at all where race was concerned. The result was a leveling critique which denied any distinction between the Jim Crow era (or even the whole *longue durée* of racism beginning with European conquest and leading through racial slavery and Jim Crow) and the present. Similarly, if the prejudice component of racism were so deeply inbred, it became difficult to account for the apparent racial hybridity and cultural interpretation that characterizes civil society in the United States, as evidenced not only by the shaping of popular mores, values, language and style, for example, but also by the millions of people, white and black (and neither white nor black), who occupy interstitial and ambiguous racial positions. The result of the 'inflation' of the concept of racism was thus a deep pessimism about any efforts to overcome racial barriers: in the workplace, the community, or any other sphere of lived experience. An overly comprehensive view of racism, then, potentially served as a self-fulfilling prophecy.

Yet the alternative view, which surfaced with a vengeance in the 1970s and urged a return to the conception of racism held before the movement's 'radical turn,' was equally inadequate. This was the neo-conservative project, which deliberately restricted its attention to injury done to the individual as opposed to the group, and to advocacy of a 'color-blind' racial policy. Such an approach reduced race to ethnicity, and almost entirely neglected the continuing organization of social inequality and oppression along racial lines. Worse yet, it tended to rationalize racial injustice as a supposedly natural outcome of group attributes in competition (Sowell 1983).

Thus have we arrived at today's dilemmas. In the post-civil rights era U.S. society has undergone a substantial modification of the previously far more rigid lines of exclusion and segregation, permitting real mobility for more favoured sectors (that is, certain class-based segments) of racially-defined minority groups. This period has also witnessed the substantial diversification of the North American population, in the aftermath of the 1965 reform of immigration laws. Panethnic phenomena have increased among Asians, Latinos, and Native Americans, reconstituting the US racial panorama in a multipolar (as opposed to the old bipolar) direction. Racial identity has been problematized (at least somewhat) for whites—a fact which has its dangers but also reflects progress—and the movements to which the black struggle gave initial impetus, notably feminism and gay liberation in their many forms, have developed to the point where a whole range of cross-cutting subjectivities and tensions (as well as new alliances) have been framed.

But the post-civil rights era has also witnessed a significant racial reaction. The racial reaction has rearticulated the demands for equality and justice made by the black movement and its allies in a conservative discourse of individualism, competition and *laissez-faire*. We must recognize that it is this 'new right' discourse which is hegemonic today, and that in these terms racism is rendered invisible and marginalized. It is treated as largely an artifact of the past.

Racism Today

Today, then, the absence of a clear 'common sense' understanding of what racism means has become a significant obstacle to efforts aimed at challenging it. As usual there are different interpretations, different racial projects, in conflict with one another over the very meaning and structure of racism. It is common to find the view, especially among white people (but also among non-whites), that we must somehow get 'beyond' race in order to overcome racism. For example, I often hear in my classes comments such as 'I don't care if someone is black, white, green or purple; a person's just a person to me . . .,' etc. This implies that racism is equivalent to color-consciousness and consequently non-racism must be a lack of color-consciousness. We should recognize that this type of idea, however naive, is a true product of the civil rights era, notably the movement's early, 'liberal' years.

On the other hand, I hear from other students (from my black and brown students particularly, but by no means only from them), that racism is a 'system of power.' This idea implies that only whites have power, and thus only they can be racists. We should also recognize the origins of this idea, which exhibits a different but no less dangerous naïveté—for it is highly problematic to assert that racially-defined minorities are powerless in the contemporary US—in the radicalized later years of the civil rights era.[1]

Given this crisis of meaning, and in the absence of any 'common sense' understanding, does the concept of racism retain any validity? If so, what view of racism should we adopt? Is a more coherent theoretical approach possible? I believe it is.

Recall my discussion of racial formation theory at this point. Let us recognize that, like race, racism has changed over time. It is obvious that the attitudes, practices and institutions of the epochs of slavery, say, or of Jim Crow, no longer exist today. Employing a similar logic, it is reasonable to question whether concepts of racism which were developed in the early days of the post-civil rights era, when the limitations of both moderate reform and militant racial radicalism of various types had not yet been encountered, could possibly remain adequate to explain circumstances and conflicts a quarter-century later.

Racial formation theory also allows us to differentiate between race and racism. The two concepts should not be used interchangeably. Omi and I have argued that race has no fixed meaning, but is constructed and transformed sociohistorically through competing political projects, through the necessary and ineluctable link between the structural and cultural dimensions of race in the United States. This emphasis on projects allows us to refocus our understanding of racism as well, for racism can now be seen as characterizing some, but not all, racial projects.

Today, a racial project can be defined as racist if it creates or reproduces a racially unequal social structure, based on essentialized racial categories; if it essentializes or naturalizes racial identities or significations, based on a racially unequal social structure; or both.

This approach recognizes the importance of locating racism within a fluid and contested history of racially based social structures and discourses. It allows us to recognize that there can be no timeless and absolute standard for what constitutes racism, because social structures undergo reform (and reaction) and discourses are always subject to rearticulation. This definition therefore does not invest the concept of racism with any permanent content, but instead sees racism as a property of certain political projects that link the representation and organization of race—that engage in the 'work' of racial formation. Such an approach focuses on the 'work' essentialism does for domination, and the 'need' domination displays to essentialize the subordinated.[2]

It is also important to distinguish racial awareness from racial essentialism. Attribution of merits or faults, allocation of values or resources, and/or representations of individuals or groups on the basis of racial categories should not be considered racist in and of themselves. Such projects may, in fact, be quite benign. Of course, any of these projects may be considered racist, but only if they meet the criteria I have just outlined: in other words, essentialization and/or subordination must be present.

Consider the following examples. First, a discursive one: the statement 'Today, many Asian Americans are highly entrepreneurial.' Second, a structural one: the organization of an association of, say, black accountants. The first racial project, in my view, signifies or represents a racial category ('Asian Americans'), and locates that representation within the social structure of the contemporary U.S. (in regard to business, class issues, socialization, etc.). It does not, however, essentialize; it is qualified in time ('today') and in respect to overgeneralization ('many').

The second racial project is organizational or social structural, and therefore must engage in racial signification. Black accountants, the organizers might maintain, have certain common experiences and characteristics, can offer each other certain support, etc. The effort to organize such a group is not in and of itself antagonistic to other groups; it does not aim at others' subordination, but only at members' well-being and uplift. So as I have posed them, neither of these racial projects can fairly be labeled racist. Of course, racial representations may be biased or misinterpret their subjects, just as racially-based organizational efforts may be unfair or unjustifiably exclusive. If such were the case, if for instance in our first example the statement in question read 'Asian Americans are naturally entrepreneurial,' this would by my criterion be racist. Similarly, if the effort to organize black accountants had as its rationale the raiding of clients from non-black accountants, it would by my criterion be racist as well.

What if my discursive example cast a particular racially-defined group in a *positive* light, however essentialist?[3] A clear problem here is 'racial lumping.' Apart from the tendency of essentialism on which I have already remarked—viz., the 'work' that it can do in the service of racial hierarchy—here is another, often discussed characteristic of racism: the denial of variety, the tendency to stereotype.

What if my organizational/structural example involved a white group rather than a black one? What if the interests it sought to mobilize (and thereby signify collectively) were privileged, dominant? Obviously, an effort to construct or perpetuate a white accountants' society would be a 'horse of a different color,' so to speak, than an attempt to mobilize black accountants. Today, and still for the foreseeable future, it would embody an exclusivist logic that a black association would not, given ongoing black underrepresentation in the profession; in a word, it would be supremacist, hierarchical.

Proceeding with this standard, to allocate values or resources—let us say, academic scholarships to racially-defined minority students—is not racist, since no essentializing/subordinating standard is at work here. Scholarships are awarded to Rotarians, children of insurance company employees, and residents of the Pittsburgh metropolitan area. Why then should they not also be offered, in particular cases, to blacks or Chicanos or Native Americans? The latter categories are no more suspect than the former ones.[4]

What if scholarships were offered only to whites? Such action *would* be suspect, not on the grounds of essentialism, but on those of domination and subordination, since the logic of such a racial project would be to reproduce an existing racial hierarchy.

Let us take an example that is much on our minds today: the effort to invalidate affirmative action programs on the ground that these constitute 'reverse discrimination.' This project would, I think, be vulnerable to criticism under the criterion of racism that I am developing here. This is because, as we have learned in the post-civil rights era, it is possible to reproduce racial categories even while ostensibly repudiating them. The preservation of racial hierarchy may operate through an essentializing logic that dissembles or operates subtextually:

The scenario . . . reads as follows: when science apologizes and says there is no such thing, all talk of "race" must cease. Hence "race," as a recently emergent, unifying, and forceful sign of difference in the service of the "Other," is held up to scientific ridicule as, ironically, "unscientific." A proudly emergent sense of ethnic diversity *in the service* of the new world arrangements is disparaged by white male science as the most foolish sort of anachronism (Baker 1985, p. 385; emphasis original).

The familiar 'code word' phenomenon, that is, the subtextual signification of race, has much the same effect. Thus the claim, first made in 1896 and recently elevated to nearly hegemonic jurisprudential doctrine, that 'our Constitution is color-blind,' can in fact be understood in two ways. It can mean, as Justice Harlan evidently intended in his ringing dissent in the *Plessy* case (the infamous 1896 Supreme Court decision that accepted the legality of 'separate but equal' racial policies, that is, segregation), and as the early civil rights movement clearly understood it as well, that the power of the state should not be used to enforce invidious racial distinctions. But it can also mean that the power of the state should not be used to uproot those distinctions either. Based on the criteria I have advanced here, I suggest that despite its anti-essentialist appearance, the 'color-blind' denial of the significance of race is, in fact, an essentializing representation of race, an 'erasure' of race, so to speak, which in the present-day United States is generally linked to the perpetuation of racial hierarchy. It is,

then, a form of racism, a type of racist project (Gotanda 1995).

In order to identify a social project as racist using the criterion I have proposed here, one must demonstrate a link between essentializing representations of race and hierarchical social structures. Such links will vary in directness and intensity, and there will inevitably be ambiguous cases. How might such ties between signification and structuration be revealed? Most often pragmatically: through the consequences of a particular policy, argument, or principle (for example, 'our Constitution is colour-blind'). Sometimes we can still see fairly explicit efforts to protect dominant interests, framed in racial terms, from democratizing racial initiatives. For instance: changing to at-large voting systems when minority voters threaten to achieve significant representation. More often, in the post-civil rights era, the hallmarks of racist projects will not be so obvious; they are not explicit any longer.

Nor does this approach rule out racist projects of non-white provenance, for example: melanin theories of racial superiority (Welsing 1991), or the racial ontology of the Nation of Islam with its mad scientist Dr. Yacub. Racism is not necessarily white, though in the nature of things, it is far more often so. It inheres in those political projects that link racial essentialism and racial hierarchy, wherever and however that link is forged.

Racism and Racial Formation

Although we can conclude that racism is not invariably white, we must also recognize that today, as in the past, there is a hegemonic racial project—that of the 'new right'—which in general defends white racial privilege. It employs a particular interpretive schema, a particular logic of racial representation, to justify a hierarchi[c]al racial order in which, albeit more imperfectly than in the past, dark skin still correlates with subordination, and subordinate status often, though not always, is still represented in racial terms.

Furthermore, as I have already noted, a key problem of racism, today as in the past, is its denial, or flattening, of difference *within* the categories it represents in essentialist fashion. Members of racially-defined subordinate groups have for a long time faced practices of exclusion, discrimination, and even of outright extermination. Such groups are thus forced to band together in order to defend their interests (if not, in some instances, their very lives). Following this argument, such 'strategic essentialism' cannot be equated with the essentialism practiced in the service of hierarchical social structures. Nor would it prevent the interrogation of internal group differences, though these are sometimes overridden by the imperative for group 'conservation,' to use Du Bois's term.

Obviously, any abstract concept of racism is severely put to the test by the untidy world of reality. Yet I believe that it is imperative to meet that test at the level of theory, and indeed at the level of practice that ought to flow from theory, just as we must meet the test in our everyday lives.

Today we live in a situation in which 'the old is dying and the new cannot be born,' in which formerly unquestioned white supremacy is now questioned. It is a situation in which an anti-racist counter-tradition in politics and culture has made significant gains. But despite all the changes wrought by this anti-racist project, this radical democratic initiative which derives from the postwar black movement, it has not been possible to overthrow the deeply rooted belief that the United States is still, as the phrase goes, a 'white man's country.' It has not been possible fully to transform the social, political, economic and cultural institutions that afford systematic privileges to whites. It has not been possible to alter the displacement of the burdens and problems of the society (such as unemployment, under-education, poverty and disease) onto the shoulders of non-whites.

Thus, the racial dualism that Du Bois identified nearly one hundred years ago continues to operate. Recall that he characterized the black experience as a conflict between '. . . two souls, two thoughts, two unreconciled strivings' (Du Bois [1903] 1995). This now applies, albeit in very different ways, to everybody. The full exposition of this point is beyond the scope of this essay, but I have discussed it more fully elsewhere (Winant 1994; 1997). Suffice it to say here that, as a society and as individuals, we both uphold and resist white supremacy. We experience both our particular privilege or subalternality, and, to the extent that we can, we resist it.

Confronting racism in such a situation is difficult. It is a moving target, a contested terrain. Inevitably, as a society, as political movements and as individuals, we have to make lots of mistakes; we have to see our action and our thought, our praxis, in pragmatic terms. Because racism changes and develops, because it is simultaneously a vast phenomenon framed by epochal historical developments, and a moment-to-moment experiential reality, we can never expect fully to capture it theoretically. Nor can we expect that it will ever be fully overcome. That does not mean, however, that we are free to desist from trying.

Acknowledgements

Previous versions of this article were presented in the Working Papers Lecture Series of the Afro-American Studies Program at Princeton University, and in the Rockefeller Lecture Series in Comparative American Cultures at Washington State University. Particular thanks to Eduardo Bonilla-Silva, Michele Lamont, Wahneema Lubiano, and Paul Wong, as well as two anonymous readers.

Notes

1. Bob Blauner has argued that the central point distinguishing the two foregoing positions is the centrality afforded to race in one's worldview. For those to whom race is central, racism remains very present. And for those to whom race is less central, racism too is seen as 'a peripheral, nonessential reality' (Blauner 1992).

2. By essentialism I mean a belief in unchanging human characteristics, impervious to social and historical context (Fuss 1989).

3. As several students (of various racial belonging) told me some years ago at Berkeley, they tended to avoid classes with 'too many Asians,' not because of a belief in any inferiority of such potential classmates, but out of competitive anxiety at these students' putative academic superiority: 'Asians drag the grading curve up too high,' one said.

4. A reader has raised the question of whether the provision of scholarships to white students by historically black or Native American colleges, presumably in the interests of diversity, would on these criteria be racist. In my view it would not, but might still suffer from a certain irony in a society such as ours, in which white 'life chances' still exceed black and Native American ones to a significant degree.

References

ADORNO, T. W. *et al.* 1950 *The Authoritarian Personality,* New York: Harper and Bros

ALLPORT, GORDON W. 1954 *The Nature of Prejudice,* Cambridge, MA: Addison-Wesley

BAKER, HOUSTON A., Jr 1986, 'Caliban's triple play,' in Henry Louis Gates, Jr. (ed.), *'Race,' Writing, and Difference,* Chicago, IL: University of Chicago Press

BECKER, GARY 1957 *The Economics of Discrimination,* Chicago: University of Chicago Press

BLAUNER, BOB 1992 'Talking past one another: Black and white languages of race.' *The American Prospect,* vol. 10

DU BOIS, W. E. B. [1897] 'The conservation of races,' in David Levering Lewis (ed.), *W. E. B. Du Bois: A Reader,* New York: Henry Holt, 1995

___ 1903 'Of our spiritual strivings,' in David Levering Lewis (ed.), *W. E. B. Du Bois: A Reader,* New York: Henry Holt, 1995

FUSS, DIANA 1989 *Essentially Speaking: Feminism, Nature, and Difference,* New York: Routledge

GOTANDA, NEIL 1995 'A critique of "Our Constitution is Color-Blind,"' in Kimberlé Crenshaw *et al.* (eds), *Critical Race Theory: The Key Writings That Formed the Movement,* New York: The New Press

MERTON, ROBERT K. 1949 'Discrimination and the American Creed,' in Robert W. MacIver (ed.), *Discrimination and the National Welfare,* New York: Harper and Brothers

MILES, ROBERT 1989 *Racism,* New York: Routledge

OMI, MICHAEL and WINANT, HOWARD 1994 *Racial Formation in the United States: From the 1960s to the 1990s,* 2nd edn, New York: Routledge

ROSE, ARNOLD M. 1948 *The Negro in America,* New York: Harper and Brothers

SOWELL, THOMAS 1983 *The Economics and Politics of Race: An International Perspective,* New York: Quill

THUROW, LESTER 1969 *Poverty and Discrimination,* Washington DC: The Brookings Institution

WELSING, FRANCES CRESS 1991 *The Isis Papers: The Keys to the Colors,* Chicago, IL: Third World Press

WINANT, HOWARD 1994 *Racial Conditions: Politics, Theory, Comparisons,* Minneapolis, MN: University of Minnesota Press

___ 1997 'Racial dualism at century's end,' in Wahneema Lubiano (ed.), *The House That Race Built,* New York: Random House

Winant:

1. Winant notes that racism is socially constructed and politically contested. Discuss what he means by this.

2. Discuss the two positions of race, that it is subjective and objective. What is positive and negative about understanding race in these two ways? How does Winant's position differ from these other two understandings?

3

The New Face of Race:
The Metamorphosis of Racism
in the Post-Civil Rights Era United States

Amy E. Ansell

In recent years, there has emerged a claim from various quarters that we are living in a postracist society. Academics celebrate the end of racism, journalists and political pundits laud the emergence of the black middle class as evidence that racism is no longer a barrier to socioeconomic advancement, and so-called angry white males bemoan what they perceive to be their new victim status in a racial spoils system that disfavors them. When confronted with clear evidence suggesting the persistence of racial inequality, adherents of the postracism consensus attribute continuing patterns of black disadvantage to the failings or pathologies of black people/culture or, more troubling yet, assert that such inequalities are simply a reflection of natural racial differences.

But the United States is far from a postracist society; rather, it is a society in which the form and operation of racism has been transformed. The aim of this essay is to chart the ways in which racism has metamorphosed in the post-civil rights era, with a particular focus on the critical role that new players on the right wing of the political spectrum (what is referred to throughout as the "new right") have played in the reorganiza-

tion of key elements of right-wing racial discourse. An understanding of these new forms of racial discourse is essential if those concerned about the growth of racism and right-wing power are to more effectively intervene in contemporary debates about controversial issues related to affirmative action, immigration, multiculturalism, welfare, and traditional/family values.

E-Racing Race

There can be little serious doubt that there is much that is new in the politics of race and racism in the contemporary United States. More traditional notions of race and racism, dependent as they were on notions of biological hierarchies of inferiority and superiority, are today largely in disrepute. The explicit rejection of equal opportunity and civil rights for people of color is now virtually an absent political discourse except at the very fringes of national political debate. Even the militia movements and the likes of David Duke, former Grand Wizard of the Ku Klux Klan, avoid overt race-baiting in favor of a more sanitized and coded challenge to the role of government in mandating racial equality.

The fact that our understanding of race and racism is fluid and ever-changing should not come as a surprise to those who have developed even the least bit of a sociological imagination. Shifts in language about race and racism reflect the deeper sociological truth that race is not an essence, not something fixed outside of history, but rather, in the words of Michael Omi and Howard Winant (1986), "an unstable and 'decentered' complex of social meanings constantly being transformed by political struggle" (p. 55). Throughout history, racial ideologies have gone through important transformations, both in terms of their internal form and content and in terms of the role they play in the policy formation process.

The form that racism has taken in the present historical context has been labeled alternatively as the "new racism" (Ansell 1997; Barker 1982), "cultural racism" (Seidel 1986), "differentialist racism" (Taguieff 1990), "neo-racism" or "post-racism" (Balibar and Wallerstein 1991), "symbolic racism" (Dovidio and Gaertner 1986; Sears 1988), "modern racism" (McConahay 1986), "smiling racism" (Wilkins 1984), and even "anti-anti-racism" (Murray 1986). Four features of contemporary racial ideology can be identified that justify considering it a departure from racist ideologies of the past. These features are (1) a sanitized, coded language about race that adheres to more than it departs from generally accepted liberal principles and values, mobilized for illiberal ends; (2) avid disavowals of racist prejudice and intent; (3) rhetorical circumvention of classical antiracist discourse; and (4) a shift from a focus on race and biological relations of inequality to a concern for cultural differentiation and national identity.

Racialized political language is today much more sanitized and indirect when compared to racial ideologies of the past, and new right racial discourse very much reflects this trend. Racial discourse is, for the most part, no longer mean-spirited or derogatory in nature. In fact, the very category "race" is intentionally avoided so the contemporary right can distance itself from the racial extremism of the past. Code words revolving around ostensibly nonracial social categories—such as "welfare" and "crime"—have been mobilized to exploit the racial anxieties of white Americans without recourse to an explicitly racial discourse. In this way, the racial dimension of a range of social issues is effectively conveyed in an implicit racial subtext, without attacking the racial gains of previous decades directly. As is demonstrated subsequently, democratic discourse and illiberal effects are not mutually exclusive categories: The two can coexist symbiotically in racial discourse that denies that it is about race at all.

New rightists are keenly aware of the charges of racism commonly attributed to previous right-wing movements and consistently and proactively respond by insisting that their views do not represent racism but realism. The apparently benign nature and sanitary coding of their language superficially supports their claim of support for "true" "nonracism." Racism is understood by new rightists as an irrational attitude of racial prejudice held by the individual and, as such, condemned. Whether this condemnation is genuine is impossible to judge, and beside the point. The intentions of the speaker are less important to analyze than the effects of the speech, that is, the way in which the contradictory nature of the new forms of racialized political language both renders charges of racism difficult to sustain and provides ample scope for those supporters who wish to discover an implicit racist message.

The new forms of racialized political discourse work by circumventing classical antiracist discourse and appropriating it for the right. Popular civil rights movement slogans related to colorblindness and the necessity of judging persons by the "content of their character" and not the color of their skins have been co-opted by the right as part of its effort to identify its vision of society as the true legacy of the civil rights movement against those who abuse it. It is a circumvention that rests on the new right's assertion that antiracist programs themselves are largely to blame for the continued oppression of black people, as well as the persistence and even intensification of racial animosities. Hostility is here shifted away from people of color themselves, as in conventional forms of racism, to the activities of antiracist bureaucrats. In this sense, the new racism is in some ways more appropriately labeled "anti-anti-racism" (Murray 1986).

The fourth and final feature that justifies the characterization of new right racial discourse as "new" is the substitution of race with the ostensibly nonracial categories of culture and nation. This trend is particularly marked in studies of racial discourse in Europe, as explicit defenses of racial domination based on assumed biological hierarchies of inferiority/superiority have given way to the more benign notions of cultural difference and national identity (Barker 1982; Taguieff 1990; Wetherell and Potter 1992). For example, European anti-immigrant sentiment no longer relies on justifying the lack of civil/political rights of the black immigrant as it does on legitimating the "natural" desire of (white) Europe to remain "itself," to preserve the homogeneity of the nation's "way of life," and to exclude those who undermine the shared sense of customs, history, and language that constitutes national identity. This shift from race to culture is also evident in U.S. racial discourse, most often in the vein of debates over the so-called culture of poverty and the underclass. According to underclass warriors, the fatal flaws of people of color lie not in their genes, as asserted in traditional forms of prejudice, but rather in their antisocial behavior, pathological family structures, or dysfunctional value systems. Such a shift from genes to culture or nation is not only more rhetorically acceptable in the sanitized post-civil rights political culture; it

also meaningfully elides the operation of power and domination in a way that justifies the pursuit of ever more brutal blame-the-victim strategies and illiberal policy initiatives.

Together, these four innovations in racial discourse render conventional antiracist politics problematic. The more sanitized forms of racial discourse and the circumvention of classic antiracist themes make charges of racism difficult to sustain, whereas definitions of racism linked to essentialist (or biologically bound) doctrines are incapable of challenging the new culturalist forms of racism championed by the new right (whereas, ironically, many factions of antiracists do operate on the basis of essentialist claims; Smith 1994). In this respect, analysis of the new forms of racialized political language demands that we rethink the very concept of racism and do so with a keen awareness of the connection between the newness of the doctrines articulated by the new right and the novelty of the historical and sociopolitical context which has given them purchase.

Racism without Racists

Tackling the issue of racism head-on is crucial for a project of this kind, although much of the literature on the subject of race and the right has managed to avoid doing so. Indeed, we have seen what is new about new right racial discourse, but the question that remains is whether these new features of racialized political language in fact constitute racism. Have the forms of racial discourse been modified to such a degree that they no longer deserve the label racism? Is what we are seeing a new racism without race or racists, or simply new forms of racialized political language that are not racist in form and content but nevertheless carry the potential of tapping into a latent popular and even state racism?

These questions are more complex than they first appear and surely will be the subject of continuing debate—a useful debate, however, because the conventional definition of prejudice + power = racism is a product of the 1960s and now quite outdated. The goal of defining racism provides an opportunity to think through all sorts of analytic difficulties: Is it possible to define a political project as racist when participants deny it and speak the language of antiracism? Is it possible to define a political project as racist when the language is in accord with mainstream liberal values of tolerance and freedom? Is it possible to define a political project as racist when the language praises difference and the political practice includes various people and communities of color? In short, what does it mean to characterize a political project or ideology as racist?

For reasons of space, I attempt to simplify the matter by drawing a distinction between what I label the *restrictive* and the *dominance* approach to the study of racism and the right. Supporters of a restrictive conception of racism would take seriously new right disavowals of racism and point out that race is not even an explicit or primary concern for the new right movement as a whole.[1] New rightists themselves would certainly challenge claims that their movement is racist and would reserve the term instead for those political projects (such as black nationalism) or policies (such as affirmative action) that employ race either to discriminate against or give advantage to an individual on the basis of the color of his or her skin. However, the main contention of this restrictive conception is that racism must refer to a content with specific criteria so as not to become so broadly applied that its critical edge is blunted. This is the view of Omi and Winant (1986) in *Racial Formation in the United States.* Having evaded the issue of racism in the first edition, the authors attempt in the second to explain what it means to characterize a political project as racist by offering the following advice: "A racial project can be defined as racist if and only if it creates or repro-duces structures of domination based on essentialist categories of race" (Omi and Winant 1986:71).

By this standard, the new right's racial project is clearly not racist. Omi and Winant seem more comfortable in arguing that the current hegemonic racial project is about the retreat of social policy from any practical commitment to racial justice and the manipulation of white racial anxiety and resentment toward alleged "special treatment" of people of color. Although not racist because it does not rely on essentialist doctrines, this hegemonic racial project, they argue, nevertheless "exhibits an unabashed structural racism all the more brazen because at the ideological or signification level, it adheres to a principle of 'treating everyone alike'" (Omi and Winant 1986:75). Other works on race and the right influenced by the code word approach, such as *Chain Reaction* by Thomas and Mary Edsall (1991), also implicitly advocate a restrictive definition of racism by avoiding use of the term racism and instead focusing on the manner in which conservative right-wing politicians have mobilized the racial anxieties of the public for partisan and electoral ends. Writing in a comparative vein, Stephen Small (1994) argued that the right's development of more sophisticated forms of racialized political language and activity certainly contributes to racialized hostility but is not best described as racism. True, politicians fan the flames of popular racism that already exists independently "out there," but this political use of racism is quite distinct from arguing that the race-neutral political discourse of the new right is itself racist.

The restrictive conception of racism has merit in the sense that it is anti-expansionist, that is, by linking racism with a particular content, the term retains its critical edge and so avoids the leveling effects of those who, as a function of focusing on structural outcomes, either ignore the study of meaning and discourse altogether or unwittingly conflate racism with mainstream meritocratic, liberal ideology. There can be no racism without race, according to the restrictive conception, for this would obscure the real qualitative differences between the racist discourse of the political right during the Jim Crow era, for example, and the colorblind discourse of today's conservatives.

Those who advocate a dominance approach to the study of racism, as I do subsequently, object to the restrictive conception's focus on the content of new right discourse. Of course, it is important to study the ways in which the content of racial discourse has changed over time, but such a task is of limited value if we recognize the degree to which the changed content nevertheless serves to justify the same old exclusionary practices, albeit in a new form. Today more than ever it is imperative to explore the connections between race-neutral discursive practices and the maintenance of institutional relations of racial domination. If the changed content of racialized political language and the new right's avid disavowals of racist intent blind us to the dynamism of racism and the variety of discursive garbs in which it can appear, we will unwittingly abandon the study of the cultural and ideological (as opposed to the structural) dimensions of racism, except in its most exceptional forms, and so effectively absolve today's conservatives from blame for increasing racial inequality, prejudice, and violence, as Wetherell and Potter (1992) noted:

Given this flexibility of the enemy, and the way the debates move on, it seems sensible not to commit oneself to one exclusive characterization of racist claims. There is a danger of being silenced when racist discourse continues to oppress but no longer meets the main characteristics of social scientific definitions of racism. (P. 72)

The dominance approach is grounded in a broader approach to the study of ideology that emphasizes not the false content of the ideas but rather the process by which meaning is mobilized in the service of power (Thompson 1990). With this compass of power in hand, it is possible to define racism in a way that avoids the pitfalls of the restrictive approach. According to the dominance approach, a discourse is racist to the extent that it establishes, justifies, and/or sustains practices that maintain systematically asymmetrical relations of racial domination. In this conception, there is no need to try to specify the propositional claims of ideology in advance. Most importantly, it allows for the operation of racist discourse without the category "race." The dominance approach locates the problem of racism not within the prejudiced mentalities of individuals but rather within the competing cultural frames and rhetorical resources available in a liberal society for articulating notions of the public good. Such an insight creates an analytic space for studying the ways in which the rhetoric of colorblindness and equal opportunity—for example, lacking anti-black affect—nevertheless replaces the ideological function of old-fashioned racism—the organization and defense of white privilege.

The dominance approach provides a way to overcome what David Wellman (1993) identified as a theoretical bifurcation in sociological studies of race and racism. In the updated introduction to the second edition of *Portraits of White Racism,* Wellman usefully summarized the literature as falling roughly into two camps: the *structuralist* camp, which explains the organization of racial privilege as a function of social location and economic organization, eschewing any concept of white racism; and the *ideological* path, which corrects the structuralist's neglect of the centrality of race by focusing on processes of racial signification and processes of racialization, but to the deficit of an understanding of the structural organization of racial advantage. Neither approach, Wellman quite rightly pointed out, is up to the task of understanding the new forms in which racism now appears. Sociological studies of race and racism must aim to overcome this theoretical divide between structural and ideological accounts and, within one conceptual approach, seek to understand the link between cultural codes, meaning systems, and processes of signification and the establishment and maintenance of existing relations of racial domination. It is with this object in mind that I now turn to a critical discourse analysis of the new racism of the new right in the United States.

New Right Racial Discourse: A Critical Analysis

Defining *racism* as a dynamic sociohistorical symbol rather than a static set of prejudices implies the need to examine the internal forms of new right racial ideology via critical discourse analysis. My research agenda has been to identify the primary assumptions—or what I label "key categories of meaning"—that render coherent new right ideas on race. Toward this end, I collected hundreds of direct-mail letters, research papers, newspaper articles, and policy statements produced by the new right. Interviews with key new right personalities also were conducted. The key categories of racial meaning identified at the core of the new racism of the new right in the United States are colorblindness, equality, individualism, the "American way of life," and "reverse racism."

The most overarching category identified is that of colorblindness. The notion of colorblindness implies the belief that government should disregard race as a factor when determining policy, a position taken by Charles Murray, neoconservative author of *Losing Ground* and, most recently, coauthor of (1984) *The Bell Curve:*

My proposal for dealing with the racial issue . . . is to repeal every bit of legislation and reverse every court decision that in any way requires, recommends, or awards differential treatment accord-

ing to race. . . . We may argue about the appropriate limits of government intervention in trying to enforce the ideal, but at least it should be possible to identify the ideal: Race is not a morally admissible reason for treating one person differently from another. Period. (P. 223)

The Director of the Free Congress Foundation, Paul Weyrich (1991), commented on the 1991 Civil Rights Act:

The time is right to seize the initiative and chart a new course for the future. That course should be a bold policy agenda of opportunity based on a foundation of nondiscrimination. America must say no once and for all to the notion that race is a legitimate basis for decisions in employment, government benefits, housing, education and the like. Discrimination on the basis of race is immoral, and if it is morally wrong, it cannot be politically right. (P. 35)

The colorblind approach rests on the argument that in order for racial discrimination and inequality to be eliminated, it is necessary that government policy treat individuals qua individuals, that is, on the "content of their character," not the color of their skin. This means that, in formulating policy, rewards must be based on personal merit—and penalties according to the lack of it—irrespective of the individual's race. The implicit assumption of the colorblind approach is that racism is the product of individual prejudice. It follows from such an attitudinal definition that to combat racism, government need only guarantee individual equality of opportunity.

The colorblind approach is conceived by the new right as the opposite of color consciousness. The color-conscious approach shares the colorblind vision of the good society wherein racial differences will be of no significance or consequence, but it differs over the question of the means to achieve such a society. For the advocate of color-conscious policies, it is necessary to pay attention to race as a means of eradicating it as a differentiating factor, that is, only when policies are pursued that positively aid subordinated racial groups in achieving parity with their white counterparts will the material basis for the perception of racial difference—a perception that itself helps to maintain the system of racial inequality—be eliminated. Thus, rather than being based on the absence of the ability to see color, the color-conscious approach emphasizes presence—that is, the ability to view an individual as part of a racial group. Only with such an ability, argues the advocate of color-conscious remedies, is it possible to address compelling social needs (i.e., the elimination of racial inequality).

The appropriation of colorblind discourse is ironic, indeed. Although the undeniable intention of the colorblind demand in the decades prior to the civil rights era was to eliminate the institutional and legal barriers to racial inclusion, the function of that colorblind demand in recent decades is arguably to put at least some of those obstacles back in place. This is the import of the new right insistence that the government's commitment to pursue equality for subordinate racial groups has gone too far in making real this commitment via the pursuit of equal results or statistical parity. True to the spirit of the new racism, the rhetorical tool of anti-discrimination, absent anti-black sentiment or prejudice, allows new rightists to oppose key items on the black agenda and to adhere to dominant constitutional principles and cultural codes.

Closely linked to the key category of colorblindness is that of equality. New rightists in the United States make what they consider to be a crucial distinction between contending interpretations of the concept. The need for government to equalize individual opportunities for all is affirmed, yet so-called preferential treatment for blacks is opposed. A distinction is thus drawn between *equal treatment* defined in terms of individual opportunity and *equal outcome* defined in terms of group rights for black people.

This distinction forms the basis of the position elaborated by the Heritage Foundation in its 1981 publication titled *Mandate For Leadership: Policy Management in a Conservative Administration* (Heatherly and Pines 1980). In this document, an argument is put forward that it is correct for government to seek to protect the civil rights of black people as legislated in Title VII of the 1964 Civil Rights Act, yet it is misguided for it to strive for racial parity via the redistribution of economic, political, and/or educational resources as mandated by the 1965 Executive Order 11246 (i.e., affirmative action). New rightists insist that the duty of government is to remove the barriers obstructing the road to racial equality, not guarantee that racial equality be achieved in fact. As Charles Murray (1984) quipped, "Billions for equal opportunity, not one cent for equal outcome" (p. 233).

New rightists believe in a society in which individuals rise and fall in the social hierarchy on the basis of individual merit. Indeed, the acceptance of inequality as a social inevitability, even a social good, is a definitive hallmark of the right wing. Irving Kristol (1977), another leading neoconservative social critic and editor of *The Public Interest,* warned, "The kind of liberal egalitarianism so casually popular today will, if it is permitted to gather momentum, surely destroy the liberal society" (p. 42). In *The Bell Curve,* Herrnstein and Murray (as quoted in Wellman 1996) wrote, "Affirmative action, in education and the workplace alike, is leaking poison into the American soul. . . . It is time for America once again to try living with inequality, as life is lived" (p. 1).

It is from this wider perspective that the new right opposes affirmative action guidelines that impose quotas, goals, or timetables, and that thereby deem underuse or underrepresentation sufficient proof of discrimination. The point of such guidelines is to ensure effort on the part of employers, but new rightists charge that such guidelines run counter to the ideal of equal protection. According to Tom Wood (as quoted in *The American Experiment* 1995), head of the California Association of Scholars and co-architect of the California Civil Rights Initiative, "Affirmative action fundamentally violates the principle that everyone deserves equal protection under the law without regard to membership in any group" (p. 8).

In the last few years, the attempt to circumvent the meaning of liberal egalitarianism has given way to a frontal assault on the very notion that equality should be an aim of public policy, thus exposing the morbid underside of the new right's defense of equal opportunity. The publication of *The Bell Curve* by Richard Herrnstein and Charles Murray is only the most extreme example of the argument that intellectuals and policymakers have overlooked the role intelligence plays in determining wealth, poverty, and social status. Although the so-called dependency culture previously served as the ideological articulator of the conservative assault on the welfare state and its associated democratic values, now it is the alleged genetically constituted intelligence deficit of the black and Hispanic underclass that is justifying more aggressive policies of benign neglect. Evoking what he calls a "wise ethnocentrism," Murray (as quoted in Morganthau 1994) cheerily imagined "a world in which the glorious hodgepodge of inequalities of ethnic groups . . . can be not only accepted but celebrated" (p. 50).

Although conservatives like Ronald Reagan and Barry Goldwater opposed the 1964 Civil Rights Act on the ground that it trampled individual rights, today's new right opposes liberal race equality policies with the same argument. The new right interprets civil rights legislation as granting rights to individuals and not social categories. Indeed, within the individualistic logic of the American Constitution, such an interpretation makes perfect sense. The corollary to the new right insistence that individual citizens (not groups) possess rights is that individuals should be judged on the basis of merit and not group membership, as explained by Carl Cohen (1979), Professor of Philosophy at the University of Michigan:

Rights do not and cannot inhere in skin-color groups. Individuals have rights, not races. It is true, of course, that many persons have been cruelly deprived of rights simply because of their blackness. Whatever the remedy all such persons deserve, it is deserved by those injured and because of their injury; Nothing is deserved because of the color of one's skin. (P. 44)

Ironically, it is the new right that has succeeded in presenting itself as heir to Martin Luther King's call that society judge an individual by the content of his character, not the color of his or her skin, as seen by quota critic Frederick Lynch (1990), author of *Invisible Victims: White Males and the Crisis of Affirmative Action:*

The academic and intellectual communities which once embraced Martin Luther King's call to judge an individual by the content of his character, not the color of his skin, now do precisely the opposite. They bow reverentially to the gods of tribalism. (P. 44)

This is the central thesis of the national bestseller written by Shelby Steele (1990) titled *The Content of Our Character*. Steele, a prominent black neoconservative, wrote, "Race must not be a source of advantage or disadvantage for anyone" (p. 17).

New rightists urge that we stop looking to white racism as an explanation for black poverty and instead focus on the behavior and attitudes of black people themselves. Walter E. Williams (1980), a black neoconservative and Hoover Institution scholar, wrote, "Somebody should tell the emperor that he has no clothes on. For years now, black 'leaders' have been pretending that all the problems of black people can be attributed to white racism" (p. 3). In *The End of Racism*, Dinesh D'Souza (1995) goes one step further by arguing that black deviancy perpetuates what he regards as a rational form of white racism.

Nothing strengthens racism in this country more than the behavior of the African American underclass which flagrantly violates and scandalizes basic codes of responsibility and civility. . . . If blacks as a group can show that they are capable of performing competitively in schools and the workforce, and exercising both the rights and responsibilities of American citizenship, then racism will be deprived of its foundation in experience. (P. 268)

In the context of the failure of black self-development, D'Souza (1995) argued, "The prejudice is warranted. . . . A bigot is simply a sociologist without credentials" (p. 268).

Although it is in all ways valid (and certainly not racist) to call attention to manifest patterns emerging in poor communities of color, such as low educational achievement or rising crime rates, new rightists of all stripes do so without relating such patterns to material circumstances, the objective opportunity structure, or the continued reality of institutional racism. In this way, through the symbolic construction of individual blame and responsibility, the key category of individualism enables the new right to oppose affirmative action and other items on the black agenda without appearing to be mean-spirited racists. Relations of class and racial inequality are thereby legitimated at the same time as the pursuit of larger, more structurally oriented political solutions are foreclosed. In all of this, the new right affirms its conviction that color-conscious antiracist initiatives run counter to individual freedom and thus counter to the "American way of life."

Individualism coexists in new right ideology with the apparently contradictory category of the American way of life. In other words, not only does the new right portray society as an aggregate of isolated individuals (as in the neoliberal category of individualism) but also as a social whole that requires social order, authority, and the viability of traditional units such as the family, neighborhood organizations, and ethnic communities. Such concerns form the heart of the neoconservative category of the American way of life.

In the recent past, new right discourse regarding national values has tended to focus less on the invasion of outsiders, as in European right-wing anti-immigration discourse, and more on the domestic threat posed by progressive educators and liberal "new class" bureaucrats. Indeed, American new right discourse on the "enemy within" has been most successful in the arena of education, specifically involving the alleged subversive intentions of liberal educators with concern to such controversial issues as school busing, "political correctness," school textbooks, multiculturalism, and affirmative action admission policies. The new right's campaign against political correctness (PC) in the late 1980s and early 1990s is especially revealing of the link between the myriad educational campaigns in which the new right is involved and the politics of the new racism. According to anti-PC ideologues, it is not racism (or sexism) that is the real threat to tolerance and freedom on campus, but rather the creed of political correctness itself. On the one hand, political correctness is presented as being totalitarian in character. In an article denouncing multicultural education as a form of political correctness, neoconservative author Irving Kristol (1991) asserted, "Multiculturalism is as much a 'war against the West' as Nazism and Stalinism ever were" (p. 15). On the other hand, political correctness is presented as being a tool of the revolutionary left, as seen in the writing of Walter Lammi

(1991), National Association of Scholars member:

According to the theorists of curriculum change, the real purpose of education for difference is not academic success but "empowerment." Empowerment means learning how to struggle relentlessly against the oppression of the "dominant culture," in other words, Western civilization, capitalism, and almost every aspect of mainstream American culture and politics. (P. 37)

Lammi concluded with a plea of tolerance for the people of the West, reminding his readers that tolerance means accepting people of all cultures. Armed with this double move, the symbolic construction of the PC enemy has allowed new rightists to erode progressive antiracist gains in the sphere of higher education while speaking in the name of tolerance and free speech.

Interjecting itself into the middle of the culture wars in the mid-1990s is what could be regarded as a shift from the project of eroding liberal policies such as multiculturalism in the name of constitutional principles of fairness to a more bold defense against challenge of the dominant (white) culture. Signaling a convergence of sorts with European new right discourse about the "alien wedge," new rightists in the United States are beginning to address the conflation of race and nation head-on, even to celebrate it. In the policy arena of multiculturalism, new rightists no longer simply attack liberal educators as enemies of tolerance but rather assail the very assumption that all cultures are equal, all the while holding up the ideal of white culture as the standard by which all others are judged, as seen in *The End of Racism* by D'Souza (as quoted in Walker 1995):

The pathologies of black culture suggest that the racists were right all along. . . . What blacks need to do is to act white . . . to abandon idiotic back-to-Africa schemes and embrace mainstream cultural norms so that they can effectively compete with other groups. (P. 9)

Indeed, the new right is engaged in an attempt to reconstruct white as a nonracist cultural identity.

A constituent element of this new narrative of whiteness is a fresh boldness on the part of a certain faction of the new right coalition to take on the issue of immigration. The paleo-conservative faction of the new right coalition in particular is demonstrating a new willingness to introduce into the public debate the question of the racial and ethnic composition of the United States. A number of paleo-conservative intellectuals—most notably John O'Sullivan (editor of *National Review*) and Peter Brimelow (senior editor of *Forbes*)—have begun to lay the bases for a new ideological war that transcends conservative policy proposals to combat illegal immigration and instead challenges the heart of the national creed of America as a nation of immigrants. Sounding suspiciously similar to right-wing populists in Europe, such paleo-conservatives warn that, in the context of census projections that the majority of the U.S. population will become "nonwhite" by the year 2050, current high levels of black and Hispanic immigration will drastically alter the U.S. national identity and, in fact, lead the United States down the road to national suicide (Brimelow 1995). In warning against this "alien nation," Brimelow and others advocate a new willingness to embrace an identity defined in explicitly racial and ethnic terms.

Despite this attempt on the part of paleo-conservatives to bridge the new/far right divide, support for anti-immigrant initiatives such as Proposition 187 (successfully passed on the 1994 ballot in California) remains a minority perspective in the new right coalition as a whole. Demonstrating the continuing tension between those new rightists concerned with liberal free market policies and limited government and those who advocate cultural conservatism and a racial-nationalist agenda, deep internal divisions within the new right coalition over the issue of immigration signal a likely strategy of evasion in the near future. This means that the enemies of the "American way of life" will probably continue to be "illegals" who break the law and the impersonal liberal social policies such as welfare that destroy the fabric of society, and the racially coded symbol of the black and/or Hispanic immigrant will remain subtextual, there for those who wish to discover it.

The final key category of meaning identified within American new right discourse is what is alternatively identified as "affirmative racism," "reverse discrimination," "reverse racism," or "affirmative discrimination" (Glazer 1975; Murray 1984; Allen 1989; Cohen 1986:24–39). The argument that antiracist initiatives constitute a new form of racism—that is, against white people—is especially prevalent in neoconservative discourse on the subject of affirmative action.

In making the argument that antiracist policies discriminate against white people, neoconservatives play on the central contradiction that although such policies are social in conception (in that they are geared to address a compelling social need), they are necessarily individual at the point of implementation. This is a real contradiction that deserves serious attention. The neoconservative critique of affirmative action (and other policies) cannot therefore be convincingly written off as simply a code word or semantic strategy to hide alleged racist intent. Neoconservative opposition to affirmative action as a form of reverse racism is, in fact, a logical culmination of the set of key categories of meaning outlined previously.

According to new rightists, positive action for people of color beyond the guarantee of individual equality of opportunity (1) discriminates against the (white) majority and so constitutes "reverse racism"; (2) creates a special class of people protected by the law and so makes black citizens more equal than others; (3) harms the very groups that it sets out to help; (4) perpetuates, rather than diffuses, racial conflict and polarization; and (5) fuels the tyranny of the new class of government bureaucrats.

At issue is the question of the legitimate means to redress racial inequality. Armed with the set of assumptions previously discussed, new rightists deem racial discrimination (defined in an individualistic rather than institutional manner) as a thing of the past, that is, as eradicated by the Civil Rights Act of 1964. It follows from this assumption that the only legitimate means for the redress of inequality in a liberal society is to ensure the individual right to compete in a "fair" system. The demand for more than this in the form of positive action is understood by new rightists as being not about the elimination of institutional racism but about power—about the power of (black) special interests as against those of whites or universal interests.

In breaking with the principle of color-blindness, so the argument goes, color-conscious policies create in their wake new victims of racial injustice. According to new right ideologues, affirmative discrimination is tantamount to saying "no whites or males need apply." In making such an argument, quota critics are exploiting very powerful sentiments. Indeed, social scientific evidence suggests that there is a growing sentiment on the part of relevant social groups that the white male is being treated unfairly at the hands of women and people of color—that is, that the men are in fact the new victims of discrimination.[2] Such symbolic construction of victimhood on the part of white males and the blatant hypocrisy it evokes was captured in an editorial cartoon published in June 1995 following a series of Supreme Court decisions limiting affirmative action. The cartoon showed a white man bounding down the steps of the Supreme Court shouting "Free at last. Free at last. Thank God almighty, free at last" (Carr 1995:5).

In advancing the claim that white males are the new victims of reverse racism, the new right is not simply disguising racist attitudes now in disrepute but rather addressing the important question of the meaning of equal protection of the law in a multiracial society. New rightists answer this question in a way that makes symmetrical and ahistorical that which is profoundly asymmetrical and historical—relations of racial dominance—so that the politics of antiracism is equated with the politics of the old racism (i.e., against people of color). For example, in an article appearing in *Conservative Digest* titled "The New Racism Is the Old Power Grab," William Allen (1989) equated the racism of Jim Crow with that of affirmative action and concluded, "The racism of racial preference remains the same old racism, whether it places American whites at the top of the scale, or at the bottom" (p. 17).

The new right's brand of anti-anti-racism has allowed conservatives to claim moral authority on the subject of civil rights and to bash the Democrats as racist because they are race-conscious. For example, Rush Limbaugh (1994) taints the Democrats as bigots for opposing the California Civil Rights Initiative (or Proposition 209 as it was labeled on the 1996 California ballot):

This is such a great thing because it points out the truth here about who's racist and who's not, who's bigoted and who's not. And guess who it is that's sweating this out, guess who it is that's biting their nails? . . . It's Democrats. . . . What are we going to call them? Bigots. They will be bigots. The people who oppose ending discrimination.

The symbolic construction of the key category of meaning of reverse racism allows new rightists to deny the systemic and continued reality of racism in American society by directing attention to both the (alleged) new victims of reverse racism (i.e., white males) and the new enemies of racial equality (i.e., the antiracist new class). In so doing, new

rightists present themselves as the true champions of equality and individual liberty, and they present the set of policy proposals that they advocate as true "nonracism."

Conclusion

As this essay has demonstrated, racial ideology is less explicit today than it was in the past and is submerged beneath a broader range of issues. Most important, racial ideology today has less to do with the articulation of a set of prejudiced attitudes, coded or not, than with the rearticulation of very general philosophical tenets long found in the American liberal tradition. The new racism is not so much an aberration from prevailing ideologies or the result of the infiltration of individuals with racist ideas aligned with the far right than a modified variant of widespread and generally accepted beliefs already in circulation in U.S. society and politics. Identification of the new racism therefore need not entail a search for the bizarre, the meanspirited, or the irrational. Quite the contrary, as this essay has revealed, the most basic and apparently common sense underlying cultural and political assumptions has become a key stake of symbolic conflict.

The new racism enables new rightists and their supporters to justify the benefits that they historically have derived, and continue to derive, from institutional relations of racial inequality without significantly appearing as mean-spirited racists. It allows them to reconcile their commitment to an idealized version of a liberal-democratic society with their fear of the challenge to their socioeconomic and cultural position posed by a militant "underclass," one that is profoundly racialized in the popular political imagination. It is precisely this combination of supporters" respect for existing institutions and dominant values with the perceived threat to their economic and social status posed by minority demands that produces an authoritarian, and in this case specifically racialized, response. New right symbolic conflict over the meaning of race provides a legitimate means to rationalize the denial of social rights to people of color as well as to justify supporters' own positions of relative advantage.

It is precisely because the new racism is characterized by public disavowals of racist prejudice and avoidance of overt discriminatory practices that outcomes-orientated public policies such as affirmative action are so needed in the post-civil rights era. If racial equality is to be pursued as a societal goal, then it is more essential than ever to address ideas and practices that are fair in form but discriminatory in operation. If public ire, government policy, and judicial action are targeted exclusively on combating more traditional forms of racism and discriminatory exclusion, as recent evidence suggests is the case, then the silence that speaks so loud in the face of the new forms of racism and indirect exclusion will facilitate a deterioration into an increasingly undemocratic public arena more interested in protecting the nonracist self-image of the dominant society than in building a truly open, nonracist, democratic society.

Notes

1. This is the view of Sara Diamond, for example, as communicated to the author in several personal interviews.

2. For examples of this evidence in that sociological literature, see Sniderman and Piazza (1993). For examples of this evidence as propounded by new rightists, see Lynch (1990, 1991).

References

The American Experiment (Spring, 1995), p. 8.

Allen, William. 1989. "The New Racism Is the Old Power Grab." *Conservative Digest* July/August:16–21.

Ansell, Amy E. 1997. *New Right, New Racism: Race and Reaction in the United States and Britain.* New York and London: Macmillan/New York University Press.

Balibar, Etienne and Immanuel Wallerstein. 1991. *Race, Nation, Class: Ambiguous Identities.* London: Verso.

Barker, Martin. 1982. *The New Racism: Conservatives and the Ideology of the Tribe.* London: Junction.

Brimelow, Peter. 1995. *Alien Nation: Common Sense about America's Immigration Disaster.* New York: Random House.

Carr, Leslie. 1995. "Colorblindness and the New Racism." Presented at the 1995 American Sociological Association annual convention, August, Pittsburgh, PA.

Cohen, Carl. 1979. "Why Racial Preference Is Illegal and Immoral." *Commentary* 67(June): 40-52.

———. 1986. "Naked Racial Preference." *Commentary* 81(March):34–39.

Dovidio, J. F. and S. L. Gaertner. 1986. *Prejudice, Discrimination and Racism.* San Diego, CA: Academic Press.

D'Souza, Dinesh. 1995. *The End of Racism: Principles for a Multiracial Society.* New York: Free Press.

Edsall, Thomas with Mary Edsall. 1991. *Chain Reactions: The Impact of Race, Rights, and Taxes on American Politics.* New York: Norton.

Glazer, Nathan. 1975. *Affirmative Discrimination: Ethnic Inequality and Public Policy.* New York: Basic Books.

Heatherly, Charles L. and Burton Yale Pines, eds. 1980. *Mandate for Leadership: Policy Management in a Conservative Administration.* Washington, DC: Heritage Foundation.

Kristol, Irving. 1977. "Thought on Equality and Egalitarianism. P. 35-42 in *Income Redistribution,* edited by C. D. Campbell. Washington, DC: American Enterprise Institute.

———. 1991. "The Tradegy of Multiculturalism." *Wall Street Journal,* July 31, p. 15.

Lammi, Walter. 1991. "Nietzsche, the Apaches, and Stanford: The Hidden Agenda of Education for Difference." *Academic Questions* Summer:37.

Limbaugh, Rush. 1994. *The Rush Limbaugh Show,* September 14.

Lynch, Frederick, R. 1990. "Surviving Affirmative Action (More or Less)." *Commentary* August:44–47.

———. 1991. *Invisible Victims: White Males and the Crisis of Affirmative Action.* New York: Praeger.

McConahay, John B. 1986. "Modern Racism, Ambivalence, and the Modern Racism Scale." Pp. 91-125 in *Prejudice, Discrimination, and Racism,* edited by J. F. Dovidio and S. L. Gaertner. San Diego, CA: Academic Press.

Morganthau, Tom. 1994. "IQ: Is it Destiny?" *Newsweek,* October 24, p. 50.

Murray, Charles. 1984. *Losing Ground: American Social Policy 1950–1980.* New York: Basic Books.

Murray, Nancy. 1986. "Anti-Racists and Other Demons: The Press and Ideology in Thatcher's Britain." *Race and Class* 3(Winter): 1-19.

Omi, Michael and Howard Winant. 1996. *Racial Formation in the United States.* New York: Routledge.

Sears, David. 1988. "Symbolic Racism." Pp. 54-58 in *Eliminating Racism,* edited by P. Katz and D. Taylor. New York: Plenum.

Seidel, Gill. 1986. "Culture, Nation and 'Race' in the British and French New Right." Pp. **107-135 in** *The Ideology of the New Right,* edited by R. Levitas. Leeds, UK: Beyond the Pale Collective.

Small, Stephen. 1994. *Racialised Barriers: The Black Experience in the United States and England in the 1980s.* New York: Routledge.

Smith, Anna Marie. 1994. *New Right Discourse on Race and Sexuality.* Cambridge, UK: Cambridge University Press.

Sniderman, Paul and Thomas Piazza. 1993. *The Scar Race.* Cambridge, MA: Harvard University Press.

Steele, Shelby. 1990. *The Content of Our Character: A New Vision of Race in America.* New York: Harper Perennial, p. 17.

Taguieff, Pierre. 1990. "The New Cultural Racism in France." *Telos* 83(Spring):109–122.

Thompson, John B. 1990. *Ideology and Modern Culture.* Cambridge, MA: Polity.

Walker, Martin. 1995. "Right, White, and Prejudiced." *Guardian,* October 11. P. 9.

Wellman, David. 1993. *Portraits of White Racism.* 2d ed. New York: Cambridge University Press.

———. 1996. "Minstrel Shows, Affirmative Action Talk, and Angry White Men: Marking Racial Otherness in the 1990s." Presented at the American Sociological Association annual convention, August, New York.

Wetherell, Maragaret and Jonathan Potter. 1992. *Mapping the Language of Racism: Discourse and the Legitimation of Exploitation.* New York: Columbia University Press.

Weyrich, Paul. 1991. "Civil Rights at a Crossroad." *New Dimensions* July, p. 35.

Wilkins, Roger. 1984. "Smiling Racism." *The Nation* 239(November 3): p. 437.

Williams, Walter. 1980. "The Emperor Has No Clothes." *Moral Majority Report,"* November.

Ansell:

1. Ansell asks whether what we are seeing is a new racism without race or racists or simply new forms of racialized political language. Given what you have read, how would you answer this question?

2. Why, according to Ansell, is "prejudice + power = racism" an outdated conception of racism?

4

White Racism:
A Case Study from the Heartland

Joe R. Feagin and Hernán Vera

Over the course of many conversations about our university life, we gradually realized that the racist torment regularly reported by our black students and other students of color is very costly for them and for their white persecutors. These students of color are forced to spend much human energy dealing with subtle and blatant racist attacks and slights at the hands of white students, faculty members, and administrators. They have wasted many hours recovering from, and fighting back against, the discriminatory treatment they often endure. Much time and energy are also devoted to this mistreatment by their white tormentors, although they are unlikely to realize this.

As analysts of U.S. society, we had until recently failed to see how much human energy is wasted in various types of social practices, both in the United States and around the globe. Consider wars and the massive amounts of resources and lives wasted therein over the twentieth century. Ponder the billions upon billions of dollars the United States and other nations still spend for death-dealing armaments. Think of the untold waste from the sexist oppression inflicted by men on women around the globe. Consider the class oppression faced by many low-wage workers under the now global arrangements of modern capitalism.

The ancient Aztecs sacrificed, according to their religious beliefs, as many as 20,000 captives in a single day just to keep the sun burning. For this, they had an elaborate organizational apparatus, a corps of priests, and elaborate rituals. From the contemporary viewpoint, this seems like catastrophic waste. Yet, much closer to home, the racial discrimination that students and faculty of color daily experience at the hands of white students, faculty, and administrators represents a complex and catastrophic type of human sacrifice, one forced on its victims by an array of white tormentors.

As we examined many case studies of racism in writing this chapter, we came to view racist thought and practice as a special and protracted form of social waste and human sacrifice. Isn't the organized exclusion of people of color from the full privileges and benefits this nation has to offer a well-organized, deliberate form of destructive and irrational sacrifice? Aren't the amount of energy and resources this nation allocates to its racist practices also a catastrophic form of human waste? Developing a sociology of human waste in the tradition pioneered by Georges Bataille, we answer these questions with an emphatic "Yes." What if we could persuade this nation's leadership and rank-and-file citizens that the resources and energies devoted to the practice of racism could be much better spent in positive ways, for individual growth and collective improvement? Systemic racism of the U.S. type is highly destructive, not only for the people of color it sacrifices but also for its perpetrators and for the society as a whole.

Racism in the Farmbelt: The Dubuque Case

During the 1980s and 1990s, cross burnings in a number of U.S. communities conjured up images of a racial past that most white Americans had considered long dead, a violent past in which a powerful Ku Klux Klan left a trail of brutality directed against the nation's black citizens. Who would want to resurrect such despicable symbols and acts, and why? Do these recent events indicate that the tradition of anti-black hostility and violence never died? For the United States as a nation, the answers to these questions are very important.

The Events

Built in the 1830s on the Mississippi River, Dubuque is a city with numerous church spires and a population of about 58,000 people in 1990; it seldom has been in the national spotlight. The city was chartered in 1841, when its population numbered 2,987, including 72 African Americans (Iowa Advisory Commission 1993:1). Today, the city has a tiny black population of 331; black Dubuquers constitute less that 1 percent of the total population (Iowa Advisory Commission 1993:2).[1] In recent decades, several of the city's major employers have been connected to the agricultural industry. Although

the region's troubled agricultural sector suffered substantial job layoffs in the early 1980s, by the early 1990s, its economy had recovered. New jobs were being created in the service sector, although they were usually not equivalent in pay to the jobs lost. Still, Dubuque was weathering the national economic recession better than most cities (Dubuque Chamber of Commerce 1991).

In 1991, some of the city's whites engaged in racist attacks on black residents. Crosses were burned, and black residents were the targets of hate messages and other verbal and physical harassment. Even though cross burnings were not new for Dubuque,[2] the city's white leaders expressed surprise, for most did not view their city as having racial problems like those in larger cities or the South (Wilkerson 1991).

The trigger for the unexpected anti-black explosion in Dubuque was a city council recruitment plan. In spring 1991, the Dubuque Human Rights Commission unanimously approved a plan proposed by the local Constructive Integration Task Force (1991). Titled "We Want to Change," the plan was designed to attract about 20 black families annually, for a total of 100 families by the mid-1990s. The plan was in part a response to the burning in October 1989 of one local black family's garage, in which a cross and "KKK lives" graffiti were found. Perhaps reflecting the national liberal concern about multiculturalism, the task force members felt the city should make a symbolic gesture of recruiting black families to overcome Dubuque's lack of diversity. Private employers were to execute the plan and lure black workers to jobs in the city. Initially, some city money was to be used to subsidize the newcomers' mortgages and rents, but this part of the plan was dropped after some whites protested. A modest version of the plan was submitted to the city council. One white council member, Donald Deich, voted against the plan because he reportedly saw it as benefiting only "a select minority," not those truly in need. The watered-down version of the task force plan that was passed by the city council specified private job recruitment only where job vacancies existed (Harney 1991; "Racial Intolerance in America's Heartland" 1991; see also Chaichian, forthcoming).

Reaction to the modest city council plan came swiftly. Aggressive white responses included a dozen cross burnings and bricks thrown through the windows of black homes. Cross burnings also occurred in other Iowa cities, including Des Moines, Waterloo, Jefferson, and Iowa City. The meanings of the cross burnings for white and black Dubuquers were dramatically different. The white men arrested for the Dubuque incidents saw the crosses as symbols of the white community's alarm at the job losses that the perpetrators assumed would result from the recruitment plan. However, the only black school principal in the city, who had seen a cross burned across from his predominantly white school, commented:

My dad used to often tell us about when he was a boy, how the crosses would be burned up on the hills and how they could stand out late at night and watch it, watch the Ku Klux Klan people. . . . I'm living in 1991, and I'm seeing the same thing. ("Welcome to White America," 1991)

He added that the cross burnings gave him the sense of being "personally violated." Another black resident explained that for African Americans the burning of crosses symbolizes exclusion and "death" ("Welcome to White America" 1991; see also Times Wire Services 1991).

In Dubuque, as in other cities, the burning crosses signaled a community's fear: white residents' fear of losing their jobs, black residents' fear for their lives. African Americans' historical experiences with the burning cross symbol explain the depth of their personal fear, but how is one to interpret the fear of whites, a fear so strong that it justified sending fellow black Dubuquers a message of death?

In addition to the smoldering crosses and racialized vandalism, hate letters and racist graffiti were directed at local black residents and white supporters of the recruitment plan. The dozen black students at overwhelmingly white Dubuque Senior High School (which had 1,471 white students) were racially harassed; police officers patrolled the halls to keep whites from violence. The high school principal reported that white students were thinking in zero-sum terms: They felt "their parents would lose their jobs and homes to minorities" (Hull 1991:39; Times Wire Services 1991:A1).

Dubuque's racist incidents quickly became more than a local problem. Representatives of national white supremacy organizations descended on the city to exploit its interracial tensions. The long-standing agenda of these organizations includes stirring up local black-white conflict; some of their leaders even envision an open war that will polarize the entire nation into racial camps. Thom Robb of Arkansas, national director of the Knights of the Ku Klux Klan and a Christian Identity (another supremacy group) minister, held a white unity meeting in Dubuque attended by about 200 whites. An even larger segment of the white community supported at least some white supremacy views. A white labor leader commented, "You hear people saying that the Klan sounds kind of reasonable, and that's scary." The Klan leader's rhetoric apparently had the desired effect of persuading whites who were not normally Klan supporters to adopt aggressive, "throw the blacks out" sentiments (Hull 1991:39). The city's mayor, James Brady, noted that in earlier years he had "heard local union members brag that they had no black people in their union and never would have them as members" (Iowa Advisory Commission 1993:13). Although local unions were initially opposed to black recruitment, they agreed to endorse the plan after the deletion of a job-security provision that disregarded union seniority regulations.

A Mississippi attorney, Richard Barrett, leader of the neo-Nazi Nationalist Movement, also came to Dubuque to exploit tensions. The day before the national holiday on the birthday of Martin Luther King, Jr., Barrett held a public meeting that was attended by about 50 people, among whom were young white men wearing T-shirts that bore the initials NAAWP, the acronym for David Duke's National Association for the Advancement of White People. Barrett's message that "Kingism means loser take all" was a clear articulation of racial relations as a contest in which whites only lose as blacks advance. He proposed that "Kingism" be destroyed and replaced with his white "Americanism" (Diebel 1992:F1). Bringing whites' half-conscious fears of African Americans into public view, the white supremacists rationalized the explosion of opposition to an increase of black residents in Dubuque as a war against black encroachment on the "white way of life."

How widespread was local support for anti-black views and actions? The evidence suggests that anti-black sentiments were fairly common. For example, in 1991 and 1992 the local *Telegraph Herald* carried a number of hostile and ill-informed letters opposed to the recruitment of, or even the presence of, black families.[3] The paper also ran a recurring advertisement opposing the plan. A *Des Moines Register* poll suggested that, throughout Iowa, more whites opposed the plan than supported it. Half the Iowans responding to the poll believed the plan to be a bad idea; only a third favored it (see Anderson 1992:30). More than 2,000 whites in Dubuque signed a petition against the recruitment plan circulated by a local business leader, who was quoted as saying "to wholesale integrate this town because 'by God we're going to integrate' is not fair" (Hull 1991:39). Code words such a "quota" often have been used by conservative political leaders, including high officials like former President George Bush, as an effective political device to generate opposition to programs for black advancement. In Dubuque, local opposition to remedial programs reflected similar debates on the national scene.

A Question of Jobs?

One of the most prevalent white objections to black recruitment was phrased in terms of the threat to white jobs. This racialized thinking had a distinct social class dimension, for it was white workers' jobs that were supposedly threatened. Major employers seemed supportive of the plan, perhaps welcoming job competition. The original plan's specific declaration that it was not a program of preferential employment but recruitment for new or unfilled positions across the entire spectrum of employment, including professional jobs, did not alleviate "the unnecessary fear of employees that they will lose their present job to people of color" (Constructive Integration Task Force 1991:2). An unemployed firefighter complained, "I can't get a job and now I want someone else to come in and compete against me?" (Worthington 1991:C25). Speaking even more forcefully, a white auto mechanic told a *New York Times* reporter that it was bad enough to have to complete with a white man for a job, and then added, "But a black guy? It would mean you lost a job to someone that everybody knows is lower than you" (Wilkerson 1991:1). Such comments underscore an important function of white racial attitudes: Black workers often serve as a gauge of where the status floor is. Some white workers feel better, no matter how poorly they are doing, if they are doing better than black workers.

Economic experts often attribute attacks on black workers and their families in cities like Dubuque to severe unemployment problems.[4] Yet Dubuque's employment situation was more complex than this simple explanation suggests. Large-scale layoffs by major employers in the late 1970s and early 1980s created high unemployment rates for a time. However, during the two-year period before the outbreak of anti-black hostility and cross burnings, the Dubuque unemployment rate had dropped to 6 percent, a figure lower than that for the nation as a whole. Rather than reacting to present-day unemployment, white workers may have been concerned that they were not doing as well as they had a few years before. Most jobs lost earlier were better-paid, skilled jobs, and many laid-off workers had to leave the city or move into less-skilled service jobs. Competing for these generally lower-wage jobs and frustrated over loss of status, many whites targeted black individuals and families as scapegoats. In the United States, working-class and middle-class whites often seek a racial explanation for local economic problems; they are less likely to condemn the corporate executives responsible for most capital flight and urban deindustrialization. Indeed, most white workers have yet to seriously question the capitalist system and its corporate elite. Understanding modern racism requires an understanding of the fictional black threat to jobs and how it is constructed in the white mind. Racialized images may be fictional, but their consequences are nonetheless real.

The proposed number of black families to be invited to the city was extremely small. Even if all stages of the plan had gone into effect over the projected period of several years, the total number of black individuals invited would have been some 300 to 400 people in 100 or so families. This influx might have brought the total number of black men, women, and children in Dubuque to 700, or about 1 black person for every 83 white inhabitants, hardly the flood envisioned by many local whites. In addition, task force supporters of the plan explicitly took the position that they wanted to draw black professionals to the city. Indeed, one recent black entrant was a badly needed medical doctor.

Regardless of how widely the myth was believed, no significant job threat existed. In addition, implementation of the recruitment plan probably would have created some jobs for whites in businesses (for example, health care and real estate) serving the new residents.

Many white Americans, from presidents to average citizens, have accepted the view that race is declining in significance in the United States. A white counselor at a local high school who was a member of the task force that drafted the plan commented that some local residents she talked with wondered how there could be "a race problem when we don't even have minorities?" (Wilkerson 1991:1). The events in Dubuque invalidated assumptions that black population concentrations or interracial interaction are necessary prerequisites for significant racist thoughts or actions. The eruption of infectious white racism in a nearly all-white heartland city with no history of extensive legal segregation confirms that this problem is neither confined to the Deep South nor a creature of the distant past.

The national context of events in Dubuque is important because the period from 1980 through the early 1990s was an era of increased white attacks on African Americans and of white insensitivity to the realities and pain of racism. During the 1980s, President Ronald Reagan spoke of "welfare queens" (a coded critique of black women) and opposed most new civil rights laws and expanded enforcement efforts. Reagan cabinet member Terrell Bell, a moderate Republican, complained that middle-level white aides in the Reagan White House told racist jokes; referred to Dr. Martin Luther King, Jr., as "Martin Lucifer Coon"; spoke of Arabs as "sand niggers"; and called Title IX the "lesbian's bill of rights" (Bell 1988:104). Most members of the administration, some of whom (including former attorney general Edwin Meese) labeled Bell "Comrade Bell," had little commitment to the enforcement of civil rights laws. Dubuque's National Association for the Advancement of Colored People (NAACP) chapter president summarized the impact of the national context on Dubuque: "Reagan made it okay to hate again" (Diebel 1992:F1). This trend continued when, in 1988, presidential candidate George Bush made use of a racially stereotypical series of advertisements in his campaign. After his election, Bush, too, opposed an aggressive expansion of civil rights enforcement and only grudgingly signed a civil rights bill that had overwhelming congressional support.

Local White Attitudes and Beliefs

Most whites in Dubuque and in Iowa undoubtedly would support "liberty and justice for all" in the abstract. On the surface, most local residents appear to support racial tolerance. Some 88 percent of the (mostly white) respondents to a 1991 Dubuque-area opinion survey were favorable to "racial and ethnic diversity"; 86 percent felt that "positive attitudes" on racial issues were important (Anderson 1992:30). However, as opinions expressed in the statewide *Des Moines Register* poll indicate, support for the implementation of racial diversity was not so strong among Iowans. Half of those who responded to the poll believed the Dubuque recruitment plan to be a bad idea.

Stereotypes about blacks, openly expressed by numerous whites in Dubuque, revealed whites' general lack of understanding of black people. The white mayor of Dubuque stated on an ABC television program that he knew whites who thought all successful blacks were athletes. Some local whites expressed ignorance about African Americans in letters to the newspaper ("Welcome to White America" 1991). Images of black people as criminals and welfare recipients, which some whites revealed in media interviews, suggested deep fears and contributed to whites' hostile reactions to the diversification of the city. Some whites cited the negative images of black men on television and in movies. One white resident writing to the *Telegraph Herald* explained that local whites were "frightened and for a good cause.... We want to keep our town just like it is, a great place to raise a family, not frightened enough to stay in at night and close our windows." Another writer imagined that the plan would precipitate a flood: "Five families a year will bring in 25 more families of friends or cousins, and the latter will not be educated, housed and with jobs" (Cerney 1991:3A).

For a city whose population included such a small proportion of black residents, the range of anti-black myths that surfaced seems substantial. One local rumor warned that armed gangs were coming to Dubuque from Chicago, and in the language of racism "gang" can become code for "any group of young black men" (Wilkerson 1991:1). Several young white Dubuque men interviewed by a *Toronto Star* reporter about their support for the white supremacist movement spoke in stereotyped terms of blacks threatening the purses of older women, of black male advances to "white" women, and of black vandalism. A territorial view of the United States as a white country that should not include people of color seemed indisputable to some, including a construction worker: "I love my country. And they're taking control of it little by little." Echoing this white nationalism, a laid-off worker said, "Every time a white person stands up for his rights, it's called racism" (Diebel 1992:F1). A local white supremacist and member of the NAAWP who reportedly had a criminal record himself told a *Time* magazine reporter, "Blacks have higher crime rates, welfare rates, and birthrates. Why should we change our life-styles to give blacks preferential treatment?" (Hull 1991:39; "Welcome to White America" 1991). An older white resident complained, "They come in fast enough now. Why bring in more trouble?" (Times Wire Services 1991:A1).

Although only small numbers of whites engaged in racial violence, the behavior of other whites revealed a supportive or indifferent attitude toward such acts. Fellow workers reportedly congratulated and applauded some of the young men who burned crosses when they returned to work after short jail terms. Local judges gave relatively lenient sentences to several cross burners. In addition, the U.S. Department of Justice delayed enforcing national civil rights laws until spring 1992, when one young white man was finally indicted for violating the civil rights of a black Dubuque woman in a cross-burning incident. By mid-1993, the federal government had secured convictions of six whites in connection with the cross burnings. Among these were William and Daniel McDermott, two local men who reportedly were activists on behalf of white supremacy causes. They were convicted of burning a cross and violating black Dubuquers' civil rights. A modest measure of justice finally had been secured for the city's black community ("Man Indicted in Cross Burning" 1992; see also McKenzie 1993).

White Isolation

As noted previously, Dubuque's population and institutions are overwhelmingly white. Only a tiny percentage of the city's population is black. Although never officially segregationist, Dubuque has long been known as unfriendly to new black families. In the 1940s and 1950s, white police officers, using a tactic then common in certain midwestern cities, told black travelers who ventured off the train at the local station not to stay. This practice gave Dubuque a negative image among potential black immigrants in some southern communities. Then, as today, the benefits to whites of discouraging blacks from residing in the city seem to have been more ideological and psychological than material. During the 1940s and 1950s, there were no more than five black families in the city,

who, as one white observer put it, "all put their heads down when they were stared at" (Times Wire Services 1991:A1).

In the early 1990s, with fewer than 400 black residents, Dubuque was one of the whitest cities in the nation. The police force and fire department were all white. Virtually no blacks held positions of power in any major institution—there were no black teachers, politicians, or corporate leaders, and only one black school principal. As in most cities, a majority of whites in Dubuque seem to live in an isolated bubble segregated from regular contact with African Americans. Mayor Brady described the city as a place where "people can go all their lives without seeing a black person" (Hull 1991:39). The head of the city's Human Rights Commission, a Nigerian-born newcomer, remarked that whites in Dubuque had little chance to associate with people of different cultures: "The real reason for these problems is deep down racism" (Times Wire Services 1991:A1). When Dubuque's black principal, the only black educator in the public schools, was offered a job in 1991, he was told that no white barber in the city would know how to cut his hair. The principal told *Time* magazine, "This is a white person's town. On my first day at school, a kid asked me whether I was Bill Cosby" (Hull 1991:39).

Everyday Black Experience

Although local whites and many in the white media tended to see the recent racial violence in Dubuque as unprecedented, there were ample warning signals that some whites in the city were hostile to African Americans. The social waste that is racism had long been evident to the black citizenry. After the recent incidents, black residents began to speak about earlier harassment, cross burnings, and other hate crimes. One black woman, who had come to Dubuque in the 1980s, discussed an incident that occurred when her two granddaughters were walking to a store to buy ice cream. A group of white men attempted to spit at the children and called out, "Niggers get out." She added, "You're afraid to walk in the streets because you're harassed." Street safety is a major issue for many whites, yet street harassment faced every day by African Americans receives little attention. This grandmother went on to point out the moral dilemma that whites' anti-black propensities pose: "The ones that I have the hardest problem with are the ones that go to church every Sunday and then won't sit on the pew beside you" ("Welcome to White America" 1991).

Black residents also talked about the pain they experienced when whites made racial remarks in their presence with no apparent regard for their feelings. The black principal recalled some whites openly "telling nigger jokes" at a local hotel ("Welcome to White America" 1991). At best, such an action reveals callousness; at worst, it denies the existence of the black listener. The pain engendered by racist jokes and comments can be severe and long-lasting. The local NAACP president told a *Toronto Star* reporter that her 21-year-old daughter refused to reside in Dubuque and spoke of the lasting scars her 13-year-old son bore: "He was just a little boy. He went with his dad to take the car in for repair. . . . And a couple of mechanics came out and my boy heard one of them say, 'That's that nigger's car'" (Diebel 1992:F1).

Reactions in the Media

Because of its scale, the racism expressed in Dubuque attracted state and national media attention. A white city council member, who supported the black recruitment plan, worried that media coverage of the cross burnings and white supremacy gatherings was "fanning the flame." In his view, the "glare of the national press is going to encourage people to take sides and become more polarized" (Times Wire Services 1991:A1; see also Anderson 1992:30). Some outsiders were calling Dubuque the "Selma

of the North," and the *Des Moines Register* ran a front-page headline referring to Iowa's "new racist image." Most major national newspapers and several national television programs ran stories on events in the city. National coverage was generally negative regarding cross burnings and supremacist rallies but failed to explore the implications of these events for the problem of white racism in the nation.

Some reporters of the conservative press took up the side of the anti-black Dubuquers. They played down the racist incidents as the work of a few extremists, an approach that was sometimes taken in the liberal media as well. Stating that Dubuque was no more racist than the rest of the state, a *National Review* article blamed the disturbance on a numerically insignificant "fringe element" of "young bloods." The writer argued that "bigotry is hardly rampant" in the city and that Iowa's mass media had exaggerated racism in Dubuque. The writer also took liberal national newspapers to task for "tiptoeing" around the black crime issues in assessing Dubuque's racial crisis. Suggesting that one reason for white opposition to the recruitment plan was fear of increased crime, the *National Review* reporter tried to make the case that white fear was realistic by citing data on black overrepresentation in crime in other Iowa cities (Anderson 1992:30). However, most of the crime in Iowa and in Dubuque is committed by whites, yet white newcomers were not the target of overt protests.

A City Responds to Racism

Some local whites did protest the violent expressions of racism in Dubuque. One counter-rally held by whites protesting cross burnings and the Klan rally drew hundreds of people. Girl Scouts, with the aid of some businesses, passed thousands of black and white ribbons to local residents as a sign of commitment to better relations between racial groups in the city. Sermons in local churches accented tolerance. Billboards sponsored by whites concerned about bettering conditions asked, "Why Do We Hate?" Some whites wrote letters of apology to black victims of violent acts. Three hundred local businesses ran an ad in the local newspaper supporting the black recruitment plan. The local school system expanded multicultural education (Bean 1991:A18; "Anti-Klan Protestors Outnumber Ku Klux Klan" 1992).

Yet these actions seem too modest to reach to the depths of racism. Anti-black actions in Dubuque, as in other American cities, have revealed a significant breakdown in many whites' capacity to empathize with the feelings and interests of members of the black out-group. We have found no evidence in published reports of the Dubuque incidents that whites collectively have made large-scale efforts to deal aggressively with the persistence of everyday racism since the more violent expressions of racism subsided.

Interpreting Rituals of Racism

The anti-black actions of whites are often repetitive and formalized. Burning a cross is a ceremony that needs the propitious darkness of the night, some technical knowledge, certain materials, and, in some cases, ritual costumes. Whites spitting at black children or adults and yelling "Niggers, get out" are using traditional words and engaging in ritualized actions that have been performed many times before. Whites who refuse to share a pew with blacks in church, those who tell or laugh at "nigger jokes," and those who refuse service or provide service of inferior quality to black customers are engaging in the ritualized behavior of racism.

Such acts are rituals, because no matter how private they appear, when enacted inside a church, a mechanic's shop, a high school corridor, or in the dark of night, they are preeminently traditional and social affairs. Such actions define socially acceptable practices and socially relevant knowledge for the community, including its youth. Whites acquire tacit understandings about black and white people and about racist attitudes and actions through these rituals (Berger and Luckmann 1967:138–39). The French sociologist Emile Durkheim, who intensively studied social rituals, sometimes referred to the degree to which people have a common life filled with rituals as "moral density." Yet it is clear that racist rituals are divisive as well as integrating. Although such rituals may bind together whites in a celebration of a socially invented "whiteness," they alienate blacks from the common life shared by the dominant white community. In this sense, the racist rituals provide an "immoral density" ultimately destructive of the broader social fabric of a community.

Apparently, the class composition of extreme white supremacist groups has varied over the course of Dubuque's history, as have the targets of racial and ethnic hostility. During the 1920s, Ku Klux Klan members came from the white working and middle classes and also from the business community. The Klan's targets then were usually Catholic Americans, especially German Catholics. In recent years, the majority of Dubuque's extreme white supremacists have been drawn from the white working class.[5] Prejudiced individuals in the business and middle-class segments of the white community who expressed opposition to the black recruitment plan appear to have chosen less extreme acts, such as circulating or signing a petition.

Most of the active participants in Dubuque's racial crisis were white men. Those yelling "nigger" and those lighting up the crosses functioned as "officiants" in the rites, but active officiants require, indeed even recruit, a large number of acolytes and passive participants. Those who sign petitions or who passively observe aggressive racist acts without protest are as much a part of the racialized rituals as are those who officiate.

These rituals can have a significant impact on a community's children. Only a few of

Dubuque's white children and teenagers officiated in the cross burnings or engaged in overt racial harassment. Yet, regardless of the degree of their disapproval of the racist actions or their empathy with the victims, most white youth, like most of their elders, did not speak out. Such passivity is a first step in learning to ally oneself with white victimizers against black victims. Remaining passive during one incident may make it harder to actively oppose racism in the future.

Across the United States, millions of whites become passive participants in white racism as they witness anti-black violence by way of the media. They have been socialized to remain more or less impassive in the face of police and Klan abuse of these black "others." The fact that anti-black violence seldom provokes an eruption of white citizen solidarity to eradicate such actions is evidence of the national proportions of the breakdown in human empathy across the arbitrary color line.

As we have noted previously, the process of denying humanity to a person of color betrays the moral principles of equality and justice on which this nation is theoretically founded. Making African Americans habitual objects of white abuse is a brutal dissipation of human talent and energy. Such abuse modifies the moral status of the person who accomplishes it: the discriminator is affected by the discrimination (Hubert and Mauss 1968:205–206). Those who exclude and segregate, torture, burn crosses, and otherwise intimidate or deny legitimate rewards to fellow human beings may realize some material or psychological benefits. They may decrease job competition or feel racially superior. But they assume an immoral position directly counter to the American ideology of "liberty and justice for all." That position is tolerated, even privileged, by the complementary role played by passive white participants.

White observers may be tempted to view violent racist acts as the work of marginal elements. This common response allows many white individuals to distance themselves from societal racism. However, the ritual character of recurring anti-black acts indicates that they have become a traditional part of white communities and of the larger white society. Individuals who engage in cross burning, one of the most painful and threatening of all white actions to black citizens, can remain in good standing at their workplaces, in their churches, and in their families. The American Civil Liberties Union has defended as legitimate speech the right to engage in some cross burning; the U.S. Supreme Court has ruled that such acts are protected by the First Amendment. The court granted immunity to one white teenager, who had burned a cross on a black family's lawn, by striking down a St. Paul, Minnesota, law banning such hate crimes (Marcus 1992:A1).

Fear has been cited as a driving force behind racist violence like that in Dubuque. Who or what did many whites fear? The few black families in Dubuque were no real threat to white jobs or centers of power. It seems probable that few whites knew any black people well enough to fear them. The objects of this white fear appear to be stereotyped images and the unknown. White workers tend to direct their anxiety over personal or social problems, such as unemployment, recession, or crime, toward society's subordinate racial or ethnic groups; far less often, they focus their concern on the actual sources of their discomfort. Some studies, for example, have found that many white workers who are laid off because of plant closings believe that their employers could not make a profit primarily because the employers were required to hire minority workers, and thus these white workers blame the job losses on blacks or Latinos. Yet there is no empirical evidence for this white notion (Roediger 1994:10).

By definition, U.S. capitalism is a system of great inequality. Ordinary workers have less power, receive less income, and own less wealth than do managers and employers. Conceivably, Americans could defend this class inequality by arguing that "people who receive higher rewards deserve them by virtue of their noble birth" (Wallerstein 1991:86). Yet most do not. Americans tend to believe that class position is based on merit. Similarly, whites could attribute their more privileged position vis-à-vis blacks to the fact that they were born white. However, most white Americans do not accept this explanation for racial inequality. Instead, whites have developed defenses of inequality that hide stark racial realities behind a language of "equal opportunity": "Because blacks already have equal opportunity, their lack of prosperity relative to whites is the result of poor values and a weak cultural heritage." Whites who hold such a view tend to believe that black Americans are much less hard-working, more inclined to welfare, and more likely to be criminal or violent than are whites. These white rationalizations of privilege provide, Immanuel Wallerstein has suggested, "the only acceptable legitimation of the reality of large-scale collective inequalities" (Wallerstein 1991:87).

Still, white workers have much to gain from a recognition that their racial fictions and rationalizations blind them to the economic realities of social class. White workers' anger against African or Latino Americans might better be directed against the white actors and institutions directly responsible for troubled economic conditions. White workers who blame or attack subordinate minority groups as scapegoats for these conditions either do not understand how modern capitalism works or do not know how to protest capitalist-led restructuring and deindustrialization. The white economic elites who are usually responsible for capital and job flight are seldom critically analyzed in mainstream media or scholarly analyses of economic changes. U.S. workers have no widely available conceptual framework, such as the class analysis found in Europe's leftist media, to explain the restructuring and other vagaries of U.S. capitalism. In contrast, the racist ideology is readily available for white workers to use in explaining their economic and social problems. Indeed, the corporate elite has on occasion encouraged suffering white workers to adopt anti-black interpretations of such problems. The psychological comfort that white workers experience because some black workers are lower on the ladder may be real, but it serves employer interests by keeping the workforce divided—thereby weakening union activity and keeping wages down for all workers.

Progressive racial change in Dubuque is not synonymous with losses for whites. On the contrary, lifting the heavy curtain of racism would empower whites as well as blacks. Whites could use the time, energy, and resources they now waste on racist actions and emotions to confront their economic and political problems. The price that whites of all classes pay for racist attitudes and incidents rarely has received comment or analysis. Many whites in Dubuque expended great energy debating the modest recruitment plan. Political, court, and police officials spent energy and resources dealing with the racial upheaval. Those who burned crosses or yelled "nigger" might have had a cathartic experience, but what might they have achieved had they devoted the same time and energy to self- or societal improvement? What would the lives of all citizens in Dubuque be like if there were less racial fear and hatred?

How have Dubuque's racial problems affected the city's future? Will industry seek this pristine white town? Will local companies want to risk a boycott of products by blacks and sympathetic whites? Indeed, one meat-packing executive told *Newsweek* reporters that some shoppers in other cities had already boycotted products labeled "Dubuque." Concern over the city's negative image and the implications of that image for the business climate has influenced Dubuque businesspeople to create a new Council for Diversity, although some local observers have viewed this council as an attempt to displace the original Constructive Integration Task Force (1991) plan just as it was about to be implemented. Significantly, the new council's goals do not include racial "integration" (McCormick and Smith 1992:71).

Events like those in Dubuque may seem ephemeral: a few months of burning crosses, some street demonstrations, a petition drive, several heated city council meetings, and modest attempts at multiculturalism in the schools. After a few months, the dramatic events passed, and the media moved on to other stories. But Dubuque's black community still has great cause for concern about racist thought and action. In January 1993, more than a year after the last cross burnings, black Dubuquers held a demonstration at the county courthouse protesting white police harassment and brutality. The demonstrators also were distressed that the police department still had no minority officers (Wiley 1993). The burden of white racism for black Dubuquers is still heavy in all arenas of their daily lives. Each racist act moves the city—and this nation—backward and makes clear how much remains to be done on America's equality agenda.

Notes

1. According to the 1990 census, there are also 370 Hispanics, 368 Asian Americans, and 69 Native Americans.

2. Roger Maiers, who chaired the Dubuque Human Rights Commission from July 1989 to July 1991, listed a number of anti-black and anti-Asian incidents between June 1982 and October 1989 in his presentation to the Human Rights Commission Training Seminar, Omaha, Nebraska, August 26–28, 1993.

3. The *Telegraph Herald,* on November 11, 1991, announced that "because of the high number of letters to the editor submitted in reaction to the racial issue in Dubuque, the *Telegraph Herald* on Tuesday will present an additional page of commentary." We examined the letters that ap-

peared between July 11, 1991, and January 31, 1992.

4. See the comment of Katherine Newman, a Columbia University professor, in Worthington (1991), p. C25.

5. Letter to the authors from Professor Mohammad A. Chaichian, University of Iowa, November 16, 1993.

References

Anderson, Lorrin. 1992. "Crimes of the Heartland." *National Review,* February 17, p. 30.

"Anti-Klan Protestors Outnumber Ku Klux Klan at Rally." 1992. *United Press International,* BC Cycle, May 30.

Bean, Joe P. 1991. "Hate Politics: Iowa Town Finds Hope." *San Francisco Chronicle,* December 14, p. A18.

Bell, Terrell. 1988. *The Thirteenth Man: A Reagan Cabinet Memoir.* New York: Free Press.

Berger, Peter and Thomas Luckmann. 1967. *The Social Construction of Reality: A Treatise in the Sociology of Knowledge.* New York: Anchor.

Cerney, Mary. 1991. "Many Dubuquers Afraid To Speak Out" [Letters to the Editor]. *Telegraph Herald,* August 20, p. 3A.

Chaichian, Mohammad A. Forthcoming. *Racism in the Heartland: Dynamics of Race and Class in Dubuque, Iowa, 1800–1993.* Champaign-Urbana: University of Illinois Press.

Constructive Integration Task Force. 1991. *We Want To Change.* Dubuque, IA: Author.

Diebel, Linda. 1992. "Darkest Iowa." *Toronto Star,* February 23, p. F1.

Dubuque Chamber of Commerce. 1991. *Brief History of Dubuque.* Dubuque, IA: Author.

Harney, James. 1991. "Iowa City Confronts Racism, but Racism Refuses to Die." *USA Today,* November 18, p. 10A.

Hubert, Henri and Marcel Mauss. 1968. "Essai sur la nature et la fonction du sacrifice" [Essay on the Nature and Function of Sacrifice]. Pp. 205–206 in M. Mauss, *Works.* Paris: Les Editions du Minuit.

Hull, Jon D. 1991. "Race Relations: A White Person's Town?" *Time,* December 23, p. 39.

Iowa Advisory Commission. 1993. *A Time to Heal: Race Relations in Dubuque, Iowa.* Washington, DC: U.S. Commission on Civil Rights.

"Man Indicted in Cross Burning." 1992. *United Press International*, BC Cycle, March 27.

Marcus, Ruth. 1992. "Supreme Court Overturns Law Barring Hate Crimes." *Washington Post*, June 23, p. A1.

McCormick, John and Vern Smith. 1992. "Can We Get Along?" *Newsweek*, November 9, p. 71.

McKenzie, Stacey. 1993. "Some Dubuque Residents Feel Hate Crime Convictions Will Help City." *Des Moines Register*, as cited in Gannett News Service, April 22.

"Racial Intolerance in America's Heartland." 1991. *Larry King Live*, CNN, November 15.

Roediger, David. 1994. *Towards the Abolition of Whiteness*. London: Verso.

Times Wire Services. 1991. "Racial Tension Smolders in City Once Tagged 'Selma of the North.'" *Los Angeles Times*, November 24, p. A1.

Wallerstein, Immanuel. 1991. *Unthinking Social Science: The Limits of Nineteenth Century Paradigms*. Cambridge, UK: Polity Press.

"Welcome to White America." 1991. *20/20*, ABC News, December 20.

Wiley, Debora. 1993. "Dubuque Still Trying to Get Rid of Stigma." *Gannett News Service*, January 28.

Wilkerson, Isabel. 1991. "Seeking a Racial Mix, Dubuque Finds Tension." *New York Times*, November 3, p. A1.

Worthington, Roger. 1991. "Hate Flares as Iowa City Courts Blacks." *Chicago Tribune*, November 17, p. C25.

Feagin and Vera:

1. Feagin and Vera ask whether the tradition of hostility and violence toward blacks ever died after the civil rights movement. After reading this chapter, how would you answer that? Provide evidence for your position.

2. Discuss why you think people are more likely to view people of different races, ethnicities, or genders as the cause of economic hardship when competing for jobs rather than viewing the decisions made by corporate executives as problematic?

5

Mongrel Monstrosities

Abby L. Ferber

Mongrelization of the White race is the single greatest danger facing the world today. It is a far greater threat than an atomic attack from Russia or a depression. We could make a comeback from such temporary disasters, but we could never again rebreed the White Race out of interracial mongrels.[1]

Interracial sexuality threatens the borders of white identity, and mixed-race people become the living embodiment of that threat. White supremacist publications are filled with images of "mongrels"—feared and despised because they straddle and destabilize those racial boundaries essential to securing white identity and power.

Gender and race are not identities imposed upon bodies; bodies only become culturally intelligible as they become gendered and racialized. At the same time, however, the regulation of heterosexual and racially pure reproduction produces a domain of abjection, a realm of the culturally unintelligible. As Judith Butler points out, it is

important to recognize that oppression works not merely through acts of overt prohibition, but covertly, through the constitution of viable subjects and through the corollary constitution of a domain of unviable (un)subjects—abjects, we might call them. . . . Here oppression works

through the production of a domain of unthinkability and unnameability.[2]

Throughout this discourse, the realm of abjection includes a number of figures: the mixed-race individual and the Jew, as well as the feminized male and the masculinized female described by Butler. These figures are produced to safeguard white male hegemony. Each of these figures symbolizes some wrong identification and serves as an image of boundary confusion and chaos. The regulation of interracial sexuality, then, is a continuous effort at boundary maintenance, producing properly racialized and properly gendered subjects as well as this realm of unintelligibility.

The Threat to Racial Identity

The properly racialized, gendered subject must repeatedly disassociate itself from the abject to construct itself as a subject.

It is this repeated repudiation by which the subject installs its boundary and constructs the claim to its "integrity." . . . This is not a buried identification that is left behind in a forgotten past, but an identification that must be leveled and buried again and again, the compulsive repudiation by which the subject incessantly sustains his/her boundary . . . subject-positions are produced in and through a logic of repudiation and abjection.[3]

Figures of abjection are essential to the production of racialized, gendered subjects. The construction of stable racial identities can only occur in relation to the production and regulation of the impure.

It is through the construction and maintenance of racial boundaries, and the demarcation of "whiteness" as a racially pure identity, that the white subject is constructed. While those who are discovered to be of mixed black/white ancestry are usually defined as black in the United States, they nevertheless represent a potential threat to the construction of racial identity based on the illusion of white racial purity. More important, mixed-race people signal the instability and permeability of racial boundaries; the regulation of interracial sexuality is required in order to secure the borders. Blackness, as long as it is carefully separated and subordinated to whiteness, poses no threat to the existence of a white identity; in fact, blackness is necessary to the definition of whiteness. White and black form a binary opposition, and white identity requires its relationship to blackness. Those who are mixed-race, however, threaten the white/black binary; they signify the instability of that opposition. Recently mixed-race people have increasingly organized under the banner of mixed-race identity, refusing to accept the predominant system of single-race categorizations. This development is particularly troublesome for white supremacists. Mixed-race people announce that the boundaries are permeable and put at risk the possibility of a racially pure identity. They threaten the binary opposition itself and the continuation of difference. If subjects only become culturally intelligible in this discourse as they become racialized, mixed-race people cannot be granted subject status; they symbolize the realm of the unlivable, "the very limit to intelligibility."[4]

The production of properly racialized and gendered subjects depends on the power of the threat of racial and gendered punishment, and throughout this discourse that threat emerges again and again. Mixed-race individuals serve as illustrations of racial punishment, figures of abjection. The terms used to refer to these people question their humanity. They are referred to as mongrels, monsters, half-breeds, etc., terms that put in question their humanity. Mongrels do not meet the racialized norm "which qualifies a body for life within the domain of cultural intelligibility."[5] In *The Turner Diaries*, readers are warned,

The enemy we are fighting fully intends to destroy the racial basis of our existence. No excuse for our failure will have any meaning, for there will be only a swarming horde of indifferent, mulatto zombies to hear it. There will be no White men to remember us.[6]

Not only is race at stake, but what it means to be human. As Michael Omi and Howard Winant and Butler have suggested, the construction of human subjects occurs through the construction and regulation of intelligible racial and gender identities. The above passage suggests that there will be no humans left, only "mulatto zombies." Without a stable racial identity, one can have no human identity in this discourse. Butler explains,

the "coherence" and "continuity" of "the person" are not logical or analytic features of personhood, but, rather, socially instituted and maintained norms of intelligibility . . . the very notion of "the person" is called into question by the cultural emergence of those "incoherent" . . . beings who appear to be persons but who fail to conform to the gendered [and racialized] norms of cultural intelligibility by which persons are defined.[7]

This incoherence is emphasized in a *New Order* article describing mixed-race individuals as

Malformed pieces of humanity sporting a combination of wooley negroid hair, white complexion and slanted mongol eyes. They call themselves "black people," but they are neither black, white or yellow, but all and none of these races. These are the children of integration. They have no culture, no common heritage, no identity and no pride. What would *you* call them? Half-castes? Hybrids? Monsters?[8]

Mixed-race persons are defined as defective or degenerate, monsterlike; their humanity is put in question. Similarly, articles in *White Power* refer to them as "mongrel monstrosities."[9] Interracial sexuality is constructed as a threat to both racial and human identity, producing *incoherent* beings—brown zombies.

Mixed-race people are referred to as "negroidal mongrels who on their own could not build a pyramid or modern city."[10] Elsewhere, we are told that "a mulatto or mongrel race is a shiftless, lazy, mindless, leaderless and slave-like race which must have a racially superior 'boss-man' to tell them what to do."[11] White supremacist discourse suggests that mixed-race people are inhuman, incapable of surviving on their own or of creating anything worthwhile. A *New Order* article warns that interracial sexuality will result in a "race-mixed and totally dead America."[12]

Throughout contemporary white supremacist discourse, in order to exist as a culturally intelligible being, one must be racialized. To have no pure race makes living impossible—"mongrels" occupy the realm of impossibility and unlivability. According to *The New Order,* "a fate worse than death . . . is what mongrelization is all about. It is a living death."[13]

If white identity is dependent upon racially pure reproduction, and its place on one side of the binary opposition of white/black, it is essential for white supremacists to be able to recognize who is white and who is not. Their own identity depends upon it. In order to engage in racially pure reproduction and not pollute their own bodies through sexual contact with nonwhites, it is imperative that whites be able to recognize who is and is not white. Race is constructed through the reiteration of physical differences that are visible and knowable, and the existence of mixed-race individuals is represented as a threat to this surety. In a *National Vanguard* article entitled "Beware the Almost Whites!" readers are warned that interracial sexuality produces

a continuous range of mongrels between the two racial extremes. Near the White end of the spectrum there will be some who . . . will be almost indistinguishable from the true Aryans. Drawing the line between what is Aryan and what is not becomes more and more difficult.[14]

An article in *The New Order* further explains, "The 'murder by miscegenation' device works all too well when . . . 'almost Whites' . . . can gain acceptance when a nigger cannot."[15] The existence of "almost whites" poses a threat to the constructed surety of racial identity and symbolizes the insecurity and permeability of racial boundaries, threatening the possibility of racially pure reproduction.

In white supremacist discourse, mongrelization is depicted as leading the genocide of the white race. A typical article describes it as "the genocide of the White race by irreversible downbreeding with a hopelessly inferior race."[16] Mongrelization, the result of interracial sexuality, is synonymous with genocide. A National Socialist White People's Party recruitment flier accuses, "race-mixing and integration mean White genocide." Mongrelization is equated with genocide because it means the loss of the illusion of purity upon which whiteness is predicated. As an article in *The Thunderbolt* explains,

Mongrelization is the worst form of "genocide." If you kill 99% of a race, but leave the other 1% pureblooded, they will in time restore the race; but when you mongrelize them, you have destroyed that race eternally. Once mixed with the

Black or Yellow Races, the White Race would be totally and forever destroyed.[17]

Another article asserts, "any large scale intermarriage . . . would mean the . . . abolition of the White Race. We would simply cease to exist in the world of the future."[18] A race once polluted with the decadent genes of the lower, backward, and underdeveloped races of the world is lost forever. White supremacists see race-mixing as even deadlier than outright war because "even a global war in which the Jews were victorious, would leave few Whites to breed back the race. Their final solution is MONGRELIZATION. A mongrel can only breed more mongrels."[19] Similarly, a *New Order* article asserts, "there is one sure way of killing a nation—to destroy or fatally dilute the blood of its creators."[20]

If subjects only become living and viable as they become racialized, mongrelization, then, is death. Properly racialized subjects are the only subjects that qualify for life in this discourse. Interracial sexuality threatens to erase not only racial difference but the actual continued existence of the white race and humanity.

The Threat to Gender Identity

Light skin has always garnered privilege in America. E. Franklin Frazier first made this argument, pointing out that mulattoes received advantages denied darker-skinned blacks. Mulattoes were most often house servants and were more likely to be emancipated during slavery by their white fathers, and after slavery they continued to reap the benefits afforded by light skin, achieving higher levels of education and occupational and economic success.[21] Recent work by Kathy Russell, Midge Wilson, and Ronald Hall and Vera M. Keith and Cedric Herring demonstrates that complexion is "more strongly related to stratification outcomes than were such background characteristics as parental socioeco-

nomic status."[22] Keith and Herring conclude that "the effects of skin tone are not only historical curiosities from a legacy of slavery and racism, but present-day mechanisms that influence who gets what in America."[23]

American ideals of female beauty are also based on skin color, and white women have remained the standard. Light skin, straight, smooth hair, and thin features are still the ideal, evident in billboards, magazines, movies, and television.[24] It is no surprise that these ideals are enthusiastically embraced in white supremacist discourse. What is interesting, however, is the way in which these ideals are used in the service of the difference versus equality framework.

Because white female beauty is constructed as a sign of racial difference, interracial sexuality is represented as a threat to that defining feature of whiteness. Interracial sexuality threatens not only racial identity but gender identity. One typical article implores,

Look at Hawaii today. One-third of all whites marry nonwhites. California is right behind. Remember the "California girl" stereotype of the late '60s? Tall and lean, with blond hair and a tawny body. Well, *Newsweek* ran individual photos of the graduating class at Bakke's medical school in California, and of some 100 students, only five or six had blond hair![25]

Another article provides a fictional account of a white survival demonstration, where protestors chant,

"Sweden is going Brown." "No more Ingrid Bergman." "America is going brown." "No more Cheryl Tiegs." "France is going brown." "No more Catherine Deneuve." . . . "What is the solution?" "White separatism!"[26]

Interracial sexuality is constructed as eliminating difference, making everyone the same inhuman brown, and because white female beauty is defined as a distinguishing feature of whiteness, interracial sexuality is depicted as a threat to that beauty and white aesthetic standards. Readers of white supremacist publications are implored to join the movement to preserve superior white physical features.[27, 28] Images of white children and white women are presented, along with captions such as "Endangered Species." White female beauty, we find, is often used as a measurement to gauge the extent of racial destruction. As summarized elsewhere, "As the race goes, so goes beauty."[29] Another article explains,

Mix these aliens into the population and, sure, you'll still have plenty of individuals with blond hair or with blue eyes or with ultrafine complexions or with classical facial features or with lithe, clean-limbed bodies, but you'll rarely find an individual who combines them all. . . . There won't be any more Greta Garbos. . . . Already in America, there is a frantic male rush after the fast dwindling supply of really Nordic women. You see it all around you in the urban areas and on TV. Today there are hardly enough blonde beauties in all Scandinavia to satisfy the appetites of a few Arab shiekdoms.[30]

Saving the white race is equated not only with saving white female beauty, but with maintaining the sexual availability of white women for white men. The preservation of the white race is refigured as the preservation of white females for the service of white male desire.

In an ongoing debate in *Instauration* about the preservation of Nordic genes, one writer suggests that white sperm be frozen in sperm banks to be brought back in the future when whites are on the brink of extinction. In response, in an article entitled "A Survey of Possible Hiding Places on Earth and Away From Earth: Where to Cache Northern European Genes," the author objects to this self-preservation plan because "while the blondie genes are twiddling their thumbs on the sperm bank shelf, they are not walking around in stuffed shorts and halters to be visually enjoyed."[31] Here, the preservation of the race

becomes equated with a voyeuristic desire for preserving white female beauty.

As Anne Flintoff argues, this sexualization of women serves to "reinforce the 'naturalness' of heterosexuality, and a construction of male sexuality based on objectification and conquest."[32] The threat to white female beauty is simultaneously a threat to white male identity and heterosexual gender relations.

Interracial sexuality is posited as a threat to racial differences and, equally important, as a threat to white heterosexual gender relations and the fulfillment of white male desire. As another racial warrior warns,

Believe me, the time is only a few years off when every attractive blonde woman in the world, in Shakespeare's words, may "fall in love with what she feared to look on," and have the chance to marry a dark millionaire.[33]

A threat to one part of the natural order is a threat to the entire natural order. The male/female binary accords males primacy, control, and superiority over the other side of the opposition, females. Male identity is constructed through this opposition: to be a male in this discourse is to have control over women. Interracial sexuality represents the loss of this control. An *Instauration* article, for example, defines that threat:

When a Northern male sees a female of his race involved in a sexual relationship with a non-Northern male it is evocative, on a racial level and on racial terms, of [what] the male would experience on the individual level upon learning that his wife was being unfaithful to him with another man. The latter is a crime against the individual. The former is a crime against the race . . . to which they are bound by bonds of nature and creation infinitely deeper, stronger and longer-lasting than the mere legal bonds of marriage.[34]

As the above article assumes, white women are considered bound by nature to white males; all white women belong to all white men, and these ties are even greater than the legal ties of marriage. White men have natural rights to white women. The threat to this right is summarized in another article:

healthy White men are discovering that some of their rightful biological partners are becoming hideous to behold. The skin of these women still gleams like ivory, their bodies as voluptuous as ever. The hideousness comes from the male hand intertwined with one of theirs. The hand is black.[35]

This discourse suggests that interracial sexuality threatens not only to destroy race and human identity, but to destroy gender identity as well. It threatens to destroy what it means to be a man, because what it means be a man is intimately tied up with race. To be a man is to be a white man who has rights of access to and protects white women. Race and gender identity are absolutely inseparable here; the construction of one depends upon the other. The following excerpt demonstrates this further:

To further their deracination Northern females are exposed to a culture which is so hostile that films and literature commonly portray Northerners as weak, decadent and degenerate while portraying their non-Northern European counterparts and adversaries as strong and noble. So far has this process gone that non-Northern males are even portrayed as the protectors of Northern females against Northern males, thereby totally usurping the natural role and rights of the Northern male and robbing him of one of his most basic natural functions.[36]

This article, as well as others, asserts that the media's portrayal of interracial sexuality as normal and acceptable behavior, and nonwhite males as the protectors of white women, is a threat to the natural gender order, a threat to the natural role of white men as the protectors of white women.

The breakdown of gender identity and what has been constructed as natural gender relations is frequently represented through images of the improperly gendered. For example, the masculinized female is portrayed as castrating males, assaulting masculinity. These images of gender impropriety are always tied to images of interracial sexuality, reinforcing the notion that a threat to either gender or racial identity is a threat to the other. For example, a *National Vanguard* article depicts

the castrating female: the militant feminist who wants every male within shrieking distance to know that she is quite capable of taking care of herself and neither needs nor wants any man's support or protection.... There are a great many more "liberated" women, who, while not shrill man-haters by any means, through their aggressive assertiveness and their manifest independence tend nevertheless to have a castrating effect on the men in their lives ... [the husband whose wife works, even out of economic necessity] feels less a man because of it.... All the brave, new talk about marriage today being a partnership of equals does not change the basic, biological natures of men and women. Those natures have fitted them for *complimentary* [sic] roles, not for the *same* role.... [He is no longer] the master in his house.... [In the past,] when a father had some authority over his daughter, and a husband over his wife, another male approached either at his peril. Not only did female dependence carry with it the need for protection, but it also stimulated in the male the desire to provide that protection. The entire community was behind the man who drew his sword or his gun in defense of his womenfolk.[37]

In this article, improperly gendered females are a threat to male identity as well. Any threat to gender hierarchy and white male dominance is an assault upon gender difference and identity and, as described later in this article, leads to interracial sexuality.

Feminists are often depicted as women taking on the characteristics and behaviors attributed to men in this discourse. This gendered boundary confusion is represented as a danger to both gender and racial identity. Additionally, interracial sexuality comes to represent white males' loss of control over white women, putting their masculinity at risk. Images of abject gender go hand in hand with interracial sexuality.

[Previous] articles suggested that threats to gender identity and the natural gender order led to interracial sexuality. Here, we see the opposite trajectory: interracial sexuality is depicted as leading to the breakdown of gender relations and gender identity. Racial and gender identities are absolutely intertwined throughout this discourse, and produced through and against the realm of the abject: the improperly raced and gendered. The mongrel symbolizes the breakdown of racial borders; the masculinized female and the feminized male symbolize the breakdown of gender borders. Interracial sexuality is linked to both abject race and gender imagery against which both racialized and gendered subjects are produced. The maintenance of the boundaries that are supposed to prevent interracial sexuality actually produce racialized, gendered subjects.

The Jew: Boundary Mediator and Destroyer

Jews are the imagined masterminds behind this grand plot to race-mix the white race out of existence. Jews are constructed as the ultimate enemy. According to *The New Order,*

The single serious enemy facing the White man is the Jew. The Jews are not a religion, they are an Asiatic *race,* locked in mortal conflict with Aryan man which has lasted for millennia, and which will continue until one of the two combat peoples is extinct.[38]

As *The Thunderbolt* proclaims, it is a "WAR OF EXTERMINATION—God's seed against Satan's seed. ONLY ONE WILL SURVIVE."[39]

Jews are racialized in this discourse. However, according to Christian Identity theology, subscribed to by a number of the publications reviewed here, Jews are not simply different genetically and biologically, but are the children of Satan rather than God.

Christian Identity theology defines Jews as nonwhite and claims that they are not merely a separate race, but an impure race, the product of mongrelization.[40] As explained in an article in *The Thunderbolt* entitled "Satan's Children vs. God's Children," Cain was cast out of Eden and married an "Asiatic" woman.

His offspring continued mixing with Asiatics, many of whom had previously mongrelized with Negroes, and they continued this miscegenation down through the years. This Cainite line had Satan's spirit, not God's. . . . The genetic function of their existence is to do the works of their father (Satan) by destroying the White Adamic Race. . . . This Cainite race (if you can call mongrels a race) became the people, who today, are known as JEWS . . . over 80% of today's Jews are descendants of the Khazars, who were phallus worshippers before converting to Judaism. . . . Khazars . . . were of Turk-Mongol blood mixed with White Europeans.[41]

Jews are confined to the fate of mongrelization and symbolize all that goes along with that designation. The position of Jews is ambiguous throughout this discourse, because while Jews are defined as mongrels, they are also produced as a distinctive race in a way that mixed-race people more generally are not. Jews are defined as a distinct race, although the product of intermixture, while other mixed-race people are defined as raceless. White supremacists often note that Jews today do not allow intermarriage for themselves. For example, a *Thunderbolt* article explains that they are advocating [interracial sexuality] for White Christians and members of the colored races but not for members of the Jew race. . . . They have long realized that the fusion of all the other races (while maintaining the purity of the Jew race) will produce a race of mongrels more subservient to their domination.[42]

Curiously, Jews are defined as simultaneously mongrels and a pure race. They are produced as a race whose central racial identity *is* impurity, mongrelization, mixture, etc. The pure essence or racial core of the Jew represents all that is antithetical to the meaning of a healthy race in this discourse. According to Zygmunt Bauman, this has traditionally been the role assigned Jews in anti-Semitic discourse:

The conceptual Jew was a semantically overloaded entity, comprising and blending meanings which ought to be kept apart, and for this reason a natural adversary of any force concerned with drawing borderlines and keeping them watertight. The conceptual Jews was *visquex* (in Sartrean terms), slimy (in Mary Douglas's terms)—an image construed as compromising and defying the order of things, as the very epitome and embodiment of such defiance.[43]

Jews are constructed as symbolizing this site of impossibility and chaos, and the behavior of Jews is described as an extension of that position. Almost every discussion of race-mixing, whether it is school busing or intermarriage, attributes it to Jews. A multitude of articles, found throughout all of the various periodicals, attempts to demonstrate that Jews are responsible for integration and race-mixing. For example, *The Thunderbolt* has published articles with titles like "Jewish Leaders Supporting Race-Mixing," "Jews Finance Race-Mixing Case," "Jewish Organizations Back Interracial Marriage," and "Why Do Jews Support Race-Mixing?"[44] According to the *NSV Report,* Aryans are facing "an or-

ganized mutiny of biologically inferior people, led by the Jews against the White race."[45]

Because Jews are consistently presented as the driving force behind integration and race-mixing, it is assumed that if Jews were out of the picture, separation of blacks and whites would be assured. Recalling the articles discussed earlier, we see that blacks are depicted as stupid and apelike, merely following the lead of the Jews, and without the Jews it is believed that blacks would no longer demand equality. [A picture from *The Thunderbolt*] provides another stark example: inside the head of the black man is a Jew.[46] The Jew is repeatedly depicted as a puppeteer, controlling the black man's actions.

Instauration articles explain that the Jew serves as the mediator between non-Jewish groups. A book entitled *The Mediator,* by Richard Swartzbaugh, is published by the press that publishes *Instauration,* and *Instauration* articles frequently discuss this book, referred to as an "underground classic." Swartzbaugh

shows how this mediating role becomes a necessity in cases where mutually antagonistic groups are to be found within the same living space and where some sort of accommodation is desired. That is why the Jews have always done their best artificially to create such situations. However, the mediator's role becomes superfluous when the groups either merge or split asunder irrevocably. Consequently, the Jew would be in danger if a new American populism united the American majority, North and South, farmer and worker.[47]

This work suggests that Jews have always served the role of mediator between races and benefit from and thrive on the breakdown of racial boundaries. Once again, this is seen as Jewish nature—it is part of their racial essence. As an *NSV Report* article explains,

It is the Jews who are the purveyors of death! Jews are a very negative people. They cannot help it. It is their racial personality. They will destroy your nation, race, culture, civilization, family and whatever you value.[48]

Jews are constructed as a race that by nature disrupts and destroys.

This discourse suggests that the Jew, who symbolizes and embodies the unnatural, the chaotic, and the destruction of the natural order, is disrupting the natural racial order of separation and white superiority and control. As an article in *The Thunderbolt* explains, "When misled liberals and Jews constantly tell negroes that they are equal to (or better) than [*sic*] Whites, hatred and violence erupts when they are unable to compete."[49] While the black man is frequently presented as a dangerous threat, whether as a criminal or rapist of white women, it is often suggested in this discourse that racial order and white male hegemony could be restored if the Jews and their brainwashed white liberals were out of the picture and American society returned to its "natural" racial order of segregation and "old-fashioned justice."

The breakdown of natural racial boundaries is depicted as leading inevitably to interracial sexuality, part of the Jewish plan to exterminate the white race. According to the *NSV Report*, "Jewish parasites . . . race-mix our people into oblivion."[50]

Newsletters often publish cartoons depicting the awesome power and control attributed to Jews, ranging from the media to the banking and finance industries.[51] The United States is often referred to as the "Zionist Occupied Government" (ZOG) or the "Jewnited States." A *White Power* article entitled "Race-Mixing in the Movies" asserts that Hollywood and the motion picture industry were created by, and are controlled by, Jews and have "taken a leading position as a promoter of race-mixing and miscegenation. . . . This medium is now being systematically used to undermine our Aryan values and destroy our White identity."[52] Another article

suggests that the "Jew controlled media" is brainwashing children and teens into accepting interracial sexuality and homosexuality so that "White kids see miscegenation and homosexuality portrayed as the 'in' thing, and anyone who opposes this sort of filth is castigated as a 'racist' or a 'prude.'"[53]

The feminist movement is also linked with the Jewish plan to divide the white race and increase interracial sexuality. Jews are considered the driving force behind feminism, "never less than a third of the leadership of feminist organizations."[54] Similarly, a *White Power* article confirms that

the "Women's Movement" which evolved out of the social turmoil of the 1960s had a distinctly Jewish approach and leadership . . . they seem to be less interested in securing equal rights for women than in turning men and women into unnatural rivals, each struggling against the other for supremacy instead of working together.[55]

Because it is supposedly inherent in Jewish nature to disrupt and threaten difference, Jews are assumed to be behind all movements for racial or gender equality.

Racist publications warn that white genocide and world domination are the end goal of this Jewish conspiracy. A *Thunderbolt* article proclaims

They hope that our seed will vanish into the Jewish contrived "melting pot" with the negroes, Puerto Ricans, Asians and Mexicans in order to create a brown skinned non-White world of the future. The Jews are waging a fierce battle to stop intermarriage within their own race. If the Jews are the last race able to retain their own racial identity they will be able to use their money power to control any mentally dulled race of mongrelized zombies that might eventually be the majority.[56]

According to a *White Power* article entitled "Jews Planning White Genocide," "world

Jewry's chilling Final Solution [is] the physical and spiritual genocide of the White race they despise."[57]

Gender Punishment

Jews serve as figures of abject racial identity, similar to the mongrel, occupying a site of impossibility and chaos. However, Jews also symbolize abject sexuality and gender confusion. The Jew destabilizes not only racial boundaries, but gender boundaries as well.

Throughout this discourse, Jews represent "unnatural" sexuality. Christian Identity theology establishes Jewish origins among the "phallus" worshiping "Khazars." Jews are also frequently associated with homosexuality. The "rabid sex-perverted Jew"[58] is held responsible for the moral decay of America. Throughout the publications I reviewed, Jews are blamed for the pornography industry, which is characterized as an exploiter primarily of Nordic women. According to *The Thunderbolt,* "90% of the pornography in America is produced by Jew owned businesses."[59] According to *Instauration,* "America's juiciest . . . sex scandals often involve Jews," and these scandals are reported in detail in each newsletter, including stories involving homosexuals, sadists, and the seduction of Aryan women.[60]

The issue of circumcision is also mined to support the charge that Jews are a threat to "normal" sexuality and a particular threat to Aryan men. An article in *Instauration* entitled "Foreskinning" exclaims that "slicing off babies' foreskins cannot be described as anything but forms of mutilation" performed by "savages."[61]

As Butler suggests, the construction of properly gendered subjects occurs through the regulation of heterosexuality and the abjection of homosexuality. In this discourse, Jews are not constructed as properly gendered. They not only occupy the site of abject racial, but gender identity as well. Because they are associated with homosexuality and other forms of "perverse" sexuality, the masculinity of Jewish men and the femininity of Jewish women are put into question. Homosexuality and gender chaos are linked. For example, *Instauration* repeatedly refers to homosexuals as "the third sex."[62] If proper gender positions are assumed through the regulation of heterosexuality, homosexuals in this discourse are not produced as proper males or females. Normal gender identity requires heterosexuality.

Jessie Daniels found that Jewish men are represented as feminizing, whether it be other men or the nation as a whole. An article in *WAR* asserts that "One of the characteristics of nations which are controlled by the Jews is the gradual eradication of masculine influence and power and the transfer of influence into feminine forms."[63] Jewish men are portrayed as feminine and feminizing, and the frequent references to circumcisions implies their castration.

Conversely, caricatures of Jewish women portray them as "'mannish' or masculinized."[64] One drawing discussed by Daniels depicts "Miss Israel of 1989" with a hairy body and male genitalia. The association of Jewish women with feminism is also used to suggest that Jewish women are aggressive and unfeminine, even antifeminine. As Daniels surmises, there is "no mention of the women's movement that does not make reference to the Jewish leaders of the movement."[65] When Jewish women are discussed in this discourse, it is usually as either feminists or lesbians, who have become synonymous in this discourse. An *Instauration* article claims, "There is an enormous overlap between the American homosexual and feminist movements, in terms of membership, activities, tactics and ideology."[66] The Jewish woman serves as a threat of gendered punishment, representing abject gender and sexuality. An *Instauration* article argues that feminism is motivated by Jewish women jealous of white women's beauty and femininity:

the leading spokewomen for "feminism" have been—by their own admission—frustrated Jewesses. . . . The entire Jewish tradition has favored mental abstraction over mind-body harmony and instinct for thousands of years—and has actually selected *against* feminine grace—so it is no wonder the Jewesses feel shortchanged in a Nordic country. . . . It isn't America's "macho" males who are under these Jewesses' skins so much as the blonde "shikses." Since they can't beat them in the body department, the Abzugs and Friedans declare the entire sacred domain of fertility/nurture/physical quality to be secondary in life when it should be primary.[67]

The Jewish woman is presented as gender-confused, overly masculine, and (usually) lesbian.

These portrayals have Jewish men and women straddling the boundaries of the male/female binary opposition. Jews are not constructed as properly gendered subjects, but are instead produced as a *threat* to heterosexual relations. For white supremacists, Jewish men and women threaten the natural gender order, putting the masculinity of white men and the femininity of white women at risk. Jews are the ultimate enemy because they destroy the boundaries through which race and gender identities are produced.

These improperly gendered images of Jews serve as figures of abjection, like the mongrel. The Jew and the mongrel represent abject racial identities and serve as threats to enforce properly racialized identities. Similarly, the improperly gendered Jew serves as the "'threat' that compels the assumption of masculine and feminine attributes."[68] The image of Jews as improperly gendered serves as a threat of the punishment for transgressing racial and gender boundaries and failing to follow the regulations for a racially pure heterosexuality. As Bauman suggests,

the conceptual Jew performed a function of prime importance; he visualized the horrifying consequences of boundary-transgression. . . . *The conceptual Jew carried a message; alternative to this order here and now is not another order, but chaos and devastation.*[69]

Notes

1. *The Thunderbolt* January 1979, 12.

The Thunderbolt (1974–1984): published by the National States Rights Party (NSRP), founded in 1958, and edited by J. B. Stoner and Edward Fields, "among the most extreme anti-black, anti-Semitic hatemongers in the U.S." (Anti-Defamation League, 1988a, 29). The ADL describes the NSRP as "ideologically hybrid . . . a bridge between the Ku Klux Klan and the American Nazi groups. *The Thunderbolt* has long been the most widely read publication among the Klans and other hate groups" (Anti-Defamation League, 1988a, 44). Problems began for the organization in 1983, when Stoner, party chair, was jailed for conspiracy involving the bombing of a black church in 1958. In the 1960s, the NSRP was considered "the most militant organized foe" of the civil rights movement (Anti-Defamation League, 1988a, 159). Stoner was a political candidate for numerous offices in Georgia throughout the 1970s, including a run for lieutenant governor in 1974, which garnered him 71,000 votes, over 10 percent of the votes cast for twelve different candidates. By 1987 the NSRP dissolved. Fields continued publishing *The Thunderbolt*, but the publication faced financial ruin.

2. Butler 1991, 20.
3. Butler 1993, 114.
4. Butler 1993, xi–xii.
5. Butler 1993, 2.
6. Macdonald 1978, 2.
7. Butler 1990, 17.
8. *The New Order* September 1979, 7.

The New Order (1979–1983): published by Gerhard Lauck, in Lincoln, Nebraska. Lauck heads the neo-Nazi National Socialist German Workers Party (known as NSDAP-AO). "The NSDAP-AO's circulation is so widespread that it allegedly is recognized by the West German government as the primary source of propaganda materials to [their] underground" (Klanwatch 1993, 8). *The New Order* is widely read and distributed by various white supremacist groups because "membership and distribution materials are easy to obtain" (Klanwatch 1993, 9). Still growing strong, the NSDAP-AO has benefited from the recent surge in neo-Nazi activity throughout Europe.

9. *White Power* February 1973, 3.

White Power (1969–1978): published by the National Socialist White People's Party, which changed its name to the New Order in 1982. This organization is headed by Matt Koehl, with headquarters in Arlington, Virginia, and later New Berlin, Wisconsin. This organization is the direct descendent of the original American neo-Nazi organization, the American Nazi Party, founded in 1958 by George Lincoln Rockwell. The New Order has attempted to form a National Socialist community, called "Nordland," in Wisconsin. According to the ADL,

the New Order is more than just the oldest neo-Nazi group in the U.S.: it is also the most stable and is ahead of the others in organization, discipline, and experience . . . it has sought to adapt its "Aryan" doctrines somewhat, emphasizing white racism as much as anti-Semitism. Still, the New Order is the most direct descendent of Hitler's party among the neo-Nazi groups. (Anti-Defamation League 1988a, 50)

Koehl has also led the World Union of National Socialists, which provides international connections among neo-Nazi groups.

10. *The Thunderbolt* August 1979, 9.

11. *The Thunderbolt* no. 297, 3.

12. *The New Order* March 1979, 8.

13. *The New Order* Spring 1982, 2.

14. *National Vanguard* August 1979, 5.

National Vanguard (1978–1984): published by the National Alliance, in Mill Point, West Virginia, a neo-Nazi racist group headed by William Pierce and founded in 1970. The National Alliance originated from the Youth for Wallace campaign in 1968, run by Willis A. Carto, but split from Carto in 1970 and became the National Alliance, run by former members of George Lincoln Rockwell's American Nazi Party. William Pierce had edited Rockwell's *National Socialist World,"* and after Rockwell's death in 1967, he became leader of the American Nazi Party, subsequently renamed the National Socialist White People's Party, led by Matt Koehl. In 1984, Pierce established a 346-acre compound in West Virginia called the Cosmotheist Community Church.

15. *The New Order* March 1979, 2.

16. *White Power* March 1972, 4.

17. *The Thunderbolt* 25 April 1975, 10.

18. *The Thunderbolt* 30 May 1975, 8.

19. *The Thunderbolt* January 1974, 10.

20. *The New Order* March 1979, 2.

21. Frazier 1957; Keith and Herring 1991; Russell, Wilson, and Hall 1992.

22. Keith and Herring 1991, 777.

23. Keith and Herring 1991, 777.

24. Russell, Wilson, and Hall 1992.

25. *Instauration* January 1980, 14.

Instauration (1976–1983): "Seemingly intellectual," racist and anti-Semitic magazine published by Howard Allen Enterprises, in Cape Canaveral, Florida. Little is known about this corporation. Edited by Wilmot Robertson, pen name of the author of *The Dispossessed Majority*, *Instauration* has been advertised as "essentially a monthly update" of *The Dispossessed Majority*. *Instauration* is concerned with putting "'Northern Europeans back on the evolutionary track' and 'the consolidation, security and advancement of the Northern European peoples.'" John Tyndall, leader of Great Britain's neo-fascist National Front, has called *Instauration* "a highly articulate and stimulating monthly . . . enjoying growing popularity among . . . the National Front" (Anti-Defamation League 1988a, 152).

26. *Instauration* June 1980, 18.

27. *White Power* December 1980, 9.

28. *National Vanguard* May 1978, 1.

29. *Instauration* November 1980, 19.

30. *Instauration* January 1980, 14.

31. *Instauration* June 1980, 14.

32. Flintoff 1993, 83.

33. *Instauration* January 1980, 14.

34. *Instauration* June 1980, 8.

35. *National Vanguard* May 1979, 11.

36. *Instauration* June 1980, 8.

37. *National Vanguard* January 1983, 17.

38. *The New Order* March 1979, 3.

39. *The Thunderbolt* January 1974, 10.

40. Barkun 1994.

41. *The Thunderbolt* January 1974, 10.

42. *The Thunderbolt* no. 297, 3.

43. Bauman 1989, 39.

44. *The Thunderbolt* no. 297, 1; *The Thunderbolt* no. 297, 3.

45. *NSV Report* April/June 1983, 5.

NSV Report (1983–1993): quarterly newsletter of the National Socialist Vanguard, started in 1983, and headed by neo-Nazis Rick Cooper and Dan Stewart, former National Socialist White People's Party members. This group has closely aligned itself with the Church of Jesus Christ Christian Aryan Nations, a Christian Identity church, in Coeur d'Alene, Idaho. Cooper has declared, "I am in this movement for life and I am willing to risk exposure, ridicule and various types of harassment for my beliefs and actions" (Anti-Defamation League 1988b, 46).

46. *The Thunderbolt* June 1975, 8.

47. *Instauration* April 1979, 28.

48. *NSV Report* January/March 1989, 1.

49. *The Thunderbolt* August 1979, 8.

50. *NSV Report* October/December 1988, 2.

51. *Crusader,* Special Introductory Sampler Issue, 3.

Crusader (no dates): subtitled "the voice of the white majority," the *Crusader* was published by the Knights of the Ku Klux Klan, led at the time by Grand Wizard David Duke, out of Metairie, Louisiana. While the newsletters contain no dates, the issues I reviewed were published in the 1970s.

52. *White Power* June/July 1969, 3.

53. *White Power* February 1973, 3.

54. *National Vanguard* January 1983, 17.

55. *White Power* no. 105, 4.

56. *The Thunderbolt* January 1974, 7.

57. *White Power* February 1973, 3.

58. *The Torch* July 1977, 4.

The Torch (1977–1979): published by the White People's Committee to Restore God's Laws, a division of the Church of Jesus Christ, a Christian Identity church.

59. *The Thunderbolt* no. 301, 6.

60. *Instauration* February 1982, 21.

61. *Instauration* December 1979, 17.

62. *Instauration* vol. 2, no. 3(February), 13.

63. *WAR* vol. 8, no. 2(1989), 14 in Daniels 1997, 112–13.

64. Daniels 1997, 116.

65. Daniels 1997, 117.

66. *Instauration* March 1984, 9.

67. *Instauration* June 1984, 16.

68. Butler 1993, 102.

69. Bauman 1989, 39.

References

The Anti-Defamation League of B'nai B'rith. 1988a. *Extremism on the right: A handbook.* New York.

———. 1988b. *Hate groups in America: A record of bigotry and violence.* New York.

Barkun, Michael. 1994. *Religion and the racist right: The origins of the Christian Identity movement.* Chapel Hill: University of North Carolina Press.

Bauman, Zygmunt. 1989. *Modernity and the holocaust.* Ithaca, N.Y.: Cornell University Press.

Butler, Judith. 1990. *Gender trouble: Feminism and the subversion of identity.* New York: Routledge.

———. 1991. Imitation and gender subordination. In *Inside/out: Lesbian stories, gay theories,* edited by Diana Fuss. London: Routledge.

———. 1993. *Bodies that matter: On the discursive limits of sex.* New York: Routledge.

Daniels, Jessie. 1997. *White lies: Race, class, gender, and sexuality in white supremacist discourse.* New York: Routledge.

Flintoff, Anne. 1993. One of the boys? Gender identities in physical education initial teacher education. In *'Race,' gender and the education of teachers,* edited by Iram Siraj-Blatchford. Philadelphia: Open University Press.

Frazier, E. Franklin. 1957. *The Negro in the United States.* New York: Macmillan.

Keith, Vera M., and Cedric Herring. 1991. Skin tone and stratification in the black community. *American Journal of Sociology* 97, no. 3: 760–78.

Klanwatch. 1993. The Midwest's top neo-nazi: Gerhard Lauck and the NSDAP-AO. In *Klanwatch Intelligence Report*. Montgomery, Ala.: The Klanwatch Project of the Southern Poverty Law Center. 66(April):8–9.

Macdonald, Andrew [pseudonym of William Pierce]. 1978. *The Turner diaries*. Hillsboro, Va.: National Vanguard Books.

Russell, Kathy, Midge Wilson, and Ronald Hall. 1992. *The color complex: The politics of skin color among African Americans*. New York: Doubleday.

Ferber:

1. Discuss the ways in which white supremacists maintain their boundaries or construct stable racial identities to produce "properly racialized and properly gendered subjects."

2. Discuss how Jews are considered to be both pure and impure.

6

Caught in the Middle:
Korean-African American Conflicts

Pyong Gap Min

Members of an ethnic group tend to join ranks in internal solidarity when they encounter threats from the outside world. Several groups have posed threats to Korean merchants, the most serious undoubtedly being the danger of physical violence, murder, arson, boycott, and looting in Black neighborhoods. Therefore, Korean-African American conflicts have more strongly fostered Korean internal solidarity than have any other type of business-related intergroup conflict. Korean merchants in Black neighborhoods have established local business associations to try collectively to solve problems with Black customers and residents. Black boycotts of Korean stores in New York and other cities and the destruction of Korean stores during the Los Angeles riots have threatened Korean immigrants' economic survival itself. Thus, these hostile actions have led not only Korean ghetto merchants but also other Korean immigrants to be concerned about their common fate and marginal status in this country. This chapter focuses on how Koreans' ethnic solidarity has been affected by the 1990–91 Brooklyn boycott of two Korean stores and the victimization of Korean merchants during the riots. In addition, it will examine Koreans' responses to Ice Cube's "Black Korea."

Ice Cube's "Black Korea"
and Koreans' Responses

At the end of October 1991, Ice Cube, a Los Angeles-based Black rap singer, released a new album entitled *Death Certificate*. "Black Korea," a controversial song included in this album, reflects African Americans' hostility toward and violence against Koreans in such phrases as "they make a nigger mad enough to cause a little ruckus" and "pay respect to the black fist or we'll burn / your store right down to your crisp." In his interview with the *Los Angeles Times,* Ice Cube stated that the song reflected African Americans' and Koreans' mutual hatred rather than his own contempt for Koreans (Hunt 1991).

Naturally, Koreans were seriously concerned about the negative impact of this song on Koreans' image and Korean–African American relations. Since the song included many incendiary phrases, they worried it would encourage Black youngsters to use violence and arson against Korean merchants. As soon as the album was released, Korean community leaders in Los Angeles and New York had a series of meetings to discuss what measures to take to protest it. Both the Korean Embassy in Washington and the Korean

Consulate General in Los Angeles were gravely concerned about its possible negative impact (*KCDNY*, November 9, 1991). Interestingly, the album also included a song, "No Vaseline," that encouraged the murder of Jerry Heller, Ice Cube's Jewish former manager. For this reason, the Simon Wiesenthal Center, a Jewish human rights organization, called on four national record chains to stop selling *Death Certificate* (Philips 1991).

Korean community leaders in Los Angeles, led by the Korean Consulate General, tried with no success to stop the distribution of the album by pressuring the record company, Priority Records. The St. Ice Beer Company, which used Ice Cube in their commercials, partly depended on Korean grocery and liquor retailers to distribute their merchandise. The Korean-American Grocers Association of Southern California threatened to boycott the company if it did not stop using Ice Cube as a model (*KTLA*, November 20, 1991). When there was no positive response, KAGROSC began a boycott. The boycott prompted the company to run an advertisement in Korean dailies in Los Angeles, emphasizing their difficulty in influencing Ice Cube and asking Korean grocers to stop the boycott. However, the National Korean-American Grocers Association, which has its office in Orange County, influenced other local KAGROs, including KAGRO New York, to increase the pressure on the St. Ice Beer Company, using the boycott as a lever for negotiation (*SGT*, November 14, 1991).

The grocers' boycott inflicted severe monetary damages on the beer company; the former president of KAGROLA told me that the company lost approximately $7 million from seven days of Koreans' boycotts. On the seventh day, the company acceded, firing Ice Cube as a model. They also asked him to make a formal apology to the Korean community. Under pressure from the St. Ice Beer Company, Ice Cube apologized to Korean merchant leaders in Los Angeles for his inflammatory lyrics in April 1992, just prior to the eruption of the Los Angeles riots (Kim 1992). Ice Cube arranged meetings with the president of the National Korean-American Grocers Association (Yang Il Kim) and the president of KAGROLA (David Kim), in which he told them, "I respect Korean Americans. It was directed at a few stores where I and my friends have had actual problems" (Kim 1992). He later sent copies of a letter of apology to the Korean community and to members of the media. Though Korean merchants failed to stop the sale of the album, by pressuring their supplier they at least succeeded in making the singer formally apologize.

Effects of the Los Angeles Riots

The Los Angeles riots marked a turning point in history for Korean Americans, much as the internment experience did for Japanese Americans. The riots brought about significant changes in the Korean community in Los Angeles. The material and nonmaterial damages inflicted by the riots have enhanced community solidarity to a far greater extent than any other major case of business-related intergroup conflict that Korean immigrants have experienced. The victimization of many innocent Korean merchants during the riots increased Koreans' political consciousness and political development. Finally, the riots heightened second-generation Korean Americans' sense of ethnic identity and increased their influence and power in the Los Angeles Korean community.

Overall Community Solidarity

Threats from the outside world generally increase internal unity, and thus the riots, as major external threats, strengthened internal solidarity in the Korean community in Los Angeles. Koreans were angry about the large-scale destruction that the Korean community suffered during the riots, and they were even more outraged by what they believed to be the White conspiracy behind the destruction than by the destruction itself. Many Koreans believed that the U.S. media intentionally focused on Korean-Black conflicts to direct Blacks' frustration toward Korean merchants. Angry about the biased media coverage, a number of Koreans sent letters of protest to the American media and to the *Korea Times Los Angeles* (see the English section of the *Korea Times Los Angeles,* May 11, 1992). On May 3, about one thousand Korean students rallied at the local ABC-TV affiliate to protest the station's biased coverage (Hwangbo 1992).

Many Koreans also considered the failure of the police to respond to Koreans' desperate calls for help to protect Koreatown part of the White conspiracy to use Koreans as scapegoats. There was widespread speculation in the Korean community during the riots that the police allowed Koreatown to be burned and destroyed to protect Beverly Hills, a wealthy White community. After hearing the radio report that Koreatown was being attacked without defense, many Korean former marines and young men volunteered to defend Koreatown. One of the volunteers, eighteen-year-old Edward Lee, died and two others were injured during cross fire on the second night of the riots. The Korean self-defense team guarded Koreatown for several weeks after the riots.

In February 1993, Korean former marines and other war veterans who helped protect Koreatown during the riots created Tae Kuk Bang Bum Dae, a crime prevention patrol (*KTLA,* February 12, 1993). The team, consisting of nine men, patrols the heart of Koreatown in two cars between noon and 8 P.M. to protect Koreatown businesses and residents from crimes. Few areas in Los Angeles have as high a rate of crime as Koreatown. Though a police box is located in Koreatown, the department lacks the resources to combat panhandling, robberies of businesses, and other crimes there. The president of the Korean Veterans Association donated $200,000

to establish Tae Kuk Bang Bum Dae (*KTLA,* January 4, 1993), which was also intended to protect Koreatown from a similar riot occurring again. In fact, the rumor about another riot in Los Angeles following the second verdict in the Rodney King case led to the creation of the patrol team in a hurry.

Koreans in Los Angeles held a solidarity and peace rally at Ardmore Park in Koreatown on May 2, just one day after the riots ended. About 30,000 Koreans from all over the Los Angeles area participated, the largest Korean meeting ever held in the United States (Sunoo 1992). Though the rally was hurriedly organized and not well publicized, many Koreans came to protest the unfair treatment of Korean Americans by the media and the police during the riots and to show Koreans' solidarity. Marching through the ravaged portions of Koreatown and wearing white headbands, the demonstrators called for peace, requested justice for Rodney King, and vowed to rebuild Koreatown and the destroyed Korean stores. A large number of second-generation Koreans participated in the rally, sharing the grief and agony of first-generation immigrants.

Throughout the month of May 1992, a number of well-known American and Korean politicians visited Koreatown, held meetings with Korean community leaders, and listened to their grievances. These leaders included President Bush, Bill Clinton, Jesse Jackson, a delegation from the U.S. Civil Rights Commission, and Dae Joong Kim, a long-time opposition party leader in South Korea. Their visits provided Korean community leaders with the opportunity to express their views concerning the injustice done to Korean Americans by the media, the police, politicians, and rioters. In addition, the meetings with top-level politicians helped Korean community leaders learn political skills and heightened their political consciousness.

In the wake of the Los Angeles riots, Koreans showed solidarity in their efforts to help riot victims. Korean Americans all over the country participated in fund-raising campaigns. As a result, more than $5 million was collected from the Korean American community, and another $4.5 million was donated from South Korea (*KTLA,* July 23 and 29, 1992; April 30, 1993). Though large Korean corporations were responsible for much of the funds raised in Korea and the United States, many Korean immigrants individually donated money. Even Mindan, a pro-South Korean Korean-Japanese organization, contributed $200,000 to help fellow Koreans in Los Angeles (*SGT,* May 12, 1992).

Though Koreans in both the United States and Korea showed solidarity by generously donating money to help riot victims, these large sums also created problems. There were several sources of conflict over the donated money. First, because the donations were collected by a dozen ethnic organizations—primarily the ethnic media—the Korean Riot Victims' Association (KRVA) had difficulty in subsequently getting all the funds forwarded from these various organizations. Leaders of the KRVA complained that some organizations did not release all the donations they had received. Responding to their complaints, the Korean C.P.A. Association of Southern California audited the ethnic organizations involved. Furthermore, the Korean Consulate General in Los Angeles, which handled the donations from Korea, was reluctant to transfer the money to the KRVA. Though the consulate finally did so, KRVA leaders accused the consul general and some others of taking some of the donated money for personal use (*KTLA,* August 14, 1992; *SGT,* October 27, 1992). Riot victims demonstrated in front of the Korean Consulate General building several times.

Second, riot victims could not agree on who should be eligible to receive the donated money, since some victims lost their entire businesses whereas the stores of others suffered only minor damage. Some of the self-identified riot victims, who were eliminated from the list of "victims eligible for receiving the distribution of the donations," sought redress in the Los Angeles Municipal Court. In November 1992, accepting their claim as justified, the court ordered the KRVA to pay all who had been eliminated from eligibility (approximately two hundred merchants) the amount of $2,500, which the other victims had received as the first distribution of the donations (*KTLA,* November 7, 1992).

Third, Korean community leaders and riot victims in Los Angeles did not agree on how to use the donated money. Whereas riot victims argued that all the donated money should be distributed to them, Korean community leaders representing professional associations (the Korean-American Bar Association of Los Angeles and the Korean C.P.A. Association of Southern California) maintained that part of the donated money should be used for long-term community programs (*KTLA,* July 15, 1992). As of April 1993, they still had $1.8 million from the donations, which will most likely be used for the construction of a community center (*KTLA,* April 30, 1993). In July 1994, the Korean-American Relief Fund Foundation that managed the unused fund opened an escrow to buy a $2 million building located in Koreatown to be used as a Korean community center (*KTLA,* July 30, 1994). In September 1993, the South Korean government provided financial support with $1.25 million to be used for reconstruction of the Los Angeles Korean community. The Korean Consulate General at Los Angeles turned it over to the Korean American Scholarship Foundation, established in memory of the victimization of Koreans during the Los Angeles riots (*KTLA,* October 4, 1993).

Before these riots, Korean immigrants did not generally use protest as a means of achieving their goals.[1] However, having lived through the outrage and pain over the unprecedented destruction and looting of their businesses, they now readily accept this technique as a means of getting their messages across to government officials. When President Bush met with Korean community leaders at Radio Korea Los Angeles in Koreatown, approximately five hundred Koreans rallied outside the building, chanting slogans such as "We Need Compensation" and "Where Is My Tax?" In the middle of June 1992, Korean riot victims started a rally at the Los Angeles City Hall (*KTLA,* June 17, 1992). For the next month, an average of two hundred victims participated daily in the rally. The president of the KRVA even went on a hunger strike for a few days.

In order to make their demands in a more concerted manner, Korean riot victims established the Korean 4.29 Riot Victims Association. In their meetings with Mayor Bradley, other city and state government officials, and lawmakers, its representatives demanded (1) that the Los Angeles City government apologize to victims for what happened, (2) that victims be compensated for their losses, (3) that the association send a representative to the Los Angeles City Reconstruction Committee, (4) that the bylaw requiring Korean liquor stores in Black neighborhoods to get permission from the residents for reopening be abolished, (5) that SBA loan application procedures be simplified, and (6) that the Los Angeles City government expand loan programs for riot victims (*SGT,* July 7, 1992). In mid-July, when Mayor Bradley promised to accept some of their demands, they stopped the month-old rally (*KTLA,* July 12, 1992).

Koreans' Political Consciousness

Many Koreans in Los Angeles and other cities felt that their lack of political power was mainly responsible for Koreans' becoming innocent victims of the Black-White racial conflict during the riots. Thus, the Los Angeles riots have heightened Korean Americans' political consciousness. Koreans in Los Angeles, in particular, have made efforts to exercise political influence to make the government compensate Koreans for their losses during the riots and to protect Koreans' overall interests. The Korean-American Bar Association of Los Angeles held several meetings to discuss the possibility of suing the government for neglecting to protect Koreatown during the riots (*KTLA,* June 15, 1992). In July 1992, a group of Korean lawyers in Los Angeles also organized the Korean American Legal Advocacy Foundation, a nonprofit organization, to protect Koreans' human rights against assaults by the government and other groups. With their central office in Los Angeles and local chapters in several other Korean communities, this organization plans to play a role in the Korean community similar to the role that the Anti-Defamation League and the Mexican American Legal Defense and Education Fund play in other ethnic communities (*KTLA,* July 25, 1992).

The post-riot political consciousness among Korean Americans is not limited to specific Korean ethnic organizations. Before the riots, Korean immigrants were preoccupied with politics in South Korea. However, there is evidence that after the riots Korean immigrants in general and those in Los Angeles in particular became more keenly aware of their need to improve their political position in this country.[2] A survey in New York City indicates that the number of Koreans who took the citizenship test dramatically increased from March to June 1992 (*KTNY,* June 17, 1992). According to the Korean Federation of L.A. as well, the number of Korean immigrants who inquired about the citizenship test noticeably increased after the riots (*SGT,* September 29, 1992). Before the riots, the ability to bring over their family members was Korean immigrants' main motive for gaining citizenship. However, in the wake of the riots more and more Korean immigrants seem to have applied for citizenship to be able to exercise their right to vote. Paralleling this increase in acquiring citizenship, Koreans' voter registration increased significantly in 1992. For example, a study based on county voter registration records estimates that 2,400 Koreans in Orange County registered to vote in 1992 alone, accounting for 30% of the Koreans who had registered since 1983 (*KTLA,* October 31, 1992).

During the 1992 presidential election year, Jay Kim (whose Korean name is Kim Chang Joon) was elected to the House of Representatives from the 41st District in California, becoming the first Korean congressional member in American history. In 1992, three other Koreans became members of the Washington, Oregon, and Hawaii state legislatures (*KTLA,* November 5, 1992). Kim and the Washington and Oregon state representatives were elected mainly because, as members of the Republican Party, they received support from conservative White voters. However, Koreans' support, not only as voters but also as helpers in election campaigns, contributed to their success. In particular, Jay Kim received enthusiastic support from Korean Americans in the first post-riot election (*KTLA,* November 15, 1992). Even a large number of Koreans in New York responded generously to a fund-raising party for Kim, for in the aftermath of the riots they were keenly aware of Koreans' lack of political power.

Younger-Generation Koreans' Ethnic Consciousness

Korean immigrants feel a sense of brotherhood with co-ethnics partly because of their commonalities in culture—the Korean language, customs, and Confucian values. They also feel connected to one another because they share common historical experiences. Their memories of major historical events that occurred in twentieth-century Korea, such as Japanese colonization, the Korean War, and the subsequent division of Korea

into two halves, have strengthened their ethnic ties. However, until the tragedy of the Los Angeles riots, younger-generation Koreans in the United States had not lived through major historical experiences together as Korean Americans. The Los Angeles riots were the first major event that provided 1.5- and second-generation Koreans with an opportunity to think about their common fate as Korean Americans. They witnessed their parents being targeted by rioters simply because they were Koreans. They realized that they, too, could be targets of attack by another group simply because they were Korean Americans. Edward Lee, the only Korean who died in cross fire during the riots, was an eighteen-year-old second-generation Korean who had volunteered to protect Koreatown businesses from attack by rioters. His funeral drew a large number of Korean mourners.

Young Koreans suspected that the police did not care about protecting Koreatown from attacks by rioters, primarily because Korean Americans were a powerless minority group. Thus, the Los Angeles riots heightened younger-generation Koreans' ethnic consciousness and identity. In an essay written almost two years after the riots, Julie Lee, a 1.5-generation Korean American, described how experiencing the riots wakened her ethnic identity (Lee 1994):

My Korean-American heritage was something I took for granted until the 1992 riots forced me to re-evaluate my identity. "Wasn't I an American?" I asked myself when witnessing the destruction of so many stores and businesses belonging to other Korean-Americans. Why have we been singled out? I kept wondering, thinking that we were no different than any other ethnic groups that came to this nation to work, endure and find our place in American history. . . .

I didn't know—until the riots. Watching the flames rise from Korean-American businesses, listening to frightened friends and relatives, then hearing the voices of the angry rioters, accusing

Korean-Americans of exploiting them in the lower-income neighborhoods that were being destroyed, I sensed that I was Korean and I was an American.

Young Koreans quickly responded to the riots by writing articles in major English dailies in California; they attacked the media bias and the police failure to protect Koreatown and defended the position of the Korean community. For example, Thomas Chung, a political science major at UCLA, responded to an interview by a *Korea Times* reporter (Ha 1992):

Korean Americans felt abandoned by the police and the whole justice system. It is really hard for me to watch the news because this is where I grew up and it was on fire everywhere. The culmination of the whole thing is just anger.

Before I felt alienated because I wanted to support the African American community, but the Korean American was targeted purposely, and I felt like we were being used as scapegoats to channel their anger. On Saturdays, when I went to the Koreatown rally, I was so glad I was there. After that, I realized that we all have to pitch in.

A large number of 1.5- and second-generation Koreans participated in a solidarity rally held at Ardmore Park, Koreatown, on May 2, making it a truly multigenerational event. On May 3, about a thousand Korean American students rallied at the local ABC-TV station to protest the station's unfair coverage of Korean Americans. On May 6, over three hundred UCLA Korean American students on campus voiced their anger and concern about losses the Korean American community had suffered during the riots (Chung 1992). Also, many young Koreans volunteered at relief centers to help Korean riot victims. Second-generation Koreans in Los Angeles, in other cities, and on college campuses have held a number of seminars on the causes of the riots and on the Korean community in general. They agreed that the riots exposed the political weakness of first-generation Koreans and that it was their obligation to protect their parents' interests (*KTNY,* May 16, 1992; *SGT,* May 15, 1992). In July 1993, Los Angeles's Korean American Coalition, the Coalition of Korean-American Voters in New York, and several other 1.5- and second-generation Korean American organizations in other cities established a national coalition organization, similar to the Japanese American Citizens League. The national coalition plans to coordinate local Korean associations in campaigning for voter registration and bilingual voting, aiding Koreans' political development, lobbying lawmakers for Korean interests, and resolving interracial conflicts (*SGT,* November 27, 1992; *KTLA,* July 28, 1993).[3]

We noted [previously] that younger-generation Koreans held views about Korean-African American conflicts different from those of Korean immigrants, particularly Korean immigrant merchants. This generational difference emerged clearly when various groups explained the riots and the victimization of Korean merchants during them. Korean merchants and even many Korean pastors emphasized the criminality of the riot participants in general and Black gang members in particular. In contrast, as is clear from many interviews and letters cited in this chapter, younger-generation Koreans directed their attack toward the mainstream media and the police, who they believed allowed and even encouraged the rioters to target Korean stores. Younger-generation Korean community leaders were careful not to criticize African Americans for victimizing Korean merchants,[4] and some second-generation Koreans emphasized the need for a Korean-African American alliance to fight against the White system. However, it is significant that the victimization of Korean merchants during the riots stimulated younger-generation Koreans' ethnic consciousness as much as it increased the solidarity of Korean immigrants. Younger-generation Koreans realized that their parents were scapegoated and victimized by the White system mainly because of lack of power and that as a powerless minority group they, too, are vulnerable to victimization in the future.

A number of scholars have indicated that major historical events such as the Holocaust and the internment of Japanese Americans during World War II have played an important role in the persistence of ethnicity. The victimization of innocent Korean merchants during the riots is another such event, and it will have an impact on the ethnic identity of Korean Americans for many years to come. Young Koreans are already talking about the 4.29 movies, 4.29 arts, and 4.29 literature. These artistic works, focusing on the theme of the victimization of Korean merchants during the riots, will serve as a symbol for Korean ethnic identity in the future. In 1992, artistic works reflecting the experiences of Japanese Americans in relocation camps during World War II were displayed at the UCLA campus to celebrate the fiftieth anniversary of the Japanese Americans' internment. In the year 2042, similar artistic works may be displayed at the same campus in commemoration of the fiftieth anniversary of the victimization of Korean merchants during the riots, and they will enhance third- and fourth-generation Koreans' ethnic identity.

Notes

1. Koreans' unwillingness to use the technique of protest is deeply rooted in their Confucian cultural tradition. Confucianism puts great emphasis on the individual's conformity to society and discourages individuals from challenging any authority, whether it be parents, teachers, or the government.

2. The democratization in South Korea also contributed to the shift in Korean immigrants' political interest from their home country to the United States. When South Korea was under military rule before the popular election in 1987, there

were many antigovernment political organizations in the Korean American community. These political organizations, which focused on homeland politics, have since gradually disappeared.

3. I interviewed a staff member of the Korean American Coalition in the summer of 1994 and asked about the progress of the national Korean American Alliance. He told me that because of its lack of financial resources, the association had not undertaken any significant activities.

4. In the summer of 1993, Stanley Karnow, a freelance journalist, visited the Korean American community in Los Angeles and interviewed several second-generation Korean community leaders, including Angela Oh, for an article on the Korean American community. He told me that the younger-generation Koreans whom he interviewed initially refused to accept that Black rioters shared responsibility for victimizing Korean merchants during the riots, but that when pressed hard they reluctantly agreed that Blacks bore some blame.

References

Chung, Suzie. 1992. "300 KAs Rally for Justice at UCLA." *Korea Times Los Angeles* (English edition), May 18.

Ha, Julie. 1992. "Reactions from KA Students at UCLA." *Korea Times Los Angeles* (English edition), May 11.

Hunt, Dennis. 1991. "Outrageous as He Wants to Be." *Los Angeles Times,* November 3.

Hwangbo, Kay. 1992. "Korean Americans Organize and Mobilize." *Korea Times Los Angeles* (English edition), May 11.

Kim, Sophia Kyung. 1992. "Ice Cube the Peacemaker." *Korea Times Los Angeles* (English edition), May 4.

Lee, Julie. 1994. "Defining 1.5 Generation." *Korea Times Los Angeles* (English edition), April 6.

Philips, Chuck. 1991. "Wiesenthal Center Denounces Ice Cube's Album." *Los Angeles Times,* November 2.

Sunoo, Paik Brenda. 1992. "Out of Ashes, Solidarity." *Korea Times Los Angeles* (English edition), May 11.

Korean Language Dailies and Magazines

Korea Central Daily New York (KCDNY).

— 11/9/1991. "The Korean Community Considers a Number of Measures against 'Black Korea.'"

Korea Times Los Angeles (KTLA).

— 11/20/1991. "Koreans' Anger against 'Black Korea' Spread Quickly."

— 6/15/1992. "Preparing Law Suits against Governments."

— 6/17/1992. "Korean Victims of the Riots Will Continue Their Demonstration for Three Months."

— 7/12/1992. "One-Month-Old City Hall Rally Ended."

— 7/23/1992. "$4,752,571 Was Raised in the U.S."

— 7/25/1992. "Korean-American Legal Advocacy Foundation to Be Established Soon."

— 7/29/1992. "Conflict over Use of Funds Settled."

— 8/14/1992. "Korean Riot Victims Demonstrated against Korean Consul General and Mr. Ki Hwan Ha."

— 10/31/1992. "2,400 Koreans In Orange County Registered for Voting in 1992 Alone."

— 11/5/1992. "The New Era in the 100-Year Korean American History."

— 11/7/1992. "Payment to 200 Additional Riot Victims Is Inevitable."

— 11/15/1992. "The Meaning of Jay Kim's Election to the U.S. House of Representatives."

— 1/4/1993. "Koreatown Security Patrol Team to Be Created in February."

— 2/12/1993. "Koreatown Security Patrol Team Established."

— 4/30/1993. "Results of the Audit of Donations for Riot Victims Disclosed."

— 7/28/1993. "The National Korean-American Alliance Established."

— 10/4/1993. "The Entire Amount of Korean Government's Financial Support Turned Over to the Korean American Scholarship Foundation."

— 7/30/1994. "An Unused Korean Riot Victims Fund to Be Used for Construction of the Korean Community Center."

Korea Times New York (KTNY).

— 5/16/1992. "It's Time We Second-Generation Koreans Work for the Protection of Korean American Interests."

— 6/17/1992. "Koreans Who Took the Citizenship Test Greatly Increased after the Riot."

Sae Gae Times (SGT).

— 11/14/1991. "St. Ice Beer Company Asked to Stop Supporting Ice Cube."

— 5/12/1992. "Mindan Contributed $200,000 for Riot Victims."

— 5/15/1992. "1.5- and 2nd-Generation Koreans Actively Participating in the Korean Community."

— 7/7/1992. "The Los Angeles City Government Owes an Apology to Koreans."

— 9/29/1992. "LA Koreans' Citizenship Applications Have Rapidly Increased."

— 10/27/1992. "LA Korean Consul General Took a Large Proportion of Donations from Korea."

— 11/27/1992. "A National Korean-American Civil Rights Organization Is Being Established."

Min:

1. Given what you have read in this essay, why do you think blacks and Koreans have historically been unable to work together in Los Angeles?

2. Discuss the factors that led to the increase in identity politics for Koreans in Los Angeles.

7

Urban Rioting in Los Angeles:
A Comparison of 1965 with 1992

David O. Sears

The nation is rapidly moving toward two increasingly separate Americas. Within two decades, this division could be so deep that it would be almost impossible to unite: a white society principally located in suburbs, in smaller central cities, and in the peripheral parts of large central cities, and a Negro society largely concentrated within large central cities.

—Kerner Commission (1968, p. 407)

I read [the] report . . . of the 1919 riot in Chicago, and it was if I were reading the report of the investigating committee on the Harlem riot of '35, the report of the investigating committee on the Harlem riot of '43, the report of the McCone Commission on the Watts riot. I must again in candor say to you members of this Commission—it is a kind of Alice in Wonderland—with the same moving picture re-shown over and over again, the same analysis, the same recommendations, and the same inaction.

—Kenneth B. Clark (In Kerner Commission report, 1968, p. 29)

Many commentators have referred to the police brutality verdict and rebellion as a strong "wake-up call." . . . Sadly, our data provide no substantial indication that this "wake up call" has been heard.

—Bobo et al. 1994, p. 133

Can we all get along?
—Rodney King, 1992

At 7 PM on August 11, 1965, a black man, Marquette Frye, having had several "screwdrivers" celebrating his brother's return to Los Angeles from military service, was weaving his way home down the freeway at a speed exceeding the legal limit. A motorcycle officer of the California Highway Patrol pulled him over at 166th Street and Avalon Boulevard, in the heart of the Los Angeles neighborhood known as "Watts." Frye's behavior was somewhat boisterous, though humorous and cooperative, but it attracted a crowd on a hot summer evening. Frye later became belligerent, as did the crowd, and other officers were summoned. His brother and mother arrived, and before long all three Fryes were on their way to jail, and the police departed leaving behind a wake of thrown rocks and bottles and bricks.

So began the "Watts riot" of 1965. Soon an area larger than the city of San Francisco was cordoned off by the National Guard as a "curfew zone." Nevertheless, the rioting continued for six days, leaving 34 dead, over 1000 injured badly enough to require treatment, nearly 4000 arrested, and 1000 buildings damaged or destroyed, at a probable loss, in 1965 dollars, of $40 million (Sears and McConahay, 1973). Local white officials denounced the rioters as inspired by "outside agitators," while black leaders tended more to see it as a racial protest.

Nearly 27 years later, on April 29, 1992, the acquittal in Simi Valley, California, of four Los Angeles Police Department officers of charges related to the widely televised beating of Rodney King, a black motorist, set off more rioting in South Central Los Angeles. The police were wholly unprepared for the outbreak. The Chief was at a fundraiser in the posh suburb of Brentwood when it began, and did not leave it for some time. The police were wholly outnumbered and outgunned during the first evening, and lost control of great stretches of the city. After the first night, the entire city of Los Angeles was placed under a dusk-to-dawn curfew. Again the riot itself lasted six days. Nearly 14,000 law enforcement personnel from outside the city were required to stop it. Over 16,000 people were arrested, 52 lost their lives, and nearly $1 billion in property had been damaged or destroyed.

Initially the events seemed quite similar to those of the Watts riots in 1965, in that the rioters were predominantly black, the area of the rioting similar, the local police again quickly lost control and had to be supplemented by the National Guard, while the Chief of Police made hard-line, inflammatory statements about the rioters. As a result, initially the events were interpreted in famil-

iar terms. Some once again saw street hoodlums (this time local gang members, not "outside agitators") as using the pretext of political events to pillage, loot, and injure the innocent, and so it was a "riot." Others saw another in a long line of black protests against social injustice, and so it was a "rebellion" or an "insurrection" of an oppressed people. But was it a 1960's ghetto riot all over again? Or was it, as some of these authors maintain, "a new form," "the first urban unrest of the 21st century"? This essay sketches out some of the similarities and differences between the two events, in an effort to understand both the meaning of the events themselves, and the social conditions underlying them.

Watts in 1965 and the Politics of Violence

Soon after the Watts riots of August, 1965, a group of social scientists at UCLA embarked on an ambitious multi-disciplinary research effort on the rioting. Much of it was published in a volume edited by Nathan Cohen (1970), the leader of the team. Our own account appeared in more detailed form as *The Politics of Violence: The New Urban Blacks and the Watts Riot* (Sears and McConahay, 1973). A simple approach to the comparison of these two events begins with a review of the main conclusions of the latter book.

Causes of the Riot

The theory of the riot's causes had three parts. First, we saw the broader white context as characterized by both a high degree of racial isolation and a new "symbolic racism" that had replaced the old-fashioned Jim Crow racism of the old South. A striking level of racial isolation did exist, due not to formal segregation but to the great geographical dispersion of the LA basin, the relatively small numbers of blacks, combined with the *de facto* segregation typical of Northern and Western American urban areas, and black invisibility in the media (Johnson, Sears, and McConahay, 1971). The new form of racism we proposed—symbolic racism—was described as a blend of traditional (and race-neutral) American values such as individualism with "the mild stereotyped white prejudice common to northern whites . . ." (Sears and McConehay, 1973, p. 199). A second component was a collection of long-standing grievances widespread among blacks in Los Angeles, including police brutality toward blacks, gouging by merchants, perceptions of racial discrimination (especially in the schools), and the negative attitudes held toward the black community by such public leaders as the Mayor and Police Chief. These grievances tended not to divide along demographic lines among blacks; rather, they tended to be fairly widely distributed throughout the black community. The riot itself was triggered by "a typical 'grievance,' involving an individual black who felt maltreated by an unsympathetic institution, largely managed and staffed by whites, following its standard operating procedures" (Sears and McConehay, 1973, p. 198).

The third component was a theory of the "new urban blacks." The great migration of blacks from the South to Los Angeles had occurred during the 1940's and 1950's, so the first generation of young Los Angeles natives was coming into maturity only in the mid-1960's. This new generation of natives [was] urban and Northern-socialized, better educated and more politically sophisticated than their largely rural, Southern, and migrant forebears, and more angry, disaffected, anti-white, and proud of being black as well.

The data analysis indicated that the rioters tended to reflect these last two components: they were more aggrieved than non-rioters, and they tended to be young, Northern and urban-reared, anti-white, pro-black, disaffected, and frustrated. These data were interpreted as supporting the view that the rioting

had been, to some substantial degree, a racial protest against bad local conditions, as well as reflecting more general support among the coming generation of young Northern blacks for confronting racial inequality directly.

A series of other theories of rioting were also tested and rejected. Most prominently, the rioters did not fit the widely heralded profile of the "riff-raff" or urban underclass—they were somewhat more likely to be unemployed than non-rioters, but they were not less educated, or from broken homes, or Southern newcomers. Nor did they did fit Banfield's (1970) "rioting for fun and profit" theory. They were not especially Southern-socialized; genuine discontents seemed to have motivated much of the rioting, rather than mere rampaging or foraying for pillage; and the "racial protest" interpretation of the rioting common throughout the area proved, as best we could tell, not to be mere post hoc rationalization. Whereas social contagion was no doubt widespread and accounted for some of the rioting, the data argued against its being the *principal* or primary explanation (Sears and McConehay, 1973, p. 201).

The Legacy of "Watts"

The riot had a strongly polarizing effect on blacks and whites. Our analysis uncovered the spread throughout the black community, in the months following the riot, of what we called a "riot ideology"—the belief that it had been a racial protest founded on realistic grievances, that it was likely to have useful effects, combined with some sympathy for the rioters. This ideology was especially prevalent among the young, and indeed Southern newcomers seemed to be increasingly socialized to this new view of things.

Local white leaders at the time of "Watts" took a hard law enforcement line, but the liberal Democrats then in charge of the state and federal government were more sympathetic. The white public responded with ambivalence: many also viewed it as a racial protest, and expected that it would lead to greater white awareness of blacks' problems, but supported the authorities and thought it would increase the gap between the races.

This presaged the ambivalent white response to the ghetto riots throughout the 1960's. On the one hand, elites often responded sympathetically, as in the McCone Commission report in Los Angeles or the Kerner Commission report nationally. These were followed by many active policy responses, such as school integration, affirmative action, and many efforts to reduce poverty in inner cities. Yet they also led to the spread of a strong "law and order" mentality among moderate and conservative whites throughout the country, and to the reactive conservative political campaigns of George Wallace and many local leaders (such as the then-Mayor of Los Angeles, Sam Yorty; see Kinder and Sears, 1981).

We concluded with four general predictions for the future:

1. Increasing ghetto tensions, based on the continuing existence of social conditions giving rise to realistic grievances, combined with increasing black sophistication.

2. Some continuing increase in violence as a strategy for dealing with those grievances. We did not expect further mass violence in the short run, but perhaps activities more akin to guerrilla action or conventional crime. We also anticipated increasingly creative and widely varying political strategies, and increasingly effective use of conventional electoral politics.

3. In terms of the white institutional response, we underlined the combination of anger and sympathy noted above. This threatened to make race an increasingly polarizing political issue (as it has become; see Carmines and Stimson, 1991; Edsall, 1993). And in doing so, we feared it might jeopardize one area of optimism shared by blacks in the 1960's—hopeful attitudes toward a federal government that had been favorably disposed toward blacks' aspirations through the administrations of FDR, Harry Truman, JFK, and Lyndon Johnson.

4. Finally, increasing racial isolation threatened America's urban areas, for two reasons: some increase in blacks' racial pride, and whites' fears of blacks (especially in terms of crime). School integration seemed at the time to be the most difficult looming issue.

What Had Changed?
The Broad Context

So what, if anything, had changed in the intervening 27 years?

Blacks in South Central Los Angeles

The area of the rioting seems superficially similar: South-Central Los Angeles. To be sure, the heart of the rioting in 1965 was "Watts," an area around 103rd Street and Central Avenue, whereas in 1992, its heart was some distance to the northwest. But in both cases, the rioting was centered in areas that had been predominantly black since World War II.

Had the social and economic status of the black population improved in that period? Not dramatically. Americans in general were, in 1965, in the midst of the great postwar economic surge. It was an era that had finally and irrevocably integrated the European immigrant groups of the late 19th and early 20th century into mainstream American society, many into the middle class. Blacks were the major non-integrated group, and the most disadvantaged. In 1992 this was still true. More young black men were in prison than in college, unemployment was soaring, most black children were being raised in female-headed households, etc. etc. etc.

At a larger level, many macroeconomic changes had impacted severely on blacks in the area (and in most other inner cities as well). The globalization of capital and labor had resulted in the loss of hundreds of thousands of industrialized jobs in areas close to South Central Los Angeles in the 1970's and 1980's. As a result, unemployment and welfare dependency skyrocketed. Even the great economic development that had taken place in Los Angeles in that period had been concentrated downtown and in West Los Angeles, bypassing South Central. On top of all that, the Bush and Reagan administrations had systematically dismantled many public welfare and safety services, leaving the area with fewer resources for dealing with its serious social and economic problems.

Ethnic Change

But the area had changed more than this implies. As of 1965, the American population had been ethnically stable for many years, after the large flows of immigration from Eastern and Southern Europe were cut off in 1924. In 1965, South Central Los Angeles was almost all African-American, and had been for two decades. One source of cleavage was between the recent black migrants from the South and blacks who had been living there for a decade or more. But even the "newcomers" came from the same culture that the older residents (or their parents) had originally come from, and were of the same race.

In 1992, America was in the midst of another surge of immigration, most visibly from Asia, Mexico, and Central America, but from many other nations as well, as wide-ranging as Iran, Russia, and India. Los Angeles was in the front lines of this wave, and so its demographic makeup had changed sharply, from overwhelmingly white (71% in 1970) to decidedly mixed (41% white in 1990, 38% Latino, with as many Asians as blacks). And the change had been abrupt. Over the prior decade, the Latino population

had increased by 1.3 million, and the Asian population had doubled, while the black population had remained about constant and the number of whites had actually diminished. South Central Los Angeles in particular had changed; by 1992, it was almost half Latino. Another major concentration of new Latino immigrants was in the Pico-Union district just to the north.

These changes generated considerable ethnic conflict. Latinos had long shared the conventional prejudices against blacks (e.g., Oliver and Johnson, 1984; also see Mexican-Americans' negative responses to the Watts rioting, in Sears and McConahay, 1973). But the recent massive influx of Latinos had exacerbated these tensions. They themselves had come from quite a variety of nations and cultures, not just Mexico. So the cultural clashes between blacks and groups moving into historically black neighborhoods were potentially even sharper than they might have been had the latter been of longer standing and from more familiar backgrounds.

And blacks and Latinos were struggling for the same piece of the small, and shrinking, economic pie in South Central Los Angeles—the flight of jobs, the influx of immigrants willing to work for less, and increasing demand for shrinking public services. In this struggle, Latinos seemed to have some advantages. Absent the legacy of slavery and a century of subsequent discrimination, they were less angry and violent, and whites often tended to trust them more. And they were often willing to work for lower wages and to forego unionization (Miles, 1992).

In 1965, the area's merchants had largely been either white (often Jewish) or black. By 1992 they came from a much greater variety of nations, including many from various Asian nations, especially Korea. Severe conflicts existed between blacks and Koreans, surrounding the latter's commercial successes (see Light and Bonacich, 1988). Blacks often felt Koreans exploited them, overcharging for goods and refusing to hire black employees, and were too ready to accuse blacks of shoplifting and other criminal behavior. The Asians rarely lived in South-Central (less than 1% was Asian in 1990), but inhabited a number of neighborhoods ringing that area, such as "Koreatown," in the Wilshire District between South-Central and Hollywood. This exacerbated the tension: Asians were prominent as local shopkeepers, but did not live in the area or play any other role in it.

The black-Korean conflicts came to a head in 1991 with a Korean merchant's (ultimately televised) shooting of the black teenager Latasha Harlins in the back of the head, and then with the shooting of another black in a liquor store. In both cases the courts gave no jail time to the persons responsible for the shooting. This led to boycotts by blacks of Korean merchants. The blacks felt they were not respected by the Koreans; the Koreans felt outrage in turn because they felt little attention was paid to the dangers they faced, including the shooting of Korean merchants. The Koreans struggled with their own racism, but it was quite real, and blacks often did not understand or appreciate Korean culture. So cultural misunderstanding was rife. Underlying much of this conflict also was blacks' anger about being denied access to the American dream; once again African-Americans were being passed by, as ambitious immigrants from many lands and cultures found fertile economic ground in America.

Political Context

What about the political context? The rioting in 1965 occurred at the end of the civil rights decade's rollback of the centuries-old system of white racial dominance in the South. Optimism abounded; the national government seemed sympathetic, as did much of the white population of the nation (at least outside the South). Locally, very little white support for formal segregation existed (Sears and Kinder, 1971), and nationally (Schuman, Steeh, and Bobo, 1985), whites had become

considerably more sympathetic to blacks' search for equality. Moreover, many whites understood the persisting impact of racial discrimination on maintaining racial inequality.

Moreover, by 1992 blacks seemed much more politically powerful than they had been in 1965. One of the most powerful political figures in the state was the black Speaker of the state Assembly, Willie Brown. Locally, the conservative midwestern white, Sam Yorty, had long since been replaced in the mayor's office by the moderate black, Tom Bradley.

Nevertheless, a number of warning signals existed. Racial isolation continued: "white flight" drove many white schoolchildren out of the mammoth Los Angeles school district in the 1970's and 1980's, and white adults followed. Conventional racial stereotypes damaging to blacks persisted: in 1992, blacks were regarded as the least intelligent and the most likely to be welfare-dependent of the four major ethnic groups, and the least welcome in Angelenos' own neighborhoods. The 1988 and 1990 national elections had presented blacks in their oldest and most degrading stereotypical form, in advertising such as the Willie Horton ad or in Jesse Helms' blunt attacks on affirmative action for blacks. The national administration seemed responsive to blacks only in putting a fervent black foe of affirmative action and civil rights on the Supreme Court. And Bradley's own support had waned somewhat, first in the black community as he cultivated Westside white liberals and the downtown business community in two decades of economic development, and then in the broader community as political scandals mounted.

Finally, the Los Angeles Police Department had been perhaps the single most aggravating element for blacks in 1965, particularly symbolized by its hardline longtime Chief, William Parker. Little had changed. The LAPD was responsible for the beating of Rodney King in 1991, and acquittal of those officers triggered the disturbances in 1992.

The then-Chief, Daryl Gates, was fully as outspoken and uncompromising as Parker ever had been. The LAPD's investment in elite units rather than grassroots, community-based patrolling only exacerbated that.

The Events Themselves: Comparison with the Watts Riot of 1965

So how [did] 1992 differ from the Watts Riot of 1965? First of all, the level of violence and scope of destruction were considerably greater, and the entire city was placed under curfew. Still, perhaps it is fairest to say bigger, but a similar event, in these terms.

However, the catalytic agent in 1992 was quite different, both more noteworthy and more sympathetic. The individual black drunk driver whose failed arrest by the CHP began the Watts riot was little noted and quickly forgotten. In contrast, Rodney King's beating was broadcast throughout the world, as was the jury verdict that stimulated the rioting. Opposition to the King verdict was overwhelming in all ethnic groups; over 60% of the whites in Los Angeles disagreed with it.

The participants in the rioting in 1965 were almost all black. Mexican-Americans were not seen as major players in the social drama. The small sample of Mexican-Americans interviewed after the 1965 rioting received only brief summary treatment, and in any case their attitudes were almost identical to those of whites (even exceeding whites' praise for the authorities' handling of the riot; see Sears and McConahay, 1973, pp. 164–66). In 1992, by contrast, over half of those arrested were Latino (51%, with only 36% black). This change paralleled the dramatic increase in Latino residents of South Central Los Angeles (from 80% black to 45% Latino), though obviously it was not compelled by that demographic change.

The targets of looting and burning in 1965 were not thoroughly documented. But in 1992 the violence was obviously quite systematically aimed at Korean merchants. No other ethnic group came remotely close in terms of loss: 54% of those businesses that were totally lost had been owned by Koreans, of whom the largest number sold apparel. Some organized vigilante Korean defense forces literally fought off invaders at gunpoint, and other Koreans simply abandoned their properties in the face of the intense hostility toward them.

Attitudes toward the authorities were quite different in the two years. In 1965, the races polarized quite sharply, whites supporting them and blacks feeling they were ineffective or worse. Blacks were overwhelmingly unfavorable toward both the white mayor and the police chief (Sears and McConahay, 1973). In 1992, all ethnic groups felt the LAPD was ineffective, and were vehemently negative toward Police Chief Gates (e.g., only 18% of the whites supported him). The mayor again polarized the races, but in the reverse direction: this time blacks supported the mayor, who was black himself. Most important, though, blacks' estrangement from the criminal justice system continued; most felt that it treated them unfairly.

In 1965, the dominant view in each ethnic group was that it was a black protest (though fewer whites than blacks used such political terms as "rebellion" or "insurrection" to describe it: 13% compared to 38%; see Sears and McConahay, 1973). In 1992, only blacks saw it as "mainly a protest" (68% did); whites, Asians, and Hispanics saw it mainly as "looting and crime." Unhappily there are no day-by-day data on this point; many observers felt that it initially looked like a racial protest of the King beating and verdict, but evolved into looting and chaos later on.

Finally, several of the immediate effects of the riots seem to me noteworthy. First, the King verdict seems to have increased blacks' belief in racial discrimination, greater belief that blacks are treated unfairly, and more black alienation. Blacks much more than other ethnic groups believe that the rioting was a racial protest. Second, Asians became more pessimistic and more negative toward blacks, and there is no evidence of a "wake-up call" having been received by whites. Blacks remained the group most often bearing the brunt of negative stereotypes and discrimination. Third, the entire community did show a marked loss of confidence in the police and especially Chief Gates, a loss of confidence that contributed to the passage of a later ballot proposition cutting the power of the police chief and increasing civilian control over the police. And fourth, the worldwide news reporting capacities of CNN sped the word of the King verdict, the Denny beating, and the rest of the events around the globe in an instant. Yet, surprisingly, there was little spread of the rioting, much less than in, for example, 1967 or 1968. Perhaps these effects help us to understand the modesty of the "rebuilding" efforts that have occurred in the area subsequent to the riots.

Systematic Theories of the Rioting

The events thus soon turned from a stark and tragic but simple political stimulus, eliciting the usual interpretive suspects, to a vast and complex Rorschach card, yielding an equally diverse set of explanations for the rioting.

Social Contagion and Rioting for Fun and Profit

The version of social contagion theory that grew out of the 1960's ghetto riots was described as the "assembling process" (McPhail, 1971). Collective violence emerges from the assembling of crowds of people who simply happen to be close by. No crowds, no violence. Some of the current authors allude to this: the densely populated neighborhoods of South Central Los Angeles provided such crowds of available participants with a "large number of young men at liberty," "with time

on their hands," who could readily get caught up in some rioting.

Edward Banfield (1970) popularized the notion that the ghetto riots of the 1960's were carried out "for fun and profit," by young men with excess energy who "rampaged" through the ghetto, taking such goods as liquor and television sets for pure pleasure. In 1992 the TV coverage of the riot gave rise to much of this, whether the wholly arbitrary and senseless and brutal beatings of innocents (such as Reginald Denny) or the pictures of healthy young men loading up their pickup trucks with any goods they could pry loose from retail stores. [Some] saw the rioters as an available and unoccupied "pool of young men" hanging around the streetcorners in South Central Los Angeles; "the resulting explosion of human energy lacked political focus" rather than serving as the vanguard of an insurrection against abominable social conditions.

A related notion was the "criminal element" or "riff-raff" theory of ghetto riots so popular among conservatives in the 1960's. This theory alluded to the breakdown of the black community in the inner city, indexed by gangs, drugs, female-headed households, illegitimacy, and crime. Various data are presented to support this view: the arrestees were disproportionately adolescent and young adult males, had high unemployment rates, often lived in single-parent families, often had criminal histories, tended to be dropouts from school, and were asserted to have histories of drug and alcohol abuse.

Whether or not the point is correct, these data are not very persuasive. There is rarely an appropriate non-arrested comparison group, there are no controls, there are alternative explanations in some cases, and so on. Yet some authors confidently conclude that these young men represented "a critical mass ... [with] ... little reason to feel bound by social rules," and that looting, rather than political rebellion, was their major motive.

A Black Protest

Perhaps the dominant interpretation of the 1960's rioting was that they were black protests against police brutality, racial discrimination, poverty, and other social conditions that impacted particularly on them (see Sears and McConahay, 1973; Kerner Commission, 1968; McCone Commission, 1965).

At the outset, the 1992 Los Angeles riot certainly paralleled those earlier outbursts, and at least initially gave rise to a similar interpretation. The patent unjustness of the treatment of Rodney King himself (first his televised beating, and then his police assailants' walking free) were viewed as typical of a long line of outrages committed against African-Americans, whether [by] slaveowners, lynch mobs, or brutal police officers. But to blacks in Los Angeles the King events had a special meaning, because the Los Angeles Police Department had a longstanding reputation for insensitivity to minority residents of the city (and indeed a rather insular and quasiparanoid attitude toward the community as a whole). So, it (1) was triggered by an event highlighting conflict between blacks and the police; the King beating and verdict quickly became symbols of police misconduct toward blacks, (2) it was initiated within the predominantly black ghetto by blacks, (3) it resulted again in much burning and looting of local businesses, and (4) most of those killed were blacks. The local television coverage of beatings and burnings in South Central Los Angeles, most seemingly perpetrated by blacks, quickly gave rise to the impression that it was predominantly a black-white conflict.

But as time went on, the evident complexity of the events overwhelmed this interpretation. The Mayor was a black man, not the usual conservative white; he himself had denounced the unfairness of the jury verdict, and was openly critical of the Chief of Police.

After the first night, intensive television coverage of the looting and burning revealed the extensive participation of Latinos, not all poor and oppressed, but backing innumerable vans and pickup trucks up to store after store and relieving them of truckloads full of merchandise. And the rioting quickly reached a scope far beyond the evening of any conceivable local scores; the longstanding poverty of East Los Angeles, entry point for generations of immigrants to Los Angeles, gave rise to very little destruction and looting, whereas numerous commercial establishments in Hollywood, some distance from any real poverty areas, were stripped clean; and the widespread attacks on relatively new and quite modest Korean-owned businesses seemed inconsistent with a rebellion against longstanding white racism. So with time, the "black protest" interpretation too looked more and more like an oversimplification.

The Rainbow Coalition

This evidence of broad participation of Latinos as well as blacks then suggested to some a "bread riot" engaged in by the disadvantaged of all minority groups, the coming together of a rainbow coalition of all people of color, who truly needed the food, the diapers, and everything else that was taken. Perhaps this was the harvest of a decade-long orgy of self-aggrandizement participated in by the white capitalist class, protected and encouraged by the Reagan administration, that progressively impoverished minorities and the working class, while redistributing wealth up the social pyramid.

There were two major problems with this explanation. Whereas minorities may all have had dissatisfactions, they were quite divided politically; both the long history of black-Latino conflict and the short history of black-Asian conflict have been alluded to, to say nothing of sharp conflicts among Latinos on both political and nationality grounds, and great differences among Asians from different nations. Moreover, whites were quite unlikely to coalesce around a politically conservative position. Of all the major groups in Los Angeles, whites are the most split ideologically, with the most educated whites the most split. In fact white liberals formed the core of the coalition that had succeeded in electing, and reelecting four times, the first black mayor in Los Angeles. So the "rainbow coalition" theory does not fit the actual data very well, either.

The Bladerunner Scenario

The "Bladerunner" syndrome heralded the final breakdown of civilized society, finally driven into criminal anarchy by the racial underclass, drug lords, and hardened criminals. Not only were the streets no longer safe at night in some neighborhoods, but the entire city had been taken over by street criminals, mostly but not exclusively racial minorities. Since the "Bladerunner" metaphor models reality on a movie, there is the inescapable and ever-popular "blame it on television" variant: blacks took the King videotape as the "smoking gun" they had long awaited to nail the LAPD where it lived.

Yet this scenario should not be dismissed too readily. It does reflect a more general fear of the breakdown of the American political system. As turnout sags, and public cynicism grows, and whites, money, and power flee to the suburbs, and even a black mayor is seen as a sell-out to downtown business interests, the process of electoral politics is often seen as irrelevant to the problems of the inner city and the poor. The Los Angeles Police Department gave fuel to this scenario by its quite evident lack of preparedness for the events, symbolized by the Chief's Nero-esque fiddling at a fundraiser throughout the first evening of the riots while his police force swiftly lost control of major portions of the nation's second largest city. And television technology had made enormous strides since 1965, reflected in both the King videotape and the zoom lenses in helicopters that allowed for close-up coverage of the rioting from a safe distance.

Multiethnic Conflict

Others saw it as an interethnic conflict. To be sure, Rodney King, a black man, was beaten badly by white officers of the LAPD, who then were acquitted of any wrongdoing. But many blacks attacked Korean-owned stores, and indeed engaged in pitched battles in the streets with Koreans. And more Latinos than blacks were involved in the rioting and looting and burning. The triggering grievances were not only the black-white conflicts surrounding Rodney King, but the black-Korean conflicts manifested in the shooting of Latasha Harlins. The Koreans in turn emphasized their roles as hard-working and misunderstood immigrants targeted by street criminals. The growing role of Latinos in Los Angeles, displacing blacks from traditional black neighborhoods and from traditionally black-held jobs, also began to receive some attention.

These facts led some to talk about the riots as "a new form," "the first multiethnic riot," or "the first urban unrest of the 21st century." Other[s] described it as a "violent interminority confrontation." The local demographic situation was "ripe for unrest." In the end this led many to a realistic group conflict explanation (see Olzak, 1986, and others). The notion of "ethnic enclaves" or "territorially-based ethnic tensions" is described as "the future." True, the intense fighting between blacks and Korean merchants had some parallel to the attacks on Jewish shops in the black ghetto of the 1960's, but somehow the level of violence against the Koreans themselves, not merely their shuttered and empty shops at 2 AM, took it to another level.

It seems apparent to me that no simple or single interpretation fits the 1992 events very well. It might be more appropriate to describe the events as several riots of different kinds occurring more or less simultaneously, rather than trying to fit any one theory to them. In that sense each of these theories probably has some merit. This is not to open the door to post-modernist license, wherein any configuration painted on an empty canvas is regarded as equally valid (see several essays in Gooding-Williams, 1993, for expressions of a contrary view). Rather, it is to recognize the true complexity of the events and of the circumstances that gave rise to them.

Conclusions

What are the lessons to be learned from the rioting in Los Angeles? In one sense, they may be rather limited; the rioting did not spread much beyond Los Angeles, for example, and there is reason to believe that much of it was specific to the particular actions and reputation of the Los Angeles Police Department regarding the black community in Los Angeles.

But there are broader lessons in it. One is surely to underline the difficulties that American cities are facing. The globalization of labor and capital often referred to in discussions of Los Angeles affect[s] all cities, and in similar ways: high levels of unemployment among unskilled, semi-skilled, and skilled blue collar workers; deterioration of such infrastructural elements as public school and public health systems; family disorganization, and so on. The squeeze on public sector revenues induced nationally during the Reagan years, and in California by recession and a series of short-sighted ballot measures, has further drained resources that might help rejuvenate the cities.

A larger lesson might be of the precariousness of public order, perhaps a lesson that needs to be relearned by every generation in every nation anew. Nothing so destructive as the ethnic cleansing in Bosnia occurred in Los Angeles, but for a few days we all got a taste of how close to the precipice we always live.

Finally, it seems evident that one cannot simply describe the rioting as a "black protest" and stop there. But there is some truth to that characterization. And the comparison with the Watts riots of 1965 must lead us to think in longer historical terms than if we focused solely on the cruelties and indignities visited on Rodney King. So another major lesson continues to be the tragic legacy of slavery.

It is not written in stone that the descendants of Africans must be poor, violent, rejected. They are not all, nor are they always, nor are they everywhere and in every context. Yet it is a powerful truth that in America, they are more at risk than any other group in almost every respect one can think of—for incarceration, educational failure, hypertension and heart disease, murder, teenage pregnancy, alcoholism, drug addiction, racial discrimination, police mistreatment. And now comes "the chosen alternative" from Mexico and Central America, less threatening and willing to work for less.

One of the great successes of black life in this country was the overthrow of Jim Crow segregationism in the South in the 1950's and 1960's. One of the ironic side effects of that success was that it quickly became the model for a whole host of other claimants, groups of every stripe claiming they had been oppressed through the centuries just like blacks. This came at an unfortunate time, when America[n] intellectuals were just beginning to shake off the self-censuring effects of a generation of World War patriotism and anti-Communist vigilantism. A lot of family skeletons suddenly came to light, perhaps distracting many from the close scrutiny required to distinguish true cadavers from mere odoriferous embarrassments.

In many quarters, blacks became thought of as just another complaining special interest group that really should just get a hold of themselves, work hard, and get ahead. But blacks are not just another special interest group. Article I, Section 2 of the United States Constitution placed them in a separate category from other Americans: free persons were to be counted as whole persons, and African slaves at three-fifths apiece.

We continue to reap the diseased harvest of decisions made in the 17th and 18th century. And American society has not, in over 300 years, figured out what to do about it. We have on our hands a very longstanding, very difficult, and terribly costly social problem. The society at large has played a large role in creating the problem and continues to play a large role in nurturing it, in many and complex ways. So the society at large has to take an equally large role in trying at least to ameliorate its worst effects. Many writing about the rioting somewhat wishfully describe it as a "wake-up call." Well, maybe. Somebody keeps pushing the snooze button. And what we cannot afford is trying to wish it away, or the illusions either that segregation will work or that black self-help will be sufficient. There is no simple solution. But it is a serious problem, and it will not go away all by itself.

References

Banfield, Edward C. 1970. *The unheavenly city.* Boston: Little, Brown.

Bobo, Lawrence, Camille L. Zubrinsky, James H. Johnson, Jr., and Melvin L. Oliver. 1994. "Public opinion before and after a Spring of discontent." Pp. 103-133 in Mark Baldassare, ed., *The Los Angeles Riots: Lessons for the Urban Future.* Boulder, CO: Westview.

Carmines, E. G., and J. A. Stimson. 1989. *Issue evolution: Race and the transformation of American politics.* Princeton, N.J.: Princeton University Press.

Cohen, Nathan (Ed.) 1970. *The Los Angeles riots: A socio-psychological study.* New York: Praeger.

Edsall, T. B., with M. D. Edsall. 1992. *Chain reaction: The impact of race, rights, and taxes on American politics.* New York: W. W. Norton.

Gooding-Williams, Robert (Ed.). 1993. *Reading Rodney King reading urban uprising.* New York: Routledge.

Governor's Commission on the Los Angeles Riots [McCone Commission]. 1965. *Violence in the city—an end or a beginning?* Los Angeles: College Book Store.

Johnson, P. B., David O. Sears, and John B. McConahay. 1971. "Black invisibility, the press, and the Los Angeles riot." *American Journal of Sociology, 76,* 698–721.

Kinder, D. R., and David O. Sears. 1981. "Prejudice and politics: Symbolic racism versus racial threats to the good life." *Journal of Personality and Social Psychology, 40,* 414–431.

Light, Ivan and Edna Bonacich. 1988. *Immigrant entrepreneurs: Koreans in Los Angeles, 1965–1982.* Berkeley and Los Angeles: University of California Press.

McPhail, C. 1971. "Civil disorder participation: A critical examination of recent research." *American Sociological Review, 36,* 1058–1073.

Miles, J. 1992. Blacks vs. Browns. *Atlantic Monthly,* October.

National Advisory Commission on Civil Disorders [Kerner Commission]. 1968. *Report of the National Advisory Commission on Civil Disorders.* Washington D.C.; U.S. Government Printing Office.

Oliver, Melvin, and James H. Johnson. 1984. "Interethnic conflict in an urban ghetto: The case of blacks and Latinos in Los Angeles." *Research in Social Movements: Conflict and change. 6,* 57–94.

Olzak, Susan. 1986. "A competition model of ethnic collective action." Pp. 17–46 in S. Olzak and J. Nagel (Eds.), *Competitive ethnic relations.* Orlando: Academic Press.

Schuman, Howard, Charlotte Steeh, and Lawrence Bobo. 1985. *Racial trends in America: Trends and interpretations.* Cambridge, MA: Harvard University Press.

Sears, David O., and D. R. Kinder. 1971. "Racial tensions and voting in Los Angeles." Pp. 51-88 in W. Z. Hirsch (Ed.), *Los Angeles: Viability and prospects for metropolitan leadership.* New York: Praeger.

Sears, David O., and John B. McConahay, 1973. *The politics of violence: The new urban blacks and the Watts riot.* Boston: Houghton-Mifflin.

Sears:

1. Compare and contrast the "Watts" riots of 1965 to the L.A. riots of 1992. What is similar and different between the two time periods?

2. Discuss the five theories of rioting. Which parts of each are beneficial in understanding the 1992 L.A. riots?

Drawing Conclusions—Part I

On the basis of what you have read in these essays, and based on personal experience in your school, on the job, or in your community, how would you describe the most important features of the new racial fault lines. To answer this question, you need to consider how serious a problem you think racism actually is and how it most typically manifests itself. You need to think about how serious is the threat posed by white supremacists. You also need to sort out your sense of the emerging structure of race relations in an increasingly multiracial society.

Representations of Race and the Politics of Identity

The selections in Part II focus on race as a socially constructed identity, and in so doing they reveal the ways dominant and subordinate groups attempt to carve out distinctive identities, while locating themselves vis-à-vis other groups. According to most sociologists today, even though there are differences in physical characteristics that one can point to in distinguishing among various groups, these differences are less significant than the meanings that are attached to them. Thus, race as a social phenomenon is distinct from the physical dimension, and the former is more important than the latter insofar as it actually plays a major role influencing and shaping people's lives.

For this reason, sociologists are interested in the social construction of race, especially in the ways people—individually and collectively—engage in this process of construction. Race needs to be considered as something that is created—imagined, constructed, invented, articulated, formulated—in the context of events past and present. As such, race is not merely an unchanging given, or what sociologists refer to as an ascriptive identity. Rather, it is an accomplishment. But identity is not created out of whole cloth. People are not entirely free to pick and choose what identity to embrace or what that identity looks like. This is because there are external social limits that set constraints on the construction process. It is shaped by ideological worldviews, which arise in situations in which hegemonic groups have more power to shape racial representations. Thus, those with the most power have the most to say about identities—theirs and everyone else's. However, as the essays in this part suggest, subordinate groups are not simply passive recipients of the definitions of others. Rather, they have varying levels of ability to define their own identities and varying levels of interest in doing so.

Given all this, it would be a mistake to think of identities as extremely fluid, where everything seems subject to revision at a moment's notice. Racial categories would not work—they would not be meaningful—if they did not have a certain staying power. Thus, it is typical for people to employ racial categories and then to act on the meanings that correspond to those categories with a conviction that such categories are simply givens, taken-for-granted understandings of a naturalistic order. However, during periods of dramatic social change, that which has been uncritically accepted is called into question. The post-civil rights era is such a time. Thus, today there is considerable fluidity, ambiguity, and contestation about racial identifications. Both at the individual and group level, a renegotiation of received definitions is under way. As can be seen in the essays contained herein, this is not merely an exercise in personal introspection; it has pronounced social, cultural, and political implications.

The section begins with F. James Davis's exploration into black identity. This essay is an outgrowth of his book in which he asks, "Who is Black?" In the United States, that question has been answered from an early point in our history by recourse to the "one-drop" rule, which states that if a person has any black ancestry whatsoever, that person is black. By operating in this way, an either-or situation is created, and no classificatory recognition is made of the reality of mixed-blood people. This is unlike nations such as Brazil and much of the Caribbean, where a variety of interstitial categories, such as mulattos and quadroons, are recognized. After tracing the detrimental sociopolitical implications of such a definition, Davis goes on to examine the phenomenon of blacks embracing this bifurcated definition of race and discusses some of the reasons such a view has taken hold in the black community.

The following two articles look at the overt politicization of racial representation. Joane Nagel explores the conflicts and controversies surrounding efforts to determine what an authentic ethnic identity is for American Indians. On the one hand, this process is part of an effort to gain complete control over the process of identification from forces outside the group. On the other hand, within the Indian community, there is a wide range of competing perspectives on this matter. Individual efforts to embrace Indianness are complicated by the ability of tribal groups to serve as arbiters of what constitutes an authentic Indian identity. Moreover, the contested role of the federal government as an arbiter in determining many matters related to tribal identities further confounds matters. Not surprisingly, as Nagel illustrates, the quest for determining authenticity rather easily produces contest and controversy. Shifting groups and the focus somewhat, Joseph T. Rhea addresses the issue of historical memory. He does so by examining the efforts of Mexican Americans in Texas to redefine hegemonic public memories regarding the historical significance of the Alamo. By advancing alternative truth claims, he suggests, Mexican Americans can be seen as attempting to reconstruct history in the interest of advancing what Rhea refers to as "racial pride." In an effort to combat notions of Anglo superiority, this is a paradigmatic instance of the current politics of identity.

Sara K. Dorow's essay looks at identity formation from a different, less obviously political, perspective in her study of transnational adoption. Her concern is with the microlevel. She explores the family as a site where children acquire a sense of selfhood, including a sense of ethnic and racial identity, as a consequence of particular experiences of socialization. Dorow reveals something of the complicated nature of constructing an identity for Chinese children who have been adopted by whites, exploring the various ways in which parents, more or less consciously, make decisions about emphasizing or de-emphasizing the racial and ethnic differences between parents and child. In so doing, she reveals the range of choices available to parents as well as the external constraints that pose limits to those choices.

The three concluding essays in Part II turn to the topic of racial representation in various facets of popular culture. Justin Lewis and Sut Jhally, authors of an influential book on the highly successful *Cosby Show,* assess television's portrayals of African Americans. The authors focus on the complex and sometimes contradictory effects of television programming on representations of black identity. Lewis and Jhally are particularly interested in the intersection of social class and race and on how that intersection yields both negative and positive images. Charles Fruehling Springwood and C. Richard King are interested in spectator sports. The focus of their essay is the historical use of racialized team names and mascots by sports teams and, in particular, ones that make use of Native American imagery. The continued use of such mascots as the University of Illinois' "Chief Illiniwek" and team names such as the Cleveland Indians has in recent years provoked protests from Native American groups, who see their use as offensive and demeaning. The authors discuss the inability of many whites to comprehend the criticisms of Native Americans, and they indicate some of the reasons that changing names is so fraught with controversy. Finally, Rocky L. Sexton's essay turns to popular music. He provides us with a discussion of the similarities and differences between zydeco and Cajun music, the former rooted in the black community and the latter in the white French American community. Although both types of music have appeal at the national level, these are regional genres rooted in the particularities of the racial character of Louisiana. Sexton reveals how these musical genres afford insights into race relations in the region. Moreover, by revealing how through music the two groups seek to define boundaries and a sense of distinctiveness, Sexton also shows how over time these boundaries have proven to be permeable—with both subcultures incorporating aspects of the other's popular music—and what this means for the preservation or transformation of existing racial categories.

Collectively, the essays contained in this part reveal something of the contested nature of creating, maintaining, revising, and challenging representations of race. In so doing, they offer insights into the salience of identity politics in the contemporary United States. The fluidity of identities, the desire of minority peoples to play a major role in shaping their identities, and the ambiguities associated with the various choices people actually have in making choices about identity all suggest that, for the foreseeable future, racial representation will remain a highly charged issue.

8

Black Identity in the United States

F. James Davis

Among the novels and films that moved me during my formative years as a rural white boy in the upper Midwest were a few that dealt with the identity of racially mixed people. Mark Twain's *Pudd'nhead Wilson* (1922) was an eye-opener. Edna Ferber's *Showboat* (1926), dramatizing the maxim that one drop of "black blood" makes you black in the South, became a popular stage play and movie. These depictions made me uneasy and curious to know more.

My first course on race relations, in 1940, was under a demanding sociologist whose early publications had included a book on American mulattoes (Reuter 1918). The following year, I began graduate study, but World War II intervened. Years later, when I returned to academe from military duty to pursue doctoral study in sociology and law, Gunnar Myrdal's *An American Dilemma* (1944) was available. This landmark study of race relations in the South included discussion of race mixture and the definition of a black person. That aspect of the study, however, received relatively little attention from most scholars. Later, the subject of miscegenation got lost in the civil rights, black power, and black history movements, with a few notable exceptions (Bennett 1962; Berry 1963, 1965; Johnston 1970; Blassingame 1972, 1973).

In my teaching and writing, convinced that the definition of who is black is an important key to understanding race relations in the United States, I gave increasing attention to the topic. The publication of historian Joel Williamson's superb book *New People* (1980) validated my search and spurred me on. Not until after my retirement was I able to complete a book on the subject (Davis 1991), at a time when the multiracial identity movement was growing.

A Nation's Definition

What is the definition of a black person in the United States? We can gain perspective on this question by focusing briefly on the experiences of two well-known Americans.

Walter White, President of the NAACP from 1931 to 1955, had blue eyes, fair hair, and light skin. Anthropologists have said that White was no more than one sixty-fourth African black, yet his own black identity was very firm. He had experienced segregation and violence while growing up as an African in the Deep South (White 1948:3–13). The black community was outraged by White's marriage to his second wife, a brunette white. He had married across the ethnic group barrier. When the Whites toured the world on an American goodwill mission, they were publicized as an interracial couple. Puzzled foreigners often asked White how he happened to marry a colored woman (Cannon 1956:12–14).

When singer Lena Horne's parents separated, she lived for a time in rural Georgia with an uncle who was a red-haired, blue-eyed African American teacher. There she was called a "yellow bastard" by the black schoolchildren and asked why she was so light (Horne and Schickel 1965:21–32). Early in her career, white audiences complained that Lena looked white and sang white love songs, not the blues. When a white male screen agent tried to get her to pass as a Latin white, she was horrified. She was embarrassed and hurt when film directors tried a darker shade of makeup to make her look "more black." It took decades for Lena Horne to achieve a clear sense of her black identity (Horne and Schickel 1965:267–87; Buckley 1986).

These illustrations dramatize the country's definition of a black person. The ancestry may be less than half African black, much less, and the person may even look white. In fact, "a black person has long been defined in the United States mainland as someone with any known African black ancestry" (Myrdal 1944:113–18; Berry and Tischler 1978:97–98; Williamson 1980:1–2). This definition was forged in slavery and Jim Crow segregation, but it emerged from the South to become the nation's definition, accepted in the end by whites and blacks alike (Bahr, Chadwick, and Stauss 1979:27–28).

In the South, this social construction became known as the "one-drop rule." It also has been known as the "one black ancestor rule," and some courts have called it the "traceable amount rule." Anthropologists use the term "hypo-descent rule," meaning that persons with mixed ancestry are assigned the social status of the subordinate group (Harris 1964:56). Whatever the name, this cultural definition of who is black has been taken for granted as readily by teachers, employers, affirmative action officers, public officials, and black leaders as by Ku Klux Klansmen.

African Americans are the only minority in the United States subject to a one-drop rule. Persons whose ancestry is one fourth or less Native American generally are not defined as Indians unless they want to be. They are perceived instead as assimilating Americans and can be proud of being part Native American. The same implicit rule evidently governs for Japanese Americans, Filipino Americans, other peoples from East or South Asia, and for Mexicans with Central American Indian ancestry.

The one-drop rule always has been associated with ideas about racial purity. I use the term "unmixed African black" to refer to a person whose entire ancestry was derived from a population in sub-Saharan Africa. I do not mean to suggest that pure races exist. Race groups such as those identified at mid-century by anthropologists Kroeber, Hooton, and Coon are, at best, overlapping statistical groupings based on combinations of visible anatomical traits. These traits are biologically superficial and they vary independently rather than being transmitted in genetic clusters (Berry and Tischler 1978:34–35). The focus has shifted to differences in the frequencies of gene markers for single traits. The latest evidence suggests that there is a continuum of genetic variation around the world rather than separate races (Marshall 1998: 654).

The Birth and Spread of the Rule

Miscegenation between white indentured servants and African black slaves became extensive in the Chesapeake area in the mid-1600s. Although there was some uncertainty for a time, these mixed persons generally were assigned the status of slaves and the same racial identity as African blacks (Williamson 1980:6–14). By the early 1700s, the one-drop rule had become the social definition of who is black in the upper South, and it spread southward from there. By the time of the American Revolution, there were slaves on southern plantations who looked white.

A competitor to the one-drop rule also originated in the 1600s, in South Carolina and Louisiana, where free mulattoes had an in-between, buffer status. Allied with whites, these free mulattoes were not considered to be blacks (Williamson 1980:14–24). Until the 1840s in South Carolina, with support from the courts, both visible and known mulattoes could become white by behavior and reputation and could marry into white families (Catterall 1926–1937, vol. 2:269). Miscegenation was widespread and tolerated in lower Louisiana, which accepted the intermediate status of mulattoes and rejected the one-drop rule. The Louisiana Civil Code of 1808 prohibited "free people of color" from marrying either blacks or whites (Dominguez 1986:23–26).

In other states in the antebellum South, there were occasional court cases in which persons known to have as much as one fourth "Negro blood" were declared legally white. The United States had not yet lined up solidly behind the one-drop rule. For more than two centuries, this in-between rule was in competition with the one-drop rule. However, the South came together in firm support of the one-drop rule in the 1850s to preserve slavery (Williamson 1980:73–75). The competing rule was put down, although for decades there were court decisions and statutes that limited the definition of black persons to at least one fourth, one eighth, or some other fraction of ancestry.

The alienation of mulattoes from whites was accelerated by the Civil War and the Reconstruction. Whites made it clear that mulattoes of all shades would be defined as blacks, and the one-drop rule gained support in the North as well as the South. The rule was further strengthened by the passage of the Jim Crow laws in the southern states at the turn of the twentieth century. These segregation laws were reinforced by extralegal threats and terrorism. Lynching of blacks peaked from 1885 to 1909, and light blacks were as likely as darker ones to pay the ultimate price for alleged violations of the master-servant etiquette—for "getting out of their place" (Vander Zanden 1972:162–63). As a result, the peak of passing occurred during this period, although most of those who could pass permanently did not do so (Burma 1946:18–22; Eckard 1947:498). By World War I, the one-drop rule was backed uniformly by American whites.

The one-drop rule was crucial to maintaining Jim Crow segregation, in which widespread miscegenation, not racial purity, prevailed. The racial double standard of sexual relations gave white men access to black women but protected white women from black men. A mixed child living in a white home would threaten the entire system of white domination. Mixed children fathered by white males, defined as black by the one-drop rule, stayed with the mother in the black community (Myrdal 1944:60–67; Rose 1956:24–26; Blaustein and Ferguson 1957:7–8).

The Rule and American Law

The one-drop rule generally has had the support of law, especially for the past century. There were many court challenges to the rule in the nineteenth century and earlier but relatively few in the twentieth. *Plessy v. Ferguson* (1896), the separate-but-equal precedent case, was decided by the U.S. Supreme Court. Homer Plessy, whose ancestry was one eighth African black, challenged the Jim Crow statute requiring segregated seating on trains in Louisiana. Plessy also contended that he could pass as white and was therefore entitled to ride in the white seats. Although the court did not rule directly on the one-drop rule, it simply took it for granted that Plessy was a Negro.

State courts generally have upheld the one-drop rule. A 1948 case in Mississippi involved Davis Knight, who was less than one sixteenth black and who said he was unaware he had any black ancestry. The state proved that his great-grandmother was a slave girl, and Knight was convicted and sentenced to five years in prison for violating the antimiscegenation statute. State laws defining who is black, either in terms of various fractions or an explicit one-drop rule, generally have been rescinded in recent decades. However, the courts have not invalidated the one-drop rule.

A district court in Louisiana, in *Jane Doe v. Louisiana*, upheld the one-drop rule in 1983 in a suit brought by Susie Phipps, whose application for a passport had been denied because she checked "white" as her race. She looked white, had always lived as white, and thought she was white (Trillin 1986:62–63, 71–74). Lawyers for the state produced evidence in court that Mrs. Phipps was three thirty-seconds black. The decision was upheld on appeal in Louisiana. In 1986, the U.S. Supreme Court refused to review this decision, stating only, "The appeal is dismissed for want of a substantial federal question" (107 Sup. Ct. Reporter, interim ed. 638).

A Louisiana statute defining a Negro as anyone with a "trace of black ancestry" was challenged in court a number of times from the 1920s on. In 1970, a lawsuit was brought on behalf of a child whose ancestry was allegedly only one two-hundred-fifty-sixth black. The statute was then revised to define a black as someone whose ancestry is more than one thirty-second black (La. Rev. Stat. 42:267; La. Enacted Acts, 1970, no. 46). After the Phipps trial caused widespread adverse publicity about this 1970 revision, the one thirty-second criterion was abolished in 1983 (La. Repealed Acts, 1983, no. 441; Trillin 1986:77). Parents were given the right to change classifications on birth certificates if they could

prove the child is white by a "preponderance of the evidence" and to designate the race of newborns. This 1983 statute did not abolish the "traceable amount rule," however, as shown by the state and federal outcomes when the Phipps decision was appealed to higher courts.

Black Support for the Rule

As African Americans moved to the cities in growing numbers during the late 1920s, the Harlem-based Black Renaissance movement emphasized black unity and pride. Mulattoes led this renaissance, allying themselves more firmly with blacks than ever before. The African American community had fully accepted the one-drop rule by 1925.

The civil rights movement of the 1950s and 1960s ended the Jim Crow laws and got major civil rights legislation passed, but it did not challenge the one-drop rule. In fact, the white backlash to the civil rights movement prompted stronger African American support for the rule than ever. Lighter blacks often felt heavy pressure to affirm their blackness (Williamson 1980:190).

Miscegenation has taken place between European and African black populations in the United States for more than three and one-half centuries, usually by means of coercion against black women and without benefit of marriage. Probably more than nine tenths of African Americans have white ancestry, and one fourth or so have Native American forbears. Apparently from one fifth to one fourth of the genes in the African American population came from white ancestors (Reed 1969:765). This large-scale mixing, in combination with the one-drop rule, has produced extremely wide variation in color, hair texture, and other visible traits in the African American community.

We have traced the experiences that eventually convinced the black community that it has an important vested interest in a rule that was imposed to preserve slavery and legalized segregation. The rule forced all shades of racially mixed persons into the African American community where, over time, white oppression and other common experiences created a common culture and forged a sense of ethnic unity and pride (Davis 1991:124–39). The one-drop rule became strongly self-perpetuating in the black community in the twentieth century, as shown by hostility to passing and to the marriage of light blacks to whites.

Alex Haley's book *Roots* (1976) and the immensely popular television series based on it dramatized the acceptance of the one-drop rule by African Americans. Haley discovered the village in Gambia, West Africa, where his ancestor, Kunta Kinte, was captured into slavery as a youth. It seemed quite natural to Americans, black and white, for Haley to identify with his African roots rather than his Scots-Irish ones. Haley's later book *Queen* (1993) did focus on his white forbears, but it received comparatively little attention. Kunta Kinte's story came as a great symbolic victory to the African American community because, unlike most slaves, he had managed to keep alive his African name and identity for his family and descendants.

The National Association of Black Social Workers strongly upheld the one-drop rule in 1972 when it passed a resolution against the adoption of black children by white parents (Day 1979:99–100). Objecting to the terms "biracial" and "racially mixed," the Association insisted that mixed children be taught to acknowledge their blackness and raised to survive as blacks (Ladner 1977, chap. 7). "Cross-racial" adoption was almost stopped by the mid-1970s, and by 1987, at least 35 states had a policy against it. The issue has been revived, but the Association has not changed its position.

Studies of very young mixed-race children adopted by white families generally have found few problems with racial identity or personal adjustment (Zastrow 1977:83–86;

Grow and Shapiro 1974:188; Simon and Alstein 1977:71–162). However, a follow-up study of one sample showed that 10- to 15-year-olds had an increasing sense of racial identity, more ambivalence about race, and more emotional and behavioral problems. Experiences outside the home evidently had confronted the children with the fact that other children and adults defined them as black, yet the majority of these older children seemed well adjusted (Simon and Alstein 1981:13–19). In another study of older adoptees, about three fourths of the children identified themselves racially the same way their adoptive parents saw them. For instance, most adoptees of parents who preferred a human label to a racial one held the same view, although some of them identified as blacks (McRoy and Zurcher 1983:126–36).

Although the one-drop rule generally is accepted by both whites and blacks, there are examples of rejection of it in both communities (Daniel 1992:91–107). Some light children of mixed marriages, as well as some African American children adopted by white families, reject the black-only identity. Many Hispanic Americans with some black ancestry resist the rule if they can and embrace a Latino ethnic identity. For example, a majority of Puerto Rican immigrants have some African ancestry, but relatively few of these were identified as black when they were on the island (Jorge 1979:134–41). Many Creoles of color in New Orleans and the vicinity still reject both the black and the white identity (Dominguez 1986:163–64).

Native Americans with some African ancestry generally try to avoid the one-drop rule, usually by staying on a reservation (Bennett 1962:268–71). Those who leave the reservation are often treated as blacks. In Virginia, persons who are one fourth or more Native American and less than one sixteenth African black have been defined as Indians while on the reservation but as blacks when they leave (Berry 1965:26). There are complex differences by state and tribe in the definition of who is Indian. Some 200 small, tri-racial communities in the East and South have long attempted to evade the rule by remaining isolated (Berry 1963:193–95).

Professional golfer Tiger Woods publicly rejected the one-drop rule after winning the Master's Championship in 1997. When asked how it felt to be the first black to win the tournament, he replied that he is not only African American. His mother, he pointed out, is from Thailand. His ancestry is apparently one fourth Thai, one fourth Chinese, one fourth black, one eighth Native American, and one eighth white. As he was growing up, Woods coined a label for himself: Cablinasian.

Examples of deviation from the one-drop rule are conspicuous because of their relative rarity. Both in the black and the white community, the typical response to such deviation is to condemn it and affirm the rule. As French sociologist Emile Durkheim emphasized, deviant acts and statements call attention to a violated rule and thus strengthen the consensus that supports it (Durkheim 1960:102). For most African Americans, including many if not most of the lightest, the rule gets such constant reinforcement that it provides a clear sense of black ethnic identity.

Other Status Rules

The one-drop rule is unique to the United States mainland, reflecting our history with slavery and segregation (Williamson 1980, chap. 1). Elsewhere in the world, persons whose ancestry is part African black are generally perceived as mixed, not as members of one parent group only. However, there is great variation in the status position mixed persons occupy in different societies. Remember that the one-drop rule assigns all racially mixed persons the same racial identity and status as that of the socially subordinate group.

A second rule assigns persons of mixed heritage an in-between status, as illustrated by the mulattoes in South Carolina and Louisiana before 1850. Another example, in which the racially mixed are defined as an in-between group that is neither black nor white, is the Coloreds in the Republic of South Africa (Watson 1970:10–24; Van den Berghe 1971:37; Williams 1992:280–303). People in this tenuous position, like all middleman minorities, are politically powerless, and their status may change drastically in times of crisis (Blalock 1967:79–84).

A third rule assigns persons of mixed ancestry a status lower than that of either parent group, as in the case of the Métis of Canada, once a middle group between whites and Native Canadians. Other examples are the mulattoes of Uganda, the Eurasians in India, and the Amerasians in Korea and Vietnam (Berry 1965:192, 275–76; Gist and Dean 1973; Valverde 1992:144–61).

A fourth rule assigns mixed persons a status higher than that of either parent group, as experienced by the Mestizos of Mexico or the mulattoes of Haiti, Namibia, or Liberia (Stoddard 1973:59–60; Nicholls 1981: 415–27).

A fifth rule allows the status to vary widely between the parent groups, depending more on education and wealth than on race, as in lowland Latin America and most of the Caribbean (Wagley 1963:143–48; Harris 1964: 57–61; Solaún and Kronus 1973:3–9, 33–35; Fernandez 1992:132–35).

A sixth rule confers a status equal with that of all parent groups, as in Hawaii (Berry 1965:138–42; Adams 1969:82–90; Howard 1980:449–51; Nordyke 1988:247–53).

A seventh status is that of an assimilating minority, following the implicit rule for racial minorities in the United States other than African Americans. This means in practice that persons with no known African forbears and one fourth or less ancestry in such groups as Native Americans, Chinese Americans, or Mexican American mestizos are perceived as assimilating Americans. Such persons are not subjected to a one-drop rule, have no need to "pass," and can acknowledge their different ancestries (Davis 1991:12–14, 117–19).

These seven status rules are social constructions that reflect the histories and social structures of different societies. International comparisons of the racial composition of countries or of racial differences in rates of diseases can be extremely misleading. For instance, most African Americans would be classified as some degree of colored in Brazil and in Latin America generally, where only unmixed Africans are defined as black. A person defined as black in the United States might well be classed as colored rather than black in Jamaica, Ghana, or South Africa, and as white in Puerto Rico (Hoetink 1967:xii, 39–41).

Costs of the Rule

Different status rules for racially mixed populations all have their costs. Problems engendered by the one-drop rule are complex, some painfully distressing, and are borne primarily by the African American community. The level of public concern about these costs has not been high because the rule is so taken for granted in both the white and the black community. The problems all stem from defining as black a population ranging from ebony to white.

There are conflicts in African American families and communities over differences in color, hair, and other traits. Although darker and "nappier" blacks are most likely to be the targets of stinging criticism of their appearance, the lightest ones also are often harassed and humiliated (Gwaltney 1980:71–86). The most desired skin color, especially since the 1960s, has become light brown (Williamson 1980:190–92). As Spike Lee has shown in his 1988 film *School Daze* and later in *Jungle Fever,* some of the most intense conflicts over color and hair in the black community accompany dating, sexual relations, and marriage. However, color discrimination by blacks against blacks also occurs in the work-

place, in the media, and in other areas (Russell, Wilson, and Hall 1992:151–62). This "colorism" is a product of white racism and the one-drop rule.

The ambiguity of the racial identity of light African Americans leads to everyday strains and embarrassments, traumatic experiences, and sometimes to deep dilemmas of identity. In the mid-1950s, a 10-year-old white boy in a middle-class family in Virginia got the jolt of his life. After the family suffered financial reverses and a broken marriage, the boy's father took him and his younger brother to live in his home neighborhood in Muncie, Indiana. En route there by bus, the father disclosed to the boys that he had passed as white. Living in the black community in Muncie as "white black," the boys were discriminated against and harassed by whites and blacks alike. After many painful experiences and against great odds, the talented older boy eventually became a law professor and dean of a major law school (Williams 1995). Despite his white appearance, he developed and retains a firm African American identity.

Another northern law professor, a white-appearing African American woman, has relatives who range in skin color from dark brown to light brown to white. Sometimes she feels she is a black passing for white and sometimes that she is a white passing for black. Once, when she was in a taxi that hit a car, the investigating policeman checked her race as white. She informed the white officer that she is black. His bored response was "Sure lady, if you say so," as if she had arbitrarily invented the centuries-old one-drop rule (Scales-Trent 1995:74–75).

Light blacks adjust to these problems of marginality in different ways, among which are (1) by accepting the black identity but trying to reduce color conflicts within the black community; (2) by embracing the symbols of blackness and striving to prove their black pride; (3) by becoming preoccupied with expressing strong hatred of all whites

(Gwaltney 1980:71–72); (4) by becoming civil rights activists committed to reducing discrimination by whites against blacks; (5) by adopting a marginal identity between the black and the white community; (6) by rejecting any kind of racial identity and focusing on a professional or some special-interest role; or (7) in rare instances, by deciding to risk the painful consequences of passing permanently as white. A person may switch from one style of adjustment to another and also may adopt more than one at a time. In her long struggle over her identity, Lena Horne seems to have experienced all these modes of adjustment except the seventh (Horne and Schickel 1965).

Among still other problems are collective anxieties of whites about "invisible blackness" (Williamson 1980:90–108) and of blacks about persons who "deny their color." Many white parents of mixed children worry about the suppression of the white ancestry. There is profound anxiety about passing as white to gain greater opportunities. There are complex administrative and legal problems in implementing the one-drop rule. The rule seems to cause gross misperceptions of the racial identity of very large populations in Asia and the Middle East and of racially mixed populations in Latin America and elsewhere. Finally, the rule poses problems of sampling and interpretation in medical and other scientific research on racial differences (Davis 1991:156–67).

A Challenge to the Rule

A movement to allow mixed-race persons to embrace a biracial or multiracial identity has developed considerable momentum. A national umbrella organization called the Association of Multiethnic Americans (AMEA) and the *Interrace* and *New People* magazines emerged in the 1980s to coordinate the efforts of groups in 30 or more cities (Grosz 1989:24–28). Campus groups have been or-

ganized at many colleges and universities. Rather than attacking the one-drop rule directly, the emphasis is on the freedom to affirm one's whole self by acknowledging all of one's ancestries (Nakashima 1992:177–78). The movement includes all racial blends, not just those with African black ancestry. Although neither Asian nor Native American ancestry has been subject to a one-drop rule, this rule for African American ancestry has kept the multiracial option off the official lists of categories.

The largest response to my book *Who Is Black?* (Davis 1991) outside of academe has been from persons of mixed racial heritage or their parents, especially from leaders and supporters of the multiracial identity movement. The Gustavus Myers Center recognized the book with its award for an Outstanding Book on Human Rights, and the mass media have shown considerable interest. I have given many interviews and have participated in radio and television newscasts, talk shows, and conferences. Other programs and a number of recent autobiographies and articles have raised public awareness of the experiences of racially mixed persons. The one-drop rule has entered the national vocabulary.

The backbone of the multiracial identity movement has been parents and children of interracial marriages, which have increased significantly since the 1960s. However, the movement faces determined opposition. Many African Americans fear that persons who want to affirm their European, Native American, or Asian roots want to deny their African ancestry (Bates 1993:38–39). There is also fear that whites who support the movement want to divide the black community, reduce its numbers, weaken black political power, and undermine affirmative action and other civil rights remedies (Daniel 1992:335–41).

In spite of opposition, the movement has had some success. PROJECT RACE (Reclassify All Children Equally), headquartered in Atlanta, has persuaded several state legislatures to consider requiring the multiracial option on all state forms. Some states have passed laws to this effect. Some school districts in several states have added the multiracial category (Graham 1995:185–89). In June 1993, both PROJECT RACE and the AMEA gave written testimony in favor of the multiracial option to the Subcommittee on Census, Statistics and Postal Personnel of the U.S. House of Representatives. Later, these organizations gave similar testimony to the Office of Management and Budget (OMB), which defines racial categories for all levels of government in the country, including the public schools (Fernandez 1995:191).

Much of this policy debate was centered on the possible use of the multiracial option on the Census Bureau forms for the year 2000. Early in 1998, the OMB rejected this proposed category. Instead, the traditional instruction to check only one racial category was changed to "check all that apply," a major victory for the multiracial identity movement. Because most households now fill out their own census questionnaires, this instruction allows those who wish to do so to indicate two or more racial ancestries. This will very likely reduce the number of "other" checks on census forms. Experience since the 1960 census suggests that most African Americans probably will continue to check only the "black" box.

Do these successes of the multiracial identity movement portend the beginning of the end of the one-drop rule? Or, instead, will they join the several patterned deviations that call attention to the rule and reinforce it? Some states are finding it difficult to implement statutes that legitimate the multiracial option. These laws and the instruction to "check all that apply" might not hold up in the courts or, if they do, judges might be reluctant to extend the precedents to other situations. Strong African American support for the one-drop rule probably will diminish only if white racism declines a great deal more.

On the other hand, exceptions can become so numerous that a rule becomes obsolete. A social construction created to support slavery and solidified to enforce Jim Crow segregation is incongruous in a nation dedicated to liberty and equal opportunity for all. Increasingly, especially since the national origins immigration quotas were abolished in the 1960s, the United States is becoming a multiracial, multi-ethnic society. The civil rights movement may yet be extended to persons who wish to resist the pressure to identify with only one of their racial heritages (Daniel 1992:334).

Unlikely as it now seems, the mainland United States might some day move toward the Hawaiian approach as the most feasible alternative to the one-drop rule. Mainlanders who move to Hawaii seem able to accept the island pattern, different as it is, within a few months (Adams 1969:86–87). African Americans, Hispanic Americans, Asian Americans, and Native Americans have all moved toward the goal of egalitarian pluralism in preference to total assimilation. The Hawaiian rule, which confers on racially mixed persons a status equal to that of all parent groups, is consistent with egalitarian pluralism (Davis 1995:125–31). Whether this is the path America eventually follows, the one-drop rule may not be forever.

References

Adams, Romanzo. 1969. "The Unorthodox Race Doctrine of Hawaii." Pp. 81–90 in *Comparative Perspectives on Race Relations,* edited by M. Tumin. Boston: Little, Brown.

Bahr, Howard M., Bruce A. Chadwick, and Joseph H. Stauss. 1979. *American Ethnicity.* Lexington, MA: D. C. Heath.

Bates, Karen Grigsby. 1993. "Color Complexity." *Emerge* June:38–39.

Bennett, Lerone, Jr. 1962. *Before the Mayflower: A History of the Negro in America, 1619–1962.* Chicago: Johnson.

Berry, Brewton. 1963. *Almost White*. New York: Macmillan.

———. 1965. *Race and Ethnic Relations*. 3d ed. New York: Houghton Mifflin.

Berry, Brewton and Henry L. Tischler. 1978. *Race and Ethnic Relations*. 4th ed. New York: Houghton Mifflin.

Blalock, Hubert M., Jr. 1967. *Toward a Theory of Minority-Group Relations*. New York: Capricorn Books.

Blassingame, John W. 1972. *The Slave Community: Plantation Life in the Antebellum South*. New York: Oxford University Press

———. 1973. *Black New Orleans, 1860–1880*. Chicago: University of Chicago Press.

Blaustein, Albert P. and Clarence Clyde Ferguson, Jr. 1957. *Desegregation and the Law*. New Brunswick, NJ: Rutgers University Press.

Buckley, Gail Lumet. 1986. *The Hornes: An American Family*. New York: Knopf.

Burma, John G. 1946. "The Measurement of Passing." *American Journal of Sociology* 52(July):18–22.

Cannon, Poppy. 1956. *A Gentle Knight: My Husband, Walter White*. New York: Rinehart & Co.

Catterall, Helen T., ed. 1926–1937. *Judicial Cases Concerning American Slavery and the Negro*. 5 vols. Washington, DC: Carnegie Institute.

Daniel, G. Reginald. 1992. "Beyond Black and White: The New Multiracial Consciousness." Pp. 333–41 in *Racially Mixed People in America*, edited by M. P. P. Root. Newbury Park, CA: Sage.

Davis, F. James. 1991. *Who Is Black? One Nation's Definition*. University Park, PA: Pennsylvania State University Press.

———. 1995. "The Hawaiian Alternative to the One-Drop Rule." Pp. 115–31 in *American Mixed Race: The Culture of Microdiversity*, edited by N. Zack. Lanham, MD: Rowman and Littlefield.

Day, Dawn. 1979. *The Adoption of Black Children: Counteracting Institutional Discrimination*. Lexington, MA: Lexington Books.

Dominguez, Virginia R. 1986. *White by Definition: Social Classification in Creole Louisiana*. New Brunswick, NJ: Rutgers University Press.

Durkheim, Emile. 1960. *The Division of Labor in Society*. Translated by G. Simpson. New York: Free Press.

Eckard, E. W. 1947. "How Many Negroes Pass?" *American Journal of Sociology* 52(May):498–503.

Ferber, Edna. 1926. *Showboat*. New York: Doubleday.

Fernandez, Carlos A. 1992. "La Raza and the Melting Pot." Pp. 126–43 in *Racially Mixed People in America*, edited by M. P. P. Root. Newbury Park, CA: Sage.

———. 1995. "Testimony of the Association of Multi-Ethnic Americans Before the Subcommittee on Census, Statistics, and Postal Personnel of the U.S. House of Representatives." Pp. 191–210 in *American Mixed Race: The Culture of Microdiversity*, edited by N. Zack. Lanham, MD: Rowman and Littlefield.

Gist, Noel P. and Roy Dean. 1973. *Marginality and Identity*. Leiden, The Netherlands: Brill.

Graham, Susan R. 1995. "Grassroots Advocacy." Pp. 185–89 in *American Mixed Race: The Culture of Microdiversity*, edited by N. Zack. Lanham, MD: Rowman and Littlefield.

Grosz, G. 1989. "From Sea to Shining Sea: A Current Listing of Interracial Organizations and Support Groups across the Nation." *Interrace* 1:24–28.

Grow, Lucille J. and Deborah Shapiro. 1974. *Black Children—White Parents*. New York: Child Welfare League of America.

Gwaltney, John Langston. 1980. *Drylongso: A Self-Portrait of Black America*. New York: Vintage.

Haley, Alex. 1976. *Roots: The Saga of an American Family*. Garden City, NY: Doubleday.

Haley, Alex and David Stevens. 1993. *Queen*. New York: Avon.

Harris, Melvin. 1964. *Patterns of Race in the Americas*. New York: Norton.

Hoetink, H. 1967. *Caribbean Race Relations: A Study of Two Variants*. New York: Oxford University Press.

Horne, Lena and Richard Schickel. 1965. *Lena*. Garden City, NY: Doubleday.

Howard, Alan. 1980. "Hawaiians." Pp. 449–52 in *Harvard Encyclopedia of American Ethnic Groups*, edited by S. Thernstrom. Cambridge, MA: Harvard University Press.

Jane Doe v. Louisiana. 479 S. 2d 369–72 (D. La. 1983).

Johnston, James Hugo. 1970. *Race Relations in Virginia and Miscegenation in the South, 1776–1860*. Amherst: University of Massachusetts Press.

Jorge, Angela. 1979. "The Black Puerto Rican Woman in Contemporary American Society." Pp. 134–41 in *The Puerto Rican Woman*, edited by Edna Acosta-Beléen. New York: Praeger.

Ladner, Joyce A. 1977. *Mixed Families: Adopting across Racial Boundaries*. Garden City, NY: Anchor/Doubleday.

Marshall, Eliot. 1998. "DNA Studies Challenge the Meaning of Race." *Science* 282:654–55.

McRoy, Ruth G. and Louis A. Zurcher. 1983. *Transracial and Inracial Adoptees: The Adolescent Years*. Springfield, IL: Charles C Thomas.

Myrdal, Gunnar, assisted by Richard Sterner and Arnold M. Rose. 1944. *An American Dilemma.* New York: Harper & Row.

Nakashima, Cynthia L. 1992. "An Invisible Monster: The Creation and Denial of Mixed-Race People in America." Pp. 162–78 in *Racially Mixed People in America,* edited by M. P. P. Root. Newbury Park, CA: Sage.

Nicholls, David. 1981. "No Hawks or Pedlars: Levantines in the Caribbean." *Ethnic and Racial Studies* 4:415–31.

Nordyke, Eleanor C. 1988. "Blacks in Hawaii: A Demographic and Historical Perspective." *Hawaiian Journal of History* 22:241–55.

Plessy v. Ferguson. 1896. 163 U.S. 537.

Reed, T. Edward. 1969. "Caucasian Genes in American Negroes." *Science* 165:762–68.

Reuter, Edward Byron. 1918. *The Mulatto in the United States.* Boston: Badger.

Rose, Arnold M. 1956. *The Negro in America.* Boston: Beacon.

Russell, Kathy, Midge Wilson, and Ronald Hall. 1992. *The Color Complex: The Politics of Skin Color among African Americans.* Orlando, FL: Harcourt Brace.

Scales-Trent, Judy. 1995. *Notes of a White Black Woman: Race, Color, Community.* University Park, PA: Pennsylvania State University Press.

Simon, Rita J. and Howard Alstein. 1977. *Transracial Adoption.* New York: John Wiley.

——. 1981. *Transracial Adoption: A Follow-Up.* Lexington, MA: D. C. Heath.

Solaún, Mauricio and Sidney Kronus. 1973. *Discrimination without Violence.* New York: John Wiley.

Stoddard, Ellwyn R. 1973. *Mexican Americans.* New York: Random House.

Trillin, Calvin. 1986. "American Chronicles: Black or White." *New Yorker,* April 14, pp. 62–78.

Twain, Mark. 1922. *Pudd'nhead Wilson.* New York: Harper and Brothers.

Valverde, Kieu-Linh Caroline. 1992. "From Dust to Gold: The Vietnamese Amerasian Experience." Pp. 144–61 in *Racially Mixed People in America,* edited by M. P. P. Root. Newbury Park, CA: Sage.

Van den Berghe, Pierre L. 1971. "Racial Segregation in South Africa: Degrees and Kinds." Pp. 37–49 in *South Africa: Sociological Perspectives,* edited by H. Adam. New York: Oxford University Press.

Vander Zanden, James W. 1972. *American Minority Relations.* 3d ed. New York: Ronald.

Wagley, Charles, ed. 1963. *Race and Class in Rural Brazil.* 2d ed. Paris: UNESCO.

Watson, Graham. 1970. *Passing for White: A Study of Racial Assimilation in a South African School.* London: Tavistock.

White, Walter. 1948. *A Man Called White: The Autobiography of Walter White.* New York: Viking.

Williams, Gregory Howard. 1995. *Life on the Color Line: The True Story of a White Boy Who Discovered He Was Black.* New York: Dutton.

Williams, Teresa Kay. 1992. "Prism Lives: Identity of Binational Amerasians." Pp. 280–303 in *Racially Mixed People in America,* edited by M. P. P. Root. Newbury Park, CA: Sage.

Williamson, Joel. 1980. *New People: Miscegenation and Mulattoes in the United States.* New York: Free Press.

Zastrow, Charles H. 1977. *Outcome of Black Children-White Parents Transracial Adoptions.* San Francisco: R&E Research Associates.

Davis:

1. Given Davis's essay, speculate on why you think it is that African Americans are the only group to be affected by the one-drop rule? Why is it that some groups are able to self-identify whereas others (i.e., African Americans) have not had the option to do so.

2. Discuss what it means with regard to the social construction of race to be able to reclassify race on birth certificates or to designate race of newborns. What are the political implications for being able to do so?

9

The Politics of Ethnic Authenticity: Building Native American Identities and Communities

Joane Nagel

No one knows for sure how many indigenous North Americans were present when Columbus landed in 1492, although estimates suggest that numbers were in the several millions. Over the next 400 years, there was a dramatic decline in the native population; by the end of the nineteenth century, the U.S. Census Bureau counted fewer than 250,000 Native Americans in the United States.[1] The decrease in the number of native people was accompanied by a marked reduction in the number of native societies or "tribes." Distinct language and dialect communities at the time of contact were estimated at more than 1,000 (Swanton 1952).[2] This number has dwindled to around 320 Indian groups or "entities" in the lower 48 states that are officially recognized by the U.S. Department of the Interior in the 1990s.[3]

In spite of these declines, the twentieth century has seen a remarkable increase in the American Indian population, from its nadir of 237,196 in 1900 to 1,874,536 in the 1990 census (Snipp 1989; U.S. Census Bureau 1991). This growth is summarized in Table 9.1. As we can see, native population figures for the past 90 years represent a reversal of 4 centuries of decline in the North American Indian population: beginning with fewer than one half million at the turn of the century, climbing back up to nearly 2 million in 1990. Although these trends reflect a tragic pattern of death and decline, they also reveal an extraordinary trend toward recovery and renewal. The twentieth century resurgence of the American Indian population is a truly remarkable story of ethnic survival and rebirth.

Population projections undertaken by the U.S. Office of Technology Assessment (OTA) in 1986 suggest that Native American demographic recovery is far from over. The OTA projected the American Indian population for the next century using as a base population the number of Indians in 1980 living in 32 states with federal reservations according to various degrees of native ancestry (so-called blood quantum). Table 9.2 shows these projections.

As we can see from Table 9.2, the total increase in the Indian population during the next century is expected to be twelvefold,

Table 9.1

American Indian Population—1890–1990

Year	Number	% Change
1890	248,253	
1900	237,196	–5
1910	276,927	17
1920	244,437	–13
1930	343,352	40
1940	345,252	1
1950	357,499	4
1960	523,591	46
1970	792,730	51
1980	1,364,033	72
1990	1,873,536	38

Sources: 1890–1970: Russell Thornton, *American Indian Holocaust and Survival* (Norman: University of Oklahoma Press, 1987), p. 160; figures for 1980 and 1990 are from U.S. Census Bureau, *U.S. Bureau of the Census Releases 1990 Census Counts on Specific Racial Groups* (Census Bureau Press Release CB91–215, Wednesday, June 12, 1991), Table 1.

growing from 1.3 million in 1980 to 15.8 million in 2080. What is especially interesting about these projections is the changing internal composition of Native America. Snipp (1989) reported on the projections made by the OTA using Bureau of Indian Affairs blood quantum data and taking "into account the prevalence of racial intermarriage among Indians based on data from the 1980 census" (p. 166).

The OTA projection begins in 1980 with 1.1 million individuals with 50 percent or more Indian ancestry (blood quantum), 120,068 with 25 percent to 49 percent native blood quantum, and 46,636 with less than 25 percent native ancestry. A century later, the demographic picture would look very different. By 2080, the OTA projects a stable number of Indians with blood quanta of 50 percent or more (1.3 million in 2080). However, the OTA predicts a tremendous growth in the other two categories, with 5.2 million individuals with blood quanta ranging from 25 percent to 49 percent and 9.3 million native people with less than one quarter Indian ancestry. This population explosion of Indians of mixed ancestry reduces the percentage of the native population with 50 percent or more Indian ancestry from 86.9 percent of the native population in 1980 to only 8.2 percent of the native population in 2080. Concomitantly, the percentage of the Indian population with 25 percent to 49 percent blood quantum rises from 9.5 percent in 1980 to 32.9 percent in 2080, and the percentage of the Indian population with less than 25 percent blood quantum increases the most, rising from 3.6 percent of the population in 1980 to 58.9 percent in 2080.

What do these predicted changes in the ancestry of American Indians mean? This future portrait of Native America painted by the OTA is one of increased racial diversity, with more and more Native Americans of mixed Indian/non-Indian ancestry. The implications of this mixing are important for understanding what it will mean to be an

Table 9.2

Office of Technology Assessment: Indian Population Projections (1980–2080)

Year	Percent Indian Ancestry (Blood Quantum)			
	50% and above	25%–49%	Less than 25%	Total
1980	1,125,746 (86.9%)	123,068 (9.5%)	46,636 (3.6%)	1,295,450 (100.0%)
2080	1,292,911 (8.2%)	5,187,411 (32.9%)	5,187,411 (58.9%)	15,767,206 (100.0%)

Source: C. Matthew Snipp, *American Indians: The First of This Land* (New York: Russell Sage Foundation, 1988), p. 167.

American Indian in the next century, in particular in light of contemporary controversies about Indian authenticity and debates over what constitutes legitimate claims to Indian ancestry and group membership.

The puzzle of why the American Indian population increased so dramatically in the last decades of the twentieth century and the implications of the racial diversity of future generations of Native Americans are two of the main reasons for my interest in American Indian history and contemporary political and social life. For a sociologist, both puzzles and change pose a challenge. Puzzles are to be solved, and change is to be understood. My solution to the rising numbers of American Indians in the post-Second World War era can be summarized as a combination of factors involving the urbanization, education, and political activism of American Indians, all of which led to an increased sense of ethnic pride and thus an increased likelihood of identifying oneself as "American Indian" (for a full explanation, see Nagel 1996). My analysis of the implications of past and future racial diversity among Native Americans is that Indian ethnicity will be a subject of debate and controversy for the foreseeable future. Questions about native ethnic group membership and who has a right to American Indian identity and resources are the focus of the remainder of this chapter.

American Indian Ethnic Diversity

Since the 1970s, more than half of all American Indians have lived in cities (Sorkin 1978; U.S. Census Bureau 1992a, table 44). Although tribal origin and affiliation continue to have enormous currency among these often first-generation native urban immigrants, demographic differences inevitably have emerged between urban and reservation Indians in education, health, income, lifestyle, interests, and perspective. These differ-

ences reflect the worldwide impact of urbanization on formerly rural populations: increased income and employment, higher levels of education, lower rates of fertility, more intermarriage, and native language loss.[4]

Despite a great deal of reservation-urban circular migration, differences between urban Indians and those residing on reservations represents an important ethnic boundary between the two groups, one characterized by some strain and suspicion. One source of this tension is the concern of reservation Indians that their urban coethnics have lost touch with reservation needs and concerns while having disporportionate access to power and influence in national arenas governing Indian affairs. In an article titled "So Who Really Represents Indian Tribes?" one commentator criticized the prominent role played by "urban Indians" in federal Indian policy, arguing that, although educated, urban Indians are "thoroughly grounded . . . in municipal bonds, capital formation, and other esoteric topics. . . . They do not understand the perspective of tribal leaders, or of Indian people" who must contend with such reservation problems as health, education, housing, cultural preservation, environmental protection, or language preservation (Chavers 1993:A5).

Urban-reservation differences, although obviously important, represent but one source of diversity among a socially, economically, politically, linguistically, and culturally plural Native American population. Tribal distinctions represent an even greater source of variability. More than 350 Indian tribes and communities in the lower 48 states are separately recognized by federal and state authorities.[5] Each has its own government, legal system, justice system, educational system, and economic, social, and cultural organization (for an overview of many tribal political differences, see O'Brien 1989). These differences are reinforced by geographic distances among tribes and the isolation of many reservations. Historical patterns of conflict, competition, or cooperation also remain a legacy that shades contemporary intertribal relations, as does the fact that Indian communities often see one another as competitors for scarce federal funding or federally regulated resources. Competition can become especially bitter when federally nonrecognized groups seek access to Indian resources. Challenges to tribal authenticity can result.

For instance, in 1979, the Samish and Snohomish tribes of Puget Sound in Washington State were judged by the federal government to be "legally extinct" and were excluded from native access to the region's fishing economy. Recognized tribes who had won rights to half the annual salmon catch in the landmark federal district court "Boldt" decision in 1974 opposed the Samish and Snohomish efforts. "It boils down to trying to protect tribal fisheries from groups which the Tulalips [a recognized tribe] view as not genuine Indians" (Egan 1992:8).[6] The importance of resource competition in intertribal relations can be seen in the situation of the Lumbees of North Carolina. One of the largest tribes in the 1980 census, numbering 26,631 (U.S. Census Bureau 1989, table 1:26), the Lumbees have long sought federal recognition, only to receive limited acknowledgment with the proviso that the tribe would receive no federal services (Blu 1980). There are many such tribes seeking social and federal acceptance as legitimate Indian communities. Their presence represents another level of complexity in Indian ethnicity.

Debates over Indian Ethnic Authenticity

Challenges to authenticity can be leveled against individuals and their claims to ethnic group membership. For instance, in 1982 I visited an American Indian[7] community center in an eastern city. I was greeted by the di-

rector, a man wearing jeans and a plaid shirt, whose dark hair was woven into braids bound by beaded ties. He told me about the Indian center's history and about its current activities, which were designed to provide a sense of community for the city's several thousand American Indian residents. The most successful undertaking, he reported, was a summer camp program, where local Indian children from diverse tribal backgrounds, most of whom had been born and lived their lives in the city, were sent to spend 2 weeks on his home reservation more than a thousand miles away to learn about reservation life and their native heritage. I found the conversation interesting and informative. Several months later, while I was visiting a Bureau of Indian Affairs office in Washington, DC, the Indian center director's name came up in conversation. To my surprise, I was told matter-of-factly by a person working there (who identified himself as a member of a recognized Indian tribe) that the director, Sam Smith (not his name), was "not really an Indian." When I inquired into this statement, the official said, "Well, maybe his grandmother had some Indian blood," but, he reiterated, "Sam Smith is not really an Indian."

Reading the Indian affairs literature and listening to native people, the question of who is really an Indian comes up again and again. The query is often made in an atmosphere of skepticism and sometimes bitter contention.[8] The question is posed to tribes as well as to individuals. For instance, in an "open letter" to the Governor of Georgia, Cherokee Nation of Oklahoma Principal Chief Wilma Mankiller denounced the state's decision to officially recognize two groups claiming Cherokee ancestry, expressing concern these groups were "using the Cherokee Nation's name, history, culture, and reputation . . . and posing as Indian tribes" (Mankiller 1993:A4).[9] Such concerns often arise because of the potential loss of scarce tribal resources to an ever-increasing pool of collective and individual recipients.

Individual Indian ethnicity is at least as problematic as that of groups, due to wide variability in the criteria and standards of proof of Indian ancestry and Indianness. Again, the doubts and suspicions seem greatest when ethnically tied resources are at stake and when benefits are seen to accrue to individuals who claim Indian ancestry or special Indian knowledge. This challenge to authenticity is extended to a wide variety of authors, artists, scholars, and activists, and individuals claiming Indian identity or interests.[10] Again, although the debate here focuses on American Indian ethnic boundaries and issues of authenticity, similar debates can be found in other ethnic communities (African Americans, Asians, Latinos, to name a few) and among other bounded social groups (age, gender, disabled, veterans). In some of these cases, the issues do not center so much on lineage or biology—who is *really* black or who is *really* female; rather, the focus is on what kind of upbringing, class position, or life experience qualifies an individual to speak for or represent the interests of the group. In other cases, the issues center more on actual personal characteristics (ability to speak Spanish or not; having been in combat or not; degree of disability).[11] In the case of American Indians, the authenticity debate often centers on ancestry (see Gates 1991),[12] namely, just how much and what kind of Indian background qualifies individuals or groups to have the rights of American Indians.

Another source of controversy concerns how an individual acquires authentic Indian ethnicity—through self-definition or by the acknowledgment of others. Again, resources seem to be a key issue. For instance, at its annual meeting in Phoenix, Arizona, in 1993, the Association of American Indian and Alaskan Native Professors (AAIANP) issued a statement on "ethnic fraud," stressing the importance of official tribal recognition of individuals' Indianness in classifying university students and faculty. The statement was intended to register the organization's concern about

ethnic fraud and offer recommendations to ensure the accuracy of American Indian/Alaska Native identification in American colleges and universities . . . and to affirm and ensure American Indian/Alaska Native identity in the hiring process. We are asking that colleges and universities: Require documentation of enrollment in a state or federally recognized nation/tribe with preference given to those who meet this criterion (AAIANP 1993).[13]

David Cornsilk, assistant director of admissions at Bacone College in Muskogee, Oklahoma, provided this rationale for such a policy:

I believe in membership as the foundation of sovereignty. . . . I believe the authority of the tribe, the right of the tribe, stems from the group, the community. . . . I don't believe in the right of self-identification. I believe that's an assault on the right of the group. (Reynolds 1993:A3)[14]

Tim Giago, editor of *Indian Country Today* and *The Lakota Times*, affirmed the tribal membership approach to establishing Indian authenticity and underlined the issue of resources in making distinctions between "real" Indians and others who claim Indian ancestry.

It was in the 1970s that people claiming to be Indian began to take jobs intended for Indians and to write books claiming to be authorities on Indians. These instant "wannabes" did us far more harm than good. Not only did they often give out misleading information about Indians, they also took jobs that left many qualified genuine Native Americans out in the cold. . . . Before you can truly be considered an Indian you must become an enrolled member of a tribe. I think most Indians would agree that this is the only way you can truly be accepted as Indian. (Giago 1991:3)

Alphonse Ortiz echoed these concerns about scarce resources allocated to self-identified recipients:

These are people who have no business soaking up jobs and grants, people who have made no claim to being Indian up to their early adulthood, and then when there's something to be gained they're opportunists of the rankest stripe, of the worst order. . . . We resent these people who just come in and when the going's good skim the riches off the surface. (Reynolds 1993:A1)

Although convincingly argued, this emphasis on official enrollment (membership) in recognized tribes in determining Indian ethnicity is at odds with the way in which most Americans (and perhaps most American Indians) acquire their ethnicity. Though estimates vary, somewhere between two thirds and one half of American Indians counted in the 1980 and 1990 census were enrolled members of recognized tribes.[15] Thus, the official enrollment rule would throw into question the ethnicity of a significant proportion of Americans who designated their "race" as Indian in the U.S. census, not to mention the millions more who identified an Indian ethnic ancestry on census forms. This restrictive approach to constructing Native American ethnic boundaries is not typical of strategies used by most ethnic groups in contemporary America, who often seek to widen ethnic self-definitions to compete more effectively in local, state, and national political arenas. Indeed, the AAIANP's reliance on external (tribal) ascription represents a challenge to the widely held notion in American society that ethnicity is, at least in part, a private, individual choice (a notion that is shared by the U.S. Census Bureau).

These debates can be trying to the targets of authenticity inquiries, as critical author and activist Ward Churchill's comments reveal:

I'm forever being asked not only my "tribe," but my "percentage of Indian blood." I've given the matter a lot of thought, and find that I prefer to make the computation based on all of me rather than just the fluid coursing through my veins. Calculated this way, I can report that I am precisely 52.5 pounds Indian—about 35 pounds Creek and the remainder Cherokee—88 pounds Teutonic, 43.5 pounds some sort of English, and all the rest "undetermined." Maybe that last part should just be described as "human." It all seems rather silly as a means of assessing who I am, don't you think? (Jaimes 1992:123)[16]

Although many methods of calculating individual Indian or tribal authenticity are often ludicrous and sometimes offensive (analyses of urine and earwax, chemical tasting abilities; Snipp 1989:30–31), unfortunately, the enterprise is by no means capricious. It turns out to be deadly serious in the many cases in which individual and community life-sustaining resources hang in the balance as judgments of "real" Indian authenticity are decided. These cases routinely involve such important matters as child custody rights, health benefits, scholarships, legitimate means of livelihood, land claims, mineral and resource rights and royalty payments, political and criminal jurisdiction, taxation, and myriad other personal and financial matters. The truth is embedded in the common sociological fact: Although ethnicity is socially and politically constructed and is thus arbitrary, variable, and constantly negotiated, it is no less real in its consequences.

Changing Definitions of Indianness

Embedded in many discussions of Indian authenticity and membership regulations is a question about whether the rules defining Indianness and tribal membership should be relaxed or tightened, that is, made more inclusionary or more exclusionary. For instance, Trosper (1976) described the adoption of tighter, more exclusionary enrollment rules by the Flathead Tribe of Montana in response to pressures to "terminate" the tribe (i.e., dissolve the federal trust relationship) in the 1950s. Federal officials charged that Flathead's Salish and Kootenai tribal members were acculturated and no longer needed federal services or protection. This prompted a move by tribal leaders to pursue a kind of ethnic purification strategy by adopting a stricter set of blood quantum rules to designate membership. Thornton (1987) reported an opposite, loosening or inclusionary strategy on the part of some nonreservation-based groups, mainly in Oklahoma, where groups such as the Cherokees or Choctaws face less competition among members for shares of tribally held or land-based resources (Thornton 1987). In these instances, inclusion can have positive political consequences in an electoral system, because a relatively large percentage of the Oklahoma population is American Indian.[17]

Some critics call for the entire abolishment of ancestry or blood quantum regulation of tribal membership, arguing that such rules, particularly when applied by the federal government, tend to heighten tension among Native Americans, creating disunity and suspicion. For instance, activist Russell Means raised questions about the meaning and legitimacy of ancestry tests of Indianness:

Our treaties say nothing about your having to be such-and-such a degree of blood in order to be covered. . . . When the federal government made its guarantees to our nations in exchange for our land, it committed to provide certain services to us as we defined ourselves. As nations, and as a *people.* This seems to have been forgotten. Now we have Indian people who spend most of their time trying to prevent other Indian people from being recognized as such, just so that a few more crumbs—crumbs from the federal table—may be available to them, personally. I don't have to

tell you that this isn't the Indian way of doing things. The Indian way would be to get together and demand what is coming to each and every one of us, instead of trying to cancel each other out. We are acting like colonized peoples, like subject peoples. (U.S. Census Bureau 1991:139)

Like Means, Stiffarm and Lane (1992) challenged the assumptions underlying ancestry and blood quantum tests of Indianness and tribal membership, asking whether American Indians

will continue to allow themselves to be defined mainly by their colonizers, in exclusively racial/familial terms (as "tribes"), or whether they will (re)assume responsibility for advancing the more general and coherently political definition of themselves they once held, as *nations* defining membership/citizenship in terms of culture, socialization, and commitment to the good of the group. (P. 45)

They wonder whether American Indian tribes cannot take seriously their semisovereign status with regard to citizenship, bringing "'outsiders' . . . into their membership by way of marriage, birth, adoption, and naturalization" (Stiffarm and Lane 1992:45).

Such a strategy certainly would open the door to an expansion of Indian ethnic membership, as well as tribal citizenship, which might be resisted by Indian communities faced with distributing already scarce resources and by a federal bureaucracy attempting to keep the lid on or reduce Indian expenditures.[18] However, many tribes may be forced to come to terms with their own blood quantum rules in the very near future. The rate of racial intermarriage for American Indians is the highest of all American racial categories, with fewer than half of American Indians marrying other Indians, compared with racial endogamy rates of 95 percent and higher for whites, blacks, and Asians (Snipp 1989:157; see also Sandefur and McKinnell 1986; Thornton, Sandefur, and Snipp 1991).

The consequence of this intermarriage is an increase in the number of Indian/non-Indian offspring with ever-diminishing degrees of Indian ancestry. One result of tribal blood quantum restrictions, even as low as one quarter, is that an increasing proportion of these children will not qualify for tribal membership even though one or both of their parents are tribal members, and despite their having lived on the reservation since birth.[19]

Conclusion

As we saw at the beginning of this chapter, the Native American population is expected to continue to grow during the next century, and that growth will produce an increasingly racially mixed, urban Indian population. Contemporary tensions between reservation and urban native communities and current debates about the rules for determining authentic Indian identity, rights, and tribal membership have enormous implications for the descendants of today's native people. A case from history might be useful in exploring these implications.

The Yamasees were an indigenous group living in the southeastern United States at the time of European contact with North America. They no longer exist as an identifiable tribe, and few individuals report Yamasee tribal affiliation.[20] The Cherokees, in contrast, have several federally recognized, state-recognized, and nonrecognized communities, and, in the 1980 census, they surpassed the historically numerically dominant Navajo Nation as the most populous tribe in the United States. Young (1987) noted that the Cherokees have been described as acculturated, of mixed ancestry, and successful at adopting white economic and political practices. Young challenged the underlying disparagement of these characteristics: "Cherokee people today still have a tribal identity, a living language, and at least two government

bodies.... That's more than one can say of the Yamasee" (p. 81).

It is instructive to keep this comparison in mind as we contemplate the future demographic shape of Native America. As we saw in Table 9.1, the 1980 census reported a 72 percent increase in the number of Americans who identified their race as "American Indian." The question has arisen: Are the roughly one half million new Indians in the 1980 census (not to mention the 6 million respondents who reported some degree of Indian ancestry; Snipp 1989) really Indians? Thornton et al. (1990) asked a similar question about the contemporary Cherokee population—a group whose numbers have increased dramatically in recent years (more than 300 percent from 1970 to 1980), increases that account for a good deal of the growth in the total Indian population.[21] His answer fits our question as well:

Common to all the Cherokees is an identity as Cherokee. All of the 232,344 individuals described here—fully 17 percent of all American Indians in the United States in 1980, according to the census definition and resulting enumeration—identified themselves as Cherokee. So they are. (Thornton et al. 1990:175)

This answer will not be satisfying to those concerned with Indian racial purity and the potential cultural change that many fear will result from the growth and racial mixing of the Indian population (Deloria 1986:3–4, 7–8). There is no doubt that native population growth has mixed consequences for American Indian ethnic and cultural survival and change. On the one hand, Indian population increases guarantee the demographic survival of Native American communities and ethnicity.[22] On the other hand are those pitfalls identified by Ron Andrade (1980), a former head of the National Congress of American Indians, who defended tribal membership restrictions (mainly involving degree of Indian ancestry) to avoid a loss of tribal resources to individuals living off-reservation and to protect against what he viewed as the dilution of tribal cultures and traditions (Andrade 1980:13).[23] Yet, as the comparison of the Yamasees and Cherokees suggests, although there may be social, economic, political, and cultural changes caused by Indian population growth and a relaxation of ethnic boundaries, the costs these changes incur may be considerably less than the price of failing to make them.

Notes

1. Estimates of the number of North American Indians at the time of European contact range from 18 million (Henry Dobyns 1983) to fewer than 1 million (Alfred Kroeber 1939). C. Matthew Snipp (1989) reported that most estimates range between 2 million and 5 million (p. 10).

2. For two reasons, this is a conservative estimate of the number of precontact tribes in the lower 48 states. First, the figure is based on coding procedures that included only separate linguistic groups and their major dialectic and/or regional subdivisions. Villages or bands often were quite autonomous (Driver 1961; Dobyns 1983), but they were not included as separate tribes in the coding. Second, Swanton (1952) used the early 1600s (more than a century after first contact) as his starting point. Many researchers believe that the first century following contact dramatically altered traditional Indian lifestyles and affected the viability of many tribes due to the virulence of Old World diseases that swept across the continent ahead of the waves of European settlers (Dobyns 1983).

3. In 1988, the U.S. Department of the Interior listed 309 recognized tribes in the lower 48 states ("Indian Tribal Entities Recognized" 1988). In 1992, the Bureau of Indian Affairs, Division of Tribal Government Services, identified another 9 recently recognized tribes not appearing on the 1988 list: the Coquille Tribe of Oregon; Kickapoo Traditional Tribe of Texas; San Juan Paiute Tribe of Arizona; Ponca Tribe of Nebraska; Scotts Valley

Band of Pomo Indians, California; Lytton Rancheria of California; Guidiville Rancheria of California; Aroostook Band of Micmac Indians of Maine; and Mechoopda Indian Tribe of Chico Rancheria, California (personal correspondence, August 3, 1992, from Bureau of Indian Affairs).

4. See Snipp (1989) for a survey of rural/urban, metropolitan/nonmetropolitan, and reservation/nonreservation characteristics in the American Indian population; for a case study of one urban Indian community, see also Weibel-Orlando (1991).

5. In addition to the 318 federally recognized tribes in the lower 48 states, more than a dozen tribes are recognized by individual states (e.g., the Shinnecocks of New York and the Schaghticokes of Connecticut).

6. In an interesting twist in this case, Samish leaders discovered that Judge Boldt died from Alzheimer's disease in 1984. They believe he was suffering from the disease in 1978, a year before he declared their tribe to be legally extinct. Other recognized tribes fear that if the Samish pursue this issue in court, the important (and unpopular with non-Indian fishermen) 1974 Boldt decision guaranteeing native tribes' fishing rights also might be thrown into question. See also Miller 1993).

7. I use the terms "American Indian," "Native American," "Indian," and "native" interchangeably in this chapter. This varying usage is consistent with formal and informal designations of Americans of indigenous ancestry by themselves and others, and these terms are used widely and interchangeably by both native and non-native researchers and writers (see, e.g., Snipp 1993, footnote 1).

8. For instance, see the introduction and first chapter of James Clifton's edited work *The Invented Indian: Cultural Fictions and Government Policies* (1990), as well as the chapters by some of his contributors (especially David Henige and Stephen Feraca) for a particularly virulent challenge to the ethnic authenticity of a variety of American Indian individuals and groups; his earlier *Being and Becoming Indian* (1989) is a somewhat less acrid inquiry into Indian identity using biographical sketches.

9. Ironically, even the Cherokee Nation itself has been challenged on occasion because of the patterns of intermarriage and cultural blending practiced by many members (see Baird 1990).

10. An interesting exception to this is reflected in the enthusiasm of Mashantucket Pequot tribal member Joseph J. Carter's response to tribal growth following casino gambling successes. "He savors the flood of would-be Indians. . . . 'Hey, everybody wants to be a Mashantucket'" (Clines 1993, p. A18).

11. For an interesting discussion of the emergence of deaf culture and "ethnicity," with its own language, culture, outlook, and boundary disputes, see Dolnick (1993).

12. In addition, questions of upbringing, membership in an Indian community, lifestyle, and outlook also can arise.

13. The notion of ethnic fraud appears to be gaining some attention. In an October 1993 conference sponsored by the American Council on Education in Houston, Jim Larimore (Assistant Dean and Director of the American Indian Program at Stanford University) and Rick Waters (Assistant Director of Admissions at the University of Colorado, Boulder) presented a session titled "American Indians Speak Out Against Ethnic Fraud in College Admissions." The session was designed to "identify the problem and its impact on the American Indian community . . . [and to] discuss effective institutional practices for documenting and monitoring tribal affiliations" (American Council on Education 1993).

14. These concerns about ethnic fraud parallel a wider skepticism about ethnic claims in general (not just those of Native Americans) when rights, jobs, and resources are at stake. In discussing the minority status of a particular individual, a fellow academic once told me, "I don't know if s/he's really a(n)_____, or has just found a horse to ride to tenure."

15. The Indian Health Service conducted a survey of federally recognized tribes to obtain tribal enrollment figures in 1986 and counted 746,175 enrolled members in 213 tribes in the lower 48 states (see Lister 1987). This is a signifi-

cant undercount, because there are more than 350 recognized tribes. However, most of the more sizable tribes (e.g., the Navajos and Cherokees of Oklahoma) were included in the survey. The 1980 and 1990 census figures for American Indians were 1,364,033 and 1,873,536, respectively (see U.S. Census Bureau 1992b).

16. Churchill has been singled out for particularly virulent attacks on his ethnic authenticity (see the series of articles, columns, and letters in *Indian Country Today*, beginning with the September 8, 1993 issue). Partly to defuse the issue of his ethnicity, in spring 1994, Churchill became an officially enrolled member of the Keetoowah Cherokee Tribe (personal communication, Ward Churchill, May 1994).

17. The proportion of Oklahomans who are Indian was 12.9 percent in 1990 (U.S. Census Bureau 1991).

18. For instance, in 1986, the Reagan administration put forth a proposal to adopt an official one quarter blood quantum definition of "Indian" for the purpose of receiving services from the Indian Health Service. Tribal organizations, led by the National Congress of American Indians, protested and lobbied effectively to stop the effort. There is no reason to believe that will be the last such attempt (see Jaimes 1992, p. 133).

19. Despite a growth in the number of Native Americans of less than one half or one quarter Indian ancestry, estimates of the total American Indian population over the next century predict increases among those whose ancestry is more than 50 percent native (U.S. OTA 1986).

20. For example, in both published and unpublished lists of tribal affiliations coded from the 1980 census, there were no Yamasees, although I have seen some native scholars report their ancestry as Yamasee.

21. The number of Cherokees increased from 1970 to 1980 by 166,194. Although this number is considerably less than the 571,000 increase in the total Indian population during the 1970–1980 period, Cherokee population growth represents 29.1 percent of the total increase (Thornton, Snipp, and Breen 1990, appendix).

22. Even without massive ethnic conversions from non-Indian to Indian, Snipp (1989) reported that the OTA's projections of the American Indian population from 1980 to 2080 show continued growth in the Indian population: Those with 50 percent or more Indian ancestry ("blood") are projected to grow slightly during the century (an increase of about 170,000); those with one quarter to one half Indian ancestry, to increase from 123,000 in 1980 to 5.2 million in 2080; those with less than one quarter Indian ancestry, to increase from 47,000 to 9.3 million; and a total American Indian population growth from 1.3 million in 1980 to 15.7 million in 2080 is projected (Snipp 1989, p. 167).

23. Andrade referred to individuals seeking to profit financially from Indian tribal membership but not willing to participate in tribal life and reservation development as "Indians of convenience." In contrast, critics of restrictive tribal enrollment criteria point out that tribal councils and enrolled tribal members also can be seen to profit personally from their participation in tribal life and reservation development (M. Annette Jaimes, personal communication, April 1994).

References

American Council on Education. 1993. *Educating One-Third of a Nation IV: Making Our Reality Match Our Rhetoric.* Washington, DC: American Council on Education.

Andrade, Ron. 1980. "Are Tribes Too Exclusive?" *American Indian Journal* IV:13.

Association of American Indian and Alaskan Native Professors. 1993. "AANIAP Statement on Ethnic Fraud." Press release, June 28, Washington, DC.

Baird, David. 1990. "Are There 'Real' Indians in Oklahoma: Historical Perceptions of the Five Civilized Tribes." *Chronicles of Oklahoma* 6:4–23.

Blu, Karen L. 1980. *The Lumbee Problem: The Making of an American Indian People.* Cambridge, UK: Cambridge University Press.

Chavers, Dean. 1993. "So Who Really Represents Indian Tribes?" *Indian Country Today,* May 19, p. A5.

Clifton, James. 1989. *Being and Becoming Indian.* Belmont, CA: Dorsey.

———, ed. 1990. *The Invented Indian: Cultural Fictions and Government Policies.* New Brunswick, NJ: Transaction Publishing.

Clines, Francis X. 1993. "With Casino Profits, Indian Tribes Thrive." *New York Times,* January 31, p. A18.

Deloria, Vine, Jr. 1986. "The New Indian Recruits: The Popularity of Being Indian." *Americans Before Columbus* 14:3–8.

Dobyns, Henry. 1983. *Their Number Become Thinned.* Knoxville: University of Tennessee Press.

Dolnick, Edward. 1993. "Deafness as Culture." *Atlantic,* September, pp. 37–53.

Driver, Harold E. 1961. *Indians of North America.* Chicago: University of Chicago Press.

Egan, Timothy. 1992. "Indians Become Foes in Bid for Tribal Rights." *New York Times,* September 6, p. 8.

Gates, Henry Louis, Jr. 1991. "'Authenticity,' or the Lesson of Little Tree." *New York Times Book Review,* November 24, pp. 1, 26–28.

Giago, Tim. 1991. "Big Increases in 1990 Census Not Necessarily Good for Tribes." *Lakota Times,* March 12, p. 3.

"Indian Tribal Entities Recognized and Eligible to Receive Services from the United States Bureau of Indian Affairs." Fed. Reg. 52829–52834 (1988).

Jaimes, M. Annette. 1992. "Federal Indian Identification Policy: A Usurpation of Indigenous Sovereignty in North America." Pp. 123–138 in *The State of Native America: Genocide, Colonization, and Resistance,* edited by M. Annette Jaimes. Boston: South End.

Kroeber, Alfred. 1939. "Cultural and Natural Areas of Native North America." *American Archaeology and Ethnology.* No. 38. Berkeley: University of California Press.

Lister, Edgar. 1987. "Tribal Membership Rates and Requirements." Washington, DC: U.S. Indian Health Service. Unpublished table.

Mankiller, Wilma. 1993. "An Open Letter to the Governor of Georgia." *Indian Country Today,* May 26, p. A4.

Miller, Bruce G. 1993. "The Press, the Boldt Decision, and Indian-White Relations." *American Indian Culture and Research Journal* 17:75–97.

Nagel, Joane. 1996. *American Indian Ethnic Renewal: Red Power and the Resurgence of Culture and Identity.* New York: Oxford University Press.

O'Brien, Sharon. 1989. *American Indian Tribal Governments.* Norman: University of Oklahoma Press.

Reynolds, Jerry. 1993. "Indian Writers: Real or Imagined." *Indian Country Today,* September 8, p. A1.

Sandefur, Gary D. and Trudy McKinnell. 1986. "American Indian Intermarriage." *Social Science Research* 15:347–71.

Snipp, C. Matthew. 1989. *American Indians: The First of This Land.* New York: Russell Sage Foundation.

———. 1993. "Some Observations about the Racial Boundaries and the Experiences of American Indians." Paper presented at the University of Washington, Seattle, April.

Sorkin, Alan. 1978. *The Urban American Indian.* Lexington, MA: Lexington Books.

Stiffarm, Lenore A. and Phil Lane, Jr. 1992. "The Demography of Native North America: A Question of American Indian Survival." Pp. 23–53 in *The State of Native America: Genocide, Colonization, and Resistance,* edited by M. A. Jaimes. Boston: South End.

Swanton, John. 1952. *The Indian Tribes of North America.* Washington, DC: Smithsonian Institution Press.

Thornton, Russell. 1987. "Tribal History, Tribal Population, and Tribal Membership Requirements." (Newberry Library Research Conference Report No. 8: "Towards a Quantitative Approach to American Indian History"). Chicago: Newberry Library.

Thornton, Russell, Gary D. Sandefur, and C. Matthew Snipp. 1991. "American Indian Fertility Patterns: 1910 and 1940 to 1980." *American Indian Quarterly* 15:359–67.

Thornton, Russell, C. Matthew Snipp, and Nancy Breen. 1990. "Appendix: Cherokees in the 1980 Census." Pp. 178–203 in *The Cherokees: A Population History,* edited by Russell Thornton. Lincoln: University of Nebraska Press.

Trosper, Ronald. 1976. "Native American Boundary Maintenance: The Flathead Indian Reservation, Montana, 1860–1970." *Ethnicity* 3:256–74.

U.S. Census Bureau. 1989. *Census of the Population, Subject Reports, Characteristics of American Indians by Tribes and Selected Areas: 1980,* Vol. 2, Section 1. Washington, DC: Government Printing Office.

———. 1991. "Census Bureau Completes Distribution of 1990 Redistricting Tabulations to States." Press Release CB91–100, March 11.

———. 1992a. "Census Bureau Releases 1990 Census Counts on Specific Racial Groups." Press Release CB91–215, June 12.

———. 1992b. *Census of the Population, General Population Characteristics: United States, 1990,* PC–1–1. Washington, DC: Government Printing Office.

U.S. Office of Technology Assessment. 1986. *Indian Health Care.* Washington, DC: Government Printing Office.

Weibel-Orlando, Joan. 1991. *Indian Country, L.A.: Maintaining Ethnic Community in Complex Society.* Champaign: University of Illinois Press.

Young, Mary. 1987. "Pagans, Converts, and Backsliders, All: A Secular View of the Metaphysics of Indian-White Relations." Pp. 75–83 in *The American Indian and the Problem of History,* edited by C. Martin. New York: Oxford University Press.

Nagel:

1. Why is there a controversy over who is authentically Native American?

2. Discuss the significance of being defined as a "true Indian." What are the benefits and disadvantages of doing this successfully? What are some of the political reasons for altering definitions of Native-Americanness?

10

Race Pride, Mexican Americans, and the Alamo

Joseph T. Rhea

American society in 1965 offered little public recognition of the value of minority cultures and identities. Worse, negative images of minority heritages continued to legitimate racial inequality in this country. Although the Civil Rights Act of 1964 and the Voting Rights Act of 1965 dramatically expanded legal representation in America, those laws could do nothing to redress the cultural exclusion that continued. Thus, just as the laws of the land had to change to include the politically disenfranchised, so too the cultural identity of the nation would have to change to include the culturally disenfranchised.

Beginning in the mid-1960s, a generation of minority activists turned to the task of gaining cultural representation. Black Power, which emerged in 1966, was the first expression of this cultural activism. Its adherents fought to change American perceptions of black identity, in large part by changing national perceptions of black history. Black Power, manifested in such groups as the Student Non-Violent Coordinating Committee (SNCC), also inspired other minority groups to try to affirm their heritages. By the end of the 1960s, similar identity movements developed among Indians, Asian Americans, and Latinos.[1]

The various assertions of minority cultural identity since the mid-1960s constitute a distinct social movement, referred to here as the Race Pride Movement. Race Pride was a diffuse movement comprised of relatively autonomous groups working toward the common goal of achieving national cultural recognition. Although the activists of each racial and ethnic group sought recognition for their own particular culture, the net result of their efforts was the cultural transformation of a nation that already had witnessed a major legal revolution. Minority activists carried the struggle for cultural inclusion into museums, history sites, universities, and other culture-producing institutions. All across America, collective memory (conceived as the publicly presented past) was changed by people engaged in a cultural revolution that had no single leader but which nevertheless dramatically transformed American identity.

Despite its organizational diffuseness and diverse membership, a basic pattern in the Race Pride Movement emerges. As with the civil rights movement, there was a period of agenda setting and cultural awakening. Before Race Pride activists could go on the offensive, they had to ask some hard questions about themselves. To counter the established interpretations of American history, these activists first had to decide what visions of the past they wanted represented in the national arena. This was no simple matter of asserting self-evident truths that had been suppressed by white hegemony. On the contrary, the assertion of identity in the late 1960s involved the rediscovery of heritage by minorities themselves, intense debates about which history mattered, and then more debates about how to interpret that history. The book *Race Pride and the American Identity* (Harvard University Press, 1997), from which this essay is drawn, describes the modern identity expressions of a variety of groups. The focus here, however, is solely on the Mexican American experience.

Mexican Americans

The Race Pride expressions of Mexican Americans reflect the diversity of contemporary self-understanding among Mexican Americans. In the 1990 census, 51 percent of Mexican Americans identified themselves as white, 1 percent as black, and 48 percent as "Other Race."[2] With no agreement about their racial identity in the present, it is not surprising that Mexican Americans also hold diverse views about their heritage. Many Mexican Americans are attracted to histories that portray them primarily as a Spanish-ancestry people, whereas others respond more to histories that emphasize an Indian or *mestizo* heritage. The advocates of the former historical vision often refer to themselves as Hispanics, and proponents of the latter often describe themselves as Chicanos.

The Race Pride Movement has encouraged Mexican American efforts to reform national memory, but continuing ambivalence and disagreements about how to characterize their contemporary identity often have made it difficult for Mexican Americans to assert a vision of the past forcefully. This truth is well illustrated by an examination of the Mexican American efforts to change the interpretation of the past presented at the most famous of all southwestern history sites, the Alamo.

Remembering the Alamo

The defense of the Alamo in San Antonio against the forces of Mexican General Santa Anna in 1836 is certainly one of the most famous events in American history. It gave rise to heroic images of Captain Travis, Jim Bowie, Davy Crockett, and their volunteer force fighting to the last man against a much larger Mexican army. But the siege of the Alamo was only one fight in the Texas War for Independence that had begun 5 months earlier at the Battle of Gonzales and that ended 2 months after the Alamo fell with the crushing defeat of Santa Anna at San Jacinto. These 7 months of 1835 and 1836 constitute the Southwest's Revolutionary War. As in the Revolutionary War in the East 60 years earlier, the fight began as an assertion of territorial rights by colonists and eventually became a struggle for national independence.

Although the people and events of both wars were heavily mythologized by later generations, there is one major difference in the memory of the two wars. The Revolutionary War in the East was remembered by later generations as a contest between two peoples of similar racial stock—that is, as a purely political struggle. In contrast, American memory of the Alamo traditionally has pitted Alamo defenders, falsely believed to be all Anglos, against Mexicans, who were characterized as foreign browns, as historian Paul Andrew Hutton rightly observed:

[A] creation myth does not pander to liberal sensibilities. The lines of good and evil are always razor sharp. The story is meant to give to a people a strong and unique self-image. It does not cater to the enemy in any way. Thus the myth of the Alamo is often stunningly racist.[3]

The Alamo became a symbol of racism to many people not so much for what happened in 1836 as for how later generations of Anglos, who controlled the site, chose to remember the conflict.

The defense of the Alamo was made in 1836, but it was only during the heightened nationalism of the late nineteenth century that Americans began to take an active interest in preserving the battle site and interpreting it for future generations.[4] The buildings most people visit in San Antonio today became Texas state property in 1905. At that time, the state granted the right of care for and interpretation of the Alamo to an organization that had been active in the preservation of the site for more than a decade, the Daughters of the Republic of Texas (DRT).[5] Founded in 1891, the DRT is a genealogical society that has maintained tight control of the interpretation of the Alamo to this day. The Alamo is thus unusual for a national historic site in that it is state-owned but is run and interpreted by a private organization.

Although dedicated to promoting the preservation and representation of all Texas heritage, the DRT's membership is determined strictly by genealogy:

Any woman wishing to be a Daughter must be . . . able to trace ancestors to the early Anglo colonists of the 1820s or prove that her ancestors in Texas "aided in establishing the independence of Texas or served the Republic of Texas in maintaining its independence" prior to its annexation to the United States in 1846.[6]

Thus, all descendants of the Anglo settlers, whether they fought for the cause or not, are eligible for membership, whereas only descendants of those Mexican Americans who can prove active assistance to the cause of In-

dependence qualify. Not surprisingly, the Daughters are nearly all Anglos. The history that the DRT has traditionally presented has downplayed the fact that the Alamo was the Mission San Antonio de Valero for 250 years before 1836.

All of the Alamo defenders the DRT has chosen to glorify by name were Anglos. Few today remember the names of any of the Mexicans who died inside the Alamo. Furthermore, despite clear evidence that many Alamo defenders were fighting for their constitutional rights as Mexican citizens, the Daughters have interpreted the battle in light of the later achievement of Texas Independence. The effect has been to simplify the tensions at work in Texas history.

The DRT's message that the Alamo is an Anglo history site is reinforced by the types of activities the DRT allows at the site. In particular, the DRT permits only two other groups to make use of the Alamo—the San Antonio Cavaliers and the Order of the Alamo. The Cavaliers are an elite, all-Anglo, group that meets annually to elect one of its members "King Antonio" for the Fiesta San Antonio, the city's major self-celebration.[7] The Cavaliers are a spinoff of an earlier organization, the Order of the Alamo, that was founded in 1909. The Order remains active, with much membership overlap with the Cavaliers, and elects the "Queen Angelina" for the Fiesta, always a daughter of one of the men of the Order.[8]

The DRT's monopolization of the Alamo sends a powerful message to the city's non-Anglo residents. The resultant tensions can be seen in the celebrations that have centered around the Alamo. The Fiesta de San Antonio is held annually during the week of April 21, the anniversary of the victory of Sam Houston's forces over Santa Anna. The Fiesta began as a tourist attraction in the 1890s, but has always been an occasion for the symbolic enactment of civic power. From 1913 until the late 1940s, the Fiesta was known as Fiesta San Jacinto.[9] Although San

Jacinto was a glorious victory for the Texans, it may also have been an outright massacre of Mexican troops (9 Anglo and 600 Mexican dead). The celebration of that event thus had a racial tinge that kept local Mexican Americans away for decades. Only when the festival name was changed to Fiesta de San Antonio, suggesting inclusion of the whole city, did Hispanic groups become involved.

In 1947, the League of United Latin American Citizens (LULAC) began electing its own alternative King for the Fiesta, the Rey Feo.[10] Each year, the Rey Feo is the man who raises the most money for LULAC's scholarship fund. Although the Rey Feo and King Antonio now open the Fiesta together in front of the Alamo, they represent two very different heritage camps. That their symbolic point of contention continues to be the Alamo is clear from the fact that although King Antonio is invited to the crowning of the Rey Feo at San Fernando Cathedral each year, the Rey Feo is not allowed to witness the crowning of King Antonio inside the Alamo.

Mexican Americans and the Alamo

Since the mid-1960s, affirmations of race and ethnic group pride have altered American memory radically. Recent events in San Antonio suggest that a major change is about to occur at the Alamo as well. However, given that the Race Pride Movement began more than 25 years ago, it is first necessary to explain why change is coming so late in San Antonio.

One reason for the durability of Anglo control is institutional. As noted previously, the Alamo is unusual among major American history sites in that, although state-owned, it is operated by a private genealogical society. The DRT has complete control of the Alamo. The DRT maintains an armed private security force at the site and allows no on-site protests.[11] This arrangement strongly discourages individuals and groups who might challenge the DRT's vision of the past.

The second reason for the continuity of Alamo interpretation has to do with the general political climate of San Antonio. Hispanics constitute 56 percent of the population of San Antonio and have never been excluded from the franchise. They are culturally separate from the Anglo elite but at the same time constitute a powerful force in politics. Mexican Americans in San Antonio are well represented in government.[12] Numerous nationally prominent politicians come from the area: Henry Gonzáles, Albert Peña, Henry Cisneros, and others.

Despite this political integration, San Antonio has long been marked by Anglo-Hispanic tension, manifested in, among other things, sharp residential segregation. Most Anglos, for example, live on the North Side, and Hispanics live on the West and South Sides, leaving the black population to the East. Not surprisingly, money is also a major source of contention. The average income for Hispanics is little more than half that of San Antonio Anglos.[13]

Although San Antonio lacks a manufacturing base, there is enough economic opportunity that Hispanics are not forced to unite around purely ethnic politics. Preoccupation with economic mobility rather than the symbols of identity has long marked members of the San Antonio Hispanic community, some of whom say "Forget the Alamo!" Establishment of the Hispanic Rey Feo in 1947 in fact signaled the emergence of a distinct Hispanic middle class. Gilberto Hinojosa, a Mexican American activist and professor at Incarnate Word College in San Antonio, described that time: "There was definitely a 'we have arrived' kind of thing that prevented any kind of single-action demonstration [against the symbolism of the Alamo]."[14] Economic opportunities and political integration have thus discouraged purely ethnic politics.

As important as these factors are in explaining the stability of Alamo interpretation, it is the sheer complexity of Tejano (Mexican Americans of Texas) identity that exerts the greatest barrier to single-issue activism within the community. Although American culture encourages Mexican Americans to define themselves as either white or non-white, Mexican Americans in San Antonio experience an ambivalence about this division that has made it difficult for them to unite against Anglo assertions of heritage at the Alamo. Hinojosa described the identity experience of many San Antonians:

It's ambivalence in a number of ways. First, Mexican Americans do not have a clear race view of themselves. The reason is the mixture of races is so profound and so thorough that it is very difficult to clearly designate, you know, Spanish, Mexican, Indian features. You can tell extremes but there's this whole group in the middle that is hard to pinpoint. Even within my own family, I'd like to point out, one of my daughters is lighter than I am. The other is darker. So the race thing is difficult to pinpoint.

Second, immigration from Mexico has continued and thus Mexican Americans find themselves at different stages of acculturation and assimilation. So the ambiguity of race plus the ambiguity of assimilation and acculturation make it difficult for Mexican Americans to form a clear sense of who they are either racially or ethnically.[15]

This ambivalence about race and ethnic identity can be found throughout local Mexican American organizations, even in those ostensibly devoted to promoting a specific conception of their heritage. Take, for example, the Granaderos de Galvez, a Spanish heritage organization in San Antonio. Its president, Robert Benavides, is also past president of the Canary Islanders Descendants Association, a genealogical group that traces its ancestry to the founding Spanish elite of San Antonio. Despite his strong emphasis on Spanish heritage, Benavides displays a reluctance to embrace a simple white ethnic view of his own past:

You have those who trace [their ancestry] back to clearly Spanish colonizers. . . . Naturally they are going to relate to the white ethnic identification. But they also have to relate, if they have any intermarriage with anybody from Mexico, to being a Mexican. Now when you go into the Mexican situation, it's a matter of, well, was he a Creole Mexican or was he a mestizo, was he half Indian and then all the variations on that, maybe even black.

Attitudes about this stuff change. The identification with the Indian [among local Hispanics] is probably the most recent of all sociological events. To be proud of your Indian heritage is now fine, just like I'm proud of my particular one.[16]

One might expect the Canary Islanders Association in San Antonio to emphasize white racial purity. Yet Benavides maintains a willingness to expand the white ethnic narrative: "There are people who overplay the Canary Islander thing. But there is a lot of choice here. Now, when do you stop being white and become something else?" Benavides acknowledges that he could identify with his Indian ancestry but opts to identify himself as a white ethnic. He emphasizes choice.

Resistance to the simplistic white/non-white dichotomy is also found among many of those San Antonians who choose to identify themselves as Indians. Gary Gabehart, President of the Inter-Tribal Council of Texas and an enrolled Chickasaw Indian, expresses this well when, after applauding the increased interest in Indian heritage among Mexican Americans, he goes on to discuss his relationship to the Canary Islanders Descendants Association: "There is a Spanish heritage group here, the Canary Islanders Descendants Association. These guys are really into being Spanish. You know my brother is head of that group now."[17] Gabehart expresses a certain nonchalance about his identification with the Indian side of his ancestry, but he takes care to differentiate himself from those who believe there is a single cultural essence to Indian identity: "My group are essentially urban Indians. And we are not into the pow-wow road wooly boogerism and New Age stuff you often see these days."[18]

The complexity of Tejano race/ethnic identity explains the local inability to directly engage the Anglo elite on the issue of heritage. Although unhappy with the exclusion of all things non-Anglo, the local Mexican American population has been divided on what, in fact, the alternative should be. This division was particularly noticeable in the varied reactions to the opening of the IMAX film *Alamo . . . The Price of Freedom* in a permanent theater across the street from the Alamo in 1988.

IMAX hired Hispanic consultants for the film, but problems remained. For example, although scholarly opinion has it that the Alamo defenders likely fought under a Mexican flag with 1824 (the year of the Mexican Constitution) painted on it, the producers of the IMAX film intentionally created a new flag to downplay the defenders' connection to Mexico.[19] Moreover, the film concluded with a silhouetted image of Mexican soldiers mutilating Jim Bowie. This final image, and the film's negligible coverage of Tejano defenders, triggered the first major local protest at the Alamo, a protest that illuminated the divisions among local Mexican Americans.

At the theater's opening, held on the 152nd anniversary of the fall of the Alamo, about 75 local Hispanics protested the film and called for a boycott of the organization that underwrote the cost of production. Professor Hinojosa wrote a statement that protesters handed out at the premier. In it, he lamented that "viewers will get the same message they received from previous versions of the Alamo story: Mexican Americans, the cultural descendants of those Tejanos, are not full members of our society."[20] In an interview, Hinojosa explained how the protest also mirrored the divergent conceptions of identity among local Mexican Americans:

You had this situation where you had Mexican Americans being consultants for the IMAX film, Mexican Americans doing the protest, and Mexican Americans crossing the line to go in and see the film. Again, this is a good example of the local ambivalence about how to define the Hispanic identity.[21]

Robert Benavides, one of the Hispanic consultants for the film, chose to attend the premier despite some misgivings. He later explained his ambivalence about the event:

I was approached by a group of 90 percent Hispanic protesters. I said, "You guys write down the name of the Tejanos, the native Mexicans that died in the Alamo, then I'll join you. Until then how the hell can you claim that this movie does not represent the truth." Of course, the movie had all kinds of problems, but the protesters outside were just about as ill-informed as the people inside.[22]

The divisions made manifest within the Hispanic community during the film protest also suggest that it is unlikely that a Hispanic equivalent of Davie Crockett, Jim Bowie, or William Travis will ever emerge. Reflecting on how those heroes became prominent during the nationalist period of 1890 to 1910, Professor Hinojosa said, "I am not sure modern society can do that for any person, Hispanic or otherwise."[23]

The IMAX film turned out to be a beginning, not so much of Hispanic unity but of opposition to the total control of the Alamo by the DRT. Enough local Hispanics were provoked by the DRT's endorsement of *The Price of Freedom* to question publicly the right of the DRT to control what is, after all, a state-owned historic site. Members of

LULAC even suggested that they take administrative control of the Alamo for a period. Their proposal was quietly dropped, but questions continued to be asked about the DRT's monopoly.[24]

Initially, it appeared that the only way to challenge the DRT's control of the Alamo would be to pass legislation repealing the agreement the state had signed with the DRT in 1905. The first action toward this end was a failure. The year after the IMAX opening, a black state representative from Houston, Ron Wilson, proposed a bill in the Texas State Legislature to put the Alamo under the direct control of the Parks and Wildlife department, which runs all other state-owned historic sites. The bill was easily defeated. Looking back on the episode, Wilson reflected on the quixotic idea of taking the Daughters out of the Alamo: "They exercise tremendous political clout out here [in Austin]. They're definitely a formidable opponent. I have the highest regard for them. . . . [T]hey literally kicked my butt."[25] Wilson's failure confirmed, for anyone who was in doubt, that the Anglo elite had firm control of the site. Opponents of the DRT continued to look for a way to crack that control. Oddly, the opening turned out to be in front of the Alamo itself.

The Alamo that most Americans know today was only a small part of the larger Mission San Antonio de Valero that originally extended out into the area in front of the compound now run by the DRT. Most of the outer walls of the compound that visitors now see at the Alamo were put up in the 1930s by the Works Progress Administration. In addition, restaurants and shops now line a street that passes over one of the Alamo's original walls. These developments obscure the fact that the Alamo compound originally extended well into the plaza in front of the current structure.

During the Spanish period, the Mission was a center of activity, and many of the community members were buried nearby. Most of these residents were Indians, a fact that took on particular importance in 1994. Early in that year, the Intertribal Council of American Indians announced that they believed Indians were buried near the site of an old wall that is now under the street in front of the DRT's compound. These remains, Intertribal Council Chairman Gary Gabehart claimed, were subject to a new federal law, the Native American Graves and Protection and Repatriation Act (NAGPRA).[26] With this legislation behind them, the small Intertribal Council was able to shut down all traffic on the street that passes in front of the Alamo. Gabehart commented on both the graves and the past problems of Hispanics with the DRT: "I think we've got troubled ground. We've had cars, buses and horses running over that cemetery for years. And what goes around, comes around."[27]

Interestingly, the information that enabled Gabehart to insist on the traffic shutdown around the Alamo came from John Leal, a local Hispanic scholar who wanted to see Spanish heritage better represented in the area. In 1988, he had expressed his unhappiness with the DRT to a researcher: "They're trying to erase us, and we refuse to be erased."[28] Leal translated a series of colonial burial records and discovered evidence that suggested the location of Indian graves. Under NAGPRA, evidence of a grave site provided all those opposed to the DRT with leverage over the Alamo Plaza area. Thus, it became unnecessary for locals with wildly different views of themselves and of the past to unite around a single counterinterpretation of the past.[29] Those Tejanos who emphasized their Spanish heritage and those who emphasized their Indian heritage were able to find common ground in a legal measure that expanded the physical space, and thus the interpretation, of the Alamo, to include both Indians and Spaniards.

The San Antonio City Council responded to the crisis by establishing the Alamo Plaza Study Committee in March 1994. The Committee's stated purpose was to "determine the best way to design the closing of Alamo Plaza East on a permanent basis."[30] The Plaza Committee met regularly from March to October and included representatives from all groups with an interest in the interpretation of the Alamo, from Indians to blacks to Anglos. It was, in fact, the first time in San Antonio history that every faction with an interest in interpreting the Alamo sat down to discuss the past. Some participants were no doubt eager to challenge the DRT's control of their land, but Committee Co-Chairmen Howard Peak and Roger Perez kept the Committee focused on the restoration of the original Mission San Antonio de Valero plaza.

Several members of the Committee commented that the discussion of interpretation worked well because it was understood that there would be more space than just the DRT's present site. Peak, for example, stressed that he made a conscious effort to keep discussion away from the DRT's historic control of the "Alamo" compound:

We really would have started having trouble with the Committee if we had gotten into the management aspects of the Alamo. And that's why I was very clear and had to remind folks from time to time that we were talking about Alamo Plaza.[31]

The Committee's final report, issued in October 1994, called for the inclusion of several interpretive themes in the expanded Alamo Plaza, including "the story of the environment and the Native Americans," the area's Spanish heritage, the battle of 1836, and the modern development of San Antonio.[32]

At this writing, the city is just beginning the process of calling for design proposals, some of which will suggest moving buildings to expand the plaza. Several Mexican American Committee members expressed optimism about expanding the interpretation of the past in the near future, as Gilberto Hinojosa explained:

We have to move the battle outside of the present Alamo complex. And if the story is told outside then the Daughters are not the only ones who can tell it. . . . They are now fighting even the closing of the street. They are threatening to sue the city for violation of the 1974 or 1976 [actually 1975] agreement with the DRT to leave those streets open. Because even the possibility that the streets would be closed would bring the possibility that the battle would come outside. . . . My purpose is to chip away at that.[33]

Robert Benavides echoed these sentiments: "I found if you're going to be successful [in changing interpretation], don't talk about history. Talk about legalities of how the site runs."[34] Thinking back on the advances of the last year, Gary Gabehart of the Inter-Tribal Council also affirmed that "if we had been the kind of people who hold protests and make a lot of noise, nothing would ever have gotten done."[35]

Unable to unite around a single vision of themselves and their history, Mexican Americans in San Antonio have been able to undermine Anglo interpretive hegemony of the Alamo through a legal assault on the land around the area controlled by the DRT. Thus, it appears that in the near future the Alamo will look much more like the rest of San Antonio: historically and racially diverse.

Postscript on Fieldwork

For the book *Race Pride and the American Identity,* I conducted interviews with minority activists at several heritage sites, focusing most on the Little Bighorn battlefield, the Martin Luther King, Jr., National Historic Site, the Manzanar internment facility, and the Alamo. The interviews were loosely structured and intended to stimulate general discussions of motives, obstacles, and accomplishments. Before I began the field research, many academics warned me that as a white male (and a Southerner, to boot!) I might be poorly received. The field research was exactly the opposite of what my colleagues feared. Literally all of the people I interviewed were happy to have the opportunity to talk about their experiences. For my part, I was greatly moved by the real generosity and openness with which people responded to my sometimes rather personal queries. The anxiety that so many academics have about interviewing across race/ethnic lines is misplaced. People of all backgrounds love to talk about themselves. Just listen.

Notes

1. The scholarly literature on these identity movements is quite extensive. As an introduction, see Joane Nagel, *American Indian Ethnic Renewal: Red Power and the Resurgence of Identity and Culture* (New York: Oxford University Press, 1996); William Wei, *The Asian American Movement* (Philadelphia: Temple University Press, 1993); Carlos Muñoz, Jr., *Youth, Identity, Power: The Chicano Movement* (London: Verso, 1989); and Clayborne Carson, *In Struggle: SNCC and the Black Awakening of the 1960s* (Cambridge, MA: Harvard University Press, 1981).

2. Peter Skerry, *Mexican Americans: The Ambivalent Minority* (New York: Free Press, 1993), p. 17.

3. Paul Andrew Hutton, introduction to Susan Prendergast Schoelwer with Tom W. Glaser, *Alamo Images: Changing Perceptions of a Texas Experience* (Dallas: DeGolyer Library and Southern Methodist University Press, 1985), p. 6.

4. For a discussion of this period's fascination with history, see Part 2 of Michael Kammen's *Mystic Chords of Memory: The Transformation of Tradition in American Culture* (New York: Knopf, 1991).

5. For more information on the DRT, see the chapter "Matronly Daughters" in Holly Beachley Brear, *Inherit the Alamo: Myth and Ritual at an American Shrine* (Austin: University of Texas Press, 1995).

6. Brear, 1995, p. 84.

7. For a detailed history of these organizations, see Brear's *Inherit the Alamo* (1995). Brear reported on the membership of the Cavaliers on p. 110.

8. Her full title is "Queen of the Order of the Alamo" (Brear 1995, p. 19).

9. Before 1913, the festival was known as the Battle of the Flowers (Brear 1995, p. 13).

10. Rey Feo is "a Fiesta personality based on the medieval Ugly King crowned by peasants of southern Europe to mock their established royalty" (Brear 1995, pp. 21–22).

11. This assertion is based on a review of the "Protests" file that the DRT keeps in their archive at the Alamo. The only protest within the DRT's compound I could find record of was a trivial incident involving three self-proclaimed Maoists who scaled the walls in 1980.

12. Skerry (1993) provided data on the political representation of Hispanics in San Antonio city government (pp. 105–106).

13. Skerry, 1993, p. 39.

14. Gilberto Hinojosa interview, March 1995.

15. Ibid.

16. Robert Benavides interview, March 1995.

17. Gary Gabehart interview, March 1995.

18. Ibid.

19. For a discussion of the flag issue, see Albert A. Nofi, *The Alamo and the Texas War of Independence* (New York: Da Capo, 1994), p. 129.

20. Flyer in files of the Daughters of the Republic of Texas.

21. Gilberto Hinojosa interview. Holly Brear (1995) also described the IMAX protest (pp. 115–16, 119–20).

22. Robert Benavides interview, March 1995.

23. Gilberto Hinojosa interview, March 1995.

24. Hector D. Cantu, "LULAC Surrenders Alamo Bid," *San Antonio Light,* May 15, 1988, pp. B1, B4.

25. J. Michael Parker and Stefanie Scott, "DRT Gears Up for Another Fight with State over Alamo," *San Antonio Express-News,* March 2, 1993; in the files of the Daughters of the Republic of Texas. Wilson resubmitted his proposal in 1993 and 1995.

26. Jim Hutton, "Indian Group's Entry on Scene a Surprise," *San Antonio Express-News,* February 20, 1994, pp. 1A, 8A.

27. Marty Sabota, "Alamo Burial-Record Finding Sprang from Search for Roots," *San Antonio Express-News,* January 26, 1994, p. A8.

28. Brear (1995), p. 113.

29. Sabota (1994), p. A8.

30. Cover sheet summary of the Alamo Plaza Study Committee's *Report and Recommendations to City Council* (October 20, 1994).

31. Howard Peak interview, March 1995.

32. Alamo Plaza Study Committee, *Report,* p. 7.

33. Gilberto Hinojosa interview, March 1995.

34. Robert Benavides interview, March 1995.

35. Gary Gabehart interview, March 1995.

Rhea:

1. Discuss the relation between the rewriting of history and identity politics.

2. What does Rhea mean when he says that "affirmations of race and ethnic group pride have altered American memory radically"?

11

Narratives of Race and Culture
in Transnational Adoption

Sara K. Dorow

All identity is individual, but there is no individual identity that is not historical or, in other words, constructed within a field of social values, norms of behaviour and collective symbols.

—*Etienne Balibar*[1]

We'll ask her, "Do you want to hear a story?"
And she'll say, "Yeah, China."
So we tell her the story about China.
—*Adoptive parent*[2]

After Chet and Nancy Cook[3] adopted a young girl from China in the early 1990s, Nancy quickly set to work assembling a memory book for her. In telling me the story of their daughter's adoption, Chet and Nancy proudly placed this album in my lap for viewing. I opened its red cover to the simple but telling first page, whose centerpiece was a flattened Chinese take-out box—the white cardboard kind with a pagoda stamped in red ink on the side—surrounded by bright stickers of fans and pandas. The words TAKE OUT were written in big block letters below this montage, only the word OUT was cheerfully but definitively crossed out and the word HOME pasted above it. Two shiny

American flags stood guard around this emended headline. Following this bold opening statement were many pages of carefully assembled photos of the Cooks' adoption journey in China, with accompanying narrative. On the final page, below two pastel cutouts of airplanes, the phrase NEXT STOP AMERICA! announced the end of the album—and the beginning of their daughter's story in a white suburban home on the West Coast (10/31/98).[4]

These front and back pages, and the photos in between, represent a tumble of interlocking issues that speak directly to the central question of this chapter: How are culture and race constructed in the stories that parents tell to and about their children adopted from China? In other words, having crossed racial, cultural, and national boundaries to build a family, how do parents make sense of their children's identities in the context of racial and ethnic structures in the United States? Three assumptions about identity form the foundation of this discussion: first, identities are not "natural" and fixed but socially constructed; second, one important way identities are constructed is through the experiences and ideas people relate in the stories they tell to and about each other; and third, identity formation is enabled and constrained by social structures in particular times and places. Identity formation is a matter of choices and assumptions embedded in specific cultural, political, and socioeconomic contexts.

Because it crosses a number of boundaries simultaneously, international adoption is a useful case for examining the social construction of racial and ethnic identities. The transnational adoptive family is often made up of people of differing race, class, and national origin, thus highlighting the tensions and possibilities that arise when diverse peoples come together in close physical and psychological proximity. Children adopted from China might be seen as "others within," or what Zygmant Bauman refers to as "strangers" and Stuart Hall has coined "the rest in the West."[5] All of these terms refer to the ways in which the intimate presence of those perceived as outsiders disrupts assumed categories of belonging. By virtue of adoption, children from China are part of a family narrative that demands a certain level of cohesion and normalization. But by virtue of national origin, class, cultural heritage, and usually racial marking, they are "strangers." The notion of the other within further highlights how global processes increasingly interact with local meanings and practices of race and ethnicity, of which international adoption from China is a pertinent case.

China Adoptions in the United States

Adoption of Chinese children in the United States began in earnest in 1994. Although before this a small number of Chinese children were adopted through formal and semi-formal channels, in 1993 the Chinese government revised its laws and created a centralized system for international adoption. Since that time, the numbers have grown significantly, and China (along with Russia) is now one of the two largest source-nations of children adopted internationally into the United States; more than 3,500 Chinese children were adopted by U.S. families in 1997.[6] Although families who adopt from China do not constitute a statistically significant number of American families, in this chapter, I want to foreground the theoretical significance of the Chinese adoption case for examining constructions of race and culture in the United States.

The China program is popular for several reasons, including its relative predictability, regulations that allow nonmarried and "older" people to adopt, and the availability of healthy infant girls. How does the process of adopting from China work? Although each family's experience is different and procedures are continually undergoing some changes, I provide the following sketch to help the reader envision the general process. In China, many thousands of "abandoned" children, usually girls, are brought to local rural and urban child welfare institutions each year.[7] Some of these institutions send information on selected children to Beijing—usually a simple health report and a photo—for matching with international adoptive families who have been approved by the central adoption agency.[8] On the U.S. end, families work through a local agency to complete paperwork required by both domestic and Chinese authorities. Agencies usually employ or contract with go-betweens (often native Chinese speakers) who work with the Chinese government to match children with families and then escort groups of families to China to officially adopt their children. From start to finish, the process for adoptive parents may take 1 year or more and can cost up to $20,000.[9]

Background to the Project

That this project is about adoptions from China, as opposed to other transnational adoption programs, is a matter of serendipity, practicality, and theoretical interest. I worked in the field of Chinese adoptions for several years and then stumbled into the opportunity to write a book for children adopted from China. These experiences provided me not only with some understanding of adoptive families but also professional and personal connections to those families—a matter of no small consequence when conducting ethnographic fieldwork, which requires close interaction with people in their everyday worlds. The China case is substantively and theoretically interesting as well, in part because it is currently one of the largest and fastest-growing international programs in the United States, and because parents who adopt from China are middle or upper class and most often white.[10] Finally, "catching" these parents while their children (and the adoption program) are young allows me to establish a baseline for future related research.

Gaining access to adoptive families may have been aided by my previous connections, but this complicated my role as researcher when parents saw me as a trusted ally. One interviewee even said to me, "I'm glad someone is finally going to get the story right." This assertion made me ill at ease, because "getting the story right" raises the question of whose side, if any, I as a researcher am on. I am interested in understanding the power relations of race and culture in the life of the adopted child and how parents negotiate these relations. This entails treating parents as actors who are both constrained by racialized, classed, and gendered structures as well as agents of and/or against them. If, following Alvin Gouldner,[11] I were to place my sentiments with anyone in this project, I would, along with adoptive parents, place them with their children—those whose early biographical trajectory is determined, in large part, by the choices of others.

The best way to access the choices and constraints experienced by adoptive parents is via ethnographic fieldwork. I used both interview and participant-observation methods in two large metropolitan areas in the United States—one (located on the West Coast) I call Westmetro and the other (located in the Midwest) I call Midcity—to begin to understand how parents with children from China negotiate issues of race and ethnicity. By "negotiate," I mean construct their own ideas about race and culture as well as deal with external racialized structures. I conducted formal open-ended interviews of 1 to 3 hours each with 10 adoptive families in the two sites during 1997 and 1998. Four of the families I interviewed were single women, and 6 were couples; in 3 of these two-parent families, both spouses were white, and in the other 3, one spouse was white and the other Chinese American.[12] Their Chinese daughters ranged from ages 2 to 8. Asian American people and resources are more numerous and a more established part of the cultural landscape in Westmetro than in Midcity. About one third of families in Westmetro adopting from China include at least one Asian American spouse (many of whom are Chinese American), whereas in Midcity the vast majority of adoptive parents are white, and Asian Americans make up less than four percent of the city's population.[13]

In Midcity, I supplemented interviews with several months of participant observation in a variety of settings related to adoption from China: a large adoption agency I call Adoptagency, a support organization for adoptive families (China Families), and an Internet bulletin board for China adoptive families (China Mail). The beauty of combining interviews with participant observation is the ability to triangulate evidence—to look for consistencies as well as inconsistencies between the more controlled atmosphere of the interview and the more "natural" activity of the observation site. The pieces of data I gathered from various fieldwork interactions all contribute to understanding the case of constructions of race and culture in international adoptions from China. What better way to get those stories than by spending time with adoptive parents and their children, in their kitchens, backyards, playgroups, and cultural and educational events?

Stories and Identities

I began this chapter with a description of Nancy and Chet Cook's photo album because of the story it tells. The album not only tells the Cooks' daughter about her "origins," it also reflects an approach to culture that is inflected with particular notions of belonging and difference. As I have said, I was interested in understanding how racial and cultural identities were constructed through stories told to and about Chinese adopted children. But why stories? Because narrative and identity are integrally and sociologically related. Narratives both form and are formed by people's lived experiences, and therefore they create meaning; a story, in fact, may be defined as the instance in which meaning is created.[14] I particularly like Widdershoven's definition of narrative identity as "the unity of a person's life as it is experienced and articulated in stories that express this experience."[15] He sees stories as telling us who we are—and stories are not just conveyed through the spoken or written word. Important to this project is that I take the idea of

narrative identity to be formed and expressed in a variety of ways, including the photos, objects, and activities through which stories are socially transmitted.

Narrative identities in the adoptive family are consciously and unconsciously about bringing coherence to change and difference. The conscious character of this narrative process illustrates Stuart Hall's point that identities are created, not fixed. In fact, Hall prefers to refer not to *identity* but to a process of *identification* that "entails discursive work, the binding and marking of symbolic boundaries, the production of 'frontier-effects.' It requires what is left outside, its constitutive outside, to consolidate the process."[16] But, for the international adoptive family, what is "outside"? What boundaries are drawn in the construction of identity, and what conditions make them necessary or preferable?

I approached parents' stories looking for what kinds of racial and cultural boundaries were being crossed and created.[17] But as parents often reminded me, many of their struggles stemmed from the biographical and emotional gaps left by adoption itself. International adoptive family life often begins without much knowledge about the beginning of the child's biography. Parents expressed to me the distress caused by trying to explain to their children why and how they were left, found, and adopted. As Laura Vigdahl, a single parent, put it, "I haven't gotten into the extent of letting her know what happened in China. I don't think she's old enough yet to comprehend that. I have a problem with it, because how are you going to tell her that she was abandoned?" (5/4/97). Some parents waited to address these gaps until their children started to ask questions. Others created a story that they told to their daughters from an early age, like this story told by Victor and Theresa Huang:

We tell her a bedtime story, lay in her bed and we say our prayers. And we tell her a story about how mommy and daddy wanted a little girl named

Katya so they asked baby Jesus for one, and we waited and waited, and she didn't come, so they started asking everybody, "Where's Katya? Where's Katya?" And then we asked our social worker and she said, "I'll bet she's in China because a lot of girls go to China on their way down from heaven and forget to come home." So mommy got on a plane and went to China, and sure enough, there was Katya. (4/12/97)

This story, infused with fantasy, illustrates that the complexity of creating identity through narrative, of restating the past as conditioning for the future, "can be observed with particular clarity in the everyday world of the adoptive family."[18] The absence of information on the adopted child's biography, and her origins in a place distant from the adoptive family, bring to the surface the constructed nature of identity. Although parents have the power to create consciously a particular version of their child's story, they do so within the context of perceived racial, cultural, and class differences. Thus, my question becomes one of how the complexities of giving shape and meaning to race and culture commingle with the biographical and emotional ruptures of adoption in the formation of "narrative identity."

Negotiating Culture

Contemporary adoption wisdom holds that it is important for families that adopt internationally to acknowledge and embrace their children's birth culture. Indeed, the Chinese government explicitly asks that international adoptive parents teach their children about Chinese history and culture. But what does this mean? Does it mean, as in the case of the Cooks' photo album, that "culture" is about the consumption of Chinese take-out food, a set of symbols employed when convenient for making sense of their adoptive family? In this section, I examine the variety of ways in which parents thought about and used im-

ages and objects they thought represented Chinese culture; the following section then suggests how these approaches to culture became a pivotal point for understanding the issues of race and racism.

The Cooks' use of take-out food as a metaphor for adoption is a reminder that choice and consumption are a part of the adoption story. Global processes of border-crossing and consumerism appear to indicate that ethnic identities are created through choice—that individuals and groups both "invent" and "consume" tradition at will from a kind of cultural smorgasbord.[19] This is echoed in the book *Ethnic Options,* in which Mary Waters concludes that ethnicity matters to white middle-class Americans

only in voluntary ways—in celebrating holidays with a special twist, cooking a special ethnic meal (or at least calling a meal by a special ethnic name), remembering a special phrase or two in a foreign language. However, in spite of all the ways in which it does not matter, people cling tenaciously to their ethnic identities: They value having an ethnicity and make sure their children know "where they come from."[20]

Identity is created and reproduced by choosing particular ways to celebrate one's cultural heritage, namely, by creating flexible but meaningful ethnic boundaries.

I found a variety of attitudes and practices among adoptive parents regarding the incorporation of objects and images from Chinese culture into their family narrative. Often, what constituted "Chinese culture" was based on what seemed interesting, pleasing, or accessible. For many, the trip to China was not just about getting a Chinese daughter but acquiring something of her cultural heritage that they could then carry back home. The travel orientation session at Adoptagency included parent panelists who suggested to those waiting to travel what they might do and buy in China as mementos of their children's culture, such as silk clothing or watercolor paintings—objects that then could be woven into the child's narrative (3/1/97). This selective incorporation of things Chinese into the adoptive family narrative continued after families returned to the United States, as seen in the words of Liz Nickels, who, with her partner Meg, parented both African American and Chinese children (both parents are white):

I feel like we've pulled out certain things about those two cultures that we can access more easily. So with our Chinese daughter, you'll notice we don't have a lot of African American art, but we have a lot of Asian, actually Chinese, artwork. But we listen to more African American music, because Chinese music isn't as accessible to us in a pleasing way. . . . And we do more Chinese eating than we do African southern. (4/16/97)

Food was a fairly common denominator. Laura told me, "I could have Chinese food all the time, with maybe a few breaks now and then for a hamburger and fries," and said that her daughter loved noodles and rice. The Leisters, a white couple living in a rural area outside of Midcity, made a point of going into the city for Chinese food on occasion. Although Larry Leister was not especially fond of Chinese food, he and his wife Linda saw this as an easy way to bring Chinese culture into their family (4/27/97). Food, thought Victor Huang, was probably the most obvious piece of his own Chinese American upbringing to pass on to his daughter. This was echoed by George Lou, third generation Chinese American:

Where I grew up, that's a lot of how we got Chinese culture—from watching Chinese cooking shows. . . . A lot of people get back to their roots just because they see a Chinese cooking show. So we stir-fry a lot, even though our daughter doesn't really like it that much. (10/3/98)

The act of crossing cultural and national borders meant having to reconstruct the fam-

ily narrative, to find cultural practices and objects that families thought worked for them. Always underlying these stories was the question of "how Chinese" adoptive families could or wanted to become.[21] An emotional thread of postings on the Internet bulletin board China Mail debated this question, and parents I interviewed often felt quite strongly about defending the choices they had made. The Cooks, whose adopted Chinese daughter was very involved in a Scandinavian song and dance group, thought that too many adopted children had Chinese culture "crammed down their throats." Chet said, "I don't think that we have to preserve the Chinese Chineseness at all costs!" Marion and Joyce, also white, were adamant in their response to this position. Their daughter was enrolled in a Chinese language school, and they had deliberately found a Chinese-speaking caregiver for her. As Joyce put it, "We see it as providing an opportunity rather than cramming anything down her throat. And I mean, she's ethnically Chinese" (11/22/98).

The narrative identity Marion and Joyce were attempting to construct was aided by the accessibility of Chinese American people and resources in Westmetro. But even there, I found it rare for families to be aiming for immersion in Chinese culture and language. The approaches to culture taken by most families I interviewed and observed in both Midcity and Westmetro seemed to fall into one of three types.[22] The first of these is a "multicultural, one-world" approach, in which Chinese culture is just one of many cultures to be celebrated.

This position of *celebrating plurality* was illustrated by the stories of both couples made up of white mothers and Chinese American fathers. They wanted to make Chinese culture one of many equally interesting ethnic choices. Victor Huang enjoyed cooking not just Chinese but German food, and his daughter's Russian name was chosen to reflect his wife's ethnicity. George Lou and his wife Patty insisted that their daughter would be exposed to all manner of ethnic celebration. George Lou looked out at Westmetro and saw not an abundance of Chinese American resources but a display of diversity: "We've become such a polyglot, just a melting pot. If our daughter wants to go study Zen Buddhism, we'll read up on it. *And* we'll explore things like Oktoberfest." Although he and Patty had adopted an infant in part "so that she would grow up as an American," being "American" was equated with the freedom multiculturalism seemed to allow.

The spatial boundaries of this position are important to note. Although the Lous and Huangs envisioned drawing on the resources of a multicultural nation, others saw plurality in more local terms. Jackie Kovich, a white single mother, wanted her daughter to be able to celebrate the multiple ethnicities of the working-class immigrant neighborhood where she lived. She was thrilled that they recently had attended a local Vietnamese celebration and it "didn't matter" that her daughter was the only Chinese child there (10/17/98). For other families, plurality was located within family tradition itself. In an ongoing China Mail discussion, parents discussed ways to bring their children up as both Chinese and Jewish, or Chinese and Irish, as seen in the words of one prospective adoptive mother:

I will be able to tell my daughter about my parents. . . . Dad would have sung her Irish ballads and spun wonderful stories; Mom would have made Polish pastries and taught her to dance a graceful, lively polka. My point is, these little windows that we open can lead to whole worlds. . . . Somehow, we must take elements from all the cultures that will inform our kids' lives. (2/14/97)

The celebrating plurality position normalized the interracial, intercultural adoptive family by envisioning a glorified global family of "different but equal." A second response on China Mail normalized by imagining an *assimilation* that tried to ignore or erase ethnic difference, sometimes with the assumption of assimilating to a white middle-class lifestyle:

If I get her a Chinese care-taker and make a special effort to keep her in touch with her Chinese roots, won't this make her feel different from her playmates who probably won't all be Chinese? Won't emphasizing her "Chineseness" within my mongrel family make her stand out even more than she already will? (3/31/96)

The Leisters and Cooks, like this parent, thought it important that their daughters knew they were Chinese, but more importantly that they were American. The Leisters felt that Adoptagency pushed heritage too much. Larry said, "I want to make sure they know they're American first, you know, and that's their heritage, but they've got a background that's Chinese, or German, or French, or whatever, you know."

Naming adopted children became one way to approximate assimilation. Linda Leister explained that they decided not to keep their daughter's Chinese name because it "was not very easy to spell, or easy to say, and she'd have to pronounce it all the time. So we said no, I'd like to make it easier for her." The Cooks chose an Anglicized name for their daughter that would look good on a business card someday, so that naming became a tool for assimilation. In the same vein, a parent at the China Families playgroup remarked that adoptive parents seemed to give their children "traditional American names" to lend some kind of "normalcy" to a situation of difference (2/8/97).

The Leisters' and Cooks' approach made Chinese heritage into a thing of the past that was woven into the narrative of the present in very selective ways. Travel to China did not necessarily give it a central place in the adoption narrative, and perhaps contributed to what Fabian calls "the denial of coevalness."[23] Other parents also seemed to make this kind of spatiotemporal distinction between China as "past" and the United States as "present," as did this China Mail parent: "While I do think a sense of heritage is important, our daughters' sense of identity won't come from constantly looking back to China, it will come from making them feel at home in our homes" (4/8/96). China and Chinese culture were mapped in the past, whereas the present was about assimilation into an American culture that was often tacitly white and middle class.

The response I see as constituting a third position used the map in a different way. This position attempted a *balancing act* between same and different by positioning the child and others on a kind of interactive map. Liz and Meg recently had placed a world map on their kitchen wall, with dots marking places where the family had traveled, where the children were born, and where special friends lived. The map could serve as an everyday normal part of the children's narrative identities yet gave particular and special meaning to China and other places with specific importance for their family. Cultural identification in this household connected to real and contemporaneous places and experiences and gave prominence but not dominance to Chinese heritage.

Several of the single mothers I interviewed, all of whom were white, seemed to strive for this balancing act as well. Often, their narratives referred to a double identity, as when Lisa Carter explained how she named her daughter: "One of the reasons I named her after my mom is because I wanted for her name to be continued, because she's a Carter. And she has a Chinese middle name because we're not pretending she's not Chinese" (10/20/98). Lisa wanted her daughter to be connected to the local Chinese American community, but not at the expense of exposure to the ethnic diversity of Westmetro. Similarly, Sharon Anderson sent her daughter to a bicultural Chinese American school and her house was decorated with Chinese objects, but she expressed discomfort with

immersing her daughter in too much Chinese language and culture:

But how much do you try to expose your child to? I mean, I don't speak Chinese so she wouldn't have a place to practice it really. I mean, they live in this part of the world, and there are a lot of other things going on. Obviously she's in the bicultural school because she's Chinese, but I like the idea that there are African Americans in her class, and an Iranian boy, and a Filipino girl.

Each of these three types was an attempt to construct a particular kind of family narrative through selective cultural consumption. And each position was surrounded with tensions and emotions, belying the notion that identities are constructed through the free and fluid exercise of choice. Parents felt they had choices in how much to explore their children's cultural heritage, and even had fun with it. On the other hand, even parents who chose not to emphasize Chinese ethnicity felt constrained to make at least some effort to engage with things Chinese—not only because adoption experts urged this but also because a variety of factors put pressure on their choices.

One of these factors was the place of gaps and ruptures in the adopted child's story, as I discussed previously. In the context of missing information about a child's early life history, and of information that was difficult or painful, connecting to Chinese culture could give children a piece of their story and thus a narrative identity that bridged those gaps. As Joyce put it, "Because our daughter can't ever know who her birth parents were, or what the circumstances were, it's like the most we can give her is her birth *country,* kind of?" Although this is an area for further exploration, I found that parents' treatment of culture was related to their approach to the adoption story itself. Those attempting a balancing act generally wove positive images of China and Chinese birth parents into their narratives from early on, whereas families striving for assimilation found it easier to ignore or even to vilify birth parents. The Cooks had no interest in making "a culture that throws its kids away" part of their narrative.

Nevertheless, these families made concessions to the incorporation of Chinese objects and events, in part because narrative identities are not created via parental choices alone. Children, even from an early age, contributed to and modified their narratives. They asked about their "tummy mommies," related scattered memories of orphanage life in China, or developed interests in Chinese objects or activities. The Cooks, for example, were taken by surprise when a friend gave their daughter a Chinese dress and she loved it.

As children got older, the construction of a cultural narrative was not only increasingly shaped by them but also by racialized categories and the realities of racism in the United States. Parents' decisions about ethnic identity were not simply a matter of free choice and cultural play. They were bound up with understandings of and experiences with race and racism. As Mary Waters finally acknowledged in the last chapter of *Ethnic Options,* the freedom of choice, flexibility, and pleasure associated with white ethnicity are not necessarily associated with being non-white: "The social and political consequences of being Asian or Hispanic or black are not symbolic for the most part, or voluntary. They are real and often hurtful."[24]

Narrating Race and Racism

Reference to cultural diversity or ethnic options sometimes masks global and national hierarchies built on racial categories that have real effects. It ignores the limitations of cultural representation within racist structures, an important omission given that race is used in American society as a cultural marker to give clues about who a person is. These are important ideas in critical race theory, which focuses quite specifically on the centrality of

hierarchical racial formation to the social and institutional life of the United States. Its theorists strive to unmask the codes, strategies, and policies through which racism has operated.[25]

In critical race theory, race is defined neither as objective and real nor as meaningless and illusory. It is a sociohistorical process that attaches both symbolic meaning and institutional consequences to supposedly observable physical traits. As Omi and Winant put it, "Race is a concept which signifies and symbolizes social conflicts and interests by referring to different types of human bodies."[26] Racism, then, "creates or reproduces structures of domination based on essentialist categories of race."[27] The question for this section is how adoptive parents talked about and responded to racial categories and racism. How did notions of race and racism figure into the construction of their children's identities, particularly in relation to cultural narratives?

Adoptive parents often related stories to me of encounters based on the differing racially marked bodies of parent and child. Both Jackie and Sharon, single white parents, told me about strangers who looked from mother to daughter and back again, inquiring whether perhaps the child's father was Chinese. Sharon reported hesitating only slightly before slyly answering, "Yes!" Marion and Joyce told the story of a white "hippie-looking" adoptive father who had been stopped twice by police in Westmetro wanting to know what he was doing with a little Chinese girl. Theresa Huang often took Katya to a playground visited by many Chinese Americans, who were upset to see them together until they were told that father Victor was Chinese American. As Patty Lou put it, "Well, people look twice if it's just her and me. But if the three of us are together, they just figure I got left out of the gene pool!" Mary Chang and Tom Mining said they had no encounters like this, but they added that usually if their daughter was with just one parent, it was Mary, who as a Chinese American "racially matched" their daughter (10/16/98).

Even more pertinent to the understanding of narrative identities is race-culture matching. Racial difference constrains the construction of identity because American society expects racial difference to mean cultural difference.[28] Some parents may have felt it ridiculous to incorporate things Chinese into a household parented by white European Americans, but others felt it equally strange for a child racially marked as Asian to not know an Asian heritage. To cross cultural borders may be enjoyable, but to cross racialized borders may be impossible.

Ben, an adoptive parent at a China Families playgroup, related a story that illustrates this point. He told me he had initially resisted "doing the Chinese culture thing" not only because it seemed somewhat ridiculous, but also because he just didn't find Han Chinese culture very interesting. He stood at the smorgasbord and saw nothing he cared to reconstruct for his daughter's cultural narrative. After all, he said, he had not chosen to call himself "German American," just "American." But Ben was reconsidering, as my notes from the event indicate:

Ben tells me he is still not convinced, but after talking to people and watching what other parents do, he is beginning to think they should be doing some things with Chinese culture. He just doesn't want to go overboard (like some parents, is the implication), and calls it a "matter of degree." I ask him why he thinks this is changing for him. One thing he says is that he has realized that although he had the option of not being German American, because of his daughter's racial difference, she will not have that option. (4/12/97)

Although I should emphasize that racial and cultural narratives did not perfectly map onto each other, the realities of race-culture matching and of racism overall seemed most acknowledged by those parents who did a cultural balancing act. Sharon admitted that if she had adopted a Russian child, she might not have thought about culture as much: "I mean, it happens in this country in general, that unless you're European, the focus is always on the other ethnic group. Like what does it mean to be Chinese American? Essentially, you're the different one." Liz anticipated race-culture matching expectations not only from whites but also from Chinese Americans. She introduced Chinese art, stories, holidays, and foods into her daughter's life "so that when she meets other Chinese American kids who do grow up in a Chinese American home, she's not completely out of the loop."

These women acknowledged the ubiquitous existence of racism, and they tried to use cultural tools to help ward off its effects. They wanted to instill both cultural and racial pride in their daughters. Liz related to me a story of her frustration with what classic Barbie represented—white as normal, female as blonde and beautiful—after she and Meg decided it was okay to take "the Barbie plunge" with their oldest daughter. I asked Liz what kind of Barbie their daughter wanted:

A blonde Barbie, don't you know. Well, because the others aren't *really* Barbie. *Barbie* is blonde. But even when she got a number of them—she got an African American, and an Asian, and a blonde—she would only play with the blonde one. She refused to play with the dark-haired ones. And we kind of talked it through. . . . But it's insidious. It's very insidious in this culture. (4/16/97)

One way to deal with this was to narrate a pride around Asian racial markings. Liz even considered sending her daughter to a school across Midcity attended by many Vietnamese students to help lend some normalcy to looking Asian. And Sharon adopted from China in part because she had Japanese American relatives "so it seemed like there would at least be an Asian connection." A second part to this approach conceived of cultural identity as a tool against racism. Several women expressed sentiments similar to Joyce's assessment of the relation between race, racism, and culture:

Because people will see our daughter as Chinese American when they look at her, she needs to have some sense of what that means, I think. Race—people notice that very first thing. So she has to have something of Chinese language and culture. I would think that kids that are given no opportunity to kind of explore those issues are going to have a harder time.

The paradox of these approaches is that they imagine that race-race and race-culture matching, practices that might themselves be seen as outcomes of racist structures, are tools to fight racism.

The *cultural plurality* approach was mixed in its racial narrative, but sometimes it saw race as a colorful and interesting adjunct to culture. Jackie Kovich hoped that her daughter would "not just see other Asians, but see everybody." And dolls of many types normalized and celebrated racial differences on this China Mail posting:

We have a variety of dolls in our house. Some look Asian, we have African American dolls, brunettes, blondes. I tell my children that the world is like a flower garden and it takes all the flowers to make the garden beautiful. I truly believe that our international families, for that is what we are, will help lead the rest of society to understand and appreciate our global community. (2/15/97)

Parents who framed race in this way sometimes found it interesting and exotic to adopt a child that was racially different from them. Jackie thought she had never seen an ugly Asian child and said that children in the orphanage in China looked like "little Buddhas. And I wanted one of them." One woman at the China Families playgroup admitted that she was momentarily disappointed when her daughter turned out not to have the unique "red-cheeked country look" she had envisioned and even hoped for on the face of a child from rural China (4/12/97). Her daughter did not fit into the colorful *National Geographic* panorama of global faces.

Although this approach embraced what it saw as the beauty and wonder of racial diversity, it did not always acknowledge structural racial inequalities and racism. When I asked the Huangs and the Lous about racism, for example, they both described their racially mixed home and circle of friends, insisting that racism was not an issue in their lives, nor did they expect it to be for their daughters. As an extension of this narrative, George Lou was averse to the idea of his daughter embracing what he called "a racial identity" later in life.

Although a plurality standpoint saw race but not always racism (a tricky stance), the assimilation approach was slightly more extreme in that it tried to erase race and normalize whiteness. The very term "American" implied "white" in the narratives of some of these families. The Leisters, perhaps in part because they lived in a small and overwhelmingly white community, were typical of the assimilation approach to race. The cover of the children's book they used to tell the story of adoption to their daughter showed a smiling, blond, blue-eyed girl. When I asked the Leisters about racialized or racist encounters, they insisted that strangers' interest in their child was simply because she was so adorable. As for potential future experiences with racism, Linda Leister beamed at her daughter and said, "You're just too cute for teasing." And the Cooks repeatedly emphasized that they were raising good little American citizens for whom racial constructions did not or should not matter.

Nevertheless, underlying this blindness to racial classification and racism lay a festering discomfort with differences in racially marked bodies. The Leisters believed their daughter might be Eurasian, and Larry had me observe how their daughter's hair showed red highlights in the afternoon sun coming through their window. A few minutes later we had the following exchange:

[Their daughter hands me a toy plastic tea pot.]

Me: Thank you. I'm going to brew my tea. Is it tea from China?

Larry: You can say tea, can't you. You like iced tea.

Me: She likes iced tea?

Larry: Yeah, weird! Yeah, it's something. . . . Still, I just can't believe she's all Chinese.

The Leisters used physical and behavioral clues to create a narrative identity that erased "pure" difference, helping them leap over the racialized boundaries with which they were uncomfortable. And the Cooks, despite their desire to erase race, acknowledged a problem:

Nancy: Our daughter is very involved in Scandinavian dancing and really has a talent for it. She's growing so tall and long-legged, and that adds to it. We may or may not encounter prejudice in that.

Me: Are there other—

Nancy: Not too many. Most are little blond-haired Scandinavian girls.

Me: Why do you think it's there that she might encounter prejudice?

Nancy: I don't know that it's there, but it's just that if anywhere in her life where we are right now, that would be the highest possibility. I think just because it's, *Scandinavian* dancing. So it kind of makes one think that Scandinavian people would be doing it. And we just tell her that judges don't always see every good thing you do. . . .

Me: So are you saying that you think it's possible the judges aren't marking her fairly because she doesn't "match" what the part should look like?

Nancy: Well, I guess Chet and I think there's that potential.

The various ways in which racial and cultural narratives were intertwined point to the complexity of their relation. For some parents, the practice of race-culture matching, which gave their daughters a piece of their rightful birth heritage, served as a tool for fighting off racism. The problem is that racism may itself be based in part on the assumption that such matching is naturalized. On the other hand, ignoring or celebrating racially and culturally marked bodies potentially served to deny the existence of everyday racism that is practiced through that physical demarcation. Clearly this is contested terrain.

Concluding Thoughts

As is probably true for all of us, the kinds of cultural and racial stories adoptive parents construct is a product of interpersonal and structural conditions, everyday experiences, and social expectations. In the case of transnational and transracial adoptive families, the presence of "the other within" highlights the processes through which identities are socially constructed. As I hope this chapter has demonstrated, racial identities are tied to ideas about culture and ethnicity in intriguing and sometimes paradoxical ways. Some parents attempted to make sense of racial difference by unmasking the kind of racial coding, such as multiculturalism or assimilation, discussed by Omi and Winant. Others used these existing codes of racial formation to celebrate or downplay racial difference. But, almost always, racially marked bodies and cultural images mutually signified each other.

Creating narratives across boundaries of race, culture, and national origin was complicated by the ruptures and difference represented by the adoptive family. This often led to slippages between nature on the one hand and race and culture on the other. Consider the exchange I had with the Lous when I asked why they had wanted to adopt an infant:

Patty: There was no issue of culture, different country, different language than she was used to. We just brought her home and she was ours! We want her to know, of course, that she's adopted, and that she's Chinese but also American.

Sara: How do those things fit together for you, that she's both Chinese and American?

Patty: It's not an issue. Because if we had a natural, a biological child, it would be half Chinese, half Caucasian.

Patty's remarks illustrate the complexity of creating a cohesive family narrative that is the result of crossing national and racial boundaries. It also foregrounds the desire to be a "normal" family protected from the hurtful meanings attached to the construction of difference. As Theresa Huang said in frustration to my line of inquiry about her child's identity, "She's just our kid!" Indeed, the families I interviewed were just trying to go about the everyday business of being a family. Nevertheless, the power of socially constructed racial and cultural differences came through in parents' narratives. Whether they tried to whitewash those differences through an assimilation as easy as ordering Chinese takeout, or tried to meet difference head-on by embracing it, all struggled with an ongoing, dynamic process of narrative identification.

Notes

1. Etienne Balibar, "The Nation Form: History and Ideology." Pp. 6-106 in *Race, Nation, Class: Ambiguous Identities*, edited by E. Balibar and I. Wallerstein (London: Verso, 1988), p. 94.

2. Interview with Victor and Theresa Huang, April 12, 1997.

3. All names from my interviews and observations are pseudonyms.

4. Dates in parentheses indicate the date of the interview or field notes from which data is ex-

cerpted. I include these dates only the first time any particular person is cited.

5. See Zygmant Bauman, "Modernity and Ambivalance," *Theory, Culture and Society* 7:(2–3, 1990):143–169; and Stuart Hall, "Cultural Identity and Diaspora," pp. 53-79 in *Questions of Cultural Identity,* edited by S. Hall and P. duGay (Thousand Oaks, CA: Sage, 1996).

6. Tamar Lewin, "New Families Redraw Racial Boundaries," *New York Times,* October 27, 1998, pp. A1, A18.

7. I do not delve here into the complex issue of why and how children in China are abandoned and orphaned. In general terms, a combination of state family planning and gendered cultural processes might be said to be responsible. According to Kay Johnson (1993) in "Chinese Orphanages: Saving China's Abandoned Girls," *The Australian Journal of Chinese Affairs* 30:61–87, there are at least several hundred thousand and probably many more children in more than 5,000 "welfare homes" throughout China. It is important to note that there is really no formalized, legal way for birth parents to place their children for adoption, so most of these children are left in public places where they will be found and taken to a welfare institution.

8. There are a large number of domestic Chinese adoptions as well, perhaps half a million each year, many of these informal and within kin groups (Johnson 1993).

9. These fees are just somewhat higher than average for international adoption. They are difficult to compare to domestic adoption fees, which vary widely.

10. According to Richard Tessler, Gail Gamache, and Liu Liming, *Bi-Cultural Chinese-American Child Socialization Study: Summary Report* (Amherst: Social and Demographic Research Institute, University of Massachusetts, 1996), families adopting from China earn a median income of more than $70,000.

11. In a 1967 article titled "Whose Side Are We On?," *Social Problems* 14(Winter):239–47, Howard Becker suggested that because the social science researcher cannot be truly objective and value-free, she must end up taking the standpoint

of the superior or the underdog. See Alvin Gouldner, "The Sociologist as Partisan: Sociology & the Welfare," pp. 27–68 in *For Sociology: Renewal & Critique in Sociology Today* (New York: Basic Books, 1973), for Gouldner's impassioned response to Becker, in which he argued that Becker's approach is overly simplistic. Gouldner wrote that a sociologist has an obligation to attend to needless suffering, but that suffering at the hands of institutional structures and processes can happen at all levels. Attending to this possibility means taking a standpoint that is distinguishable from the actors one is studying. Understanding of those actors will be aided by the recognition that such a standpoint is both partisan and unique.

12. None of these families had biological children, an issue that might affect decisions regarding cultural and racial narratives in the family.

13. This chapter does not focus on a comparison of the two research sites, but I refer to location when it is particularly important for placing data in context.

14. See Norman Denzin, "The Sociological Imagination Revisited," *The Sociological Quarterly* 31(1990):1–21; also see Guy Widdershoven, "The Story of Life: Hermeneutic Perspectives on the Relationship Between Narrative and Life History," pp. 1-20 in *The Narrative Study of Lives,* edited by R. Josselson and A. Lieblich (Newbury Park, CA: Sage, 1993).

15. Widdershoven (1993), p. 7.

16. Hall (1996), p. 3.

17. A researcher's interests do not always overlap with what the people she studies think is salient. This is a rich and complicated part of the research process—realizing that whatever one "discovers" is the combined effort of the researcher and the people whose lives and stories one is trying to understand.

18. Christa Hoffmann-Riem, *The Adopted Child: Family Life with Double Parenthood* (New Brunswick, NJ: Transaction Publishing, 1990), p. 223.

19. See Jonathan Friedman, *Cultural Identity and Global Process* (Newbury Park, CA: Sage,

1994). Bauman (1990) also noted that ethnic distinctions are increasingly seen as a matter of private choice exercised on the basis of commercialism, aesthetics, and pleasure.

20. Mary Waters, *Ethnic Options: Choosing Identities in America* (Berkeley: University of California Press, 1990), p. 147.

21. I have not yet interviewed families in which either a single parent or both spouses in a couple are Chinese American. Anecdotal evidence suggests that for some of these families the question of culture is not any more or less of an issue than it would be if they had given birth to their daughters.

22. See also Tessler et al. (1996) on similar categories found in their open-ended survey question.

23. In Johannes Fabian, *Time and the Other* (New York: Columbia University Press, 1983). Coevalness refers to events occurring in the same time period.

24. Waters (1990), p. 156.

25. See, for example, Michael Omi and Howard Winant, *Racial Formation in the United States* (New York: Routledge, 1994); David Roediger, *The Wages of Whiteness: Race and the Making of the American Working Class* (London: Verso, 1991); and Patricka Williams, *Alchemy of Race and Rights* (Cambridge, MA: Harvard University Press, 1991).

26. Omi and Winant (1994), p. 55.

27. Ibid., p. 71.

28. Ibid., p. 71.

Dorow:

1. What were some of the structural constraints that the parents Dorow interviewed faced when constructing the identity of their adopted children?

2. Discuss the three different approaches to cultural identity that the families took.

12

Television and the Politics of Racial Representation

Justin Lewis and Sut Jhally

One of the abiding concerns in contemporary North American culture has been the many attempts to deal with race and racial inequality. Because racism is often understood as a perception dependent on negative or stereotypical images, debates about race often have centered on the issue of representation, with analytical glances increasingly cast toward television, as the main image-maker in our culture.

To make sense of the many competing claims about the way black people are represented on television, we carried out an extensive study based on a content analysis of prime time television together with a series of 52 focus group interviews (made up of 26 white, 23 black, and 3 Latino groups) from a range of class backgrounds. The interviews were designed to probe attitudes about race and the media representation thereof. To facilitate these discussions, each interview began with the viewing of an episode of *The Cosby Show.*

The Cosby Show was chosen because it has, in many ways, changed the way television thinks about the portrayal of African Americans. During the time it took for *The Cosby Show* to go from being innovative to institu-

tional, African Americans became a fairly common sight on network television in the United States. And not just any African Americans: Our content analysis confirmed that we now see a plethora of middle- and upper-middle-class black characters populating our screens. Major black characters—from *ER* to *Sportsnight*—are now much more likely to be well-heeled professionals than blue-collar workers. In this sense, Bill Cosby can be credited with spurring a move toward racial equality on television. Fictional characters on U.S. television always have tended to be middle or upper-middle class—and since the late 1980s, black people have become an equal and everyday part of this upwardly mobile world.

The Cosby Show was, in this sense, more than just another sitcom. It represents a turning point in television culture, to a new era in which black actors have possibilities beyond the indignities of playing a crude and limited array of black stereotypes, an era in which white audiences can accept TV programs with more than just an occasional "token" black character. There is, it seems, much to thank Bill Cosby for. He has, quite literally, changed the face of network television.

At first reading, our study suggested that the upward mobility of black representation precipitated by *The Cosby Show* was an unambiguously positive phenomenon. It appeared, from our focus groups, to promote an attitude of racial tolerance among white viewers, for whom black television characters have become ordinary and routine, and to generate a feeling of pride and relief among black viewers. But *The Cosby Show* and the new generation of black professionals on U.S. television are caught up in a set of cultural assumptions about race and class that complicate the political ramifications of such a trend.

It is true that, in recent decades, the size of the black middle class in the U.S. has grown. This much said, the social success of black TV characters in the wake of *The Cosby Show* does not reflect any overall trend toward black prosperity in the world beyond television. On the contrary, the period in which *The Cosby Show* dominated television ratings—1984 to 1990—witnessed a comparative decline in the fortunes of most African Americans in the United States. The racial inequalities that scarred the United States before the civil rights movement could only be rectified by instituting major structural changes in the nation's social, political, and economic life—an idea informing Great Society interventions in the 1960s and 1970s. Since the election of Ronald Reagan in 1980, both Republican and Democratic administrations generally have withdrawn from any notion of large-scale public intervention in an iniquitous system, committing themselves instead to promoting a global free enterprise economy. This laissez-faire approach has resulted in the stagnation or gradual erosion of advances made by black people during the 1960s. For all the gains made in the fictional world of TV, by almost all demographic measures (such as education, health, levels of incarceration, income, and wealth), the United States remains a racially divided society.

As William Julius Wilson (1987) has documented, maintaining these divisions are a set of socioeconomic conditions that keep most people in their place. The "American Dream" of significant upward mobility is an aspiration that few can or will ever realize. It is an idea sustained by fictions and by anecdotes that focus on the exceptions rather than the rules of class division. If we are to begin any kind of serious analysis of racial inequality in the United States, we must acknowledge the existence of the systematic disadvantages that exclude most people on low incomes in poor neighborhoods—a condition in which black people in the United States have disproportionately been placed—from serious economic advancement.

Left unchecked, it is the laws of free market capitalism—rather than more overt, individual forms of racial discrimination—that reproduce a racially skewed class structure. Most major institutions in the United States have officially declared themselves nonracist and invited black citizens to compete alongside everyone else. This is important but insufficient. If three white people begin a game of Monopoly, a black player who is invited to join the game halfway through enters at a serious disadvantage. Unless blessed by a disproportionate degree of good luck, the black player will be unable to overcome these economic disadvantages and compete on equal terms. This is, in effect if not in intention, how the United States has treated most of its black citizens: It offers the promise of equal opportunity without providing the means—good housing, good education, good local job opportunities—to fulfill it.

There is a wealth of evidence about the operation of these structural inequalities (see, e.g., Wilson 1987; Hacker 1992). What is remarkable about our culture is that it refuses to acknowledge the existence of class structures, let alone understand how they influence racial inequalities. And yet, at certain moments, we do accept these things as obvious. We expect rich white children to do better than poor black children. We expect it, because we know that they will go to better schools, be brought up in more comfortable surroundings, and be offered more opportunities to succeed. And our expectations would, most often, be proved quite right. The child who succeeds in spite of these odds is a glamorous figure in our culture precisely because he or she has defied these expectations. Unfortunately, our culture teaches us to ignore these social structures and offers us instead a naive obsession with individual endeavor. Instead of a *collective* war on poverty, we have welfare reforms that increase poverty and homelessness in the name of *individual* responsibility.

We would argue that U.S. television—and popular culture generally—is directly culpable for providing an endless slew of apocryphal stories that sustain a cultural refusal to deal with class inequalities and the racial character of those inequalities.

The Upscale World of Television Fiction

Television in the United States is notable for creating a world that shifts the class boundaries upward. If the path to heaven is more arduous for the rich than the poor, the opposite can be said of entry to the ersatz world of television. Data from the University of Pennsylvania's Cultural Indicators project suggest that, in recent decades, television gives the overwhelming majority of its main parts to characters from middle- and professional class backgrounds, whereas significant working class roles are few and far between (Jhally and Lewis 1992). This is in notable contrast to the norms of other English-speaking television programs from countries like Britain and Australia, where working-class characters are much more commonplace. In the United States, the TV world is skewed to such an extent that the definition of what looks normal on television no longer includes the working class. This bias is neither obvious nor clearly stated. On the contrary, television's

professionals are generally universalized so that the class barriers that divide working class viewers from upper-middle TV characters melt away. As some of our working class viewers said of Cliff Huxtable, he may be a doctor, but he's not as aloof as some of the real doctors they encounter in the non-TV world. This is seen in the words of two respondents:

I guess he doesn't really seem professional, you know, not the way a doctor would be. The ones I meet are very uppity and they really look down on the lower class.

They don't play the status they are in the show. You expect them to be living a much higher class, flashing the money, but they're very down to earth.

Television's characters are thus well-off but accessible. These are pictures of the American Dream, and they are paraded in front of us in sitcoms and drama series night after night. On television, most people, or most people with an ounce of merit, are making it.

But surely, it is only television, isn't it? Most people realize that the real world is different, don't they? Well, yes and no. Our study suggested that the line between the TV world and the world beyond the screen has become, for most people, exceedingly hazy. Many of the respondents in our study would shift from immersion in television's world to critical distance in the same interview, praising *The Cosby Show* at one moment for its realism and criticizing it at another for its lack of realism. Thus, for example, one respondent began with an endorsement of the show's realism: "I think that Cosby is much more true to life; you can put yourself right into the picture. Just about everything they do has happened to you, or you've seen it happen."

Later in the interview, the same respondent criticized the show:

It's totally a fantasy to me, a fairy tale.... I think if you bring in the real humdrum of what really life is all about, it would be a total bore. I would much prefer to see a little bit of fairy tale and make-believe.

It seems we watch at one moment with credulity and at another with disbelief. We mix skepticism with an extraordinary faith in television's capacity to tell us the truth. We know that the succession of doctors, lawyers, and other professionals that dominate television's stories is not real, yet we continually think about them as if they were. We have thereby learned to live in the dreams of network executives.

Exceptions to this—perhaps the most notable in recent television history being *Roseanne*—become conspicuous because (at least until the last show in the series when the family wins the lottery) they defy this norm. Simply by being sympathetic and assertively working class, the characters in *Roseanne* stood out from the sea of upscale images that surrounded them. In the United States, there are nearly twice as many janitors as all the lawyers and doctors put together, and yet, on television, the legal or medical professions are run of the mill, whereas to portray a major character as a janitor seems "ostentatiously" class-conscious. The negative response to *thirtysomething* in the 1980s was, in this context, extremely revealing. Here was a show that dealt, fairly intimately, with the lives of a group of middle- and upper-middle-class people. In demographic terms, these characters were the standard fare offered by network television, where most characters of any importance are middle or upper-middle class. Why, then, was this show in particular invariably described, often pejoratively, as a yuppie drama?

The answer tells us a great deal about the way class is represented on television. The show *thirtysomething* was unusual not because it was about young professionals but because it was self-consciously about young professionals. It was difficult to watch an episode without being aware that this was a group of people who were, in class terms, fairly privileged. Here was a show that was conspicuously and unapologetically class-conscious. When most TV characters display a liberal concern for the poor or the homeless, we are invited to applaud their altruism. When characters on *thirtysomething* did so, we were more likely to cringe with embarrassment at the class contradictions thrown up by such philanthropic gestures. Thus, *thirtysomething*'s principal sin was not that it showed us yuppies, but that it made them appear part of an exclusive world that many people will never inhabit. With its coy realism, *thirtysomething* was killjoy television, puncturing the myth of the American Dream.

Although we see echoes of this class consciousness on shows like *Frasier*, they are represented in ways that tend to elide rather than confirm class distinctions. It is not just that Frasier and Niles Crane's high cultural, upper-middle-class affectations are often parodied, but the constant presence of their working-class father reminds us that class background is unimportant.

The prosperous, comfortable world in which most television characters live is generally welcoming, and it is into this world that upscale black characters—from the Huxtables onward—fit like the proverbial glove. It is, we would argue, hard to underestimate the significance of this in the politics of representation. Thus, we can say that to be "normal" on television—the prerequisite for a "positive image"—black characters are necessarily presented as middle or upper-middle class. Indeed, *The Cosby Show* itself used two of television's favorite professions—what, after all, could be more routine than a household headed by a lawyer and a doctor? But unlike *thirtysomething*, it also had to look normal, to portray these wealthy professionals as a regular, "everyday" family. The respondents in our study suggested that the show was particularly skillful and adroit in absorbing this contradiction; indeed, its popularity depends on this combination of accessibility and affluence. Professionals and blue-collar workers can both watch the show and see themselves reflected in it. Social barriers, like class or race, are absent from this world. They have to be. To acknowledge the presence of such things would make too many viewers uncomfortable. Television has thereby imposed a set of cultural rules on us that give us certain expectations about the way the TV world should be.

The bombardment from this image world makes it very difficult for people schooled in the evasive language of North American television to comprehend the world around them seriously. If a serious analysis of class structures is generally absent from our popular vocabulary, then that absence is confirmed by a television environment that makes upward mobility desirable but class barriers irrelevant. As a consequence, when our respondents tried to make sense of class issues thrown up by a discussion of *The Cosby Show*, many were forced to displace the idea of class onto a set of racial categories. This was often the case for our black respondents, who often became enmeshed in the debate about whether the show was "too white" (an idea that, incidentally, the great majority repudiated). Yet, we would argue, the very terms of such a debate involve a misleading syllogism, one that declares that because black people are disproportionately less likely to be upper-middle class, if they become so they have not entered a class category (upper-middle class) but a racial one (white). One of our black middle-class respondents revealed the confusion involved in this way of thinking when he said, "What's wrong with showing a black family who has those kind of values? I almost said *white* values, but *that's not the word I want*" (italics added). The context of a portrayal like *The Cosby Show* is not so much "white culture" (whatever that may be), but "upper-middle-class culture." It is partly by echoing the stilted discourse of U.S. television that many of our respondents found it difficult to make such a distinction.

In creating *The Cosby Show*, Bill Cosby can hardly be blamed for playing by the rules of network television. Indeed, what our study makes clear is that it was only by conforming to these cultural limitations that he was able to make a black family so widely acceptable to white TV viewers. The discomfort or distance that most of the white viewers in our study expressed about black television characters was articulated not only in racial terms, but also—albeit indirectly—in class terms. What many white viewers found off-putting about other black sitcoms was not blackness per se but working-class blackness:

I mean it's not a jive show, like *Good Times*. I think those other shows are more jive, more soul shows, say as far as the way the characters are with making you aware that they are more separate. Where Cosby is more of American down the line thing, which makes everybody feel accepted.

I remember that it (*The Jeffersons*) was a little bit more slapstick, a little bit more stereotypical. They were concerned with racial issues. And it was much more interested in class, and the difference between class, middle-class versus working class.

They talk with the slick black accent, and they work on the mannerisms, and I think they make a conscious effort to act that way like they are catering to the black race in that show. Whereas Cosby, you know, definitely doesn't do that. He's upper middle class and he's not black stereotypical. There's a difference in the tone of those shows, completely.

The Price of Admission and its Political Consequences

Although there may be dimensions to this race/class inflection that go beyond television, the difficulty some white viewers have in inviting black working-class characters into their living rooms is partly a function of television's class premise, in which normalcy is middle and upper-middle class and where working-class characters are, to some extent, outsiders. In terms of the politics of representation, our study raises a difficult question: If black characters must be upscale to be accepted into this image world, is such an acceptance worth the price of admission? To answer this question, we must consider the broader consequences of this representational move.

Among white people, the repeated appearance of black characters in TV's upwardly mobile world gives credence to the idea that racial divisions, whether perpetuated by class barriers or by racism, do not exist. Most white people are extremely receptive to such a message. It allows them to feel good about themselves and about the society of which they are a part. The many black professionals who easily inhabit the TV world suggest to people that, as one of our respondents put it, "There really is room in the United States for minorities to get ahead, without affirmative action."

If affirmative action has become a hot issue in contemporary politics, it is because the tide has turned against it, with states and universities (including our own) buckling under to pressure to abandon the policy. As Gray (1996) suggested in his analysis of the Reagan years, conservatives are able to use their opposition to such policies as a way of mobilizing white votes. Indeed, our study reveals that the opposition to affirmative action among white people is overwhelming. What was particularly notable was that although most white people are prepared to acknowledge that such a policy was once necessary, the prevailing feeling was that this was no longer so.

I think I've become less enamored of it. I think that when the whole idea was first discussed, it was a very good idea. . . . In recent years, I don't think it's necessarily getting anybody anywhere.

I think in a lot of respects it's carried too far and that it results in reverse discrimination because

you have quotas to meet for different job positions and that kind of stuff, it's like, a white person no longer has equal opportunity towards a job because you have to fill a quota.

Well, I think it has gone too far, where the white people don't have the opportunities. I think it has come to a point where people should be hired now, not because of their color or their race, but because of what they're able to do. I mean there are people who are much better qualified but can't get hired because they are white, and I don't think that's right. Maybe in the beginning, they needed this . . . but it has gone too far.

There are, of course, circumstances in which a qualified black person will receive a warm reception from employers concerned to promote an "equal opportunities" image. Any cursory glance at social statistics, however, demonstrates that this is because employers are sheepish or embarrassed by current levels of inequality in the workplace. Almost any social index suggests that we live in a society in which black and white people are not equal, whether in terms of education, health, housing, employment, or wealth. So why is affirmative action suddenly no longer necessary? Partly, we would suggest, because our popular culture tells us so.

During our content analysis of the three main networks, we came across only one program that offered a glimpse of these racial divisions. What was significant about this program, however, was that it did not take place in the present, but in the past, during the early days of the civil rights movement. TV was only able to show us racial divisions in the United States by traveling back in time to the "bad old days." Most of the black characters in television's here-and-now seemed blissfully free of such things. Attempts by Hollywood to deal with racial inequality adopt the same strategy. Racism, whether in *Driving Miss Daisy, The Long Walk Home,* or *Amistad,* is confined to the safe distance of history. There are some notable exceptions—such as

Spike Lee's work—but the general impression is clear: The social causes of racial inequality are behind us.

Television, despite—and in some ways because of—the liberal intentions of many who write its stories, has pushed our culture backward. White people are not prepared to deal with the problem of racial inequality because they are no longer sure if or why there is a problem. James Patterson and Peter Kim (1992) conducted a survey of contemporary American belief systems:

In the 1990s, white Americans hold blacks, and blacks alone, to blame for their current position in American society. "We tried to help," whites say over and over, "but blacks wouldn't help themselves." This is the basis for what we've called the new racism. Everything flows from it. It is a change from the hardcore racism that existed in our country's earlier years. It is also a dramatic contrast to the attitudes of the 1960s, when many whites, from the President on down, publicly stated that black people were owed compensation for centuries of oppression. (P. 183)

The use of upscale black television characters, our study made increasingly clear, is an intrinsic part of this process. Television becomes Dr. Feelgood, indulging its white audience so that their response to racial inequality becomes a guilt-free, self-righteous inactivity. This has saddled us, as Patterson and Kim (1992) suggest, with a new, repressed form of racism. For although television now portrays a world of equal opportunity, most white people know enough about the world to see that black people achieve less, on the whole, than do white people—a discourse emphasized by television news (Entman 1990). They know that black people are disproportionately likely to live in poor neighborhoods, drop out of school, or be involved in crime. Indeed, overall, television's representation of black people is bifurcated—a Jekyll-and-Hyde portrayal in which the bulk of ordinary working-class black Americans have few images of themselves outside of those connected with crime, violence, and drugs.

Media Images: Accentuating the Positive and the Negative

The most striking aspect of the interviews with black Americans in our study was the ubiquity of comments about the role that media images play in how white America looks at them—of how stereotypical images of blacks as criminals affected their own everyday interaction with white society and institutions, as one person put it:

Nobody can believe that you can actually have the intelligence, the fortitude, the dedication and determination to go out and earn a decent living to afford you some nice things. The mentality today is that if you're black and you get something, you either got it through drugs or through prostitution.

The role that the media played in the cultivation of this perception was clearly understood. As another of our respondents stated, "We seem to be the only people in the world that TV tries to pick out the negative to portray as characteristic of us. What television is doing to us, I think, is working a hell of a job on us."

For minority groups, then, living in the kind of residential and social apartheid that characterizes much of contemporary America, media images are vital, as they are the primary way that the broader society views them. Black America, after all, is well aware of what white perception of black males in particular can lead to. In the Rodney King case, an all-white suburban jury acquitted four LAPD officers for a brutal beating on the basis that the person receiving the beating was, in the words of one of the jurors, "controlling the action." When your image of black people is as subhuman criminals, muggers, drug addicts, gang members, and welfare cheats, then even when a black man is lying hog-tied on the ground, he is still dangerous, and any action to subdue him becomes justified.

It is not surprising, in this framework, that Bill Cosby's self-conscious attempt to promote a series of very different black images was so well received by the black respondents in our study. But if it is a kind of representational rescue mission, it is one with an almost fairy-tale script. Thus, we can move from news images of black criminals to fictional images of black lawyers and judges in a matter of network minutes.

In this way, media images turn real and complex human beings into crude one-dimensional caricatures, which then come to define minority populations for the majority. Perhaps the apotheosis of this bifurcated imagery was the figure of O. J. Simpson. If many white Americans were bemused by the degree to which black Americans felt they had a stake in the innocence of a rich TV celebrity, it was because they did not understand the representational issues at stake. The rush to a judgment of innocence was a mechanism of self-defense against a popular culture that offers a limited and bifurcated view of black life, one that can be symbolized by two characters in the recent history of black representation: Bill Cosby and Willie Horton.

The Cosby Show epitomized and inspired a move in network television toward the routine presentation of black professionals in drama and situation comedy. The flip side to this is the world of the news or so-called reality programming (like *Cops*), in which it is blacks as violent criminals, drug dealers, crackheads, and welfare mothers that dominate the screen. Perhaps the embodiment of this side of the story is Willie Horton, the image used by the Bush presidential campaign in 1988 to scare white America away from voting for Mike Dukakis. (In a now infamous TV campaign ad that is credited with turning the election around, Horton was represented as a crazed murderer, whom the Dukakis

prison furlough program, in a moment of foolish liberal do-goodery, allowed out of prison.)

These are the two predominant images of black Americans with which the majority of white people are familiar. The O. J. case was pivotal, as Simpson came to be located precisely at the conjuncture between the two. He *was* Bill Cosby (affluent, friendly, smiling, cultured). If he was guilty of a brutal double murder, he would *become* Willie Horton. The representational identity of black America as a whole, given the incredible visibility of the case, was the prize at stake.

Writer Anthony Walton (1989) commented on what is at stake in these battles over representation:

I am recognizing my veil of double consciousness, my American self and my black self. I must battle, like all humans, to see myself. I must also battle, because I am black, to see myself as others see me; increasingly my life, literally, depends upon it. I might meet Bernard Goetz in the subway. . . . The armed security guard might mistake me for a burglar in the lobby of my building. And they won't see a mild-mannered English major trying to get home. They will see Willie Horton. (P. 77)

In this context, it is little wonder that black Americans took the Simpson case so personally. His innocence would, in some ways, maintain the representational progress forged by Bill Cosby, whereas his guilt would tilt it back to Willie Horton. He *had* to be innocent because African Americans, like all people, want the world to recognize their humanity and their dignity. In a context in which their identity is at stake, the "evidence" had little relevance. Any story—however implausible—of conspiracy and racism would eradicate the forensics, the DNA tests, and so forth. That is precisely what Johnny Cochran offered the jury and black America, and it was accepted with thanks.

But for white viewers, how can sense be made of this bifurcated world? How can black failure in reality programming be reconciled with television's fictions, so replete with images of black success? How to explain racial inequalities in the context of the racial equality of television's upscale world? Without some acknowledgment that the roots of racial inequality are embedded in our society's class structure, there is only one way to reconcile this paradoxical state of affairs. If black people are disproportionately unsuccessful, then they must be disproportionately less deserving. Although few of our respondents were prepared to be this explicit (although a number came very close), their failure to acknowledge class or racial barriers means that this is the only explanation available. The consequence, in the apparently enlightened welcome white viewers extend to television's black professionals, is a new, sophisticated form of racism. Their success casts a shadow of failure across the majority of black people who, by these standards, have failed. Television, which tells us very little about the structures behind success or failure (Iyengar 1991), leaves white viewers to assume that the black people who do not match up to their television counterparts have only themselves to blame.

In a rather different way, the effect of *The Cosby Show* on its black audience is also one of flattering to deceive. The dominant reaction of our black viewers to the show was "for this relief, much thanks." After suffering years of negative media stereotyping, most black viewers were delighted by a show that portrayed African Americans as intelligent, sensitive, and successful:

I admire him. I like his show because it depicts black people in a positive way. It's good to see that black people can be professionals.

Thank you Dr. Cosby for giving us back ourselves.

The problem with this response is that it embraces the assumption that, on television,

a positive image is a prosperous image. This dubious equation means that African Americans are trapped in a position in which any reflection of more typical black experience—which is certainly not upper-middle class—is "stereotypical." As one of our black respondents said, even though he was painfully aware that *The Cosby Show* presented a misleading picture of what life was like for most black Americans, "There's part of me that says, in a way, I don't want white America to see us, you know, struggling or whatever." On TV, there is no dignity in struggling unless you win.

This analysis of stereotyping dominates contemporary thought. It is the consequence of a television world that has told us that to be working class is to be marginal. Thus, it is that viewers in our study were able to see the Huxtable family on *The Cosby Show* as both "regular" and "everyday" *and* as successful, well-heeled professionals.

For black viewers, this deceit amounts to a form of cultural blackmail. It leaves two choices, either to be complicit partners in an image system that masks the deep racial divisions in the United States or forced to buy into the fiction that, as one respondent put it, "there are black millionaires all over the place," thereby justifying *The Cosby Show* as a legitimate portrayal of average African American life.

The Structural Confines of Network Television

If our study tells us anything, it is that we need to be more attentive to the attitudes cultivated by "normal" everyday television. In the case of representations of race, these attitudes can affect the way we think about "issues" like race and class and, in so doing, even influence the results of elections.

As we have suggested, it does not have to be this way. There is no reason why TV characters cannot be working class and dignified, admirable—or even just plain normal. Bill Cosby's more recent sitcom—*Cosby*—is one attempt to do this, although his enormous popularity as a performer gives him a license that other shows, such as the short-lived *Frank's Place*, do not have. Other television cultures have managed to avoid distorting and suppressing the class structure of their societies; why can't we manage it in the United States?

The American Dream is much more than a gentle fantasy; it is the dominant discourse in the United States for understanding (or misunderstanding) class. It is a cultural doctrine that encompasses vast tracts of American life. No politician would dare question our belief in it, any more than they would publicly question the existence of God. Even though politicians of many different persuasions pay lip service to the dream (it is, in conventional wisdom, "what's great about America"), it is not a politically neutral idea. It favors those on the political right who say that anyone, regardless of circumstance, can make it if they try. In such an egalitarian world, the free market delivers a kind of equity, making public intervention and regulation an unnecessary encumbrance. For government to act to eradicate the enormous social problems in the United States is to defy the logic of the dream. Intervention implies, after all, that the system is not naturally fair, and opportunity is not universal.

The American Dream is, in this context, insidious rather than innocent. It is part of a belief system that allows people in the United States to disregard the inequalities that generate its appalling record on poverty, crime, health, homelessness, and education. It is not surprising that the more fortunate cling to the self-justifying individualism the dream promotes. One of the saddest things about the United States is that sometimes, the less fortunate do too.

The ideological dominance of the American Dream is sustained by its massive presence in popular culture. The television and film industries churn out fable after fable, thereby reducing us to a state of spellbound passivity in which decades of stagnating incomes for many Americans have been accepted with little protest. The success we are encouraged to strive for is always linked to the acquisition of goods, a notion fueled by the ubiquitous language of advertising, in which consumers do not usually see themselves in commercials; rather, they see a vision of a glamorous and affluent world to which they aspire. Underlying the preponderance of middle- and upper-middle-class characters on display is the relentless message that this is what the world of happiness and contentment looks like. In this context, ordinary settings seem humdrum or even depressing. Not only do we expect television to be more dramatic than everyday life, but, in the United States, we also expect it to be more affluent. We do not just want a good story; we want a "classy" setting.

I liked the background. I like to look at the background on a TV program, I enjoy that. The setting, the clothes, that type of thing. I don't enjoy dismal backgrounds.

"This is nice, it looks good and it's kind of, you accept it; they have a beautiful home and everything is okay.

This is the language of advertising. It is also, now, the discourse of the American Dream. This language is now so much a part of our culture that these attitudes seem perfectly natural. It is only when we look at other television cultures that we can see that they are not.

Few other industrial nations leave their cultural industries to be as dependent on advertising revenue as they are in the United States. In the United States, very little happens in our popular culture without a commercial sponsor. This takes place in a lightly regulated free market economy in which cultural industries are not accountable to a notion of public service but to the bottom line of profitability.

Apart from tiny grants to public broadcasting, the survival of radio and television stations depends almost entirely on their ability to sell consumers (viewers or listeners) to advertisers. Moreover, broadcasters in the United States are required to do little in the way of public service. There are no regulations that encourage quality, diversity, innovation, or educational value in programming. This means that the influence of advertising is twofold. Not only does it create a cultural climate that influences the form and style of programs that fill the spaces between commercials; it also commits television to the production of formulaic programming. Once cultural patterns are established, it is difficult to deviate from them without losing the ratings that bring in the station's revenue.

This is not merely a tyranny of the majority and the logic of the lowest common denominator. A ratings system driven by advertising does not so much favor popularity as the quest for the largest pockets of disposable income. The 1999 season of *Dr. Quinn, Medicine Woman* was cancelled by CBS even though it was regularly the most popular show on television during its Saturday night time slot. The problem was simply that its viewers were generally not wealthy enough to be of interest to advertisers. The ad-driven chase for well-heeled demographics thereby gives network television an in-built class bias, creating a climate in which portrayals of working-class black characters may make good television but are an unlikely way to attract television's most sought-after demographic group.

Which brings us back to the many representational offshoots of *The Cosby Show*. To be successful and to stay on the air, *The Cosby Show* had to meet certain viewers' expecta-

tions. This, as we have seen, meant seducing viewers with the vision of comfortable affluence the Huxtables epitomized. Once television has succumbed to the discourse of the American Dream, where a positive image is a prosperous one, it cannot afford the drop in ratings that will accompany a redefinition of viewers' expectations. TV programs that do so are necessarily short-lived. Programs like *Frank's Place, Cop Rock,* or *Twin Peaks* all deviated from a norm, and, although still watched by millions of viewers, they did not attain the mass audience required to keep them on the air. This puts us on a treadmill of cultural stagnation. It is a system in which the bland repetition of fantasies tailored to the interests of wealthier viewers makes sound business sense.

In such a system, *The Cosby Show*'s survival depended on meeting the demands of a formula that pleases as many people as possible and especially its more upscale audience. Our study suggests that it did so with consummate success, pleasing black and white people, blue-collar workers and professionals, all in slightly different ways. The more blue-collar *Cosby* has been less universally embraced, and in this context we should applaud Bill Cosby's attempt to use his popularity to offer audiences a less upscale image.

When our book *Enlightened Racism: The Cosby Show, Audiences, and the Myth of the American Dream* was first published in 1992, we were widely credited with holding *The Cosby Show* responsible for promoting the routine fiction of effortless black success. But this was not the thrust of our argument. *The Cosby Show* and the many black professionals portrayed in its wake are genuine attempts to make television's upscale world more racially diverse. The problem is not with individual instances of black success but with a television environment whose structural conditions make a wider array of images less profitable.

References

Entman, R. 1990. "Modern Racism and the Images of Blacks in Local Television News." *Critical Studies in Mass Communication* 7(4, December): 332-345.

Gray, H. 1996. *Watching Race: Television and the Struggle for Blackness.* Minneapolis: University of Minnesota Press.

Hacker, A. 1992. *Two Nations: Black and White, Separate, Hostile, Unequal.* New York: Scribner.

Iyengar, S. 1991. *Is Anyone Responsible?* Chicago: University of Chicago Press.

Jhally, S. and J. Lewis. 1992. *Enlightened Racism: The Cosby Show, Audiences, and the Myth of the American Dream.* Boulder, CO: Westview.

Patterson, J. and P. Kim. 1992. *The Day America Told the Truth.* New York: Dutton.

Walton, A. 1989. "Willie Horton and Me." *The New York Times Magazine,* August 20, section 6, p. 77.

Wilson, W. J. 1987. *The Truly Disadvantaged.* Chicago: University of Chicago Press.

Lewis and Jhally:

1. What are the consequences of a bifurcated representation on television of blacks in the United States?

2. What is positive and negative about *The Cosby Show* with regard to race relations in the United States?

13

Race, Power, and Representation in Contemporary American Sport

Charles Fruehling Springwood and C. Richard King

To commemorate the appearance of the University of Tennessee in the National Championship Game at the Fiesta Bowl, *The Knoxville Sentinel* produced a special section. Emblazoned on the front was a (supposedly) humorous cartoon by R. Daniel Proctor. The image dramatizes the pending competition between the University of Tennessee Volunteers and the Florida State University Seminoles. At the center of the cartoon, a train driven by the volunteer in a coonskin cap plows into a buffoonish caricature of a generic Indian. As he flies through the air, the Seminole exclaims, "Paleface speak with forked-tongue! This land is ours as long as grass grows and river flows . . . Oof!" The Volunteer retorts, "I got news, pal. . . . This is a desert. And we're painting it orange!" Beneath this hateful drama, parodying the genocide, lies, and destruction associated with the conquest of North America, Smokey, a canine mascot associated with the University of Tennessee, and a busty Tennessee fan speed down Interstate 10, here dubbed "The New and Improved Trail of Tears." They sing, "Oh give me land, lots o' land, full of starry skies above. . . . Don't de-fence me in."

Four years earlier, in February 1995, events at Rutgers University echoed the sentiments embedded in Proctor's cartoon. In a meeting with faculty, Francis L. Lawrence, the university president, reportedly after reading *The Bell Curve*,[1] commented that Africans Americans were "a disadvantaged population that doesn't have the genetic heredity background" to succeed in higher education. Once made public, his repugnant remarks sparked a national controversy. At the local level, black students responded to Lawrence not in letters to the editor, nor through an occupation of the administration building. Instead, they interrupted a men's basketball game between Rutgers University and the University of Massachusetts on the evening of February 7. The audience, assembled to watch the largely black teams compete, rather than applauding the actions of the protesters, insisted that the game resume, yelling "Niggers and spics. . . . Go back to Africa."

These two instances nicely foreground the articulations of race, representation, and power in contemporary American athletics. Although rarely as overt or politically charged, sports has become an increasingly important space in which individuals and institutions struggle over the significance of race. It simultaneously facilitates efforts to reproduce, resist, and recuperate naturalized or taken-for-granted accounts of difference, culture, and history. Too often, fans, media, coaches, and players fail to recognize the significance of sports stories. Indeed, scholars and spectators frequently think of sport as a fun diversion, a pleasurable release, a cultural time-out that is mere entertainment. The celebration of sports as the ideal, if not the only, instance of racial harmony in postintegration America exacerbates the difficulties of thinking about representations of race in association with sports. These views, in our opinion, (dis)miss the centrality of athletics to popular interpretations of race and race relations, formulations of identity and difference, and efforts to create public culture.

Here, we want to challenge these "commonsense" understandings by examining the interplay of redness, whiteness, and blackness in athletic performances. We direct attention, on the one hand, to the practice of "playing Indian at half-time," the use of stereotypical images of Native Americans as mascots, and, on the other hand, to the "pleasures" of gazing at black bodies at play, that is, by an overwhelming margin, the most prevalent of "human" mascots characterize Native American peoples and histories, and yet Native Americans play a seemingly insignificant role—as athletes, spectators, coaches, and owners—in the national sports industry. This conspicuous *presence* of Indian signs and symbols, underscored by a relative *erasure* of Native Americans on the field, contrasts in a curious fashion with what is, ostensibly, a sustained *presence* of the African American athlete, albeit characterized by a virtual *absence* of black mascots. This provocative tension between the inverted representations of racial presence/absence illuminate the ways in which America—largely a European America—has constructed and experienced

its own "imperial" identity in terms of imagined allegories of racial difference. Indeed, the way in which Indian mascots have emerged as central to the identity of sports teams, and the way in which black American participation in sport has grown, suggests that contemporary athletics stage—perhaps unwittingly—particular, often stereotypical, images of race and racial difference. The cultural and racial differences embodied within these images serve to communicate something about the identities of those people who created them in the first instance—European Americans.

Linking Euro-American identity simultaneously to redness and blackness foregrounds the irony and contradiction of racial sign-systems, noting, for example, that within athletics the predominance of one sign (the red body) curiously plays off of the relative absence of Native people in commercialized sport. Meanwhile, although it would be unthinkable to invent a sports mascot that embodied such African American stereotypes as "Sambo," the ubiquitous black athlete is celebrated in ways both more subtle and more obvious than half-time show spectacles. The tradition of identifying athletic teams with Indian symbols is well established (if not also weakening), but why did largely Euro-American sporting clubs in the late 1800s and early 1900s not remake themselves in the prevailing image of the African American? Answering this seemingly simple question promises to be a great deal more complicated and provocative than one might expect. Indeed, to arrive at an answer, the tangled symbols of American redness, whiteness, and blackness must be teased apart.

This analysis is built around an understanding of *power* that considers systems of racial classification to be predicated on notions of racial *difference*. These systems of commonly imagined and fantasized differences are produced always in a context of asymmetrical relations of social power. The creation of such racialized images as Native

American mascots or blackface minstrel clowns is a mode of the power to control space, style, value, and broadly, to "name." As Jordan and Weedon[2] argued, colonial relationships usually are enacted by a series of signifying "regimes of naming," such as the power to label a group of people in official discourse (e.g., wild Indian, female hysteria, African American "mammy"); the power to mimic (e.g., playing Indian, blackface performances); and the power to tell a story from one's own perspective (e.g., Thanksgiving, Columbus Day).

Driving this analysis is the belief that social identities are inseparable from performance, history, and power, and that mascots and athletes are engaged by spectators in such a way that they produce contradictory systems of knowledges of, for, and about others. This is not to say that somebody watching the Atlanta Braves and their Tomahawk-chopping fans will somehow gain genuine knowledge about the lives of Native Americans. Following Michel Foucault,[3] the knowledge produced by this play of signs and symbols is a more subtle form of common sense. The American citizen knows as common knowledge the categories implicit in mascot representations and already appreciates that Indians make for popular mascots, whereas French peasants or African Americans do not. She already knows the stereotypical characteristics that predispose the Indian to serve as an athletic totem. What are the implications of such knowledge? Where do such representations come from? What are the means and meanings of "playing Indian" at half-time? What does it mean for two sports teams with all African American players, each team "inspired" by an Indian mascot, to perform before a largely Euro-American audience?

Team Spirits

Native American mascots pervade American culture, an ubiquitous feature of athletic events, individual identities, and imagined communities. Dozens of professional and semiprofessional sports teams have employed such symbols. A quarter of a century after Stanford University and Dartmouth College retired "their" Indians, the National Coalition on Racism in Sports and Media reports that more than 80 colleges and universities still use Native American mascots.[4] And countless high schools still retain such imagery, referring to themselves as the Indians, the Redskins, the Braves, the Warriors, or the Red Raiders.

Euro-American individuals and institutions initially imagined themselves as Indians for myriad reasons. Whereas some institutions, like Dartmouth College, had historically defined themselves through a specific relationship with Native Americans, more commonly, especially at public universities, regional histories and the traces of the native nations that formerly occupied the state inspired students, coaches, and administrators to adopt Indian mascots, as in the University of Utah Running Utes or the University of Illinois Fighting Illini. Elsewhere, elaborations of a historical accident, coincidence, or circumstance seem to account for the beginnings of playing Indian. St. John's University, for instance, was known as the Redmen initially because their uniforms were all red; only later did fans and alumni transform this quirk into a tradition of playing Indian. Whatever the specific origins of these individual icons, Euro-Americans were able to fabricate Native Americans as mascots precisely because of prevailing sociohistorical conditions, that is, a set of social relations and cultural categories made it possible, pleasurable, and powerful for Euro-Americans to incorporate images of Indians in athletic contexts. First, Euro-Americans have always fashioned individual and collective identities for themselves by playing Indian. Native American mascots were an extension of this long tradition. Second, the conquest of Native America simultaneously empowered Euro-

Americans to appropriate, invent, and otherwise represent Native Americans and to long for aspects of their cultures destroyed by conquest. Third, with the rise of public culture, the production of Indianness in spectacles, exhibitions, and entertainment proliferated, generating new symbolic configurations in sporting contexts.

Importantly, across the United States and Canada, individuals and organizations, from high school students and teachers to the American Indian Movement and the National Congress of American Indians, have challenged Native American mascots, forcing public debates and policy changes. In 1999, a group of Native Americans sued the Washington Redskins of the National Football League for the social and psychological damage generated by their nickname. Colleges and universities arguably have been more responsive to public concern. A handful of institutions, including the University of Utah and Bradley University, have "revised" their use of imagery, whereas others, including St. John's University, the University of Miami (Ohio), Simpson College (Iowa), and the University of Tennessee at Chattanooga, have "retired" their mascots. And many schools without such mascots, including the University of Iowa, the University of Wisconsin, and the University of Minnesota, have instituted policies prohibiting their athletic departments from scheduling games against institutions using Indian icons. At the same time, numerous communities and school boards have struggled with this issue. Many, including the Minnesota State Board of Education and the Los Angeles and Dallas school districts, have required that schools remove these mascots. Of course, many other schools have retained them, often generating intense protest and controversy, such as the highly visible struggle continuing to unfold at the University of Illinois at Urbana-Champaign. Importantly, the media have detailed numerous local and national struggles, opening a crucial space of public debate about mascots in countless opinion pieces.

For all of the recent changes, we argue that playing Indian at half-time persists as a way of staging racial difference in terms as a (neo)colonial fantasy. They continue to be inspired by imperial idioms and identities of nineteenth-century colonialism. In particular, the cultural narratives that have endowed mascots with significance tend to reproduce images of the colonial past in the postcolonial present. These exhibitions freeze Native Americans, reducing them to rigid, flat renderings of their diverse cultures and histories. At the same time, they constitute a Euro-American identity in terms of conquest, hierarchy, and domination.[5]

Taking Scalps

Simpson College, a small liberal arts college and alma mater of George Washington Carver, located in Indianola, Iowa, originally dubbed its teams the Red Men because of the brilliant colors the local maples turned in autumn. Later, students elaborated a tradition drawing on their interpretations of Native Americana, writing a victory cheer, popularly known as "The Scalp Song." This song not only was sung at sporting contests after 1910 but also reached a wider audience through annual radio broadcasts coinciding with the school's homecoming, and it even was included in a musical program broadcast in New York City in January 1928.

A scalp, a scalp, a scalp to hang up
on the trophy wall!
The foe, the foe, the wretched foe was
taken to a fall!
Victoria! 'Round the glare of mighty fires dancing
figures, great and small,
Will hoot and yell, as warriors there assemble at
the call.
Jah, Jah, Jah,

Jah, Jah, Jah.

***

We'll broil, we'll broil, we'll broil them on the grid-iron 'till they're done!
Their hides, their hides, their hides we'll tan as covers for our drum!
A banquet! Hollow skulls will serve as drinking cups to toast the victory won,
Then to our tents at rising of the early morning sun.
Hi, jah, jah, hi, jah, jah,
Hi, jah, jah, hi, jah, jah,
Hi, jah, jah, hi, jah, jah.

In retrospect, the racism and stereotypes enacted in this song are readily apparent. Native Americans, far from being understood as equals, peers, or even moral persons, are compressed in a series of well-worn cliches—cannibalism, savagery, wildness, inhumanity. Surely, such texts enabled racial identity, fostering Euro-American subjectivities through the imagined Indians.

The Invention of Chief Illiniwek

At some point during each University of Illinois home football game, a male student dressed in what appears to be a Plains Indian outfit, with a breastplate and a feathered headdress weighing some 25 pounds, moves to the midfield area.[6] His entrance and subsequent performance is accompanied by song—stereotypical "Indian" music marked by a rhythmic, percussive beat. The audience stands, and "Chief Illiniwek" runs quickly but elegantly in bare feet to his place in the center. The crowd cheers, drums sound, and Chief Illiniwek—the pride of the University—performs a dance characterized by several running "split-jumps" wherein the feet are brought up to shoulder level, a number of double-steps in time to the music, a few long sprints across the playing surface, punctuated

by three high kicks. He does not smile; rather, his face advertises a stoic, understated bellicosity. He is stealthy, solitary, and brave.

The University of Illinois became known as the Fighting Illini in the early 1920s when campus football hero Robert Zuppke identified the "spirit" of his University in the historic/mythic space of the Native Americans who once lived in central Illinois. At a pep rally, he said, "Illini is the name of a tribe of Indians and the word 'Illiniwek' means the complete Indian man, the physical man, the intellectual man, and the spiritual man."[7] Seeking to "embody" his school's proud Illini tradition, Lester Leutwiler—a student with a long interest in Native Americans nurtured by his membership in Urbana Boy Scout troop 6—put together an Indian outfit and prepared a series of dances to bring the otherwise extinct Illini back to life in the form of Chief Illiniwek. Leutwiler—who once organized a "powwow" for a high school project—recreated "Redskin heritage" during half-time of the 1926 football game between the University of Illinois and the University of Pennsylvania, described in an anonymous document in the university archives:

Just as the Illinois Football Band (so named in those days) was about to march into the formation PENN, Chief Illiniwek ran from his hiding place just north of the Illinois stands and took over the leadership of the band with a genuine lively Indian dance. Halted in the center of the field, the band played "Hail Pennsylvania," Pennsylvania's alma mater song. As Chief Illiniwek saluted the Pennsylvania rooters, William Penn . . . came forward and accepted the gesture of friendship offered by the Indian chief and joined him in smoking the peace pipe. At the close of the half-time ceremony, William Penn and Chief Illiniwek walked arm in arm across to the Illinois side of the field to a deafening ovation.[8]

At a variety of levels, this performance must be read as a "rendering" of past events and is emblematic of dramatic practices that reproduce the historical process as unmarked by violence or oppression. Of course, William Penn, the Quaker founder of the state of Pennsylvania, probably never met a chief of an Illinois tribe, not to mention one named Chief Illiniwek. Nevertheless, the event staged on the athletic turf served to effectively and ritually resolve the historical conflicts between the Indian and the Euro-American and confirm the dominance of the latter. In retrospect, then, it was a moment of colonial kitsch theater; but, in the eyes of Leutwiler and supporters of Chief Illiniwek, it was pious drama.

Importantly, Leutwiler had not recreated the Illinois by piecing together aspects of their material culture or elements of their performative repertoire. Instead, he fashioned Chief Illiniwek from the manner of dress associated with the native nations of the Plains and an amalgam of movements identified as "Indian." Four years after the invention of Chief Illiniwek, efforts were made to more systematically authenticate the mascot and its performances. Once again, those involved turned away from fashions and signs of the Illinois peoples, instead embracing fashions from the northern Plains Indians to "imagine" Chief Illiniwek. Webber Borchers, who succeeded Leutwiler in portraying the mascot in later seasons, insisted that a new, "authentic" costume made by "traditional" Native Americans was needed to enhance the value of and significance of his performances. Borchers approached local businessman and Illini supporter Isaac Kuhn, who agreed to finance the fabrication of a new costume if Borchers "would personally see to the proper authenticity of the regalia."[9] During the summer of 1930, he hitchhiked to South Dakota, arriving at the Pine Ridge Reservation in August. Through the agent and local traders, he located an elderly Oglala woman, whom Borchers claimed "as a girl she had helped mutilate the dead of Custer after the battle of Little Bighorn."[10] She agreed to supervise the making of the outfit by three young women. Borchers paid $500 for the costume, overseeing the process at Pine Ridge during the summer. When completed some 3 months later, according to a press release, the ensemble was quite impressive:

It is all white calfskin. The breastplate is made of deer bones and porcupine quills and the war bonnet has real eagle feathers. The shirt has beaded insignia over the shoulders and so do the trousers, which are made in white man's style because of the activity involved in the Illiniwek dance.[11]

On November 8, 1930, the authentic "Indian" attire debuted in a parade down Fifth Avenue prior to a football game played against Army. A member of the ROTC cavalry on campus, Borchers trained a horse named Pinto so that he could ride bareback onto the field and then leap off to begin his dances.

Choreographing Colonialism

The invention of Chief Illiniwek was also extremely ironic, made possible by ambivalent and contradictory appropriations of indigenous cultures and histories. In fact, Native American forms of dance were perceived as wild, dangerously spontaneous, hypersexual, and transgressive, and these perceptions drove a colonial fear of the native as volatile and primitive. Native American forms of dance as well as other bodily practices of celebration or worship were mythologized by ambivalent European settlers as eroticized performances that inverted, ostensibly, a social order characterized by reform, hierarchy, passivity, and submission.[12]

In 1924, Horbert Work, Secretary of the Interior, reaffirmed the U.S. government's longstanding policy opposing indigenous cultural forms. In response to the Tewa Indians of San Ildefonso Pueblo, who voiced concerns about encroachment on their traditions, he expressed the acceptability of "any dance that has religious significance, or those given for pleasure and entertainment, which are not degrading. . . . There are certain practices, however, that are against the laws of nature, or moral laws." These laws were not drafted by Euro-Americans:

They were ordained by that Supreme Being who created all of us. . . . It is contrary to these moral laws to exaggerate the sex instinct of man . . . and the Indian, no more than the white man, cannot afford to contribute to his own spiritual and physical downfall by indulging in such practices which appeal to lower animal emotions only.[13]

In 1926, the year Chief Illiniwek first appeared, a *Kansas City Times* newspaper article portrayed a Friday night dance at the football stadium of an Indian boarding school in Lawrence, Kansas. The headline, "Like Birds and Beasts," framed the students as exotic and wild:

It seemed tonight as if the slinking animals of field and forest and the birds of mountain crag and wood, possessed of demons, came out into the area of the Haskell stadium to dance frog noises from the Wkarusa and the sobbing cadence of wind. . . . Aye-yah-aye-hay sing the Osages, Pawnees. . . . Only the must colored blankets around rounded backs are seen, but the measure excites the heart. . . . Feathers become tumultuous. Knees bent grotesquely; moccasined feet descend toe downward; arms rise and fall. Beribboned weapons are twirled and swung menacingly. But the dance is stopped before ecstasy comes. Enough is enough.

The journalist proceeds to literally demonize these Native American students:

The animals and birds, squaws and children, sweep over the shadowy field in an inter-tribal dance, the combined tom-toms thundering, the

grandstands echoing. It is Custer's last stand, the Halloween of beasts and birds. There is madness in the air. It would not be weird in the sunlight, but in a strip of dim light on a dark night and the air clouded with fogs of a thousand cigarettes, it was diabolism.[14]

Laced with a complex of desire and fantasy about Native American bodily movement, the words seem to suggest some imagined magical powers emergent in these performances.[15]

The tradition of reframing the Native American as a dancing, brave Indian who could inspire the basketball or football team to victory has served to "dramatize" and "reconcile" a dominant pattern of violence—ethnocide and genocide—marking the history of white America in its relations with Native Americans. Such dances are social rituals grounded in a long tradition of colonial mimicry of the colonized Other. In this case, the one indispensable material instrument needed to practice the ritual is the body—a body that mimics/signifies "Indianness" as this category has been invented by Euro-Americans. Of course, it is not the body of a "real Indian," but rather the social body of all Native Americans, enacted by a young white student. The individual members of the audiences of these dramas, largely non-Indian people, are able to participate in a ludic encounter with history. In fact, using this invented Indian body as a ritual map, they are able to participate in the remaking of the colonial past in the postcolonial present.

These meanings inscribed onto the Chief's performance—and literally, his body—arise from the "romance" implicit in the mythology of Empire that turns on the social ambivalence of colonial subjectivity and colonial terror. An odd mix of adventure, promise, guilt, and sorrow structures this subjectivity, often giving rise to forms of "imperial nostalgia."[16] Simply, this is a nostalgia in which a group mourns for the loss of a people it was—itself—implicated in oppressing or destroying. The invention of a white man's Indian—an embodied, political sign—serves to constrain the ability of the white imagination to know and engage contemporary and genuine historical Native Americans.

Of Black Bodies and White Power

In spite of the imperial idioms associated with playing Indian at half-time, Americans have come to know and think of themselves as a freer, more racially harmonious society largely through sport and discourses that boast of a postintegration sporting world. The dominant narrative has been, for some time, that America has been desegregated and racially united through sport. Of course, Jackie Robinson's breaking of the color barrier, joining the Brooklyn Dodgers in 1948, is regarded as the epiphanic act breaking down walls and paving the way for others. But other teams and other games did not embrace this movement with equal degrees of enthusiasm. Beyond occasional ritual celebrations and anniversaries of these early moments of desegregation, this set of "postintegration" discourses, oddly, seems to avoid any mention of race and the racialization of sporting social relations.

Although the common understandings acknowledge "race" as merely a "years-gone-by" moment of desegregation and tend to voice the notion that beyond anecdotal difficulties, race is no longer a problem, we suggest that racial difference animates much of the popular aesthetics of sport. Indeed, sport, as a social field characterized by a series of mediated spectacles, has opened a privileged space for the elaboration, accentuation, and reformulation of racial difference, often from the point of view of the Euro-American spectator. The final portion of this essay attempts to better understand the predominance of the African American athlete, whose pres-

ence in sport—we feel—significantly constitutes not only the social identity of black Americans but also of white Americans. But, as we argue, as a historical construction of white fantasy, the meanings of "blackness" always have contrasted—systematically—with the meanings of "Indianness."

Conditions of Impossibility

Repeatedly, defenders of Native American mascots insist that these feathered and painted sporting totems do nothing other than honor the American Indian. In response, one might ask why, in fact, other peoples of color are not similarly "honored"? Indeed, a "modest proposal" might submit that America owes great debt and gratitude to African Americans, upon whose enslaved shoulders a substantial portion of the United States' great wealth was accumulated. Surely, if it is deemed not only appropriate but necessary to erect mascots of reverence to Native Americans, then it only follows that black Americans should be similarly honored. Elaborating this proposal to its logical, if not ludicrous, end, one could even claim that—in masses—sporting teams should recreate their images in terms of African American mascots, because clearly, the number of historically notable black athletes exceeds similar Native American achievement. Because teams have embraced the image of—ostensibly—"whole" "races," such as the Cleveland Indians and the Washington Redskins, why not design a team identity such as the Chicago Blackmen?

In the preceding paragraph, these playful, outlandish suggestions foreground the contradictory symbolic structures that exist for exhibiting blackness and Indianness. Clearly, the contemporary social and political climate would render impossible any effort to fashion an athletic team in the imagined likeness of African Americans. The point is, however, that such a climate never really existed. As understandings and images of Native Americans were being remade and deployed as team mascots, wild west show thespians, and even decorations for coin currency, how did a colonizing European America engage "blackness"?

On at least one occasion, Euro-Americans have fashioned an African American mascot. In 1891, Yale and Princeton met yet again to continue their great football rivalry. According to a *New York Times* article, Yale students paraded their bulldog across the field only to be followed—a brief while later—by an impromptu Princeton mascot, designed to match the school colors of orange and black:

Princeton was not going to be outdone in that way. . . . Pretty soon came out old Nassau's mascot, and the boys of the blue had to confess that they of the orange had scored a point. Princeton's mascot was a comely young colored girl. She was dressed in a flaming orange dress, with an orange bonnet and an orange parasol. She walked around the field eating an orange and apparently entirely unconscious of the tremendous sensation she created.[17]

Clearly, and fortunately, this performance failed to generate any momentum for a broad tradition of black mascots. But it remains a most poignant and very early example of the "economy" of racial spectacle in sport.

Stereotypes and Spectacles

Although imperialist nostalgia for the Indian centered on courage, a sexualized wildness, bellicosity, and warring aggression, a particular nostalgia also emerged surrounding black Americans. Although these white discourses of racialized longing overlapped in some ways in the white imagination—for example, both the black and Indian body were hypersexualized—blackness arguably was ever more "grotesque" and polluting than was Indianness. Scholars have shown that prevailing nineteenth- and early twentieth-century representations of blackness emphasized the African American as not only a clown[18] but as a symbol of "the multiple, bulging, over- or under-sized, dirty, protuberant and incomplete."[19] Such images of black bodies and lifestyles served to define a white bourgeois society in terms of a projected opposite. Black people were imagined to be what white people were not.

During the nineteenth century, white America invented a new way to gaze on the black American as the tradition of blackface minstrel performances grew increasingly popular. To the amusement of paying audiences, particularly in urban centers, white men staged theatrical, caricatured portrayals of blacks. The minstrel show obscured the explicit and implicit terror that characterized the social institution of slavery by animating the slave as a silly, generally happy buffoon.[20] Furthermore, these exhibitions embodied various black expressive traditions, such as song and dance, into passive, complacent, childlike figures who would then signify a sentimentality for the "good ole days" of plantation life.[21] Indeed, icons emerging from this tradition linger into the present, from such subservient grocery emblems as Uncle Ben and Aunt Jemima to the folk narrations of Uncle Remus and Little Black Sambo. Although imperialist nostalgia for the Indian turns on bravery, magic, stoicism, and wildness, the tropes of the grinning, banjo-strumming, tap-dancing comic or of a happy, maternal, or avuncular servant have characterized white nostalgia for blackness.[22]

Read against this backdrop, contemporary sport becomes a troubling racial drama. Increasingly in the wake of integration, mass-mediated spectacles return the white gaze to the black body. As with imagined Indians, performance paces the significance of blackness—physicality, aesthesized play, and control of the body.

Better Bodies

More recently, white America more has expressed a fascination, indeed preoccupation, with an emerging "knowledge" of blackness. This knowledge concerns the perceived excessive athletic agility, speed, and strength of the black body.[23] Films, such as Hollywood's *White Men Can't Jump* or the independent *Hoop Dreams,* illustrate this intense interest in the athletic "essence" of the African American, an engagement no doubt linked in part to the relative success of the black athlete in televised sport. For example, approximately four out of every five National Basketball Association players are African American. But talk about imagined black athletic superiority is typically a taboo topic on sports telecasts, in locker rooms, and on playing fields. Indeed, sport continues to be celebrated as a model of integration, wherein black people and white people do not have to carry their "race" onto the court.

And yet, we argue, the African American athlete is constituted by the national media and the everyday spectator as a "racialized" spectacle. The largely unstated but ubiquitous white fascination with the natural black athlete, seemingly "born to dunk," was epitomized in the 1980s by Al Campanis, then vice president of the Los Angeles Dodgers baseball club, when he told ABC's Ted Koppel that blacks "are gifted with great musculature and various other things. They're fleet of foot. And this is why there are a lot of black major league ballplayers."[24] Many scholars have suggested this preoccupation with natural strength and speed is too easily and too often transmuted into a projection of criminality and intellectual inferiority.[25] African American athletes have emerged at the center of a multibillion-dollar collegiate and profes-sional sports industry, and the black athlete has been transformed into an aesthetic commodity, "controlled" by the gaze of a largely white but also African American consumer.[26]

"I Want to Be Like Mike" . . .

This "gaze" has assumed global contours as well, revealed, for example, in Harajuku—the *hautemonde* district of Tokyo. In the early 1990s, consumers could pay approximately $60 an hour to "rent" a basketball court for an hour. Customers would then move onto a tarnished black asphalt court decorated by messy graffiti, for a "pick-up" game, and shoot at backboards with rusty rims and chain-link nets.[27] These Japanese were, in essence, playing out the ambivalent, "White Men Can't Jump" fantasy by occupying a simulated American "hood with hoops." Indeed, this East Asian fantasy preceded *Hoop Dreams,* the film that so dramatically portrayed the American commodification of the poor, black ghetto youth. Although the documentary seemed to move toward a critique of the notion that young black boys and their social spaces engender dreams of escape and financial success though achievement on the basketball court, the narrative was celebrated by the public as a celebration of this dream rather than a critique of the political economy of urban athletes and professional and collegiate sport.[28]

This popular valorization of the African American athlete mediates a knowledge that sport is now a province of racial and class equality. Sports black heroes, such as Michael Jordan, offer white spectators who otherwise carry racist baggage an opportunity to see, love, and "know" a black man, but in this instance, they see a black spectacle. The popular understandings of sport and race, although clearly not ignorant of the conspicuous racial stratification of "big-time" college and professional sport, render impossible a broad critique of those structures of power, resources, opportunity, and exploitation that constrain the ability of the low-income student athlete of color to commit to modes of achievement that transcend sport. Given the tremendous flow of capital that now motivates college sport, the race to recruit promising athletes and to secure their "letters of intent" has intensified to the point that their educational needs are neglected. Indeed, the philosophy of the system seems to be that it is essentially worthwhile to invest in a system of attraction and recruitment of collegiate athletes that might—for every 1,000 children it encourages to dedicate essentially all of their energy and inspiration into achieving their "hoop dream"—provide only a handful with an education and financial security.

No Dancing

Previously, we described nineteenth-century religious impulses and government forces that conspired to oppress expressions of Native American dance and performance. These efforts signaled a conjectural moment in U.S. history, out of which emerged a large number of highly manufactured Indian images produced for the pleasure of Euro-Americans. A key strategy in this essay has been to consider how the "means and meanings" of playing Indian intersect with the experiences and perceptions of black athletes. Having outlined the ironic ways in which Native American dance has been both challenged and celebrated, we address here much more recent efforts to control and eliminate another form of "dancing," the end zone celebrations that emerged with great popularity in college and professional football in the 1980s and 1990s.

"Look at those jungle-bunnies jumping around, slapping each other silly!" exclaimed an acquaintance of one of the authors while watching a Washington Redskins football

game in the late 1980s. The blatantly racist remark was a reaction to several of the Redskins players—all African Americans—performing what is known as an end zone celebration. To celebrate a touchdown, several players gathered in the end zone to enact an obviously choreographed "dance" of sorts. Such orchestrated and extended expressions of victory and triumph became increasingly common in the 1980s and 1990s. Vernon Andrews concluded that, generally, African American players performed the longest and most elaborate of these end zone dances.[29] Researchers have argued that Black expressiveness—characteristically more colorful, improvisational, expansive, deliberate, and self-conscious—is a prevailing African American cultural mode of communication and style.[30]

The National Football League, partly in concert with spectator opinion, attempted to control and, indeed, erase such colorful expressions of triumph by asserting that they were unsportsmanlike displays. The league amended its rules in 1984 and 1991 to temper "any prolonged, excessive, or premeditated celebration by individual players or groups of players."[31] John Fiske claims that such struggles to control these embodied displays of success are in essence a struggle over racial power:

The argument is not *what* constitutes sportsmanlike conduct, but over *who* controls its constitution. . . . Because the issue is not one of behavior but one of control, in different social conditions, the same expressive behavior can be viewed by the power-bloc quite differently. In its TV commercials for the World Football League (which is the NFL's attempt to spread US football to Europe), the NFL relies largely on images of black expressiveness that it attempts to repress back home. [For European audiences, presumably] the expressive black body signals not a challenge to white control but an American exuberance, vitality, and stylishness which European sport lacks.[32]

Once again, the Euro-American reaction to both the expressive and spontaneous bodies of the non-white Other is decidedly ambivalent, characterized by adulation on the one hand and discomfort on the other. As coauthor Springwood and his friend watched a group of Redskins wide-receivers celebrate a touchdown, noted previously, the situation on the television screen revealed a highly complicated set of colliding images of race, sport, and history. The largely black Redskins offensive unit—fondly nicknamed "the Posse"—enacted a stylistic, effusive display of triumph as the Redskins' "unofficial" mascot—a black spectator garishly adorned in a feathered headdress and face paint—danced gleefully in the background. Ironically, celebratory displays such as those that defined the Posse were confronted by a disapproving league eye, which viewed these actions as rude, undisciplined, and transgressive modes of expression.

Conclusion

We underscore the significance of racial symbols and spectacles in American sports with one final, complicating irony. At the University of Mississippi, whiteness, not redness or blackness, energizies the choreography of body and society. At the center of these productions stands "Colonel Reb," a mascot embodying popular stereotypes of a nineteenth-century plantation owner. Completing the spectacle, at the school's football games, the Confederate flag is displayed and the marching band plays "Dixie." Taken together, this is a nostalgic statement about race and power, a romantic yearning for the Old South, complete with its structures and relations, arguably including even slavery. At 'Ole Miss, the stagings of whiteness contrast sharply, on the one hand, with the mimicry and oppression giving rise to playing Indian at half-time and, on the other hand, with the celebration (and regulation) of black bodies at play. For

all of the local differences, it also affirms our findings about the articulations of race, representation, and power in American sports. In recent years, there have been calls to stop these traditions, and, in fact, the football coach pleaded with the university to change things because "he sensed the atmosphere was harming his ability to recruit top black athletes." Finally, in the face of intense opposition, the university chancellor banned all flag sticks in fall 1997 to keep Rebel banners out of the stadium. Yet, predictably, on the first Saturday after the ban, more than 1,000 Confederate banners were unfurled in the stands.[33]

At this particular moment in the history of the United States, an analysis of sport reveals an array of odd racial juxtapositions, alliances, and contradictions. For example, how can a school, such as the University of Illinois, reconcile its continued robust support for an Indian mascot broadly challenged by Native American students and faculty and the weak graduation rates of both its black and white student athletes who wear the Chief Illiniwek images with its ostensible philosophy of a humane education? How could a southern university, for so many years, ignore the means and meanings of enacting 'Ole Miss football pride, Rebel-style?

An Indian mascot "works" because it is an emptied representation of the Native American in that it elides, even dislocates, the terror of the Native American relationship to the United States. The desire for these mascots locates the non-Indian self within a space of impossibility, wherein spectators fail to recognize the uneven, historical significance of the convergence and then slippage of professional sports, the American university, scholastic athletics, the embodiment of the Indian, the predominance of the black body of African American athletes, and the absence of Native American students and faculty.

What kinds of racialized meanings and experiences are constituted by the predominance of the African American athlete on the fields and courts where so many of these collegiate Indian and other mascots prevail? Those occasions in which African American students have allied themselves with Native American, Euro-American, and Latino students to protest these mascots and other issues confronting minority students assume monumental significance when contextualized by the plight of the African American athlete whose opportunities have been created and whose body has been exploited by the very same structures of imperial power that produce mascots. Given the location of the black athlete within this system, we have little confidence that possibilities exist for him, or student athletes of any color, to voice opinions—especially of dissent—in regard to the controversies portrayed in this chapter.

Notes

1. Richard Herrnstein and Charles Murray, *The Bell Curve: Intelligence and Class Structure in American Life* (New York: Free Press, 1994).

2. Glenn Jordan and Chris Weedon, *Cultural Politics: Class, Gender, Race and the Postmodern World* (Oxford, UK: Blackwell, 1995), pp. 11–15.

3. Michel Foucault, *The Birth of the Clinic.* (London: Tavistock, 1973); *Histoire de la Sexualité* [The History of Sexuality], vol. 1, *La Volonté de Savior.* (Paris: Gallimard, 1976); "Truth and Power," in *Power/Knowledge: Selected Interviews and Other Writings, 1972–1977,* edited by C. Gordon. (New York: Pantheon, 1980), pp. 109–33.

4. Roberto Rodriguez, "Plotting the Assasination of Little Red Sambo," *Black Issues in Higher Education* (June 11, 1998), pp. 20–24.

5. See C. Richard King, *Colonial Discourses, Collective Memories, and the Exhibition of Native American Cultures and Histories in the Contemporary United States* (New York: Garland, 1998); Charles Fruehling Springwood and C. Richard King, "Race, Ritual, and Remembrance Embodied: Manifest Destiny and the Symbolic Sacrifice of Chief Illiniwek," in *Exercising Power: The Making and the Re-Making of the Body,* edited by

C. Cole, M. Messner, and J. Loy (Albany: State University of New York Press, forthcoming).

6. This section draws substantially from King (1998) and Springwood and King (forthcoming).

7. "Chief Illiniwek Tradition," undated document, University of Illinois Library Archives.

8. Undated, untitled document, University of Illinois Library Archives.

9. Webber A. Borchers, untitled letter, University of Illinois Archives, 1959, p. 2.

10. Borchers, 1959, p. 2.

11. "An Illinois Illustrated Newsfeature," undated document, University of Illinois Library Archives.

12. See also C. Richard King and Charles Fruehling Springwood, "Choreographing Colonialism: Athletic Mascots, (Dis)Embodied Indians, and EuroAmerican Subjectivities," in *Cultural Studies: A Research Volume,* vol. 5, edited by N. Denzin (Greenwich, CT: JAI, forthcoming).

13. Quoted in Francis Paul Prucha, *The Great Father: The United States Government and the American Indians.* 2 vols. (Lincoln: University of Nebraska Press, 1984), vol. II, p. 803.

14. "Like Birds and Beasts," *Kansas City Times,* October 30, 1926.

15. Indeed, these embodied activities were often read and misread as "tribal" practices of magic. For example, see Ella Stratton, *Wild Indians and Their Deeds: Containing a Full Account of Their Customs, Traits of Character, Superstitions, Modes of Warfare, Traditions, Etc.* Philadelphia: S. L. Publisher, 1902).

16. See Renato Rosaldo, *Culture and Truth: The Remaking of Social Analysis* (Boston: Beacon, 1989), p. 70.

17. Cited in Michael Oriard, *Reading Football: How the Popular Press Created an American Spectacle* (Chapel Hill: University of North Carolina Press, 1993), pp. 229–30.

18. See Eric Lott, *Love and Theft: Blackface Minstrelsy and the American Working Class* (New York: Oxford University Press, 1993); Grace Elizabeth Hale, *Making Whiteness: The Culture of Segregation in the South, 1890–1940* (New York: Pantheon, 1998).

19. Wayne Mellinger and Rodney Beaulieu, "White Fantasies, Black Bodies: Racial Power, Disgust and Desire in American Popular Culture," *Visual Anthropology* 9(1997):117–47.

20. Lott (1993).

21. Hale (1998).

22. Lott (1993); Mellinger and Beaulieu (1997); Hale (1998); Gerald Early, *The Culture of Bruising: Essays on Prizefighting, Literature, and Modern American Culture* (Hopewell, NJ: Ecco, 1994), pp. 155–62.

23. Laurel Davis, "The Articulation of Difference: White Preoccupation with the Question of Racially Linked Genetic Differences among Athletes," *Sociology of Sport Journal* 7(1990):179–87; Billy Hawkins, "The Black Student Athlete: The Colonized Black Body," *Journal of African American Men* 1(3, 1995/1996):23–35; Jillian Sandell, "Out of the Ghetto and into the Marketplace: Hoop Dreams and the Commodification of Marginality," *Socialist Review* 25(2, 1995):57–82; John Hoberman, *Darwin's Athletes: How Sport Has Damaged Black America and Preserved the Myth of Race* (Boston: Houghton Mifflin, 1997).

24. Cited in Davis (1990), p. 180.

25. See Davis (1990); Hoberman (1997); David Andrews, "The Fact(s) of Michael Jordan's Blackness: Excavating a Floating Racial Signifier," *Sociology of Sport Journal* 13(2, 1996):125–58; David Andrews, " Just What Is It That Makes Today's Lives So Different, So Appealing? Commodity-sign Culture, Michael Jordan, and the Cybernetic Postmodern Body," in *Exercising Power: The Making and Re-making of the Body,* edited by C. Cole, J. Loy, and M. Messner (Albany: State University of New York Press, forthcoming); Cheryl Cole, " American Jordan: P.L.A.Y., Consensus, & Punishment," *Sociology of Sport Journal* 13(1996):366–97; Cheryl Cole and David Andrews, "Look—It's NBA Show Time!": Visions of Race in the Popular Imaginary," in *Cultural Studies: A Research Volume 1,* edited by N. K.

Denzin (Greenwich, CT: JAI, 1996), pp. 141–81; Cheryl Cole and H. Denny, "Visualizing Deviance in the Post-Reagan America: Magic Johnson, AIDS, and the Promiscuous World of Professional Sport," *Critical Sociology* 20(3, 1995):123–47; Vernon Andrews, "Race, Culture, Situation, and the Touchdown Dance," unpublished manuscript, University of Wisconsin–Madison, Sociology Department, 1991; Vernon Andrews, "Black Bodies—White Control: The Contested Terrain of Sportsmanlike Conduct," *Journal of African American Men* 2(1, 1996):33-59.

26. Cole and Andrews (1996); V. Andrews (1996).

27. See Patrick Smith, *Japan: A Reinterpretation* (New York: Pantheon, 1997), p. 205.

28. See Sandell (1995).

29. V. Andrews (1991).

30. John Fiske, *Power Plays/Power Works* (London: Verso, 1993); James Jones, "Racism: A Cultural Analysis of The Problem," in *Prejudice, Discrimination and Racism,* edited by J. Dovidio and S. Gaertner (San Diego: Academic Press, 1986), pp. 279–314; D. Andrews (1991, 1996).

31. Cited in Fiske (1993), p. 60.

32. Fiske (1993), p. 62.

33. See Mike Butler, "Confederate Flags, Class Conflict, a Golden Egg, and Castrated Bulls: A Historical Examination of the Ole Miss-Mississippi State Football Rivalry," *The Journal of Mississippi History* 59(2, 1977):123–39.

Springwood and King:

1. Discuss the similarities and differences in the presentations of Indians and blacks in sport.

2. Discuss why having representations of Native Americans during half-time programs is not considered to be a way of honoring them.

14

Zydeco Music
and Race Relations
in French Louisiana

Rocky L. Sexton

Black and white relations in American society are a complex issue. Since the civil rights movement, there have been obvious signs of improvement in this area. There are also clear indications of continuing distrust, dislike, and segregation between races. Race relations are often articulated as a black/white dichotomy; however, these racial categories are crosscut by ethnic divisions. This chapter examines the musical genre zydeco to illuminate the complexity of race relations through time within subsets of the broader black/white population: Creoles and the Cajun-French. The varying attitudes of Cajuns toward zydeco and the degrees of segregation at venues for the music demonstrate continuity, change, and variety, in appreciation of race-linked musical styles and racial interaction. These dynamics are shaped in part by broader trends in American society that have influenced ethnic minorities throughout the twentieth century.

The French Louisiana Region

Louisiana is a complicated region. The term "French Louisiana" is frequently used in ref-

erence to the southern portion of the state due to its Gallic heritage. However, the actual cultural pedigree of French Louisiana is more intricate. It originally was colonized by the French, including settlers from Canada and the Caribbean. African slaves were introduced at an early date. Also to be considered are Native Americans in the area. In this frontier setting, a blending of African, European, and Native American cultural elements was manifested in creolization—the emergence of new cultural forms. The result was what Hall has referred to as Afro-Creole culture, whose primary carriers were slaves but that influenced other residents of the colony.[1] Because of sexual liaisons between white masters and slave women, a population of mixed racial ancestry emerged. Many of these people were freed, educated, and even given property (even slaves) by their white fathers. These light-skinned *Gens de Couleur Libre* (Free People of Color) occupied a privileged middle social category between whites and dark-skinned slaves. The Free People of Color (also called Creoles or Creoles of Color) persisted as a distinct social category until the antebellum era, when Emancipation blurred the socioeconomic boundaries in Louisiana's African American population.[2] Anglo-Americans who assumed sociopolitical dominance of the territory following the Louisiana Purchase used a rigid black/white racial dichotomy, in contrast to the fluid, multilevel system of classification of the colonial French and Spanish. They were far less inclined to acknowledge diversity in the African American population or accord special status to subsets of this group. Although the descendants of free people of color attempted to maintain themselves as distinct from other African Americans, by the late twentieth century these differences had blurred and Creole has emerged as the common label for the Afro-French in general.

In 1763, Louisiana was ceded to Spain, which controlled the area until 1802. The territory was then briefly returned to France, which sold it to the United States in the Louisiana Purchase. During Spanish control of Louisiana, Acadian exiles moved into Louisiana. These were the descendants of French settlers who had colonized present-day Nova Scotia and New Brunswick in Canada beginning in the 1630s. In ensuing years, this population developed a unique ethnic identity and ethnic label, Acadian (in French, *Acadien*), which was derived from the name Acadia (in French, *Acadie*) applied to the region.[3] Many Acadians were deported from Acadia by the British (who had acquired the area in 1713) during the Seven Years War (1755–1763). Large numbers of Acadians arrived in Louisiana and were settled in various areas of the colony.[4] Their traditional culture was modified by adaptation to Louisiana and Afro-Creole influences.[5] By the late nineteenth century, there was a blurring of ethnic boundaries between Acadians and other white French, and the label Cajun (a derivation of *Cadien,* the shortened version of *Acadien*) was broadly applied to many white French inhabitants of Louisiana.[6]

The Genesis of a Research Project

In 1989, I was a graduate student at Louisiana State University (LSU) researching Cajun culture. While attending the Plaisance, the Louisiana zydeco music festival, I discussed the event with a fellow graduate student from LSU whom I encountered there. At some point, I commented that most of the musicians or their parents had been born within a 50-mile radius of the festival site, an interesting fact considering the broad regional, national, and international popularity of zydeco music. My colleague, a geographer, replied that this would be an interesting topic of study considering that we were both zydeco music fans but knew little about it. Within a few days, we were collaborating on research on zydeco music.[7] This project was peripheral to my thesis project. However, because Cajuns and Creoles and their musical styles coexist in the same region, I hoped to kill the proverbial two birds with one stone.

Cajun and Afro-French Musical Genres in French Louisiana

The accordion is the instrument that came to distinguish the folk music played by both Cajuns and Creoles. It was invented in Austria in 1822 and was introduced to Louisiana in the mid-nineteenth century. Although various versions of the accordion were developed, the single-row button accordion (now labeled the "Cajun accordion" by scholars) was the model that became common in Louisiana.[8] By the early twentieth century, the accordion had replaced the violin as the dominant instrument played at house dances and dance halls especially in the prairie region of southwest Louisiana. Whereas Cajun music retained the violin as a backup instrument, it became increasingly rare among Creoles.[9]

Creole music was also distinguished by the *frottoir* (rubboard), a portable instrument used to scrub clothing, as a rhythm instrument, and the triangle fulfilled a similar function for Cajun musicians. Some scholars have suggested that the rubboard's antecedents were rasps and notched gourds used in Afro-Caribbean music, which eventually were replaced by a rubboard rubbed with thimbles, spoons, or bottle openers.[10]

Creoles shared many dance forms with their Cajun neighbors such as the waltz and two-step. However, Creoles were distinguished by a faster, upbeat version of the two-step known as the "La La." Eventually, the term La La was linked to both Creole music and the house dances in which it was played in the early twentieth century.[11] Despite the shaky assertion that early Cajun and Creole music were nearly identical,[12] La La was in many respects faster, more highly syncopated, with upbeat rhythms, highly repetitive song texts, and the use of the rubboard. The variation in musical styles of blacks and whites was due to Afro-French music retaining African melodic and rhythm styles. There was also a noticeable blues influence on Afro-French music, which is not surprising considering the nearby Mississippi Delta, where blues was common, and considering the commercial distribution of blues recordings. There was also considerable interaction in Louisiana between Afro-French and Anglo-African Americans who had moved into the region in large numbers during the late nineteenth and early twentieth centuries to work in rice agriculture.[13] Elderly Creoles also recall working on sugar plantations with Anglo-African Americans from adjacent states who provided seasonal labor during the sugar cane harvest. Although Creoles were increasingly attracted to blues music, it was often considered to be barroom music and inappropriate for respectable settings like neighborhood dances. Consequently, Creole musicians converted favorite blues tunes into acceptable dance forms like waltzes.[14]

Although Cajun and Creole music shared similarities, they followed increasingly different trajectories of development due to different popular music influences. Cajuns integrated swing, country, and later rock-and-roll music into their style.[15] Creole La La music was increasingly influenced by blues and progressive urban rhythm and blues. This was especially true in the World War II era, when Creoles began to move from the countryside to work in industrial centers in Louisiana and Texas.[16] The term "zydeco" became strongly linked to La La music after World War Two. Although some link it to African linguistic influences,[17] the term zydeco is generally attributed to the folk expression *Les haricots sont pas salé* (The beans are not salted). The saying reflects hard times, with the connotation that people are so poor that they cannot even afford to flavor their beans with a cheap piece of salt pork or bacon. In French pronunciation, the combination of the "s" from *Les* and the "h" from *haricot* creates a "z" sound, thus forming *zarico*, which eventually developed into zydeco and similar phrasings. For example, the Texas blues musician Lightning Hopkins used *Zolo Go* in a song recorded in Houston in 1949, and this reflected his interaction with Creole musicians who had moved into the area.[18] Beginning in 1950, the guitarist Clarence Garlow, a native of southwest Louisiana who had relocated to Texas, recorded a series of songs that discussed the *zadacoe* that he identified as the traditional Creole weekend house dances in southwest Louisiana. This association is understandable considering that the term *les haricots* was a recurring theme in pre-World War II Creole music. For example, pioneering field recordings of Creole music in the 1930s include several songs from different areas of southwest Louisiana that feature the expression *les haricots sont pas salé.*[19]

It was during this period that Clifton Chenier, a Creole who had moved to east Texas, emerged as the dominant figure in zydeco music. He adopted the piano accordion apparently because it was well suited for his repertoire of songs that included basic La La, songs with bilingual lyrics, and standard blues selections. Building on his southwest Louisiana La La musical heritage, interaction with blues musicians, and personal innovation, Chenier defined the sound that he popularized as zydeco in his dance hall performances and recording sessions in both Texas and Louisiana.

Although some scholars mistakenly limit modern zydeco's development to Texas,[20] this process included not only strong overlap between Louisiana and Texas, as represented by Clifton Chenier and others, but also activities by Creole musicians based in Louisiana. For example, a southwest Louisiana accordionist named Boo Zoo Chavis, who previously had performed with only a single-row button accordion and rubboard, collaborated with a local rhythm and blues band in 1955 to produce *Paper in My Shoe,* a bilingual regional hit that reputable scholars credit as a strong influence on the evolution of zydeco music.[21]

Given varied instrumentation, popular music influences, and traditional musicological distinctions, contemporary Cajun and zydeco music are different in many respects. As a result of Clifton Chenier's popularity, the keyboard accordion became identified with zydeco music. However, as with earlier this century, the single-row button accordion and even triple-row button accordion are more common. In contrast, the vast majority of Cajun musicians use only the single-row button accordion. Zydeco is still characterized by the rubboard, which is not widely used by Cajun bands, who still favor the triangle. The violin is nearly absent in zydeco bands, whereas it is still the primary backup instrument to the accordion in Cajun music. Given the rhythm and blues and even jazz influences, zydeco bands also consistently include the electric guitar and, to a lesser extent, the saxophone in their instrumental repertoire. Zydeco song texts are highly repetitive. The post-World War II trend toward bilingual lyrics in zydeco music has become more pronounced. In fact, most younger musicians tend to perform almost entirely in English, albeit with the occasional French word or phrase thrown in. In contrast, most Cajun bands emphasize French lyrics or bilingual songs in conjunction with waltzes and two-steps. In distinguishing the two styles musicologically, Spitzer noted, "Zydeco music places less emphasis on melodic development and is rhythmically faster and more complex than Cajun music."[22]

Early Twentieth Century Race Relations

Because of long-term mutual cultural influences, Cajuns and Creoles can be viewed as culturally similar and socially distinct.[23] This social distinction is rooted in racial difference. Despite a traditional hierarchy that accorded higher social status to light-skinned Creole residents of the region, they still were viewed as subordinate to whites. Since the late nineteenth century, racial classification has been largely transformed into a basic black/white dichotomy similar to that of the south in general, although there is obvious ethnic diversity in these categories. As with the rest of the south, a primary feature of this racial hierarchy has been segregation. Blacks and whites traditionally have occupied separate neighborhoods in towns and have formed their own discrete population clusters in the countryside,[24] a pattern that is still common in south Louisiana. However, as a reflection of traditional stratification in the African American population that survived beyond the nineteenth century, communities also could be divided based on light versus dark phenotype.[25]

Despite segregation, there are documented instances of Cajun and Creole musicians performing together, albeit under specific controlled circumstances. For example, the legendary Creole accordionist Amede Ardoin, hailed as a major influence on both zydeco and Cajun music, played regularly at Cajun house dances but strictly in the role of performer (as opposed to guest), often in the accompaniment of white musicians, and with the consent of hosts.[26] Many of Ardoin's commercial recordings of the late 1920s and 1930s were in a duo with Dennis McGee, a legendary Cajun violinist with whom he frequently performed at Cajun dances. Misconceptions about Cajun and early zydeco being identical[27] may be attributable to Creoles altering their performance styles for a white audience. For example, one author asserts that following Ardoin's performances at white dances, he would appear at Creole events and play in a much different manner.[28] This altering of style for different audiences is reported by other Creole musicians who played for Cajun audiences during the pre-World War II era. They recall playing primarily waltzes and two-steps rather than the La La and recall that they did not use the rubboard at such events.[29] Given the strong segregation of the time, however, Creole performers were not universally accepted at Cajun dances, and any breaches of racial boundaries in these contexts were subject to severe sanctions. For example, Amede Ardoin was severely beaten after he allegedly allowed a white woman to wipe sweat from his brow during a performance, a clear articulation of existing taboos limiting contact between African American men and white women.[30]

Contemporary Race and Musicological Perspectives

Strong racial segregation was clearly present in French Louisiana earlier this century. However, one must consider the extent to which race relations have changed since the civil rights movement of the 1960s. Correspondingly, it is interesting to evaluate change in terms of attitudes toward Cajun and Creole musical styles and the contexts in which they are performed. I encountered strong attitudes about segregation and differing musical aesthetics in moving back and forth between Cajuns and Creoles during my research. These are frequently linked to negative race-based attitudes toward Creoles. As Frederik Barth noted, the ascription of particular cultural and behavioral traits to oneself and others is a primary means of articulating and maintaining ethnic boundaries,[31] an observation that is applicable to racial groups. Obviously, these perceptions are frequently negative and represent stereotyping, the linkage of particular unflattering traits to an entire group. As scholars attest, stereotypes are generally erroneous and are acquired secondhand rather than through actual experience.[32]

The stereotypes that color race perception and inhibit black/white interaction in Louisiana and in broader American society are articulated by the reluctance to enter locations where the racial "other" is in control. This dichotomy can create dilemmas for the researcher who works in segregated settings. Several instances of this occurred while I was simultaneously conducting research in Cajun bars, the topic of my master's thesis,[33] and in zydeco clubs for my secondary project. My primary methodology was participant observation combined with interviews of Cajuns and Creoles. One episode during my research, which is indicative of other experiences, occurred shortly after I had visited a zydeco dance hall. While I was at a Cajun bar for a brief visit, one of the regulars stated, "I've heard where you've been. . . . Jack told me that you've been hanging out at nigger clubs." The ensuing conversation included references to a nearby zydeco dance hall whose owner was known by several of my Cajun friends. Although he had invited some of them to visit the club, the invitation was never accepted because of anxiety about entering an all-black establishment. In fact, one informant stated, "I don't want to go into that place, I wouldn't get out of there." This attitude was held because of the belief that the establishment was a violent place where whites would be in danger. This attitude was unwarranted because the owner was anxious to bring in a mixed audience, and he had even gone so far as to advertise a "white night" to encourage white patronage. A decade after my original research, I encountered similar attitudes in the course of organizing a field tour of southwest Louisiana in conjunction with an academic conference, which included a stop at a Creole dance hall. When I told a middle-aged Cajun friend that I planned to take the all-white tour group to a local zydeco dance hall, his reaction was that of utter disbelief. He voiced the same concerns that I had heard before about what he perceived as the clear danger inherent in such an undertaking. Despite my assurances that I had visited the establishment on several occasions individually and with small groups of whites and had in fact felt safer there than in many Cajun clubs, he remained unconvinced. The attitude of whites toward my ventures into the world of zydeco represent racial stereotyping of Creoles. This is especially true considering that those most opposed to attending zydeco performances are the very people who have never been in these settings. However, no matter how invalid such perceptions may be, they have a strong influence on the degree and nature of race relations.

Although general apprehension about the racial unknown is a significant factor in race relations, one also must consider differences in musical "taste" linked to race. In American society, there has been a tendency to perceive music as totally separate race-linked genres that have developed in a vacuum. Thus, there is often a failure to acknowledge that differing styles continually influence one another, as noted by Garafalo:

The identification of music with race, which has tended to exclude African-American artists and others from certain marketing structures in the music industry, makes the task of unearthing an accurate history of U.S. popular music [and I would argue folk music as well] quite difficult and encourages serious underestimates of the degree of cross-cultural collaboration that has taken place.[34]

Broad stereotypes about music obscure complex processes of interplay among musical forms. Subsequently, there has been a creation of rigid categories emphasizing race and with corresponding negative value judgments attached to them. For example, until 1949, *Billboard* magazine used the designation "race music" as the official designation for rhythm and blues.[35] Real and imagined notions of aesthetic difference are evoked in articulating notions of racial difference. Early critics of rock-and-roll derided it as "nigger music" because of the pronounced African American musical influence, which was viewed as unsuitable for a mainstream (i.e., white) audience because of its "insistent rhythms and suggestive content" and the fact that many key figures were African American.[36]

A similar aesthetic, as reflected by the comments of Cajuns who were aware of my zydeco research, has been applied to zydeco because it reflects a historical blues influence and is continually influenced by contemporary African American genres like rhythm and blues, reggae, and even rap music. Differences in instrumentation serve as visual clues about variation between Cajun and zydeco. For example, many Cajuns readily recognize the piano accordion and rubboard as major points of distinction even though many zydeco musicians use the "Cajun" accordion. There are also differences in dance styles. Zydeco bands play few waltzes, a staple of Cajun music performances, and Creoles prefer faster, upbeat dances like the La La, the swing out, and the zydeco shuffle, a modified version of the Harlem shuffle. These differences were articulated in a recent publicized controversy in which an out-of-state African American visitor was refused entrance to a popular Cajun dance hall. In response to the ensuing outcry, a patron of the club articulated the Cajun/Creole contrast: "All the coloreds got their own clubs, and the whites got their own clubs . . . and the coloreds don't dance the way the whites do."[37]

For some, the difference in musical styles and their linkage to race results in harsh commentary on zydeco similar to that directed toward earlier African American music. For example, during a recent conversation with an elderly white man at a Cajun dance in southwest Louisiana, I stated that I was en route with a tour group to hear zydeco music at a local dance hall. He stated, "I hate that nigger music, and that's what it is, nigger music." Other Cajuns are less harsh in their criticisms and simply may criticize the repetitive nature of the lyrics of many zydeco songs by stating, "They say the same thing over and over." One could argue that increasing anglicization of zydeco lyrics and overt manifestations of overwhelming contemporary black popular music influences create greater stylistic (and, by extension, racial) distance between zydeco music and "traditional" Cajun music as recognized by middle-aged and elderly Cajuns who view it as superior to zydeco. In terms of attitudes toward race and music, the mind-set for many such people is that of once prevalent attitudes of the pre-civil rights era and dominant musical aesthetics of one or more generations past.

Differing perspectives are found among younger Cajuns whose primary frame of reference is popular American music, and they are less likely to dwell on differences in Cajun and zydeco music or to racialize such differences. A common trend in American music and race relations has been one in which older generations have derided African American musical forms while components of the younger generation have embraced

them or have at least been strongly influenced by them.[38] Such developments are evident in Louisiana, in that younger Cajuns are increasingly attracted to zydeco music for the same reasons that their elders dislike it: hard-driving sound, increasing emphasis on English lyrics, and incorporation of popular African American influences. As with their Anglo-American counterparts, young Cajuns are among the enthusiastic consumers of rap music, hip hop, and rhythm and blues that have shaped zydeco's development in recent years. Subsequently, increasing numbers of Cajuns will incorporate the work of popular zydeco artists into their music collections. One also must consider that many younger Cajun bands have borrowed from zydeco music both stylistically and in a superficial sense. For example, the Cajun musician Wayne Toups labels his hard-driving style (without the violin) "ZydeCajun." Other Cajun musicians occasionally perform songs while playing the accordion in a zydeco rhythm or integrate lyrics and themes from zydeco songs. There also have been examples of collaboration between zydeco and Cajun artists, primarily in the neutral setting of the commercial recording studio.

The increasing appreciation of zydeco by some Cajuns and continual mutual influences between zydeco and Cajun music must be contextualized by examining the complexity in racial segregation at contemporary venues for zydeco and Cajun performances. In a general sense, one can think of three levels of segregation involving the primary locations where zydeco and Cajun music are played: traditional bars and dance halls, restaurant/dance halls, and regional festivals.

In traditional bars and dance halls, patronage is still limited by race. This segregation is maintained by unspoken rules and previously discussed concerns about the racial "other." As I noted in an earlier study, Creoles are often only welcome at Cajun establishments if they come individually as the guest of a prominent Cajun patron.[39] Even in these instances, there can be tension. For example, in a recent incident in southwest Louisiana, many patrons at a Cajun bar became upset when a local zydeco musician attended a dance there in the company of a local Cajun band. Another establishment in the same town canceled an upcoming performance by the band because it was feared that the Creole musician would perform with them. On the other hand, Creole establishments, especially dance halls, are more tolerant of white visitors. However, given Cajun attitudes about African American-controlled space, the small number of white patrons at any given Creole dance hall is generally made up of out-of-state tourists.

In recent years, many combined restaurant/dance halls have been built to exploit the growing ethnic tourism industry in Louisiana. These cater to both local residents and tourists. However, nearly all of these emphasize Cajun music and attract only limited Creole patronage. This may be due to the fact that many Creoles are as unappreciative of Cajun music as Cajuns are of zydeco music.

Louisiana has many festivals that feature French Louisiana culture. Many of these originated with the start of a Cajun ethnic revival in the 1950s. As such, their primary goal has been to promote and preserve Cajun culture, and they traditionally have been Cajun-controlled events that attract a predominantly white audience. As the term Cajun has become popularized in popular culture, it increasingly has become a catchall term for cultural elements shared with Creoles.[40] Subsequently, there is considerable confusion surrounding French Louisiana culture. Zydeco musicians and their music are frequently referred to as Cajun. Creole musicians are often featured at Cajun festivals but as a subset of the Cajun population.[41] In response to this "Cajunization," Creoles initiated their own cultural revitalization movement in the 1980s. Creole efforts included the emergence of the organization C.R.E.O.L.E., with the specific goal to promote Creole culture and identity. This entailed an economic aspect, considering that ethnic tourism is a flourishing industry in Louisiana, and Creoles desire a share of the market. Like that of Cajuns, Creole revival involved the organization of festivals, some of which are openly viewed as Creole alternatives to Cajun-dominated public events.[42] In these settings, zydeco music is the most important ethnic marker to be showcased as symbolic of broader creole identity. Attendance by Cajuns is rare at festivals controlled and numerically dominated by African Americans. For example, the Plaisance zydeco festival is operated entirely by Creoles, occurs on the site of an African American-owned farming cooperative, and features zydeco music exclusively. Its annual attendance of more than 10,000 is perhaps only 10 percent white. Even younger Cajuns who appreciate zydeco music are not particularly inclined to attend such events for the same reasons that contribute to segregation of bars and dance halls. Therefore, as with Creole dance halls, most whites in attendance are out-of-state tourists or non-Cajuns living in nearby cities. Thus, in recent years, there seems to be a trend toward greater segregation of certain festivals linked to particular ethnic/racial associations.

Conclusion

Cajuns and Creoles are culturally similar but socially distinct. Their differing musical forms are rooted in traditional differences compounded by differential popular music influences throughout the twentieth century. Despite marked advances in race relations over the last generation and outward appearances of desegregation in broader society, less overt forms of segregation continue to divide French Louisiana society in many settings. This can be seen through unspoken but widely known rules and individual choices that result in forms of self-segregation. As it pertains to musical venues, this segregation may be attributed to different musical preferences with associated value judgments. However, there seems to be less tendency for younger Cajuns to racialize zydeco music in the same manner as do their elders. But they continue to racialize many of the settings where zydeco is performed. Thus, the primary factor that inhibits racial interaction in musical venues continues to be apprehension about entering spaces controlled by a racial "other" to whom race-related stereotypes are attributed.

Notes

1. Gwendolyn Midlo Hall, *Africans in Colonial Louisiana* (Baton Rouge: Louisiana State University Press, 1992).

2. James Dormon, ed., *Creoles of Color of the Gulf Coast South* (Knoxville: University of Tennessee Press, 1995).

3. Barry Ancelet, Jay Edwards, and Glen Pitre, *Cajun Country* (Jackson: University Press of Mississippi, 1990).

4. Carl Brasseaux, *The Founding of New Acadia* (Baton Rouge: Louisiana State University Press, 1987).

5. Rocky Sexton, *Cajuns, Germans, and Les Americains: A Historical Anthropology of Cultural and Demographic Transformations in Southwest Louisiana, 1880 to Present* (Ph.D. dissertation, University of Iowa, 1996).

6. James Dormon, *The People Called Cajuns* (Lafayette: University of Southwestern Louisiana, Center for Louisiana Studies, 1983).

7. Robert Kuhlken and Rocky Sexton, "The Geography of Zydeco Music," *Journal of Cultural Geography* 12(Fall/Winter 1991):27–38.

8. Malcolm Comeaux, "The Cajun Accordion," *The Louisiana Review* 7(1977):117–28.

9. Nicholas Spitzer, *Zydeco and Mardi Gras: Creole Identity and Performance Genres in Rural French Louisiana* (Ph.D. dissertation, University of Texas, 1986).

10. Barry Ancelet and Mathe Allain, *Travailler, C'est Trop Dur: The Tools of Cajun Music* (Lafayette, LA: Lafayette Natural History Museum Association, 1984).

11. Spitzer (1986); Kuhlken and Sexton (1991).

12. John Minton, "Houston Creoles and Zydeco: The Emergence of an African-American Urban Popular Style," *American Music* 14(1996): 480–532.

13. Rocky Sexton, "Rice Country Re-Visited," *Louisiana History* (forthcoming).

14. Barry Ancelet, "Zydeco/Zarico: The Term and the Tradition," in *Creoles of Color of the Gulf Coast South*, edited by J. Dormon (Knoxville: University of Tennessee Press, 1996), pp. 126–43.

15. Barry Ancelet, *Cajun Music: Its Origins and Developments* (Lafayette: University of Southwestern Louisiana, Center for Louisiana Studies, 1989).

16. Kuhlken and Sexton (1991).

17. Ancelet (1996).

18. Michael Tisserand, *The Kingdom of Zydeco* (New York: Arcade, 1998).

19. Ancelet (1996).

20. Minton (1996).

21. Barry Ancelet, "Introduction," in *Cajun Music and Zydeco*, edited by P. Gould (Baton Rouge: Louisiana State University Press, 1993).

22. Spitzer (1986), p. 301.

23. Spitzer (1986).

24. Carl Brasseaux, Claude Oubre, and Keith Fontenot, *Creoles of Color of the Bayou State* (Jackson: University Press of Mississippi, 1994).

25. Spitzer (1986); Joseph Jones, *The People of Frilot Cove: A Study of a Racial Hybrid Community in Rural South Central Louisiana*, (Ph.D. dissertation, Louisiana State University, 1950).

26. Spitzer (1986); Tisserand (1998).

27. Minton (1996).

28. Tisserand (1998).

29. Spitzer (1986).

30. Spitzer (1986); Tisserand (1998).

31. Frederik Barth, *Ethnic Groups and Boundaries: The Social Organization of Cultural Difference* (Boston: Little, Brown, 1969).

32. Jack Nachbar and Kevin Lause, *Popular Culture: An Introductory Text* (Bowling Green: Bowling Green State University Popular Press, 1992).

33. Rocky Sexton, "Passing a Good Time in Southwest Louisiana: An Ethnohistoric and Humanistic Approach to the Study of Cajun Bars/Clubs as Place." 1990. M.A. thesis, Department of Geography and Anthropology, Louisiana State University, Baton Rouge.

34. Reebee Garofalo, *Rockin' Out: Popular Music in the USA* (Boston: Allyn & Bacon, 1997), p. 12.

35. Garofalo (1997).

36. Garofalo (1997), p. 76.

37. Tisserand (1998), p. 6.

38. Garofalo (1997).

39. Sexton (1990).

40. Rocky Sexton, "Cajun Mardi Gras? Cultural Objectification and Symbolic Appropriation in a French Tradition." *Ethnology* (forthcoming).

41. Mark Mattern, "Let the Good Times Unroll: Music and Race Relations in Southwest Louisiana," *Black Music Research Journal* 17(1997):159–68.

42. Sylvie Dubois and Megan Melancon, "Creole Is, Creole Ain't," *Language in Society* (forthcoming).

Sexton:

1. How do Cajuns and Creoles make distinctions between themselves? How do they define self and other? What tools are used to make distinctions? How are these distinctions supported by sociohistorical context? What social structures help to sustain those distinctions?

2. Discuss how Creoles and Cajuns complicate a dichotomous conception of race and ethnic relations.

Drawing Conclusions—Part II

To suggest that racial identities are socially constructed implies that individuals and groups make use of various tools in order to claim, revise, challenge, or otherwise create an identity. Based on the articles in this part, what are some of the tools used in these efforts? In what ways are individuals and groups limited in their ability to construct their identities? Finally, if racial identity is socially constructed, does this mean that there is no such thing as an authentic or "true" identity?

PART III

African Americans since the 1960s: Gains, Losses, and Contested Social Policies

Over a half century ago, the Swedish economist Gunnar Myrdal oversaw the collection of a massive body of empirical data that was designed to assess in a most comprehensive way the circumstances of African Americans. Out of this project, *An American Dilemma* was published. This classic in race relations research revealed a wealth of information about the impact of a legacy of centuries of black oppression by whites. It also provided insights into the varied ways that the black community had sought to respond to discrimination and exploitation. The dilemma that defined black/white relations, from Myrdal's point of view, was that the nation's highest ideals, which included placing a premium on freedom and equality, flew in the face of the reality of a legacy of racial exploitation. Simply put, racial injustice constituted a refusal to live up to those ideals. Myrdal, as many critics have suggested, was overly optimistic in believing that whites would become increasingly uncomfortable with this dilemma and would takes steps to overcome it. Although it was an important attempt to capture the essence of race relations just before World War II, in light of the events of over a half century since he arrived at this conclusion, it is clear that Myrdal failed to appreciate how difficult it is to undo the past. He also underestimated the role that blacks would play in promoting social change.

Throughout the nation's history, African Americans have been the largest racial minority in the United States. They have been extremely consequential in shaping its political, economic, and cultural history. Therefore, it is not surprising that the relationship between blacks and whites establishes the template in which other racial minorities must be located. In other words, to understand race relations in this multiracial society, it is first necessary to ascertain the nature of black/white relations. It is also important to understand the evolution of the black community. Part III is devoted to precisely this task, looking at the status of African Americans three decades into the post-civil rights era.

In our Overview, we discussed the growth of the black middle class and, with that, the growing divide since the 1960s between blacks who are making it economically and those who are not. We begin here with Jennifer L. Hochschild's analysis of rich and poor blacks. One of the problems with attempts intended to determine how much progress African Americans have actually experienced in recent times is that it becomes increasingly difficult to generalize about the group as a whole. Rather, the role of social class divisions in the black community has become more pronounced, and the life circumstances and chances of African Americans increasingly depend not simply on their race but also on their particular class locations. Hochschild offers a snapshot of this situation in her review of various measures of well-being, including occupational status, educational attainment levels, income, and life expectancy. This essay is intended to contextualize those that follow.

Andrew Hacker examines the economic position of blacks by focusing on their income levels vis-à-vis their white counterparts. He looks at blacks as a whole, and not in terms of class differences within the black community. In addition to merely describing the persisting racial income gap, Hacker asks how much of the disparity between black and white incomes is due to racial bias or to other factors, such as economic restructuring. Although he concedes that various nonracially specific factors must be seen as causes in perpetuating the income gap, he also contends that it would be a serious mistake to conclude that racism no longer plays a role in maintaining this disparity. Indeed, he sees it playing considerably more than a residual role. As such, his essay offers empirical evidence refuting those—recall Dinesh D'Souza in the Overview—who claim that we can now speak about the end of racism.

The next three articles do take cognizance of the class divide in the African American community. William Julius Wilson explores the dilemmas of many poor and working-class blacks in finding work, Cheryl L. Cole and Samantha King look at the meaning of the allure of professional sports for many young black males, and Sharon M. Collins examines the world of successful blacks who have entered the corporate hierarchy. Wilson's contribution is based on a research project conducted in his research "laboratory" of many years, Chicago's South Side, one of the largest urban enclaves of African Americans in the country. He observes the precipitous decline of manufacturing jobs in the area since the 1960s and describes the deleterious impact of the disappearance of work on individuals and the community at large. Without claiming that racism does not play a role in the difficulties many blacks have in finding employment, a central focus of Wilson's account has to do with the loss of jobs due to deindustrialization. Cole and King look at poor young people rather than adults. They do so in a very different way, analyzing the portrayal of aspiring basketball players who are featured in the highly acclaimed film *Hoop Dreams*. Although their interest is in the way blacks are portrayed by whites, and the ways blacks respond to those portrayals, they highlight themes dovetailing with those of Wilson. Professional sport is a funnel through which very few make it. For the vast majority of those left behind, the future is frequently that described by Wilson.

Collins, looking at the other end of the stratification system, examines the world of black executives in white-controlled corporations. Although in many ways these executives look like models of success, Collins notes not only that their achievements have been hard-won, but she also discovered that blacks confront many problems and challenges to their positions that whites need not confront. A sense that they need to deal with a lingering resentment on the part of whites who might think they have been accorded special treatment or a realization that in some ways they have not been fully accepted by their white peers is a part of everyday life. Collins describes the ways these executives cope with the stresses brought about by their life in the corporation.

C. Eric Lincoln and Lawrence H. Mamiya shift the focus of Part III to the institutional structure of the black community. Specifically, they seek to assess the continuing relevance of what traditionally has been the most powerful institution in the black community: the church. Noting the prominent role the church played during the civil rights movement (think, for example, of the importance of the organization headed by Martin Luther King, Jr., the Southern Christian Leadership Conference), Lincoln and Mamiya ask whether the church has a similarly important role to play in the post-civil rights era. They proceed to suggest some of the new challenges the church confronts, but they answer their own question by suggesting some of the ways it will continue to have an important cultural and political role in the twenty-first century.

The three concluding essays in this section examine public policy as it relates to black civil rights. More specifically, they look at various initiatives on the part of the federal government to devise social policies intended to remedy inequities and injustices inherited from the past. Although a variety of policies have proven to be highly controversial, including court-mandated busing to achieve school integration, certainly the most controversial program today is affirmative action. Two articles are devoted to affirmative action, in part because it is evident that not only is it important, but it is also little understood. John David Skrentny has perhaps done more than anyone to help us understand the history behind affirmative action. In this essay, he sketches a brief overview of the origins of affirmative action plans, noting that for a variety of reasons, what ultimately emerged as policy was not necessarily what anyone in the formative period intended, particularly during the writing of the Civil Rights Act of 1964 (where the main legislative basis for affirmative action was articulated). This is the irony of affirmative action. Stephen Steinberg offers a more polemical essay in which he contends that during the 1960s liberals tended to be supportive of this interventionist form of social policy. However, more recently—especially during and since the conservative climate of the Reagan years—they have turned their backs on such activist federal policy. In particular, they have repudiated the race-specific nature of affirmative action. The result, in his view, is that the achievements of the civil rights movement are under assault.

The third article on social policy, by Kevin Fox Gotham, turns to federal housing policy, and specifically to two related programs designed to provide affordable housing to low- and moderate-income families: Section 235 and Section 8. These programs also have been seen as tools to promote residential integration. As alternatives to public housing, which became equated in the public's mind with black ghetto housing, these programs made use of private landlords and thus made possible the integration of inner-city residents into other neighborhoods. However, both programs generated considerable resistance from whites hostile to residential integration. Based on a case study of Kansas City, Missouri, Gotham reveals not simply that the results have been far from successful; in addition, he indicates how they were in part responsible for the perpetuation of racial and class segregation. Collectively, these three essays raise serious questions about what role government will play in the future in attempting to remedy racial inequities.

15

Rich and Poor African Americans

Jennifer L. Hochschild

The impression arose that the Negro community might be dividing. A middle class was clearly consolidating and growing, and yet the overall indicators continued to worsen, not precipitously but steadily. These two things could not be true unless a third fact—that things were falling apart at the bottom—was also true. And that meant trouble in the Northern slums.

—*Daniel P. Moynihan, 1967*

As Daniel Moynihan pointed out almost three decades ago, understanding the African American class structure requires us to attend to four phenomena: the "overall indicators" of relative positions held by blacks and whites; the "consolidating and growing" middle class; the "falling apart at the bottom"; and the fact that "the Negro community . . . [is] dividing." In conjunction, these phenomena "mean . . . trouble in the Northern slums"—but not only there, and not only trouble.

The Overall Indicators

African Americans are in many, but not all, ways better off than their forebears were. Whether they are also better off in comparison to white Americans depends on what is measured and how it is measured. Let us consider, respectively, arenas of unambiguous improvement, ambiguous improvement, and deterioration.

Unambiguous Improvements

African Americans' average occupational status has improved over the last few decades no matter how it is measured. Table 15.1 shows changes in blacks' and whites' "socio-economic index score," which ranges from 7 for domestic servants and day laborers to 74 for professionals. All four race and gender groups enjoyed higher job statuses in 1980 than in 1940. In addition, blacks' job status improved relative to whites' status among both men and (especially) women.[1] The ratio of black to white men's occupational status rose from .53 to .72; the corresponding rise for women was from .36 to .84.

For years of schooling, too, the results are unambiguous. In 1940 whites averaged about nine years of education and blacks about six.

Table 15.1

Average Job Status for Employed Adults, by Race and Gender, 1940–1980

	1940	1960	1980
Socio-economic Index			
Black men	16	21	31
Black women	13	21	36
White men	30	36	40
White women	36	39	43

Source: Farley and Allen (1987: 264–265).

In the succeeding fifty years, whites gained over three years and African Americans about five. Thus African Americans' absolute gain in years of formal education is large, and the relative gap between the races has declined from three years to one year.[2] Fewer students of either race drop out of high school now than did twenty years ago, and the decline in dropping out is steeper among blacks than among whites.[3]

What children learn in school matters more than how many years they sit in a classroom. Here too improvement in the "overall indicators" is clear. Blacks always score lower than whites on nationwide standardized tests, regardless of the subject, students' age, or test year. But the racial gap is getting smaller. Whereas, for example, white students' reading and mathematics scores improved somewhat between 1971 and 1990, African American students of all ages showed significant improvements. A weaker version of the same pattern obtains for science and civics. Thus the gap between whites' and blacks' proficiency in all four fields diminished.[4]

Finally, blacks are more involved in the formal political system than they were four decades ago. Barely one-tenth of southern blacks could vote for the president in 1952, but by 1984 about 55 percent did. The proportion of all voters who are black increased from 8 percent in 1964 to 10 percent in 1992.[5] Largely as a consequence, the number of black elected officials has risen from the ludicrous number of thirty-three in 1941 to over eight thousand in 1993, changing the proportion of elected officials who are black from a minute fraction to almost 2 percent.[6]

Mixed Results

Despite occupational, educational, and political gains, African Americans are not unambiguously better off than they used to be. Consider incomes: in 1967 black per capita income was about $5,400 (in 1992 dollars); the corresponding figure for whites was about $10,100. In 1992 blacks received $9,300 and whites $16,000.[7] Thus African Americans clearly have more money than their parents had. But are their incomes now more equal to whites'? In relative terms, yes, since the ratio of black incomes to white incomes increased from .53 in 1967 to .58 in 1992. In absolute terms, no, since the discrepancy in income rose from $4,700 to $6,700.[8]

Measures of wealth give similarly mixed results. The mean net worth for white households in 1991 was $112,000, compared with a paltry $27,900 for black households. But black households held only 4 to 21 percent of the net worth of white households in the 1960s and 1970s, compared with 25 to 33 percent as much at present.[9] African Americans remain dramatically less wealthy than whites, but the gap is slowly closing.

African Americans, like whites, are healthier than they used to be and live longer, as Table 15.2. shows. Black women can expect to live longer than white men; thus several decades ago "the gender gap in the life span became larger than the racial gap." However, "the racial gap in mortality, after declining between [the] 1940s and the 1960s, has not gotten much smaller. . . . An extrapolation of current trends implies that the death rates of blacks will continue to be higher than those of whites into the future."[10]

Table 15.2

Life Expectancies at Birth, by Race and Gender, 1940–1990 (in years)

	1940	1970	1990
Black men	51	61	65
Black women	69	77	78
White men	62	68	72
White women	82	81	83

Source: Farley (1992: chap. 1, fig. 1).

Mobility across generations is yet another overall indicator that cuts both ways. Among white men, those born during the 1920s were upwardly mobile compared with their fathers; those born during the Great Depression have moved down as well as up the mobility ladder; and those born after 1936 are on balance downwardly mobile. In contrast, "successive cohorts of black men have had higher levels of occupational status relative to their fathers." Furthermore, young white men are not reaching the job levels that their background and education would lead them to expect; older white men and black men of all ages are. However—and herein lies the ambiguity—"intergenerational gains in status among blacks have been consistently lower than those enjoyed by any cohorts of white men at any age."[11]

Persistent Racial Disparities

African Americans are unambiguously gaining on white Americans in job status, education, and political involvement; they are or are not gaining economically and demographically, depending on how one interprets the data. But by some measures they are unambiguously losing ground.

Many people (some of whom are not real estate agents) consider owning one's home to be a central component of the American dream. Fewer blacks than whites own their own homes, and the disparity is growing. In 1950, 35 percent of nonwhite and 57 percent of white heads of households were homeowners; forty years later, only 9 percent more nonwhites and 11 percent more whites were. A smaller fraction of African Americans owned houses in 1990 than did whites in 1920. Houses owned by blacks are worth on average barely more than half of houses owned by whites, and the value of the former, but not of the latter, may be declining.[12]

Blacks also remain about half as likely as Latinos or Asians to live in suburbs. And despite their consistent preference for residential integration, blacks in almost all central cities remain highly segregated from non-Hispanic whites.[13] They are more racially isolated from whites than are Latinos and Asians, and high incomes or levels of education make it no easier for African Americans to move into white neighborhoods.[14]

Finally, African Americans are much more likely to become and remain unemployed than are white Americans, and the disparity is growing. Through the 1940s and early 1950s, the ratio of nonwhite to white unemployment was below 2; in the twenty years after 1955, it hovered around 2.2. But since 1977 the black/white unemployment ratio has risen as high as 2.4. Even if the earliest ratio partly reflects hidden unemployment among farm laborers, we have no grounds for supposing that the ratios are moving or will move toward equality. Jobless blacks also stay unemployed longer than jobless whites do.[15]

Thus one can tell almost any story one chooses about whether African Americans are moving toward parity with whites in their ability to pursue their dreams. They are gaining in nonmaterial resources, perhaps holding their own with regard to money, and losing in living conditions. Is that an improvement? Probably, compared with even more consistent deterioration during the previous half-century, but not certainly.

What that equivocal conclusion implies is the need to disaggregate. African Americans can pursue their dreams in some arenas of

Table 15.3

Household Income, by Race, 1967–1992 (in constant 1992 dollars; percent making each amount)

	1967		1977		1987		1992	
	Black	*White*	*Black*	*White*	*Black*	*White*	*Black*	*White*
0–$15,000	45.6	23.4	41.9	22.0	41.8	20.5	42.7	21.6
$15,000–35,000	38.3	39.5	35.3	33.3	32.4	31.0	31.5	31.8
$35,000–50,000	10.2	19.8	13.0	20.1	12.4	18.5	12.8	17.7
Over $50,000	5.8	16.8	9.9	24.4	13.5	30.0	13.0	28.9
Total	100.0	100.0	100.0	100.0	100.0	100.0	100.0	100.0

Source: U.S. Bureau of the Census (1993a: B-3, B-4).

Note: Income is measured before taxes; it includes cash transfers but not in-kind benefits. These are the earliest and latest years, respectively, for which these data are available.

life better than in others. Similarly, some African Americans can pursue any dream more readily than can others. Let us turn, then, to the other trends that Moynihan identified in 1967 in order to make sense of the "overall indicators."

The Middle Class— Consolidating and Growing

Ebony magazine recently celebrated the "new Black middle class" as "young, vibrant, on the go, with new interests and orientations, and a bumper crop of MBA's and high-tech managers." It distinguished these "salaried workers in high-level occupations that serve the society at large" from "the old Black middle class" of "ministers, educators, doctors and small businessmen who served primarily the Black community."[16] It is this new middle class, firmly if uneasily planted in what whites consider to be the mainstream of society, that comprises most of the best-off third of blacks.[17]

Improving Status

The growth of the black middle class is most simply described in terms of income.

Table 15.3 shows the changes over the past three decades. The first and second lines of the table show that the proportion of blacks who are poor or almost poor has declined by almost 10 percent, but the third and fourth lines are of most interest here. The third line shows a slightly larger percentage of African Americans now enjoying middle-class incomes than was the case in 1967; the opposite is the case for whites. The fourth line shows over twice as many well-off blacks now as twenty-five years ago, a proportionally greater rise among blacks than among whites. In all, one in four black households, compared with just under half of white households, now receives an income that provides comforts or luxuries.

African Americans who earn enough to acquire comforts or luxuries also hold more wealth than other African Americans, not only absolutely but also in comparison with whites. The median black household owns just over one-tenth as much as the median white household, but households in the top two quintiles of black income own up to 40 percent as much as white households earning a comparable amount.[18]

Measures of job status show the same pattern: the black middle class has grown considerably and is slowly gaining on the white middle class, even though it remains far smaller. In 1950, 5 percent of employed blacks were professionals or managers; by 1990, about 20 percent were. Another 20 percent held clerical or sales positions in 1990, also up from 5 percent in 1950. Thus up to two-fifths of black workers, depending on how stringently one defines a middle-class occupation, are in the middle class.[19]

An increasing number of African Americans also have middle-class educations, although here too the proportions lag behind those of whites. In 1960, 3 percent of black and 8 percent of white adults had completed college; by 1992, the comparable figures were 12 and 22 percent. In the lower grades, black students from "advantaged" communities are gaining on "advantaged" whites in their reading ability. The proportion of students taking the Scholastic Assessment Test (SAT) who are black is rising, and the disparity in SAT scores between whites and blacks has dropped since 1972.[20]

Mobility across Generations

One has not really succeeded in America unless one can pass the chance for success on to one's children. Until the 1960s even those few African Americans who comprised the old black middle class had great difficulty in doing so. A massive survey in 1962 found race to be "such a powerful variable that even the more modest of the class effects that stratified whites were cancelled by the skin color of blacks." Blacks, in other words, "experienced a perverse sort of egalitarianism"—neither the disadvantages of poverty nor the advantages of wealth made much difference in what they could achieve or pass on to their children.[21] Discrimination swamped everything else.

Between 1962 and 1973, however, class position began to affect mobility for blacks as it had always done for whites. "Upward mobility . . . was greatest among [black] men from the most advantaged socioeconomic back-

grounds"; well-off black men thus could begin for the first time in American history to expect their success to persist and cumulate.[22] Since 1973 these trends have continued, although less dramatically.

Thus the black middle class is growing, is narrowing the gap between itself and the white middle class, and is increasingly stable across generations. Roughly one-third of black families can reasonably be called middle class, compared with well below one-tenth a few decades ago and about half of white families now. The best-off third of blacks, in short, is vastly better off than the best-off third of blacks has ever been before in American history.[23]

The Poor—Falling Apart at the Bottom

Unchanging or Deteriorating Status

No sentient being can doubt the existence of a group of deeply impoverished African Americans. In 1959, 55 percent of blacks and 18 percent of whites had incomes below the poverty line; in 1992, the figures were, respectively, 33 and 12 percent. The ratio of black to white poverty has remained at 3—hardly a victory in the war on racially disproportionate poverty. Absolute numbers tell the same story: there are now about four million fewer poor whites than thirty years ago, but 686,000 *more* poor blacks.[24]

It is bad enough to be poor, but it is worse to be deeply poor or poor for a long time. One-quarter of black children, compared with 6 percent of white children, lived below half of the poverty line in 1988. (The number of destitute children declined from 1960 to 1980 but has risen since then.)[25] Black children's poverty is long as well as deep: during the past twenty years about one-third of black children remained poor for six or more years, and the number is slowly rising.[26]

Poor African Americans lack wealth as well as incomes. Although even the poorest fifth of whites have a median net worth of $10,300, the net worth of the poorest fifth of blacks is 0.[27] Furthermore, blacks with little wealth are even less likely to attain any than poor whites. Seventy-seven percent of black men in the poorest quintile of wealth holders in 1966, compared with 57 percent of comparable white men, were still in the poorest quintile in 1981.[28]

Measures of occupation, or lack thereof, tell an equally dismal story. An increasing number of men, especially black men, have no job at all. In 1960, 17 percent of civilian men of both races were unemployed or looking for jobs; by 1993, an additional 7 percent of white men and 14 percent of black men were out of the labor force. In 1968 four-fifths of poorly educated central-city black male residents held jobs; by 1992 fewer than half worked. Barely a third held full-time jobs. In the poorest neighborhoods of large cities, four-fifths of young male high school dropouts have no work.[29] As a consequence, between 1967 and 1992 an increasing proportion of black men, compared with a decreasing proportion of white men, reported receiving no income.[30]

Even holding a job does not ensure an escape from poverty. In 1992, 15 percent of African American and 6 percent of white job holders did not earn enough to get above the poverty line. To be a single mother of preschool children is itself a full-time job. But of those single mothers with young children who also worked full-time outside the home, one-fifth of blacks and one-tenth of whites were rewarded for their extraordinary efforts with incomes below the poverty line.[31]

As those figures suggest, even when they work blacks still hold a disproportionate share of the least desirable jobs. In 1950, 61 percent of black men and 72 percent of black women workers were service workers, domestics, laborers, or farm laborers, whereas 25 percent or fewer of white men and women workers were similarly employed. In 1990, about one-third of both male and female black workers were service workers or laborers, compared with two-tenths of white workers.[32]

Poor blacks come no closer to achieving their dreams of a nice place to live than of a decent income or job. Television has shown all of us the filthy, burned-out blocks of northern cities and the sewerless, tarpaper shacks of southern countrysides, and the cold data of government surveys confirm the hot images of television stories. One-third of poor black households, compared with one-seventh of poor white households, lived in substandard housing in 1985.[33] To be deemed substandard, housing must, among other criteria, show "evidence of rats" (57 percent of such units were occupied by Latinos and blacks in 1985), have "holes in the floor" (51 percent were occupied by Latinos and blacks), or have "exposed wiring" (33 percent were occupied by Latinos and blacks).[34]

Poor African Americans are increasingly likely to live among other people with such dismal housing conditions. In the 100 largest central cities, the proportion of poor non-Hispanic blacks living in neighborhoods where more than 40 percent of their neighbors were also poor rose from 28 percent in 1970 to 42 percent in 1990.[35] A likely consequence of being poor in a poor neighborhood is attending a low-quality school, with predictable consequences. In 1988 about 30 percent of poor black eighth graders were "below basic" in their reading proficiency, and about 37 percent had less than basic math proficiency. (Seven percent fewer poor whites were "below basic" readers, and 4 percent fewer were "below basic" in math.)[36] Fully half of the non-Hispanic black (and white) adults living in extreme poverty areas of large cities have not completed high school.[37]

Another likely consequence of being poor in a poor neighborhood is being a victim of crime. On average, Americans are safer now than they were twenty years ago. But suburban and rural dwellers are becoming safer from theft and household crime (although not from violence) at a faster ra e than are urban residents, who over the san e period were increasingly likely to be people of color. The ratio of urban to suburban theft increased from 1.0 to 1.3 between 1973 and 1992, and the ratio of urban to suburban household crime increased from 1.2 to 1.6. City dwellers have become even more likely than rural residents to suffer from crime; the victimization ratios rose from 1.4 to 1.6 for theft, and from 1.6 to 1.9 for household crimes.[38]

Mobility across Generations

For the well-off, being able to pass on one's status to one's children is a critical element of the American dream. For the poor, *not* passing on one's status is equally critical. But it is an element of the dream that eludes many poor African Americans. In 1962, 43 percent of the grown sons of white men who had held "lower manual" jobs held similar jobs; by 1973, that figure had declined by 3 percent. Among blacks, the decline was steeper but the absolute level remained much higher: 71 percent of laborers' sons in 1962 and 61 percent in 1973 were also laborers. One-third of a 1978 sample of young adults were black, but almost half of the bottom quintile were.[39] Finally, parents who are poor enough to need welfare are disproportionately likely to have dependent children; the probability that the daughter of a black recipient of aid to families with dependent children (AFDC) has a child and receives welfare herself is .486, compared with a probability of .136 for the daughter of a nonrecipient.[40]

The Dividing Community

The gap between haves and have-nots widened strikingly; and the most rapid widening was among Negroes—between those outside the slums who were rising, beginning finally to cash in on the American dream, and those still in the hard-core ghetto, on limited rations of income an l hope.... Not only dis :ance is building up between the two poles, but t :nsion as well—as with electrodes approaching a sparking point.

—*Walter Williams, 1967*

Although these words depict Cleveland from 1960 to 1965, they could, slightly modernized, be my own. Growing inequality is not the problem. After all, only a fanatical egalitarian would oppose the move from equally shared poverty to inequality caused by the fact that some have gained wealth. But polarization—improving conditions for some accompanied by or at the expense of deteriorating conditions for others—*is* the problem, and not only in Cleveland.

We can begin to examine this point by comparing the share of aggregate income held by various fractions of the population at different times (Table 15.4). Three points are important with regard to the table: first, rich blacks have always held a larger share of their race's income than have rich whites, and poor blacks have always held a smaller share of their race's income than have poor whites. Second, the disparities within both races are increasing. Third, and most important here, the income disparity among blacks is increasing at a faster rate. The Gini indices summarize that phenomenon, and the rest of the table demonstrates it more precisely: the richest fifth of whites lost, then gained income and have ended up 3 percent better off than they were forty years ago. The poorest fifth of whites gained, then lost income and are now 10 percent worse off. African Americans followed the same trajectories, but at a faster rate. By 1992 the poorest quintile had lost 30 percent of its meager 1947 income, and the richest quintile had gained 8 percent over its comparatively high 1947 income.[41]

Table 15.5 translates abstract shares of aggregate income into actual dollar amounts.

Table 15.4

Share of Families' Aggregate Income Held by Richest and Poorest Fifths, by Race, 1947–1992

	1947		1967		1987		1992	
	Nonwhite	White	Black	White	Black	White	Black	White
Poorest fifth	4.3	5.5	4.7	5.8	3.3	5.1	3.0	4.9
Richest fifth	45.3	42.5	44.6	40.9	47.7	43.1	48.8	43.8
Gini index	.406	.366	.400	.349	.447	.380	.462	.389

Sources: 1947: U.S. Bureau of the Census (1989: 42–43); 1967–1991: U.S. Bureau of the Census (1993a: B-13, B-14).

In the first period the richest and poorest quintiles gained equally as a proportion of their previous income, although the wealthy gained much more in absolute dollars. Blacks gained proportionally almost as much as whites, but their actual incomes grew much less. Thus this period can be interpreted as moving either toward equal overall improvement or away from racial and class equality, depending on which set of figures one looks at.

The second period allows for no ambiguity of interpretation. The poor, especially among African Americans, lost substantial ground, while the wealthy barely held their own. This was a period of unambiguous growth in inequality.

The third period, from 1983 to 1992, saw yet another step away from equality, into polarization. The poorest fifth of African Americans *lost* almost as large a share of their income as the richest fifth *gained* of theirs. The wealthiest fifth gained a large amount in absolute terms as well. Well-off blacks did as well proportionally, although not absolutely, as well-off whites. Poor whites gained a little, whereas well-off whites surged ahead. In short, whites became more unequal; blacks polarized.[42]

Table 15.5

Income Gains of Top and Bottom Quintiles of Families, by Race, 1967–1992 (in 1992 dollars)

	Black		White	
	Income Gained	% Increase over Period	Income Gained	% Increase over Period
1967–1972				
Bottom fifth percentile	$711	13%	$1,619	16%
Top fifth percentile	7,064	14	10,797	15
1973–1982				
Bottom fifth percentile	−1,426	−23	−1,402	−11
Top fifth percentile	1,098	2	2,953	3
1983–1992				
Bottom fifth percentile	−558	−12	570	5
Top fifth percentile	8,950	15	12,966	15

Source: U.S. Bureau of the Census (1993a: B-13, B-14).

Table 15.6

Crime Victimization, by Race and Class, 1976–1992 (per 1,000 people)

	Violence				Theft			
	1976	1981	1986	1992	1976	1981	1986	1992
Total	32.6	35.3	28.1	32.1	96.1	85.1	67.5	59.2
Blacks								
Poor	50.5	57.3	44.4	60.1	64.5	71.4	55.3	59.2
Well-off	40.5	34.2	19.6	35.0	137.6	116.4	82.8	70.2
Whites								
Poor	39.1	45.2	46.0	44.7	81.5	74.7	69.1	60.3
Well-off	26.6	28.2	19.9	20.7	117.8	104.1	75.9	70.0

Source: U.S. Department of Justice (1994: 247, 267), and earlier years of the same volume.
Note: "Violence" includes rape, robbery, and assault (but not homicide, which represents about 1% of all violent crime). "Theft" includes personal larceny. No comparable data are available for "household crimes," which include burglary, larceny, and motor vehicle theft. These are the earliest and latest years, respectively, for which these data are available.

Other indicators of well-being show the same pattern of growing polarization between well-off and poor African Americans. Consider housing, for example: in 1980 the index of residential dissimilarity between classes was higher among blacks (.50) than among whites (.39). Residential separation by class had increased slightly among African Americans during the 1970s, even though it decreased slightly among whites, Asians, and Latinos.[43] Or jobs: white employers penalize black applicants for low-skill jobs for being black even after all of their specific traits are taken into consideration, but they reward black applicants for high-skill jobs for being black. Furthermore, African American men in the top fourth of the occupational status distribution have seen a consistent improvement in the prestige of and rewards accruing to their jobs over the past two decades. But the job quality of those in the bottom quartile has fallen from their already very low starting points.[44] Even controlling for experience, the wage gap between black and white women with twelve or fewer years of education grew between 1973 and 1989, whereas it declined between black and white women with a college education.[45]

Polarization is also occurring in the likelihood of being a victim of crime, as Table 15.6 shows. The number of well-off Americans who are victims of violence is steadily *decreasing*, while the number of poor Americans who are victimized by violence is steadily *increasing*. The pattern holds for both blacks and whites, although the former are always more likely to be victims of violence than are the latter. Poor blacks not only began the period with the highest rates of victimization from violence, but they are also suffering from the greatest increase. (The pattern is different for theft. The well-off used to be dramatically more likely than the poor to suffer from theft; they are now only slightly more likely to be victimized, and all groups suffer from less theft now than they did two decades ago. Here is a pattern to celebrate.)

African Americans are becoming more disparate politically and demographically as well as economically and socially. Through the 1960s and 1970s, poorly educated blacks outvoted poorly educated whites (mainly because black women voted at very high rates). But by the late 1980s that disparity was reversed. Furthermore, although overall participation rates dropped from the 1960s to the 1980s, the decline in voting among the poorly educated was greater than the corresponding decline among the well-educated. Well-educated blacks vote, campaign, organize, and petition at the same rates as well-educated whites. Thus the worst-off in general are losing political influence, and the worst-off blacks in particular are losing the most.[46]

Even birth and death are increasingly affected by the interaction of race and class. "The effects of age, family structure, and socioeconomic variables on age at first childbirth are stronger among blacks than among whites.... An increased internal stratification of the black population [with regard to child-bearing] may be taking place." At the other end of life, in the two decades after 1960, the disparity in mortality rates between well-educated and poorly educated black men doubled. It rose by 30 percent between well-educated and poorly educated black women. (The growth in disparity was the same for white as for black men but lower for white than for black women.)[47]

Improvement at the top combined with worsening at the bottom is a disaster for the American dream. It radically undermines the first and second tenets and raises the stakes for the third and fourth. It adds class conflict within races to racial conflict across and within classes. Polarization is especially disastrous for the dream if it is concentrated in the race that is already most tenuously attached to the dominant ideology. And that is what is occurring.

Notes

1. See also Wright et al. (1992).

2. Farley (1992: chap. 2, fig 1).

3. Hauser and Phang (1993:15–21); Harrison and Bennett (1995: 170–72).

4. US Department of Education (1990; 1994: 15, 19).

5. Jaynes and Williams (1989: 230); Farley (1992: chap. 7). Rosenstone and Hanson (1993: 219–24) explain the rise, and recent fall, of black voting.

6. Joint Center for Political and Economic Studies (1994).

7. U.S. Bureau of the Census (1993a: B–38).

8. See Jencks (1991: 46–47) and Rae et al. (1981: 104–29) on relative and absolute comparisons. Comparing blacks' and whites' earnings over the past few decades, Card and Krueger (1993: 85–85) and Sorensen (1991) both find convergence before the 1980s, but no change and divergence, respectively, since 1980.

9. Data for 1991 are in U.S. Bureau of the Census (1994: xiii); see also Oliver and Shapiro (1989); O'Hare (1983). Data for the 1960s and 1970s are in Terrell (1971: 364); Browne (1974: 35); Birnbaum and Weston (1974: 105); James Smith (1975: 360–61); Henretta (1979: 72); Sobol (1979: 586); Blau and Graham (1990); Soltow (1972). Jianakoplos and Menchik (1992: 16, table 15) and Steckel and Krishnan (1992) analyze changes in wealth by race over time.

An often-cited study for the Federal Reserve Board (Kennickell and Shack-Marquez 1992) contradicts the Census Bureau on changes in median net worth by race during the 1980s. But it appears to have changed its definition of "non-white" between 1983 and 1989 so I do not report those figures.

10. Farley (1992: chap. 1, pp. 4–5).

11. Hauser (1990: 15–16, 19–26); see also Grusky and DiPrete (1990: 624–25).

12. On homeowners, see U.S. Bureau of the Census (1993b: 724); Wachter and Megbolugbe (1992). On housing values, see Farley and Allen (1987: 291–92); Kennickell and Shack-Marquez (1992: 10–11); U.S. Bureau of the Census (1986: 14, 22; 1994: 3, 9).

13. Massey and Denton (1988: 605; 1993). On preferences for desegregated neighborhoods, see,

for example, Farley et al. (1993); CBS News/*New York Times* (1978: vars. 27, 43).

14. Farley and Allen (1987: 139–50); Massey and Denton (1987; 1988); Jaynes and Williams (1989: 140–46); Alba and Logan (1993); Harrison and Bennett (1995: 157–64).

15. Data on unemployment derived from *Economic Report of the President* (1994: 314); General Accounting Office (1994:19–20).

16. *Ebony* (1987: 27). Throughout this book, I use the term "class" to refer to points along a continuum of stratification rather than to dichotomous categories of owner and worker. My reasons are pragmatic: that is how most data are organized and how most Americans think of social divisions. I also mostly ignore, as not material for my purposes, the issue of whether blacks mean the same thing by "middle class" as do whites. See Williams (1964: 251); Jackman and Jackman (1983: 22–41, 81–86); A. Wade Smith (1985); Landry (1987); Boston (1988); Vanneman and Cannon (1987: 225–56); and Stricker (1982) on the latter point.

17. Six in ten blacks held jobs serving their own community in 1960; four in ten did a decade later (Hout 1986; see also Landry 1987).

18. U.S. Bureau of the Census (1994: xiii). See also U.S. Bureau of the Census (1986: 5); Oliver and Shapiro (1989:12); Wolff (1993: 19).

19. In 1950 about 20% of whites were professionals or managers, and another fifth held clerical or sales jobs. In 1990 three-tenths of whites were in each category (Ferleger and Mandle 1991: 6).

20. U.S. Bureau of the Census (1993b: 153); Jones (1987: 7–8); U.S. Department of Education (1993:54, 244).

21. Quotations from Hout (1984: 308); and Hogan and Featherman (1978: 101). See also Siegel (1965); Blau and Duncan (1967); Duncan (1969).

22. Hout (1984: 308); see also Featherman and Hauser (1976; 1978); Hogan and Featherman (1978). Class origins of white men began to have *less* effect on their outcomes during this period than they did earlier. There are no data on women. For a less sanguine view, see Oliver and Glick (1982).

23. Smith and Welch (1989) give the most optimistic recent assessment of the growth of the black middle class.

24. U.S. Bureau of the Census (1993c: 2–3).

25. Eggebeen and Lichter (1991: 809); see also Rodgers and Rodgers (1991: 352). A mother and three children living under 50% of the poverty line have less than $7,000 a year to spend.

26. About 5% of the white children are poor for six or more years (Duncan and Rodgers 1991: 543). See also Bane and Ellwood (1986: 17, 21); Ruggles (1989: 19); Ashworth et al. (1994: 673–74).

27. U.S. Bureau of the Census (1994: xiii; 1986: 5).

28. Jianakoplos and Menchik (1992: tables 6, 7).

29. *Economic Report of the President* (1994: 312). Women are moving in the opposite direction; in 1960, 48% of black women and 36% of white women were in the labor force, whereas in 1993, 58% of both races were working or seeking work. Kasarda (1995) gives the best and most recent treatment of the structural causes of rising black unemployment.

30. In 1967, 11.8% of black men and 7.1% of white men reported no income. In 1992, the comparable figures were 12.7% and 4.4% (U.S. Bureau of the Census 1993a: B–28, B–29).

31. U.S. Bureau of the Census (1993c: 85, 86).

32. Ferleger and Mandle (1991:6).

33. Lazere and Leonard (1989: 15); see also Lazere et al. (1991: 24); Leonard and Lazere (1992) for later years.

34. Lazere and Leonard (1989: 15).

35. Kasarda (1993: 266–68); see also Nathan and Dommel (1987: A–2); Jargowsky and Bane (1991: 252–53); Danziger and Gottschalk (1987: 213–14). Nathan and Adams (1989) and Ledebur and Barnes (1992) show that the disparities between central cities and their suburbs have grown steadily and sharply since 1970.

36. Virtually no well-off students of either race were below basic in math or reading proficiency (Burbridge 1991: 7, 9). In the mid-1980s poor urban black students at all ages read better than their predecessors did, but the two youngest

groups (ages nine and thirteen) were no longer gaining on poor urban whites (Jones 1987: 7–8).

37. Kasarda (1993: 272–73). In 1970, however, three-quarters of black and white residents of severely poor neighborhoods were high school dropouts.

38. Data from U.S. Department of Justice (1994a: 16–18); 1973 and 1992 are the first and last years for which these data are available. DiIulio (1989) portrays the implications of these data in one representative city.

39. Data for 1962 and 1973 are from Featherman and Hauser (1978: 89, 326); 1978 data are from Cohen and Tyree (1986).

40. The corresponding problem for white daughters of recipients and nonrecipients are .261 and .066 (Gottschalk et al. 1994: 106; see also McLanahan 1988: 12–14; Gottschalk 1992).

41. See also Levy and Michel (1991); Karoly (1993: 45, 64–65); Villemez and Wiswell (1978).

42. See also Hochschild (1988:177–81); Lichter and Eggebeen (1993: tables 4, 5); Morris et al. (1994:212–15).

43. Massey and Eggers (1990: 1170–74).

44. Braddock and McPartland (1987: 16–17); Hauser (1990:24–25).

45. Card and Lemieux (1993: table 5). Among men, both well-educated and poorly-educated blacks lost wages compared with similar white men over this period. Darity and Myers (1993:8–12) show polarization by education in the labor force participation rate, especially among black men.

46. Olsen (1970); Greeley (1974); Farley (1992: chap. 7, 15–17); Kleppner (1982: 114–22); Nie et al. (1988:11–14, fig. 3).

47. On births, see Hogan and Kitagawa (1985: 829); on deaths, see Pappas et al. (1993:106). See also Menchik (1993: 435).

References

Alba, Richard, and John Logan (1993) "Minority Proximity to Whites in Suburbs," *American Journal of Sociology* 98, 6: 1388–1427.

Ashworth, Karl, et al. (1994) "Patterns of Childhood Poverty," *Journal of Policy Analysis and Management* 13, 4: 658–80.

Bane, Mary Jo, and David Ellwood (1986) "Slipping Into and Out of Poverty," *Journal of Human Resources* 21, 1: 1–23.

Birnbaum, Howard, and Rafael Weston (1974) "Home Ownership and the Wealth Position of Black and White Americans," *Review of Income and Wealth,* series 20, no. 1: 103–18.

Blau, Francine, and John Graham (1990) "Black-White Differences in Wealth and Asset Composition," *Quarterly Journal of Economics* 105, 421, Issue 2: 321–39.

Blau, Peter, and Otis Dudley Duncan (1967) *The American Occupational Structure* (John Wiley).

Boston, Thomas (1988) *Race Class, and Conservatism* (Unwin Hyman).

Braddock, Jomills II, and James McPartland (1987) "How Minorities Continue to Be Excluded from Equal Employment Opportunities," *Journal of Social Issues* 43, 1: 5–39.

Browne, Robert (1974) "Wealth Distribution and Its Impact on Minorities," *Review of Black Political Economy* 4, 4:27–37.

Burbridge, Lynn (1991) "The Interaction of Race, Gender, and Socioeconomic Status in Education Outcomes" (Wellesley College, Center for Research on Women).

Card, David, and Alan Drueger (1993) "Trends in Relative Black-White Earnings Revisited," *American Economic Review* 83, 2: 85–92.

Card, David, and Thomas Lemieux (1993) "Wage Dispersion, Returns to Skill, and Black-White Wage Differentials" (Princeton U., Dept. of Economics).

CBS News/*New York Times* (1978) "The Kerner Commission—Ten Years Later," Feb 16–19.

Cohen, Yinon, and Andrea Tyree (1986) "Escape from Poverty: Determinants of Intergenerational Mobility of Sons and Daughters of the Poor," *Social Science Quarterly* 67, 4: 803–13.

Danziger, Sheldon, and Peter Gottschalk (1987) "Earnings Inequality, the Spatial Concentration of Poverty, and the Underclass," *American Economic Review* 77, 2: 211–15.

Darity, William, and Samuel Myers (1993) "Racial Earnings Inequality and Family Structure," paper at annual meeting of Western Economics Association, Lake Tahoe, NV.

DiIulio, John Jr. (1989) "The Impact of Inner-City Crime," *Public Interest* 96: 28–46.

Duncan, Greg, and Willard Rodgers (1991) "Has Children's Poverty Become More Persistent?" *American Sociological Review* 56, 4: 538–50.

Duncan, Otis (1969) "Inheritance of Poverty or Inheritance of Race?" in Daniel Moynihan, ed., *On Understanding Poverty* (Basic Books), 85–110.

Ebony (1987) Special Issue on "The New Black Middle Class": 42, 10.

Economic Report of the President (1994) (U.S. Government Printing Office).

Eggebeen, David, and Daniel Lichter (1991) "Race, Family Structure, and Changing Poverty among American Children," *American Sociological Review* 56, 6:801–17.

Farley, Reynolds (1992) "The Changing Status of Blacks and Whites, Men and Women" (U. of Michigan, Population Studies Center).

Farley, Reynolds, et al. (1993) "Continued Racial Residential Segregation in Detroit: 'Chocolate City, Vanilla Suburbs' Revisited," *Journal of Housing Research* 4, 1: 1–38.

Farley, Reynolds, and Walter Allen (1987) *The Color Line and the Quality of Life in America* (Russell Sage Foundation).

Featherman, David, and Robert Hauser (1976) "Changes in the Socioeconomic Stratification of the Races, 1962–1973," *American Journal of Sociology* 82, 3: 621–51.

——— (1978) *Opportunity and Change (Academic Press).*

Ferleger, Lou, and Jay Mandle (1991) "African Americans and the Future of the U.S. Economy," *Trotter Institute Review* 5, 1: 3–7.

Gottschalk, Peter (1992) "Is the Correlation in Welfare Participation across Generations Spurious?" (Boston College, Dept. of Economics).

Gottschalk, Peter, Sara McLanahan, and Gary Sandefur (1994) "The Dynamics and Intergenerational Transmission of Poverty and Welfare Participation," in Sheldon Danziger, Gary Sandefur, and Daniel Weinberg, eds., *Confronting Poverty* (Harvard U. Press), 85–108.

Greeley, Andrew (1974) "Political Participation among Ethnic Groups in the United States," *American Journal of Sociology* 80, 1: 170–204.

Harrison, Roderick, and Claudette Bennett (1995) "Racial and Ethnic Diversity," in Reynolds Farley, ed., *State of the Union: America in the 1990s, Vol. 2: Social Trends* (Russell Sage Foundation), 141–210.

Hauser, Robert (1990) "Changes in Occupational Status among U.S. Men from the 1970s to the 1980s" (U. of Wisconsin, Center for Demography and Ecology).

Hauser, Robert, and Hanam Phang (1993) "Trends in High School Dropout among White, Black, and Hispanic Youth, 1973 to 1989" (U. of Wisconsin, Institute for Research on Poverty).

Henretta, John (1979) "Race Differences in Middle Class Lifestyle: The Role of Home Ownership," *Social Science Research* 8, 1: 63–78.

Hochschild, Jennifer (1988) "The Double-Edged Sword of Equal Opportunity," in Ian Shapiro and Grant Reeher, eds., *Power, Inequality, and Democratic Politics* (Westview Press), 168–200.

Hogan, Dennis, and David Featherman (1978) "Racial Stratification and Socioeconomic Change in the American North and South," *American Journal of Sociology* 83, 1: 100–126.

Hogan, Dennis, and Evelyn Kitagawa (1985) "The Impact of Social Status, Family Structure, and Neighborhood on the Fertility of Black Adolescents," *American Journal of Sociology* 90, 4: 825–55.

Hout, Michael (1984) "Occupational Mobility of Black Men: 1962 to 1973," *American Journal of Sociology* 49, 3: 308–22.

——— (1986) "Opportunity and the Minority Middle Class," *American Sociological Review* 51, 2: 214–23.

Jackman, Mary, and Robert Jackman (1983) *Class Awareness in the United States* (U. of California Press).

Jargowsky, Paul, and Mary Jo Bane (1991) "Ghetto Poverty in the United States, 1970–1980," in Christopher Jencks and Paul Peterson, eds., *The Urban Underclass* (Brookings Institution), 235–73.

Jaynes, Gerald, and Robin Williams, eds. (1989) *A Common Destiny: Blacks and American Society* (National Academy Press).

Jencks, Christopher (1991) "Is the American Underclass Growing?" in Christopher Jencks and Paul Peterson, eds., *The Urban Underclass* (Brookings Institution), 28–100.

Jianakoplos, Nancy, and Paul Menchik (1992) "Wealth Mobility" (Michigan State U., Dept. of Economics).

Joint Center for Political and Economic Studies (1994) *Black Elected Officials, 1993* (University Press of America).

Jones, Lyle (1987) "Trends in School Achievement of Black Children" (U. of North Carolina, Institute for Research in Social Science).

Karoly, Lynn (1993) "The Trend in Inequality among Families, Individuals, and Workers in the United States," in Sheldon Danziger and Peter Gottschalk, eds., *Uneven Tides: Rising Inequality in America* (Russell Sage Foundation), 19–97.

Kasarda, John (1993) "Inner-City Concentrated Poverty and Neighborhood Distress: 1970 to 1990," *Housing Policy Debate* 4, 3: 253–302.

——— (1995) "Industrial Restructuring and the Changing Location of Jobs," in Reynolds Farley, ed., *State of the Union: America in the 1990s, Vol. 1: Economic Trends* (Russell Sage Foundation), 215–67.

Kennickell, Arthur, and Janice Shack-Marquez (1992) "Changes in Family Finances from 1983 to 1989," *Federal Reserve Bulletin,* Jan.: 1–18.

Kleppner, Paul (1982) *Who Voted? The Dynamics of Electoral Turnout, 1870–1940* (Praeger).

Landry, Bart (1987) *The New Black Middle Class* (University of California Press).

Lazere, Edward, and Paul Leonard (1989) "The Crisis in Housing for the Poor" (Washington, D.C.: Center on Budget and Policy Priorities).

Lazere, Edward, et al. (1991) *A Place to Call Home: The Low Income Housing Crisis Continues* (Washington, D.C.: Center on Budget and Policy Priorities and Low Income Housing Information Service).

Ledebur, Larry, and William Barnes (1992) *City Distress, Metropolitan Disparities, and Economic Growth* (Washington, D.C.: National League of Cities).

Leonard, Paul, and Edward Lazere (1992) *A Place to Call Home: The Low Income Housing Crisis in 44 Major Metropolitan Areas* (Washington, D.C.: Center on Budget and Policy Priorities).

Levy, Frank, and Richard Michel (1991) *The Economic Future of American Families* (Urban Institute Press).

Lichter, Daniel, and David Eggebeen (1993) "Rich Kids, Poor Kids: Changing Income Inequality among American Children," *Social Forces* 71, 3: 761–80.

Massey, Douglas, and Nancy Denton (1987) "Trends in the Residential Segregation of Blacks, Hispanics, and Asians: 1970–1980," *American Sociological Review* 52, 6: 802–25.

——— (1998) "Suburbanization and Segregation in U.S. Metropolitan Areas," *American Journal of Sociology* 94, 3: 592–626.

Massey, Douglas, and Mitchell Eggers (1990) "The Ecology of Inequality: Minorities and the Concentration of Poverty, 1970–1980," *American Journal of Sociology* 95, 5: 1153–88.

McLanahan, Sara (1988) "Family Structure and Dependency: Early Transitions to Female Household Headship," *Demography* 25, 1: 1–16.

Menchik, Paul (1993) "Economic Status as a Determinant of Mortality among Black and White Older Men" *Population Studies* 47, 3: 427–36.

Morris, Martina, et al. (1994) "Economic Inequality," *American Sociological Review* 59, 2: 205–19.

Nathan, Richard, and Paul Dommel (1987) "Needed—A Federal Safety Net for Communities," statement to U.S. Senate Committee on Governmental Affairs, Subcommittee on Intergovernmental Relations, June 25.

Nathan, Richard, and Charles Adams, Jr. (1989) "Four Perspectives on Urban Hardship," *Political Science Quarterly* 104, 3: 483–508.

Nie, Norman, et al. (1988) "Participation in America: Continuity and Change," paper at the annual meeting of the MWPSA, Chicago.

O'Hare, William (1983) *Wealth and Economic Status: A Perspective on Racial Inequality* (Washington D.C.: Joint Center for Political Studies).

Oliver, Melvin, and Mark Glick (1982) "An Analysis of the New Orthodoxy on Black Mobility," *Social Problems* 29, 5: 511–23.

Oliver, Melvin, and Thomas Shapiro (1989) "Race and Wealth," *Review of Black Political Economy* 17, 4: 5–25.

Olsen, Marvin (1970) "Social and Political Participation of Blacks," *American Sociological Review* 35, 4: 682–97.

Papas, Gregory, et al. (1993) "The Increasing Disparity in Morality Between Socioeconomic Groups in the United States, 1960 and 1986," *New England Journal of Medicine* 329, 2: 103–9.

Rae, Douglas, et al. (1981) *Equalities* (Harvard U. Press).

Rodgers, John, and Joan Rodgers (1991) "Measuring the Intensity of Poverty among Subpopulations," *Journal of Human Resources* 26, 2:338–61.

Rosenstone, Steven, and John Mark Hansen (1993) *Mobilization, Participation, and Democracy in America* (Macmillan).

Ruggles, Patricia (1989) "Short and Long Term Poverty in the United States" (Washington, D.C.: Urban Institute).

Siegel, Paul (1965) "On the Cost of Being a Negro," *Sociological Inquiry* 35, 1: 41–57.

Smith, A. Wade (1985) "Social Class and Racial Cleavages on Major Social Indicators," *Research in Race and Ethnic Relations* (JAI Press), 4: 33–65.

Smith, James (1975) "White Wealth and Black People," in James Smith, ed., *The Personal Distributions of Income and Wealth* (Columbia U. Press), 329–63.

Smith, James, and Finis Welch (1989) "Black Economic Progress after Myrdal," *Journal of Economic Literature* 27, part 1, 2: 519–64.

Sobol, Marion (1979) "Factors Influencing Private Capital Accumulation on the 'Eve of Retirement,'" *Review of Economics and Statistics* 61, 4: 585–93.

Soltow, Lee (1972) "A Century of Personal Wealth Accumulation," in Harold Vatter and Thomas Palm, eds., *The Economics of Black America* (Harcourt Brace Jovanovich), 80–84.

Sorensen, Elaine (1991) "Gender and Racial Pay Gaps in the 1980s" (Washington, D.C.: Urban Institute).

Steckel, Richard, and Jayanthi Krishnan (1992) "Wealth Mobility in America" (National Bureau of Economic Research).

Stricker, Lawrence (1982) "Dimensions of Social Stratification for Whites and Blacks," *Multivariate Behavioral Research* 17, 2: 139–67.

Terrell, Henry (1971) "Wealth Accumulation of Black and White Families," *Journal of Finance* 26, 2: 363–77.

U.S. Bureau of the Census (1986) *Household Wealth and Asset Ownership: 1984,* P70–7 (U.S. Government Printing Office).

——— (1989) *Money Income of Households, Families, and Persons in the United States, 1987,* P60–162 (U.S. Government Printing Office).

——— (1993a) *Money Income of Households, Families, and Persons in the United States, 1992,* P60–184 *(U.S. Government Printing Office).*

——— (1993b) *Statistical Abstract of the United States 1993* (U.S. Government Printing Office).

——— (1993c) *Poverty in the United States: 1992,* P60-185 (U.S. Government Printing Office).

——— (1994) *Household Wealth and Asset Ownership: 1991,* P70–34 (U.S. Government Printing Office).

U.S. Department of Education (1990) *The Civics Report Card,* by Lee Anderson et al. (Princeton: Educational Testing Service, National Assessment of Educational Progress).

——— (1993) National Center for Education Statistics, *The Condition of Education, 1993* (U.S. Government Printing Office).

——— (1994) *Report in Brief: NAEP 1992 Trends in Academic Progress* (Office of Educational Research and Improvement).

U.S. Department of Justice (1994a) Bureau of Justice Statistics *Criminal Victimization in the United States: 1973–92 Trends.*

——— (1994b) *Sourcebook of Criminal Justice Statistics—1993* (U.S. Government Printing Office).

Vanneman, Reeve, and Lynn Cannon (1987) *The American Perception of Class* (Philadelphia: Temple U. Press).

Villemez, Wayne, and Candace Wiswell (1978) "The Impact of Diminishing Discrimination on the Internal Size Distribution of Black Income, 1954–74," *Social Forces* 56, 4: 1019–34.

Wachter, Susan, and Isaac Megbolugbe (1992) "Racial and Ethnic Disparities in Homeownership," *Housing Policy Debate* 3,2: 333–70.

Williams, Robin Jr. (1964) *Strangers Next Door: Ethnic Relations in American Communities* (Prentice-Hall).

Wolff, Edward (1993) "The Rich Get Increasingly Richer: Latest Data on Household Wealth during the 1980s" (Washington, D.C.: Economic Policy Institute).

Wright, Eric, et al. (1992) "The American Class Structure," *American Sociological Review* 47, 6: 709–26.

Hochschild:

1. Discuss the ways in which black Americans are better off, worse off, and experiencing mixed results in comparison to their white counterparts.

2. What explanations can you discuss that would account for the discrepancies between black and white measures of well-being?

16

The Racial Income Gap: How Much Is Due to Bias?

Andrew Hacker

Since their first arrival, and continuing after they started receiving wages, black Americans have figured disproportionately among the nation's poor. Of course, differences in incomes can have explanations apart from race. After all, a lot of white people are poor, and a number of blacks are very visibly rich. Even so, after other factors have been accounted for, race still seems to play a role in how people fare financially. A recurrent theme of this chapter will be how being black or white affects economic opportunities and outcomes.

Any discussion of incomes and earnings will depend strongly on statistics. While we cannot measure equity with precision, numerical disparities represent real facts about the races. Each year, the census asks a national sample of Americans to estimate their total incomes during the previous year.[1] Table 16.1 gives some of the results from the 1990 survey, reported first as median incomes and then by how much blacks received for every $1,000 that went to whites. (This means of comparison will be used extensively throughout this chapter.)

The listings for families and for all men and women include every sort of income, ranging from pensions and welfare payments to disability benefits and capital gains. The figures for employed men and women reflect

only the earnings of individuals who held full-time jobs throughout the year. The relative incomes for black families as a group and for black men are embarrassingly low, in particular when compared with those for the earnings of black women.

In 1990, the most recent figures available at this writing, personal income received by everyone living within the country added up to a grand total of $3.6 trillion. While black Americans made up 12.1 percent of the tabulated population, they ended up with only 7.8 percent of the monetary pie. Earnings by some 134 million gainfully employed persons accounted for $2.8 trillion of the income total. Black workers comprised 10.1 percent of that employment force, but received only 8.0 percent of all earnings. This chapter will focus on the conditions causing these gaps.

White households are more apt to have both a husband and wife present, which raises the likelihood of multiple incomes. In fact, 59 percent of white families have two or more earners, while only 47 percent of black families do. As it happens, among married couples, a smaller percentage of white wives work: 61 percent have jobs, compared with 68 percent of black married women. Since the earnings of black men tend to be lower, fewer of their families can afford the luxury

Table 16.1

Incomes and Earnings (1990 Medians)

	White	Black	Ratio*
Families	$36,915	$21,423	$580
All Men	$21,170	$12,868	$608
All Women	$10,317	$8,328	$807
Employed Men	$30,598	$22,167	$725
Employed Women	$20,759	$18,838	$907

*Incomes of blacks per $1,000 for whites. Earnings for Year-Round Fulltime workers.

Table 16.2

Education and Earnings (Earnings of Blacks per $1,000 for Whites)

	Men	Women
High School Not Finished	$797	$974
4 Years of High School	$764	$942
1 to 3 Years of College	$825	$925
4 Years of College	$798	$1,002
5 + Years of College	$771	$973

of full-time housewives. When white wives work, they are more likely to take part-time jobs and their paychecks tend to be supplemental; whereas among black families, the husbands' and wives' earnings are often of equal value. And since more black families are headed by single women, a higher proportion of their households must make do with only one income. Moreover, when black single mothers work—and the majority do—it is generally at a job paying relatively low wages.

So the question arises whether income ratios would change if black families had the same mixture of single parents and married couples as white households now do. If this became the case, then many more black homes would have someone bringing in a man's earnings. Were this change to occur, the income ratio for black families would only rise from $580 to $732, not exactly an impressive improvement. The reason is that while having more men's incomes would help, it would not accomplish very much since black men still make considerably less than white men. Moreover, even if more black households had a man in residence, some of the men would be unemployed or removed from the labor force for other reasons. So emulating the white family structure would close only about half of the income gap.

On the whole, increased education tends to bring in higher incomes. While we can always find exceptions, for most people most of the time, staying in school does pay off. The figures in Table 16.2 show how the rule works along a racial continuum. To make the comparisons as firm as possible, the table covers only individuals who worked full time throughout the entire year.

A steady economic progression is evident for all four groups: among black and white men and women, incomes ascend with added years of school. The catch is that even when black men reach the same academic level as white men, their incomes stay several steps behind. Thus among men with four years of college, blacks still earn only $798 for each $1,000 going to whites in that educational stratum. Even worse, black college men end up just a few dollars ahead of whites who went no further than high school. When black men persevere to graduate school, they still receive only $771 compared with their white counterparts, even less than for black men who never finished college. Hence the advice so often offered to blacks, that they should stay in school, seems valid only insofar as it informs them that with additional education they will move ahead of others of their own race. There is little evidence that spending more years in school will improve their positions in relation to whites.

Of course, the table also shows that black women come much closer to parity with their white counterparts, making between $925 and $1,002 for each $1,000 earned by white women at their level. The greater equity among women results largely from the fact that few women of either race rise far in the earnings hierarchy. The comparative status of black women warrants only a muted cheer: achieving equality is easier within an underpaid cohort. Yet there remains the question of why black men are denied even the limited equity that black women enjoy.

If we want to find out how much income disparities result from racial bias, then we must do our best to compare similar groups, since additional elements like age and experience can distort comparisons. A census study that examined the earnings of male attorneys between the ages of thirty-five and forty-five found that black lawyers averaged $790 for every $1,000 made by their white counterparts. Given that these men are in the same age range and have the same level of education, it could be argued that race accounts for at least part of the $210 earnings gap. Of course, we would have to know a lot more about the individuals in question. Factors like talent, intelligence, and temperament could affect the equation. Or the variance in earnings might reflect different law schools the men attended and how well they did there. After all, it hardly needs mentioning that not all educations are comparable. If more of the white lawyers in the cohort went to Harvard, while the black lawyers were apt to have studied at Howard, then some people might want to argue that some part of the $210 difference is justified.

As it happens, black *women* lawyers in the same age group make $930 for every $1,000 going to their white colleagues. Moreover, this similarity holds even though black women attend the same spectrum of law schools as black men. So a question must arise: if black women in the legal profession are paid nearly as much as white women, then why don't black men make almost as much as white men? A suspicion cannot help but arise that some of the racial earnings spread among men stems from the fact that black men are given fewer opportunities to rise to better-paid positions.

Measured in economic terms, the last two decades have not been auspicious ones for Americans of any race. Between 1970 and 1990, the median income for white families, computed in constant dollars, rose from $34,481 to $36,915, an increase of 8.7 percent. During these decades, black family income barely changed at all going from $21,151 to $21,423. In relative terms, black incomes dropped from $613 to $580 for each $1,000 received by whites. As it happened, the incomes of white men dropped during this period, so if white families recorded a modest rise, it was because more of them had wives who could go to work.

However, medians—like averages—can conceal important variations. The four configurations in Figure 16.1 show how incomes were distributed among black and white families in 1970 and 1990. The shapes for both races changed in revealing ways. In 1970, the black incomes depicted at the bottom left took the form of a classical pyramid, beginning with a fairly broad base and tapering at each subsequent level. Twenty years later, the base had become much wider, and families were arrayed more evenly among the higher brackets. This change reflects not only the much-heralded growth of a black middle class, but also a significant shift in black America's social structure, signaling a separation of better-off blacks from those at the lowest level.

In 1970, the white distribution shown at top left had the shape of a chunky column, with a heavy girth in the middle ranges. By 1990 aggregate income had moved toward

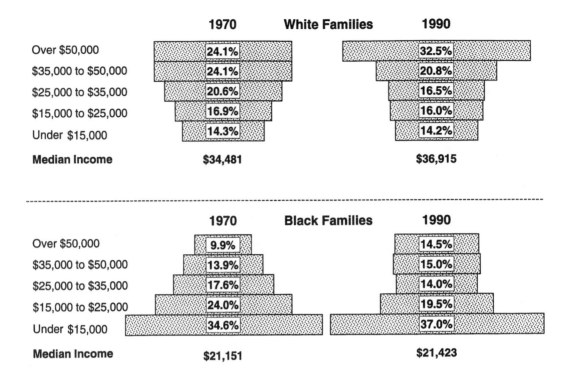

Figure 16.1. Income Distributions

the top. The figure had become an inverted pyramid, with more than half of the homes in the two top tiers. The rise in better-off households came in part from a growth in highly paid positions during the 1980s; but the principal reason was that by 1990 many more white homes had two earners. At the same time, between 1970 and 1990, the size of the two bottom tiers had barely changed. However, there had been a shift in the composition of the white poor. In 1970, it consisted largely of the elderly, or employed persons working for very low wages. By 1990, low-income white households were more apt to be those headed by women.

During the two decades, the proportion of black households with incomes over $50,000 expanded by 46 percent, while the share of white homes at that level rose by only 35 percent. Even if whites were not advancing as fast, they were not falling behind; so it cannot be argued that blacks were replacing whites in better-paid positions.

Nor does the fact that more black families enjoy incomes of over $50,000 mean that many black men and women have jobs paying at that level. Indeed, only 3.4 percent of all black men make $50,000 or more; most $50,000 homes result from two or more sets of earnings. In contrast, 12.1 percent of white men receive over $50,000, and many more of them are the sole or dominant earners in their households. So while there is now a much larger black middle class, more typically, the husband is likely to be a bus driver earning $32,000, while his wife brings home $28,000 as a teacher or a nurse. A white middle-class family is three to four times more likely to contain a husband earning $75,000 in a managerial position, which allows him to support a nonworking wife. It is not easy to visualize these two couples living on the same

Table 16.3

Poverty Percentages

	White	Black	Multiple
All Persons	8.8%	31.9%	3.63
All Children	15.9%	44.8%	2.82
All Families	8.1%	29.3%	3.62
Female Headed Households	37.9%	56.1%	1.48

Where Poor Americans Live

	White	Black
Central Cities	32.7%	60.3%
Suburbs	35.2%	17.5%
Nonmetropolitan	32.1%	22.2%
	100%	100%

block, let alone becoming acquainted with one another.

Some thirty years ago, federal officials devised a formula to designate which Americans could be considered poor. The poverty threshold is adjusted every year, to keep pace with the cost of living. In 1990, an older woman living by herself would fall in the poverty cohort if her income fell below $6,268. A single mother with two children was counted as poor if their income was lower than $10,530. In most parts of the United States, $6,268 spells not simply poverty, but a good chance of malnutrition. Nor is it possible to bring up, say, two teenagers on $10,530 a year. Even adding in the dollar value of school lunches, food stamps, and medical benefits, the formula understates the number of Americans who are truly poor. Another problem is that the figures ignore variations in living costs. A widow might manage on $6,268 in rural Arkansas, but that would barely pay her rent in Boston or Brooklyn. Still, if we make appropriate adjustments, the official poverty percentages can tell us a lot about who is poor and why.

As Table 16.3 shows, 44.8 percent of black children live below the poverty line, compared with 15.9 percent of white youngsters. So black children are almost three times as likely as whites to grow up in poor surroundings. The ratio runs higher for all black families, and is somewhat similar for black people as a whole. However, the poverty figures have a much closer ratio (1.48) among households headed by women. Indeed, the proportion in poverty among white single mothers (37.9 percent) exceeds that for the black population as a whole. For women who must raise children on their own, being white loses much of its advantage.

The poverty figures also show that some two thirds of poor white Americans live in suburbs or rural areas. Anyone who has traveled along the back roads of outlying America has seen the homes of people who are white and poor. However, their homes are less likely to be clustered together in slum neighborhoods, unless one applies that description to decaying trailer parks. Among the poor white families who do live in urban areas, less than a quarter of them reside in low-income tracts. This suggests that there are relatively few white ghettos. Urban black families below the poverty line are more visibly segregated: no less than 70 percent of such households are concentrated in low-income neighborhoods.

Of course, there is a white underclass.[2] Its members can be found among the addicted and the homeless, among men who have never held steady jobs, and women who have spent many years on welfare. The nation's prisons still have plenty of white criminals, some of whom are quite vicious and others who have made careers in small-time larcenies. Even so, neither sociologists nor journalists have shown much interest in depicting poor whites as a "class." In large measure, the reason is racial. For whites, poverty tends to be viewed as atypical or accidental. Among blacks, it comes close to being seen as a natural outgrowth of their history and culture. At times, it almost appears as if white poverty must be covered up, lest it blemish the reputation of the dominant race. This was not always the case. In the past, sociology textbooks dilated at length about families like the Jukes and the Kallikaks, who remained mired in squalor from generation to generation. In earlier days, too, white people could be "trash," whether along the tobacco roads or in pellagra-infested pine barrens. While class bias prompted these discursions, at least they granted that white people could occupy the lowest stratum of society.

Apart from people who are independently wealthy and those with generous pensions, enjoying the modest comforts of life requires having a decent job. Altogether, about 80 percent of Americans' personal income comes from wages and salaries or other gainful earnings.

Between 1939 and 1959, the earnings of black men relative to whites improved by over a third. Those who made the move to Northern cities relocated in search of employment. They were willing to take blue-collar positions once reserved for immigrants,

Table 16.4
Black Workers' Earnings (per $1,000 for Whites)

	Men	Women
1939	$450	$379
1949	$596	$434
1959	$612	$664
1969	$694	$819
1979	$715	$925
1989	$716	$919

but which newer generations of whites were beginning to spurn. This period saw the emergence of a stable black working class, underpinned by two-parent families and orderly neighborhoods. If many saw themselves as "poor," that status did not have the connotations conveyed by "poverty" today. The earnings of black women also grew during this period, as they turned from domestic employment to better-paid occupations.

However, during the past twenty years, as Table 16.4 shows, the relative earnings of black men has tapered off. Between 1969 and 1989, their ratio in relation to whites has improved by only $22, and of that only a rise of a single dollar came during the second decade. (And this was a period when affirmative action supposedly gave blacks preferences in hirings and promotions.) The decline in blue-collar employment hit black men especially hard. Each year found the economy offering fewer factory jobs, while more were being created in the white-collar sector.

If black women have fared better, it is because more of them have been seen as suitable for office positions. Professional and clerical occupations generally call for attitudes and aptitudes associated with the white world. For reasons that will be considered later, black women apparently satisfy employers on these counts more readily than black men. Even so, by 1979, it became clear that black women would still fall short of parity with their white female colleagues.

While white women were later in entering the labor force in large numbers, their arrival on the scene brought pressures to move them into professional and supervisory positions, which has in turn increased the pay gap between white and black women.

Black men, women, and children were brought to this country for a singular purpose: to work. Indeed, the demand for their labor was so great that slaves continued to be smuggled in even after that traffic had been banned by the Constitution. In the years following emancipation, former slaves found that their services would not necessarily be needed. Their labor, like that of other Americans, would be subject to the vagaries of a market economy. The capitalist system has been frank in admitting that it cannot always create jobs for everyone who wants to work. This economic reality has certainly been a pervasive fact of black life. For as long as records have been kept, in good times and bad, white America has ensured that the unemployment imposed on blacks will be approximately double [that] experienced by whites. Stated very simply, if you are black in America, you will find it twice as hard to find or keep a job.

The ratios in Table 16.5 make it clear that black Americans get jobs only after white applicants have been accommodated. In periods of prosperity, when the economy requires more workers, blacks who had been unemployed are offered vacant positions. But as last hired, they can expect to be the first fired. In bleak times, the jobless rate among blacks can approach 20 percent, as it did in 1983. Since 1974, unemployment rates for blacks have remained at double-digit levels, and they have not fallen below twice the white rate since 1976. Even more depressing, the gap between the black and white figures grew during the 1980s, suggesting that the economy has little interest in enlisting black contributions.

It is frequently remarked that many black men and women lack the kinds of skills that modern employment requires. However,

Table 16.5
Unemployment Rates

Year	White	Black	Multiple
1960	4.9	10.2	2.08
1961	6.0	12.4	2.07
1962	4.9	10.9	2.22
1963	5.0	10.8	2.16
1964	4.6	9.6	2.09
1965	4.1	8.1	1.98
1966	3.3	7.3	2.21
1967	3.4	7.4	2.18
1968	3.2	6.7	2.09
1969	3.1	6.4	2.06
1960s Average			2.11
1970	4.4	8.2	1.86
1971	5.4	9.9	1.83
1972	5.0	10.0	2.00
1973	4.3	8.9	2.07
1974	5.0	9.9	1.98
1975	7.8	14.8	1.90
1976	7.0	13.1	1.87
1977	6.2	13.1	2.11
1978	5.2	11.9	2.29
1979	5.1	11.3	2.22
1970s Average			2.01
1980	6.3	14.3	2.27
1981	6.7	14.2	2.12
1982	8.6	18.9	2.20
1983	8.4	19.5	2.32
1984	6.5	15.9	2.45
1985	6.2	15.1	2.44
1986	6.0	14.5	2.42
1987	5.3	13.0	2.45
1988	4.7	11.7	2.49
1989	4.5	11.4	2.53
1980s Average			2.37
1990	4.1	11.3	2.76

these charges are hardly new. They were also common in the past, when blacks were shunted to the end of the line even for laboring jobs. And today, whites who barely make it through high school continue to get the first openings in the building trades. Moreover, blacks who do stay in school soon learn there is no assured payoff. Those who finish college have a jobless rate 2.24 times that for whites with diplomas, an even greater gap than that separating black and white high school graduates.

Exacerbating the situation today is the fact that millions of jobs are being filled by legal and illegal aliens, largely from Latin America and Asia. Few of the positions they take call for special skills, so the question arises as to why these places haven't been offered to native-born black Americans. This issue is not new, since it has long been argued that immigrant labor takes bread from the mouths of citizens. In most cases, though, aliens and immigrants acquiesce to wages and working conditions that black and white Americans are unwilling to accept. Indeed, newcomers often put up with what are essentially Third World terms of employment to gain a foothold in the American economy. And if these workers are exploited, it is often by employers or supervisors of their own origins who arrived here not much earlier. Nor is it likely that the pay for such jobs can be raised appreciably.

What black Americans want is no more nor less than what white Americans want: a fair chance for steady employment at decent pay. But this opportunity has been one that the nation's economy continues to withhold. To be black in America is to know that you remain last in line for so basic a requisite as the means for supporting yourself and your family. More than that, you have much less choice among jobs than workers who are white. Entire occupations still remain substantially closed to people who were born black.

That black Americans are willing or required to do arduous work cannot be questioned. When a new hotel announces that it will be hiring porters and chambermaids, a line largely composed of black men and women can be seen curling around the block. Black youths sign on for the armed services in disproportionate numbers because this is the only promising job they can get. And other young men and women can be found on sordid streets in all hours and weathers, selling illicit services or merchandise. The baleful consequences aside, the fact remains that what they are doing is unquestionably *work*. For each one who sports a fancy car, dozens more serve as "stashers" or "spotters" in hopes of picking up a few dollars.

All in all, a greater proportion of black Americans lack regular employment than at any time since the 1930s Depression. Many of those who have jobs are needed for less than a full day's work or for only part of the year. And in addition to men and women who are officially recorded as unemployed, at least an equal number have given up the search. Because this is now a substantial group, the Bureau of Labor Statistics has created a category it calls "discouraged workers." These are individuals who say they would like to work, but have ceased looking because they have become convinced that they will never find a job. So they have been dropped from the "labor force" category and are no longer even counted among the unemployed.

On a typical day in 1990, the bureau was able to locate almost a million of these "discouraged workers." The true total has to be considerably higher, since many in this plight cannot be found for interviews or refuse to give out information about themselves. Of the recorded "discouraged workers," close to 30 percent are black, a much higher proportion than on the official list of the unemployed who say they are actively looking for work. As was just noted, some of these "nonworkers" support themselves on the streets by providing products and services in the underground economy. Others resort to theft, which means that sooner or later they will join yet another cohort of the nonemployed: the growing number of Americans who languish in this nation's prisons.

It is frequently proposed that the economy should create more semiskilled jobs at decent wages, which will be made available to black men. Just what kinds of positions they would be are seldom specified. As hardly needs mentioning, machines now perform many of the tasks once handled by human beings, while a lot of factory work once done within this country is being contracted overseas. Moreover, recent trends have expanded the sectors of the workforce open to women. Even if special jobs were devised, it is not clear how they could pay what today's men regard as a living wage. For at least a decade, newly created positions have been offering wages and salaries lower than those of the jobs they replaced. As a result, they are usually taken by women or teenagers or immigrants, who are willing to work at those rates because they have no other option. Put another way, many native-born men cannot see how they can work for such wages and still maintain a self-respect integral to their identity.

But the larger point is that this country cannot revert to a sweat-and-muscle economy of earlier eras. More than that, to contrive blue-collar jobs for black men would not only rouse charges of preferential treatment but accusations of racism as well, since it would imply that work requiring physical skills is all that black men can be expected to do.

Notes

1. *Money Income of Households, Families, and Persons in the United States,* Series P-60, No. 174. Washington, DC: Bureau of the Census, 1991. The date in this chapter derive from this document.

2. See, for example, Jay MacLeod, *Ain't No Making It.* Boulder, CO: Westview Press, 1987.

Hacker:

1. How would you answer Hacker's question of whether the black to white income ratios would change if black families had the same mixture of single parents and married couples as white households do?

2. Discuss some of the consequences that Hacker raises for the disparities between black and white incomes for race relations in the United States.

17

When Work Disappears: Societal Changes and Vulnerable Neighborhoods

William Julius Wilson

The disappearance of work in many inner-city neighborhoods is partly related to the nationwide decline in the fortunes of low-skilled workers. Although the growing wage inequality has hurt both low-skilled men and women, the problem of declining employment has been concentrated among low-skilled men. In 1987–89, a low-skilled male worker was jobless eight and a half weeks longer than he would have been in 1967–69. Moreover, the proportion of men who "permanently" dropped out of the labor force was more than twice as high in the late 1980s than it had been in the late 1960s. A precipitous drop in real wages—that is, wages adjusted for inflation—has accompanied the increases in joblessness among low-income workers. If you arrange all wages into five groups according to wage percentile (from highest to lowest), you see that men in the bottom fifth of this income distribution experienced more than a 30 percent drop in real wages between 1970 and 1989.

Even the low-skilled workers who are consistently employed face problems of economic advancement. Job ladders—opportunities for promotion within firms—have eroded, and many less-skilled workers stagnate in dead-end, low-paying positions. This suggests that the chances of improving one's earnings by changing jobs have declined: if jobs inside a firm have become less available to the experienced workers in that firm, they are probably even more difficult for outsiders to obtain.

But there is a paradox here. Despite the increasing economic marginality of low-wage workers, unemployment dipped below 6 percent in 1994 and early 1995, many workers are holding more than one job, and overtime work has reached a record high. Yet while tens of millions of new jobs have been created in the past two decades, men who are well below retirement age are working less than they did two decades ago—and a growing percentage are neither working nor looking for work. The proportion of male workers in the prime of their life (between the ages of 22 and 58) who worked in a given decade full-time, year-round, in at least eight out of ten years declined from 79 percent during the 1970s to 71 percent in the 1980s. While the American economy saw a rapid expansion in high technology and services, especially advanced services, growth in blue-collar factory, transportation, and construction jobs, traditionally held by men, has not kept pace with the rise in the working-age population. These men are working less as a result.

The growth of a nonworking class of prime-age males along with a larger number of those who are often unemployed, who work part-time, or who work in temporary jobs is concentrated among the poorly educated, the school dropouts, and minorities. In the 1970s, two-thirds of prime-age male workers with less than a high school education worked full-time, year-round, in eight out of ten years. During the 1980s, only half did so. Prime-age black men experienced a similar sharp decline. Seven out of ten of all black men worked full-time, year-round, in eight out of ten years in the 1970s, but only half did so in the 1980s. The figures for those who reside in the inner city are obviously even lower.

One study estimates that since 1967 the number of prime-age men who are not in school, not working, and not looking for work for even a single week in a given year has more than doubled for both whites and nonwhites (respectively, from 3.3 to 7.7 percent and 5.8 percent to 13.2 percent). Data from this study also revealed that one-quarter of all male high school dropouts had no official employment at all in 1992. And of those with high school diplomas, one out of ten did not hold a job in 1993, up sharply from 1967 when only one out of fifty reported that he had had no job throughout the year. Among prime-age nonwhite males, the share of those who had no jobs at all in a given year increased from 3 percent to 17 percent during the last quarter century (Buron et al., 1984).

These changes are related to the decline of the mass production system in the United States. The traditional American economy featured rapid growth in productivity and living standards. The mass production system benefited from large quantities of cheap natural resources, economies of scale, and processes that generated higher uses of productivity through shifts in market forces from agriculture to manufacturing and that caused improvements in one industry (for example, reduced steel costs) to lead to advancements in others (for example, higher sales and greater economies of scale in the automobile industry). In this system plenty of blue-collar jobs were available to workers with little formal education. Today, most of the new jobs for workers with limited education and experience are in the service sector, which hires relatively more women. One study found that the U.S. created 27 clerical, sales, and service jobs per thousand of working-age population in the 1980s. During the same period, the country lost 16 production, transportation, and laborer jobs per thousand of working-age population (McKinsey and Co., 1994). In another study the social scientists Robert Lerman and Martin Rein (forthcoming) revealed that from 1989 to 1993, the period covering the economic downturn, social service industries (health, education, and welfare) added almost 3 million jobs, while 1.4 million jobs were lost in all other industries. The expanding job market in social services offset the recession-linked job loss in other industries.

The movement of lower-educated men into the growth sectors of the economy has been slow. For example, "the fraction of men who have moved into so-called pink-collar jobs like practical nursing or clerical work remains negligible" (Nasar, 1994, A7). The large concentration of women in the expanding social service sector partly accounts for the striking gender differences in job growth. Unlike lower-educated men, lower-educated women are working more, not less, than in previous years. The employment patterns among lower-educated women, like those with higher education and training, reflect the dramatic expansion of social service industries. Between 1989 and 1993, jobs held by women increased by 1.3 million, while those held by men barely rose at all (by roughly 100,000).

Although the wages of low-skilled women (those with less than twelve years of education) rose slightly in the 1970s, they flattened out in the 1980s, and continued to remain below those of low-skilled men. The wage gap between low-skilled men and women shrank not because of gains made by female workers but mainly because of the decline in real wages for men. The unemployment rates among low-skilled women are slightly lower than those among their male counterparts. However, over the past decade their rates of participation in the labor force have stagnated and have fallen further behind the labor-force-participation rates among more highly educated women, which continue to rise. The unemployment rates among both low-skilled men and women are five times that among their college-educated counterparts.

Among the factors that have contributed to the growing gap in employment and wages between low-skilled and college-educated workers is the increased internationalization of the U.S. economy. As the economists Richard B. Freeman and Lawrence F. Katz (1994) point out:

In the 1980s, trade imbalances implicitly acted to augment the nation's supply of less educated workers, particularly those with less than a high school education. Many production and routine clerical tasks could be more easily transferred abroad than in the past. The increased supply of less educated workers arising from trade deficits accounted for as much as 15 percent of the increase in college-high school wage differential from the 1970s to the mid-1980s. In contrast, a balanced expansion of international trade, in which growth in exports matches the growth of imports, appears to have fairly neutral effects on relative labor demand. Indeed, balanced growth of trade leads to an upgrading in jobs for workers without college degrees, since export-sector jobs tend to pay higher wages for "comparable" workers than do import-competing jobs. (P. 46)

The lowering of unionization rates, which accompanied the decline in the mass production system, has also contributed to shrinking wages and nonwage compensation for less skilled workers. As the economist Rebecca Blank (1994) has pointed out, "unionized workers typically receive not only higher wages, but also more non-wage benefits. As the availability of union jobs has declined for unskilled workers, non-wage benefits have also declined" (p. 17).

Finally, the wage and employment gap between skilled and unskilled workers is growing partly because education and training are considered more important than ever in the new global economy. At the same time that changes in technology are producing new jobs, they are making many others obsolete. The workplace has been revolutionized by technological changes that range from the development of robotics to information highways. While educated workers are benefiting from the pace of technological change, involving the increased use of computer-based technologies and microcomputers, more routine workers face the growing threat of job displacement in certain industries. For example, highly skilled designers, engineers, and operators are needed for the jobs associated with the creation of a new set of computer-operated machine tools; but these same exciting new opportunities eliminate jobs for those trained only for manual, assembly-line work. Also, in certain businesses, advances in word processing have increased the demand for those who not only know how to type but can operate specialized software as well; at the same time, these advances reduce the need for routine typists and secretaries. In the new global economy, highly educated and thoroughly trained men and women are in demand. This may be seen most dramatically in the sharp differences in employment experiences among men. Unlike men with lower education, college-educated men are working more, not less.

The shift in demand has been especially devastating for those low-skilled workers whose incorporation into the mainstream economy has been marginal or recent. Even before the economic restructuring of the nation's economy, low-skilled African-Americans were at the end of the employment queue. Their economic situation has been further weakened because they tend to reside in communities that not only have higher jobless rates and lower employment growth but lack access to areas of higher employment and employment growth as well. Moreover, they are far more likely than other ethnic and racial groups to face negative employer attitudes.

Of the changes in the economy that have adversely affected low-skilled African-American workers, perhaps the most significant have been those in the manufacturing sector. One study revealed that in the 1970s "up to half of the huge employment declines for less-educated blacks might be explained by industrial shifts away from manufacturing toward other sectors" (Bound and Holzer 1993, p. 395). Another study reported that since the 1960s "deindustrialization" and the "erosion in job opportunities especially in the Midwest and Northeast . . . bear responsibility for the growth of the ranks of the 'truly disadvantaged'" (Bluestone et al., 1991, p. 25). The manufacturing losses in some northern cities have been staggering. In the twenty-year period from 1967 to 1987, Philadelphia lost 64 percent of its manufacturing jobs; Chicago lost 60 percent; New York City, 58 percent; Detroit, 51 percent. In absolute numbers, these percentages represent the loss of 160,000 jobs in Philadelphia, 326,000 in Chicago, 520,000—over half a million—in New York, and 108,000 in Detroit.

Another study examined the effects of economic restructuring in the 1980s by highlighting the changes in both the variety and the quality of blue-collar employment in general. Jobs were grouped into a small number of relatively homogeneous clusters on the basis of job quality (which was measured in terms of earnings, benefits, union protection, and involuntary part-time employment). The authors found that both the relative earnings and employment rates among un-skilled black workers were lower for two reasons: traditional jobs that provide a living wage (high-wage blue-collar cluster, of which roughly 50 percent were manufacturing jobs) declined, as did the quality of secondary jobs on which they increasingly had to rely, leading to lower relative earnings for the remaining workers in the labor market. As employment prospects worsened, rising proportions of low-skilled black workers dropped out of the legitimate labor market (Gittleman and Howell 1993).

Data from the Chicago Urban Poverty and Family Life Survey show that efforts by out-of-school inner-city black men to obtain blue-collar jobs in the industries in which their fathers had been employed have been hampered by industrial restructuring. "The most common occupation reported by respondents at ages 19 to 28 changed from operative and assembler jobs among the oldest cohorts to service jobs (waiters and janitors) among the youngest cohort" (Testa and Krough 1995, p. 77). Fifty-seven percent of Chicago's employed inner-city black fathers (aged 15 and over and without undergraduate degrees) who were born between 1950 and 1955 worked in manufacturing and construction industries in 1974. By 1987, industrial employment in this group had fallen to 31 percent. Of those born between 1956 and 1960, 52 percent worked in these industries as late as 1978. But again, by 1987 industrial employment in this group fell to 28 percent. No other male ethnic group in the inner city experienced such an overall precipitous drop in manufacturing employment. These employment changes have accompanied the loss of traditional manufacturing and other blue-collar jobs in Chicago. As a result, young black males have turned increasingly to the low-wage service sector and unskilled laboring jobs for employment, or have gone jobless. The strongly held U.S. cultural and economic belief that the son will do at least as well as the father in the labor market does not apply to many young inner-city males.

Joblessness and declining wages are also related to the recent growth in ghetto poverty. The most dramatic increases in ghetto poverty occurred between 1970 and 1980, and they were mostly confined to the large industrial metropolises of the Northeast and Midwest, regions that experienced massive industrial restructuring and loss of blue-collar jobs during that decade. But the rise in ghetto poverty was not the only problem. Industrial restructuring had devastating effects on the social organization of many inner-city neighborhoods in these regions. The fate of the West Side black community of North Lawndale vividly exemplifies the cumulative process of economic and social dislocation that has swept through Chicago's inner city.

After more than a quarter century of continuous deterioration, North Lawndale resembles a war zone. Since 1960, nearly half of its housing stock has disappeared; the remaining units are mostly run-down or dilapidated. Two large factories anchored the economy of this West Side neighborhood in its good days—the Hawthorne plant of Western Electric, which employed over 43,000 workers; and an International Harvester plant with 14,000 workers. The world headquarters for Sears, Roebuck and Company was located there, providing another 10,000 jobs. The neighborhood also had a Copenhagen snuff plant, a Sunbeam factory, and a Zenith factory, a Dell Farm food market, an Alden's catalog store, and a U.S. Post Office bulk station. But conditions rapidly changed. Harvester closed its doors in the late 1960s. Sears moved most of its offices to the Loop in downtown Chicago in 1973; a catalog distribution center with a workforce of 3,000 initially remained in the neighborhood but was relocated outside of the state of Illinois in 1987. The Hawthorne plant gradually phased out its operations and finally shut down in 1984.

The departure of the big plants triggered the demise or exodus of the smaller stores, the banks, and other businesses that relied on the wages paid by the large employers. "To make matters worse, scores of stores were forced out of business or pushed out of the neighborhoods by insurance companies in the wake of the 1968 riots that swept through Chicago's West Side after the assassination of Dr. Martin Luther King, Jr. Others were simply burned or abandoned. It has been estimated that the community lost 75 percent of its business establishments from 1960 to 1970 alone." In 1986, North Lawndale, with a population of over 66,000, had only one bank and one supermarket; but it was also home to forty-eight state lottery agents, fifty currency exchanges, and ninety-nine licensed liquor stores and bars.

The impact of industrial restructuring on inner-city employment is clearly apparent to urban blacks. The UPFLS survey posed the following question: "Over the past five or ten years, how many friends of yours have lost their jobs because the place where they worked shut down—would you say none, a few, some, or most?" Only 26 percent of the black residents in our sample reported that none of their friends had lost jobs because their workplace shut down. Indeed, both black men and black women were more likely to report that their friends had lost jobs because of plant closings than were the Mexicans and the other ethnic groups in our study. Moreover, nearly half of the employed black fathers and mothers in the UPFLS survey stated that they considered themselves to be at high risk of losing their jobs because of plant shutdowns. Significantly fewer Hispanic and white parents felt this way.

Some of the inner-city neighborhoods have experienced more visible job losses than others. But residents of the inner city are keenly aware of the rapid depletion of job opportunities. A 33-year-old unmarried black male of North Lawndale who is employed as a clerical worker stated: "Because of the way the economy is structured, we're losing more jobs. Chicago is losing jobs by the thousands. There just aren't any starting companies here and it's harder to find a job compared to what it was years ago."

A similar view was expressed by a 41-year-old black female, also from North Lawndale, who works as a nurse's aide:

Chicago is really full of peoples. Everybody can't get a good job. They don't have enough good jobs to provide for everybody. I don't think they have enough jobs period. . . . And all the factories and the places, they closed up and moved out of the city and stuff like that, you know. I guess it's one of the reasons they haven't got too many jobs now, 'cause a lot of the jobs now, factories and business, they're done moved out. So that way it's less jobs for lot of peoples.

Respondents from other neighborhoods also reported on the impact of industrial restructuring. According to a 33-year-old South Side janitor:

The machines are putting a lot of people out of jobs. I worked for *Time* magazine for seven years on a videograph printer and they come along with the Abedic printer, it cost them half a million dollars: they did what we did in half the time, eliminated two shifts.

"Jobs were plentiful in the past," stated a 29-year-old unemployed black male who lives in one of the poorest neighborhoods on the South Side.

You could walk out of the house and get a job. Maybe not what you want but you could get a job. Now, you can't find anything. A lot of people in this neighborhood, they want to work but they can't get work. A few, but a very few, they just don't want to work. The majority they want to work but they can't find work.

Finally, a 41-year-old hospital worker from another impoverished South Side neighborhood associated declining employment opportunities with decreasing skill levels:

Well, most of the jobs have moved out of Chicago. Factory jobs have moved out. There are no jobs here. Not like it was 20, 30 years ago. And people aren't skilled enough for the jobs that are here. You don't have enough skilled and educated people to fill them.

The increasing suburbanization of employment has accompanied industrial restructuring and has further exacerbated the problems of inner-city joblessness and restricted access to jobs. "Metropolitan areas captured nearly 90 percent of the nation's employment growth; much of this growth occurred in booming 'edge cities' at the metropolitan periphery. By 1990, many of these 'edge cities' had more office space and retail sales than the metropolitan downtowns." Over the last two decades, 60 percent of the new jobs created in the Chicago metropolitan area have been located in the northwest suburbs of Cook and Du Page counties. African-Americans constitute less than 2 percent of the population in these areas.

In *The Truly Disadvantaged*, I maintained that one result of these changes for many urban blacks has been a growing mismatch between the suburban location of employment and minorities' residence in the inner city. Although studies based on data collected before 1970 showed no consistent or convincing effects on black employment as a consequence of this spatial mismatch, the employment of inner-city blacks relative to suburban blacks has clearly deteriorated since then. Recent research, conducted mainly by urban and labor economists, strongly shows that the decentralization of employment is continuing and that employment in manufacturing, most of which is already suburbanized, has decreased in central cities, particularly in the Northeast and Midwest. As Farrell Bloch, an economic and statistical consultant, points out, "Not only has the number of manufacturing jobs been decreasing, but new plants now tend to locate in the suburbs to take advantage of cheap land, access to highways, and low crime rates; in addition, businesses shun urban locations to avoid buying land from several different owners, paying high demolition costs for old buildings, and arranging parking for employees and customers."

The African-Americans surveyed in the UPFLS clearly recognized a spatial mismatch of jobs. Both black men and black women saw greater job prospects outside the city. For example, only one-third of black fathers from areas with poverty rates of at least 30 percent reported that their best opportunities for employment were to be found in the city. Nearly two-thirds of whites and Puerto Ricans and over half of Mexicans living in similar neighborhoods felt this way. Getting to suburban jobs is especially problematic for the jobless individuals in the UPFLS because only 28 percent have access to an automobile. This rate falls even further to 18 percent for those living in the ghetto areas.

Among two-car middle-class and affluent families, commuting is accepted as a fact of life; but it occurs in a context of safe school environments for children, more available and accessible day care, and higher incomes to support mobile, away-from-home lifestyles. In a multitiered job market that requires substantial resources for participation, most inner-city minorities must rely on public transportation systems that rarely provide easy and quick access to suburban locations. A 32-year-old unemployed South Side welfare mother described the problem this way:

There's not enough jobs. I thinks Chicago's the only city that does not have a lot of opportunities opening in it. There's not enough factories, there's not enough work. Most all the good jobs are in the suburbs. Sometimes it's hard for the people in the city to get to the suburbs, because everybody don't own a car. Everybody don't drive.

After commenting on the lack of jobs in his area, a 29-year-old unemployed South Side black male continued:

You gotta go out in the suburbs, but I can't get out there. The bus go out there but you don't want to catch the bus out there, going two hours each ways. If you have to be at work at eight that mean you have to leave for work at six, that mean you have to get up at five to be at work at eight. Then when wintertime come you be in trouble.

Another unemployed South Side black male had this to say: "Most of the time . . . the places be too far and you need transportation and I don't have none right now. If I had some I'd probably be able to get one [a job]. If had a car and went way into the suburbs, 'cause there ain't none in the city." This perception was echoed by an 18-year-old unemployed West Side black male:

They are most likely hiring in the suburbs. Recently, I think about two years ago, I had a job but they say that I need some transportation and they say that the bus out in the suburbs run at a certain time. So I had to pass that job up because I did not have no transport.

An unemployed unmarried welfare mother of two from the West Side likewise stated:

Well, I'm goin' to tell you: most jobs, more jobs are in the suburbs. It's where the good jobs and stuff is but you gotta have transportation to get there and it's hard to be gettin' out there in the suburbs. Some people don't know where the suburbs is, some people get lost out there. It is really hard, but some make a way.

One employed factory worker from the West side who works a night shift described the situation this way:

From what I, I see, you know, it's hard to find a good job in the inner city 'cause so many people moving, you know, west to the suburbs and outs of state. . . . Some people turn jobs down because they don't have no way of getting out there. . . . I just see some people just going to work—and they seem like they the type who just used

Table 17.1

Demographic Changes in Douglas, Grand Boulevard, and Washington Park, 1950–1990

	Douglas				
	1990	*1980*	*1970*	*1960*	*1950*
Total Population	30,652	35,700	41,276	52,325	78,745
% female	58.3	57.6	55.1	52.2	52.3
% male	41.7	42.4	44.9	47.8	47.7
% age 0–4	10.5	9.0	10.2	15.1	11.0
% age 5–19	24.5	26.2	33.3	29.9	21.7
% age 20–44	34.8	36.4	32.0	33.0	43.3
% age 45–64	15.6	16.5	16.8	15.9	18.7
% age 65 +	14.7	11.9	7.7	6.1	5.3

	Grand Boulevard				
	1990	*1980*	*1970*	*1960*	*1950*
Total Population	35,897	58,741	80,150	80,036	114,557
% female	55.9	54.4	53.8	52.3	52.7
% male	44.1	45.6	46.2	47.7	47.3
% age 0–4	11.4	9.5	9.4	11.7	8.3
% age 5–19	30.0	31.5	36.4	21.3	16.8
% age 20–44	30.3	27.9	24.8	32.6	45.3
% age 45–64	14.0	17.5	18.4	25.0	24.0
% age 65 +	14.3	13.6	11.0	9.4	5.6

	Washington Park				
	1990	*1980*	*1970*	*1960*	*1950*
Total Population	19,425	31,935	46,024	43,690	56,865
% female	54.5	54.7	53.0	52.0	52.5
% male	45.5	45.3	47.0	48.0	46.8
% age 0–4	11.8	9.9	9.0	9.7	7.2
% age 5–19	28.8	30.8	31.8	18.1	15.7
% age 20–44	33.7	28.5	28.5	34.9	47.0
% age 45–64	14.9	18.8	20.3	27.6	24.5
% age 65 +	10.8	12.0	10.4	9.4	5.6

Source: 1990 Census of Population and Housing, File STF₃A; and *Local Community Fact Book—Chicago Metropolitan Area.*

to—they coming all the way from the city and go on all the way to the suburbs and, you know, you can see 'em all bundled and—catching one bus and the next bus. They just used to doing that.

Let us examine the three Bronzeville neighborhoods of Douglas, Grand Boulevard, and Washington Park. As shown in Table 17.1 the proportion of those in the age categories (20–64) that roughly approximate the prime-age workforce has declined in all three neighborhoods since 1950, whereas the proportion in the age category 65 and over has increased. Of the adults age 20 and over, the proportion in the prime-age categories declined by 17 percent in Grand Boulevard, 16 percent in Douglas, and 12 percent in Washington Park between 1950 and 1990. The smaller the percentage of prime-age adults in a population, the lower the proportion of residents who are likely to be employed. The proportion of residents in the age category 5–19 increased sharply in each neighborhood from 1950 to 1990, suggesting that the growth in the proportion of teenagers also contributed to the rise in the jobless rate. However, if we consider the fact that male employment in these neighborhoods declined by a phenomenal 46 percent between 1950 and 1960, these demographic changes obviously can account for only a fraction, albeit a significant fraction, of the high proportion of the area's jobless adults.

The rise in the proportion of jobless adults in the Bronzeville neighborhoods has been accompanied by an incredible depopulation—a decline of 66 percent in the three neighborhoods combined—that magnifies the problems of the new poverty neighborhoods. As the population drops and the proportion of nonworking adults rises, basic neighborhood institutions are more difficult to maintain: stores, banks, credit institutions, restaurants, dry cleaners, gas stations, medical doctors, and so on lose regular and potential patrons. Churches experience dwindling numbers of parishioners and shrinking resources; recreational facilities, block clubs, community groups, and other informal organizations also suffer. As these organizations decline, the means of formal and informal social control in the neighborhood become weaker. Levels of crime and street violence increase as a result, leading to further deterioration of the neighborhood.

The more rapid the neighborhood deterioration, the greater the institutional disinvestment. In the 1960s and 1970s, neighborhoods plagued by heavy abandonment were frequently "redlined" (identified as areas that should not receive or be recommended for mortgage loans or insurance): this paralyzed the housing market, lowered property values, and further encouraged landlord abandonment. The enactment of federal and state community reinvestment legislation in the 1970s curbed the practice of open redlining. Nonetheless, "prudent lenders will exercise increased caution in advancing mortgages, particularly in neighborhoods marked by strong indication of owner disinvestment and early abandonment."

As the neighborhood disintegrates, those who are able to leave depart in increasing numbers; among these are many working- and middle-class families. The lower population density in turn creates additional problems. Abandoned buildings increase and often serve as havens for crack use and other illegal enterprises that give criminals footholds in the community. Precipitous declines in density also make it even more difficult to sustain or develop a sense of community. The feeling of safety in numbers is completely lacking in such neighborhoods.

Although changes in the economy (industrial restructuring and reorganization) and changes in the class, racial, and demographic composition of inner-city ghetto neighborhoods are important factors in the shift from institutional to jobless ghettos since 1970, we ought not to lose sight of the fact that this process actually began immediately following World War II.

The federal government contributed to the early decay of inner-city neighborhoods by withholding mortgage capital and by making it difficult for urban areas to retain or attract families able to purchase their own homes. Spurred on by massive mortgage foreclosures during the Great Depression, the federal government in the 1940s began underwriting mortgages in an effort to enable citizens to become homeowners. But the mortgage program was selectively administered by the Federal Housing Administration (FHA), and urban neighborhoods considered poor risks were redlined—an action that excluded virtually all the black neighborhoods and many neighborhoods with a considerable number of European immigrants. It was not until the 1960s that the FHA discontinued its racial restrictions on mortgages.

By manipulating market incentives, the federal government drew middle-class whites to the suburbs and, in effect, trapped blacks in the inner cities. Beginning in the 1950s, the suburbanization of the middle class was also facilitated by a federal transportation and highway policy, including the building of freeway networks through the hearts of many cities, mortgages for veterans, mortgage-interest tax exemptions, and the quick, cheap production of massive amounts of tract housing.

References

Blank, Rebecca, 1994. "Outlook for the U.S. Labor Market Prospects for Low-Wage Entry Jobs. Working Paper, Center for Urban Studies, Northwestern University.

Bluestone, Barry, Mary Stevenson amd Chris Tilly. 1991. "The Deterioration in Labor Market Prospects for Young Men with Limited Schooling." Paper presented at the Eastern Economic Association, March 14, Pittsburgh.

Bound, John and Harry Holzer. 1993. "Industrial Shifts, Skill Levels, and the Labor Market for White and Black Men." *Review of Economics and Statistics,* 75 (August): 387-396.

Buron, Lawrence, Robert Haveman, and Owen O'Donnell. 1994. "Recent Trends in U.S. Male Work and Wage Patterns." Unpublished manuscript, University of Wisconsin at Madison.

Freeman, Richard B. and Lawrence F. Katz. 1994. "Rising Wage Inequality." In *Working Under Different Rules,* ed. Richard B. Freeman. New York: Russell Sage Foundation.

Gittleman, Maury B. and David R. Howell. 1993. "Job Quality and Labor Market Segmentation in the 1980s." Working paper, Bard College.

Lerman, Robert I. amd Martin Rein. Forthcoming. *Social Service Employment: An International Perspective.* New York: Russell Sage Foundation.

McKinsey and Company. 1994. *Employment Performance.* Washington, D.C.: McKinsey Global Institute.

Nasar, Sylvia. 1994. "The Men in Prime of Life Spend Less Time Working." *New York Times.* December 1, A7.

Testa, Mark and Marilyn Krogh. 1995. "The Effect of Employment on Marriage Among Black Males in Inner-City Chicago. In *The Decline in Marriage Among African Americans,* eds. M. Belinda Tucker and Claudia Mitchell-Kernan, pp. 59-95. New York: Russell Sage Foundation.

Wilson:

1. What are the reasons for the decline of the fortunes of low-skilled workers in the United States? How are these reasons intimately connected with issues of race and ethnicity?

2. What is problematic when jobs move into suburban areas? Discuss the barriers that inner-city residents face when work moves into the suburbs.

18

Documenting America:
Racism, Realism, and *Hoop Dreams*

Cheryl L. Cole and Samantha King

The 1990s witnessed a boom in the production and consumption of popular ethnographic accounts of life in America's inner cities. From Alex Kotlowitz's *There Are No Children Here* and Daniel Coyle's *Hardball: A Season in the Projects,* to Greg Donaldson's *The Ville: Cops and Kids in Urban America* and Darcy Frey's *The Last Shot: City Streets, Basketball Dreams,* the public has eagerly devoured these highly acclaimed, real-life tales of struggle and survival in some of the nation's poorest urban neighborhoods.[1] Told, for the most part, through the lives of children, these accounts are repeatedly celebrated for their ability to educate the suburban middle classes about the reality of growing up poor and black in America.

Ethnographies of the Urban

Perhaps no other media event demonstrates America's desire to know the "urban other" and America's particular fascination with urban black masculinity more forcefully than *Hoop Dreams,* a 3-hour, low-budget, independent documentary.[2] Although documentaries typically are relegated to the margins of the American film industry and popular media, *Hoop Dreams* quickly became a megahit

in the United States. Popular critics described it as "beautifully made" and "one of the best and most deeply moving American films of 1994" and used the key term "achievement" to affirm the film's "claim to truth"—a truth that ostensibly intervened in previous and more familiar documentations of the inner city, urban problems, and African American inner-city youth.

The popular reception of *Hoop Dreams* and these books are intricately bound within a historical context in which black bodies and masculinities have become highly commodified and marketable. Moreover, this historical context has shaped and has been shaped by America's fascination with and acquired knowledge of "urban problems," particularly as those problems have been rendered visible through coming of age narratives of African American male youths. Furthermore, racially coded coming of age narratives have accrued political purchase as they have been transmitted to consumers through figures such as Magic Johnson, Isiah Thomas, and Michael Jordan. National Basketball Association (NBA) superstars are created through and provided fertile ground for narratives of limited scope that emphasized mobility, transformation, transcendence, and utopic social visions through discipline. Morality tales of promise and possibility for individuals, families, and nation that circulate through the NBA celebrity zone were made even more compelling and convincing through the often invisible, but nonetheless effective, rhetorical figure of the gang member. That is, black urban masculinity was visualized through a fundamental distinction between the athlete (primarily the urban basketball player) and the criminal (typically the gang member): The tension between what is represented as two choices served as the ground for stories continually circulated and fed by the mass media industry for public consumption. Whereas gang members were seen as choosing alien and undesirable values, athletes were viewed as the embodiment of dominant, and thus desirable, values. These dominant values were displayed most prominently in assimilationist repetitions of "the desire to exit," or "find a way out" of the ghetto. As public consumer spectacle, the sport/gang dyad organized a way of seeing urban America and explaining its problems.[3]

Although America's "will to know" and these journalistic portrayals of urban life potentially intervene in public debates over federal assistance and urban problems, such analyses of urban youths' struggles, according to Michael Massing, typically are moved forward at the expense of their parents: An older generation of African Americans are held responsible for the obstacles and struggles that condition the youths' everyday lived experiences.[4] Thus, although "real" racially coded coming of age stories have increased in popularity, they have failed to introduce alternative or oppositional knowledges into public debates. For us, then, the popularity of the ethnographic urban does not simply convey an innocent cultural enthusiasm; instead, we understand America's voracious appetite for such images to be an expression of America's social subjectivity—the "nation's state of mind." Given its enormous popularity, *Hoop Dreams* provides a privileged locus for interrogating America's "state of mind" and the obsessive consumption of images of urban America as sites and effects of power, knowledge, and pleasure.

We examine the national celebratory reception of *Hoop Dreams,* keeping in mind the weight of the racist order that it would need to overcome to even simply disturb historically conditioned "ways of seeing" and not seeing so-called urban problems, racism, whiteness, and America (a term we use to designate imagined origins, community, and character). Rather than offering a powerful contrast to familiar documentations of urban America, we think that the film relies on a series of now-familiar themes, events, and figures that both enable and limit how we imagine violence, power, and our selves in late modern America.[5] We see the film and its popular representations as consistent with a national spirit and imagination inseparable from the prominence accrued by African American basketball players over the last decade. Moreover, we suggest that this prominence needs to be understood within wider global transformations that have devastated, reordered, and revitalized urban areas in ways that are indissolubly linked to the perverse profitability of transnational corporations. We consider "the urban basketball player," who is implicated in these networks, to be a subject and object of late modern forms of discipline and consumption. In Lauren Berlant's terms, these "'stars' [are] transformed into trademarks and corporate logos, prosthetic bodies that ideally replace the body of pain with the projected image of safety and satisfaction that commodities represent."[6] As such, these stars (NBA celebrities) are key figures in a reconfigured racism that allows American (middle-class) audiences to recognize themselves as compassionate and ethical subjects.

We seek to show how the self-recognized ethical and compassionate subject is produced through a series of exclusions and displacements.[7] To a great extent, these exclusions and displacements are embodied in the "origin stories" (which revise history) promoted by the mainstream media. Moreover, we contend that the film's primary figure of exploitation and social wrongs, "Gene Pingatore," functions as a figure for displacements, that is, American middle-class audiences derive identification and pleasure from the film because guilt and the audience's implication in exploitative spectatorship and consumption practices are displaced onto Pingatore. We argue that such figures of exploitation and social wrongs work to protect particular understandings of America as they repress the banal violence and monstrosities that shape the everyday lives of already vulnerable populations in urban areas. Stated differently, we read *Hoop Dreams* as an expression of a national imagination and spirit that represses and displaces violence under the guise of care, compassion, social cause, and ethical superiority.

Hoop Dreams: The Film

Hoop Dreams is a 3-hour documentary filmed between 1986 and 1991. The film focuses on the high school experiences of two African American teenagers growing up in racially segregated Chicago neighborhoods. Although only 14, William Gates and Arthur Agee already demonstrate the sort of basketball skills that suggest that they will be recruited to play at the college level and possibly be employed to play in the NBA. Viewer position and context are immediately established through the opening juxtaposed images: The viewer travels the expressway north toward the Chicago skyline. As the elevated train running parallel to the expressway moves into the frame, a group of young African American men playing basketball on the court below come into view. The camera follows a player (who we later will recognize as William Gates) as he approaches the basket to shoot; the graffiti-laden concrete wall surrounding the court comes into focus. The

camera moves around a concrete high-rise, the sign of urban housing projects, to reveal "Chicago Stadium" as fans enter to attend the 38th annual NBA All-Star Game. A picture-perfect steal and dunk by the East's No. 23, Michael Jordan, is met by overwhelmingly white, exuberant spectators as they celebrate the physical achievement they have just witnessed.

As the All-Star Game (apparently) continues inside Chicago Stadium, the elevated train moves us to the Cabrini Green Housing Project, where William lives with his mother, Emma, and brother, Curtis. Although housing projects signify decay, threat, and the anti-normative in the national imagination, Cabrini Green is introduced through signs of community: Youngsters play in the high spray of an open fire hydrant; men and women mingle and engage in neighborly exchanges; two young boys play basketball on a makeshift court in the corner of the building. As the camera lingers outside the door to someone's home, the sounds of the NBA All-Star Game inside suggest that despite their geographical dispersion, the images are temporally bound. Inside, we see William intensely watching the closing moments of the game. He steps outside his apartment and onto the playground court, where we watch him, in slow motion, dunk on a netless rim.

Right now [closeup of William, expressing his aspirations through a wide smile], I want, you know, to play in the NBA like anybody else would want to be. That's who, tha's, tha's somethin I dream-think about all the time, you know, playin in the NBA.

The camera takes us to the West Garfield Park neighborhood where Arthur lives with his mother, father, sister, and brother. Again, in the intimacy of a home where the NBA All-Star Game plays on television (we hear the announcer introducing Isiah Thomas), a smiling Arthur describes his desires and imagined NBA life:

When I get in the NBA, I'm . . . ah, the first thing I'm gonna do is I gonna see my momma, I'm gonna buy her a house. I'm gonna make sure my sista and brotha's okay [met by shouts of approval from brother and sister]. Probably get my dad . . . a Cadillac, Oldsmobile, so he can cruise in the game. [Cut to Arthur's mother, Sheila] He dreams about it. . . . He look at those basketball commercials when . . . they be advertising like these Nike shoes and he'll tell, he'll tell his little small brother "Joe . . . Joe, that's me."

We watch as Arthur is "discovered" by Earl Smith on one of his "expeditions" to a park near Central and Congress Parkway. Smith, an insurance executive and "unofficial scout" for area high schools, instantly recognizes Arthur's talent and arranges for him to attend St. Joseph's summer basketball camp. St. Joseph High School, the featured education-basketball structure in the film, is a predominantly white, private Roman Catholic school in Westchester, a western suburb of Chicago. It maintains its position as one of Chicago's high school basketball powerhouses by recruiting players from across the city.

Based on his basketball skills and performance at the camp, Arthur is recruited to play for St. Joseph High School by Gene Pingatore, the head basketball coach. In a conversation with Arthur and his family, Pingatore not too cautiously promises that Arthur's chances of securing a college scholarship will be enhanced by attending St. Joseph.

If you work hard at your grades, and if you work hard at basketball, then I'll be able to help you as far as going to college. And I guarantee—I can't promise you where you're going to go and if you're going to be a star, but I guaran-*tee* that I will help you get into the school that will be best for you.

Pingatore (apparently in conversation with the off-camera filmmakers) admits un-certainty about Arthur's potential given the "playground" he sees in him. However, Pingatore claims that he sees it all—"personality, confidence, talent, intelligence"—in another new recruit, William Gates. Both Arthur and William are given partial scholarships and, like Isiah Thomas, will commute 3 hours daily by train to attend the school. Their first year, William "starts" on the varsity squad while Arthur wins the freshman team starting point guard position. Although both entered reading at a fourth-grade level, William's academic skills improve dramatically his first year. Arthur's academic work does not advance at the same rate: He appears less interested in his high school education and seems to view it as a required detour on his way to the NBA. Gene Pingatore verbalizes his hesitations about Arthur's ability to adapt to the new environment:

When Arthur first started at St. Joseph's, he was a good kid from what we saw, but he was very immature. He wasn't used to the discipline and control. He reverted back to, maybe, his environment, where he came from.

Meanwhile, through a series of upbeat, last minute, high-drama game-day scenes, we learn that William is also excelling on the basketball court and drawing attention from Division I schools and sports writers who appear on a television talk show and have identified him as the next Isiah Thomas.

A tuition increase at the beginning of their sophomore year creates potential problems for both students. Patricia Wier, President of Encyclopedia Britannica, makes a contribution to a scholarship fund that, in combination with other sources, including "Cycle" (a Cabrini Green organization), covers William's tuition. By mid-semester, Arthur is forced to leave St. Joseph's because his parents have been unable to make the required tuition payments and now owe St. Joseph's $1,500. This is due, in part, to the cycle of hiring and layoffs that Arthur's father, Bo Agee, is caught up in throughout the film. Sheila Agee, Arthur, and the coach at Arthur's new (inner-city) school, Marshall High, believe that Arthur's expulsion was due to his failure to live up to coach Gene Pingatore's expectations. Shortly after Arthur starts at Marshall, the narrator tells us that after 20 years of marriage, Bo has left the family. Forced to quit her job due to chronic back pain, Sheila Agee eventually receives welfare. She expresses her discomfort with receiving public assistance (apparently aware of, as she implicitly responds to, dominant understanding of "welfare generations") by contrasting her situation to that of her parents who always worked for a living. The impoverishment cycle continues when Arthur turns 18 (a birthday of particular significance for his mother because, as she explains, many young black men don't live to 18) and is no longer eligible to receive public aid.

Soon after, Arthur's best friend and teammate Shannon talks about the importance of his friendship with Arthur, and Bo's drug use, violent behavior, and time in jail. As Sheila explains that she has taken out a protection order against Bo, her words fade to music, and the camera sweeps over a collection of legal papers. The camera lingers on black type that allows us to read documentation of Bo's criminal record:

GUILTY—BATTERY

GUILTY—BURGLARY

SENTENCED TO IMPRISONMENT—JAIL 37 DAYS

SENTENCED TO PROBATION 2 YEARS

William's freshman and sophomore challenges were narrated around and confined to trying to lead his team to the state tournament; however, during his junior year, William injures his knee. Under doctor's instructions, he reluctantly sits out the rest of the season. Once injured, the instability of his knee most explicitly organizes William's narrative of uncertainty. Indeed, it is under the stress of his knee surgery and when his basketball career is in jeopardy that Emma Gates reveals her desire and investment in William's professional basketball career. "I really thought Curtis was gonna make it, but he didn't make it, so I just wanted this one to make it." Curtis, a high school standout and player of the decade at Colby Jr. College, developed a reputation for being difficult. Although awarded a scholarship to the University of Central Florida, he dropped out of school because of a conflict with the coach. The clips from Colby do far more than demonstrate Curtis's exceptional talent; they also make inexplicable his refusal to abide by the rules. Now working for a security firm, Curtis describes his life in terms of his disappointment in being just another guy. When he loses his job, he identifies himself as a complete failure: "I ain't amounted to nothin'."

Arthur's narration remains governed by the unpredictability of his basketball and academic skills along with the unpredictability and potential reversibility of events in his family, although at Marshall, Arthur grows taller, his game improves dramatically, and he becomes a league and local media star. Although Arthur succeeds on the basketball court, he continues to struggle with his academic work. During visits to Marshall High, teachers, counselors, and Arthur's coach express concern at his mediocre grades and attitude toward his classroom work. In the meantime, one year after he left, Bo has rejoined the family. Following the reunion of the Agee family, Arthur's mother graduates as a nurse's assistant. Arthur's team eventually makes it to the state championships in Champaign, Illinois, where Arthur leads his team to third-place position. Because St. Joseph's has yet again failed to make it to the state tournament, Gene Pingatore participates only as a spectator. Arthur is on track for a scholarship to a major university but cannot meet the SAT requirements. He receives an athletic scholarship from Mineral Area Junior College in Missouri, where he lives in "Basketball House"—a dormitory located in the middle of a field, far removed from the rest of the campus—along with six of the seven black students at the college.

In the meantime, William and his girlfriend, Catherine, have had a child, Alicia. In two scenes in which the three appear together, William and Catherine discuss the anxiety they experienced on learning of her pregnancy and the arguments caused by William being unable to attend the birth. He had an important game that day and Pingatore, William recalls later, was unsympathetic to his family commitments. Despite his recurring knee injury and struggles to attain the minimum SAT score, William performed well at the Nike summer basketball camp and received an athletic scholarship offer from Marquette University in Milwaukee, Wisconsin. The movie ends with William on his way to Marquette, but uncertain of his desire to pursue a basketball career. In a written postscript, the filmmakers tell us that Arthur graduated from Mineral Area with a "C" average and went on to study at Arkansas State University, a Division I school, where he played starting point guard: "A national basketball magazine judged the team's success to be largely dependent on Arthur's success. In his first start, Arthur hit a 30 foot jump shot at the buzzer to win the game." William, we are told, married Catherine, who moved to Marquette with their daughter. In his junior year, he became increasingly disillusioned with basketball and decided to drop out of school. His family persuaded him otherwise, and the University agreed to let him continue studying without playing basketball.

America Responds to *Hoop Dreams*

Since its premier at the 1994 Sundance Film Festival in Park City, Utah, *Hoop Dreams* received widespread and enthusiastic endorsement. It won Sundance's "Audience Award" over 16 other documentaries, it was the audience favorite at the Toronto Festival, and it was met with a 10-minute standing ovation at the New York Film Festival, as recounted by filmmaker Steve James: "The people at the festival said nothing like this had ever happened before. The audience was just standing there, clapping for the connection they felt for those families. It was the most amazing experience of my life."[8]

Mainstream reviews endlessly applauded *Hoop Dreams* for eluding and exceeding the boundaries of seductive sport clichés. *Washington Post* film critic Hal Hinson suggested that "*Hoop Dreams* provides more emotion and human drama than 10 Hollywood movies."[9] Popular critics proclaimed the film "an American epic" as they identified the two youths on whom the film is based in terms of "instant celebrity" and its filmmakers as heroes and filmic pioneers. *Hoop Dreams*, we are repeatedly told, is about something of vastly greater significance than sport: *Hoop Dreams* is about the real urban America. In the words of Michael Wilmington, "We get the true, raw emotion usually buried under the glitz and hoke of the average Hollywood-ized sports movie. . . . It isn't a slice of life—but a huge chunk of it."[10]

Indeed, reviews intimated that the youths' dreams to play professional basketball set the stage for a larger diagnostics of the inner city. The complex, realistic, and positive portrait of black inner-city life represented in *Hoop Dreams* was not, according to most mainstream reviews, typically available to middle-class America. Mainstream media accounts repeatedly implied that America was prepared for—apparently even sought—an objective account of the inner city that would challenge the dominant versions on offer. In a telling comment that punctuates the affective purchase of the documentary drama, Steve James told the *Chicago Tribune*, "White people have told us that the only contact they have with inner city neighborhoods is what they see from their high rise. But seeing a film like this, they really felt connection."[11] Despite the stereotypical racially coded mythical figures that saturate America's popular culture, "white high-rise America" was apparently able to recognize and embrace the "real thing" when they saw it. Stated differently, mainstream media accounts produced (in collaboration with *Hoop Dreams* the film), and then represented, an American consensus that designated *Hoop Dreams* the official version of real life in urban America.

Claims to the film's "social consciousness" are substantiated through declarations that distinguish the treatment of the inner city and its residents in *Hoop Dreams* from other Hollywood films. Although Patrick McGavin contends that "the film does not demonize inner-city life," academic critic Lee Jones claims that the film "decenters long held stereotypes about residents who happen to live in the inner ghetto."[12] Such pronouncements and conclusions reinforce and are consistent with what director Peter Gilbert identifies as one of the filmmakers' primary concerns: "One of the things that was very important to us is that the people in the film are human beings. That they don't fit the stereotypes of inner city life."[13]

Overall, *Hoop Dreams* was revered and imbued with the status of a vanguard film that furnished America with a unique educational opportunity—an opportunity that stimulated and satisfied its "will to know." Although such knowledge claims are most obviously made possible by the realist pretensions of documentary filmmaking, that aesthetic dimension was complemented with a narrative of integrity culled through a network of recurring themes that drew attention to the good intentions and personal virtues of its three white filmmakers: Steve James, Fred Marx, and Peter Gilbert.

Origin Stories of History and Character

Hoop Dreams' history and context are established through an origin story (the popular constructed history of the film) in which the film is represented as an unplanned and unforeseen social accomplishment. *Hoop Dreams*, we are repeatedly told, developed out of a modest project. Initially, the filmmakers undertook a 6-month project to produce a 30-minute nonprofit educational film-short about Chicago's street basketball culture. Their intent was to compare the lives of a former NBA player who had successfully made it through the system (apparently they had Isiah Thomas in mind), a "washed up" player whose dreams had not materialized, and a talented high school star who aspired to join the professional ranks. The original short film project was funded by Kartemquin Educational Films, noted for "its noble poverty."[14]

Kartemquin Educational Films is a Chicago-based production company founded in the 1960s by three University of Chicago alumni. Kartemquin survives by making for-profit films for industry to fund the production of its own documentaries. A $2,000 state arts council grant provided a base from which to begin filming the newly conceived project, while Kartemquin continued to sustain the production process by providing donations and office space. In the end, the film cost $600,000 to make and received funding along the way from the Corporation for Public Broadcasting, PBS, and the MacArthur Foundation.

According to James, it was not until the Sundance Film Festival that film distributors began to show any interest in the film and the filmmakers signed a contract with Turner Broadcasting.[15] Turner, who owns Fine Line Features, the distributor of the documentary, hired Spike Lee as executive producer and director of its made-for-television counterpart. Additionally, Turner had the capacity to cross-promote the film during its airing of NBA games. Thus, the cycle of takeovers and mergers that resulted from Reagan's deregulation policies begins to come into focus. Moreover, Fine Line Features announced that it had "taken the film as a personal cause"—a cause it advanced with an advertising budget of only $500,000. In the words of its president, Ira Deutchman, Fine Line formulated "the most complex marketing scheme we've ever pulled off."[16] The company sought to target a broad audience that included art-house patrons, sports-film fans, teenagers, and inner-city children and their parents. Nike was recruited to endorse television, radio, and billboard advertisements for the movie and subsidize promotional events (the Nike logo appears on print and movie ads). Nike also helped to establish the 800 number for local community group tickets and also was credited with persuading *Sports Illustrated* to pay for the publication and mailing costs of a student/teacher study guide that accompanied the release of the film. Nike, having never before endorsed a film, explained that it "really believed in the message of the film," a message Nike identified as about hope, spirit, sport, and family.[17]

Dominant accounts that imagine the film being plucked from a sea of independent films doomed for limited release maintain the film's commercial success as purely accidental (thereby maintaining the film and filmmakers' purity) by distancing the film from the capitalist imperatives of mainstream Hollywood production and consumer-driven individualism. Moreover, by locating and restricting stories of the financing and production of the film to the "local" level, the film's implication in the imperatives of global capitalism was erased. This erasure

helped establish the authenticity of the film both in terms of its status as an independent, small-scale, local production and in terms of its narrative integrity.

Media collaboration in the production of truth-effects, narrative integrity, and valorized identities is most easily observed in the disproportionate commentary devoted to the "actual making" of the film rather than the narrative of the film itself. We are repeatedly reminded that the filmmakers shot 250 hours of film over a period of four and one-half years, that the film was made on an extremely low budget, and that all three men accumulated huge debts in the process. As Michael Wilmington of the *Chicago Tribune* remarked, "The odds are so stacked against their [Arthur and William's] success. There's an obvious analogy with the long shot world of independent filmmaking itself."[18] Along a related theme, Steve James told the *Washington Post* that the fact that he and his colleagues drove "rust bucket cars" was an important factor in gaining their subjects' trust.[19] These unifying thematics rely on and generate easy slippages between the socioeconomic conditions of the filmmakers and the Agee and Gates families. These slippages trivialize the economic and social devastation defining the conditions of poverty in the post-Fordist inner city and the everyday lives of those who inhabit such spaces. That reviewers felt able to draw parallels between the socioeconomic situation of two African American youths from Chicago's poor inner city and the economic hardship that defines independent filmmaking is testament to the filmic and popular erasures of the historical forces shaping the lives of the urban poor.

More telling are the repetitions that portray filmmakers James, Marx, and Gilbert as acutely loyal to Arthur, William, and their families that are inseparable from those lauding them for the financial and personal sacrifices made to complete the film. In what we think are symptomatic repetitions, the filmmakers appear repeatedly through the categories of loyalty and ethical superiority. We are told that unlike others before them, these filmmakers were persistently loyal despite the difficulties Arthur and William confronted. That which the filmmakers take to be, by definition, the subject matter of the film, the predicaments encountered by Arthur and William, are narrated as "tests" of the filmmakers' character. Numerous interviews recount Steve James's depiction of Arthur's astonishment that the filmmakers continued filming him after he was expelled from St. Joseph. Similarly, several reviews draw attention to Emma Gates's initial ambivalence about the film and filmmakers and her subsequent conversion experience: It was only after the filmmakers made clear that they would not abandon William's story when a knee injury threatened his career that she came to trust them. "She realized," says Gilbert, "we weren't going to run away because things didn't fit the storybook ideal." When a different kind of trouble threatened Arthur's basketball future, "he was literally surprised when we showed up to film him," Gilbert says. "He told us, 'Why would you want to help me now?' We said, 'It's because we care about you.'"[20]

At first glance, such anecdotes may simply appear to be true, real-life, "behind-the-scene" stories or background information; yet, such anecdotes reveal America's "political unconscious" (to use Fredric Jameson's term) as they reshape America's historical consciousness and the public's reception of *Hoop Dreams*. Such repetitions suggest that the narrative is not simply about "trust"; instead, the narrative—which is most often and most explicitly organized around the unexpected material and financial success of the film and, by extension, of the filmmakers—appears to be motivated by anxieties about guilt. The origin narrative repeatedly relieves anxieties about guilt by drawing attention to innocence, good will, personal virtues, and highly principled and ethical behaviors of the filmmakers. Moreover, the concentrated atten-

tion to the philanthropy of the filmmakers reverses the critique that might have ensued through a different and more historical contextualization. For example, *Hoop Dreams*' origin story fails to account for the relationship between the rise of the NBA and its role in revitalizing America's post-Fordist cities. It neglects the correspondence between the making of the African American NBA celebrity and America's war on inner-city youth. Not coincidentally, *Hoop Dreams* was initiated the same year that Michael Jordan *and* crack became national preoccupations. Although eclipsed by the origin story, the conditions of possibility of *Hoop Dreams* (by which we mean the *Hoop Dreams* portfolio, the comprehensive *Hoop Dreams* phenomenon) are embedded in a complex of transnational corporate interests, including the media, the NBA, and manufacturers of sports apparel, which motivate the film and its popularity. The exclusions that govern the promotional *Hoop Dreams* origin story effectively designate, establish, and stabilize the narrative integrity of the film. Additionally, the "honorable filmmakers" stories allow the film to be read as a celebration of the promise of political action, social change, and racial harmony based on humanism, individual intervention, and personal interactions.

In the public response to *Hoop Dreams,* the filmmakers' friendship with the Agees and the Gateses comes to represent (for the presumed white suburban audience invited to identify with the filmmakers) a real solution to America's racial and class tensions, a fantasy that obscures questions about the deep-seated, systematic violence of racism and economic deprivation. The aesthetic and narrative work by which the film is endowed with integrity and social advocacy both relies on, and is productive of, a notion of sameness in which race (and, by extension, racism) no longer matters. The appeal to sameness, which displaces racism, allows white, middle-class America to view itself as democratic and compassionate even at a time of increased resentment and revenge directed at already vulnerable inner-city populations. But America's ability to derive pleasure from the film, to celebrate its ethical audience position, relies on the film's criticism of sport and, more specifically, the easily identifiable figure of exploitation and wrongdoing, Gene Pingatore.

Visualizing Social Critiques: Individuals and Moral Messages

In this section, we consider the ways in which *Hoop Dreams* indicts and fails to indict the economies of sport. We contend that although *Hoop Dreams* gestures toward criticizing the exploitative treatment and commodification of William, Arthur, and other urban African American youths (an exploitation endemic to the sport-entertainment complex), the criticism is ultimately directed to and displaced onto the bodies of particular social agents who are visualized as virtuous or vicious. An indictment of the sport-entertainment complex would require examining the economic, political, and cultural forces governing that system (the forces defining the post-Fordist city), a critical examination that is an unlikely filmic possibility because the film's origin story and narrative integrity are maintained through these exclusions. Rather than interrogating the sport system, the film displaces and explains racism, greed, and exploitation through individual character. In our view, such displacements work to position viewers ("white high-rise America") as apparently "discriminating" and "socially conscious" cultural critics who not only easily recognize but are distanced from the everyday violences that shape the lives of the poor in the inner city. Moreover, this dynamic aligns the viewers with "the socially conscious filmmakers": Both accrue identity and meaning as they are defined over and against figures of exploitation, defined as those involved in exploitative relations with Arthur and William. Such narrative mechanisms "relieve" the audience of the responsibility of critical reflection about their implication in exploitative spectator and consumption practices as well as the everyday conditions that structure the lives of the urban poor. The responsibility of critical reflection is relieved in the sense that it is actively discouraged.

One of the film's more obviously critical moments of the sport system occurs during William's stay at the Nike All-American Camp at Princeton, New Jersey. Also known as the ABCD (Academic Betterment and Career Development), the camp brings together 120 of the nation's top high school players for a week-long, all-expenses-paid program each summer. The camp, ostensibly designed as an introduction to student-athlete life, reserves mornings for academics and guest lectures and afternoons for games. But the camp is not, as claimed by William DuBois, the camp athletic director, solely an introduction to student-athlete life. Instead, it provides a convenient, centralized location for university coaches and scouts to assess potential recruits.

The viewers' arrival at the camp is signaled by an army of white Nike sneakers marching along the clean-swept paths of the Princeton University campus. The camera cuts to an old grand red-brick building and then to a large lecture theater filled with young predominantly African American men decked out in bright red and blue Nike polo shirts. In the front of the room, Dick Vitale, a well-known sports commentator, performs an energetic, "inspirational" speech, in which he tells his audience: "This is America. You can make something of your life." From here, the film moves to a gymnasium with several basketball games in progress. With the court action as background, the viewer is offered a series of sound bites from various coaches including Kevin O'Neill, William's future coach at Marquette, and the infamous Bobby Knight of Indiana. According to Knight, "There aren't very many kids at any level, including the NBA, that really understand what basketball is all about."

In the classroom, the young men appear bored as William DuBois claims, "We provide them with an experience they can't get anywhere else, in that we simulate what it's going to be like to be a student-athlete. The stats on Division I players graduating from college are really frightening." As we see a close-up of William's face, we hear Spike Lee:

Nobody cares about you. [The camera cuts to Spike Lee pacing around a lecture theater podium.] You're black, you're male, all you're supposed to do is deal drugs and mug women. [We see William, looking pensive.] The only reason why you're here, you can make their team win. If their team wins, these schools get a lot of money. This whole thing is revolving around money.

Back at the gymnasium, William is excelling on the court. Bo Ellis, the assistant coach at Marquette, claims that if "you look at some of these young boys' bodies . . . they've got NBA bodies already." Bob Gibbons, an independent talent scout, announces, "It's already become a meat market, but I try to do my job, and, you know, serve professional meat." In the next frame, we see Gibbons with another scout discussing the various schools (DePaul, Marquette, Indiana, Michigan) that are interested in William. Soon after, William sustains a muscle injury. Interspersed with shots of an athletic trainer examining his leg, we see coaches, including O'Neill and Knight, who apparently "look" concerned about the implications of his injury. As a result of a muscle injury, William is unable to compete for the final two days of the camp.

The progression of the scenes leading up to William's trip to Princeton establish the context that confirms the relevance and worth of the camp experience: Two scenes undermine the critical potential of the Nike Camp sequence. The first scene takes the form of a "tour" of Bo Agee's former neighborhood. As we pass by decaying buildings and garbage-strewn patches of wasteland, Bo identifies the street corners where he purchased drugs. In combined confession and testimony, he expresses regret for this period in his life and takes responsibility for Arthur's expulsion from St. Joseph's:

I think about it, had I not been on drugs when Arthur went to St. Joseph's just how good it would have been for him. He wouldn't ha' had to leave. He can just look at my life and say here's a good example of what not to do. If he had my ways, I'd be, I would be shakin [laughter] in my shoes right now.

Images of Arthur, Shannon, and a friend on a shopping trip punctuate Bo's comments. Jackets embroidered with team logos, a wall lined with sneakers, the Air Jordan silhouette on red shirts and shorts, and other signs of Nike fill the screen, as all three youths admire the display, try on various pairs of shoes, and make purchases. The camera closes in first on Arthur, as he hands $70 over the counter to pay for his goods, and then "the dollars" as they are placed in the register. As Arthur reveals that drug dealers in the neighborhood give promising ball players money to buy athletic gear and "to keep our careers going," we see a series of close-ups: sneaker after sneaker displaying the Nike swoosh; a shirt decorated with an image of a primitivized and monsterized Michael Jordan; and, finally, the brand name Nike and its signature swoosh emblazoned on shirts. A cut to the army of white Nike sneakers marching on the Princeton path follows the close-up images of Nike consumer goods.

The two scenes condense an array of issues immediately recognizable as "urban problems": drugs, gangs, drug money, family breakdown, "sneaker crimes," and insatiable consumer desires. No explanation of the issues is needed nor is it invited by the film: Extensive attention directed at these problems in both the scientific and popular realms renders them distinct, obvious, and easily intelligible. Although edited to make "Nike" the link between the camp and the sneakers purchased with drug money, Nike—and its implication in the network of inner-city poverty, deindustrialization and the global economy—escape interrogation. The camp and, by extension, Nike accrue their value and meaning in relation to what are presented in the film as alternatives. Despite the offensive attitudes displayed by some of the coaches and the meat market environment at the Nike camp, real possibility, control, and comfort are forged over and against first the menial labor that possibly awaits Arthur (the Nike camp sequence is interrupted momentarily by a scene showing Arthur and Shannon working for minimum wage at a Chicago Pizza Hut) and, more forcefully, the despair, disillusion, and dystopian possibility that Arthur might go the way of his father and environment (a prediction made by Arthur's Marshall coach earlier in the film).

Familiar narratives of social problems also overdetermine identities through which characters, regardless of whether they appear in newspaper reports or documentary films, function. In other words, because Bo Agee's identity is already overdetermined by these narratives, his admissions of failure and lack of moral worth, articulated through his claim of responsibility for Arthur's expulsion from St. Joseph's, are immediately understandable. The force of contrast and meaning in this filmic composition is established through the sport/gang dyad that governs the national imagination in general. Combined with critical attention directed to the personalities of individual coaches, audiences are discouraged from thinking about urban violence, drug use, and the late capitalist global economy and consumerism in their complexity. Corporate investments and disinvestments are never broached as potentially crucial issues.

Gene Pingatore *is* the distillation of the exploitative relationships we witness, but that distillation, which individuates and dis-

tances, is not simply revealed, nor is it easily achieved. Pingatore is positioned early and throughout the film as the embodiment of social wrongs and exploitation through the considerable time devoted to visual narratives of long, intense practice sessions in which he appears ruthless, impatient, aggressive, and loud. Moreover, Pingatore's unemotional and frank interview style supports this characterization, and it is particularly jarring when, in a matter-of-fact manner, he explains Arthur's expulsion from St. Joseph's as an unfortunate but unavoidable financial necessity. His opening conversation with the Agees, coupled with Arthur's dismissal, suggests that Gene Pingatore has feigned care and concern, which makes him an especially despicable character. Interviews with a depressed Sheila Agee, who expresses her anger at the school for expelling him mid-semester, and the Marshall High coach who argues that had Arthur fulfilled his potential, St. Joseph's would not have been so swift to force him out, heighten the impact of Pingatore's words. Pingatore appears as uncaring and parasitic in what remains a legitimate and potentially even beneficial sport system. The figure of the coach who only sees young players as a tool for victory works to eclipse the broader conditions and policies that deny Arthur as well as other inner-city youths access to a solid public school education and opportunities.

Pingatore's "obvious" questionable character is defined over and against other individuals in the system who appear caring, well-intentioned, and loyal. For example, Kevin O'Neill, the Marquette coach with whom William eventually signs, is represented as personable, committed to higher principles, and concerned with William as a person, not simply as a player. While recruiting William, O'Neill displays an unconditional commitment to William when he offers William a 4-year scholarship to Marquette that will continue to pay for his education despite prohibitive injuries. In a repetition of the sort of concern and loyalty attributed to the filmmakers, O'Neill displays the sort of loyalty and ethical superiority that both constructs white viewer identity and demonstrates the possibilities and promises of the sporting system.

Pingatore's position as the visible and locatable embodiment of guilt and wrongdoing is evident in what for the audience are two of the most satisfying scenes in the film. Because Gene Pingatore's parasitic and exploitative tendencies were apparently motivated by his endless desire to "go down state"—that is, to coach his team in the state high school championships—Arthur's trip to Champaign is experienced as particularly pleasurable. Audience satisfaction and pleasure cannot be reduced to Arthur's outstanding play during the championships. Instead, because editing effects have established the sense that we can clearly see where guilt lies, we also sense that we can clearly perceive that justice has been achieved, within allowable bounds, when it is Arthur, whom Pingatore has most betrayed, who has the honor of delivering a stinging moral message to him. Pingatore watches as Arthur realizes Pingatore's dream, leading his team to victory and a third-place finish in the state championship in Champaign's Assembly Hall. Although Pingatore did not betray William, at least not to the same degree that he betrayed Arthur, justice, within apparently proper limits, is again served when William delivers his moral message to Pingatore. As Pingatore says goodbye to William, William tells Pingatore that he decided to major in communications, so "when you start asking for donations, I'll know the right way to turn you down." Indeed, the effect of these moments suggests that the film has been edited in such a way that one of the biggest challenges presented to William and Arthur is defined in terms of Pingatore. These moments confirm Pingatore's central position in the production and stabilization of audience identity.

Conclusion

Lauren Berlant's work, which underscores how attention on youth functions to allow American audiences self-recognition in terms of compassion, care, and ethical superiority, is helpful in understanding the affective purchase of *Hoop Dreams*. She argued that the celebration of the prepolitical child and other incipient citizens are vital to the American public sphere because the image of the future, a future they convey, works to draw attention away from the more troubling issues of violence, exploitation, and equality in the present. As we see it, *Hoop Dreams* is a prominent example in a long line of representative strategies that both reflect and incite America's desire to know the "urban other" and the continued significance of the figure of the prepolitical child in this quest for knowledge. Berlant suggested that the fantasy of the American Dream, a quintessential fantasy of futurity so absolutely central to the narrative of *Hoop Dreams* and its commercial success, is a central force in the mobilization of violence in the present.

Arthur Agee and William Gates, promising basketball players of fine character, embody the fantastic future that (white) America lives for and through. The frequent references to Isiah Thomas and Michael Jordan remind the audience that William and Arthur's promise lies in their ability to become revenue-producing commodities (of course, the irony is that they already are) who bring pleasure to millions. *Hoop Dreams* celebrates and relies on futurity. The film imagines Arthur and William as highly marketable celebrities. The omnipresent Nike/NBA signs in *Hoop Dreams* signify earning potential and the possibility of leaving the ghetto.

Thus, the politics of *Hoop Dreams* are embedded in a duplicitous optimism of the future that circumvents the terror of the present.[21] This circumvention cannot be understood apart from the conventions of documentary filmmaking (clearly adhered to by the makers of *Hoop Dreams*) and photography, which deny the limits of the visual register and the significance of location and perspective by rendering them invisible. Although *Hoop Dreams'* appeal is routinely cast in terms of its realness, we see that "realness" as symptomatic of a point of view whose limits and exclusion have been naturalized and are therefore not easily recognizable—an effect of familiar and undisturbing knowledges. Although the truth-effect of documentary aesthetics exemplified in *Hoop Dreams* erases context and location, a familiar visual economy solicits a national appeal and pleasure. This dynamic is integral to the understanding of urban, consumer, racial, and national politics.

In an effort to understand the stakes in the "reality effect" of *Hoop Dreams,* we want to revisit Steve James's depiction of the 10-minute ovation that met the film's New York Film Festival debut. Again, as James characterized the moment: "The people at the festival said nothing like this had ever happened before. The audience was just standing there, clapping for the connection they felt for those families."[22]

We agree with Steve James, whose assessment suggests that the applause, at least on one level, is for the recognition of sameness, shared values, and desires. Easy slippages between the conditions of poor, primarily African American, inner-city residents who face inhumane conditions of poverty, public assistance, and employment possibilities and "white, high-rise America," slippages routinely facilitated through the category of "family," are not necessarily something to be celebrated; instead, they are indicative of the "knowledges" that govern the audience's understanding of the crisis of the inner city in ways that demonize single parents, welfare recipients, the under- and unemployed, and African American youths in general. Moreover, these slippages, particularly as they are aligned with and as they call for a reconstitution of the family, work in concert with the neoconservative agenda of empowerment—will, self-sufficiency, independence. The affective dimension of the audience's desire to recognize itself in the lives of the urban poor and to celebrate that recognition is deeply problematic and symptomatic of the position from which identity is forged and judgments made, America's quest for sameness, and America's inability to think adequately about difference and inequality. Repeated visual codes and the narrative work not only to displace guilt and implication onto easily identifiable agents such as Pingatore but also to reinforce a conservative, normalizing agenda in which the virtuous and vicious are easily distinguished. We do not mean to suggest that these easily identifiable agents are not implicated in exploitative relations; instead, our intent is to direct attention to how such figures of displacement operate in the national popular psyche to relieve guilt and to produce ethically superior subjects. In *Hoop Dreams,* "Gene Pingatore" helps mainstream audiences reconcile the conflict between inner-city poverty and the sense of themselves as compassionate, virtuous, and morally superior. Moreover, the celebration of the filmmakers and the parallels drawn between their lives and the lives of Arthur and William in America's response to *Hoop Dreams* allow questions of whiteness to be displaced onto Gene Pingatore.

Hoop Dreams refuses to trouble the familiar categories that govern knowledges of the inner city; therefore, the exclusions that lend stability to those categories remain invisible and uninterrogated. The figure of the basketball player, defined over and against the criminal (the gang member who governs America's representation of African American men in the mid-1980s to the mid-1990s and who appears explicitly and implicitly in both texts), functions as a means of displacement that reconciles middle-class America's sense of itself as compassionate while it calls for and endorses increasingly vengeful punitive programs. Again, as a project that translates subjectivity into objectivity, *Hoop Dreams* tells us less about real urban life and conditions than it does about the nation's state of mind.

Notes

1. Alex Kotlowitz, *There Are No Children Here* (New York: Anchor, 1992); Daniel Coyle, *Hardball: A Season in the Projects* (New York: Harper & Row, 1995); Greg Donaldson, *The Ville: Cops and Kids in Urban America* (New York: Anchor, 1994); Darcy Frey, *The Last Shot: City Streets, Basketball Dreams* (Boston: Houghton Mifflin, 1994).

2. Earlier versions of our discussion of *Hoop Dreams,* realism, and urban possibilities appear in Cheryl Cole and Samantha King, "Representing Urban Possibilities: Racism, Realism, and Hoop Dreams," in *Sport and Postmodern Times,* edited by G. Rail (Albany: State University of New York Press); and Cheryl Cole and Samantha King, "Documenting America: Ethnographies of Inner City Basketball and Logics of Capitalism," in *Anthropology, Sport and Culture,* edited by R. R. Sands (Westport, CT: Bergin & Garvey, 1999), pp. 147–71.

3. Cheryl L. Cole, "American Jordan: P.L.A.Y., Consensus, and Punishment," *Sociology of Sport Journal* 13(4, 1996):366–97.

4. Michael Massing, "Ghetto Blasting," *The New Yorker,* January 16, 1995, pp. 32–37.

5. For a critique of *Hoop Dreams'* mobility narrative, see Jillian Sandell, "Out of the Ghetto and into the Marketplace," *Socialist Review* 95(2, 1995):7–82.

6. Lauren Berlant, "National Brands/National Bodies: Imitation of Life," in *The Phantom Public Sphere,* edited by B. Robbins (Minneapolis: University of Minnesota Press, 1993), p. 178.

7. For an extremely useful and insightful discussion on modern power, the see-able and the say-able, and the possibility of living ethically and acting politically, see Melissa Orlie, *Living Ethically, Acting Politically* (Ithaca, NY: Cornell University Press, 1998).

8. Desson Howe, 1994, "*Hoop Dreams:* An Overtime Victory," *The Washington Post,* November 13, p. G4.

9. Hinson, Hal, "'Hoop Dreams': A Slamdunk Shot of Truth," *Washington Post,* November 4, 1994, pp. F1, F7.

10. Michael Wilmington, "When Film Dreams Come True," *Chicago Tribune,* October 2, 1994, p. 5.

11. Wilmington, 1994, p. 20.

12. Patrick Z. McGavin, "From the Street and the Gyms to the Courtroom and Beyond," *The New York Times,* October 9, 1994, p. 26; Lee Jones, "Hoop Realities," *Jump Cut* 40:8.

13. McGavin, 1994, p. 26.

14. Pat Aufderheide, "The Dream Team," *The Independent,* October 1994, p. 32.

15. A public relations and film distributor team convinced Roger Ebert and Gene Siskel to review the film prior to its showing at Sundance. In their rave review, Siskel and Ebert identified the film as an "unforgettable portrait of American urban reality" (quoted in Aufderheide, 1994, p. 33). As a result of the Siskel and Ebert review, tickets for *Hoop Dreams* were among the hottest at Sundance.

16. Glenn Collins, "Advertising," *The New York Times,* November 7, 1994, p. B21.

17. Collins, 1994, p. B21.

18. Wilmington, 1994, p. 5.

19. Howe, 1994, p. G4.

20. Ibid.

21. Ibid.

22. Ibid.

Cole and King:

1. In what ways do the messages conveyed in *Hoop Dreams* serve to perpetuate the status quo?

2. Why do Cole and King contend that *Hoop Dreams* distorts the reality of inner city life?

19

Black Mobility in White Corporations: Up the Corporate Ladder but Out on a Limb

Sharon M. Collins

Spurred in part by threats of federal sanctions, white companies during the 1960s and 1970s incorporated a new echelon of college-educated blacks into previously closed managerial job and business-related professions (Farley 1984; Freeman 1981, 1976a, 1976b; Landry 1987). Indeed, the 1960s witnessed the reversal of a longstanding pattern of declining black-white income ratios with levels of education—and the ratio of black-to-white income rose most rapidly for managers. Employed black men, in particular, were in greater demand for prestigious occupations in the labor market. In 1960, only about 7 percent of non-white male college graduates were managers, compared with 18 percent of college-educated white men (Freeman 1976b). Between 1960 and 1970, the proportion of black male college graduates employed as managers increased almost twofold over the 1960 level (Freeman 1976b). And between 1970 and 1980, the number of black men holding executive, administrative, or managerial jobs increased each year at twice the rate of white men (Farley and Allen 1987).

Yet, even after more than 30 years of social and political pressure to diversify corporate manpower and management teams, the net result is more black managers but negligible gain for black men in the decision-making strongholds of white corporate America (Chicago Urban League 1977; Heidrick and Struggles 1979; Korn/Ferry 1986, 1990; Theodore and Taylor 1991). Despite gains in entry, African-Americans clearly stagnate in their climb up the managerial hierarchy, thereby failing to make inroads into key decision-making positions and in the racial redistribution of power.

Against a backdrop of sustained inequality in corporate job allocation, this paper asks whether constraints to blacks' corporate progress are manufactured in the work process. In the 1960s and 1970s, highly educated blacks experienced less discrimination in access to higher-paying corporate jobs, yet we know little about their careers. Nkomo and Cox (1990) examine macro- and micro-level variables related to job promotion; Kraiger and Ford (1985) focus on discrimination in performance evaluation; and others survey black managers' perceptions of corporate life (Jones 1986; Irons and Moore 1985). The responsibilities and assignments accorded black managers in the post-entry period are a crucial but neglected element for analysis.

This chapter explores the problem of race and corporate mobility. It uses a unique data set: in-depth interviews with 76 of the most successful black executives employed in major Chicago-based white corporations in 1986. These black achievers in traditionally closed managerial occupations have had the greatest chance to enter into the higher echelons of organizations in functions tied to profitability. I explore the repercussions of a corporate division of labor on the career development of these managers.

Neoclassical economic theories and social structural explanations of race-based inequality in labor markets often are argued as oppositional insights. That is, human capital theory in economic literature and status attainment theory in sociology presume that economic progress among blacks is a color-blind function of supply-side characteristics such as education, ability, and individual preferences—not race conscious social forces and barriers. The lack of marketable skills, a dependent mentality, inferior education, and even relatively lower IQs are reasons for blacks' inability to gain parity with whites (Herrnstein and Murray 1994; Murray 1984; Smith and Welch 1983, 1986; Sowell 1983).

The opposing contention is that individuals' economic attainments are determined by structural aspects of the labor market. This alternate viewpoint attributes people's limited progress to the characteristics of their jobs (Doeringer and Piore 1971; Thurow 1975). Minorities and women, for example, fill occupational niches that are in decline or that do not lead to advancement (Ghiloni 1987; Kanter 1977; Reskin and Roos 1990). Consequently, powerful and prestigious jobs with career growth opportunities—managerial jobs, in particular—are much more likely to be filled by white men. In contrast, insights from my study of black managers in the white private sector cast social structure and human capital as interactive, not as mutually exclusive explanatory schemes.

In this chapter, I illustrate how a link between opportunity structure and human capital shaped subjects' abilities to achieve top jobs. In general, I view the managerial division of labor as mediating human capital. Therefore, these factors interactively influence blacks' progress in executive arenas. First, I argue that Chicago corporations deployed highly educated black labor out of mainstream positions and into "racialized" jobs. These are jobs created or reoriented during the 1960s and 1970s to carry out pro-black governmental policies and mediate black-related issues for white-owned companies. Affirmative action, urban affairs, community relations, and purchasing jobs are examples. Next, I show the impact of filling these jobs on executives' upward mobility. Initially, these jobs anointed black job holders with positive status in a company, thus attracting black talent. Over time, however, this structure of opportunity underdeveloped the human capital that corporations value. Consequently, racialized jobs marginalized the job holder's skills and, thus, the job holder. Ultimately, occupants' probability of moving into, competing for, and/or performing in, corporate areas that lead to decision-making positions (that is, general management, sales/marketing, production, finance/ accounting, and human resources) was greatly diminished.

The Study

I considered blacks to be "top executives" if: 1) they were employed in a banking institution and had a title of comptroller, trust officer, vice-president (excluding "assistant" vice president), president or chief officer; or 2) they were employed in a non-financial institution as department manager, director, vice president, or chief officer. In the mid-1980s, the respondents in this study held some of the more desirable and prestigious positions in Chicago's major corporations. About two-thirds (52) had the title of director or higher, including three chief officers, 30 vice presidents, and 19 unit directors. (The total includes three people with the title "manager" whose rank within the organization was equivalent to director.) The participants in this study were among the highest-ranking black executives in the country. Five of the executives interviewed were the highest-ranking blacks in corporations nationwide. Almost half (32) were among the highest-ranking blacks in a company's nationwide management structure.

To locate these managers, first I identified the 52 largest white corporations in Chicago using the *Chicago Reporter*'s (1983, 1986) listing of industrials, utilities, retail companies, transportation companies, and banks. Second, I asked knowledgeable informants familiar with the white corporate community in Chicago to identify blacks who met the study criteria. These same informants also identified employees of the targeted companies who might be able to provide names of higher-level black officers. I then used snowball sampling to identify a total of 87 managers. Eleven people were not interviewed because they declined to participate, because of logistical problems, or because they did not meet my criteria. Using resumes respondents forwarded to me before the interview, I explored the characteristics of each executive's job, as well as each respondent's career development and promotional opportunities.

I distinguished two types of jobs held by blacks in white corporations: racialized and mainstream. A job was coded "racialized" when its description indicated an actual and/or symbolic connection to black communities, to black issues, or to civil rights agencies at any level of government. For example, one respondent was hired by the chief executive officer of a major retailer in 1968 specifically to eradicate discriminatory employment practices used in the personnel department. I coded this job "racialized" because it was designed to improve black opportunities in the company at a time when the federal government increasingly was requiring it.

In contrast, jobs in line and support areas that lack racial implications in a company were coded "mainstream." In this category, functions relate to total constituencies, and neither explicit nor implicit connections to blacks could be found in the job description. A vice president and regional sales manager for a *Fortune* 500 company in the manufacturing and retail food industry provides an illustration of a career consisting of mainstream jobs. A *Fortune* 15 East Coast oil company hired this manager as a market researcher in 1961; his job involved marketing only to the total (predominantly white) consumer market, not to "special" (predominantly black) markets. He was not assigned to black territories as a salesman nor as a sales manager although, he said, "Those kinds of things even happen now [and once] happened a lot." This manager was not responsible for a predominantly black sales force, nor for sales and marketing to the black community when he managed geographical areas.

In this paper, the "mainstream" is the pipeline of line and support jobs leading to senior executive positions that oversee the strategic planning, human resource/personnel development, or production components of a company. For example, the manager just cited moved up the mainstream sales hierarchy from salesman to sales manager, from zone manager to district manager, from area manager to division manager and, finally, to his current position as a firm officer. Granted, the pipeline narrows as it moves upward, yet the flow of occupants into these jobs fills the executive vice president, senior vice president, group vice president, functional vice president, and corporate specialist slots that comprise company officers. The typical track to top jobs in major corporations is through profit-oriented positions, such as sales, operations, and finance or, to a lesser degree through personnel or public relations (Korn/Ferry 1990).

A Corporate Division of Labor

The corporate division of labor found among Chicago's top black executives is distinctly different than job patterns found among their white peers. In this study, African American executives with mainstream careers in the private sector stand out as the exception, not the rule. Only one-third (25) of the people I interviewed built careers that consisted entirely of mainstream jobs. On the other hand, 12 (16 percent) had one racialized job and about half (39) had two or more racialized jobs. One vice president and company director was a company ombudsman during the 1970s whose task was, he said, to "promote the visibility and good name" of the bank in the black community in Chicago. A second vice president built a career interspersed with black community relations jobs during the late 1960s and 1970s that, he said, "develop[ed] a good corporate citizenship image among blacks and . . . work[ed] with . . . local [black] agencies." A third vice president spent part of his tenure in an urban affairs job. He said:

After the civil disorders, the riots . . . there was a tremendous movement . . . to have black [representation in the company]. Basically [my] job was to work with the [company] and come up with minority candidates.

To obtain a rough comparative illustration of black and white executive careers, I conducted an informal survey of top white executives by asking 20 CEOs of major Chicago private sector companies if they ever held affirmative action or urban affairs jobs. (I asked about these jobs specifically because they exemplify racialized jobs.) Only one had (or admitted having) a job in either of these areas. Some CEOs even seemed startled by the question. The CEO that had worked in urban affairs performed different tasks than those performed by my respondents. Although this man represented the company on several city-wide committees to improve race relations, his job, unlike the black executives I interviewed, was a part-time, temporary assignment, not a full-time, permanent position. The results of my informal survey suggest that—among the managerial elite in Chicago—blacks are likely to have held racialized jobs, but whites are not.

Disparate career patterns are not attributable to educational differences. Indeed, African American respondents' educational level closely parallels that of white male senior-level executives in 1986. Ninety-four percent of top executives in *Fortune* 500 companies surveyed by Korn/Ferry (1986) had bachelors' degrees, and 42 percent had graduate degrees. Eighty-nine percent of respondents in my study had at least a bachelor's degree when they entered the private sector. Over one-third (38 percent) earned advanced degrees. Moreover, their level of education is well above the median level of about one year of college for salaried male managers in 1960 and in 1970 (U.S. Bureau of Census 1960, 1973). In addition, slightly more than one-half of the black graduates I interviewed received their college degrees from predominantly white institutions.

Career differences are not extensions of respondents' ports of entry into the private sector. Almost one-half of 45 people who filled affirmative action and urban affairs jobs started in the corporate mainstream with line positions. Therefore, black but not white managerial careers reflect a race conscious interaction with skill and education that tracked black managers into administrative jobs that emerged during the 1960s and 1970s.

The career of one man, who was succeeding in his company but then moved into an urban affairs position, exemplifies this interaction between race and career tracking. Between 1964 and 1967 this man rapidly ascended through a series of supervisory and store management slots to become an area supervisor, a middle management position.

At 23, his annual salary was more than doubled by a performance-based bonus. Yet, in the midst of this mainstream success (i.e., succeeding in the route typically traveled by the company's top executives), this man was asked to create an urban affairs program. The circumstances that led to this request were relatively straightforward: Civil rights activists had confronted the company with specific demands backed by the threat of a nationwide boycott; and the company viewed blacks as a sizeable proportion of its customer base. The respondent said, "Basically [my] job was to work with the licensee department and [come] up with minority candidates around the country to become [store owners]." After completing a strenuous series of meetings with the company's top executives—which included the head of personnel, a senior vice president, the head of licensing, the corporate legal council, and finally, the company president—he was offered, and he accepted, the assignment.

Within this operations-driven corporation, a manager with demonstrated talent for business operations generally would be considered a serious contender for a top-level mainstream position. From this perspective, slotting this man in an urban affairs job appears to be a frivolous use of talent. But in 1968, no other blacks worked at the company's corporate offices (save for one black janitor) and the company was vulnerable to racial protest. Deploying a black middle-level manager, a known commodity, into corporate urban affairs was a rational business decision. Indeed, a white vice president of personnel who worked in a major Chicago firm during the 1960s and 1970s noted that top management often filled newly created affirmative action positions with their best workers. He explained that this strategy signalled to the rank and file workers the seriousness of a company's commitment. Senior corporate managers believed that transferring an experienced black line manager into affirmative action would increase the credibility of this collateral role and enhance its effectiveness.

Black social and political unrest infused black managerial capacities with race-related purposes (Collins 1997). African Americans moved into urban affairs, affirmative action, and other racialized management jobs that required them to interact predominantly with black community organizations and/or to help white companies recruit black labor. A 53-year-old company director, who began his private sector managerial career in operations in a retail company, was deployed to set up the equal employment opportunity function for the company. He recalled that the perquisites accompanying the job were "very attractive [and] that was the place for us [blacks] to be."

Indeed, other occupants of affirmative action and urban affairs jobs who were recruited from mainstream line areas commented that black-oriented jobs appeared to be a route where talented blacks could advance rapidly. Senior-level white management, usually either senior vice presidents or chief executive officers, personally solicited 12 of the 22 recruits (55 percent) from the mainstream. Eleven (50 percent) were given salary increases, more prestigious job titles, and promises of future rewards. Nine people turned down the first attempt at recruitment because they evaluated the job to be a dead end, despite high pay and elevated titles, and were approached a second time by top management. A director of affirmative action and diversity took the job initially because, he said, "I remember the CEO saying, 'we want you to take this beautiful job. It's going to pay you all this money. It's going to make you a star.'"

Racialized Division of Labor and Mobility

What impact did this allocative process have on upward mobility in white corporations?

To compare the advancement associated with racialized and mainstream careers, I selected 64 respondents employed in the white private sector at least since 1972 to construct a career typology.[1] Three types of managerial careers—mainstream, mixed, and racialized—emerged, based on the jobs that these executives held. Respondents having no racialized jobs in their careers were coded as having mainstream careers (24 of 64). Respondents whose careers incorporated at least one, but not a majority, of racialized jobs were coded as having mixed careers (22 of 64), the careers of those with a majority of racialized jobs were coded as racialized (18 of 64).

Lowered Job Ceilings

By the mid-1980s, racialized respondents had advanced less than respondents in mainstream careers. The top executives (i.e., chief officers and senior vice presidents) spent most of their careers in mainstream areas. There was little difference in the executive job titles associated with mixed and mainstream careers, possibly because the vast majority of mixed careers had only one or two racialized jobs in them.

In contrast, 80 percent of racialized careers terminated with director or manager titles. Only 38 percent of the mainstream careers, and 46 percent of mixed careers terminated with those titles. Not one manager in a racialized career progressed above vice president.

Those who stayed in racialized jobs were ambitious people who saw themselves as doing the best they could, given blacks' historically limited job possibilities in white companies. One equal employment opportunity manager had post-graduate work in physics and engineering. He had been with the company eight years when the employee relations director approached him to set up the company's first affirmative action program. This man accepted the offer because, he said, "I wanted to get into management. That was

the first and only opportunity that I felt I was going to get." This executive weighted the jobs' perquisites against the void in managerial opportunities for blacks in white firms. Racialized managerial positions appeared to be a way to sidestep the career stagnation common among the handful of blacks who previously attained management roles but remained trapped in low-level positions. In the 1970s, such jobs seemed to offer faster mobility, greater freedom and authority, and higher visibility and access to white corporate power brokers than mainstream jobs.

I asked an affirmative action director for a major retail company in Chicago if he ever tried to move back into the mainstream after he took on equal employment opportunity functions. To my surprise he said that he turned down a buyer's job with his first employer. He said, "I was stubborn at that point. No, I didn't want that." Given that buyers were key people in that organization and that the job was a stepping stone to higher-paying positions, his refusal signals the attractiveness of racialized positions in companies in the early 1970s. He said,

Remember now, this [equal opportunity] stuff was exciting and there's a trap that you get into. Those of us who are in this kind of area talk about it all the time. It's kind of a golden handcuffs trap. We used to go on the convention circuit around the country... the Urban League and the NAACP, promoting our individual corporations. We were visible. We were representing the company. We had big budgets. I mean, you know, you go to every convention. And [you can] get yourself two or three suites and entertain all the delegates. You could spend $15,000 or $20,000 at a convention. I never had that kind of money to spend, to sign a check, so it was very attractive.

The economic rewards and social status that accompanied racialized positions were unimaginable luxuries to blacks—in this or any employment sector—in the years preceding federal legislation. With the benefit of hindsight, the affirmative action director explained:

I believe that had I stayed in operations [I would have] continued to move up and that's where the clout is. But the opportunity just wasn't there [for blacks] when I first started with that company.

After a slight pause he added, somewhat ruefully, "things changed and it is now."

Only four of 18 managers with racialized careers (22 percent) were the highest ranking black executive in a company's Chicago location. In contrast, 31 of 46 managers who had a majority of mainstream functions in their careers (72 percent) were the highest-ranking black executive in a Chicago company. Acknowledging advancement limitations associated with racialized jobs, respondents alternately described them as "dead end jobs [that had] no power," "nigger jobs," and "money-using" versus "money producing" jobs. The affirmative action director quoted above said that creating and administering the affirmative action function for his company was a misstep in his career:

If I had to go back and do it all over again, I would not stay in affirmative action. Them that brings in the dollars is where the most opportunity is. I advise my sons . . . stay out of the staff functions, although those functions are very necessary.

He went on to name people who took different routes, and who he viewed—somewhat wistfully—as "making it."

Not coincidentally, a manager's position in the corporate division of labor in 1986 coincided with his level of optimism about his future in a company (see Kanter 1977:135). About three-quarters of mainstream (19 of 26) but less than one-quarter of racialized respondents (4 of 20) believed in 1986 that their chances for a promotion or a lateral move leading to promotion in the company were "good" or "very good." Respondents in racialized careers in 1986 reported that they

were at the end of their career ladders in white companies. Sixty-five percent (13 of 20) said there would be no additional moves for them in the company, neither lateral nor promotional. Moreover, their pessimism extended to their perceptions of their opportunities for upward mobility on the open job market. The director of affirmative action quoted above summarized this shared perception of future mobility: "ascension for me is over."

The white executive elite I interviewed informally shared the opinion that African-American managers in racialized jobs were "out of the mix," in other words, not in the running for top jobs in a company. The assessment of each group—black and white—is not surprising, because racialized jobs are predominantly support positions, although these jobs can be found in sales and operations areas.[2] White executives, in general, view support functions as one of the worst routes to top jobs in a company (Korn/Ferry 1990). Nkomo and Cox (1990) indicate line positions play a highly significant positive role in individuals' promotion success. Support jobs are less desirable than line jobs because they lack influence and have shorter and more limited chains of career opportunities (Kanter 1977). I suggest further that the chain of opportunity becomes even shorter when linked to a job with racial purposes. These jobs not only impose relatively lower career ceilings, they underdevelop the talents and skills that corporations value, and therefore marginalize the job holder.

Limited Skill Development

Pressures placed on companies by federal government legislation and by protests in urban black communities made racialized jobs valuable to companies. In placating blacks and buffering corporations from racial turmoil, racialized jobs were highly unstructured; employees handled new and unpredictable contingencies. More than 80 percent of first racialized jobs were created when the respondents filled them. Ultimately, however, this managerial division of labor undermined the development of black human capital. As job content evolved, racialized jobs became routine work centered on a narrow set of administrative tasks extracted from generalist personnel functions. One manager noted that his job in the 1970s involved recruiting blacks, but not whites, into a company. Another mentioned the job was essentially "[black] number counting." A third man said the company promoted him and increased his salary because he was serving a function. He admitted he was aware, even then, that his future in the company might be limited:

You have a little stepladder . . . a logical progression [of personnel functions] you have to go through if you are to ever become a personnel director. I wasn't doing any of that. As far as I could see, the company wanted black folks to be my only responsibility.

The narrowness of the jobs' routines limited—not broadened—these people's development of knowledge and skills. An executive for a clothing manufacturer and retailer made this clear when he summarized his experience:

[The company] sent me to Chicago for a week long workshop on affirmative action. In that one week I learned all I needed to know about affirmative action, and I haven't learned much since. It's the kind of field that nothing, well, a few laws might change, but the concept doesn't. You don't branch out. There's nothing, oh, now how can I explain it? There's not a lot of specialties . . . in affirmative action. You deal with 6 or 7 basic laws, or regulations, and . . . once you know those there's not an awful lot more to learn. I'm serious about it. Since 1965 or 1972, I don't think I've learned very much more.

Racialized managers in the 1960s and 1970s initially were rewarded with mobility

in their companies. Ultimately, however, they required little or no company investment for job preparation and training. This racialized structure of mobility, therefore, created and solidified career ceilings through a cumulative work experience. Although managers' status elevated when their departments, titles, and salaries grew, respondents weren't trained in other areas. When I asked managers for job descriptions associated with various promotions, one affirmative action manager in a segregated career dismissed the question, indicating that he was "essentially doing the same thing" in each affirmative action job, although the scope of each job and his title and grade-level changed. His report distinctly contrasts with those of respondents who were promoted in mainstream personnel. In the case of personnel executives, at least six distinct components of job experience were clearly delineated—including employee relations, employment, compensation and benefits, and labor relations.

In contrast, people who ascended racialized career ladders became more specialized and increasingly secluded from generalist management areas. One manager summarized the gulf between mainstream and racialized personnel in the following way:

If you stay in affirmative action, when you go looking for a job you're going to be seen as the affirmative action person. And personnel jobs are bigger than that.

Narrowly defined racialized jobs rely on interpersonal skills and external relationships without building administrative skills and internal support networks important to advancement. For example, a manager in a manufacturing company described his urban affairs job as if he were an ambassador-at-large:

I just moved about. Traveled. Everything was coming out of the community and I was there. I'd make 10, sometimes 12, meetings [in the black community] a day.

An executive in the food industry described his affirmative action job in a strikingly similar way:

I spent most of my time in the [black] community trying to . . . let people know that there were jobs and positions available in this company. I did a lot of speaking with community groups.

An executive in a communications firm said, "Mostly I worked with local community agencies to get the word out that there were opportunities [in the company]."

A director of urban affairs linked his company with black civil rights and social service organizations and represented it in black-dominated settings. This college-educated man moved out of sales and became skilled at brokering the interest of his company, successfully "absorbing" the tensions between white companies and urban black constituencies. He said that in 1971:

[My role was to] make [the company] look good. I did what they needed done to look good in the community. They utilized me in that fashion. For eleven years I was just their spook who sat by the door, and I understood that. Certainly I was, and I charged them well for it.

Marginalized Job Holders

The structure of upward mobility became restrictive so that success in segregated areas prolonged these managers' career segregation. Prolonged career segregation, in turn, further undermined these executives' value in mainstream corporate functions. Promoting respondents in place created and solidified career barriers by conferring information about respondents' abilities. That is, racialized human capital became a factor in marginalizing respondents by limiting their value in mainstream corporate functions.

People in segregated careers faced two alternatives for enhancing their chances for upward mobility: (1) to laterally move into an entirely different corporate area associated with mainstream planning, production, or human resources administration, or (2) to move laterally to the mainstream component of the racialized area (e.g., from community relations to public relations). People who specialized in affirmative action, community relations, and other race-related jobs were stymied in both routes by real or perceived limits to their usefulness in mainstream fields.

When an affirmative action manager (and one-time comptroller) tried to re-enter the corporate mainstream, she found she was locked into her racialized niche at each turn. She said:

I tried to negotiate myself out [of affirmative action]. There didn't seem to be a lot of . . . future. I wanted to try to get back into merchandising at that point. Or go back into comptrolling or to go somewhere else in personnel. You know nothing ever came out of it. I even took a special class . . . to get accreditation in personnel, as a personnel generalist. Which I completed. [It] had absolutely no effect on me going anywhere. . . . It got to where the [job] level and the salary level to go and change fields is too high . . . to [be] able to sell me to someone else. The likelihood of me going outside of [affirmative action] at this point is pretty well zero.

The trade-off to rising in companies in racialized jobs that required specialized skills and external networks was that managers became cut off from the internal networks and skill-building that would enable them to move into, and then move up in, the corporation's job mainstream.

A community relations manager for a major electronics corporation—when noting that his company's commitment to urban affairs programs for blacks began to decrease noticeably in the 1980s—also illustrates this trade-off. Observing, as he put it, the "hand-writing on the wall," he made multiple attempts to move out of his dissolving niche in the company and into a mainstream production area. He first attempted to get into production, and next into general administrative services. Describing these attempts he said:

I was just not able to make that break. I talked to [people] in various divisions that I was interested in, and I got the lip service that they would keep [me] in mind if something opened up. As it happened, that just did not develop. I can never remember being approached by anyone. Nothing [happened]—that I can really hang [onto] as an offer. People would ask, "have you ever run a profit and loss operation?"

Finally, he described himself as taking "hat in hand" and approaching senior management in 1982 to request duties he knew to be available in a general administrative area. He said:

Frankly, this was an attempt to seize an opportunity. This time I went and I asked for a [new assignment]. We had some retirement within the company and some reorganization. I saw an opportunity to help myself. The urban affairs was shrinking. A number of jobs we created [in urban affairs] were completely eliminated. It just happened that the opportunity [to pick up administrative services] was there. It had a significant dollar budget and profit and loss opportunity . . . it was concrete and useful. So I asked for it.

Yet he was only temporarily successful in his attempt to exchange urban affairs for a more stable assignment in administrative services. One year later he was invited to resign from the company because of poor performance.

The story told by a second urban affairs manager—who tried a move to warehouse distribution in a retail company—reveals similar constraints. This manager was a department director, a position that was targeted to be cut from the company. This manager also discovered that the trade-off for

rising in a company in urban affairs was an inability to shift into any mainstream corporate function. Here is his assessment:

I was too old to do what you had to do to compete. . . . I was competing with 21 and 22 year olds to get into the system. They couldn't charge [my salary] to a store and have me doing the same thing the others [were] doing [for much less money]. You need the ground level experience. When I should have gotten it, I was busy running an affirmative action department.

Indeed, from a practical standpoint, retraining this individual would not likely reap a long-term benefit because of his age. Consequently, I asked this manager why he didn't move laterally into mainstream public relations, an area (apparently) he was more qualified to pursue. He responded:

I thought about it very seriously. I wondered where I was going with the system. It came up quite often. I talked about it when I first accepted this job. And at the end. They told me, "We don't know. We'll have to get back to you." They never did.

That his superiors never got back to him "at the end" may reflect the fact that the organization needed him precisely where he was placed. Or, it may result from the fact that he lacked a skill base and/or his superiors perceived that his skills differed from those managers who had moved up the ladder in generalized public relations. The latter point is highlighted by the comments of a manager who failed in his attempt to transfer into compensation and benefits—precisely because his past concentration in affirmative action made him underqualified for the job. He explained:

I moved over . . . as director. Now, mind you, I'm going from a corporate [affirmative action] job . . . to . . . compensation and benefits. I told the chairman of the company I didn't have any experience in that field. I might not be his man.

In short, because of limited skills and career "track records," people who were concentrated in racialized roles lacked the human capital to compete in mainstream company areas. The same skills that once made them valuable now constrained them.

Discussion

Rather than viewing human capital and structure as mutually exclusive explanatory variables, these interviews illustrate that the organization of managerial job assignments and job allocation create human capital deficits. Human capital and the structure of management occupations are not independent phenomena; they interact to mediate labor market outcomes. In the case of black managers, human capital explains the existence of a supply of black labor that companies could draw from when confronted with governmental anti-bias pressures in the 1960s and 1970s. Yet, although human capital was a necessary ingredient for entry and initial job attainments, it does not sufficiently explain who competes for and succeeds in attaining organization power. For black managers, the structure of opportunities associated with the managerial assignments looms large as an additional explanatory variable. The relationship between human capital is circular: A race-based system of job allocation creates a deficit in on-the-job training and experience, and this structurally imposed deficit, in turn, leads to human capital deficits that create barriers to black advancement.

The talent and training that these managers initially brought to their occupations were filtered through a peripheral system of jobs and cumulative work experience. As respondents moved into—and then up through—racialized management assignments, they were locked out from mainstream management jobs. The devaluation of their abilities eventually constrained their progress in executive arenas.

The observations derived from this study have several implications. The first concerns the level of analysis. Studies that rely only on aggregate level data cannot explain black progress, or the lack of progress, without a supplementary closer look at the jobs African Americans hold. This study shows that individual skill and talent is embedded in, and brought forth by, a sequence of assignments in an ongoing work process. Both Althauser (1975:143) and Freeman (1976b:146) have commented on this. Althauser suggests the need to focus on characteristics of the jobs black men hold, just as attention is now given to the job holders' characteristics. Freeman further notes that the degree to which blacks are in token (i.e., black-related) jobs, the significance of blacks' gains may be overstated. More recently, Bielby and Baron (1984, 1986) show that analyses that use detailed occupational categories reveal more occupational segregation. Yet, there are few case studies on black professional and managerial careers.

The second implication concerns the more abstract problem of how inequality is manufactured. To the extent that blacks occupy jobs cut off from core company goals, they are held back from core skill development. The interaction between an individual and the work s/he does can evolve so that a worker matures or evolves in such a way that the worker is taken out of the running. When viewed through the lens of my analysis, the often noted—but rarely explored—high concentration of blacks in corporate support implies a process of deskilling highly educated blacks through the absence of on-the-job profit-centered work experiences. How such a concentration occurred is a critical research question regarding the status of blacks in white collar occupations. In this study, the black managerial vanguard entering the white private sector was eased out of the running for top executive jobs via racialized careers because of a mix of corporate pressure, career naivete, and blacks' perceptions of race-related corporate barriers (Collins 1997).

Human capital and structural explanations of what influences black achievement generally correspond to functionalist and conflict perspectives in sociology. By extension, therefore, findings from this study are nested in a broad paradigm of inequality. Using a conflict perspective, career construction can be viewed as part of a process of social closure to defend the existing advantage of white managers (see Tomaskovic-Devey 1993). This idea is similar to Reskin and Roos's (1987) proposal that occupational sex segregation is best understood within the broader conceptual framework of status hierarchies. The corporate role in the allocation of jobs—and the assessment of their value—was not a function of objective or impersonal supply characteristics, but of a race-conscious employment discrimination. It is not clear that the subsequent deskilling of a black cohort depressed their wages, as Braverman (1974) suggested. Rather, this deskilling served a more pressing purpose. The problem for white corporate elites was how to incorporate protected groups of minorities while minimizing their impact on organizational culture and structure. The creation and allocation of racialized jobs was an efficient way to meet both goals. These jobs appeased governmental legislation and black demands for more economic resources, while reducing the threat of increased competition for mangerial power in organizations along racial lines. Initially, racialized jobs had attractive characteristics that suggested they were important to a company—faster mobility, greater freedom, and high visibility to white power brokers, but over time, racialized functions became routinized and devalued. Ultimately, the peculiar evolution during the 1960s and 1970s of careers documented in this study diminished the black executive pool in Chicago corporations that could compete to manage mainstream units in the 1980s and beyond. Consequently, many respondents over the last three decades did not—and could not—blossom into black executives in powerful decision making roles.

Notes

1. I selected the base year of 1972 because it takes about 15 to 20 years to reach upper management positions in the major companies in the non-financial sector of Chicago (Chicago Urban League 1977).

2. Sales functions involved helping white corporations orient products' positive images to black consumers. People in operations took on racialized functions when managing a predominantly black workforce and mediating black-white relationships in racially volatile employment settings.

References

Braverman, Harry. 1973. *Labor and Monopoly Capital: The Degradation of Work in the Twentieth Century.* Albany: State University of New York Press.

Chicago Reporter. 1983. Annual Corporate Survey. December:2–6.

———. 1986. Annual Corporate Survey. January:7–10.

Chicago Urban League. 1977. *Blacks in Policy-Making Positions in Chicago.* Chicago: Chicago Urban League.

Collins, Sharon M. 1997. *Black Corporate Executives: The Making and Breaking of a Black Middle Class.* Philadelphia: Temple University Press.

Doeinger, Peter B., and Michael J. Piore. 1971. *Internal Labor Markets and Manpower Analysis.* Lexington, Mass.: D.C. Heath.

Farley, Reynolds. 1984. *Blacks and Whites: Narrowing the Gap?* Cambridge: Harvard University Press.

Farley, Reynolds, and Walter R. Allen. 1987. *The Color Line and the Quality of Life in America.* New York: Russell Sage.

Freeman, Richard. 1976a. *The Black Elite.* New York: McGraw-Hill.

———. 1976b. *The Over-Educated American.* New York: Academic Press.

———. 1981. "Black economic progress after 1964: Who has gained and why." In *Studies in Labor Markets*, ed. S. Rosen, 247–295. Chicago: University of Chicago Press.

Ghiloni, Beth W. 1987. "The velvet ghetto: Women, power, and the corporation." in *Power Elites and Organizations*, eds. G. William Domhoff and Thomas R. Dye, 21–36. Newbury Park, Calif.: Sage.

Heidrick and Struggles, Inc. 1979. *Chief Personnel Executives Look at Blacks in Business*. New York: Heidrick and Stuggles, Inc.

Herrnstein, Richard J., and Charles Murray. 1994. *The Bell Curve: Intelligence and Class Structure in American Life*. New York: Free Press.

Irons, Edward, and Gilbert W. Moore. 1985. *Black Managers in the Banking Industry*. New York: Praeger.

Jones, Edward W. 1986. "Black managers: The dream deferred." *Harvard Business Review* (May-June): 84–89.

Kanter, Rosabeth Moss. 1977. *Men and Women of the Corporation*. New York: Basic Books.

Korn/Ferry. 1986. *Korn/Ferry Internationals' Executive Profile: A Survey of Corporate Leaders in the Eighties*. New York: Korn/Ferry International.

———. 1990. *Korn/Ferry Internationals' Executive Profile: A Decade of Change in Corporate Leadership*. New York: Korn/Ferry International.

Kraiger, Kurt, and J. Kevin Ford. 1985. "A meta-analysis of ratee race effects in performance ratings." *Journal of Applied Psychology* 70:56–63.

Landry, Bart. 1987. *The New Black Middle Class*. Berkeley, Calif.: University of California Press.

Murray, Charles. 1984. *Losing Ground: American Social Policy 1950–1980*. New York: Basic Books.

National Opinion Research Center, Chicago. 1986. *Closing the Gap: Forty Years of Economic Progress for Blacks*. Santa Monica, Calif.: Rand Corporation.

Nkomo, Stella M., and Taylor Cox, Jr. 1990. "Factors affecting the upward mobility of black managers in private sector organizations." *The Review of Black Political Economy* 78:40–57.

Reskin, Barbara F. 1990. *Job Queus, Gender Queus: Explaining Women's Inroads into Male Occupations*. Philadelphia: Temple University Press.

Reskin, Barbara F., and Patricia Roos. 1987. "Status hierarchies and sex segregation." In *Ingredients for Women's Employment Policy*, eds. Christine Bose and Glenna Spite, 71–81. Albany: State University of New York Press.

Smith, James P., and Finis R. Welch. 1983. "Longer trends in black/white economic status and recent effects of affirmative action." Paper prepared for Social Science Research Council conference at the National Opinion Research Center, Chicago.

Sowell, Thomas. 1983. "The Economics and Politics of Race." Transcript from "The Firing Line" program. Taped in New York City in November 1983 and telecast later by PBS.

Theodore, Nikolas C., and D. Garth Taylor. 1991. *The Geography of Opportunity: The Status of African Americans in the Chicago Area Economy*. Chicago: Chicago Urban League.

Thurow, Lester. 1975. *Generating Inequality*. New York: Basic Books.

Tomaskovic-Devey, Donald. 1993. *Gender and Racial Inequality at Work: The Sources and Consequences of Job Segregation*. Ithaca, N.Y.: ILR Press.

U.S. Bureau of Census. 1960. *Occupational Characteristics*. Series PC(2)-7A. Washington, D.C.: The Bureau of Census.

———. 1973. *Occupational Characteristics*. Series PC(2)-7A. Washington, D.C.: The Bureau of Census.

U.S. Department of Labor. 1990. *Report on the Glass Ceiling Initiative*. Washington, D.C.: U.S. Department of Labor.

Collins:

1. Discuss why Collins notes that there are more black managers but that the gains in positions of decision making have been insignificant in white corporations.

2. Discuss the two different theoretical perspectives that Collins uses in explaining the movement of blacks into corporate managerial positions. How do they differ and how do they complement each other?

20

The Black Church and the Twenty-First Century

C. Eric Lincoln and Lawrence H. Mamiya

The Challenge of Two Black Americas and Two Black Churches

The process of secularization in black communities has always meant a diminishing of the influence of religion and an erosion in the central importance of black churches. Secularization is accompanied by the twin processes of increasing differentiation and increasing pluralism that tend to diminish the cultural unity provided by the black sacred cosmos.[1] There is some evidence that the present and past central importance of the Black Church may be threatened by the virtual explosion of opportunities, which are now becoming available to recent black college graduates. An officially segregated society contributed to the dominant role black churches were able to maintain as one of the few cohesive black institutions to emerge from slavery. Talented black men and women developed their leadership skills in black churches and used them as launching pads for professional careers in the church or elsewhere in black society like education, music, and entertainment. With the breakdown of official segregation, some opportunities in previously closed professions in law, medicine, politics, and business have opened up as

never before. Also many white colleges, universities, and graduate schools have been seeking black students to bolster their black enrollment. As Freeman has pointed out in his study of black elites, recent black college graduates have been able to achieve income parity with their white counterparts for the first time in history, an occurrence beyond reach of the vast majority of black workers.[2] Even with some decline in black college enrollment during the Reagan years, the total numbers of black college graduates since the 1960s will still represent an unprecedented phenomenon in black history. How black churches and their leadership grapple with this challenge will determine whether they will be faced with the same problems of attrition and decline now affecting several white mainstream denominations. Whether black churches will have the clergy with educational training equal to that of their lay members is also in question. At one time black clergy were among the most highly educated members of the community, and a number of black colleges and universities were founded for the training of the clergy. However, that is no longer the case. With the proliferation in available professions for young people, the question of whether the ministry of the Black

Church will continue to attract the best and the brightest is still unresolved.

Some studies have pointed out the increasing bifurcation of the black community into two main class divisions: a coping sector of middle-income working-class and middle-class black communities, and a crisis sector of poor black communities, involving the working poor and the dependent poor.[3] The demographic movement of middle-income blacks out of inner city areas and into residential parts of the cities, older suburbs, or into newly created black suburbs, has meant a growing physical and social isolation of the black poor. For example, since the 1960s, 48 percent of the black population of Atlanta has moved out of the central city into surrounding counties.[4] The gradual emergence of two fairly distinct black Americas along class lines—of two nations within a nation—has raised a serious challenge to the Black Church. The membership of the seven historic black denominations is composed largely of middle-income working-class and middle-class members, with a scattering of support from poorer members, especially those in southern rural areas who tend to be among the most loyal members.[5] But black pastors and churches have had a difficult time in attempting to reach the hard-core urban poor, the black underclass, which is continuing to grow.[6] In past generations some of the large urban black churches were one of the few institutions that could reach beyond class boundaries and provide a semblance of unity in black communities.[7] The challenge for the future is whether black clergy and their churches will attempt to transcend class boundaries and reach out to the poor, as these class lines continue to solidify with demographic changes in black communities. If the traditional Black Church fails in its attempt to include the urban poor, the possibility of a Black Church of the poor may emerge, consisting largely of independent, fundamentalist, and Pentecostal storefront churches.

There also may emerge cults and sectarian forms of new religious movements among the black poor, similar to those exotic groups that emerged in the 1930s like those of Father Divine, Daddy Grace, Mother Horne, Elder Solomon Lightfoot Michaux, Rabbi Cherry, and Elijah Muhammad.[8] One of the few hopeful signs that the historic black churches will be able to provide a measure of unity beyond class boundaries involves the rise of a neo-Pentecostal movement in some black denominations.

The Challenge of Church Growth: A Case Study of the Rise of a Neo-Pentecostal Movement in the A.M.E. Church

While some recent studies have pointed to the phenomenon of a growing sector of unchurched black people, especially among black males in northern urban areas, scant attention has been paid to the rise of a neo-Pentecostal or charismatic movement that has contributed to the opposite phenomenon of church growth among some black church denominations.[9] Just as some of the white mainstream church denominations, including the Roman Catholics, have experienced a charismatic or neo-Pentecostal movement among some of their churches, a similar phenomenon has also occurred among some of the middle-class black denominations like the African Methodist Episcopal Church.[10] Rev. Dr. John Bryant, Jr., who was the former pastor of the Bethel A.M.E. Church in Baltimore until he was elected a bishop of the denomination in 1988, has been one of the central figures in leading and influencing A.M.E. pastors and laity in the direction of neo-Pentecostalism. The most significant fact about this movement in the A.M.E. Church has been the enormous church growth it has produced in almost all of the churches associated with it. For example, when Bryant took over the Bethel A.M.E. Church of Baltimore in the mid-1970s the church had about five hundred members; within ten years its membership had grown to over six thousand members, making it the largest A.M.E. congregation in the nation. Besides Bethel, several of the largest A.M.E. churches in the country associated with the movement were pastored by Bryant protégés. Rev. Frank M. Reid III of Ward A.M.E. in Los Angeles, Rev. Floyd Flake of Allen A.M.E. in Queens, Rev. Fred Lucas of Bridgestreet A.M.E. in Brooklyn, Rev. Grainger Browning of Fort Washington A.M.E., just outside Washington, D.C., and Rev. Dr. Kenneth Robinson of Payne Chapel A.M.E. in Nashville are representative. While some of the church growth took place in older, urban A.M.E. churches like Bethel, Bridgestreet, and Ward, others occurred in churches in residential working-class neighborhoods such as Allen A.M.E. in Jamaica, Queens, and in churches in newly created black suburbs such as Fort Washington A.M.E. The Allen A.M.E. Church grew from 1,400 members to over five thousand, and Fort Washington A.M.E. from twenty-five members to over a thousand members in two years.[11]

The membership of most of these neo-Pentecostal churches consists of a mix of middle-income working-class and middle-class blacks, who make up the majority of traditional A.M.E. membership and some of the black urban poor, the latter tending to be attracted by the informal, less structured, and highly spirited worship services. Neo-Pentecostalism in black churches tends to draw upon the reservoir of the black folk religious tradition which stressed enthusiastic worship and Spirit filled experiences. One of the appeals of the current movement is its emphasis upon a deeper spirituality, the need for a second blessing of the Holy Spirit. The older Holiness-Pentecostal movement of the late nineteenth century emerged out of Methodism and John Wesley's search for spiritual perfection, which was carried one step further by the Pentecostalists with their stress on another blessing of the Spirit (with its evidence of glossolalia, interpretation and prophesying, or other "gifts of the Spirit").

Another characteristic of the neo-Pentecostal movement in the A.M.E. Church concerns its curious combination of a deep Pentecostal spiritual piety and the A.M.E. tradition of involvement in progressive politics and political activism. The pastors as well as the laity associated with movement churches are caught up in the most intense, enthusiastic worship featuring the traditional Pentecostal phenomena referred to above. The lay members of these churches tend to be intensely involved with church activity on a daily basis, from prayer meetings and Bible study to adult education classes. Drums, tambourines, cymbals, and such instruments as electric guitars have also been introduced into worship services. The charismatic style of worship is much more emotionally oriented than the traditional A.M.E. emphasis upon "order and decorum." However, the A.M.E. tradition of political involvement seems unaffected. In contrast to most white churches in which the Pentecostal spirit and political conservatism seem to appear in tandem, the majority of the black pastors and their churches in the neo-Pentecostal movement tend to be politically progressive. Like Bishop Bryant, many of them were veterans of the civil rights struggle of the 1960s and this background has influenced their political views. Some of these activists felt burned out by the continuous struggle and sought a deeper, spiritual side. Under Bryant's leadership, Bethel established a private Christian school for elementary grades with future plans for a high school. It also ran a soup kitchen for the poor and it has been active in city politics by providing a forum for officials and candidates. Rev. Floyd Flake used his church base at Allen A.M.E. to conduct a successful election campaign to become congressman of his district, after the church had organized more than $20 million worth of community projects in the neighborhood. Rev. Grainger Browning of the Fort Washington A.M.E. Church calls on each family of his mostly middle-class congregation to contribute a new pair of shoes on the Sunday before Labor Day. On Labor Day the church dispenses to anyone a pair of shoes without cost. Rev. Frank Reid III of Ward A.M.E. in Los Angeles has been one of the more vocal black clergy in political affairs in Southern California, supporting black nationalists and being involved in police-community relations issues. Ward A.M.E. sponsors a prison ministry program that involves church members in Bible study and prayer sessions with inmates in prisons and halfway houses, and supplies food and clothing to their families. A program to help church members adopt black children, called "Room for One More," was devised by a laywoman at Ward.[12] Rev. Dr. Kenneth Robinson, who is also a practicing physician, has persuaded his congregation at Payne Chapel A.M.E. to hold neighborhood health fairs in Nashville, where health professionals from the church provide free medical screening and advice.

For the A.M.E. charismatics, today's neo-Pentecostalism also differs from the traditional Pentecostalism in that it combines both the "letter and the spirit," transcending the sheer emotionalism of the past. Many of the pastors and some of the laity of the new charismatic movement have had a college education and formal theological education in seminaries. Supporters argue that the merger of the letter and the spirit, the intellect and the emotions, is a corrective to traditional African Methodism, which allegedly tended to kill off the emotional side of worship and rituals prompting many to opt for other denominations like the Baptists or Pentecostals. Spirited, enthusiastic worship, they say, can attract people, and is not contrary to genuine A.M.E. tradition. In support of this argument it is said that the place where worship has the most vitality among A.M.E.s is in South Carolina where enthusiastic and spirited worship is normative, and where "there are more A.M.E.s than anywhere in the world."[13]

The neo-Pentecostal movement has been a source of spiritual revitalization among the A.M.E.s and a rich source of ministerial candidates. For example, the Bethel A.M.E. Church in Baltimore has sent more than twenty-five students to divinity schools like Howard Divinity and the Interdenominational Theological Center. Bethel has also had more than fifty assistant ministers in training, serving at the church.

While the neo-Pentecostals in the A.M.E. Church have produced enormous church growth and a revitalized energy and enthusiasm in some congregations, there are severe critics of the movement who resent the threat to traditional worship in an atmosphere of order and decorum. They also criticize the spiritual chauvinism of many charismatics who tend to view their way as the only way. The charismatic movement represents a powerful potential for the revitalization of the A.M.E. Church, but it could also produce a serious schism with the whole church ending up as the loser.

There is some evidence that this neo-Pentecostal movement has also involved black church denominations other than the A.M.E. Church, including a few churches in the A.M.E. Zion Church and some middle-class Baptist churches.[14] These churches have also exhibited similar characteristics such as rapid and enormous church growth in membership. However, the extent of this neo-Pentecostal phenomenon among black churches is unknown because it has not been examined thoroughly. Nevertheless, the challenge which neo-Pentecostalism poses for the Black Church is real, and the issue of how to benefit from this potential of church growth and spiritual revitalization without alienating the pillars of normative tradition, both lay and clergy, and without producing a crisis of schism is a challenge most black churches must inevitably address.

The Islamic Challenge to the Black Church

The resurgence of Islamic fundamentalism has been a worldwide phenomenon in recent years and it has implications for the general religious situation in the United States and for black Christian churches. Black communities have been particularly vulnerable to the Islamic challenge since the largest indigenous sector of Americans who have become Muslims are from the black population. The influence of varieties of Islam among blacks in the United States has had a long history, stemming from the African Muslims who were brought to North America as slaves and who constituted as much as 20 percent of the slave population on some large southern plantations.[15] However, much of the African Islamic influence did not survive the period of slavery, and the main bearers of that tradition came through the writings of intellectuals like Edward Wilmot Blyden, a late nineteenth-century advocate of African Islam.[16] But it was the leaders of "proto-Islamic" movements during the black urban migrations of the twentieth century who prepared the way for a much wider acceptance of Islam. Muslim advocates such as Noble Drew Ali of the Moorish Science Temple in 1913 and Master Wali Fard and the Honorable Elijah Muhammad of the Nation of Islam during the years of the Great Depression opened the door of Islam to black America with a dramatic appeal to heritage and history.[17] The Nation of Islam survived to become the nucleus of a rapidly proliferating Islamic growth in America transcending racial and ethnic boundaries.

The Nation of Islam, which was founded by Master Farad Muhammad in 1930 and led by Elijah Muhammad from 1934 until 1975, has a challenging and controversial history.[18] Under the influence of Minister Malcolm X, Elijah's national representative, the Nation made its greatest impact on the black community and American society during the 1960s and early 1970s when America was searching for change but adamantly resisting changing. Malcolm X and the Nation are credited with the primary ideological foundations that led to the development of the concepts of "black power," "black pride," and "black consciousness" which stirred black youth and reverberated all through the civil rights movement of the period. Malcolm X was more deeply aware than many less controversial leaders that the struggle for civil rights and integration [was] meaningless if the integrity and independence of black selfhood were drowned in a sea of whiteness. Malcom's biting critique of the "so-called Negro" and his emphasis upon the recovery of an independent black selfhood helped to change the language and vocabulary of an entire society from "Negro" to "black."[19]

Under Wali Fard and Elijah Muhammad the Nation of Islam was essentially a proto-Islamic religious black nationalism that was often at odds with the traditional doctrines of orthodox Islam.

Since the death of Elijah Muhammad in 1975, many members of the Nation of Islam, or the Black Muslims, have followed their new leader Imam Warith Deen Muhammad in making the transition to orthodox Sunni Islam. Warith began dismantling the exclusive black "nation" by accepting whites into the movement and then proceeded to gradually discard all the precepts and practices taught by Elijah, which he considered in violation of the spirit and the letter of orthodox Islam. "There is no black Muslim or white Muslim," he declared, "all are Muslims, all children of God."[20] Under Warith Muhammad the movement changed its name, first to the World Community of al-Islam in the West, then to the American Muslim Mission, finally finding its long-sought "true" identity in the world brotherhood of traditional Islam. Imam Warith Muhammad was recognized and accepted by world Muslim leaders, who honored him with the office of certification for Muslims from the United States who go on the annual pilgrimage, or Hajj, to Mecca. Muslim imams or leaders of the "Jummah," or Friday prayer services, are now commonly accepted as members of black ministerial alliances across the country.

An estimated 100,000 former members of Elijah Muhammad's old Nation of Islam followed Warith Deen Muhammad into Islamic orthodoxy as Sunni Muslims. Imam Muhammad's newspaper, *The Muslim Journal,* has also been one of the pioneers in using the term African American in reference to black Americans. Perhaps another 20,000 or so are led by Minister Louis Farrakhan, who continues the provincial black nationalist teachings of Master Fard and Elijah Muhammad. Farrakhan's followers retained the original designation of the Nation of Islam along with its ideology. While there have been smaller splinter groups led by rival leaders, the fluidity of membership in these groups has made it very difficult to obtain an accurate assessment of membership figures. However, over the fifty-eight-year history of the Nation and its evolution to orthodox Islam, it is estimated that several million black people, mostly black men, have passed through these various Islamic and proto-Islamic movements.[21] In 1989 the *New York Times* has estimated that about 1 million of the 6 million Muslims in the United States are African Americans, and close to 90 percent of new converts are black.[22]

Islam has proven itself to be a viable religious alternative to black Christian churches, especially for many black males, who have experienced difficulty with normative social and economic adjustments. In fact, the membership of Islamic masjids or mosques has always tended to be heavily made up of black men, a segment of the black population which black churches have had great difficulty in recruiting. The attraction of Islamic movements to black males may be due to several reasons, among them the legacy of the militant and radical black nationalist Malcolm X has been a profound influence on these young men. As a culture hero, Malcolm X was seen as the uncompromising critic of American society. Another reason is that the Muslims project a more macho image among black men. The Qur'an advocates self-defense while the Christian Bible counsels turning the other cheek. The *lex talionis,* "an eye for an eye, a life for a life," has a persuasive appeal to the oppressed whose cheeks are weary of inordinate abuse. Black sports heroes such as Muhammad Ali and Kareem Abdul-Jabbar have further legitimated the Islamic option by converting to Islam and taking on Muslim names. Black parents who are not Muslims frequently give their children Muslim names as a statement of solidarity with some features of Islam and as a way of announcing their independence from Western social conventions, or as a means of identifying with an African cultural heritage. Finally, many black men have been attracted to Islamic alternatives because the Muslims have been very active in working in prisons and on the streets where they are, a ministry which is not pronounced in most black Christian churches.

A full decade before the turn of the twenty-first century, if the estimate of 6 million Muslims in the United States is reasonably accurate, Islam has become the second largest religion in America, after Protestant and Catholic Christianity. American Judaism with a steadily declining membership is now third. While much of this Islamic growth is independent of the black community, the possibility of a serious impact on the Black Church cannot be peremptorily dismissed. The phenomenon of more black males preferring Islam while more black females adhere to traditional black Christianity is not as bizarre as it sounds. It is already clear that in Islam the historic black church denominations will be faced with a far more serious and more powerful competitor for the souls of black folk than the white churches ever were. When is the question, not whether.

"E Pluribus Unum,"
Out of Many, One?

The Challenge of Black Ecumenism

The potential power of the Black Church as a social institution has never been fully realized and it probably never will be so long as sectarianism is the norm. However, there have been men and women throughout black history who have dared to dream that out of the denominational pluralism that has characterized the situation of black churches, there might one day arise a unity, and perhaps an organic union and merger, so that the several black churches could speak with one effective voice and move with one unified spirit and singleness of purpose. They have dreamed that these churches could pool their financial, material, and human resources to better serve their people, eliminating the duplication and replication of services such as individual multi-million dollar publishing houses for each denomination. From the very beginnings of the historic black denominations there were serious discussions between black Methodist leaders of Philadelphia-Baltimore and New York City about merging into one denomination. In fact, the New York leaders of the A.M.E. Zion Church did adopt as their official name "the African Methodist Episcopal Church in America" before relationship between the communions degenerated and the word "Zion" was added to differentiate themselves from the Philadelphia- Baltimore Methodist movement that became known as the A.M.E. Church.[23] Throughout the nineteenth and twentieth centuries there have been sporadic efforts at ecumenical merger between various members of the historic black denominations. For example, the National Baptist Convention, U.S.A., Inc., was formed in 1895 through the merger of three Baptist groups, but two schisms in 1915 and in 1961 also produced two new and independent denomination, the National Baptist Convention of America, and

the Progressive National Baptist Convention. Another cooperative attempt, the Fraternal Council of Churches which was founded in 1934 by A.M.E. Bishop Reverdy C. Ransom, was active in the 1940s and 1950s.[24] The period of civil rights ferment and black consciousness has also spawned a wide variety of black ecumenical movements such as the Southern Christian Leadership Conference, the National Black Evangelical Association, and the National Conference of Black Churchmen.[25] One of the more successful ventures in black ecumenism was the Interdenominational Theological Center, founded in 1957. ITC represents the cooperative efforts of six denominational bodies, including black Episcopalians and black United Methodists, to provide a common center for theological training by pooling their separate resources and services.

During the decade of the 1980s several other major efforts in black ecumenism have emerged: Partners in Ecumenism (PIE); and the Congress of National Black Churches (CNBC). A merger of three black denominations is planned, consisting of the African Methodist Episcopal Zion Church, the Christian Methodist Episcopal Church and the Union American Methodist Episcopal Church. Both PIE and CNBC were established as ecumenical groups in 1978, although with different purposes and constituencies. Founded under the auspices of the National Council of Churches to promote social change programs through the common efforts of black and white churches, Partners in Ecumenism challenged the NCC and white denominations to be more responsive to black concerns, and provided a platform for progressive black and white clergy. In contrast, the Congress of National Black Churches, which began with a membership restricted to black denominations with a national constituency, is concerned with social and economic programs that promote institution building in black communities through such programs as collective purchasing, banking, insurance, and communications.[26] Plans call for a cooperative publishing house adequate to meet the printing and publishing needs of member denominations and secular black writers. The congress also sponsors a large-scale social program called Project Spirit which attempts to relate black churches, families, and children in after-school programs focused on developing self-esteem among the children in an enriched cultural ethos in Atlanta, Indianapolis, and Oakland.

The planned merger of the C.M.E. Church, the A.M.E. Zion Church, and the U.A.M.E. Church may be completed by the early 1990s, thereby strengthening historic black Methodism at a time when membership in some of the churches involved is beginning to decline. Merger may help to resolve some problems common to black churches such as an aging clergy, dwindling financial resources, inefficient use of duplicated church properties and personnel. However, church mergers are among the most complicated of human endeavors, and the restructuring of ecclesiastical entities seem to founder more often than they succeed. Human interests vested in positions of power and leadership must be resolved once the doctrinal and ritual preferences have been resolved. Traditions are not readily relinquished, even in the face of the obvious, and emotions sometimes speak with more authority than either reason or practicality.[27] Nevertheless, the planned merger of these three black Methodist denominations has heightened speculations about the possibility of their merger with the A.M.E. Church at some time in the future, and of the possibility that the black Baptist denominations may also consider reunion with each other. The split between the National Baptist Convention, U.S.A., Inc., and the Progressive National Baptist Convention is fairly recent and probably not irreparable, though the divisions of separation between the two older Baptist conventions have had more time to harden. But the hopes among some black and white Christians that the Black Church will eventually merge itself into mainline white Christianity seem increasingly unrealistic as these racial communions seem more and more resigned to the realities of religious separation in a society where secular separation remains the ideological norm.

As the United States moves into the technological space age of the twenty-first century, the collective efforts of black ecumenical groups will become increasingly important both to preserve their religious and cultural integrity and to oppose the subtle manipulations of an information society.

Notes

1. For general theoretical descriptions of the effects of the process of secularization on religion, see Peter Berger, *The Sacred Canopy*, chapters 2, 3.

2. Richard B. Freeman, *Black Elite: The New Market for Highly Educated Black Americans*, pp. 27–40.

3. For example, see Wilson, *The Truly Disadvantaged*. Also see the socioeconomic data of the National Urban League in the annual publication, *The State of Black America*, 1986, 1987, 1988. The descriptive terms "coping" and "crisis" sectors of the black community are derived from Professor Martin Kilson in his presentation on black clientage politics in the working group on Afro-American Religion and Politics at the W. E. B. Du Bois Institute, Harvard University, October 29, 1988.

4. Smothers, "Atlanta Still on a Roll, but New Doubts Arise," *New York Times*, July 14, 1988, p. A-21.

5. Nelson, "Unchurched Black Americans."

6. Laura Sessions Stepp, "Black Church Losing Historic Role: Drug Use, Teen Pregnancies Seen as Consequences," *Washington Post*, August 20, 1988, p. A-6.

7. Drake and Cayton, *Black Metropolis*, vol. 2.

8. See Joseph Washington, *Black Sects and Cults*. For an overview of five major groups, see

Mamiya and Lincoln, "Black Militant and Separatist Movements."

9. See Nelson, "Unchurched Black Americans." Also see Welch, "The Unchurched, Black Religious Non-Affiliates." The most recent study of the unchurched was done by George Gallup, Jr.'s organization. See Princeton Religious Research Center, *The Unchurched American ... 10 Years Later.* For a profile of the black unchurched, see Robert J. Taylor, "Correlates of Religious Non-Involvement Among Black Americans," *Review of Religious Research* 30, no. 2 (December 1988): 126–39.

10. Meredith McGuire, *Pentecostal Catholics: Power, Charisma and Order in a Religious Movement.*

11. See the unpublished in-house study by Lawrence H. Mamiya, "The Second Episcopal District," pp. 4–5.

12. *1984–1985 Annual Report,* Ward African Methodist Episcopal Church, Rev. Frank Reid III pastor, pp. 25–28.

13. Ibid.

14. For example, there is a Four Square Gospel A.M.E. Zion Church with several thousand members in Fort Washington.

15. Allan D. Austin, *African Muslims in Antebellum America: A Sourcebook.*

16. Edward W. Blyden, *Islam and the Negro Race.* Also see Hollis Lynch, *Edward Wilmot Blyden: Pan Negro Patriot.*

17. For overviews of the Moorish Science Temple and the Nation of Islam, see Mamiya and Lincoln, "Black Militant and Separatist Movements." The term "proto-Islam" was coined by C. Eric Lincoln, "The American Muslim Mission in the Context of American Social History," in *The Muslim Community in North America,* edited by Earle H. Waugh, Baha Abu-Laban, and Regula B. Qureshi.

18. For the best historical overview of the origins of the movement, see C. Eric Lincoln, *The Black Muslims in America.*

19. See Mamiya and Lincoln, "Black Militant and Separatist Movements," p. 767.

20. "Rule Switch Allows Whites as Muslims," *Nashville Tennessean,* June 19, 1975. For an exami-

nation of the reasons for the change to orthodox Islam, see Lawrence H. Mamiya, "From Black Muslim to Bilalian: The Evolution of a Movement," *Journal for the Scientific Study of Religion* 21, no. 2 (June 1982): 138–52.

21. Bruce M. Gans, and Walter L. Lowe, "The Islam Connection," in *Playboy,* May 1980.

22. Ari L. Goldman, "Mainstream Islam Rapidly Embraced by Black Americans," *New York Times,* February 21, 1989, pp. 1, B-4.

23. Walls, *The African Methodist Episcopal Zion Church,* pp. 73–84.

24. See Mary Sawyer, "Black Ecumenical Movements: Proponents of Social Change," *Review of Religious Research* 30 (December 1988), no. 2:152–53.

25. Ibid., see figure 1.

26. This section on black ecumenism is indebted to Sawyer's work, "Black Ecumenical Movements," pp. 154–55.

27. Mamiya and Lincoln, "Policy and Planning Implications of the Christian Methodist Episcopal Church Survey."

References

Austin, Allan D. *African Muslims in Antebellum America: A Sourcebook.* New York: Garland, 1984.

Berger, Peter L. *The Sacred Canopy.* Garden City, N.Y.: Doubleday, 1967.

Blyden, Edward W. *Islam and the Negro Race.* London: Edinburgh University, 1967 reprint.

Drake, St. Clair, and Horace Cayton. *Black Metropolis: A Study of Negro Life in the North.* New York: Harper and Row, 1962, revised and enlarged, 2 volumes.

Freeman, Richard B. *Black Elite: The New Market for Highly Educated Black Americans.* New York: McGraw-Hill, 1976.

Gans, Bruce M., and Walter L. Lowe. "The Islam Connection." *Playboy* (May 1980).

Goldman, Ari L. "Mainstream Islam Rapidly Embraced by Black Americans," *New York Times,* February 21, 1989, 1, B-4.

Lincoln, C. Eric. "The American Muslim Mission in the Context of American Social History." *The Muslim Community in North America.* Earle H. Waugh, Baha Abu-Laban, and Regula B. Qureshi, editors.

Edmonton: University of Alberta Press, 1983: 215–33.

———. *The Black Muslims in America*. Boston: Beacon, 1961.

Lynch, Hollis. *Edward Wilmot Blyden: Pan Negro Patriot*. New York: Oxford University Press, 1970.

Mamiya, Lawrence H. "From Black Muslim to Bilalian: The Evolution of a Movement." *Journal for the Scientific Study of Religion* 21 (June 1982), no. 2: 138–52.

———. "The Second Episcopal District of the African Methodist Episcopal Church Under the Leadership of Bishop John Hurst Adams: Evaluations of the Leadership Training Institutes and the Phenomenon of Church Growth in the District." January 1986. Study funded by the Lilly Endowment.

Mamiya, Lawrence H., and C. Eric Lincoln. "Black Militant and Separatist Movements." *Encyclopedia of the American Religious Experience.* Charles H. Lippy and Peter W. Williams, editors. New York: Charles Scribner's Sons, 1988, 2: 755–71.

McGuire, Meredith. *Pentecostal Catholics: Power, Charisma and Order in a Religious Movement*. Philadelphia: Temple University Press, 1982.

Nashville Tennessean, "Rule Switch Allows Whites as Muslims," June 19, 1975.

Nelsen, Hart M. "Unchurched Black Americans: Patterns of Religiosity and Affiliation," *Review of Religious Research* 29 (June 1988), no. 4: 398–412.

Princeton Religion Research Center. George Gallup, executive director. *The Unchurched American . . . 10 Years Later*. Princeton: Princeton Religion Research Center, 1989.

Sawyer, Mary L. "Black Ecumenical Movements: Proponents of Social Change." *Review of Religious Research* 30 (December 1988), no. 2.

Smothers, Ronald. "Atlanta Still on a Roll, but New Doubts Arise," *New York Times,* July 14, 1988, A-21.

Stepp, Laura Sessions. "Black Church Losing Historic Role: Drug Use, Teen Pregnancies Seen as Consequences," *Washington Post,* August 20, 1988, A-6.

Taylor, Robert J. "Correlates of Religious Non-Involvement Among Black Americans." *Review of Religious Research* 30 (December 1988), no. 2: 126–39.

Walls, William J. *The African Methodist Episcopal Zion Church: Reality of the Black Church.* Charlotte, N.C.: A.M.E. Zion Publishing House, 1974.

Washington, Joseph R., Jr. *Black Sects and Cults.* Garden City, N.Y.: Anchor/Doubleday, 1973.

Welch, Michael R. "The Unchurched, Black Religious Non-Affiliates," *Journal for the Scientific Study of Religion* 17 (September 1978): 289–93.

Wilson, William Julius. *The Truly Disadvantaged: The Inner City, the Underclass, and Public Policy.* Chicago: University of Chicago Press, 1987.

Lincoln and Mamiya:

1. What were some of the factors in society that contributed to the dominant role of the black church?

2. In what ways do the traditional and neo-Pentecostal black churches differ? In what ways are they similar?

21

The Origins and Politics of Affirmative Action

John David Skrentny

After examining the social science literature on American politics for a brief period of time, one usually can discern two basic views or models of how policy making works. In one model, Americans make policies following their Constitution and the basic principles laid out in the Declaration of Independence, that is, the opinions of the people are taken into account as government representatives make policies while pursuing individualist and egalitarian values.[1] In the competing, more pessimistic model, policies are made by and for the benefit of elites, usually understood as upper class, white, and male, who dominate government and business.[2] These models, of course, are simplifications. Most scholars (and Americans) only tend toward one or the other.

Still, a policy such as affirmative action presents a puzzle for even a moderate adherent of either view. For someone who supports the more democratic and egalitarian model of policy making, it would seem to fit because affirmative action generally is understood to be a policy designed to create more opportunities for the most marginalized minorities in America. But others argue that affirmative action confers benefits on the basis of ascriptive group traits, not on the basis of individuals, and so it is at variance with Ameri-can individualist ideals. Furthermore, public opinion polls, though highly sensitive to question wording, indicate that some aspects of the policy are very unpopular, and therefore the policy must have developed against the majority will.[3] This suggests that the policy was implemented with the blessing of government elites. But affirmative action also presents a puzzle for the more pessimistic model for a very basic reason: If affirmative action is meant to benefit minorities, why would the white, male, rich people who have supposedly dominated government ever create a policy that is designed to help everyone but themselves? Analyzing the origins of affirmative action illuminates the complex dynamics of policy making in the United States.

On a personal and professional level, for myself studying affirmative action had another attraction. I was interested in acquiring expert knowledge of public controversies. I wanted to do my best to bring a social scientific analysis to any interested person who wanted to get beyond the 5-minute television news debates and newspaper opinion page polemics. By analyzing the origins and politics of affirmative action, I hoped to gain some valuable knowledge that might trickle into public deliberation and improve the quality of those debates.

With that as a rationale, I reveal myself to be someone who believes that, at least sometimes, policy is made in the United States in ways that take into account public opinion and debate. But the affirmative action story is more complex and fascinating than this. I argue here that affirmative action developed because white, male elites in government wanted it. It was in their interests and justified using arguments or discourses that made sense in specific circumstances. Those circumstances were the national crisis created by ghetto riots in the late 1960s, the administrative difficulties of federal civil rights agencies, the Nixon administration's rather precarious political support, and the general reliance on appeals to tradition in the American political system, especially in the courts.

What Is Affirmative Action?

Before we continue, it is important to have an idea of what I mean by affirmative action. Critics of affirmative action policies insist that they amount to quotas or preferences intended to ensure a certain, predetermined proportion of minority group representation in employment, university or professional school admissions, or firms that contract with the government. Supporters of the policy deny this and argue that affirmative action does not mean quotas or preferences but simply minority representation goals that firms, universities, or the government use to ensure equal opportunity. The supporters are right in that affirmative action almost never means fixed, numerical quotas of minority representation that must be attained. But if it were only about ensuring equal opportunity, affirmative action would not be so controversial.

Given the complexity of the policies that go under this name and the political controversy that goes with some aspects of them, I prefer a simple, perhaps somewhat vague, definition: *affirmative action* is any government policy that gives a positive meaning to

some nonclass, noneconomic group difference.[4]

To better understand affirmative action, it is helpful to contrast it with the "colorblind" or "difference-blind" approach of the Civil Rights Act of 1964. Title VII of this law, the employment civil rights section, assumes an America where discrimination is rare, where Americans generally go about their pursuit of opportunity as equal, abstract citizens, all essentially the same. If an American feels he or she has been discriminated against on the basis of race, gender, religion, or national origin, he or she can make a formal complaint to the government to investigate the situation. Title VII created an official body for this purpose, the Equal Employment Opportunity Commission (EEOC). If the EEOC finds discrimination in a particular case, it attempts to conciliate with the employer and persuade it to stop discriminating and hire or promote the aggrieved employee. Failing that, either the individual or the government may sue an employer that has discriminated. Attention to group differences between Americans is ideally kept to a minimum.

With an affirmative action policy in place, in contrast, an employer, university, or contracting agency of the government will perceive not just "American citizens," but white Americans, black Americans, Asian Americans, Latinos, and American Indians of both genders. It directs attention away from non-Latino whites and onto the other groups and gives some pressure (from very light to firm) to hire, promote, or admit some unspecified proportional range of persons who are different from non-Latino whites. For an employer, group differences are given some positive meaning—hiring and promoting minorities in adequate numbers means the policy is being carried out successfully.

There are two primary government bureaucracies involved in affirmative action enforcement. As mentioned previously, one is the EEOC. The EEOC oversees enforcement of prohibition of discrimination in hiring and promotion. The primary mechanism of Title VII is color- and gender-blind; the EEOC investigates individual complaints of discrimination and attempts to conciliate. In late 1965, it began to require larger firms to submit the EEO-1 form, which records hiring data, separated by gender, for "white (not of Hispanic origin)," "black (not of Hispanic origin)," "Hispanic," "Asian or Pacific Islander," and "American Indian or Alaskan Native" (see Figure 21.1).[5] As I describe subsequently, the EEOC began, in the late 1960s, to use the statistical patterns gathered from the EEO-1 forms to hold public hearings, asking firms with very low percentages of minority and women workers to explain themselves. In 1972, the EEOC gained the power to sue discriminating firms, and it sometimes used statistics as evidence of discrimination, usually (though not always) in addition to individual complaints. The EEOC also issues various rulings on topics such as ability testing, employee recruitment, and litigation-proof affirmative action plans.[6]

The preeminent federal affirmative action program, however, has its legal basis in an executive order of the president. Lyndon Johnson signed Executive Order 11246 in 1965, declaring there would be no discrimination in employment in the federal government and by federal government contractors on the basis of race, religion, and national origin, and it required "affirmative action" to ensure nondiscrimination. The order created an Office of Federal Contract Compliance (OFCC[7]) in the Labor Department that would wield the power to cancel the contracts of noncomplying firms. In 1967, this order was amended to include sex discrimination.

The OFCC's 1969 "Philadelphia Plan" created affirmative action regulations that many in Congress believed required quotas: Firms competing for lucrative federal construction contracts would have to promise "good faith" efforts to hire predetermined percentages of Afro-American workers in specified occupations within specified time periods. In 1970,

the OFCC expanded the goals and timetables of the Philadelphia Plan to all government contractors. In "Order No. 4," contractors with at least a $50,000 contract and more than 50 employees were to make efforts to "correct any identifiable deficiencies" in the utilization of minorities. *Utilization* was "having fewer minorities in a particular job class than would reasonably be expected by their availability." Order No. 4 required racial hiring goals and timetables, roughly based on "the percentage of the minority work force as compared with the total work force in the immediate labor area."[8] The ambiguity of the regulations has allowed a 30-year debate: Conservatives argue that a goal is really a quota and that nonmeritocratic preferences are required to meet the goal/quota; liberals deny both claims.

In this chapter, I concentrate on affirmative action in employment for African Americans, because it is here and with this group that affirmative action began. However, universities often have affirmative action policies for college admissions, and most professional schools have some affirmative action admissions policy. Universities began to practice affirmative action without government pressure beginning in the late 1960s. There is also affirmative action in government help for small businesses (such as loans and technical assistance) and in "set-asides" in procurement. Set-asides refer to the government practice of disbursing money to states for projects such as road building on the condition that the states promise to set aside some percentage of the money to try to hire minority-owned firms to do the work.

A Word about Theory and Method

When I first began to study the origins of affirmative action, I believed that the civil rights movement fought and lobbied hard for the government to enact the policy. This hypothesis was derived less from social science

Employer Information Report: EEO-1

Joint Reporting Committee

- Equal Employment Opportunity Commission
- Office of Federal Contract Compliance Programs (Labor)

EQUAL EMPLOYMENT OPPORTUNITY

EMPLOYER INFORMATION REPORT EEO—1

Standard Form 100
(Rev. 4-82)
O.M.B. No. 3046-0007
EXPIRES 12/31/83
100-213

Section A—TYPE OF REPORT
Refer to instructions for number and types of reports to be filed.

1. Indicate by marking in the appropriate box the type of reporting unit for which this copy of the form is submitted (MARK ONLY ONE BOX).

   Multi-establishment Employer:

   (1) ☐ Single-establishment Employer Report

   (2) ☐ Consolidated Report (Required)
   (3) ☐ Headquarters Unit Report (Required)
   (4) ☐ Individual Establishment Report (submit one for each establishment with 50 or more employees)
   (5) ☐ Special Report

2. Total number of reports being filed by this Company (Answer on Consolidated Report only) _____

Section B—COMPANY IDENTIFICATION (To be answered by all employers)

	OFFICE USE ONLY
1. Parent Company	
a. Name of parent company (owns or controls establishment in item 2) omit if same as label	a.
Address (Number and street)	b.
City or town / State / ZIP code	c.
2. Establishment for which this report is filed. (Omit if same as label)	
a. Name of establishment	d.
Address (Number and street) / City or Town / County / State / ZIP code	e.
b. Employer Identification No. (IRS 9-DIGIT TAX NUMBER)	f.

c. Was an EEO–1 report filed for this establishment last year? ☐ Yes ☐ No

Section C—EMPLOYERS WHO ARE REQUIRED TO FILE (To be answered by all employers)

☐ Yes ☐ No 1. Does the entire company have at least 100 employees in the payroll period for which you are reporting?

☐ Yes ☐ No 2. Is your company affiliated through common ownership and/or centralized management with other entities in an enterprise with a total employment of 100 or more?

☐ Yes ☐ No 3. Does the company or any of its establishments (a) have 50 or more employees AND (b) is not exempt as provided by 41 CFR 60-1.5, AND either (1) is a prime government contractor or first-tier subcontractor, and has a contract, subcontract, or purchase order amounting to $50,000 or more, or (2) serves as a depository of Government funds in any amount or is a financial institution which is an issuing and paying agent for U.S. Savings Bonds and Savings Notes?

If the response to question C-3 is yes, please enter your Dun and Bradstreet identification number (if you have one): ☐☐☐☐☐☐☐☐

NOTE: If the answer is yes to questions 1, 2, or 3, complete the entire form, otherwise skip to Section G.

NSN 7540-00-180-6384

2-86

8-18-93   *Human Resources Guide*

Figure 21.1. Employer Information Report EEO-1

SF 100 Page 2

Section D—EMPLOYMENT DATA

Employment at this establishment—Report all permanent full-time and part-time employees including apprentices and on-the-job trainees unless specifically excluded as set forth in the instructions. Enter the appropriate figures on all lines and in all columns. Blank spaces will be considered as zeros.

JOB CATEGORIES		OVERALL TOTALS (SUM OF COL. B THRU K)	MALE					FEMALE				
			WHITE (NOT OF HISPANIC ORIGIN)	BLACK (NOT OF HISPANIC ORIGIN)	HISPANIC	ASIAN OR PACIFIC ISLANDER	AMERICAN INDIAN OR ALASKAN NATIVE	WHITE (NOT OF HISPANIC ORIGIN)	BLACK (NOT OF HISPANIC ORIGIN)	HISPANIC	ASIAN OR PACIFIC ISLANDER	AMERICAN INDIAN OR ALASKAN NATIVE
		A	B	C	D	E	F	G	H	I	J	K
Officials and Managers	1											
Professionals	2											
Technicians	3											
Sales Workers	4											
Office and Clerical	5											
Craft Workers (Skilled)	6											
Operatives (Semi-Skilled)	7											
Laborers (Unskilled)	8											
Service Workers	9											
TOTAL	10											
Total employment reported in previous EEO-1 report	11											

NOTE: Omit questions 1 and 2 on the Consolidated Report.

1. Date(s) of payroll period used: 2. Does this establishment employ apprentices?
     1 ☐ Yes   2 ☐ No

Section E—ESTABLISHMENT INFORMATION (Omit on the Consolidated Report)

1. What is the major activity of this establishment? (Be specific, i.e., manufacturing steel castings, retail grocer, wholesale plumbing supplies, title insurance, etc. Include the specific type of product or type of service provided, as well as the principal business or industrial activity.)

OFFICE USE ONLY

E.

Section F—REMARKS

Use this item to give any identification data appearing on last report which differs from that given above, explain major changes in composition or reporting units and other pertinent information.

Section G—CERTIFICATION (See Instructions G)

Check one
1 ☐ All reports are accurate and were prepared in accordance with the instructions (check on consolidated only)
2 ☐ This report is accurate and was prepared in accordance with the instructions.

Name of Certifying Official	Title	Signature	Date
Name of person to contact regarding this report (Type or print)	Address (Number and Street)		
Title	City and State	ZIP Code	Telephone Number (Including Area Code) Extension

All reports and information obtained from individual reports will be kept confidential as required by Section 709(e) of Title VII. **WILLFULLY FALSE STATEMENTS ON THIS REPORT ARE PUNISHABLE BY LAW, U.S. CODE, TITLE 18, SECTION 1001.**

Figure 21.1. Employer Information Report EEO-1 (continued)

research—there was virtually none on the origins of affirmative action—than from what I gathered from the public discourse on the topic. I thought I was embarking on a social movement study. I soon learned, however, that the African American civil rights movement was not demanding affirmative action in the way it was understood at the time it was created. Most black leaders supported a massive infusion of government aid to help build resources such as better schools and job training for black Americans in the years immediately after the Civil Rights Act of 1964. Leaders such as Whitney Young, for example, argued for a "Marshall Plan" for black America, similar to the Marshall Plan that channeled American aid to Europe after World War II. Martin Luther King, Jr., the preeminent civil rights leader, usually sought cross-race alliances of poor blacks and whites, and consequently, when discussing special employment regulations, he used colorblind terms. For example, he sought quota hiring for the "difficult to place," a term that could include any American in economic difficulty.[9]

Consequently, I turned to studies of the workings of government to understand why federal officials might create affirmative action without being specifically told to do so.[10] In my preliminary research on the policy, I was struck by the seemingly taboo nature of a race-conscious employment policy. In 1964, there were a few who talked about affirmative action (though not using that term at the time), but in Washington, DC—especially in Congress—affirmative action was almost unspeakable. To advocate affirmative action then was to announce to the world that you knew nothing about sensible government policy.[11] Of course, targeting in public policies is quite common. The Veterans' Preference Act of 1944, for example, adds points to the scores of veterans on the civil service exam and instructs the government to hire the veteran in the event of a tie after points are added. In Congress in 1964, there was not much explanation on this point. Having em-

ployers take race into account to help blacks was self-evidently inappropriate, wrong, unfair, and un-American. Colorblindness, or, more generally, difference-blindness, was the only way to go.

The interesting fact was that by 1969, only 5 years later, a Republican president, Richard M. Nixon, was an open defender of affirmative action. Specifically, he championed the Philadelphia Plan, and he even beat back an attempt in Congress to kill it. The research question became clear: Between 1964 and 1969, which government officials advocated affirmative action? Furthermore, if it was taboo in 1964, how did they get away with it—how and why did they "sell" the policy?

To answer the questions, I was especially attracted to a cultural variant of "institutional theory" that emphasized that actors in organizations do not consciously think through everything they do; they often follow various taken-for-granted, cultural rules of legitimacy or appropriateness that shape the way they behave.[12] One can view government as an agglomeration of different organizations: the White House administration, the Congress, various bureaucracies, the court system. My task was to search out those government actors who advocated affirmative action and study the circumstances in which affirmative action advocacy was appropriate, legitimate, and logical, rather than inappropriate, illegitimate, and taboo. At what times and to which audiences was it safe for a government official to say that affirmative action was a good idea? In a sense, the story of the origins of affirmative action is the story of how, when, and why political cultural taboos can be overcome.

My basic research question, the facts of the situation (civil rights groups did not push affirmative action onto the government), and my refinement of my research question thus shaped the nature of the study. I would have to do a study in state-centered, cultural historical sociology, venturing into government archives to examine the official papers of the

Johnson administration, the Nixon administration, the EEOC, and the OFCC. I would seek out the memoranda, letters, and reports in which some government official told another that affirmative action was a good idea.[13] Furthermore, I would interview a few key players who were there on the scene.

Overcoming Taboos: The Origins of Affirmative Action

After exploring the historical record, I was able to identify four discourses that government officials used to advocate affirmative action, and four contexts in which these corresponding discourses were appropriate, logical, and within the cultural boundaries of legitimate political action.

Crisis Management

One important part of the affirmative action story is that in the mid-1960s, national political leaders perceived that the United States was a nation in crisis. No one has ever fully explained why, but in the years between 1964 and 1969, American cities were battlegrounds, as blacks living in the poorest sections of the cities vented their frustration and anger through violence, arson, and looting. Hundreds of millions of dollars of property damage resulted; there were clashes with police, fire fighters, and National Guard forces; and tens of thousands of arrests and many deaths occurred, as well. Los Angeles in 1965 and Newark, New Jersey, and Detroit, Michigan, in 1967 probably saw the worst of it, as the conflagrations lasted several days.[14] These cities were literally out of control. Less severe violence was widespread across America.[15]

Some referred to these urban disturbances as "ghetto revolts," emphasizing their political nature. But though a distinctly political discontent was always a part, they were always unplanned, spontaneous, and disorganized, and most scholars and journalists referred to them as riots. Whatever the label, the fact remained that government officials saw them as serious threats to their control. White House documents show that government elites, including President Lyndon Johnson, were very concerned. America was in crisis. And a crisis calls for some kind of crisis management. Although the duties of modern governments are generally understood as the pursuit of justice and progress,[16] their first order of duty is the maintenance of order.

What were the options? One option was military repression. After all, ghetto rioting was obviously against the law. Some opinion polls supported repression, and all political leaders realized that being perceived as "rewarding the rioters" with government programs would not be popular with the majority of Americans.[17] But repression was not an option for President Johnson. A big part of the reason was that Johnson had to consider an audience for American actions outside the American electorate. The 1960s were part of the Cold War, the period of intense competition between the United States and the Soviet Union for influence over the emerging and developing nations of Asia, Africa, and Latin America. America's treatment toward its black citizens had become an issue in the Cold War, as Soviet propaganda highlighted American abuses of the human rights of minorities. Equal human rights and race discrimination were issues of great concern the world over, especially in Asia and Africa.[18] Consequently, Johnson did not want to risk the loss of American legitimacy; he felt he had to play according to the world cultural rules of human rights, as he wrote in his memoirs:

I knew what I had to do, but I could not erase from my mind the awful prospect of American soldiers possibly having to shoot American citizens. The thought of blood being spilled in the streets of Detroit was like a nightmare. I could imagine the inflammatory photographs appearing within hours on television and on the front pages of newspapers around the world.[19]

Therefore, the Johnson administration encouraged measures to empower inner-city blacks, not repress them (though in the short term, military force was needed to stop looting and arson). In the climate of crisis, new approaches to black inequality became appropriate and legitimate. Johnson officials quickly perceived that some kind of affirmative action was needed in the city police forces, fire departments, and state National Guards (all of which had almost all white personnel), but they did not publicize this affirmative action. Johnson also worked with business leaders to develop new programs to get around old ideas of merit, such as scores on aptitude tests and consideration of police arrest records, and to have urban employers hire more blacks. Many business owners themselves believed they should protect their businesses from being burned down by race-consciously reaching out to hire more blacks. Finally, Johnson created a National Commission on Civil Disorders to study the problem and recommend solutions. Johnson specifically instructed the Commission to reach beyond old ideas and get to the heart of the problem. Though the Commission's report generally stuck to colorblind terms such as "ghetto resident" rather than "black," it still recommended moving beyond old ideas of merit to hire new people, seconded the notion that city police forces should represent more blacks, and even argued that newspapers should hire minority reporters to report on minority issues.[20]

Administrative Pragmatism

Administrators in the EEOC and OFCC also were drawn to affirmative action. Like the Johnson administration, they moved toward affirmative action in a behind-the-scenes sort of way. They generally did not publicize what they were doing; they justified affirmative action primarily only to themselves.

The specifics of how the EEOC and OFCC moved to affirmative action were different, but the underlying logic of their action was the same. Administrators in both organizations were trying to find some pragmatic means to achieve the end of equal opportunity. It is common for government administrators to try to find efficient and effective means to show some policy success, especially when new and under the watchful eye of some constituent group.[21] EEOC and OFCC administrators believed they were not accomplishing anything by following only the procedures of colorblind methods. Though civil rights groups were not demanding affirmative action, they were demanding effective enforcement of civil rights, and this they were not getting.

At the EEOC, administrators saw the extremely cumbersome procedure of investigating complaints of discrimination as the main problem, what they called a "retail" approach to civil rights. Crippled by a small budget, an inexperienced staff, and weak leadership, the difficult job of examining each of the thousands of written, sworn complaints of discrimination flooding into the office became almost impossible. In a 60-day period, EEOC administrators were to determine if each complaint was even worth investigating, and if so, they were to send personnel to the firm or union to talk to alleged discriminators and disgruntled employees, examine hiring and promotion records, and, if discrimination was found, they were to attempt to persuade the employer to rectify the situation. In fact, many EEOC determinations and investigations were taking as long as two years. One can imagine the frustration of a victim of discrimination at this situation—the jobless, after all, need jobs. A backlog of cases numbering more that 3,000 accumulated in only one year, and by 10 years, it was 125,000 cases.[22] Civil rights advocates outside of government were labeling the EEOC administrators failures. The administrators had little to show to challenge that claim.

EEOC administrators responded in a way typical of government administrators in any field: They sought a more efficient means to demonstrate progress to their goal (in this case, equal opportunity). More specifically, they sought a "quantifiable," "wholesale" approach to civil rights. Virtually any social problem can be and is quantified in some way: drunk driving accidents, food poisonings, and workplace injuries.[23] At the EEOC, they sought some numbers to show where discrimination was occurring. They created a document, the EEO-1 form, that employers with a workforce of more than 100 would have to fill out that described the racial ("Negro" and "Oriental"), national origin ("Spanish American" and "American Indian") makeup of their workforces, broken down into various levels of employment (unskilled to professional) and separated by male and female (see Figure 21.1). They collected the statistics and, first concentrating on black employment, held hearings with representatives of various industries (e.g., textiles, pharmaceuticals) or geographic areas (e.g., white-collar employment in New York) that employed very few or even no blacks in an area where many black workers were available. It was 1967, and it was among the first broad efforts at using the federal government to encourage some race-based proportional hiring. For the firms, it meant that they should review their hiring procedures until they figured out a way to get more blacks onto their payrolls. Doing so meant the government would leave them alone; some federally determined minority backgrounds thus gained a positive meaning for them. For the government, the new policy was simply administrative pragmatism. In internal memos, bureaucrats justified the affirmative action approach as a cost-effective, efficient, and effective way to promote civil rights and equal opportunity (though the individual complaint investigations continued). Adminis-

trators were talking to administrators, speaking a discourse they all could understand. Civil rights leaders, some dubious at first, went along with the new approach.[24]

Procedures at the OFCC were different, but similarly frustrating. The executive order that created the OFCC demanded nondiscrimination by government contractors and some undefined "affirmative action" to achieve nondiscrimination. This term had no clear meaning, and administrators were not at all sure how to enforce "affirmative action." The term was borrowed from the Wagner Act (1937) dealing with discrimination against members of labor unions and seemed limited to specific, identifiable victims of anti-union activity at a particular firm. What would it mean in civil rights law?

At first, the OFCC would have firms that bid for government contract work promise not to discriminate and to take some "affirmative action" to prevent discrimination. They would even sign some forms with these promises on them. But that would be that—nothing would change. After the work was completed, a firm could have employed an all-white workforce but still have told the OFCC that they did not discriminate. They could say they wanted qualified black workers to come try for jobs, but none did. The OFCC was achieving what in the words of one administrator was "paper compliance."[25]

Over a period of two years and four construction projects (in St. Louis, San Francisco, Cleveland, and Philadelphia), the OFCC pragmatically sought a way to get beyond simple paper compliance. Finally, for the Philadelphia Plan, they achieved what they believed was a workable model, justifying their experimentation with a discourse of administrative pragmatism. Affirmative action promises would have to be more than a vague promise of extra efforts at nondiscrimination. Firms winning a federal contract would have to promise to try to achieve specific, racial hiring "goals"—percentage ranges based on availability of minorities in the workforce—and offer "timetables"—the racial hiring would occur in a specified time period. The phrase "goals and timetables" entered the American policy lexicon quietly, not with ideological fervor or in moral arguments for minority compensation, but in the technocratic language of administrative pragmatism. For many, goals and timetables would be synonymous with affirmative action. But there was a problem: In 1968, some government officials said that goals and timetables amounted to racial quotas and were illegal. The Philadelphia Plan went into limbo, its legality in question.

The Politics of Preemption

Ironically, a white male conservative, Richard M. Nixon, would resurrect the affirmative action of the OFCC's Philadelphia Plan. I believe it is a shame that research on the Nixon administration has been overshadowed by the Watergate scandal,[26] obscuring Nixon's first term, 1969 to 1972, during which some fascinating policy making took place.

It was less difficult for Nixon officials to advocate affirmative action in 1969 than it would have been even a few years earlier. A few years of crisis management and administrative pragmatism had quietly introduced race-conscious hiring into American policy making. But the specific circumstances of the Nixon administration made affirmative action advocacy logical and appropriate for other reasons.

The political scientist Stephen Skowronek has made an important point in arguing that, despite the tendency to rank presidents in terms of their leadership abilities and to describe them in terms of character traits, a crucial component of what a president does and can do is shaped by the political context in which he is elected.[27] For example, a president such as Franklin Delano Roosevelt, who is elected during a time when the prevailing ideological regime is perceived as crumbling

or exhausted (the Depression), can wield great leadership authority and accomplish great things. Resistance is weak, a greater range of new actions are legitimate and appropriate. Roosevelt, being elected during an economic calamity, or Ronald Reagan, being elected after the troubled Carter presidency and when liberalism was in decline, were able to push bold, new agendas. But presidents who represent opposition to the prevailing political order when that order is still strong (a rare occurrence, but it happens) are in for a tough time. They will want to pursue their opposition agenda but still have to play by the rules of the prevailing agenda. They tend to pursue a "politics of preemption," in which they seek new approaches in new policy areas to "preempt" the other side. In this context, presidents will take risks, and risky policy moves will have more legitimacy than otherwise would be the case.

Nixon was elected as a moderate conservative in liberal times. He barely won election in a three-way race, scoring 43.5 percent of the popular vote, compared to Democrat Hubert Humphrey's 42.7 and third-party challenger George Wallace's respectable 13.5 percent.[28] Congress remained solidly Democratic. From the early days of his campaign, Nixon was taking risks and seeking to preempt liberals on issues. For example, he gave the first public exposure to affirmative action for minority businesspersons when he called for a special program to develop "black capitalism."[29]

Ironically, he did this at the same time that he was advocating a slowdown in the area of school integration. To appeal to the South, he argued that although segregation was clearly wrong, he also believed it was wrong to bus children across towns and cities to integrate schools. Although the Deep South voted for George Wallace, the states on the border of the Deep South went with Nixon, and Nixon pursued a policy of trying to slow down busing (much of which was court-ordered) to reward the border South and win the Deep

South for the next election. For example, he fired government bureaucrats who continued to advocate busing.

All of this put him squarely at odds with powerful liberals who strongly advocated protecting civil rights. Nixon and his aides believed they had to offer something in the name of civil rights besides black capitalism. Some in the administration, including Labor Department Secretary George Shultz and Assistant Secretary Arthur Fletcher, convinced him to resurrect the Philadelphia Plan. Affirmative action needed a strong defense to remove the cloud of illegality. The Philadelphia Plan was appealing for several reasons. First, Nixon needed a civil rights policy to defend himself against charges he was anti-civil rights. Second, because the Philadelphia Plan targeted construction unions—a group that voted heavily Democratic—he would not be antagonizing any Republican voters. Nixon was always careful to emphasize that his affirmative action program was limited: "It is essential that black Americans, all Americans, have an equal opportunity to get into the construction unions."[30] And third, he would be "preempting" the liberal agenda: Democrats in Congress generally avoided discussion of and were quite troubled by a policy like the Philadelphia Plan. Because the Democratic unions hated it and the Democratic blacks would like it, congressional Democrats would have to choose sides and split their own coalition. Other reasons also played a part, including attempting to gain some votes from blacks, increasing the supply of construction workers (and thereby holding down their wages and thus holding down the rising inflation of the time),[31] and the attractiveness of getting blacks into jobs rather than having them off welfare.[32]

Democrats had not yet publicly championed the Philadelphia Plan or affirmative action's race-conscious hiring. The Johnson administration pursued limited policies for crisis management and publicly championed colorblind "War on Poverty" policies to help blacks, along with the white poor.[33] The EEOC and OFCC bureaucrats worked without considering political impacts. When Nixon came into office, he sold fellow Republicans on the idea of affirmative action in the construction industry using a discourse that expressed the logic of the politics of preemption. The Nixon administration would confound the liberal Democrats with a new liberal policy that liberal Democrats viewed without enthusiasm.

After Nixon gave his support to the Philadelphia Plan, Congress, led by Republican Representative and future President Gerald Ford, beat back challenges to its legality. The OFCC then expanded the goals and timetables of affirmative action to all government contracts with the quiet issuing of "Order No. 4."[34]

Affirmative Action as Tradition

Studying historical documents related to the origins of affirmative action, one discerns another pattern that is less dependent on specific political contexts. Advocates of affirmative action throughout the government often sold the policy by denying that it was anything new, by arguing instead that it was simply a part of American political, cultural, or legal tradition. They did this by referring to affirmative action as "civil rights," or "equal opportunity," or a "fair chance," or preceding a description of affirmative action with a recitation of the opening paragraph of the Declaration of Independence and downplaying or keeping quiet about the controversial aspects of affirmative action, its race-conscious aspects. With the discourse of tradition, advocates are essentially denying the new policy represents anything new.

One specific context in which the discourse of tradition is taken for granted and central to operation is the court system. Federal district and appeals courts, and ultimately the Supreme Court, found traditions—in law, they are called precedents—to ground the move from a colorblind discrimination law to an affirmative action model. Most importantly, in *Griggs v. Duke Power* (1971, 401 U.S. 424), the Supreme Court argued that Title VII prohibited unintentional discrimination as well as intentional discrimination. In other words, based on the text of Title VII and other federal court opinions, any firm practices that had an "adverse impact" on the numbers of minorities hired could be considered in a court of law to be discriminatory and illegal. It was an important change in civil rights law that added an element of race-consciousness into employment practices that is the hallmark of affirmative action. Firms in compliance were no longer only rooting out bigots; they also were keeping an eye on the number of minorities hired.

Policy Expansion: Other Areas, Other Groups

By 1971, then, affirmative action in employment had received the sanction of a president and the Supreme Court. While the general public was mostly distracted by other late 1960s phenomena, such as anti-Vietnam War protests and busing for school integration, affirmative action had become legitimate policy, at least for federal government elites. As it was developing in employment, affirmative action also was expanding into different areas and including new groups.

Some universities, following a crisis management logic while responding to urban unrest or unrest on their own campuses, began to lower admission requirements for minorities.[35] Organizations that conferred accreditation to medical and law schools strongly encouraged those schools to do the same.[36] The new medical school at the University of California at Davis went as far as to reserve a set number of seats for minorities, and when a white male challenged the program as a violation of the Civil Rights Act and the Consti-

tution, the Supreme Court struck down the Davis plan (*Regents of the University of California v. Bakke,* 1978, 438 U.S. 265) as an illegal racial quota, but allowed racial difference to be given consideration as a "plus factor" in school admissions. In a widely cited opinion, Justice Powell looked with admiration on the admissions policy of Harvard College, which took race into account as part of a strategy to achieve "diversity" among the student body. In this understanding, affirmative action was not about finding ways to prevent discrimination, compensate for past discrimination, or control racial unrest. The philosophy was pedagogical: All students would benefit from the presence and viewpoints of racial and (some) national-origin minorities.

Beginning in 1968, and mostly as a response to the urban rioting, the Small Business Administration began a program of offering more favorable terms on loans to minority business owners. Nixon followed through on his promise of helping to foster black capitalism by creating the Office of Minority Business Enterprise through a 1969 executive order. Beginning in the late 1970s, Congress also began to offer the contract set-aside program.[37]

All affirmative action programs began with the intention of helping blacks, but they all also quickly expanded to include other groups. When the EEOC created the EEO-1 form, administrators included four different minority groups but left off all national-origin groups, save Latinos and American Indians, and left off all religion groups. These decisions occurred with very little discussion; everyone took for granted who the minorities in America were. EEOC administrators initially concentrated on statistics of black employment. After pressure from women's groups and Latino groups for more attention (not specifically for affirmative action), the EEOC began to focus more attention on women's and Latino employment and to encourage firms to hire more American Indians.[38] At the OFCC, although the Philadelphia Plan concentrated on blacks, administrators quickly began to include Latinos, American Indians, and Asian Americans in affirmative action plans, and, after heavy lobbying from women, they began to include women as well. These same groups are also included in most affirmative action for minority businesses. Universities have left out women and, except for law school admissions, most leave out Asian Americans as well. There is amazing regularity in that almost no programs go beyond the groups on the EEO-1 form to include other groups that possibly were discriminated against, such as Arab Americans, various eastern and southern European groups (Italians, Poles, Greeks), or any religious groups. The OFCC issued a regulation for federal government contractors to use affirmative action to improve the representation of Catholics, Jews, and southern and eastern European groups, but this regulation was greatly weakened by the Nixon administration (though it remains on the books today).[39]

Effectiveness, Attempts at Retrenchment, and Resilience

As a political sociologist most interested in the policy-making process, I have not had occasion to examine fully the effectiveness of affirmative action in increasing minority representation in any area. It is a difficult question, for a variety of reasons. One is that there are a large number of variables that may explain rising minority upward mobility. Another is that the overall quality of education that blacks received improved around the time that affirmative action developed. In addition, many blacks migrated from the South to the North, where they had greater opportunities. These factors might help explain why black achievement was on an upward trend even before the civil rights policies of the 1960s.[40] In the case of women, affirmative action developed shortly after their mass infusion into the workforce. Furthermore, despite the growth of complex regulations, affirmative action enforcement often has been weak. It always has been inconsistent.

There are, nevertheless, signs of success and failure. Successes include improvements after 1964 in black representation in certain fields, especially for black men in skilled positions, which some social scientists attribute to new civil rights laws and especially affirmative action.[41] On the negative side, the black unemployment rate has remained consistently at approximately double that for whites throughout the post-1964 period. In higher education, successes are more easily measurable and seem to be considerable. Affirmative action clearly has been very important in getting more blacks and Latinos into universities. The demise of affirmative action at the University of California resulted in the admission of black students at Berkeley to fall from 547 students in 1997 to 224 in 1998; 260 were enrolled in 1997, and only 98 were enrolled in 1998. The numbers of Latinos at Berkeley in admissions and enrollments were roughly halved in the same time period. Whites and Asians and a mysterious "other" category saw their proportion rise (numbers at other universities in the UC system varied, showing a more modest decline in black and Latino admissions or even gains at Irvine, Riverside, and Santa Cruz).[42] A comprehensive study of elite universities' use of affirmative action in admissions found that black students, despite often having lower SAT scores, generally did almost as well as whites and went on to successful careers.[43]

There is very little research on the effects of affirmative action for minority business owners. In the early 1970s, the Nixon administration bragged about the results of its Minority Business Enterprise program and described the increases from 1969 to 1971 in grants and loans to minorities ($200 million to $566 million) and the growth in purchases from minority companies from $13 million to $142 million.[44] More recent data show that the federal set-aside program for minority-owned businesses works well; when federal monies carried affirmative action provisions in Missouri, for example, 15.1 percent of funds went to "disadvantaged business enterprises," but only 1.7 percent of state monies went to similar firms without the set-aside in place.[45] Further research is needed.

In recent years, affirmative action regulations have been limited and refined in the courts. *City of Richmond v. Croson Co.* (1989, 488 U.S. 469) was especially important for contract set-asides. Under the Fourteenth Amendment, the Supreme Court struck down Richmond, Virginia's minority contract set-aside program. There was no evidence of discrimination in Richmond's minority contracting, and a statistical imbalance was not enough to show discrimination. This ruling—that all race classifications were inherently suspect—was then expanded to all regulations in a 5-4 decision of 1995, *Adarand Constructors v. Peña*.[46] Also in 1995, the Fifth Circuit ruled in *Hopwood v. Texas*[47] that the University of Texas Law School's affirmative action admissions program was unconstitutional, rejected the University's "diversity" rationale (the law school claimed that racial preferences were necessary to maintain a diverse student body), and argued that a specific finding of discrimination is necessary for such a program. The court declared, "The law school may not use race as a factor in deciding which applicants to admit" (p. 933). The Supreme Court denied review of the case.

"Quotas" and "preferences" also remain unpopular with the majority of voters (the majority being mostly white), and, when asked to vote on affirmative action when framed in these terms, voters in California in 1996 and Washington State in 1998 rejected it. However, when asked to vote simply on "affirmative action" in Houston, voters (where minorities were heavily represented) affirmed the policy. Still, there are other signs that suggest affirmative action is alive and

well. Democrats have been defenders of affirmative action regulations since the 1970s, and Republican leaders in Washington and in state governments, though they often have criticized the policy, have done little to eliminate it. The Reagan administration weakened enforcement but backed off a planned rewrite of the Executive Order 11246. The Republican Congress of 1995–1996, led by Senate Majority Leader Robert Dole of Kansas, created a bill to end affirmative action, but it went nowhere. The bill was reintroduced the following session but fared no better.[48]

One reason its attackers have not followed through with their attacks on the policy is that in some elite circles, affirmative action remains very popular. Many, if not most, universities are committed to finding some policy to maintain high representation of blacks and Latinos. Perhaps more surprisingly, most big businesses are strong supporters of affirmative action. Though they at first simply complied with government regulations mandating affirmative action, when the Reagan administration lessened enforcement, human resources professionals in the largest corporations adopted a version of the diversity rationale used in universities. In the business version, racial diversity was helpful to business because it increased profits; it did so by bringing in new viewpoints and helping corporations connect with minority communities to better market products and services to those communities.[49]

Conclusion

In a word, affirmative action has become institutionalized, a taken-for-granted way of doing things in our nation's largest corporations, in many universities, and for policy makers working in civil rights. Affirmative action has come a long way since 1964, when very few in positions of power seriously considered the policy let alone openly and actively advocated it. It took extraordinary circumstances for it to overcome its taboo status, but it was not an ideological movement that put it in place. Policy and business elites supported it, including prominent conservatives. But affirmative action remains controversial. For the sociologist, this fact and its relevance to important issues of equal opportunity and social harmony make it an especially important and fascinating topic of study.

Notes

1. See, for example, the work of Seymour Martin Lipset, *First New Nation* (New York: Norton, 1979 [1963]); *Continental Divide* (New York: Routledge, 1991); *American Exceptionalism* (New York: Norton, 1996). On the importance of public opinion in policy making, see Paul Burstein, *Discrimination, Jobs and Politics* (Chicago: University of Chicago Press 1998 [1985]); Paul Burstein, "Bringing the Public Back In: Should Sociologists Consider the Impact of Public Opinion on Public Policy?" *Social Forces* 77(1998):27–62.

2. There is a large number of scholars espousing this view. Perhaps the most influential is G. William Domhoff. See his *Who Rules America?* (Englewood Cliffs, NJ: Prentice Hall, 1967), *The Powers That Be* (New York: Vintage, 1978); Richard L. Zweigenhaft and G. William Domhoff, *Diversity in the Power Elite* (New Haven: Yale University Press, 1998). Although the government remains dominated by white, upper-class males, Zweigenhaft and Domhoff do find improvement in minority group representation over the past several decades.

3. The evidence here is far from uniform—a 1995 CBS/*New York Times* poll showed that as many as a third of Euro-Americans do not even know what affirmative action is, and polls that simply ask if the public favors "affirmative action" tend to find the public evenly divided. See Jennifer Hochschild, "Race in the Culture Wars: The Symbolic Use of Affirmative Action," in *The Cultural*

Territories of Race: White and Black Boundaries, edited by M. Lamont (New York/Chicago: Russell Sage Foundation/University of Chicago Press, forthcoming). However, questions asking about support for preferences for blacks in hiring and university admissions "because of past discrimination" find Euro-Americans consistently and overwhelmingly rejecting the policy. The numbers vary between 82 percent and 90 percent opposed for questions on hiring in the years 1986 to 1994, and from 68 percent to 76 percent rejection in admissions for those same years. The strength of the economy has no discernible effect on percentages opposed. See Paul M. Sniderman and Edward G. Carmines, *Reaching beyond Race* (Cambridge, MA: Harvard University Press, 1997), pp. 28–30. In response to a question that asks for views on whether jobs and places in colleges should be based solely on ability as determined by test scores or should allow preferential treatment for women and minorities, 81 percent of men and 84 percent of women supported ability. In a 1991 *Newsweek*/Gallup poll, 72 percent of Euro-Americans disagreed that qualified Afro-Americans should get preferences for jobs and college over equally qualified Euro-Americans. Forty-two percent of Afro-Americans disagreed, and 48 percent agreed. John David Skrentny, *The Ironies of Affirmative Action: Politics, Culture and Justice in America* (Chicago: University of Chicago Press, 1996), pp. 4–5. Views vary by racial/ethnic category. Whereas 45 percent of Euro-Americans believe "affirmative action for blacks is unfair to whites" (31 percent disagree and 24 percent say neither), 34 percent of Asians agree (31 disagree), 30 percent of Latinos agree (37 disagree) and 18 percent of Afro-Americans agree (65 percent disagree). Lawrence Bobo, "Race, Interests and Beliefs about Affirmative Action: Unanswered Questions and New Directions," *American Behavioral Scientist* 41(1998):985–1003.

4. This definition is more in line with general usage of the term and not with the technical meaning. Legally speaking, affirmative action may include difference-blind actions such as simply publicizing that one is an equal opportunity employer. See Roger Clegg, "Beyond Quotas: A

Color-Blind Vision for Affirmative Action," *Policy Review* May/June 1998, pp. 12–21.

5. From the 1993 EEO-1 form. The "Hispanic" category has had different names in the past. The categories are broken down for Officials and Managers, Professionals, Technicians, Sales Workers, Office and Clerical, Craft Workers (Skilled), Operatives (Semi-Skilled), Laborers (Unskilled), and Service Workers.

6. Alfred W. Blumrosen, *Modern Law: The Law Transmission System and Equal Employment Opportunity* (Madison: University of Wisconsin Press, 1993), pp. 242–45.

7. In 1978, the OFCC became the Office of Federal Contract Compliance Programs (OFCCP).

8. Quoted in Hugh Davis Graham, *The Civil Rights Era: Origins and Development of National Policy, 1960–1972* (New York: Oxford University Press, 1990), pp. 342–43. In 1971, the OFCC's Revised Order No. 4 added women to the goals and timetables requirement.

9. Skrentny, 1996, pp. 30–34, 76–78, 96, 231–32.

10. This notion is the hallmark of the state-centered approach in political sociology. See, for example, Peter B. Evans, Dietrich Rueschemeyer and Theda Skocpol, eds., *Bringing the State Back In* (New York: Cambridge University Press, 1985). More recent modifications include Theda Skocpol, *Protecting Soldiers and Mothers: The Political Origins of Social Policy in the United States* (Cambridge, MA: Harvard University Press, 1992); Edwin Amenta, *Bold Relief: Institutional Politics and the Origins of Modern American Social Policy* (Princeton, NJ: Princeton University Press, 1998); Robert C. Lieberman, *Shifting the Color Line: Race and the American Welfare State* (Cambridge, MA: Harvard University Press, 1998).

11. See, for example, Graham, 1990, pp. 108–13.

12. From sociology, I rely on, generally, the essays collected in Walter W. Powell and Paul J. DiMaggio, eds., *The New Institutionalism in Organizational Analysis* (Chicago: University of Chicago Press, 1991); George M. Thomas, John W. Meyer, Francisco Ramirez, and John Boli, eds., *Institutional Structure: Constituting State, Society, and the Individual* (Newbury Park, CA: Sage, 1987); Frank Dobbin, *Forging Industrial Policy* (New York: Cambridge University Press, 1994). For a more recent example, see Elisabeth Clemens, *The People's Lobby* (Chicago: University of Chicago Press, 1997).

13. I mostly relied on four large collections of official documents: Michal R. Belknap, ed., *Civil Rights, The White House and the Justice Department* (New York: Garland, 1991); Steven F. Lawson, ed., *Civil Rights during the Johnson Administration* (Frederick, MD: University Publications of America, 1984); Joan Hoff-Wilson, ed., *Papers of the Nixon White House* (Bethesda, MD: University Publications of America, 1989); and Hugh Davis Graham, ed., *Civil Rights during the Nixon Administration, 1969–1974* (Bethesda, MD: University Publications of America, 1989).

14. Skrentny, 1996, pp. 70–73.

15. James W. Button, *Black Violence* (Princeton, NJ: Princeton University Press, 1978).

16. John Boli, *New Citizens for a New Society* (Elmsford, NY: Pergamon, 1989).

17. Skrentny, 1996, pp. 82–83.

18. On the Cold War effects on black civil rights, see Mary L. Dudziak, "Desegregation as a Cold War Imperative," *Stanford Law Review* 41(1988):67–88; Doug McAdam, "On the International Origins of Domestic Political Opportunities," in *Social Movements and American Political Institutions*, edited by A. Costain and A. McFarland (New York: Rowman & Littlefield, 1997), pp. 251–67; Philip Klinkner with Rogers M. Smith, *The Unsteady March* (Chicago: University of Chicago Press, 1999).

19. Lyndon B. Johnson, *The Vantage Point* (New York: Holt, Rinehart and Winston, 1971), p. 170.

20. Skrentny, 1996, pp. 96–99.

21. John David Skrentny, "State Capacity, Policy Feedbacks and Affirmative Action for Blacks, Women and Latinos," *Research in Political Sociology* 8(1998):279–310; Robin Rogers-Dillon and John David Skrentny, "Administering Success: The Legitimacy Imperative and the Implementa-

tion of Welfare Reform," *Social Problems,* forthcoming.

22. Skrentny, 1996, pp. 123–24.

23. John Kingdon, *Agendas, Alternatives, and Public Policies* (Boston: Little, Brown, 1984), p. 97.

24. Graham, 1990, p. 199. Alfred Blumrosen, *Modern Law: The Law Transmission System and Equal Employment Opportunity* (Madison: University of Wisconsin Press, 1993), p. 76.

25. James E. Jones, Jr., "The Bugaboo of Employment Quotas," *Wisconsin Law Review,* 34(2, 1970):341–403, p. 346.

26. For example, Gerald S. Strober and Deborah Hart Strober's *Nixon: An Oral History of His Presidency* (New York: HarperCollins, 1994) devotes 11 pages of interviews with administration leaders to "Domestic Issues" but approximately 250 pages to Watergate and related scandals.

27. Stephen Skowronek, *The Politics Presidents Make* (Cambridge, MA: Harvard University Press, 1993).

28. Skrentny, 1996, p. 182.

29. Maurice H. Stans, "Nixon's Economic Policy toward Minorities," in *Richard M. Nixon: Politician, President, Administrator,* edited by L. Friedman and W. F. Levantrosser (New York: Greenwood, 1991), pp. 239–46; see pp. 239–40.

30. Congressional Quarterly, *Nixon: The First Year of His Presidency* (Washington, DC: Government Printing Office, 1970), p. 27-A.

31. Judith Stein, *Running Steel, Running America: Race, Economic Policy, and the Decline of Liberalism* (Chapel Hill: University of North Carolina Press, 1998), pp. 150–52.

32. William Safire, *Before the Fall* (New York: DeCapo, 1975), pp. 266, 585.

33. When Lyndon Johnson gave his famous speech at Howard University in which he argued that blacks needed some special help to be given true equal opportunity, he had his War on Poverty programs in mind and not affirmative action. Skrentny, 1996, p. 153; Gareth Davies, *From Opportunity to Entitlement* (Lawrence: University of Kansas Press, 1996), pp. 65–72.

34. Graham, 1990, pp. 342–43.

35. John R. Hammond, "Affirmative Action in Historical Perspective," in *Affirmative Action's Testament of Hope: Strategies for a New Era in Higher Education,* edited by M. García (Albany: State University of New York Press, 1997), pp. 19–46, p. 31; Allan P. Sindler, *Bakke, DeFunis, and Minority Admissions: The Quest of Opportunity* (White Plains, NY: Longman, 1978), p. 265. In California, the state legislature also encouraged affirmative action in university admissions. John Aubrey Douglas, "Anatomy of a Conflict: The Making and Unmaking of Affirmative Action at the University of California," *American Behavioral Scientist,* 41(1998):938–59.

36. Susan Welch and John Gruhl, *Affirmative Action and Minority Enrollments in Medical and Law Schools* (Ann Arbor: University of Michigan Press, 1998), p. 80.

37. Hugh Davis Graham, "Unintended Consequences: The Convergence of Affirmative Action and Immigration Policy," *American Behavioral Scientist* 41(1998):898–912; George R. La Noue and John C. Sullivan, "Deconstructing the Affirmative Action Categories," *American Behavioral Scientist* 41(1998):938–59.

38. Statistics did not show gross underrepresentation of Asian Americans and the EEOC did not pay much attention to this group. Alfred Blumrosen, *Black Employment and the Law* (New Brunswick, NJ: Rutgers University Press, 1971), chapter 3.

39. John David Skrentny, 1998, "Affirmative Action: Some Advice for the Pundits," *American Behavioral Scientist* 41:877–86.

40. Nathan Glazer, *Affirmative Discrimination* (Cambridge, MA: Harvard University Press, 1987 [1975]); Stephan Thernstrom and Abigail Thernstrom, *America in Black and White* (New York: Simon & Schuster, 1997).

41. Andorra Bruno, *CRS Report for Congress: Affirmative Action in Employment* (Washington, DC: Congressional Research Service, 1995), pp. 29–40; Hochschild, "Race in the Culture Wars: The Symbolic Use of Affirmative Action," forthcoming; Barbara Reskin, *The Realities of Affirmative Action in Employment* (Washington, DC: American Sociological Association, 1998).

42. Ethan Bronner, "Fewer Minorities Entering U. of California," *New York Times,* May 21, 1998, p. A28.

43. William G. Bowen and Derek Bok, *The Shape of the River: Long-Term Consequences of Considering Race in College and University Admissions* (Princeton, NJ: Princeton University Press, 1998).

44. "Special Message to the Congress Urging Expansion of the Minority Business Enterprise Program, October 13, 1971," *Public Papers of the Presidents of the United States: Richard M. Nixon, 1971* (Washington, DC: Government Printing Office, 1972), pp. 1041–46. Nixon sold the preferences for minority capitalists as self-help: "The best way to fight poverty and to break the vicious cycle of dependence and despair which afflicts too many Americans is by fostering conditions which encourage those who have been so afflicted to play a more self-reliant and independent economic role" (p. 1041).

45. *Congressional Record,* March 5, 1998, p. 1401.

46. 115 S. Ct. 2097 (1995).

47. 78 F. 3d 932 (5th Cir. 1996).

48. John David Skrentny, "Republican Efforts to End Affirmative Action: Walking a Fine Line," in *The New Politics of Public Policy, Vol. II,* edited by M. Landy, M. Levin, and M. Shapiro (Baltimore: Johns Hopkins University Press, forthcoming).

49. Erin Kelly and Frank Dobbin, "How Affirmative Action Became Diversity Management: Employer Response to Antidiscrimimation Law, 1961–1996," *American Behavioral Scientist* 41(1998):960–84; Frederick Lynch, *The Diversity Machine* (New York: Free Press, 1997).

Skrentny:

1. Compare and contrast the philosophies behind civil rights (colorblindness) with that of affirmative action (color-consciousness). What are the consequences of each perspective?

2. How are "legacies" in college admissions similar to other examples of targeting in public policies such as affirmative action and the Veterans' Preference Act of 1944? What other examples can you think of that are based on the same philosophy of being conscious of difference?

Affirmative Action and Liberal Capitulation

Stephen Steinberg

It may seem strange or self-contradictory to say, but racists get too much of the blame for racism. As a system of institutionalized beliefs and practices, racism does not depend only on the virulent hatred of fervid racists (who are usually few in number). It also depends on the apathy and passivity of nonracists and on the equivocation and bad faith of those who profess commitment to the cause of racial justice. Conversely, the struggle against racism ultimately will flounder without the steadfast and vigorous support of those who repudiate racism, at least in principle. This is why it is appropriate, indeed crucial, to scrutinize not only the racists who perpetrate wrongs but also the nonracists and antiracists who, often through acts of omission, play a role in the perpetuation of the racial status quo.

This was an underlying premise of my 1995 book, *Turning Back: The Retreat from Racial Justice in American Thought and Policy,* as can be seen by looking at one passage:

As is often argued, liberals are not *the* enemy. However, this enemy depends on the so-called liberal to put a kinder and gentler face on racism. To subdue the rage of the oppressed. To raise false hopes that change is imminent. To modulate the demands for complete liberation. To divert pro-

test. And to shift the onus of responsibility for America's greatest crime away from powerful institutions that *could* make a difference onto individuals who have been rendered powerless by these very institutions.[1]

The comedian Dick Gregory put it more succinctly: "The moderate is a cat who would hang me from a low tree."

In this chapter, I again subject liberals to critical scrutiny, this time on the specific issue of affirmative action. Assuming that recent headlines are correct, and we are today witnessing "the end of affirmative action," it behooves us to ask what went wrong. Does this policy reversal reflect a liberal failure to protect the hard-won gains of the civil rights movement? To what extent have liberals been implicated in the dismantling of affirmative action policy? It is one thing to blame racists for racism. But whom are we to blame for the failure of antiracist public policy?

It is ironic that the most vehement opposition to affirmative action comes not from the corporate world—not from the companies actually subject to affirmative action mandates—but from the world of politics. At a time when even liberal journals like *The New Republic* and *The American Prospect* are trouncing affirmative action policy, one finds far more favorable treatment on the pages of *Business Week, Personnel Journal,* and *Fortune.* Corporations tout their success with affirmative action not only because it projects the "right" image but also because they have come to appreciate the importance of expanding the pool of talent and of diversifying their workforce in a global economy.

Given the contentious public debate over affirmative action, one might think that affirmative action failed as policy. On the contrary, affirmative action achieved its overriding policy objective: the rapid integration of minorities and women into occupations in which they had been excluded throughout American history. Why, then, the fierce debate? The simple answer is that affirmative action has become politicized. It is being used to deflect attention away from problems that neither political party wants to address: declining wages, a widening wage gap between more and less educated workers, and massive layoffs related to new technology and globalization. The message is: "Blacks are cheating you of jobs and opportunity. End affirmative action and your problems will be solved."

This is scapegoating, pure and simple. Ironically, all of the problems of a declining empire are being blamed on the very group that benefited least from empire. And whereas anti-affirmative action discourse always focuses on blacks, the gutting of affirmative action will have dire consequences for white women who have been the primary beneficiaries. In short, affirmative action is the sop that politicians are throwing at white men who are wracked with economic insecurity.

It would be easy to go on assailing the rogues on the right who have used affirmative action in a thinly veiled attempt to appeal to racism in their assault on the welfare state. However, I address a more thorny issue: the capitulation of liberals to the anti-affirmative action backlash. Here we are dealing not with people who have racist and reactionary tendencies but with those proverbial "friends of the Negro" who purport to be committed to the cause of racial justice.

The liberal default on affirmative action began even before the words "affirmative action" entered the political lexicon. As the civil rights revolution approached its triumphant climax in 1965, protest leaders began to realize that winning civil rights would not by itself assure racial equality. The words "compensation," "reparations," and "preference" already had crept into the political discourse, and white liberals were beginning to display their disquiet with this troublesome turn of events. In *Why We Can't Wait,* published in 1963, Martin Luther King, Jr., observed, "Whenever this issue of compensatory or preferential treatment for the Negro is raised, some of our friends recoil in horror. The Negro should be granted equality, they agree; but he should ask nothing more."[2]

Later, when affirmative action evolved as policy, liberals were in the vanguard of the attack. One of the first was Nathan Glazer who, in 1976, wrote a book mischievously entitled *Affirmative Discrimination.*[3] On the premise that rights devolve to individuals, not to groups, Glazer accused the proponents of affirmative action of engaging in a racial classification reminiscent of the Nuremberg Laws. Note the rhetorical sleight of hand as antiracist policy is portrayed as the quintessence of racism itself. In opposing affirmative action, Glazer then sanctimoniously projected himself as the champion of a colorblind society even as so-called color blindness functions as a spurious justification for maintaining the racial status quo.

Recently, Glazer has recanted his blanket opposition to affirmative action. In a recent issue of *The New Republic* (April 6, 1998), he noted that the abolition of affirmative action is already leading to sharp declines in black enrollment at major universities and concluded that the costs of ending affirmative action are "too grim to contemplate." However, this is, at best, an equivocal position. Instead of arguing that affirmative action is a necessary and just remedy for past and present discrimination, Glazer implied that blacks lack the qualifications to compete unless they are accorded preference. Nor does Glazer explain why he was able to see in 1998 what advocates of "compensatory programs" were able to see in 1965: that civil rights legislation alone would not be enough to level the playing field and to integrate blacks into jobs and universities where they have been excluded historically.

Other liberals concede that affirmative action is right in principle but that it is too costly politically. For example, in 1992 Paul Starr published an article in *The American Prospect* titled "Civic Reconstruction: What to Do without Affirmative Action." The trouble with affirmative action, according to Starr, is that it triggers a popular backlash and fragments the coalition between minorities and labor that is necessary to elect Democrats to the White House. Starr went so far as to suggest that the gutting of affirmative action might be "a blessing in disguise," in that it will allow "the formation of bi-racial political alliances necessary to make progress against poverty."[4]

This logic continues to pervade liberal discourse. In the October 1997 issue of *Mother Jones,* a progressive journal, Jeffrey Klein contended that "affirmative action has eroded liberals' moral credibility and driven away many natural allies." Like Starr, he holds that "progressives need to reassess their commitment to affirmative action and find better alternatives that can re-establish racial healing as a national priority."[5] If self-identified progressives are willing to throw in the towel on affirmative action, what can we expect of people who make no claim to racial justice?

Indeed, liberal capitulation on affirmative action is reminiscent of what happened as Reconstruction unraveled at the end of the nineteenth century. Congress and the Supreme Court had turned back the clock on rights supposedly secured by the Reconstruction amendments, and Southern "redemp-

tionists" gloated that "all the fire has gone out of the Northern philanthropic fight for the rights of man."[6] Then, as now, liberal capitulation meant that a last line of defense had crumbled and that the redemptionists could proceed with political impunity.

To make matters worse, liberal capitulation is predicated on false assumptions concerning the history, purpose, and significance of affirmative action policy. In the pages that follow, I offer a rejoinder to five arguments that are commonly advanced by liberals to justify the withdrawal of support for affirmative action.

1. **Affirmative action was cooked up by Richard Nixon in order to drive a wedge into the coalition between the civil rights movement and the labor movement.**

True, the Nixon Administration implemented the Philadelphia Plan, which was the key initiative in the development of affirmative action policy as we know it today. It is also true that contemporaneous critics of the Philadelphia Plan—notably the civil rights leader Bayard Rustin—accused Nixon of a cunning ploy to destroy the liberal coalition. This allegation has received further credence by historian Hugh Davis Graham, who claims that "Nixon wanted to drive a wedge between blacks and organized labor—between the Democrats' social activists of the 1960s and the party's traditional economic liberals—that would fragment the New Deal coalition."[7] I would submit, however, that this is a distortion of historical fact—one that has assumed mythical proportions and is invoked time and again to provide political cover for liberal capitulation to the affirmative action backlash.

The Philadelphia Plan initially was developed in President Lyndon Johnson's Department of Labor but shelved after Hubert Humphrey's defeat in 1968. It was Arthur Fletcher, the black Assistant Secretary of Labor during the first Nixon Administration, who maneuvered to resurrect the Plan. The other "unsung heroes" of affirmative action are George Shultz, then Secretary of Labor, who gave Fletcher indispensable backing; Attorney General John Mitchell, who successfully defended the Plan before the Supreme Court; and Nixon himself, who expended considerable political capital heading off a Democratic challenge to the Plan in the Senate. One of the great ironies of racial politics in the post-civil rights era is that the Philadelphia Plan was implemented by Republicans over the opposition of the famed "liberal coalition" and without notable support of the civil rights establishment.[8]

There is obvious reason for doubting Nixon's motives. Nixon got elected on the basis of a Southern strategy that appealed to popular racism, and he subsequently nominated two Southern racists to the Supreme Court. Nevertheless, there is reason to doubt Graham's account of why Nixon threw his support behind the Philadelphia Plan.

One must begin by putting this decision in historical context. In 1969, the Vietnam War was reaching a critical stage, and Nixon had to worry about an escalation of racial protest "on the home front." This was a period when memories of the "riots" following the assassination of Martin Luther King, Jr., were still fresh, when black militancy was at its height, and when there were strident job protests in Philadelphia, Chicago, and numerous other cities against racism in the construction trades. Consider Graham's own account of the job protests in the summer of 1969:

In Chicago, job protests launched by a coalition of black neighborhood organizations shut down twenty-three South Side construction projects involving $85 million in contracts. . . . The demonstrations in Pittsburgh were more violent than in Chicago, but were similarly organized and focused on job discrimination in construction. One clash in Pittsburgh in late August left 50 black protestors and 12 policemen injured. . . . Racial violence over jobs also occurred in Seattle, and black coalitions announced job protest drives for New York, Cleveland, Detroit, Milwaukee, and Boston.[9]

This was the context in which Fletcher and Shultz seized the opportunity to resurrect the Philadelphia Plan, whose main objective was to enforce the hiring of blacks in building trades controlled by lily-white unions. From the perspective of the White House, there was little political liability in "sticking it" to the mostly Democratic unions. On the other hand, there was clear political advantage in neutralizing black protest and in preempting the liberal agenda on civil rights with a policy predicated on contract compliance.[10]

Whatever tangle of motivations were at work, Nixon actively fought off a congressional attempt to pass an anti-affirmative action rider that had the support of many Democrats, and John Mitchell successfully defended the Philadelphia Plan before the Supreme Court. Subsequently, the Department of Labor issued a new set of rules that extended the Philadelphia Plan to all federal contractors, including colleges and universities. Thus, the scope of affirmative action policy expanded beyond anything contemplated when the Philadelphia Plan had been disinterred in 1969. Furthermore, the Philadelphia Plan embodied none of the "liberal" elements that were ideologically anathema to Republicans. It envisioned no new government programs, no make-work schemes, no major public expenditures.[11] However, as the backlash against affirmative action mushroomed, Nixon did an about-face and, as Graham pointed out,[12] railed against the very "quotas" that he had put into place.

2. **Affirmative action has not worked. At best, it has helped the black middle class. Therefore, we are not giving up very much.**

This argument is based totally on false premises. Affirmative action is the most important policy of the post-civil rights era, in that it went beyond civil rights to attack institutionalized inequalities on the basis of race and gender. Nor was affirmative action the invention of "a Marcusean left coalition of feminists and minorities," as Michael Lind has claimed.[13] On the contrary, affirmative action was a policy of last resort. It evolved only after it became clear that the 1964 Civil Rights Act, which proscribed discrimination in the workplace, had failed abysmally to alter entrenched patterns of racial and gender discrimination.

Furthermore, affirmative action has been a dramatic success. This is widely acknowledged in the case of women, but it is also true of blacks. Most of the black middle class is directly a product of affirmative action programs that have been in place for over 20 years in both the public and private sectors. It is simply not accurate to say, as William Julius Wilson has done, that affirmative action primarily helps the middle class.[14] Listening to the affirmative action discourse, one might think that affirmative action exists primarily for brain surgeons and literati trained at Yale. In point of fact, affirmative action has had a great impact throughout the occupational world—not only in the ranks of corporate management but also in major blue-collar industries that, for the first time in American history, have opened craft and production jobs to blacks and women.

For blacks, the impact of affirmative action has been greatest in the public sector. For decades after World War II, the only jobs open to blacks in the vast federal workforce were in the postal service. Today, 1.6 million blacks, constituting one fourth of the black labor force, are employed by government, mostly as social welfare providers in areas such as education, welfare, health, employment, and public housing. Most of these supposedly middle-class people have few assets and are only a pink slip away from poverty. To say that affirmative action mainly helps the middle class misses the point. One wants to scream: "That's *how* they came to be middle class!"

The executive orders issued by Presidents Johnson and Nixon applied to some 15,000 companies employing 23 million workers at 73,000 installations. Whatever ethereal issues one might wish to raise, there is simply no other mechanism for influencing employment practices and outcomes on a large scale. Affirmative action is no panacea, but its achievements are considerable, certainly far too great to give up in blatant appeasement of the right. As Frederick Douglass once commented, "You sacrifice your friends in order to conciliate your enemies."

3. **Affirmative action is merely a reform. Even worse, it amounts to a form of cooptation designed to buy off dissent.**

It must be conceded that affirmative action does little or nothing to alter the basis of power and wealth. Although it alleviates racial inequality, it implicitly substitutes blacks for whites, leaving structures of inequality intact. Nevertheless, affirmative action is no ordinary reform. It has helped to remedy the most grievous of all of the ravages of American capitalism—slavery and racial subordination down to the present. This is not a reform that can be dismissed with a sleight of hand.

Whatever its limitations, affirmative action enhances democracy and erodes racism. No amount of hairsplitting and political calculation can obscure this self-evident truth.

4. **Affirmative action is politically divisive, thus playing into the hands of the right. It would be far better politically, and more consistent with the left credo, to base affirmative action on class instead of race.**

The argument for a class-based affirmative action is specious on both practical and theoretical grounds. As Andrew Hacker has shown, a class-based affirmative action program would mainly benefit whites, including middle-class whites whose parents are divorced.[15] It would reach few blacks, not only because they constitute only a minority of the poor, but because they are the poorest of the poor. Besides, what evidence is there that a class-based affirmative action can be implemented on a large scale? On closer scrutiny, the argument for class-based affirmative action is only a politically respectable cover for liberal capitulation.

The idea of class-based affirmative action is also conceptually flawed. Affirmative action was designed to address the inequities of caste, not class. It is premised on a recognition that the victims of racial oppression have suffered the impediments of race as well as the disabilities of class. For all their hardships, white workers always have benefited from a system of racial preference. They do not need affirmative action to gain access to the construction trades and other coveted working-class jobs. Blacks and women do.

In arguing his case for a class-based affirmative action, Richard Kahlenberg dregs up the hackneyed argument that it is unfair to give preference to "the son of a black doctor over the son of a white garbage collector."[16] Think about it. How often is it that the son of a black doctor finds himself vying with the son of a white garbage collector? Presumably, Kahlenberg has in mind competition for admission to Berkeley or to Yale. But that son of a black doctor is likely to find himself in competition with, not the sons of white garbage collectors, but the sons of white doctors, who have not had to cope with the psychological liabilities and material disadvantages of being black in a white society. This is the rationale for giving a leg up even to the son of a black doctor.

Now let us think about that son of the white garbage collector. Granted, he has many liabilities to cope with in a society highly stratified by class. On the other hand, as a white man in a racially stratified society, he has access to coveted jobs in the blue-collar world that historically were the exclusive domain of white men. Indeed, in cities where garbage collectors were protected by union contracts, blacks could not even get hired as garbage collectors, much less as policemen or plumbers or assembly line workers.

In short, affirmative action is designed to address inequities of caste, not class. It gives recognition to the fact that, as an oppressed minority, blacks have had to deal with the impediments of race in addition to those of class. This is not to deny that there is a dire need to address the inequities of class as well as those of race. Clearly, we need both class-based and race-based affirmative action, but Kahlenberg asks us to substitute the one for the other.

One also has to beware of the argument that if we could eliminate poverty and unemployment, then blacks would benefit disproportionately. This is a seductive but fundamentally dishonest argument. The first problem, of course, is with the conditional "if." We are being asked to forsake a policy already in place, and one that has been a demonstrable success, for political goals that are unrealistic and unattainable, at least at the present time. All in the name of realpolitik!

The second problem with race-neutral programs is that they amount to a leftist variant of trickle-down economics and invariably reach blacks last and least. Race-neutral policy simply does not address the unique problems that blacks confront as a stigmatized and segregated minority that is still subject to pervasive discrimination, especially in the job market.

The significance of affirmative action is that it constitutes a frontal attack on institutionalized racism. It is the only policy that has decisively breached the wall of occupational segregation. Our choice is not between class-based or race-based public policy but between protecting the gains that have been made under affirmative action or witnessing a gradual return to old ways of doing business.

5. "You are right historically and you are right morally, but you are wrong politically." Affirmative action only triggers a popular backlash that defeats the liberal agenda.

The backlash is real, but it has been whipped up by right-wing politicians in an ideological attack on the welfare state. It is unbecoming and hypocritical for liberals to surrender to this kind of race-baiting. Besides, appeasement will not diminish reaction, but, on the contrary, it will only fuel reaction.

Eric Foner has written on the role of the left in *The Nation:*

Since the days of the abolitionists . . . the role of the left has been to put forward utopian ideas, to offer a moral and political critique of existing institutions, to worry less about what is politically possible than about what might be.[17]

The left represents a last line of defense against the current racial backlash that has engulfed the nation. A left that surrenders its principles to political expediency loses its most valuable asset: moral credibility. A left that capitulates to racial backlash loses its defining characteristic as a left.

If we are indeed witnessing the end of affirmative action, this is hardly a "blessing in disguise." The gutting of affirmative action signifies the end to the second Reconstruction and imperils the limited progress that has been made over the past several decades. The danger is that we will return to the status quo ante—the period before affirmative action when we salved our national conscience with laws on the books that did little or nothing to reverse centuries of occupational apartheid.

Notes

1. Stephen Steinberg, *Turning Back: The Retreat from Racial Justice in American Thought and Policy* (Boston: Beacon, 1995), p. 135.

2. Martin Luther King, Jr., *Why We Can't Wait* (New York: Harper & Row, 1963), p. 147.

3. Nathan Glazer, *Affirmative Discrimination* (New York: Basic Books, 1975).

4. Paul Starr, "Civil Reconstruction: What to Do without Affirmative Action," *The American Prospect,* 8 (Winter 1992), p. 14.

5. Jeffrey Klein, "The Race Course," *Mother Jones,* October 1997, p. 3. In *Dissent,* another left publication, Michael Walzer also frets about the political costs of affirmative action: "The gains we seek when we support affirmative action programs (which mostly, I think we ought to do) carry real losses with them, and it is crucial to the future of the left that the losses be acknowledged." Editor's Page, *Dissent,* Fall 1995, p. 435.

6. Neil R. McMillen, *Dark Journey: Black Mississippians in the Age of Jim Crow* (Urbana: University of Illinois Press, 1990), p. 7.

7. Hugh Davis Graham, "Race, History, and Policy: African Americans and Civil Rights since 1964," *Journal of Policy History,* 6(1, 1994), p. 23.

8. For a detailed account, see John David Skrentny, *The Ironies of Affirmative Action* (Chicago: University of Chicago Press, 1996), Chapters 4 and 7.

9. Hugh Davis Graham, *The Civil Rights Era: Origins and Development of National Policy, 1960–1972* (New York: Oxford University Press, 1990), pp. 334–335.

10. See Skrentny, 1996, Chapter 4.

11. Perhaps the most germane testimony comes from Arthur Fletcher himself:

I decided to go ahead with the Philadelphia Plan of putting specifications of minority employment goals in all contracts. I did this because my study and experience had convinced me that such targets were essential if we are to measure results in terms of minority employment. Without such targets, the paper compliance, and the indeterminable ineffectiveness of the government programs would go on. I had not come to Wash-

ington to preside over the continuation of the ineffective programs of the past. (Arthur Fletcher,
The Silent Sell-Out. New York: Third Press, 1974,
p. 65)

12. Graham, 1990, pp. 446–447.

13. Michael Lind, "Symposium on Affirmative Action," *Dissent* (Fall 1995), p. 470.

14. "To repeat, programs of preferential treatment applied merely according to racial or ethnic
group membership tend to benefit the relatively
advantaged segments of the designated groups.
The truly deprived members may not be helped by
such programs." William Julius Wilson, *The Truly
Disadvantaged* (Chicago: University of Chicago
Press, 1987), p. 115.

15. Andrew Hacker, "Symposium on Affirmative Action," *Dissent* (Fall 1995), p. 466.

16. Richard Kahlenberg, "Class-Based Affirmative Action," *New Labor Forum* (Spring 1998),
pp. 37–43. This article derives from Kahlenberg's
earlier book *The Remedy* (New York: Basic Books,
1995); an excerpt was featured as a cover story for
The New Republic under the title "Class Not Race"
(April 3, 1995).

17. "The Great Divide," *The Nation* 261 (October 30, 1995), p. 488.

Steinberg:

1. What does Steinberg mean when he notes that
   "racists get too much of the blame for racism?"

2. Discuss the five arguments that liberals use as
   an argument to eliminate affirmative action.

23

Residential Segregation and Federal Housing Policy: A Comparative Analysis of Section 235 and Section 8

Kevin Fox Gotham

In this chapter, I explore the relation between federal housing policy, racial discrimination, and residential segregation. In recent years, a number of scholars have turned their attention to explaining why racial residential segregation remains a tenacious and enduring feature of U.S. metropolitan areas, despite the passage of fair housing and a host of antidiscrimination statutes since the 1960s (Massey and Denton, 1993; Denton 1994). Much research indicates that high levels of racial residential segregation cannot be explained by individual or group housing preferences or socioeconomic differences between whites and African Americans (Horton and Thomas 1998; Farley 1995). Indeed, whereas residential segregation declines steadily for most racial and ethnic minorities as socioeconomic status increases, levels of black-white segregation do not vary by social class (Farley 1995; Denton 1994). Sociologists recognize that racial discrimination remains an institutionalized feature of the housing industry that cuts across a variety of public agencies and private firms, including land-

lords, bankers, real estate agents, and government officials (Feagin 1994; Yinger 1995). Racial discrimination in housing today is somewhat different than it was decades ago. State and federal laws make official discrimination illegal, and a few African American families now live, or have tried to reside, in historically white neighborhoods in almost all U.S. cities (Keating 1994; Darden 1994). Yet, racial residential segregation continues to be a persistent and undeniable characteristic of American society (Oliver and Shapiro 1995; Squires 1993).

This chapter examines the racially segregative effects of two federal housing programs—the Section 235 program and the Section 8 program—that originally were designed to stimulate home ownership for the poor and racial minorities and remedy racial residential segregation and inequality. As a major component of the Housing and Urban Development Act of 1968, the Section 235 program was designed provide mortgage insurance and subsidies to private lending institutions in an effort to encourage home ownership for racial minorities and the poor. The program was discontinued by the Nixon administration in 1973 amid reports of scandals in the program by private real estate firms and agents. A major centerpiece of federal housing policy since the 1970s has been the Section 8 program, established through the Housing and Community Development Act of 1974. The Section 8 program is a rental assistance program that provides certificates and vouchers to low-income people to purchase rental housing. Landlords receive rental subsidies from the federal government to keep rents at affordable levels.

This research examines the local operation and implementation of the Section 235 program and Section 8 program in Kansas City, Missouri, to illustrate how these federal housing programs reinforced and, in the case of the latter, continue to reinforce patterns of racial residential segregation. Both programs were designed and implemented after the passage of the landmark Title VIII of the Civil Rights Act of 1968, which established the national goal of fair housing and provided the first administrative mechanisms to combat housing discrimination through litigation. Prior to the passage of federal fair housing legislation through Title VIII, racial minorities, especially African Americans, were excluded officially from federal government home ownership subsidies and segregated by the Federal Housing Administration's (FHA) refusal to underwrite mortgages in predominantly minority areas. (Oliver and Shapiro 1995:39–41; Massey and Denton 1993, chapter 2). The explicit goal of the Section 235 program was to ameliorate the social problems of housing segregation and racial inequality in housing by encouraging home ownership. The Section 8 program also shares these goals but works to deconcentrate the poor and racial minorities through a system of housing vouchers and certificates that they use to purchase housing where they can find it. Using Kansas City as a case study, I focus on the racial dynamic of these federal housing programs to illustrate the connection between racial discrimination, residential segregation, and federal policy.

Racial Residential Segregation in Metropolitan Kansas City

The social problems of racial inequality and residential segregation in Kansas City have been recognized and documented by scholars and local journalists and residents, as seen in a 1991 report by the Greater Kansas City Urban League:

Housing patterns in Kansas City show a continuation of . . . efforts to control the movement of the black population. . . . Sellers of homes and landlords still use disguised tactics to prevent black families from purchasing or renting. . . . For the most part, integration of housing has flowed one way—blacks move in, whites move out. (Williams 1991:87–88)

In recent years, Kansas City has been identified by scholars as one of the nation's "hypersegregated" metropolitan areas due to the high degree of residential segregation on a number of housing indexes (Denton 1994; Massey and Denton 1993). Although Kansas City's urban core has less than 25 percent of the region's population, it is home to more than 60 percent of the region's African American residents (Mid-American Regional Council 1993). According to 1990 census data, almost four out of every 10 core residents are African American, compared with less than 1 in 10 in the suburbs. More important, more than 70 percent of Kansas City's poor African Americans live in areas where at least 20 percent of the population live in poverty (Mid-American Regional Council 1993). As in other U.S. metropolitan areas, the problems of racial inequality in employment, education, and housing are central features of the spatial organization of Kansas City.

Before going on, I should reveal that I was born in Kansas City, Missouri, in 1966 and lived in the metropolitan area most of my life (until 1997). Over the last three decades, I have observed firsthand the social problems of poverty, segregation, and inner-city disinvestment. I can recall, in my childhood, conversations my parents had with neighbors and friends about the changing racial composition and physical deterioration of neighborhoods in the city. As a high school and college student, I remember discussions in classes and with friends about whether the United States was a "democracy" given the persistent social inequalities and disparities in wealth and income—discussions that raised more questions than answers. From 1994 to 1997, I collected data on poverty-affected neighborhoods and housing conditions in the city for my Ph.D. dissertation (Gotham 1997). During 1996, I was a member of the "Housing, Neighborhoods, and Economic Development" cluster of Kansas City, Missouri, Mayor Emanuel Cleaver's Racial Relations Task Force. As a participant on this task force, I helped establish a series of focus groups with prominent public officials and local residents and developed a sophisticated survey that was distributed throughout the metropolitan area. In addition, I conducted numerous in-depth interviews with local residents and field observations on the state of race relations, housing, and economic development in the inner city.[1] Oral histories and in-depth interviews with local residents were important because much of my work is an effort to understand the struggles and concerns of inner-city residents in a metropolitan area where race and inequality are defining characteristics of everyday life. The advantage of using interviews and other qualitative data sources is that they can offer insight into the dimensions of history, human agency, and social action that typically are lost in quantitative or statistical analyses of urban poverty and residential segregation.

In his classic treatise *The Sociological Imagination,* C. Wright Mills (1959) argued that the mission of sociology is to reveal the interconnectedness of individual biography, social structure, and human history. The sociological imagination, according to Mills, is the "quality of mind" necessary to grasp the relation between "personal troubles" and "private issues" in an effort to provide "lucid summations" of what is going on in the world and why it is happening. Many of the inner-city residents I interviewed and talked with are well aware that their "personal troubles" with poverty, poor schools, and neighborhood deterioration are intimately bound up with the larger "public issues" of racial discrimination, disinvestment, and minimalist social policy. Residents have developed their own explanations and attitudes for the changes and problems they have witnessed. Resentment, bitterness, animosity, and rage were common in my interviews and conversations. Many residents saw the persistence of racial residential segregation and its negative consequences as a powerful symbol of the lack of political and economic power and opportunity for African Americans. This chapter is about applying the sociological imagination to understand the connection between federal housing policy and people's "personal troubles" with continuing racial discrimination and residential segregation. A related goal is to explain why barriers to neighborhood racial stability and integration persist, despite governmental efforts to remove them.

Section 235[2]

The 1968 Housing Act represented the beginnings of a long-term shift in federal housing policy away from dispensing aid to local housing authorities for building public housing to providing direct subsidies to the private sector to stimulate home ownership for the poor (Schafer and Field 1973; Hays 1985,

Table 23.1

Section 235 New Construction, Existing Units, and Substantial Rehabilitation in Metropolitan Kansas City, 1969–1972

	KCMO	Suburbs	Total
New Construction	361 (27.6%)	945 (72.4%)	1,306
Existing Housing	861 (93.5%)	60 (6.5%)	921
Substantial Rehabilitation	52 (89.7%)	6 (10.3%)	58
Total	1,274	1,011	2,285

Note: Table appears in Gotham (1999). KCMO = Kansas City, Missouri.
Sources: Department of Housing and Urban Development (HUD). William A. Cleaver, and Jan Alspaugh. 5/31/72. "A Statistical Study of the FHA 235(i) Program in the Kansas City Metropolitan Area." Unpublished Manuscript. X1281; Box 334. KC 250, Arthur A. Benson, II. Legal Papers. Western Historical Manuscript Collection-Kansas City.

chapter 5; Mitchell 1985). The Section 235 program of the 1968 Housing Act directed the Department of Housing and Urban Development (HUD) to relax conventional lending standards and financial barriers so that the poor could obtain mortgages for home ownership. The housing subsidy program provided lending institutions with mortgage insurance and reduced the homeowner's housing costs by making payments directly to the lenders on behalf of the owners. Home mortgages were insured by HUD through a special risk insurance fund that was intended to protect the lending institution against foreclosures. Rather than have the federal government provide direct funds and money, the Section 235 program was designed to stimulate consumer demand by extending mortgage credit and homeowner's insurance to poor people and racial minorities via private lending institutions (Schafer and Field 1973:460).

Between 1969 and 1974, HUD administered its Section 235 program throughout cities in the United States, combining single-family mortgage insurance and mortgage subsidies to lenders to enable low-income families to purchase homes. Section 235's two component programs involved "existing" (usually foreclosed) and "new" homes built by HUD-subsidized developers. Table 23.1 shows Section 235 housing by location and type of housing in metropolitan Kansas City.

According to this table, the vast majority of new construction financed through Section 235 was in the suburban areas (72.4 percent), whereas only 27.6 percent of new housing was located in central city Kansas City, Missouri. Only 6.5 percent of housing located in the suburbs was existing housing, whereas 93.5 percent of existing housing was located in Kansas City. The lack of new housing in the central city may be explained by lack of available land. However, there is no apparent reason why more existing housing was not financed through the program or located in suburban areas.

Table 23.2 shows Section 235 housing by race of purchasers in metropolitan Kansas City from August 1971 through March 15, 1972. According to this table, 80.1 percent of the participating white families, typically young couples with children, bought new homes, the majority of which were in suburban areas. In contrast, 90.4 percent of participating African American families (typically

Table 23.2

Section 235 Housing by Race of Purchasers in Metropolitan Kansas City, 1971–1972

	African American	White	Total
New Construction	56 (19.9%)	225 (80.1%)	281
Existing Housing	104 (90.4%)	11 (9.6%)	115
Substantial Rehabilitation	2 (100.0%)	0 (0.0%)	2
Total	162	236	398

Note: Information on race of purchaser is available on only 398 cases out of a total of 642 for the period from August 1971 through March 15, 1972.
Sources: Department of Housing and Urban Development (HUD). William A. Cleaver, and Jan Alspaugh. 5/31/72. "A Statistical Study of the FHA 235(i) Program in the Kansas City Metropolitan Area." Unpublished Manuscript. X1281; Box 334. KC 250, Arthur A. Benson, II. Legal Papers. Western Historical Manuscript Collection-Kansas City.

single females with children) purchased existing homes, the vast majority of which were located in central city Kansas City, Missouri. Only 19.9 percent of participating African American purchasers bought new housing, whereas only 9.6 percent of participating white families purchased existing housing under the Section 235 program. HUD began to include race of purchaser on Section 235 application forms in August 1971, and this information was reported on only 398 cases out of 642 (62 percent). Although HUD did not keep systematic data on the race of Section 235 participants, addresses of where participants located show that almost all of the existing homes in Kansas City purchased through the housing subsidy program were in virtually all-black census tracts. In contrast, addresses of almost all new homes in the suburbs purchased through the Section 235 program were in virtually all-white census tracts.

Although the Section 235 program allowed poor people, African Americans, and other non-whites to participate in a federally insured housing program for the first time, the laxity of regulations and decentralized character of the program helped foster housing abandonment and neighborhood deterioration. In a typical case, a real estate agent would purchase a number of vacant or dilapidated dwellings in a deteriorating section of the inner city. The agent then would make sufficient cosmetic repairs to make the building appear habitable and obtain an inflated appraisal from an unscrupulous HUD appraiser, occasionally for a kickback. Next, the real estate agent would find a low-income family with little knowledge of the responsibilities of home ownership. The bank would service the risk-free, federally insured loan and sell the home to the aspiring low-income family, generating a huge profit for the real estate agent. Later, the unsuspecting low-income homeowner would discover that the home had many substandard conditions that the family could not afford to repair. As the housing repairs and expenses mounted, the homeowner would abandon the home, and the dwelling would become the property of HUD (Quadagno 1994:110–14).

One long-term resident and journalist reported in 1972 that the Blue Hills neighborhood (47th to 63rd street) was littered with dilapidated HUD-owned dwellings that had been abandoned by families who gave up trying to maintain the poor houses or who were victims of foreclosure: "Most of the homes are attractive and well kept, but on nearly every block one or two stand vacant, repossessed by the [federal government]. Some have been boarded up. Some have been damaged by vandals" ("Southeast Wears FHA's Mark," 1972, p. 1). In this same neighborhood, HUD-held homes remained vacant through the 1970s and into the 1980s. During that time, HUD attempted to sell many of the foreclosed homes on an "as-is" basis but with little success because of the dilapidated condition of the homes. "Things are bad, and then you got one of those HUD as-is houses in there and that's the end of the line for a block," recalled Paul K. Whitmer, vice president of the Blue Hills Homes Corporation in 1974 ("Blue Hills Beseeches City," 1974, p. 30). By the late 1970s, HUD consistently had an inventory of almost a thousand dilapidated homes located in Kansas City city neighborhoods ("HUD Criticized," 1975, p. 1).

In addition to fostering housing abandonment, the Section 235 program helped set in motion a vicious wave of "blockbusting" and white flight. Blockbusting is a practice in which a real estate agent attempts to move a non-white, usually African American, family into an all-white neighborhood to exploit white fears of impending racial turnover and property devaluation to buy up other property on the block at depressed prices, thereby generating an immense profit in the typically victimizing and exploitive transaction (Helper 1969; Orser 1994:4). For example, real estate agents would purchase a house from a white family in a racially mixed neighborhood for a low price, secure a HUD guarantee through the Section 235 program, and then resell it to an African American family at an inflated price. Prior to the late 1960s, speculation and panic selling were unsuccessful in areas that lacked available credit for African Americans (e.g., areas where most banks ei-

ther would not lend to African Americans or lend only on the most unfavorable terms) (Hays 1985:112–20). The effect of the new Section 235 program was to relax mortgage lending standards and open a flood of credit to neighborhoods susceptible to panic selling and racial turnover. The Section 235 program made lending in these areas a risk-free venture for lenders who could get HUD approval on almost any dwelling, service the loan for a lucrative fee, and then sell the mortgage back to the federal government. If the homeowner defaulted on the mortgage, HUD covered the loss and acquired the home (Quadagno 1994:111).

The Blue Hills neighborhood underwent dramatic racial transition at the height of the Section 235 program, going from about half white, half African American at the time of the 1970 census, to about 80 percent African American four years later ("Blue Hills Beseeches City," 1974, p. 30): "After the program began in 1969, Blue Hills residents began to think almost every new black neighbor was a '235 family,'" remembered Alvin Brooks, Assistant City Manager at the time. "Every black family that moved in became a 235er" (Tammeus, 1975b, p. 1; Tammeus, 1975a, p. 1). Part of the motivation behind the formation of the Blue Hills Home Corporation was to stem blockbusting in the area fostered by the Section 235 program. As one Blue Hills resident and founder of the Home Corporation recalled in 1974, "The [corporation] has but one goal—the renewal of the Blue Hills area. The physical condition of our neighborhood has suffered greatly from an over-concentration of federal Section 235 housing and from actions of speculator types" ("Blue Hills Beseeches City," 1974, p. 30).

In effort to halt white flight and housing abandonment, a number of interracial neighborhood coalitions such as the Forty Nine-Sixty Three Neighborhood Coalition and the Marlborough Heights Neighbor Association launched door-to-door campaigns to prevent fear of rapid racial change and persuade people not to sell to profiteering real estate agents ("Neighbors Hope to End Blockbusting Fears," 1970; "Neighbors Offer Pact to Real Estate Brokers," 1970; "Neighborhood Association Sees Racial Balance as Vital," 1971, p. 1; "Goal is Working Together," 1971, p. 20; "Neighbors Brace to Accept Change," 1971, p. 6A). In August 1970, the Marlborough Heights Neighborhood Association sent a letter to HUD and a number of local and state elected officials asking for assistance in halting the Section 235 program and stabilizing the neighborhood.

Marlborough Heights Neighbors is a newly formed group whose goal is to establish a viable multiracial neighborhood. Our group is composed of black and white neighbors who are working together to minimize the possibility of panic and to preserve the comfortable character of our residential area.

The FHA 235 program as it exists today is a major stumbling block to our efforts to stabilize our neighborhood [and] could alter the middle class nature of the neighborhood by precipitating outward movement of middle class home owners, both black and white. We believe our neighborhood has absorbed, under the existing program, as many FHA 235(i) buyers as it can without crippling our efforts; the prospect of a greater influx of FHA 235(i) buyers will create panic here that may doom our effort.[3]

A number of local residents recalled how both whites and African Americans reacted to the tide of blockbusting set in motion by the Section 235 program.

Very poor families were directed into the area by unscrupulous real estate brokers, who used the program to make money. They sold homes that were in bad repair. They dropped poor people in there without guidance. . . . Some of the homes deteriorated, and the remaining whites moved out. ("Southeast Wears FHA's Mark," 1972, p. 1)

Black people really weren't aware with what was going on, white people probably weren't either. But there has been such a taboo with the races coming together, [real estate agents] would just say that "We got a black person moving into the neighborhood," and so one real estate company could sell the house that white folks were leaving to a black person, and steer the white folks to another area. You had a double-deal going on. (Interview with Cynthia Kaskins, 5/1/96)

When you got out to 40th street further south the houses weren't in bad condition. They were small but not in too bad a condition, you would find one or two bad ones in a three to four block radius. By and large they were not badly taken care of. . . . And a lot of people—white people who bought those houses got up and left, and here was FHA holding these houses, and they were in bad shape, and they were reselling them to minorities. (Interview with Jon Herman, 3/19/96)

The interviews and oral histories show that local residents were well aware of the segregative and destabilizing effects of the Section 235 program. Many people I interviewed recalled intense organization efforts including letter writing to state representatives, lobbying of local government leaders, and attempts to persuade fellow neighbors not to succumb to blockbusting. By November 1971, the deleterious effects of Section 235 had become sufficiently widespread to elicit official condemnation from Kansas City, Missouri, city council members. In a letter to the HUD area office, City Councilman Joseph Shaughnessy requested that HUD meet with the city's new Housing Advisory Commission to discuss dispersal of Section 235 Housing:

I am deeply concerned about the impact of the recently released funding for Section 235 existing housing program is having on the Southeast part of Kansas City. Real estate people are using this program to exploit homeowners fears in targeted areas, and are creating instability and turnover.[4]

In 1972, the Forty Nine-Sixty Three Neighborhood Coalition, the Blue Hills Community Association, and the Marlborough Heights Neighbors had joined together in filing a lawsuit to compel HUD to halt further 235 loans in their neighborhoods.[5] HUD's suspension of the program later that year effectively ended the lawsuit as reports from around the nation poured into Washington detailing the scandalous ripoffs and exploitative and victimizing character of the housing subsidy program (Hays 1985:112; Quadagno 1994:111–13).

Section 8

During the late 1960s and 1970s, the Section 235 program played a major role in shifting federal responsibility for providing low-income housing to the private sector. The Section 8 program of the Housing and Community Development Act of 1974 essentially replaced the Section 235 program. Like the Section 235 program, the Section 8 program moved HUD further away from its traditional role as direct actor in housing provision for low-income people to a role as facilitator and subsidizer of private sector housing production (Gotham and Wright, forthcoming). The Section 8 program works by allowing local housing authorities to issue housing vouchers to low-income renters to give to landlords, who then receive rental subsidies from HUD to keep rents at affordable levels. Participating landlords charge the approved "prevailing market rate" for apartments, low-income tenants pay 30 percent of their income for rent, and HUD pays the rest. Low-income renters use the housing voucher to search for affordable housing that meets HUD approved minimum quality standards (Salsich 1996:346). The Section 8 program has remained the major centerpiece of all federal housing policy since the 1970s (Gotham and Wright, forthcoming).

In recent years, the Section 8 program has been promoted by public officials as a promising antipoverty strategy to increase housing mobility for low-income, inner-city residents. Others have championed the program as an effective vehicle for deconcentrating racial minorities and creating racially mixed and economically mixed neighborhoods (Keating 1994). According to promoters, the Section 8 program can enable low-income residents and racial minorities to leave high-poverty areas and segregated neighborhoods to move to middle- and high-income areas and racially integrated neighborhoods. The potential benefits of increasing housing mobility through the Section 8 program supposedly include greater access to employment opportunities, quality schools, reduced crime, enhanced cultural amenities and entertainment venues, and enriched lives for white, middle-class residents through increased interaction with more diverse groups of people (Briggs 1997; Burby and Rohe 1989; Rosenbaum 1991, 1995). A number of localities, such as Camden, New Jersey, Kansas City, Missouri, Chicago, and Yonkers, New York, are experimenting with housing mobility to deconcentrate poor people and create racially mixed neighborhoods.

Despite the fanfare, there is little evidence to indicate that increasing housing mobility through Section 8 vouchers and certificates is an effective antipoverty strategy or housing desegregation strategy. On the one hand, one study found that modest racial mixing can be achieved through Section 8 if home counseling and information services are provided to recipients (Finkel and Kennedy 1992). On the other hand, in a case study of Washington, DC, Hartung and Henig (1997) found that although vouchers and certificates scatter subsidized tenants into suburbs better than does conventional public housing, these suburbanized tenants nonetheless tend to concentrate in areas whose socioeconomic status and proportions of white residents are below average. McDonnell's (1997) analysis of the Section 8 program found that the greater the size of a city's African American population, the less the likelihood of city participation in the program. Dreier (1999) found that racial minorities have trouble finding apartments with vouchers, even in markets with many vacancies, due to discrimination by landlords. Continuing racial discrimination in the private housing market, combined with landlord reluctance to rent to tenants (primarily racial minorities), has confined recipients to finding apartments in low-income areas, thereby creating "Section 8 ghettos" (Goering, Stebbins, and Siewert 1995; Fischer 1993; Keating 1994). Moreover, the Section 8 program has encountered NIMBY ("not in my backyard") protest in some cities, including Boston and Kansas City, from local residents opposed to locating subsidized housing residents in their neighborhoods (Hoffman 1996:441; Gotham 1998b).

In Kansas City, the results of the Section 8 program have been racially segregative, channeling African Americans into predominantly black neighborhoods in the inner city and dispersing whites to white neighborhoods in suburban areas. For example, in 1983, 88 percent of the Housing Authority of Kansas City's (HAKC) 1,458 certificate holders were African American, as were about 85 percent of the 2,000 persons on HAKC's Section 8 waiting list. In addition, 1983 HAKC data show that 73 percent of African American certificate holders located in census tracts that were 80 percent African American or greater, whereas 82 percent of white certificate holders located in census tracts that were less than 20 percent African American, many outside the inner city.[6] As of 1993, HAKC and HUD data indicate that less than 12 percent of the 3,757 Section 8 subsidized units were located in suburban areas of Kansas City, Missouri. More than half were concentrated in census tracts where 90 percent of the population was African American (Department of Housing and Community Development 1995). A city-by-city inventory of subsidized units compiled by the *Kansas City Star* from 1995 HUD data indicated that although the inner cities of Kansas City, Missouri (Jackson County portion), and Kansas City, Kansas, had only one quarter of the region's homes, they contained two thirds of the metropolitan area's subsidized rental units, both federally insured building and Section 8 housing vouchers. By contrast, in suburban Johnson County, subsidized housing units accounted for less than two percent of its housing stock ("Many Restrictions Confine KC's Poor to Ailing Core," 1995, p. 1).

In addition, the Section 8 program has been the target of intense criticism by housing and civil rights activists throughout the country due to persistent and multiyear waiting lists for embarrassingly few vouchers. The average waiting time nationwide for Section 8 housing vouchers is more than two years, and many housing agencies have much longer waits (Finkel et al. 1996). As of 1995, the HAKC had a three-year waiting list of more than 1,200 people waiting for Section 8 housing units. "We're taking in 400 to 500 applications a month and only turning over 50," said David Murrell, Director of the Section 8 voucher programs at the HAKC. "We can't get ahead. We're going backwards fast. The waiting list gauges the amount of pain in the community" ("U.S. Aid to House Poor Declines," 1996, p. B1). In Chicago, the waiting list is more than five years, with the number of applications running as high as 10,000 in recent years, according to a recent HUD report (U.S. Department of Housing and Urban Development 1998). The Section 8 program gives a few qualifying low-income people inadequate housing resources to compete with other needy citizens for a dwindling supply of affordable housing. Not surprisingly, studies throughout the country indicate that many residents fail to use their vouchers because of an inability to locate quality housing and the dearth of landlords willing to participate in the voucher program (Salsich 1996). In addition, although inadequate funding clearly impedes the effectiveness of the Section 8 voucher program, the program's greatest weakness is its focus on increasing the housing "choice" for low-income residents rather than addressing the problem of housing affordability that many low-income citizens face (Hartung and Henig 1997; Hoffman 1996:440–41).

Conclusion

This comparison of the Section 235 and Section 8 programs offers support for the argument that racial discrimination continues to be an important factor influencing the operation and implementation of federal housing policies and programs in the local housing market. Although both programs were designed to ameliorate racial residential segregation, the programs in fact reinforced and, in the case of the Section 8 program, continue to reinforce segregation and racial inequalities in housing. The segregative effects of these federal programs, however, go far beyond the mere restriction of African Americans to inner-city housing. All of HUD's Section 235 homes in the Kansas City area were marketed by private real estate agents who worked to unleash a destructive wave of blockbusting, housing foreclosures, and abandonment that contributed to white flight and physical deterioration in city neighborhoods from 1969 through the early 1970s. Despite the claims of government officials, the Section 8 program has not had a significant impact on patterns of racial residential segregation in Kansas City or other U.S. metropolitan areas. Although Section 8 has been designed to move people out of public housing projects and deconcentrate the poor, the program has tended to resegregate the races due to reluctance on the part of apartment owners in

white neighborhoods to open their units to Section 8.

Why does racial residential segregation persist despite the passage of federal fair housing laws and other antidiscrimination statutes over the last few decades? I suggest two reasons why fair housing laws have been a weak tool for remedying racial residential segregation and creating racially mixed neighborhoods. First, fair housing laws tend to be reactive, responding to violations of the law rather than attempting to undo prevailing discriminatory patterns through proactive or affirmative measures. Neither the federal government nor any state or local government has ever adopted racial integration as an explicit policy goal. Fair housing laws and other antidiscrimination statutes in lending and real estate do not encourage or promote racial integration. Instead, they allow individuals to sue landlords or real estate agents for violating the law and may bring monetary rewards for victims of discrimination. However, it is extremely difficult to prove violations of fair housing legislation, because individual acts of discrimination must be overt and intentional. More subtle and covert forms of housing discrimination, including efforts by real estate agents to show homes in specific areas of the city to racial minorities (racial steering), generally go unnoticed and are more difficult to uncover and document. Real estate activities that have the effect of residential segregation but are not based on overt intent to discriminate are immune from prosecution.

Second, fair housing laws in general do not challenge the institutional practices, ideology, and everyday activities of real estate agents and firms that create and reinforce racial residential segregation. Housing programs tend to perpetuate housing segregation due to the federal government's heavy reliance on the private sector to address housing problems (Gotham 1998a). Interestingly, most federally assisted housing in the United States, unlike that in other industrialized nations, is provided by the private sector (Sternlieb and Hughes 1991; Bratt and Keating 1993). In particular, the Section 8 program is based on the idea that market forces can remedy segregation if only the barriers to mobility and "choice" are removed. However, despite more than two decades of ostensibly open housing markets and antidiscrimination ordinances, in metropolitan areas throughout the United States, "markets" routinely fail to adequately provide quality housing for all citizens due to the persistence of institutionalized mechanisms of housing discrimination. Institutional housing discrimination refers to actions prescribed by the norms of public agencies, private firms, and social networks of actors within the housing industry that have a differentiated and negative impact on members of a subordinate racial group (Feagin 1994). Racial discrimination in local housing markets exists not because of a few isolated bigots but because the majority of participants in the real estate industry still harbor strong anti-black stereotypes, including the belief that racial minorities are poor credit risks and racially mixed or predominantly African American and minority neighborhoods are of lesser value than are all-white neighborhoods.

Given the persistence of institutional discrimination in the housing market, what can be done, in addition to more effective enforcement of fair housing laws, to remedy the negative effects of housing discrimination and segregation? First, there must be a clear articulation of objectives in the design and implementation of federal housing programs and a formal system of program evaluation for monitoring progress toward these objectives. Second, Congress could redistribute existing housing funds or expand funding for those who need it the most. The recent level of federal funding for housing ($136 billion in 1997) is targeted toward very wealthy and affluent citizens (through home ownership subsidies), whereas only a small proportion of the poor and middle class receive any housing aid (Dreier 1999). Third, cities could institute comprehensive training programs and hiring and promotion practices that encourage real estate firms and lenders to accept and appreciate racial and ethnic diversity, provide counseling and education on home ownership, and familiarize real estate agents and loan officers with the special needs of first-time minority customers (Reed 1994; Smith 1994). Although there is no guarantee that these efforts, by themselves, would create integrated neighborhoods, these and other policies and practices could begin to address the general problem of racial inequality in housing.

Notes

1. Using a snowball sample, I interviewed 21 individuals during 1996. Respondents included 7 white males, 3 white females, 7 African American males, and 4 African American females. The youngest person I interviewed was 39, and the oldest person was 79. Most of these interviewees were either current or former real estate agents, housing activists, civil rights activists, neighborhood coalition leaders, or city planners. Interviews generally lasted between one and three hours, and I transcribed all the interviews. To protect the confidentiality of my interviewees, I use pseudonyms for nonpublic persons whom I quote in the chapter.

2. Portions of this section are forthcoming in Gotham, "Separate and Unequal: HUD's Section 235 Program and the Housing Act of 1968," *Sociological Forum* 14.

3. Letter from Marlborough Heights Neighbors to Representative Joe L. Evans, Chairman of HUD Sub-Committee, House Appropriations Committee, and John O. Pastore, Chairman of HUD Sub-Committee, Senate Appropriations Committee, August 28, 1970, X363. Letter from Sidney L. Willens to Honorable George Romney, HUD, January 29, 1971, regarding Marlborough Heights; Letter from Sidney L. Willens to Mr.

Harry Morley, Regional Administrator, HUD, July 27, 1971, regarding 235 Exterior Maintenance Fund. Box 343, KC 250, Arthur A. Benson, II, Legal Papers, Western Historical Manuscript Collection–Kansas City (WHMC-KC).

4. Letter from Joseph Shaughnessy, Jr., Councilman at Large, 2nd District, Kansas City, Missouri, to William Southerland, Director, HUD Area Office, November 29, 1971, X1596AAA-4, Box 206, KC 250, Arthur A. Benson, II, Legal Papers, WHMC-KC.

5. Forty Nine-Sixty Three Neighborhood Coalition, April 1973, "Status Report as of April 1973," prepared by the Planning Group of the Forty Nine-Sixty Three Neighborhood Coalition. Box 3, Folder 123. KC 61. Forty Nine-Sixty Three Neighborhood Coalition Inventory of Records and Information, WHMC-KC.

6. Section 8 Certificate Holders, Distribution of Race, and Race of Census Tract in which located. Housing Authorities of Liberty, Lee's Summit, Independence, Missouri, 1983, prepared by Gary Tobin. X1481A, Box 206; Section 8 Certificate Holders, Distribution of Race, and Race of Census Tract in which located. Kansas City Housing Authority. X1481B, Box 206, KC 250, Arthur A. Benson, II, Legal Papers, WHMC-KC.

References

"Blue Hills Beseeches City to Help Reverse Decay." 1974. *Kansas City Star,* August 28, p. 1.

Bratt, Rachel G. and W. Dennis Keating. 1993. "Federal Housing Policy and HUD: Past Problems and the Future Prospects of a Beleaguered Bureaucracy." *Urban Affairs Quarterly* 29(1):3–27.

Briggs, Xavier de Souza. 1997. "Moving Up versus Moving Out: Neighborhood Effects in Housing Mobility Programs." *Housing Policy Debate* 8(1):195–234.

Burby, Raymond and William M. Rohe. 1989. "Deconcentration of Public Housing: Effects on Residents' Satisfaction with Their Living Environments and Their Fear of Crime." *Urban Affairs Quarterly* 25(1):117–41.

Darden, Joe T. 1994. "African American Residential Segregation: An Examination of Race and Class in Metropolitan Detroit." Pp. 82–94 in *Residential Apartheid: The American Legacy,* edited by R. D. Bullard, J. E. Grigsby, III, and C. Lee. Los Angeles, CA: CASS Urban Policy Series.

Denton, Nancy A. 1994. "Are African-Americans Still Hypersegregated." Pp. 49–81 in *Residential Apartheid: The American Legacy,* edited by R. D. Bullard, J. E. Grigsby, III, and C. Lee. Los Angeles, CA: CASS Urban Policy Series.

Department of Housing and Community Development. 1995. *Kansas City, Missouri's 1995 Consolidated Housing and Community Development Plan.* A Report to the U.S. Department of Housing and Urban Development. Kansas City, Missouri: City of Kansas City, Missouri. James M. Vaughn, Director, May 24, 1995.

Dreier, Peter. 1999. *The Devolution Revolution: Housing Policy and Devolution—A Delicate Balancing Act.* New York: Twentieth Century Fund.

Farley, John E. 1995. "Race Still Matters: The Minimal Role of Income and Housing Cost as Causes of Housing Segregation in St. Louis, 1990." *Urban Affairs Review* 31:244–54.

Feagin, Joe R. 1994. "A House Is Not a Home: White Racism and U.S. Housing Practices." Pp. 17–48 in *Residential Apartheid: The American Legacy,* edited by R. D. Bullard, J. E. Grigsby, III, and C. Lee. Los Angeles, CA: CASS Urban Policy Series.

Finkel, Meryl Carissa G. Climaco, Paul R. Elwood, Judith D. Feins, Gretchen Locke, and Susan J. Popkin. 1996. *Learning from Each Other: New Ideas for Managing the Section 8 Certificate and Voucher Programs.* Prepared for U.S. Department of Housing and Urban Development. Office of Policy Development and Research. Office of Public and Indian Housing. Prepared by Abt Associates, Contract HC-18374.

Finkel, Meryl and Stephen D. Kennedy. 1992. "Racial/Ethnic Differences in Utilization of Section 8 Existing Rental Vouchers and Certificates." *Housing Policy Debate* 3:463–508.

Fischer, Paul. 1993. *A Racial Perspective on Subsidized Housing in the Chicago Suburbs.* Homewood, IL: South Suburban Housing Center.

"Goal Is Working Together." 1971. *Kansas City Star,* January 25, p. 20.

Goering, John, Helene Stebbins, and Michael Siewert. 1995. *Promoting Housing Choice in HUD's Rental Assistance Programs: Report to Congress.* Washington, DC: U.S. Department of Housing and Urban Development, Office of Policy Development and Research.

Gotham, Kevin Fox. 1997. *Constructing the Segregated City: Housing, Neighborhoods, and Racial Division in Metropolitan Kansas City, 1880–2000.* Ph.D. dissertation, Department of Sociology, University of Kansas, Lawrence.

Gotham, Kevin Fox. 1998a. "Blind Faith in the Free Market: Urban Poverty, Residential Segregation, and Federal Housing Retrenchment, 1970–1995." *Sociological Inquiry* 68:1–31.

Gotham, Kevin Fox. 1998b. "Suburbia under Siege: Low-Income Housing and Racial Conflict in Metropolitan Kansas City." *Sociological Spectrum* 18(4):449–483.

Gotham, Kevin Fox. Forthcoming. "Separate and Unequal: HUD's Section 235 Program and the Housing Act of 1968." *Sociological Forum* 14.

Gotham, Kevin Fox, and James D. Wright. Forthcoming. "Housing Policy." Chapter 15 in *Handbook of Social Welfare Policy,* edited by J. Midgley, M. Tracy, and M. Livermore. Thousand Oaks, CA: Sage.

Hartung, John H. and Jeffrey R. Henig. 1997. "Housing Vouchers and Certificates as a Vehicle for Deconcentrating the Poor." *Urban Affairs Review* 32:403–19.

Hays, R. Allen. 1985. *Federal Government and Urban Housing: Ideology and Change in Public Policy.* Albany: State University of New York Press.

Helper, Rose. 1969. *Racial Policies and Practices of Real Estate Brokers.* Minneapolis: University of Minnesota Press.

Hoffman, Alexander von. 1996. "High Ambitions: The Past and Future of American Low-Income Housing Policy." *Housing Policy Debate* 7:423–46.

Horton, Hayward Derrick and Melvin E. Thomas. 1998. "Race, Class, and Family Structure: Differences in Housing Values for Black and White Homeowners." *Sociological Inquiry* 68(10):114–36.

Housing and Community Development Act of 1974, Pub. L. No. 93-383, § 201.

Housing and Urban Development Act of 1968, Pub. L. No. 90-448, 82 Stat. 476 (August 1968).

"HUD Criticized for As-Is Housing Sales." 1975. *Kansas City Star,* October 7, p. 1.

Keating, W. Dennis. 1994. *Suburban Racial Dilemma: Housing and Neighborhoods.* Philadelphia: Temple University Press.

"Many Restrictions Confine KC's Poor to Ailing Core." 1995. *Kansas City Star,* December 18.

Massey, Douglas S. and Nancy A. Denton. 1993. *American Apartheid: Segregation and the Making of the Underclass.* Cambridge, MA: Harvard University Press.

McDonnell, Judith. 1997. "The Role of 'Race' in the Likelihood of City Participation in the United States Public and Section 8 Existing Housing Programs." *Housing Studies* 12(2):231–45.

Mid-American Regional Council. 1993. *Metropolitan Kansas City's Urban Core: What's Occurring, Why It's Important and What We Can Do.* A Report of the Urban Core Growth Strategies Committee. Kansas City, MO: Author.

Mills, C. Wright. 1959. *The Sociological Imagination.* New York: Oxford University Press.

Mitchell, J. Paul, ed. 1985. *Federal Housing Programs: Past and Present.* New Brunswick, NJ: Rutgers University Press.

"Neighborhood Association Sees Racial Balance as Vital." 1971. *Kansas City Star,* January 24, p. 1.

"Neighbors Brace to Accept Change." 1971. *Kansas City Star,* January 26, p. 6A.

"Neighbors Hope to End Blockbusting Fears." 1970. *Kansas City Star,* July 30.

"Neighbors Offer Pact to Real Estate Brokers." 1970. *Kansas City Star,* August 14.

Oliver, Melvin L. and Thomas M. Shapiro. 1995. *Black Wealth, White Wealth: A New Perspective on Racial Inequality.* New York: Routledge.

Orser, W. Edward. 1994. *Blockbusting in Baltimore: The Edmondson Village Story.* Lexington: University Press of Kentucky.

Quadagno, Jill. 1994. *Color of Welfare: How Racism Undermined the War on Poverty.* New York: Oxford University Press.

Reed, Veronica. 1994. "Fair Housing Enforcement: Is the Current System Adequate?" Pp. 222–36 in *Residential Apartheid: The American Legacy,* edited by R. D. Bullard, J. E. Grigsby, III, and C. Lee. Los Angeles, CA: CASS Urban Policy Series.

Rosenbaum, James. 1991. "Black Pioneers: Do Their Moves to the Suburbs Increase Economic Opportunity for Mothers and Children." *Housing Policy Debate* 4:1179–213.

Rosenbaum, James. 1995. "Changing Geography of Opportunity by Expanding Residential Choice: Lessons from the Gautreaux Program." *Housing Policy Debate* 6(1):231–70.

Salsich, Peter W. 1996. "A Decent Home for Every American: Can the 1949 Goal Be Met?" Pp. 343–72 in *Race, Poverty, and American Cities,* edited by J. C. Boger and J. W. Wegner. Chapel Hill: University of North Carolina Press.

Schafer, Robert and Charles G. Field. 1973. "Section 235 of the National Housing Act: Homeownership for Low-Income Families?" Pp. 460–71 in *Housing Urban America,* edited J. Pynoos, R. Schafer, and C. W. Hartman. Chicago: Aldine.

Smith, Shanna L. 1994. "The National Fair Housing Alliance at Work." Pp. 237–56 in *Residential Apartheid: The American Legacy,* edited by R. D. Bullard, J. E. Grigsby, III, and C. Lee. Los Angeles, CA: CASS Urban Policy Series.

"Southeast Wears FHA's Mark." 1972. *Kansas City Star,* August 28, p. 1.

Squires, Gregory D. 1993. "The Political Economy of Housing: All the Discomforts of Home. Urban Sociology in Transition." *Research in Urban Sociology* 3:129–57. Greenwich, CT: JAI.

Sternlieb, George and James W. Hughes. 1991. "Private Market Provision of Low-Income Housing: Historical Perspectives and Future Prospects." *Housing Policy Debate* 2(2):123–56.

Tammeus, William D. 1975a. "House by House, Racial Turnover Changed Blue Hills." *Kansas City Star,* February 17, p. 1.

Tammeus, William D. 1975b. "Loss in Neighborhood Turnover." *Kansas City Star,* February 16, p. 1.

"U.S. Aid to House Poor Declines." 1996. *Kansas City Star,* June 2, p. B1.

U.S. Department of Housing and Urban Development. 1998. *Rental Housing Assistance—The Crisis Continues.* Washington, DC: Government Printing Office.

Williams, Deborah D. 1991. "The Status of Housing in Kansas City's Black Community." Pp. 81–102 in *The State of Black Kansas City, 1991* edited by S. V. Walker. Kansas City, MO: Urban League of Greater Kansas City.

Yinger, John. 1995. *Closed Doors, Opportunities Lost: The Continuing Costs of Housing Discrimination.* New York: Basic Books.

Gotham:

1. Differentiate between the purposes and effectiveness of Section 235 and Section 8 housing policies.

2. Describe what blockbusting is. How is it different from redlining? How are these different from "racial steering"? What are the consequences of all of these practices?

Drawing Conclusions—Part III

Depending on the data one looks at, blacks have either come a long way, or they have not. They either have overcome the legacies of a racist past, or they have not. Looking at the same data sometimes yields different conclusions. Optimists see a glass half-full, whereas pessimists see a glass half-empty. Making use of the essays in this part as well as your own sense of the situation, where do you stand on the issue? How do you understand the significance of the split between middle-class and poorer blacks? Do they continue to share similar problems based on race, or are their lives increasingly distinct due to their different class locations? Finally, what do you think the proper role of government ought to be in dealing with issues of civil rights in the present?

PART IV

New Immigrants and the Dilemmas of Adjustment

After a hiatus of over four decades during which large-scale mass immigration ceased, the United States once again has become a magnet for newcomers. Due to the passage of a new liberalized immigration law in 1965, during the last three decades of the twentieth century, immigration levels escalated dramatically. Thus, at the end of the century, the numbers of immigrants reached levels similar to those experienced during the early decades of the century—heretofore the period of peak migration to the nation. Given the tendency of the newcomers to settle in a select number of states, including California, New York, New Jersey, Texas, Florida, and Illinois, their presence is especially felt in these parts of the country. It is not surprising that their impact has been felt most tangibly in these locales. However, even in states with smaller levels of new immigrant settlement, their presence is often felt, whether, for example, it involves Mexican or Southeast Asian workers employed in meat processing plants or doctors from the Indian subcontinent working in hospitals and clinics.

Ronald Takaki has written about the new immigrants as coming "from different shores." He points to the fact that whereas immigration waves earlier in American history have included people from around the world, the overwhelming majority of immigrants originated from Europe. In contrast, today's immigrants come chiefly from three regions: Latin America, the Caribbean, and Asia. This does not mean that immigration from Europe has ceased. Nor does it mean that other regions, such as the Middle East, have not contributed in significant ways to this new wave. However, in terms of sheer numbers, these three places constitute the primary points of departure of the new immigrants. What this means is that a majority of the newcomers are non-white. Thus, the reconstitution of racial identities addressed in Part II is in no small part an outgrowth of this fact.

When sociologists first turned their attention to this migratory wave, they tended to focus, not surprisingly, on matters such as the push/pull factors promoting immigration. They were interested in finding what social forces in immigrant homelands served as stimuli to emigration and in looking for the precise pull factors that led people to the United States and not somewhere else. Although many parallels can be drawn between contemporary immigrants and earlier ones, there are also differences that are important to recognize. In the first place, earlier immigrants entered an economy dominated by manufacturing industries. They found work in steel mills, foundries, automobile plants, mines, and other industries associated with manufacturing. In contrast, contemporary immigrants have entered an advanced industrial society with far fewer such jobs. Those with the least amount of education and training, who earlier likely would end up in manufacturing, now tend to end up in relatively low-paying service sector jobs. On the other hand, far more "brain drain" immigrants have entered the country in recent years compared to earlier times. Doctors, nurses, educators, and other white-collar professionals enter a different part of the American economy, and, not surprisingly, their job-related experiences tend to be quite different from those located in other sectors of the economy.

Although new immigrants continue to arrive, it is not clear whether current high levels of immigration will continue to persist in the future or will taper off and decline. Demographic projections are necessarily speculative, and it is impossible to predict with certainty how long this current wave of immigration will continue. Given this uncertainty, there is much that we cannot know at present about the lasting impact of the new immigrants.

Recently, sociologists have refocused their attention on issues related to adjustment processes, concerned less with why immigrants came and more with what they—and their offspring—have done to make this their new homeland. This new focus has begun to shift attention from the immigrant generation to the second, American-born generation, as well as to the nature of the relationship between these two generations. Part IV begins with an article by Alejandro Portes and Min Zhou on the matter of assimilation—whether it is possible and whether it is desirable—for second-generation ethnics from various new immigrant communities. By looking at individuals from several different groups, the authors point to some of the more general features of coming to terms with becoming an American while also maintaining aspects of one's heritage. Portes and Zhou discuss some of the dilemmas, challenges, and frustrations all immigrants seem to encounter, along with some of the more potentially troubling aspects of the process.

The following three articles look at immigrants who have found their current niche in the United States at the lower end of the socioeconomic ladder. Roger Waldinger raises the question, "Who Gets the 'Lousy' Jobs?" In offering at least partial explanation, he looks at workers who have found employment in the service sector. One of the central issues he addresses—related to the topic of new racial fault lines—is whether the entry of new immigrants into certain occupations has been at the expense of African Americans, who historically have been highly concentrated in such jobs. Although many people do not want the "lousy" jobs Waldinger examines, not every new immigrant even manages to enter this tier of the legitimate economy. Some are consigned to live, as Sarah J. Mahler poses it, "on the margins." The purpose of her article is to reveal insights into the lives of those new immigrants who have found that the American dream can look like a nightmare. These are the greenhorns who manage to survive with difficulty and are often exploited by both fellow ethnics and native Americans. Mahler offers us perceptive insights into the worldviews of people who have failed to get a real foothold in their new environment. Joan Moore and James Diego Vigil turn from an examination of the world of work to that of community. Many poor Mexicans for generations have resided in barrios, inner-city ethnic enclaves that in many ways manage to reproduce the homeland culture but that also are beset by the problems of any neighborhood characterized by persistent poverty. The authors provide a portrait of barrios in Los Angeles that indicates the ways the present is similar to the past, as well as how the arrival of new immigrants has changed these communities in far-reaching ways.

Some immigrants are doing considerably better than others are economically. Sometimes, the immigrant generation manages to enter the middle class very quickly. At other times, it is not until the second generation comes of age that large numbers of group members become members of the middle class. In either case, what is clear is that many of the new immigrant groups have developed a significant middle class. The next two essays examine two cases. Timothy P. Fong offers an ethnographic account of the Chinese presence in Monterey Park, California, which he refers to as "the first suburban Chinatown." The focus of his chapter is not on the economic circumstances of this growing community but on the ways they have established their place in the community, as well as the difficulties and challenges they have encountered in doing so. Orlando P. Tizon's essay also offers evidence derived from ethnographic work. In this case, he examines a Filipino American Protestant church in Chicago. The focus here is not on Filipino relations with the larger society or with other groups, but on the tensions within the community over inherited cultural values. Specifically, he explores the competing views that have generated intragroup debates over gender relations, defining this in terms of traditional notions versus more contemporary American views. As Tizon observes, these debates arise in the context of generational shifts.

The following two essays look at groups that have a long history in the United States, but in the current wave constitute a smaller part of the whole. These are groups emigrating from Poland and Israel. Mary Patrice Erdmans looks at recent Polish immigrants to Chicago, which contains more Poles than any other city in the world outside of Warsaw. She is interested in exploring the relationship between this new cohort of Poles and those who have arrived earlier, whether they be the "for bread with butter" laborers of the turn of the century or the displaced persons fleeing the ravages of World War II and the communist regime that came to rule the nation. Erdmans discovered evidence of considerable strain between the new arrivals and other Polish Americans, and she offers insights into why this is the case. Steven J. Gold undertakes a similar analysis, only in this instance he does so with Jews who have emigrated from Israel. Although millions of Jews reside in America, they emigrated from Europe, not Israel. In contrast, arrivals now generally come either from Russia or Israel. In the case of the latter, one of the complicating features of their journey to this country is that for American Jews, Israel is a potent symbolic force. Many American Jews, even though they do not plan to emigrate to Israel, harbor suspicions about why Jews would choose to leave the homeland for the United States. In both of these examples, we look at groups that are not from the major areas contributing to immigration; nonetheless, the issues raised herein are relevant to those groups as well.

Part IV concludes with a comparative essay by the German political scientist Thomas Faist. He offers a comparison of the work training and employment programs in the United States and Germany, looking at the ways these programs affect the two largest immigrant groups in each country: Turks in the German case, and Mexicans in the United States. Faist is interested in assessing the respective role of the federal governments in both countries, comparing and contrasting their understanding of the proper role of the public sector in facilitating immigrant adjustment.

Together, these essays offer a flavor of the complex and fluid circumstances of the new immigrants, exploring the ways they seek to find jobs, create communities, preserve homeland cultures, and adjust to America. The chapters also provide some sense of the varied ways the native-born have responded to them. Given the impact that the new immigrants will have on the nation's cultural, social, economic, and political future, there is one thing that is certain: Sociologists will continue to devote considerable energy to expanding our knowledge of these new arrivals.

24

Should Immigrants Assimilate?

Alejandro Portes and Min Zhou

MY NAME IS HERB / and I'm not poor / I'm the Herbie that you're looking for / like Pepsi / a new generation / of Haitian determination / I'm the Herbie that you're looking for.

A beat tapped with bare hands, a few dance steps, and the Haitian kid was rapping. His song, entitled "Straight Out of Haiti," was performed at Edison High, a school that sits astride Little Haiti and Liberty City—the largest black area of Miami. The lyrics capture well the distinct outlook of his immigrant community. In Little Haiti, the storefronts leap out at the passersby. Bright blues, reds, and oranges vibrate to Haitian merengue, blaring from sidewalk speakers. Yet behind the gay Caribbean exterior, a struggle goes on that will define the future of this community. As we will see, it involves the second generation—children like Herbie—who are subject to conflicting pressure from parents and peers, and to pervasive outside discrimination.

Growing up in an immigrant family has always been difficult. Individuals are torn by conflicting social and cultural demands, while facing the challenge of entry into an unfamiliar and frequently hostile world. Yet the difficulties are not always the same. The process of "growing up American" ranges from smooth acceptance to traumatic confrontation, depending on the characteristics that immigrants and their children bring along and the social context that receives them. We believe that something quite disturbing is happening to the assimilation or, if you will, the "Americanization" of the second generation of new immigrants.

Research on the new immigration—that which arose after passage of the 1965 Immigration Act—has focused almost exclusively on the first generation, which is composed of adult men and women who came to the U.S. in search of work or to escape political persecution. Little noticed until recently is the growth of the second generation. Yet by 1980, second-generation immigrants made up 10 percent of the children counted by the U.S. Census. Another survey in the late 1980s found that 3 to 5 million American students speak a language other than English at home.

While there has been a great deal of research and theorizing on post-1965 immigration, it offers only tentative guidance on the prospects and paths of adaptation of the second generation, whose outlook may be very different from that of the first. For example, it is generally accepted among immigration experts that entry-level menial jobs are performed without hesitation by newly arrived immigrants, but that these same jobs are shunned by the immigrants' U.S.-reared offspring. The social and economic progress of first-generation immigrants often fails to keep pace with the material conditions and career prospects that their American children grow to expect.

What literature on second-generation adaptation that exists is based largely on the experience of the descendants of pre-World War I immigrants. The last sociological study of the children of immigrants seems to have been Irving Child's *Italian or American? The Second Generation in Conflict,* published fifty years ago. Conditions at the time were quite different from those that confront settled immigrant groups today. Two such differences deserve special mention. First, the descendants of European immigrants who confronted the dilemmas of conflicting cultures were uniformly white. Even if they were of a somewhat darker hue than the natives, their skin color permitted them to skirt a major barrier to entry into the American mainstream. As a result, the process of assimilation depended largely on the individual's decision to leave the immigrant culture behind and to embrace American ways. This advantage obviously does not exist for the black, Asian, and mestizo children of today's immigrants.

Approximately 77 percent of post-1960 immigrants are non-European: 22 percent are Asian, 8 percent are black, and 47 percent are Hispanic. (The latter group, which originates in Mexico and other Latin American countries, poses a problem in terms of classification since Hispanics can be of any race.)

The immigrants of recent years also face economic opportunities different than those in the past. Fifty years ago, the United States was the premier industrial power in the world. Its diversified industrial labor requirements offered the second generation the opportunity to move up gradually through better-paid occupations while remaining part of the working class. Such opportunities have grown scarce in recent years as the result of rapid national de-industrialization and—global restructuring. This process has left entrants to the American labor force confronting a growing gap between the minimally paid menial jobs commonly accepted by immigrants and the high-tech and professional jobs generally occupied by college-educated native elites. This disappearance of intermediate opportunities has contributed to the mismatch between first-generation economic progress and second-generation expectations.

Assimilation as a Problem

We see these processes occurring under particularly difficult circumstances among the Haitians of Miami. The city's Haitian community is composed of some 75,000 legal and clandestine immigrants, many of whom sold everything in order to buy passage to America. Haitians of the first generation are strongly disposed to preserve a robust national identity, which they associate both with community solidarity and with social networks promoting individual success. But in trying to instill in their children national pride and an orientation toward achievement, they often clash with the youngsters' everyday experiences in school. Little Haiti is adjacent to Liberty City, the main black inner-city area of Miami, and Haitian adolescents attend predominantly inner-city schools. Native-born black youth stereotype the Haitian youngsters as docile and subservient to whites, and make fun of the Haitians'

French and Creole as well as their accents. As a result, second-generation Haitian children find themselves torn between conflicting ideas and values: to remain "Haitian," they must endure ostracism and continuing attacks in school; to become "American" (black American in this case), they must forgo their parents' dreams of making it in America through the preservation of ethnic solidarity and traditional values.

An adversarial stance toward the white mainstream is common among inner-city minority youth, who instill in the newcomers consciousness of American-style discrimination. Also instilled is skepticism about the value of education as a vehicle for advancement, a message that directly contradicts that from immigrant parents. Academically outstanding Haitian-American students, Herbie among them, have consciously attempted to retain their ethnic identity by cloaking it in black American cultural forms, such as rap music. Many others, however, have followed the path of least resistance and thoroughly assimilated. In such instances the assimilation is not to mainstream culture, but to the values and norms of the inner city. In the process, the resources of solidarity and mutual support within the immigrant community are dissipated.

As the Haitian example illustrates, adopting the outlook and cultural ways of the native born does not necessarily represent the first step toward social and economic mobility. It may, in fact, lead to exactly the opposite. Meanwhile, immigrant youth who remain firmly ensconced in their ethnic communities may, by virtue of this fact, have a better chance for educational and economic mobility.

This situation stands the common understanding of immigrant assimilation on its head. As presented in innumerable academic and journalistic writings, the expectation is that the foreign born and their offspring will acculturate and seek acceptance among the native born as a prerequisite for social advancement. If they did not, they would remain confined to the ranks of the "ethnic" lower and lower-middle classes. This portrayal of the path to mobility, so deeply embedded in the national consciousness, stands contradicted today by a growing number of empirical studies.

A closer look at these studies, however, indicates that the expected consequences of assimilation have not changed entirely, but that the process has become segmented. In other words, the question is to what sector of American society a particular immigrant group assimilates. In the absence of a relatively uniform "mainstream" whose mores and prejudices dictate a common path of integration, we observe today several distinct forms of adaptation. One of them replicates the time-honored portrayal of growing acculturation and parallel integration into the white middle-class; a second leads straight in the opposite direction to permanent poverty and assimilation to the underclass; still a third combines rapid economic advancement with deliberate preservation of the immigrant community's values and solidarity. This pattern of "segmented assimilation" immediately raises the question of what makes some immigrant groups susceptible to the downward route and what resources allow others to avoid this course. In fact, the same general process helps to explain both outcomes. We will advance next our understanding of how this process takes place and how the differing outcomes of the assimilation process can be explained. In the final section, this explanation will be illustrated with recent empirical evidence.

Vulnerability and Resources

While individual and family variables are influential, the context that immigrants encounter upon arrival plays a decisive role in the course that their offspring's lives will follow. This context includes such broad variables as political relations between the sending and receiving countries and the state of the economy in the latter, and such specific variables as the degree to which the immigrant group meets discrimination and finds a pre-existing ethnic community. Thus, Cuban immigrants of the 1960s came under perhaps the best circumstances: they were welcomed by the government, did not meet great prejudice, and soon formed a supportive community. On all three dimensions, the contrast with the Haitians is great.

To explain second-generation outcomes and their "segmented" character, however, we need to consider in greater detail the various paths of assimilation. There are three features of the social contexts encountered by today's newcomers that create vulnerability to downward assimilation: the first is color, the second is location, and the third is the absence of mobility ladders. As noted above, the majority of contemporary immigrants are nonwhite. Although this feature may at first glance appear to be an individual characteristic, in reality it is a trait of the host society. Prejudice is not invariably suffered by those with a particular skin color or racial type, and indeed many immigrants never experienced prejudice in their native lands. It is by virtue of moving into a new social environment, marked by different values and biases, that physical features become redefined as a handicap.

The concentration of immigrant households in cities and, in particular, central cities, gives rise to a second source of vulnerability because it puts new arrivals in close contact with concentrations of native-born minorities. This leads the majority to identify both groups—immigrants and the native poor—as identical. Even more importantly, it exposes the children of immigrants to the adversarial subculture that marginalized native youth have developed to cope with their own difficult situation. This process of socialization may take place even when first-generation parents are moving ahead economically and, hence, when their children have no "objective" reasons for embracing a countercultural message. If successful, this socialization can effectively block parental plans for inter-generational mobility.

The third source of vulnerability results from changes in the economy that have led to the elimination of occupational ladders for inter-generational mobility. New immigrants form the backbone of what remains of labor-intensive manufacturing in the cities, as well as of the growing personal services sector, but these are niches that seldom offer channels for upward mobility. The new "hourglass economy" created by economic restructuring means that the children of immigrants must cross a narrow bottleneck to occupations requiring advanced training if their careers are to keep pace with their U.S.-acquired aspirations. This "race" against a narrowing middle demands that immigrant parents accumulate sufficient resources to allow their children to cross the bottleneck (and, simultaneously, to believe that they can cross the bottleneck). Otherwise, "assimilation" may be not to mainstream values and expectations, but to the adversarial stance of impoverished groups confined to the bottom of the hourglass.

We have painted the picture in such stark terms for the sake of clarity, although in reality things have not yet become so polarized. Middle-level occupations that require relatively modest educational achievement have not vanished completely. As of 1980, skilled blue-collar jobs (classified by the U.S. Census as "precision production, craft, and repair occupations") had declined by 1.1 percentage points compared to a decade earlier, but still represented 13 percent of the experienced civilian labor force, or 13.6 million workers. Administrative support occupations, mostly clerical, added another 16.9 percent of the jobs. Meanwhile, occupations requiring a college degree increased by 6 percentage points from 1970 to 1980, but still employed less than a fifth of the American labor force (18.2 percent). Even in the largest cities, occupations requiring only a high school diploma were common in the late 1980s. In New York City, for example, persons with twelve years or less of schooling held just over half of the jobs in 1987. Yet despite these figures, there is little doubt that the trend toward occupational segmentation has reduced opportunities for upward mobility through well-paid, blue-collar positions. This trend forces today's immigrants to bridge in one generation the gap between entry-level and professional positions, a distance that earlier groups took two or three generations to travel.

At the same time, there are three types of resources that ease the assimilation of contemporary immigrants. First, certain groups, notably political refugees, are eligible for a variety of government programs including educational loans for their children. The Cuban Loan Program, begun by the Kennedy administration as part of a plan to resettle Cuban refugees beyond south Florida, gave many impoverished first- and second-generation Cuban youth a chance to attend college. The high proportion of professionals and executives among Cuban-American workers today, a figure on par with that for native white workers, can be traced, at least in part, to the success of that program. Passage of the 1980 Refugee Act gave subsequent refugees, in particular Southeast Asians and Eastern Europeans, access to a similarly generous benefits package.

In addition, certain foreign groups have managed to escape the prejudice traditionally endured by immigrants. This has facilitated a smoother process of adaptation. Political refugees such as the early waves of exiles from Castro's Cuba, Hungarians and Czechs escaping the invasions of their respective countries, and Soviet Jews escaping religious persecution, provide examples. In other cases,

it is the cultural and phenotypical affinity of new comers to ample segments of the host population that ensures a welcome reception. The Irish who came to Boston during the 1980s provide a case in point. Although many were illegal aliens, they came into an environment where generations of Irish-Americans had established a secure foothold. Public sympathy effectively neutralized governmental hostility in this case, and led to a change in the immigration law that directly benefited the newcomers.

Third and most important are the resources made available through networks in the co-ethnic community. Immigrants who join well-established and diversified ethnic groups have access to a range of moral and material resources well beyond those available through official assistance programs. Educational help for second-generation youth may include not only access to college grants and loans, but a private school system geared to immigrant community values. Attendance at these private ethnic schools insulates children from contact with native minority youth, while reinforcing the authority of parental views and plans.

In addition, the economic diversification of some immigrant communities creates niches of opportunity that members of the second generation can occupy, often without need for an advanced education. Small-business apprenticeships, access to skilled building trades, and well-paid jobs in local government bureaucracies are some of the many ethnic niches documented in the recent literature. In 1987, average sales per firm of the smaller Chinese, East Indian, Korean, and Cuban enterprises exceeded $100,000 per year, and jointly they employed more than 200,000 workers. These figures omit medium-sized and large ethnic corporations whose sales and work forces are much greater. Fieldwork in these communities indicates that up to half of recently arrived immigrants are employed by co-ethnic firms and that self-employment offers a prime avenue of mobility for second-generation youth. Through the creation of a capitalism of their own, some immigrant groups have thus been able to circumvent outside discrimination and the threat of vanishing mobility ladders.

In contrast to these favorable conditions are those faced by foreign minorities who lack a community already in place or co-ethnics capable of rendering assistance. The Haitians in south Florida, cited above, must cope with official hostility and widespread social prejudice, as well as the absence of a strong receiving community. Yet in some cases the existence of a large but downtrodden co-ethnic community may be even less desirable than no community at all. That is because newly arrived youth enter into ready contact with the reactive subculture developed by earlier generations. Its influence is all the more powerful because it comes from individuals of the same national origin, "people like us" who can effectively define the proper stance and attitudes of the newcomers. To the extent this occurs, the first generation's aspirations of upward mobility through school achievement and attainment of professional occupations will be blocked.

The Case of Mexican-Americans

"Field High School" is located in a small community in central California whose economy has long been tied to agricultural production and immigrant farm labor. About 57 percent of Field's students are of Mexican descent. An intensive study of the class of 1985 by M. G. Matute-Bianchi revealed that the majority of U.S.-born Spanish-surname students dropped out by their senior year. Yet of the Spanish-surname students originally classified by the school as Limited English Proficient (LEP), only 35 percent dropped out. (LEP status is commonly assigned to recently arrived Mexican immigrants.) This drop out rate was

even lower than the 40 percent rate for native white students.

Intensive ethnographic fieldwork at the school identified several distinct categories into which the Mexican-origin population could be grouped. "Recent Mexican immigrants" were at one extreme. They dressed differently and unstylishly. They claimed a Mexican identity and considered Mexico their permanent home. The most academically successful of this group were those most proficient in Spanish, reflecting their prior levels of education in Mexico. Almost all were described by teachers and staff as courteous, respectful, serious about their schoolwork, and eager to please, as well as naive and unsophisticated. They were commonly classified as LEP.

"Mexican-oriented students" spoke Spanish at home but were generally classified as Fluent English Proficient (FEP). They had strong cultural ties with both Mexico and the U.S., reflecting the fact that most were born in Mexico but had lived in the U.S. for more than five years. They were proud of their Mexican heritage, but saw themselves as different from the first group, the *recien llegados* (recently arrived) as well as from the native-born Chicanos and Cholos who were derided as having lost their Mexican roots. Students from this group were active in soccer and the Sociedad Bilingue and in celebrations of May 5th, the anniversary of the Mexican defeat of French occupying forces. Virtually all the students of Mexican descent who graduated in the top 10 percent of their class were members of this group.

"Chicanos" were by far the largest group of Mexican descent at Field High. They were mostly U.S.-born second- and third-generation students whose primary loyalty was to their in-group, seen as locked in conflict with white society. Chicanos derided successful Mexican students as "schoolboys" and "schoolgirls" or as "wannabes." According to Matute-Bianchi:

To be a Chicano meant in practice to hang out by the science wing . . . not eating lunch in the quad where all the "gringos" and "schoolboys" hang out . . . cutting classes by faking a call slip so you can be with your friends at the 7–11 . . . sitting in the back of classes and not participating . . . not carrying your books to class . . . not taking the difficult classes . . . doing the minimum to get by.

Chicanos merged imperceptibly into the last category, the "Cholos," who were commonly seen as "low riders" and gang members. They were also U.S.-born Mexican-Americans, easily identifiable by their deliberate manner of dress, walk, and speech, and other cultural symbols. Chicanos and Cholos were generally regarded by teachers as "irresponsible," "disrespectful," "mistrusting," "sullen," "apathetic," and "less motivated," and their poor school performance was attributed to these traits. According to Matute-Bianchi, Chicanos and Cholos were faced with what they saw as a choice between doing well in school and being Chicano. To study hard was to "act white" and so be disloyal to one's group.

The situation of these last two groups exemplifies a lost race between first-generation achievements and later generation expectations. Seeing their parents and grandparents confined to menial jobs, and increasingly aware of discrimination by the white mainstream, the U.S.-born children of earlier Mexican immigrants readily join a reactive subculture as a means of protecting their sense of self-worth. Participation in this subculture erects serious barriers to upward mobility because school achievement is defined as antithetical to ethnic solidarity. Like the Haitian students in Miami, newly arrived Mexicans are at risk of being socialized into a reactive stance, with the aggravating factor that it is "other Mexicans," not native-born strangers, who convey the message. The principal protection of Mexicanos against this type of assimilation lies in their strong identification with the home country's language and values, which brings them closer to their parents' cultural stance.

The Case of Punjabi Sikhs

"Valleyside" is a northern California community in which the primary economic activity is orchard farming. Farm laborers in the area often come from India and are mainly rural Sikhs from the Punjab. In the early 1980s, second-generation Punjabis made up 11 percent of the student body at Valleyside High. Their parents were not only farm laborers; about a third were orchard owners themselves and another third worked in factories in the nearby San Francisco area. An ethnographic study of Valleyside High between 1980 and 1982 by M. A. Gibson revealed a very difficult process of assimilation for Punjabi Sikh students. According to Gibson, Valleyside is "redneck country" and white residents are extremely hostile toward immigrants who look different and speak another language:

Punjabi teenagers are told they stink . . . told to go back to India . . . physically abused by majority students who spit at them, refuse to sit by them in class or in buses, throw food at them or worse.

Despite these attacks and some evidence of discrimination by school staff, Punjabi students performed better than the majority "Anglo" students. About 90 percent of the immigrant youth completed high school, compared to 70 to 75 percent of native whites. Punjabi boys earned above-average grades, were more likely than average to take advanced science and math classes, and often aspired to careers in science and engineering. Punjabi girls tended to enroll in business classes, but were less interested in immediate career plans than in satisfying parental wishes that they first marry. This gender difference reflects the strong influence exercised by the immigrant community over its second generation. According to Gibson, Punjabi parents pressured their children to avoid too much contact with white peers who might "dishonor" the immigrants, and defined "becoming Americanized" as forgetting one's roots and adopting various frowned-upon traits of the majority—such as leaving home at age eighteen, making decisions without parental consent, dating, and dancing. Instead, Punjabi parents urged their children to abide by school rules, ignore racist remarks, avoid fights, and learn useful skills including full proficiency in English.

The overall success of this strategy of "selective" assimilation to American society is remarkable. Punjabi immigrants were generally poor when they arrived and confronted widespread discrimination. They did not benefit from either governmental assistance or a well-established co-ethnic community. In terms of our typology of vulnerability and resources, the Punjabi Sikh second-generation was very much at risk except for two crucial factors. First, immigrant parents did not settle in the inner city nor in close proximity to any native-born minority whose offspring could provide an alternative model of adaptation to white majority discrimination. In particular, the absence of a downtrodden Indian-American community composed of children of previous immigrants allowed first-generation parents to influence decisively the outlook of their offspring, including their ways of fighting white prejudice. There was no equivalent of a Cholo-like reactive subculture to offer an alternative blueprint for the stance that "people like us" should take.

Second, Punjabi immigrants managed to make considerable economic progress, as attested by the number who became farm owners, while at the same time maintaining a tightly knit ethnic community. The material and social capital created by this first-generation community compensated for the absence of an older co-ethnic group and had a

decisive effect on the outlook of the second generation. Punjabi teenagers were shown that their parents' ways "paid off" economically and this fact plus their community's cohesiveness endowed them with a source of pride that counteracted outside discrimination. Through a strategy of selective assimilation, Punjabi Sikhs appear to be winning the race against the inevitable acculturation of their children to American-style aspirations.

The Case of Caribbeans in South Florida

Miami is arguably the American city that has been most thoroughly transformed by post-1960 immigration. The Cuban revolution had much to do with this transformation, as it sent the entire Cuban upper-class out of the country, followed by thousands of refugees of more modest backgrounds. Over time Cubans in Miami have created a prosperous community. Signs of this prosperity abound: by 1987, Cubans owned more than 30,000 small businesses, which formed the core of the Miami ethnic enclave; by 1989, Cuban family incomes approximated those of the native-born population; the Cuban community has also developed a private school system oriented to its values and political outlook. In terms of the above typology of vulnerability and resources, well-sheltered Cuban-American teenagers lack extensive exposure to outside discrimination and have little contact with youth from disadvantaged minorities. Moreover, the development of a Cuban enclave has created economic opportunities beyond those in the narrowing industrial and tourist sectors on which most other immigrant groups in the area depend. Across town, Haitian-American teenagers face exactly the opposite set of conditions.

Among the other immigrant groups in Miami, two deserve mention because they face situations intermediate between those of the Cubans and Haitians. Nicaraguans escaping the Sandinista regime during the 1980s were not as welcomed in the U.S. as Cuban exiles, nor were they able to develop a large and diversified community. Yet Nicaraguans shared with Cubans a common language and culture, as well as a militant anti-communist outlook. This common outlook led the Cuban-American community to extend its resources in support of the Nicaraguans, smoothing their process of adaptation. For second-generation Nicaraguans, this has meant that the pre-existing ethnic community providing a model for their own assimilation is not a downtrodden group, but rather one that has managed to establish a firm presence in the city's economy and politics.

Members of a second group, West Indians from Jamaica, Trinidad, and other English-speaking Caribbean republics, generally arrive in Miami as legal immigrants. In addition, many bring along professional and business credentials as well as the advantage of English fluency. These advantages are diminished, however, by the fact that these immigrants are seen by whites as identical to native-born blacks and discriminated against accordingly. The recency of West Indian migration and its limited numbers have prevented the development of a diversified ethnic community in south Florida. Hence new arrivals experience the full force of white discrimination without the protection of a large co-ethnic group, and with constant exposure to the situation and attitudes of the inner-city population. These disadvantages put the West Indian second generation at risk of bypassing white or even black middle-class models and instead assimilating to the culture of the underclass.

A recently completed survey of eighth and ninth graders in the Dade County (Miami) and Broward County (Fort Lauderdale) schools by the senior author of this article and Lisandro Perez included sizable samples of Cuban, Haitian, Nicaraguan, and West Indian second-generation children. The study defined youth of the "second generation" as those born in the U.S. who have at least one foreign-born parent, and those born abroad who have lived in the U.S. for at least five years. The survey included both inner-city and suburban public schools, as well as private schools and those in which particular foreign-origin groups were known to concentrate. The sample was divided evenly between boys and girls and included children ranging in age from twelve to seventeen.

There were, as expected, large socio-economic differences among the four national groups. Cuban children in private schools had the best educated parents and those with the highest status occupations. Haitians in public schools had parents who ranked lowest in both dimensions. Nicaraguans and West Indians occupied intermediate positions, with parents whose average education was often higher than that of public-school Cubans, but whose occupational levels were roughly the same. While more than half of private-school Cuban respondents defined their families as upper-middle class or higher, only a third of Haitians and Nicaraguans did so.

Most interesting were the differences in ethnic self-identification. Less than one-fifth of the second-generation students identified themselves as non-hyphenated Americans. The proportion was highest among higher-status, private-school Cubans, but even among this group almost two-thirds saw themselves as "Cuban" or "Cuban-American." Very few Cubans opted for the self-designation "Hispanic." Nicaraguan students, on the other hand, used this label almost as frequently as "Nicaraguan."

While none of the Latin students identified themselves as "black American," roughly one-tenth of Haitians and West Indians did so. The self-identification of Haitians was similar to that of Nicaraguans in that both attached less importance to the country of origin and more to pan-national identity than did Cubans or West Indians. In total, about half of the Haitian children identified themselves as something other than "Haitian."

Aspirations were very high in all groups. Although there were significant differences in expectations of completing college, at least 80 percent in each group expected to achieve this level of education. Similarly, roughly 70 percent of the students from each nationality aspired to professional or business careers. This uniformity contrasts sharply with the wide variation in socioeconomic background and reported experiences of discrimination. The Haitians and West Indians reported discrimination two to three times as frequently as did the Cubans. Majorities of both Haitian and West Indian youth reported having been discriminated against and about 20 percent said that their teachers had done so. In contrast, only 5 percent of Cubans in private school reported such incidents; Nicaraguans occupied an intermediate position, with half reporting discrimination and 13 percent reporting discrimination by their teachers.

Unsurprisingly, Haitian and West Indian teenagers were the most likely to agree that there is racial discrimination in the U.S. economy and to deny that non-whites have equal opportunities. Interestingly, they were joined in these negative evaluations by private-school Cubans. This result may reflect the greater information and class awareness of the latter group relative to their less privileged Latin counterparts. However, all Cuban students parted company with the rest of the sample in their positive evaluation of the United States. Roughly three-fourths of second-generation Cubans endorsed the view that "the United States is the best country in the world"; only half of Nicaraguans did so and the two mostly black groups took an even less enthusiastic stance.

The results of this survey illuminate with numbers the "race" between generalized career aspirations and the widely different vulnerabilities and resources created by first-generation modes of assimilation. Aspirations are very high for all groups, regardless of origin; however, parental socio-economic background, resources of the co-ethnic community, and experiences of discrimination are very different. These factors influence decisively the outlook of second-generation youth, even at a young age, and are likely to have strong effects on the course of their future assimilation. The importance of these factors is illustrated by the enthusiasm with which children of advantaged immigrants embrace their parents' adopted country, and by the much less sanguine views of those whose situation is more difficult.

A final intriguing fact about today's second generation as revealed by this survey: the best-positioned group (private-school Cubans) is the one least likely to step out of the ethnic circle in inter-personal relationships, while the group in the most disadvantaged position (Haitians) is the most likely to do so. Overall, the three Latin groups overwhelmingly select friends who are also the children of immigrants and who are mostly of the same nationality. Less than half of Haitians and West Indians do the same.

Assimilation and the Future

Fifty years ago, the dilemma of the Italian-American youngsters studied by Child consisted of assimilating to the American mainstream and thus sacrificing their parents' cultural heritage versus taking refuge in the ethnic community and forgoing the challenges of the outside world. In the contemporary context of "segmented assimilation," the alternatives have become less clear. Children of non-white immigrants may not even have the opportunity to gain access to middle-class white society, no matter how acculturated they become. Yet joining those native circles to which they do have access may prove a ticket to permanent subordination and disadvantage. Remaining securely ensconced in their co-ethnic community may, under these circumstances, be not a symptom of escapism but the best strategy for capitalizing on otherwise unavailable moral and material resources. As the experiences of the Punjabi Sikh and Cuban-American students suggest, a strategy of paced, selective assimilation may prove the best course for immigrant minorities. But the extent to which this strategy is possible depends on the history of each group and its specific profile of vulnerabilities and resources.

Portes and Zhou:

1. Discuss the factors that could affect into which subculture young immigrants assimilate. Which of these factors increase the vulnerability of downward social movement? Which of these factors increase the likelihood that assimilation of immigrants will be easier?
2. What do Portes and Zhou mean by "selective assimilation"?

25

Who Gets the "Lousy" Jobs?

Roger Waldinger

Hotels: Who Takes Care of the Guests?

The epic story of the garment workers—with its cycles of oppression, revolt, and exploitation—captured the attention of reporters and researchers ninety years ago and has held it ever since. But most of the inhabitants of the "other New York" work in the shadows, where few social scientists or journalists go. In this chapter, I turn my attention to one of these unheralded trades, where less-skilled newcomers to New York have always managed to get a leg up—hotels. While the hotel account lacks the historical dimension of garments, it presents a more complex configuration, one that is also closely linked to New York's postindustrial future. Because hotels are connected to the city's newer economic functions, the industry has been able to grow: in contrast to the badly eroding rag trade, hotels added employment over the period 1970–1990. Like the garment industry, the hotel business is a black niche of the past, but one in which the African-American presence persisted until recent years. As black New Yorkers are but one of a varied set of groups on which the industry draws to fill its jobs, a look at current employment patterns in ho-

tels lets us observe the factors shaping the ethnic division of labor at play.

Growth and Restructuring

Unlike New York's factory sector, which has steadily eroded over the past fifty years, the jobs of low-wage service have kept their place during the postindustrial transformation. Suburbanization and sagging urban economic fortunes spelled bad times for big-city hotels in the 1950s and the 1960s. With the upswing of urban service economies, starting in the mid-1970s, and the new forms of urban agglomeration that emerged during this period, the downtown hotel took a new lease on life. The corporate service firms, whose growth fueled a massive office-building boom, thrived on their linkages with an increasingly national and international clientele. Not surprisingly, then, "companies that settled into the new downtown offices soon wanted modern hotels nearby where they could put up out-of-town clients and business colleagues in comfort."[1] A huge expansion in tourism accompanied this growth in business travel, further swelling the market for downtown hotel facilities.

An extraordinary burst in hotel construction has occurred over the past several decades. During the 1960s, hotel construction added an average of 4,000 rooms a year to the downtowns of the thirty-eight largest metropolitan areas; between 1970 and 1982, the rate increased to more than 5,400 a year.[2] Hotel construction in New York took off in the 1980s, under the stimulus of the city's boom in tourism and business and financial services, yielding many new hotels and more than 8,500 new rooms.

Renewed investment in hotels turned the job picture around. Whereas employment languished in the postwar period, as business sagged and older properties were converted to other uses, payrolls expanded during the years after 1970. Total employment increased by one-third between 1970 and 1990, a quite respectable gain for an industry that remains a cluster of entry-level jobs.

Structure of Employment

In comparison to other immigrant-reliant industries, hotels stand out in several key respects. First, the hotel is a sizable establishment that often belongs to a much larger chain. New York's largest hotel has over 2,000 rooms and employs approximately 1,400 people. Second, whether large or small, hotels maintain an elaborate division of labor. Jobs fall into either the "back" or the "front" of the house, with the latter involving activities requiring direct guest contact. Functions create further distinctions, of which housekeeping, kitchen work, stewarding, and banquet services are generally the most important in employment terms. Differentiation within these functions varies considerably, with an elaborate hierarchy among kitchen workers, for example, and virtually none within housekeeping. Alongside the major functions are a plethora of smaller departments, with a large hotel maintaining a carpentry shop, upholstery shop, machine shop, lock-smith, and so on, each one of which employs a complement of specialized workers.

These various characteristics have contradictory influences on the structure of employment. On the one hand, size and organizational form lead to a formal and elaborate employment structure along the lines of an internal labor market. Many hotels have formal training programs, developed either by the owner or the chain; job-posting systems are common, as is a preference for hiring and promotion from within. On the other hand, the distinction between the front and the back of the house, as well as the functional divisions, have the opposite effect of separating job clusters and career paths within the hotel. Although workers can move from the back to the front of the house, jobs at the front usually get filled from the outside. And outsiders rarely come from the same groups as workers in housekeeping. Hotels want workers with good communication skills and middle-class self-presentation at the front of the house, which gives the edge to whites with at least some college education. In the back of the house, kitchen workers come from differing sources: professional associations or culinary schools refer chefs and sous-chefs, while lower-level help gets recruited from other hotels, restaurants, or the open market. In either case, movement occurs via the external market.

Despite its complexity, the hotel is a large service factory from an occupational point of view. At a time when the shape of so many organizations is changing, the hotel remains the classic pyramid: in 1990, managers and professionals constituted barely 18 percent of the industry's employees in New York City. The great bulk of employment in hotels lies in one of a variety of service occupations, which engages almost 60 percent of the industry's labor force. The largest concentration of workers, approximately 25 percent, is involved in the heavy, menial work of house-keeping; approximately another 16 percent of employees work in one of a variety of food service occupations (of which waiting is the largest).

The Hotel Work Force

With an occupational structure that emphasizes manual skills and ability to do heavy, menial work, hotels have always leaned heavily on minority and immigrant workers. Hotels had already evolved into a concentration of black and Puerto Rican employment on the eve of World War II. Employment shrunk over the next thirty years, as the industry consolidated, modernized, and phased out older properties and residential hotels, but the minority share of employment grew. By 1970, African-American and Puerto Rican workers each accounted for about a sixth of the work force.

Though a major component of the hotel rank and file, blacks historically found themselves confined to a narrow tier of positions. In the years immediately after World War II, hotels were often charged with discrimination, not just in lodging but in employment practices as well. A 1956 review of complaints filed with New York State's Commission against Discrimination noted "an occasional breakthrough in the employment of Negroes as waiter, busboy, and bartender but the overall picture is not one of major or extensive advance."[3] As if the data from its files were not enough, the commission underlined the obstacles to black progress in a mid-1950s survey of the industry's employment practices that it undertook on its own. Blacks were trapped in low-skilled, low-paying, dead-end jobs in the back of the house, with few chances of moving into positions involving customer contact; two-thirds of the black labor force was crowded into housekeeping alone, a category that only employed a fifth of

the total labor force.[4] All thirty-three of the hotels that the commission studied excluded blacks from bar service and front-service departments; the thousand and some waiters and waitresses at work in the higher-end hotels included only five blacks; and the top-paying banquet jobs remained virtually closed off to blacks. African-Americans rarely gained promotion from rear to front elevators, a shift that opened the door to still better-paying jobs in the front of the house.[5] Notwithstanding an agreement to use the state employment service for referrals, as part of an antidiscrimination plan, the range of job placements did not significantly expand: "Almost two out of every three nonwhites were referred and placed in housekeeping, laundry, and maintenance jobs, whereas white applicants were referred and placed in a greater diversification of jobs . . . A higher proportion of white than nonwhite referrals was accepted in each of the four major groups."[6]

Government regulators, joined by civil rights protesters, kept up the pressure in the 1960s. Picket lines mounted in front of some of the city's best-known hotels led the industry to put a training and upgrading program in place, but the job ceiling only gradually lifted. Results from a 1964 survey, which found that "a large number of Negroes [were] employed as maids, housemen, and elevator operators, but only a few or none in building maintenance positions, and as cashiers, clerks, auditors, typists, and telephone operators," showed that little had changed since the industry had been canvassed a decade before.[7] A 1967 survey discovered that, blacks made up one of every three workers in the back of the house but only one of every ten in the front of the house. Ironically, more progress was made in the clerical and managerial positions than in the skilled and waiting jobs, where the importance of networks and a buddy system among incumbents proved much harder to reform.[8]

Table 25.1
Ethnic Employment in the Hotel Industry, 1940–1990

| | Total | Whites | | Hispanics | | Blacks | | Asians |
		Native	Foreign	Native	Foreign	Native	Foreign	Foreign
Employment								
1940	43,800	14,200	20,000	3,300	—	5,500	700	—
1950	41,486	15,094	15,773	3,595	545	5,771	652	NA
1970	19,750	5,600	3,700	3,500	2,250	3,400	1,100	200
1980	21,700	4,200	2,540	2,980	4,440	3,680	3,080	640
1990	27,176	4,840	2,375	3,153	6,076	2,625	4,613	2,987
Index of Representation								
1940		0.60	1.21	8.16	—	2.33	1.54	—
1950		0.62	1.35	3.52	1.67	1.75	1.25	NA
1970		0.50	1.38	2.55	2.64	1.12	2.84	0.82
1980		0.41	1.11	1.53	2.62	1.08	2.45	0.71
1990		0.45	1.03	1.25	2.13	0.63	2.06	1.40

Note: Index of representation = share of group in category + share of group in total economy.
Source: Census of Population, 1940–1990.

After 1970, the industry's overall complexion changed abruptly, while the legacy of its racial hiring practices shifted much more slowly. European immigrants, previously a dominant presence, seeped out of the industry; as they did so, whites' share of hotel jobs dropped from just under a half in 1970 to a little over a quarter two decades later (Table 25.1). The seventies appear to be years of transition, with newcomers pouring into the industry, while the native minorities held on to their place. The industry's recovery in the 1980s added to the vacancies created by the old-timers' exodus, but the fruits of change went to the immigrants, who grabbed the positions vacated by whites. By 1990, the transition to a new configuration had been completed. Almost 60 percent of the industry's work force was foreign-born, among the highest of all major industries in the city; Asian immigrants made the most sizable gains, making significant inroads for the first time, followed by immigrant Hispanics and

immigrant blacks, in that order. Hotels also emerged as a niche for immigrant Dominicans and West Indians. The number of African-American workers eroded by over a thousand and their share of hotel jobs declined even more severely. Those black New Yorkers who remained in hotels found themselves repositioned: while waiting and kitchen jobs remained largely closed to them, employment in housekeeping plummeted, and front-of-the-house clerical and managerial jobs opened up. Despite progress on the last front, hotels underwent the changes of other black niches of the past, evolving into an industry in which African-Americans found themselves badly underrepresented.

Labor Supply Conditions

The hotel industry exemplifies the problems afflicting America's service complex: rapidly growing employment, low productivity, and declining available labor supplies.

Nationwide, hotel employment increased from a little under 1.1 million workers in 1980 to almost 1.5 million in 1987. But in a report on labor productivity recently issued by the Bureau of Labor Statistics, hotels ranked thirty-seventh of forty-three selected industries in terms of the average annual percentage change in output per employee for the years 1982 through 1987. Between 1983 and 1988, payroll and related expenses rose from 32 to nearly 37 percent, "primarily reflecting high rates of hiring," according to a report by industry consultants.[9] Although current data are not available, the industry's most recent growth followed a decade in which local productivity declined: between 1972 and 1982, the ratio of employees to rooms rose by 18 percent.

But while the industry's payrolls are growing and its productivity is sagging, finding workers is becoming an increasingly difficult task. The hotel is a relatively low-wage, service factory; hence, many industry observers contend that the industry faces "a human resources crisis."[10] One consultant told the industry's weekly publication, *Hotel and Motel Management,* that he considered "the labor shortage in the market as the most difficult it's been in his 25 years of hotel experience and that it is 'just getting worse.'"[11]

In New York, however, "there are plenty of people in the industry," as one manager put it. "We just have to open the door." In part, the density of hotel employment means that there exists a pool of circulating, experienced labor on which all employers can draw. Moreover, the labor force lives close by, in the city, whereas many hotels near new suburban office parks have no local pool of labor. But whatever the precise explanation, labor supply conditions in New York differ sharply from the national norm. "If I didn't have the hiring hall prescreen applicants," noted one manager, "I'd have a line wrapped around the block." "We could get a hundred maids by tomorrow if we needed," commented another.

"We have a nonstop flow of people coming in for jobs."

Whereas poor quality often aggravates the problems of insufficient quantity, New York's hotels seem to do better on this count as well. "The hard-core unemployed are a small percentage of the people who apply for our jobs," one manager told me. And turnover rates, which appear to be well below the industry average, suggest a more firmly attached population as well. For example, the two New York hotels operated by a large nonunion chain enjoy the lowest turnover rates among two hundred properties. "I'm surprised," said one manager, whose prior experiences had all been out of town, "that we don't have to go into the market and recruit . . . We can spend more time to find individuals who are a cut above. This further keeps turnover down."

The Role of Immigrants

Though New York's hotels had always drawn on an immigrant labor force—and which of the city's low-wage industries had not?—hotel managers have developed a new appreciation of the importance of immigrants since they entered the 1990s. "There's constant immigration," noted one veteran manager. "There isn't one department that doesn't have newly arrived immigrants." A large hotel found that its employees spoke forty-seven different languages, ranging from Creole to Twi, with Spanish, Vietnamese, Filipino, French, Polish, Russian, Italian, and Mandarin the largest language groupings. One personnel manager, a native Spanish speaker with twenty years of experience in one of New York's largest hotels, described the new immigrant influx at length: "The population in housekeeping and stewarding increasingly comes from Haiti, Jamaica, the Dominican Republic, and Central America. Asians are starting to come: we have a tremendous number of Asians applying for jobs. Lots of Dominicans: well represented, more so than Puerto Ricans. The Dominicans have come in over the last six or seven years, mostly replacing Puerto Ricans."

While the immigrants are important for "filling jobs from which other people have moved up the ladder," they also frequently import specific proficiencies that expand their role in the industry. "Many immigrants bring skills that we want," commented one experienced manager in a large hotel, who maintained that one-fifth of his immigrant contingent had arrived with home-country experience. Often, immigrant workers have backgrounds in related trades, acquired either at home or in the United States, that can easily be transferred to hotels. In general, "ethnic cooks—Italians, Chinese, Greek specialties—seem to be always needed," according to an employment service official. Certain cooking skills—for example, experience in the preparation of cold meats and hors d'oeuvres—favor the entry of Thai and Chinese workers into specialized kitchen occupations. "Filipinos with housekeeping experience in hospitals at home become housekeepers here," related one manager. "I get calls from lots of waiters in Indian restaurants," noted another.

However important the immigrant influx, there are no signs that it has occurred in response to deliberate employer efforts. On the contrary, the hotels seem to be the passive "bellwether of what's coming into the population." "With more than enough workers," most employers are content to "satisfy needs from the applicant flow." Thus, as the city's population has diversified, new groups have spontaneously streamed into the labor force. "The ethnic group to choose from is Indians," reported one new manager in a comment echoed in other interviews. "They are the number one group of applicants." But the Indians are only one of a batch of newcomers, as I learned from the interviews, where one informant told of "all of a sudden getting lots of Irish," and another of "an influx of literate Russians and Poles, some mid-easterners."

Thus, "with different groups now entering, looking for any kind of employment," natural turnover combined with ethnic differences in predispositions for hotel work have expanded the immigrant employment base. "Blacks and Puerto Ricans are being replaced by immigrants," noted the manager of a downtown tourist-oriented hotel. "This is strictly what the market has born."

Weakly Attached Workers

The advantage of immigrants, as one personnel director pointed out, is that their "need to work is as great as our need to fill the position." But the supply of immigrants is not unlimited and, more important, their skill levels often preclude them from jobs that require communication with guests. Even housekeepers have contact with guests; as one informant noted, "95 percent of what a housekeeper does will not require English; the problem is what they do when they're stopped in the hotel by a guest." In contrast to the manufacturing sector, where sign language is sufficient for instruction and any continuing interaction with employers or workers, some English-language ability seems to be a prerequisite for employment in the hotels. One job developer for a refugee-placement program observed: "Service demands for English are much greater than in manufacturing. When I get someone an interview with a hotel personnel department, the expectation of the hotel personnel people is that the person will speak for himself, although I will accompany him. In a factory, the expectation is that I will do everything—fill out the interview, translate at the interview, explain what the job involves." Moreover, immigrants are looking for stable, steady employment, but hotels also want a labor force that can adjust to changing hours and uncertain, flexible staffing requirements.

For these needs hotels turn to actors and students, a veritable "blessing to me," exclaimed an interviewee who ran a Broadway hotel. In actors and students, the hotels secure "overqualified workers at bargain rates." "What are the advantages of employing these people?" asked one manager rhetorically. "Above-average people skills and communication skills." Another informant added that "their good educational background makes them easy to train." Where immigrants tend "not to work in guest contact areas," actors and students ideally suit these roles. They have an additional virtue as "people who want less than the traditional workday. Actors want to be available in the day, and are therefore willing to work nights." Since hotels operate as seven-day-a-week, twenty-four-hour enterprises, they have staffing requirements that many workers, especially those with families, find undesirable. If students or actors can be hired for part-time, weekend positions, it relieves the strain of having to find full-time adult employees to work during these undesirable shifts. Furthermore, hotel occupancy rates are notoriously volatile, but weakly attached workers like students and actors move out of the industry without friction. Rather than laying career workers off, hotels are able to adjust to slow seasons, such as summer, by waiting for the students and actors they employ to simply quit.

Clearly differentiated from the hotel rank and file, actors and students make attractive recruits. According to the white officials in the New York State employment service whom I interviewed, hotels prefer to fill their positions with a "younger, yuppie, white crowd. They'd like to present that image right down to the maid: a blue-eyed, blond kid." Moreover, these same recruits are unlikely to feel much sense of kinship with less-educated, more heavily minority back-of-the-house workers—a not unimportant consideration in the industry's changing industrial relations environment. Tastes in compensation and benefits also vary among these two groups in ways that work to the advantage of management. "At the Marriott," noted a former employee, now a manager with a union-

ized hotel, "actors don't want to join the union, with its $200 initiation fee and $25 monthly dues." And one large nonunion hotel with a sizable labor force of actors and students emphasizes that its employees do not have to use union clinics but can consult their own doctors—a feature more likely to appeal to workers of middle-class background than to the hotel rank and file.

Native Black Workers

Although the hotel industry has long found a sizable share of its workers among African-Americans and continues to do so today, immigrants appear to provide a preferable labor force.

The entry and recruitment of immigrants seems to have little to do with wages or the immigrants' supposed susceptibility to exploitation. Those in immigrant-dominated occupations like housekeeping receive higher pay than those in front-desk occupations, where the immigrant penetration is much lower. Still higher wages are to be found in the kitchen, where the disparity between immigrant and African-American employment levels is the greatest. Nor can a strong case be made for employers' preference for immigrants on the grounds of the latter's greater vulnerability. Pay rates in the nonunion hotels equal, when not surpassing, the union rates, and the benefit packages are often better. Moreover, obtaining actors and students is a more effective union-avoidance strategy than hiring immigrants and one that large nonunion hotels have employed.

Despite their restrained labor market role, hotel employers still appear to prefer hiring immigrants. To some extent, employers evince "the philosophy that you get an immigrant who hasn't been spoiled by the welfare system, they're a lot harder working." More important, managers perceive a congruence between the hotels' competitive strategy—which increasingly emphasizes the quality and quantity of service—and workers' assumed traits. Hotels want workers known for their "friendliness," "service-orientation," and "smiling faces"—in short, "people-oriented intangibles that make people come back." Personnel officials think that these attributes, and an orientation more accepting of menial work, are likelier to be found among immigrants than among native minority workers. "Lots of new immigrants have more acceptable work ethics," noted one manager. "Asians have a culture for dealing with people in a courteous and respectful manner. They are here to work." An official in the state employment service advanced the same view, putting employers' motivation in a less flattering light: "The industry is elitist. They look for characteristics that are intangible, gratuitously hiring Orientals because they think they're hard working."

Ultimately, African-American participation in the hotel industry reflects a broad complex of factors—of which the entry of immigrants is just one part. Most important, the structure of incentives works less favorably for blacks than for immigrants.

Differences in preferences play a part. Interviews and statistical data both suggest that African-American workers are slowly moving out of the industry's effective labor supply. "For native black Americans in the past twenty years," reflected an official in the industry's joint labor-management training program, "the idea of service as a mechanism to make a living is simply not attractive." Similarly, many of the managers I interviewed agreed that the industry's legacy as a repository of the traditional jobs to which blacks had long been confined deterred younger African-Americans from taking hotel jobs: "American-born blacks see hotel work as servitude. They don't want to be a bellperson or a waiter. They don't want to do it. They say so. They're willing to take a lower paying job if it gives them a higher level of self-esteem." (manager of a New York business hotel)

But if African-Americans judge the benefits of hotel work more harshly than do im-

migrants, they also confront problems in their search for upward mobility that further diminish the attractiveness of hotel work. To begin with, the natural starting point for movement into hotel management is the front of the house, an area in which blacks have historically been underemployed. The blatant discriminatory practices that previously kept blacks out operate with much less force than before, but the basic pattern remains in place. Until recently, African-Americans had been confined to the back of the house, which offers relatively few options for upward mobility. Currently, there are few takers for the available management positions—like executive housekeeper or executive steward—that open up: "the pay is not great for these jobs and the positions aren't great either. Managers have to fill in for workers if the latter don't show up for work: in other words, the managers have to make rooms or serve." These back-of-the-house managerial positions are also detached from the main lines of upward mobility, which are to be found in the front.

The case of food service occupations provides further insight to the barriers to black employment, especially since it highlights the difference between African-Americans and immigrants. Kitchen and catering jobs contain a range of opportunities for upward mobility, yet African-American employment in these categories remains well below parity. The kitchen, "where the average temperature is 120 degrees," is not an inherently attractive place in which to work. For those kitchen workers who start at the bottom without any skills, the appeal is diminished because "hotel kitchens don't have opportunities to train hands-on." Getting ahead in the kitchen requires entering with training, which gives other groups a leg up over African-Americans. As already mentioned, immigrants often arrive in the United States with cooking skills or else learn them in the burgeoning sector of immigrant restaurants. "Culinary schools are exploding with graduates," who, as it turns out, are mainly middle-class whites. Thus, African-Americans are the most likely to get stuck at the bottom of the kitchen hierarchy, which discourages them from starting there in the first place.

If lack of skills and exclusion from the skill-acquisition process impede access to high-paying cooking jobs, the case of banquet waiting illustrates other obstacles. Banquet waiting requires strength, quickness, and care but no skill that involves years of training. Still, it is "considered a high-prestige job," one of the industry's most desirable. Banquet waiters receive a salary supplemented by a tip, based on a predetermined percentage addition to a banquet's total costs. A worker attached to a hotel with a good volume of business can earn from $40,000 a year in a run-of-the-mill establishment in New York to over $100,000 a year in a top-of-the-line deluxe hotel, though these earnings will vary, depending on the ups and downs of a hotel's catering business.

The problem is that there is no fast road to banquet waiting in union hotels. One must have five years of prior service as a hotel waiter to apply to be sent out as a "roll-call" waiter when additional banquet staff is required; with enough seniority, one moves to a hotel's list of permanent "B" waiters, from which one eventually steps to the "A" list and serves on a more regular basis. Thus, to become a banquet waiter, one first needs to be employed in the front of the house. To maintain the long effort to gain a permanent banquet job, one also needs information about opportunities in the many different hotels, and contacts with waiters who are on the permanent A or B list. Those contacts are not equally available to all. "Banquet waiters have been cliquish," admitted one union official, himself a former banquet waiter. "Blacks and women have had a hard time breaking in. It used to be Italian; it's now more Greek and Latino." Today's cliquishness has long-standing roots: in the past, as we have seen, blacks seeking employment in a high-paying, low-skilled job like banquet waiter found few doors open, with informal practices that generally restricted access to whites. There is little evidence to suggest that things have since turned around.

Thus, the case of banquet waiting illustrates the vicious circle that keeps mobility opportunities closed. Discrimination, past and present, reduces access to this particular ladder; discrimination also lowers the probability of movement up that ladder, thereby reducing the incentive to obtain initial front-of-the-house jobs. Whereas African-Americans lack a network that might connect experienced and aspiring black banquet waiters, other groups are well-connected, possessing the contacts and ties to other waiters and banquet managers that blacks, given their history and smaller numbers, cannot possibly possess.

Other factors—limited skill backgrounds, problems in communicating, and lack of facility with computers—impede access to those front-of-the-house positions directly linked to managerial tracks. As the director of a union training program pointed out, minority workers who want to move up to front-desk jobs "must be trained explicitly for middle-class norms." Though rank-and-file hotel workers find the "front office very attractive, there's lots of competition, especially from middle-class whites." Large hotels maintain active college recruitment programs, which funnel an ample supply of new trainees from college and university hotel management programs. The Council on Restaurant and Institutional Education includes almost two hundred college hotel management programs among its affiliates and reports that the number of such programs has grown considerably in recent years. Yet, hotel schools appear to enroll a very small minority population. For example, New York City Technical College, a community college unit of the City University of New York where the student body is 87 percent nonwhite, maintains a hotel and restaurant management program in which at least half of the students are white and a high proportion of the remainder are foreign-born. Similarly, New York University runs a hotel program in its extension division, which enrolls a principally immigrant student body, while the students in the hotel program at the university's main campus are predominantly white.

Peripheralization?

Perhaps the African-American exodus from hotel work is a response to the declining wages and work standards that sometimes accompany immigration. Although that hypothesis frequently appears in the literature, the hotel case offers little support. New York is an old union town, with a powerful branch of the Hotel and Restaurant Employees Union, which established firm control over its respective markets during the heyday of labor-movement activity over half a century ago.[12] Though union-management relations in the hotel industry changed during the 1980s—with nonunion chains experiencing growth and the industry's productivity squeeze motivating cost-cutting measures— these shifts had little impact on New York. Only two of the hotels that opened in New York during the 1980s remained nonunion, a status that has entailed substantial costs in wages and benefits, which compare favorably with union standards. Consequently, even in the market of the early 1990s—when demand was weak and unemployment rising—the very newest hotels signed neutrality agreements with the hotel workers.

The recent collective-bargaining experience attests to the stability of these arrangements. Negotiations over the 1985 contract broke down, leading to a thirty-five-day strike, the industry's first in over forty years. In the settlement, the union assented to only two of the more than thirty give-backs with which management had originally come to the table. The most important concession involved a two-tier wage agreement, which in contrast to that implemented in many other industries, held for only first-year employees, who would then automatically move up to the standard rate for their classification. In return, hotel workers received sizable wage increases. In 1990, however, negotiations pivoted around health care costs. But union and management averted the conflicts that had earlier led to stoppages in private hospitals and the telephone industry, successfully restructuring their benefits plan without imposing deductions or coinsurance and signing an agreement ahead of its expiration date.

Alternatively, we might expect to see an immigrant effect on wages, which could suggest a tie-in to broader arguments about the relationships among service growth, immigration, and earnings inequality. Nationwide, real earnings for hotel and motel employees declined, falling from $181 a week in 1972 to $160 a week in 1990. But in New York, hotel workers' *real wages,* which stagnated during the 1970s, rose during the buoyant 1980s. Likewise, a look at wages for detailed occupations in unionized hotels confirms the picture of rising real wages during the 1980s, while providing no evidence of growing inequality. On the contrary, wage trends showed a slight shift toward compression between more- and less-skilled occupations. Hotel workers also moved upward relative to their counterparts in manufacturing while holding their own in the overall economy.[13]

As Figure 25.1 shows, however, the hotel industry did pay immigrants better than their native black counterparts. That advantage is hard to square with the usual claims of immigrant competition: after all, why should the hotel industry have substituted immigrants for African-Americans, if the result was a higher wage bill? But the disparity fits the argument I have made all along: that immigrants found a more supportive environment in hotels than did African-Americans, a difference that in turn helps explain the diverging supply curves between the two groups.

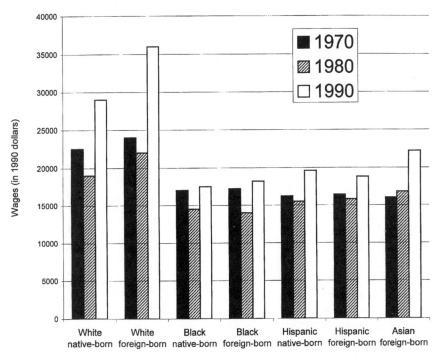

Figure 25.1. Wages of Hotel Workers in New York City, 1970–1990. (Source: Census of Population, 1970–1990.)

On Different Tracks

The portals to the bottom of New York's economy have run through the city's garment and hotel industries for the past hundred years. At midcentury, those characteristics led African-American New Yorkers to gravitate toward hotel and garment work. But now, when both industries remain concentrations of easy-entry jobs, their native black workers have largely gone. Instead, hotels and garments, like so much of New York's low-skilled sector, have reverted to the earlier pattern of immigrant domination.

The histories recounted in this chapter suggest that African-American trajectories have been shaped by a complex of interacting sociological and economic factors. The African-American experience in hotel and garment work coincides with the years of the great migration, as black workers converged on the lowest-level jobs, filling positions va-

cated by whites. In both cases, attempts to move up the hierarchy ran into the obstacle of competition with better-established white workers. Good jobs got rationed through informal ties among established workers and the younger members of their core networks. As long as white ethnics sought work as cutters, banquet waiters, cooks, or skilled seamstresses, opportunities for African-Americans remained largely foreclosed.

African-Americans subsequently moved out of both industries; the timing of those shifts casts light on the factors that triggered the outflow. The supply of native black labor began to fall short in the garment industry by the early 1950s, but not in hotels. The pace of wage change has much to do with this development, as wages in the garment industry fell behind in the city's wage hierarchy, while hotel wages pulled ahead.[14] Similarly, African-Americans' discontent with garment work conditions first showed up in the industry's recruitment problems; active protest emerged only later, toward the end of the 1950s, as the growing protest movement reflected shifting black aspirations. By the late 1960s, when the city's economy reached its postwar boom and apparel employers were searching for workers as never before, African-Americans dropped out of the industry's effective labor supply for good. Similarly drastic change did not occur in the hotel industry until the 1980s, a period of considerable improvement in the industry's real wages. As the interviews suggest, the attenuation of African-American ties was linked to the emergence of new generation that rejected stigmatized service jobs to which blacks had long been confined.

In both industries, differences in economic aspirations put African-Americans and immigrants on different tracks. But the hotel case further suggests that the structure of opportunity systematically varied between African-Americans and immigrants, in turn yielding divergent motivations and incentives to develop the relevant skills. In hotels, African-American movement beyond the entry level is hindered by a variety of factors that do not hold for immigrants. The skills needed to enter at higher levels of the blue-collar hierarchy are *more* difficult to acquire for African-Americans than for immigrants; at the lower levels of the white-collar hierarchy, African-Americans encounter substantial and effective competition from whites; and African-Americans seem more victimized by discrimination than immigrants, as indicated by black underrepresentation in food service occupations.

What about the alternative hypothesis, that cheap immigrant labor pushed African-Americans out? Timing seems to rule that possibility out. African-American employment erosion began *before* the new immigrant influx; as noted above, the most severe African-American losses seem to have occurred in the 1960s, just when employers were most desperately seeking bodies. In ho-

tels, the decline in African-American employment occurred in the 1980s, when real wages grew. The fact that relative wages for the most immigrant-dominated hotel occupations rose fastest makes the immigrant-displacement hypothesis still more implausible. In any case, African-Americans' chief competitive threat in hotels comes from actors and students, who provide the preferred sources of flexible labor, *not* immigrants.

But the seepage of African-American employment from industries like hotels and garments, and its replacement with immigrant labor, does seem to produce an irrevocable and irreplaceable loss. Once in place, immigrant networks have an inherently exclusionary bias, an effect that only grows when newcomers concentrate in an ethnic economy, as in the case of Chinese in the garment industry, or in an ethnic occupational niche, as in the case of hotel kitchens. Although the arrival of the new immigrants seems to be an instance of self-recruitment, not manipulation by employers, the evidence from the hotel industry indicates that employers prefer immigrants to African-Americans, when they have the choice. To some extent, employers also respond to the preferences of their immigrant workers, whose involvement in the struggle for place may yield an antipathy for African-Americans.

In the end, the immigrants may have hastened the African-American exodus from New York's low-skilled sectors, but if so, they only pushed along a development that was well under way before they arrived. African-Americans stopped doing New York's dirty work more than a generation ago, a change that has now run its course. Today's areas of African-American concentration are to be found in activities that require more schooling and provide much greater rewards. But this particular path of adaptation leaves behind the low-skilled. For these black New Yorkers there are no alternatives to work in the city's traditional, easy-entry industries.

Unfortunately, that option is largely fore-closed: African-American recruitment networks into low-skilled industries like garments or hotels have dried up; and the advent of immigrants means that the newcomers have a lock on those jobs.

Notes

1, Bernard Frieden and Lynn Sagalyn, *Downtown, Inc.* (Cambridge, Mass.: MIT Press, 1989).

2. Ibid.

3. New York State Commission against Discrimination, *Employment in the Hotel Industry* (New York: Commission against Discrimination, 1958), p. 11.

4. New York State Commission against Discrimination, *Hotel Industry*, p. 24.

5. Herman Bloch, "Discrimination against the Negro in Employment in New York, 1920–1963," *American Journal of Economics and Sociology*, 24, 4 (1965):365–366, 373–375; U.S. House Committee on Education and Labor, *Investigation on Extension of Coverage to Laundry, Hotel, Restaurant, Bar, and Hospital Workers*, 87th Congress, 2d sess., 1962, pp. 22–29, 53–56.

6. New York State Commission against Discrimination, *Hotel Industry*, p. 14.

7. "Americana Picketed in Racial Protest," *New York Times*, February 8, 1964, p. 11; Damon Stetson, "Hotels and Labor Spur Integration," *New York Times*, October 15, 1964, p. 20.

8. Edward Koziara and Karen Koziara, *The Negro in the Hotel Industry* (Philadelphia: Industrial Relations Unit, Wharton School, 1967), pp. 15, 29.

9. Laventhol and Horvath, *U.S. Lodging Industry* (Philadelphia: Laventhol and Horvath, 1989), p. 5.

10. T. Lattin, "Human Resources Crisis Looking for Hotel Industry," *Hotel and Motel Management*, April 3, 1989, p. 30.

11. P. LaHue, "Employee Shortage Clouds Hospitality Hiring Practices," *Hotel and Motel Management*, November 2, 1987, p. 130.

12. Morris Horowitz, *The New York Hotel Industry: A Labor Relations Study* (Cambridge, Mass.: Harvard University Press, 1960).

13. See my article "Taking Care of the Guests: The Impact of Immigrants on Services—An Industry Case Study," *International Journal of Urban and Regional Research*, 16, no. 1 (1992); and Dorothy Sue Cobble and Michael Merrill, "Collective Bargaining in the Hospitality Industry," forthcoming in Paula Voos, ed., *Collective Bargaining in the Private Sector* (Madison, Wis.: Industrial Relations Research Association).

14. Wage data from the period 1947–1955 from Segal, *Wages in the Metropolis,* pp. 178–179.

References

Bloch, Herman. "Discrimination against the Negro in Employment in New York, 1920–1963," *American Journal of Economics and Sociology*, 24, 4 (1965):365–366, 373–375.

Cobble, Dorothy Sue, and Michael Merrill, "Collective Bargaining in the Hospitality Industry," forthcoming in Paula Voos, ed., *Collective Bargaining in the Private Sector,* Madison, Wis.: Industrial Relations Research Association.

Frieden, Bernard, and Lynn Sagalyn. *Downtown, Inc.* Cambridge, Mass.: MIT Press, 1989.

Horowitz, Morris. *The New York Hotel Industry: A Labor Relations Study.* Cambridge, Mass.: Harvard University Press, 1960.

Koziara, Edward, and Karen Koziara. *The Negro in the Hotel Industry.* Philadelphia: Industrial Relations Unit, Wharton School, 1967, pp. 15, 29.

LaHue, P. "Employee Shortage Clouds Hospitality Hiring Practices." *Hotel and Motel Management.* November 2, 1987, p. 130.

Lattin, T. "Human Resources Crisis Looking for Hotel Industry." *Hotel and Motel Management.* April 3, 1989, p. 30.

Laventhol and Horvath. *U.S. Lodging Industry.* Philadelphia: Laventhol and Horvath, 1989.

New York State Commission against Discrimination. *Employment in the Hotel Industry.* New York: Commission against Discrimination, 1958.

New York Times. "Americana Picketed in Racial Protest." February 8, 1964, p. 11.

Segal, Martin. 1960. *Wages in the Metropolis: Their Influence on the Location of Industries in the New York Region.* Cambridge, MA: Harvard University Press.

Stetson, Damon. "Hotels and Labor Spur Integration," *New York Times,* October 15, 1964, p. 20.

U.S. House Committee on Education and Labor. *Investigation on Extension of Coverage to Laundry, Hotel, Restaurant, Bar, and Hospital Workers,* 87th Congress, 2d sess., 1962, pp. 22–29, 53–56.

Waldinger, Roger. "Taking Care of the Guests: The Impact of Immigrants on Services—an Industry Case Study," *International Journal of Urban and Regional Research,* 16, no. 1 (1992).

Waldinger:

1. In what ways did economic restructuring affect employment opportunities in New York for minority groups of people?

2. What are some of the tools that new immigrants have used to allow them to more easily move into hotel positions and what have been some of the consequences for non-immigrant hotel workers?

26

Immigrant Life on the Margins:
Descent into Disappointment

Sarah J. Mahler

More often than not, the brooms migrants imagined using to sweep up dollars turn into the brooms that they toil with in the rest rooms of restaurants or kitchens of the middle class. Reality swiftly eclipses their visions. Even those who had been well-informed by their relatives about life in the United States still did not anticipate how they would have to realign both their expectations and their strategies after arrival. During their early days and months, migrants' eyes are opened. They learn that the rules of life are different in the United States from what they were at home. As innocents and greenhorns, they often learn these lessons through victimization. But once having paid their dues, they also learn to play the new games to their advantage. Among the lessons migrants learn in the days following their arrival, three play crucial roles in realigning expectations with reality: (1) learning how difficult it is to produce and safeguard surplus income, (2) understanding that the drive to produce a surplus commodifies most relationships, and (3) realizing that opportunities for producing that surplus lie primarily within one's community and not outside it. To tap these opportunities, migrants must recognize and utilize their community's resources for their own benefit. Intra-community strategies become the immigrant's primary avenue to socioeconomic mobility because they are largely excluded from mainstream America, its economy and opportunities. They live segregated from the mainstream by structural forces beyond their control, forces that limit their opportunities for success. Most stagnate within this restricted sphere but some advance, learning to exploit resources found mainly within their immigrant communities.

From Subsistence to Surplus

The majority of my interviewees arrived in the United States mired in debt from their trips but with great expectations of returning home in a few years with a nest egg—several thousand dollars—in their pockets. Yet nearly everyone told me that within days of arrival they wished they had never come and wanted to go home. Most felt like Don José, who was ready to leave the United States after only a month. Their debts, their pride, and the burden of providing for their families keep them from turning back. In their first months, they swallow their disillusionment and despair because they face the daunting task ahead of finding ways to meet their obligations. In order to understand these people's despair, one must comprehend the magnitude and complexity of immigrants' financial obligations relative to their capacity to generate income. Second, it is critical to recognize that the immigrants underestimated the difficulty of meeting their obligations owing to a simple miscalculation and to the fact that most would not listen to seasoned immigrants who sent home bleak information about prospects in the United States. The miscalculation involves estimating earnings in U.S. dollars but failing to account for the costs of living in the United States.

The first task immigrants face following arrival is to find employment and to work as long and as hard as they possibly can. Work becomes life's fulcrum in the United States, qualitatively different from its function in migrant's home countries. Gilberto had known long days as a peasant in El Salvador, but he found that work there was much different from work in the United States. "There you're not obligated to work," he said. "You work out of *cariño* [love]. Sometimes you work hard but you work with more cariño because it's your own. Yes, I mean you work with more *voluntad* [willingness]. Because you work for yourself, you are happy with the work you're going to do. But here, no." "Why do you work here?" I asked him, and he responded, "Because if you don't work you won't have a place to stay, even though you don't live comfortably anyway. Sometimes you don't even earn enough to pay the rent."

When Gilberto says he feels "obligated" to work in the United States whereas at home he willingly went off to work, he articulates the dilemma facing all of my informants. Though they earn salaries that classify them among the working poor (typically four to seven dollars per hour), their incomes must stretch much further than mere survival. They are obligated to produce a surplus from their meager salaries in order to (1) repay their travel loans, INS bonds, and any other debts they incur as they start their lives in the United States, (2) remit monies homeward to sustain their families left behind and finance investments there, and (3) save a nest egg to return home with. Additionally, immigrants hope to have some savings on hand in case of an emergency or the loss of their job. Undocumented immigrants qualify for no government public cash assistance, and in only a few states do they even qualify for Medicaid to pay for emergency medical treatment. They have little if any institutional safety net (the church, soup kitchens, and a few other charities are the only sources of aid I have found) to fall back upon if they cannot meet their own needs, let alone meet the needs of their dependents and creditors.

It is difficult to convey how pressures build on immigrants, driving them to assume the nonstop work lives that they are famous for. Cándido's early experiences are illustrative. He crossed the Mexican-U.S. border in the back of a pickup truck that was detected by immigration officials who gave chase. The driver stopped the vehicle and ordered his human cargo to jump out; there was screaming and shooting as people ran for their lives into the surrounding desert. As the migrants ran, the INS officers shouted at them to stop or they would be shot, but Cándido kept running. "Me, I didn't even turn around to look at him," he said. "I said to myself, 'I owe all this money and how am I ever going to pay it off if they deport me, if they catch me?' So, I ran by myself into an area covered with vegetation and I escaped. But the rest were captured and put in the *corralón*."

Even when the pressures to repay their travel debt become less acute, their void is filled by responsibilities to families at home. When Tina was languishing in the detention center, for instance, she was beset by guilt for not being able to send money back to her family. Her sister was caring for Tina's young son and would send her letters begging for help: "Things are worse now than when you left. Just to buy milk is so expensive. If you don't send me money how will I be able to buy a tin of milk" Her sister thought that she was working; Tina had not had the heart to tell her the bad news that she had fallen into the hands of the INS. But she had no job and no income except a few dollars that she received from friends who had been released. She would send off five or ten dollars to her sister, who responded by writing, "Little sister. I am thankful for what you send me." And this partial fulfillment of her obligations eased Tina's anguish.

"You Spend What You Earn"

Immigrants communicated their pressures primarily through their actions, through their workaholic lives, not through words. The workaholism is a product of their need to generate more wealth than that required for their own sustenance. It is also the product of U.S. economic realities—the realities of a postindustrial economy that produces more minimally paid than well-paid jobs. As such, people face the task of stretching their meager salaries past self-sustenance—which many native workers cannot achieve at these wage levels—and achieving a surplus to cover debts and family obligations. For many this alone is not disillusioning, since they faced dire economic challenges in their homelands, albeit just to sustain their families. What causes them to despair so immediately upon arrival is the jolt they receive in realizing that *"lo que se gana se gasta"* (you earn [in dollars] and you spend [in dollars]).

Virtually none of my informants, however highly educated, avoided misestimating to some degree the facility of generating surplus income. The miscalculation works this way: A would-be migrant hears he can earn five dollars per hour in the United States. He then translates this five-dollar-an-hour salary into its worth back home where a worker earns

five dollars a day. He also subconsciously estimates that his cost of living in the United States will be similar to that at home. Relying on these calculations, a migrant can reasonably assume that he will achieve his goal of a nest egg in a few years. Alfredo's experience illustrates this type of planning, characteristic of what migration scholars label "target earners."

Alfredo, a schoolteacher with a university education in Peru, heard through his friends Berta and Manuel that he could earn $6 per hour on Long Island. "When they told me, 'We're earning $6 per hour. Imagine. Here we generally work twelve hours, fourteen hours, and $6 per hour.' 'Six dollars per hour,' I would say, 'in eight hours that's $48. I will make this in eight hours. I will make more than $60, $70, $80 per day. I'll work seven days a week; I don't care about Sunday, holidays, or anything like that. I will be making at least $400 or $500 per week. After a few weeks, I will have $2,000 or $2,500.'" This estimate, because it does not measure expenses in the host country's terms, dooms the new immigrant to disillusionment upon arrival. Immigrants often refer to this new realization with the saying "You spend what you earn." Migrants from urban, educated backgrounds like Alfredo's are deceived roughly as often as peasants. I found that peasants were quite savvy about avoiding migration to cities in their home countries because they understood that this would make them completely dependent on a wage economy with little hope of betterment and with no subsistence agriculture to fall back on. However, they were not necessarily able to apply the same analysis when contemplating the economics of migrating to the United States. "I thought that housing was going to be cheaper and that finding work wasn't going to be so hard," Jesús, a Salvadoran peasant and a key informant, told me when I asked him what he had expected. "But no, here it's papers, permits, and so on. And you find a little bit of work in landscaping but it's only for six months and you have to save up some money to wait until the summer comes [so you can work again]." He too miscalculated the economics and found himself shocked and dismayed by the reality.

The exigencies of earning dollars descend swiftly on newly arrived migrants as they learn the true cost of living in the United States. The stress increases as they also learn that their income must stretch further than subsistence and cover expenses that they did not incur in their homelands and often did not anticipate incurring. Suddenly, as Tina—the spunky woman from Nicaragua—explained to me, you realize that "here you earn in dollars and you buy things in dollars. You have to spend a lot here. Rent is a serious matter here. . . . You can't be without work. Not anyone will tell you to take what you need for yourself; it's easier to find someone who won't tell you that. If you don't work you don't eat. If you're sick or not sick you always have to work. If you get sick it's really hard. It's expensive to have a child here. It's fifty dollars for a [medical] visit, the least would be forty dollars. And if work is slow or if you don't earn enough then you have to find a way to survive. Just for my daughter's care I have to take fifty dollars out of my pocket. Rent is fixed and you have to buy food. When I look around there's always something I need." Tina finds rent payments most irksome because she never paid rent in Nicaragua and she never imagined it would consume a third or more of her income.

When migrants learn that "you spend what you earn," they must face the task of reestimating the time they will need to stay to meet their obligations and, perhaps, their goals. Already feeling dehumanized after their journeys, many migrants are driven to new depths of despair by this realization. Like Don José, they feel deceived and depressed, desirous of returning home. But they cannot return because this would be humiliating (they would be seen as failures at home) and, more important, because they are heavily in

debt. It is the fear of humiliation, the burden of their travel debt, and their responsibility to family left behind that figure most prominently among the conditions driving them to stay. Once they make it through the first critical months of adjustments, they are likely to become permanent, albeit undocumented and unintentional, settlers.

"People Change Here"

When I asked individuals about their first impressions of how their lives in the United States differed from their lives at home, I frequently received the response "People change here. They don't act like people do in my country. Here, they're more competitive, egotistical." They offer several reasons for this change, one they confront almost immediately upon arrival. Travelers arrive in the United States exhausted, expecting to find rejuvenation in the sight of familiar faces and a sense of home in friends' and relatives' embraces. Frequently they encounter cold shoulders and individualism instead. They find that the mutuality of immigrant life is shared deprivation more than shared provisioning. When Altagracia was reunited with her family in "Gold Coast," she anticipated hungrily the warmth of her religious, evangelical relatives. In El Salvador, they had often requested assistance from her and now she felt certain she could count on their generosity in return. "'Now it is my turn to receive,'" she told me she was thinking when she saw them. "'Now that I need them they are going to support me.'" But this is not what happened—just the opposite. Altagracia was told by her relatives to leave. "'You have to go elsewhere because, you know, you've got to find work. Food and housing are expensive,' they would say to me bit by bit. I got to see the real world as it is. . . . 'Who' I thought, 'could help me?' They didn't help me. Instead, I got help from people whom I had never even known. I received many favors from them.

The law of recompensation exists because although those whom I helped didn't come and help me, there were other people who had such faith in me—so much faith that I was very happy. But this made me think: Why would these people feel so sure of me if they don't even know who I am? . . . I realized that these were good people and I had arrived at the feeling that now there were not good people left. But these people gave me a lot. I, personally, had lost my belief in people, in all people."

Altagracia's experience illustrates both the fiction and the fact of social relations. Much to her surprise, her relatives did not fulfill her expectations for proper treatment of guests or for kinship obligations to reciprocate past favors. She is deeply disillusioned with them, but she is heartened by other unnamed individuals who did come to her aid. Altagracia's story demonstrates that cooperation and mutual assistance *do* occur, but they occur outside home country norms and cannot be assumed.

Regardless of whether they received help in the first, impressionable stage of their lives in the United States, many individuals recall this epoch as formative of their bitter views toward compatriots here. They encounter what they term "egoism" in relatives and neighbors that would have been unimaginable back home. Sister Maria and Roberto Morán employ similar language to contrast the concern and cooperation characteristic of peasant lives in El Salvador with the social disregard and individualism they witness in the United States. "Here things are not like over there," Maria explained. "Over there you eat even if it's only beans with bread. Here you don't. Here whoever has [money] eats and whoever doesn't, can't. You don't know about any groups who will help you or anything. You don't know anything. It's worse living here. Because here everyone lives for himself."

I then asked her why she thinks this happens here and not in El Salvador, and she responded, "Because over there if you don't have anything then you go next door and say, 'Señora So-and-so, don't you have some beans you could give me so I can eat them with tortillas?' But here no. They tell you to go work. This happens even within the same family. I've seen it. They don't help each other because they all work and have their own money and if they give you something they expect you to pay for it. . . . My cousin told me one day, '[Maria], we are not going to be able to help you any more because I had better have some [money] left over for me.' She couldn't [help me anymore] because the expenses were very high and only her husband worked. So she told me, 'Find a way to make your own life.'" Roberto responded to my question about differences between people's behavior in El Salvador and in the United States by voicing an ultimatum. "Here if you don't have work you can't survive. You don't have [money] to pay the rent, to eat. You could die of hunger. Over there, no. If I don't work one week it's the same. I have food to eat. And I don't pay to live. And even without money I am okay but I can't live like that here."

Roberto is a diminutive man in his mid-twenties who worked as a peasant with a rural cooperative sponsored by the Catholic Church in the La Paz Department of El Salvador. He joined their efforts out of his own desire to alleviate human suffering but was forced to flee the country when his organization was targeted as subversive by the government. He describes this action as class repression by the elites against the peasantry; but he has a more difficult time comprehending how it can be that people of his own social class have stopped supporting each other just because they now live in the United States.

Don José has spent much time analyzing the genesis of this apparent change of heart. When he himself arrived in the United States, he could not find a job and became a burden on his brother. Though not rejected by his brother, he felt humiliated by his new status since in El Salvador he had always served as a generous father figure to his siblings. "I don't want to be a burden on anyone," he insisted. "There were eleven of us children in my family and I helped every one of them. . . . I was like a father to [my brother] before. I can't tell you all the things I have done for him; I was just like his father. . . . But [in California] when others were paying rent and food for me I felt bad with each day that came and went. I got sick two times from being without work and thinking that they were supporting me. That's horrible. In El Salvador I know that because people are self-supporting—their own house, their own things, and so on—[then they can help each other out and that's] magnificent! But here everything is money; everything has to be bought. . . . I didn't feel well at all, at all. I felt humiliated, *apenado.* So I said it was better for me to leave and I did."

Unlike some other informants, Don José blames immigrants' retreat from reciprocity on their induction into an economy where everything must be paid for with money. He feels that this is not a change in their temperament, but a change in their own material conditions. A peasant who produced most of his family's needs and who enjoyed few luxuries requiring payment in hard currency, he argues, was freer to help out neighbors in times of need. But monetary demands are different in the United States—particularly the ever-pressing necessity of paying rent, which averages $300 per month for Salvadorans and $425 for South Americans, according to my survey. People react to this reality by scaling back on assistance to others even though they wish to help. During a long conversation, Don José emphatically insisted that "brotherhood among Hispanics has always existed, in El Salvador and in all the countries of the world . . . brotherhood exists. The problem is that [Gold Coast], because it is a city of millionaires, has extremely high rent. So, of course, Hispanics see themselves as obligated

not to offer shelter or housing free to anyone who has just arrived and who is unemployed and can't pay rent. [The leaseholder] wants to get people who can pay, who can help pay the rent. So perhaps they deny help to their Hispanic brothers but it is not because they don't want to, but because of circumstances beyond their control. They can't let people in for free when they have to pay more than a thousand dollars for an apartment and they need to have four or five people there who can help them pay the rent. If they let in people for free, who is going to help them make the rent? But if they have a lot of people in the apartment, the building manager will throw them out. So they see themselves obliged, perhaps bothering their conscience, not to help their brothers out. But it is not they are not willing; no, we have the desire because we have the tradition of serving others. I have helped a lot of people . . . in whatever country I'm in I want to help others. But sometimes you can't, you want to but you can't and sometimes someone who can doesn't want to. But we Hispanics, we're like this: we always help each other. But here, there aren't circumstances for doing it. The conditions put us in a position that we can't help others. If you don't have a fixed income—for instance, all the landscapers, all the construction workers who work seasonally don't have work in the winter. They are only able to make it through the winter because of the little savings they have from the working season. But if they start to donate their money to help others, they will have no way to feed themselves. For this reason they have to turn a cold shoulder to their Salvadoran or other Hispanic brothers. Many times they don't colaborate, but it is because of this—they can't help because their circumstances don't allow them."

Don José argues here that reciprocal relations often cannot be sustained given people's pressures to make ends meet. But he bases his argument on the transition migrants undergo from highly self-sufficient peasants to dependent wage earners. Does his reasoning work as well for migrants of urban backgrounds? Informants who had lived in metropolitan areas expressed dismay at how people "change" in the United States too, but they couched their complaints in terms of "competition" and "jealousy," not in the language Don José employs. Juanita's discussion of her uncle's behavior offers a sample. "Here it's competitive, completely competitive," she insisted. "I swear. . . . It's like people are happy when you have problems. I note all of this. I don't know if I'm the only one. I'm going to tell you one story from my own family. I bought myself a small car. I bought it for $350 and I walked to where it was. But I didn't have any papers and since I didn't have papers I called my uncle who has papers and insurance. I asked him to help me, I said, 'Uncle, I bought myself a car.' I called him by phone. 'Oh, good,' he said. 'Now you are going to have to find someone who can get insurance for you.' He didn't want to come and help me. So since I didn't have any way to insure the car I had to give it back."

The universality of my informants' dissatisfaction with their compatriots' demeanor in the United States leads me to conclude, in contrast to Don José, that class background, and even the commodification of social relations resulting from these individuals' greater incorporation into modernity, are insufficient to explain the suspension of home country social rules among them. Both urban and peasant immigrants were innocent of neither the globalization of capitalism nor their dependency on wage income. To a greater or lesser extent, they had been integrated into the world system prior to migration and this had not completely undermined so-called precapitalist social relations based on kinship and mutual trust. Rather, the critical difference to their experience in the United States that so radically affects the quality of their relationships is their mandate to produce a surplus above and beyond that needed to provide for their own needs. It is their transnational obligations that strain their alacrity to engage in mutual assistance with compatriots as they did at home. As I have illustrated above, newly arrived immigrants are burdened with debt and remittance responsibilities which require that they generate more income than that required to meet their own needs. As I shall document later on, they frequently must wring this surplus out of their own deprivation, forgoing everything but an ascetic existence. The fact that most immigrants retain ties to family and friends in their homelands signifies that they are beholden to social networks in two very different countries. Whereas in their premigratory lives, their social networks comprised local and regional ties, now they are stretched to fulfill transnational obligations as well, creating two competing sets of relationships.

Jesús's predicament illustrates this span. About two years after he arrived, Jesús received a letter from his compadre, René Maldonaldo, asking him to finance his own journey. Jesús borrowed money from several friends to send to René. He began the process of repaying the loans while he was working the busy summer season as a landscaper. In September, Jesús's wife called. It was an emergency; his daughter had fallen from a tree and hit her head. She urgently needed medical treatment and there was no money. Could he send some immediately? Jesús was able to assemble the funds only by suspending payment on his debts and hurriedly borrowing more money from other friends. When the end of the landscaping season came, Jesús still owed money to many of his creditors. They became irritated with him because, also unemployed, they needed the money for daily expenses. With no income of his own (undocumented workers do not qualify for unemployment insurance), Jesús could not repay them and his friendships soured as a consequence. The next time he needed to borrow money he encountered few sympathetic ears.

Because immigrants are asked to provide mutual assistance to disparate groups of people in different countries, they may not engage in reciprocal relations in the same way that they did in their homelands. More precisely, while people are called upon and do assist one another quite frequently, they are not always in a position to do so because of demands from home. There is a trade-off; they are simultaneously pulled into and away from relationships with fellow migrants. Other poor communities do not experience this divided attention; they are freer to focus on local relationships alone. This is amply evidenced within the social network literature on poor communities in Latin America (e.g., Lomnitz 1977; Roberts 1973; Brown 1977), in El Salvador (Nieves 1979), and in the United States (e.g., Stack 1974; Horowitz 1983). These authors illustrate how people, women in particular, develop and maintain reciprocal bonds, knitting nuclear and extended families together into networks that exchange many items needed for survival. Items exchanged vary from tangible resources such as money and physical amenities like televisions and clothing to less tangible resources such as child care, emotional support, and information about jobs. The circular exchange of such items functions to distribute wealth quite evenly within the cluster of participating households. Families who acquire resources that they do not wish to share are ostracized by the others. If they choose to withhold distribution of this extra income, they must cut off their networks and they may move out of the community at large. In her research among poor, rural-to-urban migrants in Mexico City, Lomnitz (1977) found that the Latin custom of *compadrazgo,* or fictive kinship, transcended its traditional religious use to include members of these social networks. Normally, compadrazgo links couples through the baptism of their children. A

couple chooses another couple to be godparents to their child, and the two couples now are linked as compadres as in the relation between Jesús and René. In Lomnitz's community, "compadre" became a term used among males linked by the networks and not limited to godparent ties. Women could also choose close friends to be "comadres." In this manner compadrazgo was adapted by the migrants to their new urban environments and the exigencies placed on individuals and social groups.

People Do Help Each Other

Compadrazgo has not been extended to friendships and networks among my informants on Long Island. That is, I did not hear friends using the terms "compadre" or "comadre" in casual bantering. I was told that where it is practiced, it has preserved its religious, baptismal function. This does not mean, however, that mutual assistance is nonexistent among these migrants. On the contrary, people help each other frequently. Cooperation *does* occur within households although it does not necessarily involve income sharing or continuous exchange networks. While informants may feel disillusioned with people who do not participate, there is little of the ostracism that Lomnitz observed in her community (1977). Rather, there is an understanding that those who can participate will, and those who do not participate either cannot or are not close associates. For example, within all the housing arrangements, cooking is almost invariably performed by individuals or in small groups of friends or kin. These same groupings buy food together and store it in their rooms or in designated areas of the kitchen. Many individuals write their names with Magic Markers on items stored in collective areas such as the refrigerator and cabinets. These are formal separations of goods. Informally, food is often exchanged among individuals who are not part of the cooking group. For instance, one group may finish cooking and sit down to eat while the next group prepares its food. Ultimately the second group may share some of its food with the first, or the first may leave food for the second. This tends to occur more frequently on Sundays when there is more time to cook and relax. Single men eat out much of the week and cook only on Sundays, when they will often prepare a favorite dish to be shared by everyone. This informal food sharing helps strengthen and solidify social ties to nonrelatives. Some groups, however, never share anything and are most likely to separate. I have noted this most often in households where groups of different nationalities coreside or where there are personality conflicts.

Assistance among coethnics is not limited to people from the same household. Margarita Flores, a Salvadoran mother in her early thirties, for instance, helped out a friend who was injured on the job and could not work for several months. The two met in the United States at a previous job and had been friends for some time before the accident. Margarita's friend later told me that she was able to make ends meet during her recuperation only because her women friends paid her rent and expenses. She considered their help to be a loan, though she did not know if she could repay them even when her disability lawsuit was settled. Margarita, who had been trained as a schoolteacher in El Salvador, also assisted a boarder in her apartment who is illiterate in Spanish. She helped him write letters to his wife and joked to me about her labors, saying, "I guess I had better start charging him for all the time it takes!"

Assistance also flows among neighboring households. When Amalia Sandoval gave birth to a son with heart trouble, her friends who live in the same building donated baby clothes and brought her food. Since she could no longer work at her hotel job, she began to sew clothes for a living. The friends not only ordered clothes from her but also helped to widen her clientele. In another example, Ana Fernández and her common-law husband Jorge Ayala share their telephone with the residents of the apartment next door. Ana and Jorge are a teenage Salvadoran couple with two small children who share their cramped quarters with Jorge's brother and uncle. But the apartment next door holds ten single men who often drop by Ana's house to converse, to use the phone, and so on. Cooperation even exists among people who deny that it does. For instance, as we have seen, Juanita was angry with her uncle when he failed to help her get insurance for her car; she held him up as an example of the competitive lifestyle that so dismayed her in the United States. Yet the same uncle had loaned her the money to come to the United States. He had also taught her how to put advertisements in the *Pennysaver* (a local free paper) to get housecleaning jobs. He made Juanita's transition to life in the United States quite smooth.

While there is ample evidence of mutual assistance among my informants, they feel that this help does not approach the degree of mutual support that they enjoyed in their home countries. There is a good reason for this disparity: at home differences in resources among interconnected households were leveled through continual exchange that strengthened social bonds. That is, the price paid for long-term reciprocity and its insurance against individual disaster was homogeneous social status. Immigrants cannot afford this price. If they followed the rules of balanced or generalized reciprocity as ordained in their home countries, their principal goal of producing a surplus would be defeated; the surplus they produced would have to be redistributed throughout their kinship networks.

As Lomnitz, Stack, and others skillfully illustrate, the centripetal force generated by exchange networks pulls people inward and impedes their escape. Individuals who attempt to extricate themselves from the network are ostracized, particularly if they try to hold onto wealth rather than redistribute it. Migrants undergo two forces simultaneously: centripetal obligations toward relations in the host country and centrifugal obligations toward those in the home country. Since migrants share the compulsion to produce surplus income, they understand that they are unlikely to be completely severed from their friends in the United States if they send home remittances instead of circulating this wealth through their networks here. But the price they pay is that there will not always be someone to help them in times of need. Thus, shortly after arriving in the United States, many people were disappointed by their relatives' behavior. The kind of hospitality and common courtesy they expected was suspended here; they saw people less as a community to rely on than as individuals to compete against for success in the immigrant game. These early experiences served as a solid introduction to the realities they would face daily.

Capitalizing on Greenhorns

There is one more early lesson that immigrants learn as they revise their idealized notions of life in the United States. They learn that their "friends" are capable not only of turning a cold shoulder to them, but also of using them to their own advantage. Many individuals told me that they came to the United States prepared to be exploited by Americans and they often were, but they did not come prepared to be taken advantage of by their own coethnic peers. They told me stories in which they figured as naive newcomers who fell easy prey to older migrants with greater expertise. Typically, this fall from innocence occurred during a time of particular vulnerability: the pursuit of the first job. (Li [1977] has documented this phenomenon among Chinese in Chicago, and Grasmuck

and Pessar [1991:185] among Dominicans in New York.) Jaime's example is a good case in point. A baseball jacket manufacturer from Lima, Peru, he arrived on Long Island in 1988 to a royal welcome. His sponsor, a Peruvian immigrant from his Lima barrio, took him in, gave him food, and provided a room for him. The next day, however, the tides turned. Jaime was put to work in his sponsor's construction business laboring fourteen hours per day, six days per week. For his efforts, he was paid $250 but docked $50 each week for the lunches that the sponsor's wife packed for him daily. In addition, he had to pay the sponsor back $200 per month in rent. Jaime remembers these first six months bitterly: "I had to separate me from myself. If I hadn't I would have cried. I had to leave behind my personality—like taking my clothes off and putting new ones on." Jaime says that he was willing to work hard, but not to be exploited, not to lose his dignity. In one short week he descended from boss to laborer, from man to mouse. As soon as he found another opportunity, he left his sponsor and now exclaims proudly, "*Yo bailo con mi propio pañuelo*" (I'm dancing to my own tune now). Determined never to be so humiliated again, particularly at the hands of a compatriot, Jaime in three short years has found a steady, union job working in a nursing home and serves as a manager for an office-cleaning firm at night. He even employs some of his own relatives now. He recently bought a house in Gold Coast and has sublet it to many fellow Peruvians, turning a profit by charging them more in rent than he pays for the mortgage.

Marco, a Peruvian sociologist, found his first job in construction. He was hired by a fellow Peruvian who held contracts in New York City. But after several weeks on the job, Marco had not been paid; when he complained to his boss, he was summarily dismissed. Roberto had a similar experience. A Salvadoran peasant and volunteer church worker, Roberto is in his twenties but has a boyish face that exudes innocence. The first job he found was painting houses and doing odd jobs for fourteen hours per day. His boss, a Salvadoran acquaintance of the man who had sponsored Roberto's emigration, refused to pay him after two weeks. Aware that he was being taken advantage of and feeling the pressure to repay his debts, Roberto quit and started a job landscaping. He has kept that job, with no raise, ever since.

First job experiences of many informants mirror the kind of frustration Jaime expresses above. Jaime's and Marco's anguish was exacerbated by their drop in status from owner and organizer to worker. Marco's treatment put him inside a world that he had previously observed as an outsider. An academic and union organizer in his native Peru, Marco only truly experienced blue-collar life once he became a worker in the United States. "I just recently began to understand why it was that workers in my country found it difficult to go to a meeting, a conference. or to read a book," he confessed one day. "Now, somehow I understand their reasons. Why? Because when you do physical work, especially when it's heavy, the person who is not used to this gets tired. He's not going to be ready to study. Being tired makes you go to bed; it's the tiredness. You don't feel pushed to study, especially complex things. I feel this. This is one of my biggest worries—that I am losing my willingness to study, the will to analyze. I am losing my desire to write. . . . When I am doing these jobs I feel strange. It's not that the things are difficult, they are just strange. They aren't undignified." Few Salvadorans feel this same drop in status; most were peasants or workers in their home country who assumed blue-collar jobs such as landscaping and factory work in the United States. But they too feel exploited and disillusioned. What piques their resentment is their exploitation at the hands of peers.

In the rigid class hierarchies of their homelands, migrants were accustomed to patron-client relationships, to being taken advantage of by people of superior class status. Thus, when they arrive in the United States, they accord Americans a similar class deference. When Americans exploit them, they recognize it but do not resent it with the same vehemence as when their compatriot equals take advantage of them. Immigrants are angered when they are exploited by gringos, but they are *embittered* when their own people exploit them. This gives them a strong resolve to learn the ropes as quickly as possible so that they will never be made to feel so vulnerable and humiliated again. "The people who come here change," Sonia insisted. "Before they come here they're naive, fools as we say, but they change once they come to this country. When they come here they become big shots, as if they were children of the wealthy and, maybe, they're really the children of poor folk."

When the innocence of neophyte immigrants is exploited by more experienced coethnics, the newcomers are introduced to the opportunity structure they will face and learn to use to their own ends. They learn that in the land of marvels the pathways to success are fewer than they anticipated; they learn the hard way that one of the best avenues available is utilizing resources within their own community to their advantage. Capitalizing on greenhorns is, quite literally, generating capital by paying them less than the value of their labors. There are many forms of expropriating wealth from within the immigrant community. But immigrants' critical and disillusioning initiation into the dog-eat-dog world they vividly describe occurs too early for them to comprehend why their friends and family behave so differently here.

References

Brown, Susan E. 1977. "Household Composition and Variation in a Rural Dominican Village." *Journal of Comparative Family Studies* 8 (2): 257–67.

Grasmuck, Sherri, and Patricia Pessar. 1991. *Between Two Islands: Dominican International Migration.* Berkeley and Los Angeles: University of California Press.

Horowitz, Ruth. 1983. *Honor and the American Dream: Culture and Identity in a Chicano Community.* New Brunswick, NJ: Rutgers University Press.

Li, Peter. 1977. "Occupational Achievement and Kinship Assistance among Chinese Immigrants in Chicago." *Sociological Quarterly* 18:478–89.

Lomnitz, Larissa Adler. 1977. *Networks and Marginality: Life in a Mexican Shantytown.* New York: Academic Press.

Nieves, Isabel. 1979. "Household Arrangements and Multiple Jobs in San Salvador." *Signs* 5 (1): 134–42.

Roberts, Bryan R. 1973. *Organizing Strangers: Poor Families in Guatemala City.* Austin: University of Texas Press.

Stack, Carol B. 1974. *All Our Kin: Strategies for Survival in a Black Community.* New York: Harper & Row.

Mahler:

1. Discuss why immigrants stay in the United States as long as they do when their goal is to make enough money for a nest egg and return to their country of origin. Discuss the additional constraints that immigrants have with their already meager salaries that they earn in the United States.

2. Discuss the conflicting forces that impede or generate exchange networks.

Barrios in Transition

Joan Moore and James Diego Vigil

Los Angeles has long been the Chicano "capital" of the United States, housing more people of Mexican descent than most cities in Mexico. Many of Los Angeles' Chicanos are poor, and virtually all of Los Angeles' increase in poverty between 1969 and 1985 was because poor Latinos increased by more than half a million (Ong 1988). Los Angeles, then, is a good place to see how well arguments that are derived from experiences with other minorities and economic structures in other parts of the country actually help explain Chicano poverty.

This chapter will focus on change in four separate Chicano barrios in Los Angeles County.[1] Reflecting their origins in labor camps as well as immigrant enclaves, they range along a continuum from central city to rural (see Figure 27.1). Only by looking at this range of settlements can we understand the complexity of Chicano poverty in the Los Angeles area. These are not the most poverty-stricken barrios: in 1980 only 5 percent of Los Angeles' Chicanos lived in communities with more than 40 percent poor (Ong 1988). But these four neighborhoods are poor: poverty levels in 1980 ranged from 20 to 35 percent of each barrio's population. Briefly, this is what they look like:

The barrio that is nearest to downtown, White Fence, is one of the westernmost neighborhoods inside the long-standing Chicano concentrations that is called East Los Angeles (see Romo 1983). In the 1920s and 1930s, the barrio's first Mexican residents came to work in brickyards, packinghouses, and railroads, building small houses in the ravines of what was then an affluent Anglo neighborhood. The barrio had a strong local identity centered on its church. By the 1970s Mexican Americans dominated the community, and it was among the poorest in the county. Today the barrio is still full of the empty lots and the dirt footpaths that mark the neglected areas of the city.

The second, Hoyo Maravilla, is also in East Los Angeles, east of White Fence, just outside the Los Angeles city limits. Settled by Mexicans in the 1920s and 1930s, it is ecologically isolated, in a "hole," or arroyo. Its early Mexican residents built shacklike homes that were periodically inundated when the "dry" riverbed flooded. By contrast with White Fence, El Hoyo Maravilla was semirural. Many of its residents worked in nearby Japanese-owned market or truck gardens. By the

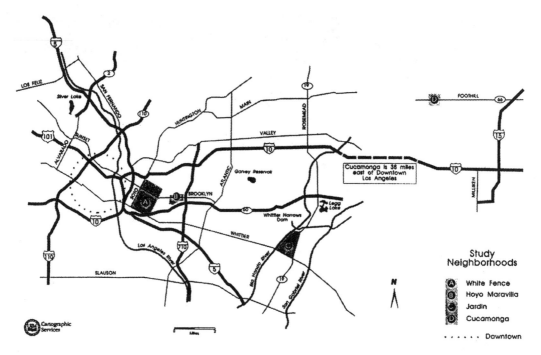

Figure 27.1. East Los Angeles, California, Area

1970s the residents of El Hoyo Maravilla were fully integrated into the urban labor market, though still among the poorest communities in the County.

The third, Jardin, is now surrounded by suburban housing in the city of Pico Rivera. For many Chicanos in East Los Angeles in the early days, Pico Rivera was "suburbia," the American Dream. Jardin started out as a low-income, Anglo housing tract in periodically flooded terrain near the Rio Hondo river, about 6 miles from downtown Los Angeles. Mexicans began to move in during the 1940s, working in the local citrus and avocado orchards, and by the 1960s it was a mixed Mexican and white working-class area. The socially mobile Chicanos living there worked hard at various agricultural and industrial jobs.

The fourth, Cucamonga, started out in the 1920s as an all-Mexican farm laborers' settlement in the middle of a vineyard, close to citrus groves just east of the Los Angeles County line on the western edge of San Bernardino County. As recently as the 1970s it was a desperately poor barrio of 2600, with dirt streets and no sewers, but surrounded by bright new middle-class housing tracts.

All four of these communities have been profoundly affected by ecological and economic changes that have altered the entire Los Angeles metropolitan area, and it is to those changes that we will now turn. First, we will flesh out our description of the barrios by discussing the population shifts in this portion of the Los Angeles metropolitan area that spreads east from downtown. Second, we will discuss the broad economic changes. There has, indeed, been economic restructuring recently, but it is not quite the same as in Rustbelt cities of the Middle West. Third, we will turn to what we see as some of the major institutional changes over the past twenty years.

Population Changes

Los Angeles grew enormously and almost continuously between 1930 and 1990, adding more than 6 million people for a total of nearly 9 million residents. From a rather small minority in 1930, Latinos[2] expanded to form almost 40 percent of the county's population by 1990.[3] Between 1980 and 1990 their numbers grew by an astonishing 70 percent, led by immigration from Mexico as well as from Central America, but also fueled by a high birth rate.

East Los Angeles, the most massive concentration of Mexican Americans, starts just east of downtown and continues for dozens of miles. The history of the White Fence, El Hoyo Maravilla, and Jardin barrios is part and parcel of the filling-in by Mexican Americans of the area east of the Los Angeles River. For example, in 1960 the general area that contains El Hoyo Maravilla was two-thirds Hispanic. By 1980 it was 94 percent Hispanic. And, further east, in 1960 the general area that includes Jardin was only 26 percent Hispanic, while by 1980 it was 76 percent Hispanic (Garcia 1985).

During the 1970s and 1980s, immigrants from Mexico settled heavily in and around Los Angeles' central city (Garcia 1985). The barrios that are immediately adjacent to downtown Los Angeles thus tend to be very poor, and home to large numbers of Mexican immigrants.[4] The neighborhoods are shabby, with people spilling out of overcrowded dwellings onto the streets. The stores and street vendors on nearby busy streets obviously cater almost exclusively to immigrants. The farther east one goes, in general, the less immigrant-dominated and the less poverty stricken the neighborhoods become, though there are still pockets of severe poverty.

White Fence and El Hoyo Maravilla, a little farther east of downtown, house larger proportions of U.S.-born Chicanos. Although recent immigrants were an increasingly significant fraction of these neighborhoods in the late 1980s, they did not dominate the scene, nor was there much overt extreme poverty. Housing in both neighborhoods was old,[5] small, and crowded, and in 1980 close to 20 percent of the homes had no heat whatsoever—a problem even in balmy Los Angeles. However, many of the homes had been up-graded by their owner-occupants. Many houses in both barrios had been recently restuccoed, and in White Fence new houses were built on the few remaining empty lots. (Close to 40 percent of the residents in these communities owned their homes in 1980). Real estate prices increased as they did in the rest of the county. Most new immigrants had jobs, and were managing reasonably well. Nearby arterial streets in White Fence, closer to downtown, catered somewhat more to recent immigrants than in El Hoyo Maravilla, farther east, but both neighborhoods were taking on a more mainstream appearance, surrounded by minimalls, chain grocery stores, and fast-food outlets. Some of the smaller mom-and-pop stores had vanished.

Nonetheless, in White Fence and El Hoyo Maravilla, there were signs that not all was well. As far back as 1980, both communities were still very poor, with more than a third of the population in poverty, compared with less than a fifth of the county as a whole.[6] Homeless men began to appear on the streets in the mid-1980s. They could be found sleeping in the park that nestles in El Hoyo Maravilla or even begging on the sidewalks of the busier streets. Many of them were older members of the barrio street gangs—former heroin users and former prisoners whose family members had died or had finally rejected them. Some were recent immigrants who had not found a niche for themselves. Jardin, still somewhat "suburban," was spared the more obvious manifestations of these problems, as was Cucamonga. Neither Jardin nor Cucamonga seemed to be deeply affected by the rapid changes that influenced the barrios closer to downtown.

If White Fence, El Hoyo Maravilla, and Jardin evolved as part of the Chicano filling-in of Los Angeles' East Side, Cucamonga, on the rural fringe of the metropolis, had quite a different history. In its early years, the Cucamonga barrio was a colony of agricultural laborers, working in the vineyards and orchards. The general area was the farming and truck-crop basket of Los Angeles. But by the mid-1970s it had become the new exurbia for Los Angeles and even for Orange County commuters. The changes in the Cucamonga barrio were thus dominated by the mobility patterns of middle-class whites. Land near the barrio was still available for new middle-income bedroom housing tracts, and the small agricultural workers' settlements were engulfed by the growth.

Immigration has always been a factor in the lives of all in these barrios, particularly those near downtown. But the massive surge in immigration during the 1980s was a major factor of change in all four barrios, and we will allude to it throughout this chapter. In Los Angeles in general, Latino immigrants are more likely to live next door to native-born members of their own group than are immigrants of any other ethnic group (White 1988). Mexican immigrants, in particular, tend to seek out Mexican American areas; many, of course, come to live with relatives.

The composition of the schools is yet another indication of the importance of continuing immigration. "Latinization" processes are at work throughout the Los Angeles area: by 1991 the city schools were 70 percent Latino. For example, Jefferson High School, in South Central Los Angeles, was once 90 percent black, and clearly recognized as African American; by 1991 it was 90 percent Latino. In 1974 most of the students in Garfield High School, the school that serves El Hoyo Maravilla youngsters, were third- and fourth-generation Chicanos, but by 1988 the student body was predominantly first and second generation. This generational transformation was also reflected in greater use of

and fluency in Spanish, and preference for "Mexican" as an ethnic identity label.

Economic Changes in Los Angeles County

Los Angeles has been the outstanding national example of a Sunbelt boom town, most recently symbolized by a spectacular rise in the cost of housing. For example, the median sales price of an existing single-family home leaped from $87,400 in 1980 to $201,034 in 1989—more than double the national average (*New York Times,* July 3, 1990; United Way 1988). Actually, Los Angeles has seen a series of economic booms. Each involved significant economic restructuring, and each involved a somewhat different mix of industries. Each had different implications for poor Chicano communities.

Before World War II, only a minority (18 percent in 1940) of Los Angeles' workers were employed in manufacturing. There was no strong, unionized, blue-collar tradition. Citrus, motion pictures, petroleum, and tourism dominated the economy. At the end of the war, Los Angeles experienced a major boom and industrial shift. Not only was there an increased demand for consumer goods, but the cold war and the Korean conflict extended the demand for the machines and weapons of war. The military industry—aerospace in particular—began to dominate manufacturing, supplying 36 percent of its employment in 1957 (California 1989). Much of the boom was based on a change from the simple production of airplanes to sophisticated aerospace, missile, and electronic technology. This involved a rapid shift from skilled to professional labor.[7] Thus by the late 1950s Los Angeles was already beginning a pattern that became familiar in the "post-industrial" 1980s—increasing proportions of professional and clerical workers and declining proportions of blue-collar workers (Meeker 1964, pp. 43–46).

At the same time, other sectors of manufacturing were also expanding. Though Chicanos and other minorities were largely excluded from the excellent high-tech jobs, they *were* being hired in more traditional manufacturing plants. Notably, in White Fence, El Hoyo Maravilla, and Jardin, these included the large-scale auto assembly, tire, auto parts, and steel factories that skirted East Los Angeles. All were unionized, "core sector" plants, with nationally recognizable names. In addition, secondary-sector enterprises, like the garment, shoe, and furniture factories, were important local employers. There were also vegetable packing and other food-processing plants, and—especially for White Fence—the slaughterhouses and cattle pens near downtown. East of the area, especially in Jardin, Mexicanos also continued to work in the citrus groves and market gardens, and some gained skills in construction industries—carpentry, masonry, and cement—that catered to 1950s and 1960s suburban housing needs.

The 1970s brought another wave of substantial economic restructuring. Combined with large-scale immigration, it had major consequences for East Los Angeles. There was a short recession following the Vietnam War. But then in the 1970s and 1980s Los Angeles experienced another boom in high-tech manufacturing and also—a new factor—a boom in the financial and managerial sectors associated with the city's emerging "Pacific Rim" orientation. This time, however, traditional core-sector manufacturing did not expand: it declined rapidly. The city saw "an almost Detroit-like decline of traditional, highly unionized heavy industry." Not surprisingly, very low-wage manufacturing and service jobs expanded (see Soja, Morales, and Wolff 1983, pp. 211ff).[8]

Effects of Economic Change on the Four Barrios

The changes in the mix of manufacturing jobs during the 1970s and 1980s had a major impact, especially on the communities we study. The heavily unionized industries that were located nearby all but vanished.[9] White Fence, El Hoyo, and Jardin are not far from the City of Commerce, which had been the home of several "good," traditional industries. Even in 1970 such firms were beginning to leave. By 1978 there were only 761 manufacturing firms in Commerce—a 25 percent drop from 1970 (TELACU 1978). Between 1978 and 1982 another 200 firms in and near East Los Angeles closed their doors, and with them went another 70,000 jobs (Kort 1990). Further, poor-paying, non-unionized jobs in manufacturing enterprises (like the garment shops) and in service industries (like restaurants and hotels) expanded dramatically. Ong calls this "low wage reindustrialization."

And in concert, the 1970s and 1980s saw a dramatic increase in immigration from Mexico and Central America to Los Angeles County (McCarthy and Valdez 1986; Muller and Espenshade 1986; Ong 1988). As always, the East Los Angeles communities like White Fence and El Hoyo Maravilla were home to many immigrants. In 1980, almost half of the residents of these communities were Mexican-born, and the proportion certainly increased during the 1980s. The most important economic effect of the large-scale new immigration was that it coincided with—and probably stoked—local economic restructuring to drastically constrict the job opportunities available to Chicanos in the area. New immigrants from Mexico and Central America could usually get work. Hispanics[10] filled virtually all of the new low-wage jobs created in manufacturing during the decade. The net effect was that by the end of the decade, the earnings of Hispanics in Los Angeles County had, on the average, declined rather substantially by comparison with Hispanics elsewhere in the nation (McCarthy and Valdez 1986, p. 44). If immigrants fail to find work, they have difficulty surviving; they are not eligible for public assistance. Many are undocumented, adding to what some authors call "perhaps the largest pool of cheap, manipulable, and easily dischargeable labor of any advanced capitalist city" (Soja, Morales, and Wolff 1983, p. 219). To put it crudely, Mexican immigrants were more likely to get jobs than were Chicanos in the same community.

Zeroing in on our particular neighborhoods, almost half of the White Fence and Hoyo Maravilla residents were still, in 1980, working in manufacturing, but these were less likely to be good jobs. White Fence is within easy commuting distance of the expanding downtown garment industry in Central Los Angeles, for example. Many of the garment factories are run as sweatshops. Conditions are not good, and workers—many of whom were immigrant women—continue to be badly exploited. Downtown also houses low-wage job opportunities in big new hotels and restaurants. In general, Los Angeles' Latinos "do not face the same spatial mismatch experienced in Black ghettos" (Ong 1989, p. 206), partly because so many Latino barrios are near downtown, and partly because, as Ong argues, the availability of cheap labor has attracted some new developments in their own barrios. In White Fence, El Hoyo Maravilla, and Jardin, the informal economy proliferated, as we discuss later.

The broader economic changes had a somewhat different effect in Cucamonga. The first generation had labored for low wages as regular/seasonal workers. Generally, low-skilled, low-paid occupations dominated these first years—grape and citrus picking, packing, and processing, work as railroad section hands or in road gangs. With the passage of time, education, relaxation of racist barriers, and familiarization with American opportunities permitted some of the second generation to secure employment in small industries, like the Frito-Lay (corn and potato chips) factory and a foundry producing auto tailpipes. Others moved up to find permanent semiskilled jobs (e.g., as janitors and cooks in schools and local busi-

nesses). However, when the housing tracts began to appear in the area, thriving grape, citrus, and railroad operations were curtailed or closed down; the foundry moved to Mexico. The largely untrained and ill-prepared population were left with few employment outlets. In addition, by the 1970s a large influx of undocumented immigrants, mostly male, appeared in the barrio and took what few vineyard and citrus jobs were available. With new housing and new people, new industries and plants also appeared. But the new industries (like so many contemporary enterprises) were concerned with service and electronics, requiring even more education and training. Thus macro-changes acted with job competition to hasten the marginalization of local Chicanos.

Institutional Changes

Thus far we have argued that the interaction of demographic and economic changes in Los Angeles had profound effects on the well-being of the poverty-level Chicanos living in these four barrios. In this section we will discuss other changes at the local level, beginning with shifts in commercial institutions and going on to shifts in other major institutions.

Commercial Institutions

In some communities throughout the nation, Latinos have been able to establish a strong economic base *within* the community itself: in Miami, for example, Cubans own and operate most of the enterprises that serve the Cuban community. This type of "enclave economy" has not developed in East Los Angeles. Instead, there is a kind of hybrid economic development. At the neighborhood level, many of the Chicano-owned mom-and-pop stores foundered, and were replaced by small businesses in new minimalls. Although local people tend to own most of the independent restaurants, bars, and drugstores, they work only as managers or lower-level employees in the small chain outlets that dominate the minimalls. At the same time, chain stores maintain an important hold on the grocery business in East Los Angeles, and one of the largest food chains in Southern California has found profit in a Mexican-style marketplace—the Tianguis supermarket located at the edge of East Los Angeles.

In White Fence and El Hoyo Maravilla, the informal economy burgeoned—particularly among immigrants following time-honored strategies for making a little money. Along the main streets bordering White Fence and El Hoyo Maravilla one could buy fresh fruit, hot corn on the cob, tamales, cigarettes, and cheap merchandise from unlicensed immigrant street vendors—estimated by one source at between 2000 and 3000 (*Los Angeles Times,* June 27, 1990). They worked under constant threat of fines and police confiscation. At most freeway ramps and many intersections vendors sold bags of fruit, and men tramped endless miles peddling ice cream along the streets of the barrios. At an estimated forty sites (Cornelius 1990), young men, mostly immigrants, clustered early every morning to sell their labor to anyone who passed by—gardeners, restaurant owners, construction contractors, homeowners. Less than a half mile from Jardin stands a construction materials yard that every morning had close to eighty immigrant workers for hire. In East Los Angeles many U.S.-born Chicanos were also working in the informal economy, usually for cash, but also for food, for services, or for furniture. Yard sales of used clothing and household goods were common. On the other side of town, in the more affluent sections of Los Angeles, Spanish phrase books to facilitate communication with one's maid or gardener were being sold in local drugstores, and immigrant labor was so plentiful that some jobs—like car washes—were being demechanized. It was cheaper, as well as more elegant, to have your car washed by hand.

Family

The intense concern about the rise in female-headed households as a result of family impoverishment seems somewhat irrelevant in the two inner-city barrios. Thus in White Fence and El Hoyo Maravilla, in 1980 close to 80 percent of the families with children under the age of 18 were headed by a married couple. That certainly is not grounds for complacency about the structure of the family, but neither is it grounds for the kind of deep concern that has been expressed about, for example, Puerto Rican families.

However, such aggregate figures conceal a good bit of internal variation. We would expect, for example, that the more Americanized Mexicans of second and third generations would show a different family structure from immigrants'. Heavy immigration means that there are still many traditional family networks, particularly of the extended family type. However, more and more Mexican American families are beginning to work out an egalitarian, dual leadership arrangement or are simply single-parent households. Finally, we would expect that some fraction of the poorest or most street-oriented families would in fact be disorganized (cf. Moore and Vigil 1987). In this regard, it may be somewhat surprising that in El Hoyo Maravilla and White Fence, even among those families that might be considered "problems" (in that their children were in gangs), almost two-thirds were headed by a married couple.[11] A more complete breakdown was possible for one segment of the Jardin barrio. Among sixty-nine families, the Mexican-born were the largest, with an average of 5.5 individuals, and the Mexican Americans were the smallest, with an average of 3.6 members. Somewhat surprisingly, the "cholos," street-oriented families, were mostly fe-male-centered and were also the largest, averaging 6.2 members. What this suggests is that immigration strongly colors, adding nuances and subtleties here and there, any analysis of Mexican family life and structure. With the addition of new immigrants to enliven and regenerate Mexican culture, the contrast in family styles and patterns is made even wider.

The Disappearance of Community-Based Organizations and the Growth of Political Representation

There were other changes, equally important, and easily overlooked by researchers who have not been familiar with these communities over time. All four of these neighborhoods were profoundly affected in the late 1960s and early 1970s by the flurry of institutional development in which the Chicano movement and the expanded "Great Society" interacted to produce a wide range of community-based organizations. One of the biggest institutional changes may have been that those programs were destroyed.

This statement requires some background. From a national perspective, the worst race riot in decades occurred in Watts, the black section of Los Angeles, in the summer of 1965. Existing institutions, along with the fledgling local offices of the War on Poverty, were slowly propelled into a series of confrontations with newly activated civil rights groups—Chicano as well as black. For example, with Chicano high school dropout rates about 40 percent in East Los Angeles schools and close to 80 percent in Cucamonga, education was long a concern among Mexican Americans, and was a prime target of change. Thus one of the first overt manifestations of the Chicano movement in Los Angeles was the dramatic staging in 1968 of a week and a half of protest-oriented "blowouts" from several schools (see Acuña 1981). The focus was on the high schools that serve

White Fence and [El] Hoyo Maravilla and surrounding barrios. Cucamonga had a similar blowout two years later, centering on elections to the Board of Education. The climax of the Chicano movement was the August 29, 1970, Chicano Moratorium march in East Los Angeles, which drew demonstrators from barrios throughout the region. The event ended in death and destruction: a crowd dispersed by police and tear gas reacted by looting and destroying stores in the commercial section of East Los Angeles.

Between 1965 and 1972 federal anti-poverty measures generated a "massive increase" in federal expenditures for social welfare (Katz 1986, p. 257). In East Los Angeles the effects were visible and important in every neighborhood. There were new community-based organizations bringing pressure not only on schools but on health and mental health-care institutions, on law enforcement, and even on the Immigration and Naturalization Service. Cucamonga, still a rural enclave, had only a multipurpose "contact" station to serve these main needs. In East Los Angeles, job training and job development programs proliferated. One (the Mexican-American Opportunity Foundation) was located right in the White Fence barrio. Teen Posts and Neighborhood Youth Corps programs began to spring up throughout the area, including an innovative out-of-school program for gang youngsters. Easily reached, culturally accessible agencies appeared in every barrio, meeting needs that had been so badly served by existing institutions that they led to the stereotype that Mexican Americans were a "hard-to-reach" population. They were *not* hard to reach: it was just that few had tried to reach them in ways that were culturally cued to community networks and habits.

Funding for even the most "radical" of the Model Cities agencies lasted through the early 1970s. Thus undocumented immigrants could get legal advice; heroin addicts, gang youth, and ex-offenders could turn to grass-roots agencies to help them reintegrate into conventional society. These agencies were generated by and supported by significant groups of "respectable" leaders within the community as well as by the newly mobilized ex-offenders (see Moore 1985 for an analysis of the fluctuation in attitudes toward street problems in East Los Angeles).

Gradually, however, the welfare state contracted again. By the late 1970s, new budget constraints combined with a series of intra-agency scandals to destroy most of the agencies dealing with street problems, leaving them to an enhanced police force. A few agencies became institutionalized—mainstreamed—offering greatly expanded mental health services, for example. Others became absorbed into existing institutions so that the visible, accessible grass-roots-staffed community-based agencies all but disappeared.

Meanwhile, beginning in the late 1970s, a growing political power had by 1991 put local Chicanos from East Los Angeles into both houses of the state legislature, into the City Council, into additional congressional seats, and, after a lengthy legal battle, into the County Board of Supervisors. But growing political representation did not compensate for the loss of community-based organizations. The welfare state had shriveled, and there was simply no money available for social programs, no matter how effective the new local politicians might be.[12]

Schools

The mainstream institutions have, in general, become somewhat more responsive over time. For example, we refer to the schools at several points during this chapter. Though leaders of the Chicano movement "blowouts" interviewed in 1988 saw little change in the schools since their protests in the 1960s (Woo 1988), it is clear that many school programs now exist that were unheard of in the earlier generation. Bilingual education has become entrenched, for example, despite problems in implementation because of a shortage of funding and of well-trained teachers, and reports of continuing resistance from older staff. Nonetheless, there are obvious problems for Chicanos in the system. White flight, combined with the increase in the Latino population, meant that the Los Angeles school system became predominantly Latino. The proportion increased from 19 percent in 1966 to 59 percent by 1988, particularly notable in the lower grades. Between 1969 and 1986 Latinos in elementary school increased by 134 percent, whereas students of other ethnicity declined by 57 percent. Performance on standardized test scores in reading and math were close to the statewide bottom for both 3rd and 12th graders in the system, and 56 percent of the Chicano students who entered the 10th grade in the fall of 1986 failed to register for 12th grade in the fall of 1988. The system had failed to attract Hispanic teachers: in 1988 only 11 percent of the teachers were Latino. Year-round schools were instituted in some overcrowded Latino areas of the system, with generally inferior results, especially for students with limited English proficiency (Castellanos et al. 1989). In an even more disturbing vein, in the early 1990s budget cutbacks in California eliminated English-language classes for immigrants who are under the amnesty program of the Immigration Reform and Control Act. From a high of $133 million in 1988 to a proposed level of $40 million for 1992, this shortfall virtually ensures that educational and employment mobility will be severely affected (*Los Angeles Times*, June 19, 1991, p. 1B).

Health and Mental Health

Similarly, by the late 1980s the nearby County Hospital was much better equipped than in the 1960s to deal with Spanish-speaking clientele, and East Los Angeles also had both a large new health clinic and a greatly expanded mental health facility. All of these new efforts were working: for example, one sensitive indicator of the health status of a population is the neonatal death rate, and in the health districts that include White Fence and El Hoyo Maravilla both the neonatal and the fetal death rates declined between 1981 and 1986.[13]

Health and mental health problems remained, of course. Many were associated with other changes in the communities. Thus immigrants were reportedly showing up with "Third World" diseases like tuberculosis and various dysentery-producing infections whose sources were unfamiliar to local physicians.[14] Local schools were overcrowded and had many transient pupils, and schools were losing control of immunization. As a consequence, there was a measles epidemic in 1990. Sexually transmitted diseases were a problem, with gonorrhea being especially troublesome. The incidence of AIDS had been quite low (in 1986 there were only 11 cases reported in the East Los Angeles Health District), but by 1991 an AIDS advocate reported that the County Hospital had close to 800 Latino patients, of whom nearly a third were immigrants. (AIDS had been detected as undocumented immigrants went through the amnesty processes.) As of 1991 the stigma surrounding AIDS was seriously inhibiting educational efforts, and local priests were opposing efforts aimed at AIDS prevention. Substance-abuse treatment programs were virtually unavailable.

Health-care advocates had been active since the 1960s and 1970s, and new ones appeared. But fiscal problems at every level of government reduced health and mental health services. Eleven County mental health clinics were closed, and El Centro Human Services Corporation, a mental health facility serving a large portion of East Los Angeles, had to curtail services for monolingual Spanish-speaking patients and to concentrate on crisis intervention, abandoning long-term approaches to therapy because of a $1 million county deficit. Despite significant accomplishments, then, both new problems and reduced funding were inhibiting health-care efforts.

Churches

One further institutional shift may be important. The Catholic churches in the area continued to attract members, and began to engage in significant social action efforts. UNO, the United Neighborhood Organization, was a social action effort organizing parishioners to press for changes in local conditions of life. The organization put pressure on a supermarket chain to improve the quality of its products and services, put pressure on insurance companies to combat high rates, put pressure on politicians for improved transportation and for elimination of a toxic waste dump, and put pressure on a corporate office park to provide new jobs.

The number of small, storefront, evangelical Protestant churches also increased dramatically, especially in El Hoyo Maravilla. Some, like the one discussed below, expanded so rapidly that they could embark on ambitious building programs. There is an extensive literature on how extended kinship networks function in poor Mexican and Chicano barrios, but the activities of these churches have been neglected. They serve important social service functions—for many very poor people, and particularly for immigrants.

In a typical instance, a Tijuana family moved to Los Angeles as members of an energetic small sect, which established its church in East Los Angeles in the early 1980s. Its members pooled their resources to build an impressive structure that looms over the freeway. The father was helped by the church to immigrate to Los Angeles. When he became seriously ill, he was joined by his family, and jobs were found for his wife and two oldest children. In time, his sisters and their families also immigrated to Los Angeles and jobs were found for their families. Of the eight family members over the age of 18, six were working. There were six children under the age of 16—all in school, and all doing well. The church is their American lifeline. They found their current two-bedroom apartment through their church. (The landlord is a fellow member.) The church helps them with food and furniture, and they supplement this help by energetic scavenging. The church helped them take advantage of the amnesty program, and by the end of the decade family members were all getting their permanent resident visas, borrowing money for the filing fee from church members. And the church helped the father of the family to get on Medi-Cal (the California version of Medicaid) when he got sick. The church is also their social lifeline. They go to church early every morning; when they have parties, it is church members rather than fellow workers or neighbors who attend; and they give quite a bit of money to the church.

Similar churches also serve significant functions for many street people in these communities. Victory Outreach, for example, is an affiliate of the Assemblies of God, which established missionary churches in various barrios of Los Angeles. Their purpose was to revitalize gang members and drug users through an evangelical process of being "born again" (see Vigil 1982).

What these pentecostal churches do *not* do is protect the immigrants from the kind of exploitation that the 18-year-old daughter in this family experiences in her job in an Asian-owned sweatshop. These churches may have provided some compensation for the vanished grass-roots community organizations of the 1970s, but the emphasis on social justice and direct action that characterized the Chicano movement is absent. In addition, community-based organizations provided a way for their workers to make their way up the organizational ladder—often into stable city jobs—and the pentecostal churches provide no such ladder.

Notes

1. We have been studying these communities for many years. The work in Jardin and Cucamonga was of long duration. Vigil worked in both barrios as a youth counselor, with intensive interaction with the youth of Jardin in 1966–1967. Later, in 1986, he returned to Jardin to compile household data for the U.S. Bureau of the Census. He began to study Cucamonga in the middle and late 1970s and utilized youth and adults from the community as field workers. Since 1974 Moore has been working in White Fence and El Hoyo Maravilla, focusing on several funding research projects in which she used a collaborative approach: former members of the quasi-institutionalized gangs in the two barrios were involved in all phases of the research (Moore 1977; Moore et al. 1978; Moore, 1991). Most of that research has concentrated on the barrio gangs, with a general interest in the community as well. Both Moore and Vigil have taken an eclectic approach, drawing on life histories, key informants, participant observation, surveys of community residents and of gang members (Moore et al. 1978; Moore 1991).

2. Wherever possible, we have reported data for Mexican-origin populations. However, in many cases it has not been possible to obtain national-origin data, and in such instances we have used "Latino" and "Hispanic" interchangeably to refer to the broader population group.

3. In the nineteenth century, of course, Mexican-origin people were the majority population of Los Angeles throughout most of the century.

4. In 1980, the majority (53 percent) of residents of the poorest predominantly Hispanic census tracts (poverty rates of 40 percent or more) were foreign-born (Ong 1989).

5. In 1980, in Los Angeles County as a whole only one-third of the housing was older than thirty years, but the majority of buildings—66 percent—in Boyle Heights (the community in which White Fence is located) and unincorporated East Los Angeles (the community in which El Hoyo Maravilla is located) were that old.

Forty-five percent of the County's dwelling units were owner-occupied in 1980: in the census tracts that formed the White Fence and Hoyo Maravilla barrios the proportions—37 percent and 40 percent, respectively—were comparable.

6. "Poverty" refers to the proportions living at or below 125 percent of the official poverty line. 1980 data were for Boyle Heights (in which the White Fence barrio is located) and unincorporated East Los Angeles (in which the Hoyo Maravilla barrio is located), and are obtained from special tabulations made by Los Angeles' United Way. We are grateful to the organization's research director, Marge Nichols, for her generosity with these data. Somewhat different figures were used by Ong (1988) to show that while the total poverty rate in Los Angeles increased from 11.0 percent in 1969 to 14.8 percent in 1985–1986, the Latin poverty rate increased from 16.6 percent to 25.3 percent.

7. Thus in 1955 three-quarters of the aerospace employees were production workers, but by 1961 only 54 percent were (Lane 1975, p. 21).

8. Thus between 1970 and 1980 low-wage manufacturing jobs accounted for 53 percent of the city's growth in employment. Moderate-wage jobs accounted for only 7 percent, and high-wage manufacturing for 11 percent (McCarthy and Valdez 1986, p. 40).

9. As Sassen notes (1988, p. 161), 75 percent of the workers in the most unionized industries lost their jobs between 1978 and 1988. These industries included auto production, rubber tires, auto glass, steel, and steel products. By contrast, some 80,000 jobs were created in the garment industry.

10. In the period discussed here, these jobs in Los Angeles were often filled by undocumented workers from Central America as well as Mexico.

11. This statement refers to a retrospective study of men and women who had been in youth gangs in El Hoyo Maravilla and White Fence during the 1970s. Sixty-four percent of this probability sample of gang members were living with both parents when they were in their early teens (Moore 1991).

12. California was particularly hard-hit because of the passage of Proposition 13, which severely limited the amount of revenues that could be raised through the property tax.

13. In the East Los Angeles Health District, which includes El Hoyo Maravilla, the neonatal death rate in 1981 was 8.3/1000 live births; by 1985 it was 7.9/1000 live births, and by 1986 it was 5.25/1000 live births. In the Northeast Heath District, which includes White Fence, the neonatal death rate in 1981 was 7.7/1000 live births; by 1985 it was 5.25/1000 live births, and by 1986 it was 4.20/1000 live births (County of Los Angeles 1982, 1986).

14. In 1985, the shigellosis rates for the East Los Angeles and Northeast Heath Districts were 60.06 and 39.8/100,000; in 1986 they were 32.4 and 35.0, respectively. In 1986, the salmonella rates for the districts were 18.3 and 26.5/100,000; in 1986 they were 28.8 and 34.1. In 1985, the tuberculosis rates for the two districts were 23.5 and 35.0/100,000, and in 1986 they were 16.2 and 32.5, respectively (County of Los Angeles 1986). Local informants reported in 1991 that there had been a recent alarming rise in tuberculosis, largely attributed to Asian immigration.

References

Acuña, Rodolfo 1981. *Occupied America*. New York: Harper and Row.

California, State of, Health and Welfare Agency, Employment Development Department 1989. *Annual Planning Information: Los Angeles-Long Beach Metropolitan Statistical Area* (Los Angeles County). Los Angeles: Employment Development Department.

Castellanos, Eulalio, Luz Echavarria, and Yvette Galindo 1989. "Educational Inequality." In Paul Ong, ed. *The Widening Divide: Income Inequality and Poverty in Los Angeles* (A Student Comprehensive Project), pp. 211–238. Los Angeles: UCLA Research Group on the Los Angeles Economy.

Cornelius, Wayne 1990. "From Sojourners to Settlers: The Changing Profile of Mexican Migration to the United States." La Jolla, CA: University of California, San Diego, Center for U.S.-Mexican Studies. Unpublished manuscript.

County of Los Angeles, Department of Health Services, Public Health Programs and Services, Data Collection and Analysis Division 1982. "Health District Profiles." East Los Angeles and Northeast Health Districts. Unpublished.

——— 1986. "Health District Profiles." East Los Angeles and Northeast Health Districts. Unpublished.

Garcia, Philip 1985. "Immigration Issues in Urban Ecology: The Case of Los Angeles." In Lionel Maldonado and Joan Moore, eds. *Urban Ethnicity in the United States,* pp. 73–100. Beverly Hills: Sage.

Katz, Michael B. 1986. *In the Shadow of the Poorhouse.* New York: Basic Books.

Kort, Michele 1990. "What Price Poverty?" *UCLA Magazine* 2:29–33.

Lane, Thomas 1975. "Report on Manufacturing Employment in the Los Angeles Region. Master's thesis, University of California-Los Angeles.

McCarthy, Kevin, and R. B. Valdez 1986. *Current and Future Effects of Mexican Immigration in California.* Santa Monica, CA: Rand Corporation.

Meeker, Marchia, with Joan R. Harris 1964. *Background for Planning.* Los Angeles: Welfare Planning Council.

Moore, Joan 1991. *Going Down to the Barrio: Homeboys and Homegirls in Change.* Philadelphia: Temple University Press.

Moore, Joan, and Diego Vigil 1987. "Chicano Gangs: Group Norms and Individual Factors Related to Adult Criminality." *Aztlan* 18:27–44.

Muller, Thomas, and Thomas J. Espenshade 1986. *The Fourth Wave.* Washington, DC: Urban Institute Press.

Ong, Paul 1988. "The Hispanization of L.A.'s Poor." UCLA, School of Planning, Photocopy.

Ong, Paul 1989. *The Widening Divide: Income Inequality and Poverty in Los Angeles* (A Student Comprehensive Project). Los Angeles: UCLA Research Group on the Los Angeles Economy.

Romo, Ricardo 1983. *East Los Angeles: History of a Barrio.* Austin, TX: University of Texas Press.

Sassen, Saskia 1988. *The Mobility of Labor and Capital: A Study in International Investment and Labor Flows.* Cambridge: Cambridge University Press.

Soja, Edward W., Rebecca Morales, and G. Wolff 1983. "Urban Restructuring: An Analysis of Social and Spatial Change in Los Angeles." *Economic Geography* 59:195–230.

TELACU 1978. "TELACU: A Framework for Greater East Los Angeles Community Union." Los Angeles: TELACU.

United Way, Planning and Resource Development Division 1988. *State of the County: Los Angeles 1987.* Los Angeles, CA: United Way, Inc.

Vigil, James Diego 1982. "Human Revitalization: The Six Tasks of Victory Outreach." *Drew Gateway* 52:49–59.

White, Michael J. 1988. "The Segregation and Residential Assimilation of Immigrants." Washington, DC: The Urban Institute.

Woo, Elaine 1988. "'60s 'Blowouts' Leaders of Latino School Protest See Little Change." *Los Angeles Times,* Part II, pp. 1–2, March 7.

Moore and Vigil:

1. What happened to the community-organized, grass roots organizations that were formed to help address the needs of Mexican Americans and immigrants?

2. What role do the churches play in assisting people to move into these barrio communities?

28

The First Suburban Chinatown:
The Remaking of Monterey Park, California

Timothy P. Fong

A New and Dynamic Community

On an early morning walk to Barnes Memorial Park, one can see dozens of elderly Chinese performing their daily movement exercises under the guidance of an experienced leader. Other seniors stroll around the perimeter of the park; still others sit on benches watching the activity around them or reading a Chinese-language newspaper.

By now children are making their way to school, their backpacks bulging with books. They talk to each other in both English and Chinese, but mostly English. Many are going to Ynez Elementary, the oldest school in town.

When a nearby coin laundry opens its doors for business, all three television sets are turned on: one is tuned to a Spanish novella, another to a cable channel's Chinese newscast, and the third to Bryant Gumbel and the *Today* show.

Up the street from the park a home with a small stone carved Buddha and several stone pagodas in the well-tended front yard is an attractive sight. The large tree that provides afternoon shade for the house has a yellow ribbon tied around its trunk, a symbol of support for American troops fighting in the Persian Gulf. On the porch an American flag is tied to a crudely constructed flagpole. Next to it, taped to the front door, Chinese characters read "Happiness" and "Long Life" to greet visitors.

These sights and sounds are of interest not because they represent the routine of life in an ethnic neighborhood but because they signal the transformation of an entire city. Monterey Park, California, a rapidly growing, rapidly changing community of 60,000 residents, is located just eight miles east of downtown Los Angeles. An influx of immigrants primarily from Taiwan, Hong Kong, and the People's Republic of China has made Monterey Park the only city in the continental United States the majority of whose residents are of Asian background. According to the 1990 census, Asians make up 56 percent of the city's population, followed by Hispanics with 31 percent, and whites with 12 percent.[1]

In the early 1980s Monterey Park was nationally recognized for its liberal attitude toward newcomers. In fact, on June 13, 1983,

---

Time magazine featured a photograph of the city council as representative of a successful suburban melting pot. The caption read, "Middle-class Monterey Park's multiethnic city council: two Hispanics, a Filipino, a Chinese, and, in the rear, an Anglo."[2] Another national public relations coup came in 1985 when the National Municipal League and the newspaper *USA Today* named Monterey Park an "All-America City" for its programs to welcome immigrants to the community.[3] Nicknamed "City with a Heart," it took great pride in being a diverse and harmonious community. But despite these accolades, there were signs that the melting pot was about to boil over.

Tensions had begun to simmer with the arrival in the late 1970s of Chinese immigrants, many of whom were affluent and well educated. New ethnic-oriented businesses sprang up to accommodate them: nearly all the business signs on Atlantic Boulevard, the city's main commercial thoroughfare, conspicuously displayed Chinese characters with only token English translations. In 1985, the same year Monterey Park received its "All-America" award, some three thousand residents signed a petition attempting to get an "Official English" initiative on the municipal ballot; a local newspaper printed an article accusing the Chinese of being bad drivers; and cars displayed bumper stickers asking, "Will the Last American to Leave Monterey Park Please Bring the Flag?"[4]

In April 1986 the two Latinos and the Chinese American on the city council were defeated in their bids for reelection. Voted into office were three white candidates, one a proponent of controlled growth, the other two closely identified with the official-English movement in Monterey Park and the state. In June the new council passed Resolution 9004, which, among other things, called for English to be the official language of the United States of America.[5] Though the resolution was purely symbolic and carried no legal weight, it was immediately branded as a deliberate

slap at the city's Chinese and Latino population. Undaunted, the council continued to take controversial actions that critics labeled "anti-Chinese," among them adopting a broad moratorium on new construction and firing the city planning commission that had approved many Chinese-financed developments. But it was rejection of the plans proposed by a Taiwanese group to build a senior housing project that prompted a rare display of public protest by the usually apolitical Chinese community. Four hundred people, mostly elderly Chinese, marched to City Hall carrying American flags and signs reading, "Stop Racism," "We Are Americans Too," and "End Monterey Park Apartheid."[6]

These high-profile controversies, lasting throughout the 1980s were not isolated or incidental cases of cultural conflict. Indeed, events in this community have received publicity in local, national, and even international media; recently, scholars too have become interested in Monterey Park, focusing primarily on ethnic politics and race relations.[7] Close study of the community is important for several reasons. To begin with, Monterey Park's Chinese residents reflect the changing pattern of Chinese immigration nationwide. Chinese newcomers to Monterey Park and elsewhere are not analogous to the historically persecuted and oppressed male laborers who came to this country in the mid-nineteenth century; they are men and women generally much better educated and more affluent than either their Chinese predecessors or their white counterparts.[8] Further, similar demographic and economic changes are occurring not just in Monterey Park but throughout southern California's San Gabriel Valley and Orange County, and in the northern California cities of San Francisco, Mountain View, and San Jose. Increasing Chinese influence is felt also in New York City's boroughs of Manhattan and Queens (particularly Flushing), in Houston, Texas, and Orlando, Florida. Outside the United States, recent examples of a rapid influx of Chinese people and capital are found in Sydney, Australia, and in Vancouver and Toronto, Canada.[9]

Next, because demographic change and economic development issues have created a complex controversy in Monterey Park, the intersection of ethnic, racial, and class conflict shows up quite clearly there. One prominent aspect of the social, economic, and political dynamics in Monterey Park is the popular call for controlled growth combined with a narrow nativist, anti-Chinese, anti-immigrant tone in debates that crossed ethnic lines throughout the community. And again, these developments too are relevant nationwide, occurring as they did at a time of increasing concern over immigration: over statistics showing that almost 90 percent of all legal immigrants coming to the United States since 1981 have been from non-European countries,[10] and over the numbers of undocumented immigrants crossing the southern U.S. borders. Documented and undocumented immigrants are rapidly changing the face of many urban centers.

Finally, the conflicts in Monterey Park took place in a period of increased anti-Asian sentiment and violence. Debate occasioned by the large trade deficit between the United States and Japan, suspicion raised by large Asian investments throughout the nation, and envy generated by repeated headlines about Asian superachievers in education all fueled the fires of resentment throughout the 1980s. The 1982 killing of Vincent Chin in Detroit, a widely cited act of anti-Asian violence, prompted a U.S. Commission on Civil Rights investigation.[11] The commission concluded that the upswing in animosity toward Asians reflected a perception that all Asian Americans, immigrants, and refugees are "foreigners" and as such are responsible for the economic woes of this country.[12]

This study of Monterey Park examines the evolution of conflict in the city and locates the beginnings of its recovery from internal strife and unwanted negative media atten-

tion. I argue that what was generally seen by the media and outsiders as a "racial" conflict was in fact a class conflict. At the same time, I demonstrate the highly charged saliency of ethnicity and race in the political arena and show how they were used to obscure class interests and to further political interests.

Effects of Chinese Immigration

As the influx of Chinese to Monterey Park began, most community leaders and residents compared the newcomers with the American-born Japanese *nisei* who had moved to the community twenty years earlier and quickly assimilated. Together they welcomed the Chinese as yet another group of hard-working people who would naturally be more than happy to settle into the established wholesome life of the community. But because these Chinese were new immigrants, expectations for their immediate assimilation proved unrealistic, and several areas of friction developed—involving business and social organizations, schools, and even supermarkets.

Divided Organizations

When it became obvious that no one could stop the influx of Chinese immigrants to the community, Eli Isenberg wrote a conciliatory column in December 1977 titled, "A Call for Open Arms," which was later translated into Chinese and republished in the [Monterey Park] *Progress:*

Twenty years ago, Monterey Park became a prestige community for Japanese. At first they settled in Monterey Hills. Today they live throughout and are active in the community. They were invited and accepted invitations to become involved. Today George Ige is our mayor, Keiji Higashi, a past president of chamber of commerce, is president-elect of Rotary. Fifty other Japanese men and women serve on advisory boards and in other leadership roles.

Today we must offer the same hand of friendship to our new Chinese neighbors. They should be invited to join service clubs, serve on advisory boards, become involved in little theater and PTA.... To become and stay a good community, there must be a structured effort to assimilate all those who want to become a part of Monterey Park. The city itself should coordinate this effort through the community relations commission and call on all organizations in Monterey Park to play their part in offering a hand of friendship to our new neighbors.[13]

Isenberg may have written partly in response to the formation of an independent Monterey Park Chinese Chamber of Commerce in September 1977—much to the chagrin of the original chamber. A great deal of animosity and criticism were leveled at this separate group for their reluctance to cooperate with established merchants. Shortly after Isenberg's column appeared, a series of meetings between the two groups resulted in the admission of the Chinese organization to the regular city Chamber of Commerce and the formation of a new Chinese American committee. "Helping keep the doors open was Fred Hsieh," recalls Isenberg. "Fred played an important role in maintaining an integrated Monterey Park Chamber of Commerce."[14]

After the proposed "Chinatown theme" was rejected in 1978, however, some dissatisfied Chinese business people resurrected the idea of a separate Chinese business organization and grumbled about other aspects of their chamber membership. For one thing, few of the Chinese businessmen spoke much English and could understand little of what was being said during meetings. Chinese merchants also resented having to seek chamber approval for business decisions; they wanted more autonomy. Furthermore, unlike Frederic Hsieh, most of the Chinese saw little to be gained by interacting with established merchants who, they felt, were antagonistic. Though they remained in the

chamber, the tension was not resolved, and flare-ups periodically occurred.

The Lions Club was even less successful at amalgamating with the newcomers. In the early 1980s an ad hoc group of Chinese asked Lions Club International to charter the Little Taipei Lions Club in Monterey Park. Given the historical prestige of the Lions Club in Monterey Park, its aging and dwindling membership was embarrassed by the formation of a separate club. Although they formally voted to sponsor the Chinese Lions organization in 1985, there was a great deal of reluctance. "The effort to recreate Little Taipei in Southern California," says Joseph Graves, was "unfortunate": "We would infinitely rather they had joined the existing, strong, long-time club with traditions." Graves spoke with pride of the original club's accomplishments, such as "screening all the children's eyes in Monterey Park.... [And] it looks like about 50 percent to 60 percent are Oriental."[15]

The projects of the Little Taipei Lions Club have been admirable, as well. Twice a year, during Chinese New Year's Day and on Thanksgiving, it sponsors a free lunch for senior citizens in Monterey Park's Langley Center, and it has raised considerable money for various non-profit organizations in the community—for example, making major donations to the city's public library to purchase Chinese-language books. But Graves objects that the Little Taipei Lions Club just gives out money rather than organizing work projects: "The Lions Club believed in the idea of going down and pouring cement to build a Memorial Bowl, or hammering nails to the roof of the pavilion at the park," he insists. "As older members, we look down our noses at any organization that doesn't get their hands dirty."[16]

In the mid-1980s the Monterey Park Kiwanis Club refused to sponsor a separate Chinese chapter, but one was formed anyway. To persistent rumors that a Chinese Rotary Club would soon be organized as well, long-time Rotary member Eli Isenberg responded in 1985: "Apartheid, whether in South Africa or in service clubs in Monterey Park, is a giant step back." In a tone quite different from that of his 1977 "Call for Open Arms," he continued: "Asians do not have a Constitutional right to form service clubs where they will be comfortable with members of their kind. All service clubs, from their international, should ban this happening. Provided, of course, that the Anglo clubs are willing to accept Asians as is the case in Monterey Park."[17]

Little Taipei Lions Club members interviewed during their Thanksgiving day luncheon in 1990, however, denied that they are separatist. While passing out plates of turkey and trimmings to senior citizens, many said they meant no disrespect toward the established Lions Club and had no intention of competing with it in service to the community. As a master of ceremonies in the background called out winning door prize numbers in both English and Chinese, one member asserted that there was plenty of room for both clubs. Another member found nothing surprising about preferring to be with people his own age who spoke his language: "What is wrong with a service club that happens to be sensitive and in touch with the Chinese community?" Angered by any perception that the Little Taipei Lions Club serves only the Chinese, he added: "Look around you. There are lots of different people here. We happily serve them [all]. . . . But we do things for the Chinese in this city that no one else would."[18]

Bilingual Education

The impact of the newcomers on the local schools also generated a great deal of tension. Brightwood Elementary School is located in the heart of one of the most heavily concentrated Asian sections in Monterey Park (census tract 4820.02), and surrounded by well maintained middle-class homes built in the

1950s. In early 1978 a Chinese bilingual education plan initiated at Brightwood School opened what the PTA president called "a bucket of worms."[19]

On January 21, 1974, the United States Supreme Court had ruled in the landmark *Lau v. Nichols* case that the San Francisco Unified School District had failed to provide necessary assistance to nearly 2,000 Chinese American students who did not speak English. The district was ordered to implement "appropriate relief," subject to approval by the court. This precedent-setting case established bilingual education in public schools for students who speak limited or no English.[20]

In 1976 the school district of which Brightwood was a part was cited by the Department of Health, Education and Welfare's Office of Civil Rights for having an inadequate English-as-a-second language (ESL) program. The department ruled that affirmative steps should be taken to correct the language deficiency of many minority children, in order to give them equal educational opportunity. The district complied the following year with a Spanish bilingual program in elementary and secondary schools and planned to phase in a Chinese bilingual program in 1978.

The proposal divided the Brightwood School—which was 70 percent Asian at the time—along English- and non-English-speaking lines. The plan called for all students from kindergarten to third grade to be taught in Chinese *and* English. Opposition to the program was led by American-born parents of Japanese and Chinese ancestry who were fearful that implementation would impede their children's educational progress in the future. Some threatened to take their children out of Brightwood and place them in private schools, or move them out of the district entirely. Supporters of the plan, mostly immigrant parents, welcomed bilingual education because they believed it would help their children maintain their native language and provide them with emotional and psychological support and the acceptance they needed within a new environment. A small third group of more moderate parents supported bilingual education but wanted the district to consider a "transitional" program that would instruct children in their native language but at the same time teach them enough English to allow their eventual transfer to a regular classroom.

During meetings to discuss the plan, the debate became intense. "Let them talk English," cried out one angry mother. "Why don't they leave the whole damn school as it is?"[21] Eventually, even supporters of the program asked the school board to delay implementation until the district could provide parents with more information and options. The delay was granted, and the bilingual program at Brightwood School did not start until early the following year. The result of months of meetings by the Brightwood Bilingual Committee turned out to be a much weaker variation of the original plan. Only one second grade class offered Chinese bilingual instruction; other Chinese students were taught English by "traveling teachers" at the parents' request.

Asian Markets

The prominence of Chinese-owned and -operated businesses in town became an even greater source of resentment. Non-Asians in Monterey Park commonly complain that Chinese merchants quickly replaced many established businesses and catered almost exclusively to an Asian and Chinese-speaking clientele. The best examples are food stores and eateries. Chinese have taken over all but two of the town's major chain supermarkets. Bok choy is more common than lettuce in produce departments, and dim sum and tea more readily available than a hamburger and coffee in the restaurants.

The first Asian grocery in Monterey Park was opened in 1978 by Wu Jin Shen, a former stockbroker from Taiwan. Wu's Diho Market proved to be an immediate success because the owner hired workers who spoke both Cantonese and Mandarin, and sold such popular items as preserved eggs and Taiwan's leading brand of cigarettes. Wu built the Diho Market into a chain of stores with 400 employees and $30 million in sales.[22] Likewise, the Hong Kong Supermarket and the Ai Hoa, started in Monterey Park, were so successful that today they operate satellite stores throughout the San Gabriel Valley.

In Monterey Park there are now half a dozen large Asian supermarkets and about a dozen medium-sized stores. Their proprietors also lease out small spaces to immigrant entrepreneurs who offer videos, newspapers, baked goods, tea, ginseng, and herbs. Together, these enterprises attract Chinese and other Asian residents in large numbers to shop for the kinds of groceries unavailable or overpriced in "American" chain stores: fifty-pound sacks of rice, "exotic" fruits and vegetables, pig parts (arranged in piles of ears, snouts, feet, tails, and innards, as well as buckets of fresh pork blood), live fish, black-skinned pigeon, and imported canned products used in Chinese, Vietnamese, Indonesian, Thai, Philippine, and Japanese menus. In these markets, Chinese is the dominant language of commerce, and much of the merchandise is unfamiliar to non-Asian shoppers.

Growth and Resentment

For many residents, the redevelopment and replacement of businesses in the Garvey-Garfield district, along Atlantic Boulevard, and throughout other areas in the city seemed sudden and dramatic. In January 1979, under the headline "Monterey Park Is Due for Big Facelift," the *Monterey Park Progress* reported that a northern portion of Atlantic Boulevard was set to "be transformed so it's unrecognizable." Construction there was to include the completion of a shopping center, office, and theater complex developed by the Kowin Development Company; groundbreaking for a new office building at the northeast corner of Atlantic and Newmark Avenue; and a hillside condominium project on the west side of Atlantic Boulevard. The article went on to state with great anticipation that "a large international concern" planned to "locate its international service center in Monterey Park," that substantial construction in anticipation of new tenants was to be done at McCaslin Industrial Park in the eastern section of town, and that several street and park improvement projects were in the works. In addition, a major city-sponsored Community Redevelopment Agency (CRA) project would erect a new civic center complex and make necessary improvements on a senior center, a school cafetorium, a community center, and the municipal library.[23]

Between the influx of new Chinese immigrants, the infusion of large amounts of capital, the rapid introduction of Chinese-owned and -operated businesses, and the disruptions caused by construction crews tearing up the city and starting new projects, rumblings of discontent among long-time established residents became quite audible.

"I Don't Feel at Home Anymore!"

At first the new Chinese-owned businesses seemed novel, innocuous, even humorous. "The gag was that if it wasn't a bank, it was going to be a real estate office, or another Chinese restaurant," says Lloyd de Llamas.[24] But as these and other Chinese businesses proliferated rapidly from 1978 on—taking over previously established merchants, displaying large Chinese-language signs, and seeming to cater only to a Chinese-speaking clientele—residents became increasingly hostile.

The famous Laura Scudder potato chip factory, converted into a Safeway store in the 1960s, became a bustling Chinese supermarket. Frederic Hsieh bought the Edwards Theater and began showing Chinese-language movies; when people complained he added such English-language films as *Gone with the Wind, Doctor Zhivago,* and *Ryan's Daughter* to the afternoon repertoire. Even the locally revered Garvey Hardware Store was sold to new Chinese owners who divided the premises into mini-shops, relegating the much-reduced hardware department to the back of the building. Kretz Motorcycle, Paris' Restaurant, and the Midtown Pharmacy were similarly redeveloped, engendering resentment among many residents, particularly older whites. For "old-timers" the loss of a familiar business could be akin to the loss of an old friend. "Just a few years before they sold Paris' Restaurant I walked in there for lunch alone," remembers Ed Rodman, "and . . . there wasn't a single person in there that I knew by name! That describes the changes in Monterey Park."[25]

Such losses were compounded when many long-time residents felt they were not welcomed by new businesses because they were not Chinese. Avanelle Fiebelkorn told the *Los Angeles Times:* "I go to the market and over 65 percent of the people there are Chinese. I feel like I'm in another country. I don't feel at home anymore." Emma Fry agreed: "I feel like a stranger in my own town. You can't talk to the newcomers because many of them don't speak English, and their experiences and viewpoints are so different. I don't feel like I belong anymore. I feel like I'm sort of intruding."[26]

Joseph Graves particularly remembers an incident that occurred in the late 1970s when he was a member of the Monterey Park Chamber of Commerce. A group of visiting dignitaries from Taiwan asked the chamber whether a statue of Confucius could be built in one of the parks to remind young Chinese to respect and honor his teachings. Graves had no objection but told them that "the people coming over here ought to be building Statues of Liberty all over town." Graves, who was born in Monterey Park the year the city was incorporated, continues to live there and says he harbors no resentment toward the Chinese. "I ride my bike everywhere and I see all these Chinese people out there taking their walks. They are so warm and friendly. How can you end up with anger? And yet, [if] I look at something they're doing that forces me to change, then I can be temporarily angry. I reserve the right to be temporarily angry as long as I don't nurse grievances."[27]

Others, however, *have* nursed grievances, and white flight has been the most obvious reaction to the changes in the community. While the Asian population in Monterey Park has grown and the Latino population has remained relatively stable, the white population has plummeted. In 1960 the 32,306 white residents made up 85 percent of the population; by 1990 the number of whites had dropped to 16,245, or just 12 percent. When former Monterey Park resident Frank Rizzo moved out, he cited the large condominium complexes on either side of his house and the people in them as reasons he could no longer stay. Prior to the influx of Chinese, Rizzo said, his neighborhood had been a quiet and friendly block of mostly single-family homes with expansive yards. But his new neighbors lived in large extended families in cramped quarters, spoke little English, and seemed unwilling to give up their traditions and settle into an American way of life. Rizzo, who sold his home to a Chinese developer, was emphatic about leaving Monterey Park: "What I might do is hang a little American flag on my truck and drive through town on my way out and wave good-bye to all my old friends. . . . I'm moving far away from here."[28]

Latinos in Monterey Park too were concerned that they were losing the integrated community they thought they'd moved into. David Barron has lived in the city since 1964 and raised his family there. Previously, he attended nearby East Los Angeles Community College and California State University, Los Angeles. He still remembers when Monterey Park was referred to as the "Mexican Beverly Hills." Fluent in Spanish and proud of his heritage, Barron thought he had found the ideal integrated community. He is still involved in many of the city's social and civic activities and has no immediate plans to move, but he misses the diversity he initially found in the town. "I would like to see a balance maintained," he explains. "I cannot live in a mono-ethnic community. I wouldn't want to live in an all-Hispanic . . . or all-Chinese . . . or all-white community. I want to live in a mixed community."[29]

Similar sentiments were expressed by Fernando Zabala, a hair stylist who grew up in East Los Angeles and also found Monterey Park a stepping-stone out of the barrio. "It was very important that my children grow up in a racially diverse community," Zabala said. "When we moved to Monterey Park, we had a little bit of everybody: whites, blacks, Latinos, and some Chinese and Japanese. But we lost that mix. In my neighborhood alone, it went from twenty-five Latino families to three."[30] Unlike Barron, Zabala sold his house and moved out.

One woman, who asked not to be identified, said that she was one of the first Mexican Americans to move into a new hillside housing tract in Monterey Park in the late 1950s and that she had worked very hard to integrate into the community. Like many whites, she expressed anxiety about the rapid change in the commercial areas in town: "It wasn't like one business changing at a time, it was like two or three at a time. When they put in the Diho [supermarket], that right away changed the appearance of Atlantic Boulevard." She recalled with particular sadness a Mexican restaurant she and her mother used to frequent. This small restaurant, greatly appreciated for its home-style cooking and family atmosphere, was forced to close when new owners bought the property. "The owner was very upset, and she put [up] a big sign. . . . 'I'm not leaving my friends because I want to, but the mall has been bought and my rent has been raised and I cannot afford it.' Things like that you would get upset about."[31]

Like the Latinos who had settled in Monterey Park, long-time Asian American residents had lived their entire lives believing in the "American Dream" that proclaimed just rewards for hard work and initiative. It was an affront to their sensibilities to see so many newcomers acquire the fruits of a material society seemingly without having to struggle. The newcomer Chinese were simply not playing by the rules of assimilation: they bought property, started businesses and banks, and built shopping malls as soon as they arrived—and many of them didn't even speak English! John Yee—whose great-great-grandfather had come to California during the gold rush, whose great-grandfather died building the transcontinental railroad, and whose grandfather and father owned a Chinese laundry business that served steel factory workers in Midland, Pennsylvania—is particularly articulate in this regard. "When I first came to L.A., I lived in Chinatown, went into the service, came out, worked in a lot of jobs, and step by step I moved to Monterey Park. It took how many years? Thirty, forty years? It seems like these immigrants ... want to live in Monterey Park as soon as they get off the boat. Not the boat, now they come by airplane. Give them another forty years, they'll be in Beverly Hills. I won't ever get to that point. . . . Maybe I'm jealous like everybody else."[32]

The resentment of the older Latinos and Asian Americans who had experienced racial segregation and witnessed the civil rights struggles of the 1960s also stemmed from a feeling that Monterey Park's new Chinese immigrants were taking for granted the equality won by the struggles of others. Yee says: "I don't mind the people too much, don't get me wrong; I am of Chinese descent. But the thing is, you get these people with this attitude. . . . they think [everything] was like this all the time. It wasn't. I hear people say, 'China got

strong and now the United States and the rest of the world has more respect for us.' Maybe so, but . . . if it wasn't for some of these guys [people of color born in the United States] who squawked about it, went into the service, these changes wouldn't happen. You got the blacks and Mexicans, they all helped change the government. . . . That attitude [among new Chinese immigrants] just burns me up."[33]

Particularly for Asian Americans born in the United States, the appearance of Chinese immigrants raised questions about their assumed assimilation and acceptance into American society. "When there were just Japanese people in Monterey Park, it was no problem because we were just like them [whites]," explains long-time resident Kei Higashi. "But now all of a sudden [with the arrival of the new immigrant Chinese] when we walk into a place and start talking perfect English, they [non-Asians] look at us like we're some foreign creature," he laughs. "That's what happened in Monterey Park."[34]

In the middle of all this are many of the Chinese immigrant professionals, who found themselves lumped together with the development- and business-oriented newcomers. Many express appreciation for the large Chinese population that makes them feel welcome, but at the same time, they say, had they wanted to live in a crowded, exclusively Chinese environment, they never would have left home. This is the case for Dr. Frances Wu, who moved to Monterey Park in 1971, after she was accepted in the doctoral program at the University of Southern California. Born and educated in China, Wu lived in Taiwan for four years following the Communist takeover; in 1953 she went to Canada to earn a master's degree from McGill University, then spent fifteen years in New York working in the Child Welfare Department.

When Wu came to southern California, she changed her social work specialty to gerontology, and shortly after earning her Ph.D. she started the Golden Age Village, a retirement center located in Monterey Park. Although the project is open to all elderly people who qualify, Wu told the *Monterey Park Progress*, "My motivation was to develop a social program for elderly Chinese and we selected Monterey Park because of its growing Chinese population," as well as its uncongested, small-town atmosphere.[35] The overall design of the Golden Age Village is obviously Asian, with its curved roofs and a courtyard that features a babbling brook surrounded by a decorative Oriental-style garden. The majority of residents are retired Chinese, many of whom speak little or no English, and the communal food garden grows bok choy and Chinese parsley among other vegetables. But the serene environment that Wu found in Monterey Park and recreated at the Golden Age Village is threatened by what she considers too much growth too fast. "I would rather keep this community a bedroom community," she says. "For retired people, we like a quiet environment. . . . People describe Monterey Park as 'Little Taipei,' but Taipei is horrible. I don't want Monterey Park to be like that."[36]

Notes

1. U.S. Bureau of the Census, "Monterey Park, City, California," 1990 Census of Population and Housing Summary Tape File 1, May 13, 1991.

2. Kurt Anderson, "The New Ellis Island: Immigrants from All Over Change the Beat, Bop, and Character of Los Angeles," *Time*, June 13, 1983, p. 21.

3. Several newspapers have incorrectly cited this honor as the "All-American" award. According to the official entry form, the term is "All-America."

4. Mike Ward, "Language Rift in 'All-American City,'" *Los Angeles Times*, November 13, 1985; Gordon Dillow, "Why Many Drivers Tremble on the Streets of Monterey Park," *Los Angeles Herald*, July 8, 1985; "English Spoken Here, OK?" *Time*, August 25, 1985.

5. Monterey Park City Council *Minutes*, June 2, 1986.

6. Mike Ward, "Racism Charged over Monterey Park Vote," *Los Angeles Times*, July 15, 1986; Ray Babcock, "'Sanctuary' Resolution Stays," *Monterey Park Progress*, July 16, 1986; Evelyn Hsu, "Influx of Asians Stirs Up L.A. Area's 'Little Taipei,'" *San Francisco Chronicle*, August 1, 1986.

7. See José Calderon, "Latinos and Ethnic Conflict in Suburbia: The Case of Monterey Park," *Latino Studies Journal* 1 (May 1990): 23–32; John Horton, "The Politics of Ethnic Change: Grass-Roots Response to Economic and Demographic Restructuring in Monterey Park, California," *Urban Geography* 10 (1989): 578–92; Don Nakanishi, "The Next Swing Vote? Asian Pacific Americans and California Politics," in *Racial and Ethnic Politics in California*, ed. Bryan O. Jackson and Michael D. Preston (Berkeley: University of California, Institute of Governmental Studies, 1991), pp. 25–54; Mary Pardo, "Identity and Resistance: Latinas and Grass-Roots Activism in Two Los Angeles Communities" (Ph.D. diss., University of California, Los Angeles, 1990); Leland Saito, "Politics in a New Demographic Era: Asian Americans in Monterey Park, California" (Ph.D. diss., University of California, Los Angeles, 1992); Charles Choy Wong, "Monterey Park: A Community in Transition" in *Frontiers of Asian American Studies*, ed. Gail M. Nomura, Russel Endo, Stephen H. Sumida, and Russell Leong (Pullman: Washington State University Press, 1989), pp. 113–26; Charles Choy Wong, "Ethnicity, Work, and Community: The Case of Chinese in Los Angeles" (Ph.D. diss., University of California, Los Angeles, 1979).

8. U.S. Commission on Civil Rights, *The Economic Status of Americans of Asian Descent: An Exploratory Investigation*, Publication no. 95 (Washington, D.C.: Clearinghouse, 1988), p. 109.

9. See Marshall Kilduff, "A Move to Ease Racial Tensions in S.F. Neighborhood," *San Francisco Chronicle*, August 11, 1986; Tim Fong, "The Success Stereotype Haunts Asian-Americans," *Sacramento Bee*, July 4, 1987; David Reyes, "'Asiantown'

Plan Taking Shape in Westminster," *Los Angeles Times,* March 22, 1987; "Chinese Enclaves Abound in New York," *Asian Week,* October 3, 1986; Kevin P. Helliker, "Chinatown Sprouts in and near Houston with Texas Flavor," *Wall Street Journal,* February 18, 1983; "$50 Million 'Orlando Chinatown' Features Hotel-Retail Complex and 30 Restaurants," *AmeriAsian News,* March–April 1987; Russell Spurr, "Why Asians Are Going Down Under," *San Francisco Chronicle,* December 7, 1988; Howard Witt, "British Columbia's Anti-Asian Feelings Suddenly Surface," *Chicago Tribune,* February 5, 1989.

10. U.S. Immigration and Naturalization Service, *1989 Statistical Yearbook of the Immigration and Naturalization Service* (Washington, D.C.: Government Printing Office, 1990), p. xiv.

11. In June 1982 Vincent Chen, a Chinese American draftsman, was beaten to death by a Chrysler Motors supervisor and his stepson. One of the assailants was alleged to have yelled, "It's because of you motherfuckers we're out of work." The two men later confessed to the crime, were fined $3,780 each, and placed on three years' probation. Neither spent a day in jail. See Ronald Takaki, *Strangers from a Different Shore* (Boston, Little, Brown, 1989), p. 481.

12. U.S. Commission on Civil Rights, *Recent Activities against Citizens and Residents of Asian Descent:* Publication no. 88 (Washington, D.C.: Clearinghouse, 1986), p. 3.

13. Eli Isenberg, "A Call for Open Arms," *Monterey Park Progress,* December 7, 1977.

14. Interview with Eli Isenberg.

15. Interview with Joseph Graves.

16. Ibid.

17. Eli Isenberg, "It Seems to Me," *Monterey Park Progress,* February 27, 1985.

18. Fieldnotes from November 20, 1990.

19. Art Wong, "Bilingual Plan Opens Up 'Bucket of Worms,'" *Monterey Park Progress,* June 7, 1978.

20. L. Ling-chi Wang, "Lau v. Nichols: History of a Struggle for Equal and Quality Education," *Amerasia Journal* 2 (1974): 16–46.

21. Wong, "Bilingual Plan."

22. See Andrew Tanzer, "Little Taipei," *Forbes,* May 6, 1985, pp. 68–71; Mike Ward, "Cities Report Growth—and Some Losses—from Asian Business," *Los Angeles Times,* April 19, 1987; and Randye Hoder, "A Passion for Asian Foods," *Los Angeles Times,* June 5, 1991.

23. Malcolm Schwartz, "Monterey Park Is Due for Big Facelift in 1979," *Monterey Park Progress,* January 3, 1979.

24. Interview with Lloyd de Llamas by Tim Fong, for the Monterey Park Oral History Project, sponsored by the Monterey Park Historical Heritage Commission, March 29, April 13, and May 11, 1990.

25. Interview with Ed Rodman by Tim Fong, for the Monterey Park Oral History Project, sponsored by the Monterey Park Historical Heritage Commission, October 17 and 24, 1990.

26. Mark Arax, "Selling Out, Moving On," *Los Angeles Times,* April 12, 1987.

27. Interview with Joseph Graves.

28. Arax, "Selling Out, Moving On."

29. Interview with David Barron by Tim Fong, for the Monterey Park Oral History Project, sponsored by the Monterey Park Historical Heritage Commission, October 9, 1990.

30. Mark Arax, "Nation's 1st Suburban Chinatown," *Los Angeles Times,* April 6, 1987.

31. Fieldnotes from August 16, 1990.

32. Interview with John Yee by Tim Fong, for the Monterey Park Oral History Project, sponsored by the Monterey Park Historical Heritage Commission, May 31 and June 4, 1990.

33. Ibid.

34. Interview with Kei Higashi by Tim Fong, for the Monterey Park Oral History Project, sponsored by the Monterey Park Historical Heritage Commission, May 7 and 30, 1990.

35. "Second Housing Project for Seniors on Horizon," *Monterey Park Progress,* Sept 13, 1978.

36. Interview with Dr. Frances Wu by Tim Fong, for the Monterey Park Oral History Project, sponsored by the Monterey Park Historical Heritage Commission, June 22 and July 6, 1990.

References

Anderson, Kurt. "The New Ellis Island: Immigrants from All Over Change the Beat, Bop, and Character of Los Angeles." *Time,* June 13, 1983.

Calderon, José. "Latinos and Ethnic Conflict in Suburbia: The Case of Monterey Park." *Latino Studies Journal* 1 (May 1990): 23–32.

Horton, John. "The Politics of Ethnic Change: Grass-Roots Responses to Economic and Demographic Restructuring in Monterey Park, California." *Urban Geography* 10 (1989): 578–92.

Monterey Park, City of. City Council *Minutes,* June 2, 1986.

Nakanishi, Don. "The Next Swing Vote? Asian Pacific Americans and California Politics." In *Racial and Ethnic Politics in California,* ed. Bryan O. Jackson and Michael D. Preston, pp. 25–54. Berkeley: University of California, Institute of Governmental Studies, 1991.

Pardo, Mary. "Identity and Resistance: Latinas and Grass-Roots Activism in Two Los Angeles Communities." Ph.D. diss., University of California, Los Angeles, 1990.

Saito, Leland. "Politics in a New Demographic Era: Asian Americans in Monterey Park, California." Ph.D. diss., University of California, Los Angeles, 1992.

Takaki, Ronald. *Strangers from a Different Shore: A History of Asian Americans.* Boston: Little, Brown, 1989.

Tanzer, Andrew. "Little Taipei." *Forbes,* May 6, 1985.

U.S. Bureau of the Census. *Census of Population and Housing Summary Tape File 1* (STF1): Monterey Park, City, California, 1990.

U.S. Commission on Civil Rights. *The Economic Status of Americans of Asian Descent.* Publication no. 95. Washington, D.C.: Clearinghouse, 1988.

———. *Recent Activities against Citizens and Residents of Asian Descent.* Publication no. 88. Washington, D.C.: Clearinghouse, 1986.

U.S. Immigration and Naturalization Service. 1990. *1989 Statistical Yearbook of the Immigration and Naturalization Service.* Washington, D.C.: Government Printing Office.

Wang, L. Ling-chi. "Lau v. Nichols: History of a Struggle for Equal and Quality Education." *Amerasia Journal* 2 (1974): 16–46.

Wong, Charles Choy. "Ethnicity, Work, and Community: The Case of Chinese in Los Angeles." Ph.D. diss., University of California, Los Angeles, 1979.

———. "Monterey Park: A Community in Transition," In *Frontiers of Asian American Studies,* ed. Gail M. Nomura, Russell Endo, Stephen H. Sumida, and Russell Leong, pp. 113–26. Pullman: Washington State University Press, 1989.

Newspapers

AmerAsian News, March–April 1987.

Asian Week, October 3, 1986.

Chicago Tribune, February 5, 1989.

Los Angeles Herald, July 8, 1985.

Los Angeles Times, November 13, 1985–June 5, 1991.

Monterey Park Progress, December 7, 1977–July 16, 1986.

Sacramento Bee, July 4, 1987.

San Francisco Chronicle, August 11, 1986–December 7, 1988.

Wall Street Journal, February 18, 1983.

Fong:

1. What was ironic about Monterey Park, California, receiving the "All-America City" award from the National Municipal League and *USA Today*?

2. Discuss what Fong describes as ethnic tensions used to obscure class and political interests.

"Destroying a Marriage to Save a Family": Shifting Filipino American Gender Relations

Orlando P. Tizon

Given the high educational level of Filipino American women as a whole and their high labor participation compared to Whites and other Asian Americans, it would seem that they would enjoy more equal relations with the men.[1] This seems to be even more plausible because Filipino women, according to some researchers, enjoy more equal marital relations compared with women in other Asian countries, for three reasons. First, Filipinos' bilateral kinship structure provides support to the women from their male kin. Second, Filipino family hierarchies are based on age, not gender. Third, women control property acquired both before and after their marriage.[2]

Through participant observation and open-ended interviews with members of Philippians Church, a Filipino American Protestant congregation, I show how traditional views and practices concerning gender relations and family strongly influence immigrant women's lives. However, contrary to what one might expect, these influences do not result in more equal gender relations, even though women in the congregation are visibly active and have gained positions of leadership in its various organizations and activities. At the same time, these women are

challenging traditional Filipino family and gender relationships in this immigrant congregation. These changing gender relations are central to the ongoing construction of Filipino American ethnicity.

As a Filipino immigrant and as a sociologist, I became interested in how the ethnicity of my coethnics is changing in their new homeland. I was surprised to find that little sociological research had been done about this ethnic group, one of the early Asian groups in the United States and now one of the largest. During my research, an important discovery was that changing gender relations in the ethnic group were an important part of ethnicity being transformed. In this chapter, I describe women's activities in Philippians Church and explore the ways that women are changing gender ideologies and practices in the congregation.

Gender Relations in Traditional Philippine Society

Filipinos in both rural and urban areas hold socially defined gender relations, which children learn at an early age. By watching their parents and gradually helping the father or the mother with daily tasks, by socializing with peers, and by interacting with relatives, elders, and other people in the community, they learn to take responsibilities, enjoy privileges, and engage in activities recognized as proper to and expected of each gender. In rural areas, besides helping her mother with household chores such as cooking, washing clothes, taking care of siblings, and feeding the animals, a young girl helps with light farm work, such as harvesting and planting. A young boy helps his father with farm work, gradually assuming the heavier work of clearing and plowing the fields and hauling produce and other materials. The boy's passage to adolescence depends less on biological age than on his participation in community and economic activities, especially his contribution to the family pot.[3] The young girl, in contrast, is oriented toward the household and the needs of nurturing and feeding the family.

Essentially, the same gender relations operate in the urban areas, the only difference being that the period of adolescence and maturation is lengthened because of educational demands. *Binatilyos* (diminutive form of *binata*, "young man") are socialized early to participate in many community affairs, such as meetings and discussions concerned with various community projects. Adolescent boys spend time with their own *barkada* (gang) or join with the men of the community in drinking sessions and other "adult" male activities. Young men generally have more freedom, are allowed to stay out late, and are seldom checked on by parents, who tend to be tolerant of their misdemeanors. Jocano referred to a comment he frequently heard in a slum community when a mother worried about her son. The father would chide her saying: "Let him alone, he is a grown-up now. Moreover, there's nothing to lose—he is a boy. Let him grow up like a man."[4]

Things are different for the *dalagita* (diminutive form of *dalaga*, "young woman"), because she has a lot to lose, her virginity. Virginity is the primary criterion for the men to choose a wife; any young women whose morals are suspect are courted only for sexual adventures. After a girl's first mens, parents become apprehensive that she might get pregnant. When young people start showing interest in each other, parents try to restrict girls' movements so that they do not go around the neighborhood alone or freely, especially at night. Although parental and community pressure restrict young women, young men have wide leeway to indulge in sexual experimentation and adventures.

Jocano noted that many adolescents, both male and female, move about freely and socialize among themselves despite parental restrictions. Young people, in fact, may be using premarital sex as a form of rebellion against family control, and it may be a barometer of subtle changes going on in Philippine society.[5]

Marriage

Filipinos look at marriage traditionally as an alliance of families; this is the reason parents and kin have had so much control over their children's choice of marriage partners. The practice, however, is changing, especially in urban areas, although the tradition of marriage as an alliance of families remains in many parts of the country.[6]

Another important aspect of traditional Filipino marriage is its orientation toward children. Just as in many cultures, children of both genders are considered gifts from God, a source of joy to parents, siblings, and relatives. Children also represent security in old age, because they are expected to care for their parents in their old age, in gratitude for a debt that can never be repaid—their birth and the care that they received from their parents. They solidify a marriage and give a sense of continuity between generations. Furthermore, men consider children a proof of their virility.[7]

In marriage, the gendered division of responsibilities is also clear. As in many cultures, the traditional role of Filipino women is that of *maybahay*, or keeper of the house. The interior of the house and the kitchen are the woman's proper sphere, even if she works outside the home at a paid job. She is also in charge of the family cash as treasurer and budgeteer. Besides all these tasks, Philippine society expects wives to bear the main responsibility for keeping the families intact. Husbands are considered the breadwinners, responsible for the family's economic support as well as heads of the house and the authority figures for the entire family. Fathers are expected to discipline the children and to represent their families in the community. In traditional Philippine society, it is not proper for a woman to "control" her husband, especially by not allowing him time to go out with his friends and indulge in his pastime. To maintain her dignity as a woman, she must take care of her sphere of influence, namely, the duties involving domestic work, because the man and the community expect her to fulfill her "womanly" duties as *babae* (woman) and her role of wife and mother, the counterpart of the man's role of provider.[8] These gender divisions of responsibilities have resulted in also fixing each gender's sphere of influence and activities—the husband's to politics and the community and his world of friends and work, the wife's to the home, the household, and her children.

Women in rural areas in the Philippines always have done paid and unpaid labor outside the home. The unpaid labor that women in rural areas do is mainly taking care of small farm animals, such as chickens and pigs, and helping with the seasonal planting, weeding, and harvesting of crops such as rice, sweet potatoes, and sugar cane. They also may work for pay or for a share of the harvest when seasonal labor is in demand.

Especially in urban areas, as in many places worldwide, women are increasingly visible in the labor market.[9] They usually work in jobs that are "culturally compatible" with their gender, such as teaching, health care, office work, and sales.[10] Women mainly work for the income they earn, rather than for the satisfaction of a "career," and this is socially accepted even by men. Seldom is the reason for the wife's work professional development or self-satisfaction, even among middle-class and upper-class women. Women still feel as their responsibility the task of building the home and caring for the family, even when carrying the load of a full-time job. As elsewhere, women carry a double burden of housework and paid work.

The Double Standard

Traditional gender practices create a double standard of sexual morality that has worked to women's disadvantage and brought problems that have plagued Philippine marriages to this day. Marriage counselors and researchers consistently have mentioned men's marital infidelity as one of the main causes of marriage crises. Further complicating the situation is the inadequacy of the legal system.[11] Divorce is not allowed in the Philippines, except for Muslims. The laws allow the legal separation of husbands and wives only with great difficulty and without the right to remarry. Divorce is a political issue in the Philippines according to Vancio, who refers to the Catholic Church's power in a country in which 85 percent of the population are baptized Catholics. The only occasion for a marriage to be dissolved, thus allowing the former partners to remarry legally, is through its annulment by a court of the Catholic Church or a civil court, procedures that are very expensive and time-consuming.

The double sexual standard is institutionalized in the legal system. Until August 1988, the law defined criminal adultery differently for married people based on their gender. A single act of intercourse was enough to convict a woman of this crime, and circumstantial evidence was sufficient to do so. Her partner became liable only if he knew that she was married. On the other hand, a married man having sexual intercourse with a single woman had no criminal liability, as long as the act was consensual and done discreetly. He would be found guilty of concubinage only if the act was scandalous or resulted in cohabitation. Furthermore, adultery was punishable by imprisonment of two years and one day to six years, whereas concubinage was punishable by imprisonment of six months and a day to four years and two months. In effect, the legal distinction between adultery and concubinage in the old law allowed men to indulge in extramarital affairs but did not give the wife legal grounds to bring the husband to court.[12]

The double standard of sexual morality, coupled with existing gender practices and marriage laws, has become fertile ground for a unique institution called the *querida* system. *Querida* or *querido* is the Spanish word for beloved and connotes a "kept woman" or "mistress." In the Philippines, it refers to a situation involving a couple legally married or socially recognized as such and a third person. The involvement with the third person—almost always the husband with another woman single or married—takes on a semipermanent arrangement because there is some degree of emotional bond and financial commitment. This can range from occasional gifts to a house or a fully furnished apartment and regular allowances for the *querida* and her children. If there are children by the *querida,* the man has to give his paternity to them by law, as long as there is no reason for doubt. The *querida* system, therefore, is different from a passing affair.

The practice goes against the teaching of many Christian churches, and most Filipinos disapprove of it, yet it remains quite widespread across classes and regions.[13] The wives strongly condemn the practice because it lessens the man's emotional and financial support and weakens family ties, but most are resigned to their husbands' infidelities and

blame "the other woman" for "tempting" their husbands. *Queridas* typically are regarded as deviants, like prostitutes and sex entertainers. There is equal if not stronger condemnation for a wife who takes a *querido.* In contrast, even women tolerate men's sexual adventures as "natural" to men, who often regard illicit sex as an expression of their virility. Typical is this husband's response in an interview by Yu and Liu. "I am a man, I would be a *bayot* (a homosexual or hermaphrodite) if I refused the others."[14]

These traditional views and practices on marriage, family, and gender relations are changing because of the influence of urbanization and global culture. Still, they have a firm hold even when Filipinos immigrate to the United States because they are internalized by men and women and are propagated by the older generation.

Women in Philippians Church

Philippians is a Protestant congregation in Chicago founded more than 25 years ago by Filipino immigrants, with more than 200 members, 99 percent of whom are Filipinos or Filipino Americans. The members envisioned and organized the church as an extended Filipino family with its extensive kinship networks providing social and moral support for Filipino immigrants. The congregation is evenly divided between men and women, and more than half are 30 years old or younger. Most are immigrants, but there is a growing number of 1.5 and second and third generation youth who were either born or raised in the United States.

Women are active in the different aspects of congregational life. The assistant pastor is a woman, Reverend Ruth, who serves the church part-time. The governing body of the church is the Board of Directors elected every two years, together with the two pastors. Five of the 12 Board members are women who have the tasks of secretary, financial secretary, and treasurer. The women are most active in the worship and music committee and Christian education committee, and the men lead the insurance, building and maintenance, and legal matters committees.

Besides the committees, there are the different organizations according to age groups, as well as the Philippians Women's Club for the elderly ladies and middle-aged women and the Young Adults organization for the younger women and men. There is a difference of age and class and a difference in the distribution of church tasks between the Philippians Women's Club and the Philippians Young Adults. The Women's Club consists of women who are high school graduates or have one or two years of college and came here as adults. The Young Adults are college-educated professionals who came here as children or young teens. The Women's Club is responsible for maintaining the church kitchen and managing the Sunday fellowship meals. The Young Adults group, the majority of whom are women, are responsible for the Christian education projects of the church. They take charge of the Bible classes and manage the Christian education projects of the church throughout the year. I also observed that the women in the Young Adults group take turns baby-sitting the infants and young children during Sunday services. After the first part of the service before the sermon, they go down with the children to the children's room in the church basement.

An important work done by the elderly and middle-aged women, mainly of the Women's Club, is managing the weekly fellowship lunch, which is an important part of the Sunday celebration. After the Sunday service, members and visitors go down to the dining hall in the church basement where two long tables stand filled with steaming rice, three or four kinds of Filipino dishes, some dessert, and soda. Before saying grace, the pastor announces the birthdays or anniversaries of important events in the lives of the members, such as weddings or deaths. Although English is the language used during the church service, here the members, except the children and teens, speak in Filipino or in their regional languages. It is clear from the relaxed atmosphere and animated conversation that they can be themselves during the fellowship lunch.

The event is not a mere lunch; it is centered on the lunch and the food that they share, but it involves the other activities of bringing the congregation together by linking each others' lives and weaving a collective memory through the ritual. The whole event rests in the hands of the women in the congregation, who plan, contact people for the potluck, buy needed food and kitchen materials, cook, set up the dining hall, and clean up the hall after lunch. I realized how important this meal was to the congregation when they held their Sunday services in a rented church after they sold their church property, shortly after I finished my research. In their temporary location, they could not hold the fellowship lunch because there were no facilities in the building. So, after the service people would mill around outside the church, chatting before going home. Even I, who was not a church member, could sense that something was lacking in their Sunday celebration.

Women in Philippians also do "emotion work." Teens would go to other women in the church for help when their own parents were not available or they needed extra support. Jenny, for example, one of the teens, considered Tess, a woman in the congregation, her "second mom," to whom she could go if she needed help.

Hulugan is another form of work that women in the congregation undertake. It is a system of retailing goods popular especially among office and factory workers in the Philippines. Coworkers or peddlers sell small items such as clothes, jewelry, and even food on an installment basis and collect monthly payments. The system is based on mutual acquaintance and trust among workers or members of a group. Women are usually the ones active in the *hulugan* system. It is a steady source of extra income and is not taxed. Items that I saw women selling were jewelry and watches, phone cards, insurance, health products, and beauty products. Besides being a source of income, *hulugan* builds trust among members and strengthens the congregation because it is not based on any collateral as a security. It is based solely on the trust that members of the congregation have for each other. I asked one of the women, "What are the terms of paying for these items?" She said, "You pay a monthly installment until you pay for the full price."

One kind of invisible work that women do in the church is kin work. It refers to the planning and the different activities needed to maintain and strengthen kin ties across households, including visits, writing letters, sending cards, and making telephone calls.[15] In Philippians, kin work includes the ties to fictive kin and the entire church congregation. According to *Aling* (a Filipino term of respect) Catalina, Pastor Lee's wife, the women in the Women's Club monitor the birthdays, wedding anniversaries, and other special occasions in the lives of the members. They inform the congregation about these through the church bulletin and announcements during the Sunday service. If the family wishes to celebrate the event with the congregation by bringing food to the fellowship lunch, the women coordinate the celebration with family members. Thus, on a given Sunday, a 5-year-old may be happily surprised to find the congregation singing "Happy Birthday" to her during the lunch.

Women also actively help in the church's mission to reach out to the Filipino immigrant community, even to people in the homeland, as seen in the words of Catalina:

When somebody needs help, for example, someone gets sick, or there's a death in the family, it's also the women who lead. [I prodded: For example, there's somebody who gets sick in the Philippines.] Yes, they'll write asking for help. We tell them that we will talk about it. Sometimes, it's not needed. If there are relatives; we approach the relatives. We can put some money together.

For many women in Philippians, the church becomes an extension of the home and the same division of work based on gender and age that they follow in the home applies in the church. Members of the church refer to themselves by using the metaphor of the family. They often say, "We are family in Philippians." This metaphor has reinforced women's role in the church as an extension of their traditional family role. The work of caring and nurturing all aspects of the individual and the church community, body, mind, and spirit belongs to the women.

Immigration and Women's Work

Immigrating has brought changes in Filipino women's situation, which has affected gender relations. Like most immigrants, Filipinos, especially professionals, are downwardly mobile.[16] When they immigrate to the United States, most, especially men, work at jobs below their education levels and work experience, at wages lower than they would expect in their home country. Moreover, their prospects for advancement in their work are extremely limited.[17] Filipino women often have better work opportunities compared with men and often end up earning more because of higher pay or because they work longer hours.

Nationwide, Filipina Americans have a labor participation rate of 72.3 percent, which is higher than the rate of non-Asian women (56.7%) and other Asian American women (60.0%); they are known to work longer hours even than White women.[18] Several factors account for this high rate of labor force participation. First, Filipino American workers earn much less than Whites and most other Asian Americans; economic necessity, therefore, drives their labor force participation. Second, their high levels of education and skill make them competitive in the labor market. Finally, Filipino cultural expectations promote women working outside the home. In Philippians, all 21 women members I surveyed were working in jobs traditionally considered women's occupations, such as nursing, medical technology, beauty treatment, sales, and teaching. Eight of the women worked in health-related occupations, such as nursing, phlebotomy, and X-ray technology. This corresponds to data from the 1990 census showing that, nationwide, Filipinas are overrepresented in the health fields, particularly nursing.[19] All the women in Philippians have regular full-time jobs outside the home, except the grandmothers, who usually do the unpaid work of the household, as cleaners and babysitters.

Many Filipinos work overtime or work at two jobs, and this is especially true of the women. In fact, working 16 hours and having double jobs have entered the terminology of the Filipino American community. *Mag-sixteen* and *mag-doboljob* are Taglish expressions (a combination of Tagalog and English) commonly heard in conversations when Filipinos get together. The reason is that most are underpaid. The other reason, I suspect, is the women's desire to be independent and not depend financially on the men. It is common for Filipino women to be earning more than the men, with the concomitant loss of status for the men who see the women becoming strong breadwinners.[20]

In the church, an example of this imbalance of incomes between husbands and wives is the case of Manuel, a church leader who was a bank manager in the Philippines. Now, he works full-time as a bank clerk, and Amelia, his wife, works at two jobs as a laboratory technician in two hospitals, earning more than he does.

Do these arrangements mean that women in Philippians enjoy greater equality with men? As I described previously, they are active in the church and play important roles, mainly as earning high incomes and becoming co-breadwinners with the men and fulfilling the responsibility of feeding and nurturing the congregation and doing the vital kin and emotion work in the congregation. Still, men assert their traditional role of authority in the church; this could be to make up for the loss of status they suffer in the wider society.[21]

The fact that the assistant pastor is a woman, or the presence of women preachers during church services, and their leadership in Christian education may hide the situation that men still hold the positions of leadership in the church. Besides, women are still responsible for the "domestic" aspects of church work like Christian education, child care, and the fellowship meals and activities.

According to Amelia, Manuel's wife, husband and wife discuss important family decisions together. I asked her, "How do you decide important financial investments, for example, buying a new car?" "Both of us discuss it." I continued, "What if you disagree, whose opinion has the final word?" "*Siyempre kay Manuel*" (Of course, Manuel's). As a college-educated professional, she has been more influenced by the modernizing and liberalizing influences of the wider society than have the grandmothers in the church. Yet, she subordinated herself to her husband's authority.

I observed similar relations in the subtle interplay between Pastor Tabay, a part-time pastor of the church, and his wife Lisa, a college-educated professional and an award-winning insurance representative. When I interviewed both of them at home, it was Tabay who talked most of the time, even when I told them that I wanted both of their opinions. Twice during the interview, when I asked them for their interpretation of certain points of Philippians history, Tabay dismissed Lisa's opinions with a wave of his left hand, when she voiced a different interpretation of a certain event in the church's history. Still, she continued talking and stopped only when she had explained her point to me, showing in a subtle way her resistance to his imposition.

During this interview, I saw that she had her own ideas and opposed him if she felt strongly enough about a certain point and disagreed with him. We were discussing the splits in the church that happened 10 years ago. Tabay's analysis was that Philippine ethnolinguistic divisions were the main cause of the splits. I turned to Lisa and asked her, "What do you think? Is that also your perception of the events?" The telling exchange between the two then began when Tabay continued speaking despite a question posed to his wife:

Tabay: In fact . . .

Lisa: [interrupting] Personalities . . .

Tabay: [cutting in again, explaining what his wife meant by recalling a certain incident in which a person named Dino tried to oust her from a church position she held. Both of them agreed that Dino, one of the early church leaders, used methods that were dictatorial. He tried to split the church, but left instead.]

I asked, "Did he have a following?"

Tabay: He had very little.

Lisa: [correcting him] Just his wife.

Tabay: Because before this . . .

Lisa [interrupting him, raising her voice] Later, even his wife didn't want to follow him.

Her tone expressed her approval of the action of Dino's wife's to not follow her husband's wrong move. Lisa was expressing her resistance to her own husband's style, which resembled that of Dino.

Changing Gender Ideologies and Practices

Until recently, the women of the congregation have accepted traditional gender roles and practices as natural and normal. But members of the younger generations are questioning and in small ways resisting. Divorce is an accepted fact of U.S. society, but I observed a certain reticence in speaking about it in Philippians among pastors and members. I did not see any explicit exclusion of divorced persons from the church, but when a divorced person applies for church membership, complications can ensue. Attitudes toward divorce show that there is a struggle emerging between the generations and between men and women.

One such case is that of Evelyn, the mother of a 15-year-old boy. She graduated as a medical technologist in the Philippines and worked for some years in a laboratory before coming to the United States in the early 1980s. On the advice of a friend, she trained for two years as an X-ray technician. She finished the training and found work in a hospital, where she met and married Gerry, a white coworker. She explained the cause of her divorce:

I was the one [who asked for the divorce]. He was Jewish and I am Christian. He would not allow any Christian expression in the house. Also we had different ideas about disciplining children and our son was getting confused.

Gerry was an avid reader and spent most of his time at home reading. On certain days, he insisted that their son spend time with him reading instead of watching TV or playing computer games. Evelyn did not consider it a problem if their son watched TV as long as he finished his lessons first. She realized that the child was "learning to lie to his father" and was getting confused because he saw that his mother had other ideas about schoolwork and activities at home.

When she divorced her husband, she kept it a secret from friends and close relatives. She went into a depression for months:

At first I told them that I was separated from my husband. It was only later that I told them that I was divorced. . . . [It was hard to tell relatives and friends] because in the Philippines there is no divorce allowed. The Bible does not allow divorce. So, I was afraid that Filipinos would ostracize me because of that. I did not tell my friends. I did not change my phone number. My ex-husband would sometimes answer the phone when friends called and he would relay the message to me. I would answer it. Sometimes I just disregarded the phone messages, not returning calls. Later I told them that we were separated but I did not mention divorce.

Why did she find it difficult to tell her friends about her marriage status even though she was living in a society in which divorce is accepted? Divorcing violates cultural standards regarding relations between husband and wife. In traditional Filipino families, the ideal wife is expected to preserve the marriage by her patience and submission, and the ideal husband is supposed to be a good provider.[22] When the marriage breaks up, the presumption is that the wife did not do her part because she has the heavier burden of nurturing the family and keeping it together. Thus, for many traditional Filipinas, divorce may be an accepted part of American society but alien to them culturally.

Evelyn used to attend two churches, a Filipino church and a black Pentecostal church in the city's South side. When the Filipino pastor told her that he did not want her attending services there, she resigned from this Filipino church. She found the weekly trip to the Baptist church too far, however, and the church overwhelmingly large with 14,000 members, although she liked the "preacher's" sermons. When a friend learned that she was looking for a church, he referred her to Pastor Lee of Philippians, who invited her to attend Sunday services. She confided to the pastor and his wife about her divorced status and found the pastor's family very accepting of her. Still, she felt apprehensive about the reactions of other members.

But her fears turned out to be baseless. She became active in the church choir and was accepted by the members, who were mostly young adults and teens. She finally realized that the congregation truly accepted her despite her divorced status. When I interviewed her in the middle of 1997, she was quite confident of her situation in Philippians and had begun to resolve some of her problems about her marital status. The following exchange indicates this.

Once I asked her if she were planning to attend a Bible class, which the pastor announced would discuss divorce. She said,

It was last Friday. I did not attend it. Mario [a divorced friend] told me that the elderly members were against divorce because it destroys families. If I were there, I would have told them that I destroyed a marriage but I did not destroy my family. My son sees his father regularly and he is close to his grandparents (from the father's side). My ex-husband and I do not fight as much anymore.

Her problem concerning her marital status was rooted in traditional religious and family culture. As I noted previously, she kept the divorce secret from friends and relatives, fearing that they would ostracize her because there is no divorce in the Philippines and the Bible does not allow divorce. Therefore, she had to settle her questions within the context of church and family and a changing culture. The proper conditions for this came when she felt that she was accepted by the congregation and had the opportunities to discuss her marital status with the members, as in the Bible class. She justified her position by saying that she saved her family at the cost of ending her marriage, so that she was a better Christian and mother after the divorce, whose relationship with her ex-husband has also improved.

Evelyn's status is now common knowledge in the church. She has been a member for two years and is very active in church affairs. She usually brings her son with her to church and she told me that the boy has adjusted to Filipino friends there. If she can stand before the older members of the church and defend her status as a divorced single mother, as she says she could, it means that she has found confidence in herself and acceptance within the congregation.

Evelyn also has helped to change the church members' notion of family and their standards of a member in good standing. In the Philippine context in which divorce is not legal, the idea of marriage is a bond that cannot be dissolved and oriented primarily to children and the family. Yet she has forced Philippians and the congregation to stretch their notions of marriage, family, and church membership by having members accept her despite her marital status and showing them that she is an active member.

In spring 1997, the church Board of Directors chose Evelyn to replace a woman Board member who was ailing. Still, it does not mean that the issue has been resolved for the church and its members. The objections to divorce that some older members expressed during the Friday Bible class show that the question is more complicated than it seems and is closely linked to other issues in the congregation. However, for the church to choose her to sit in its highest governing body means that it is changing, because some of its leaders give more importance to her practical work for the congregation than to her marital status.

Divorce is going to be a continuing issue in the church because the trend in the Filipino community is for divorce to rise. The number of divorced Filipino females has gone from 1.9 percent in 1960 to 5.1 percent in 1990. As women's divorce rate has risen, it has surpassed the rate for Filipino men. In 1960, men divorced more frequently than women (3.4 percent). By 1990, the rate was 4.2 percent.[23] This shift suggests that women are learning to use opportunities—not accessible to them in the home country—to assert their rights.

Meeting a Filipina divorced or separated from a husband in the Philippines is common among Filipino circles in big U.S. cities. Perhaps emigrating for some women, for all its risks and difficulties, is attractive to them, not only for its promises of economic advancement but also for the opportunity to dissolve a marriage that has become a burden. The high rate of separated Filipinas (2.1 percent compared to 1.5 percent for men) that comes close to the rate of separated non-Asian females (2.6 percent) might support this.[24] In Philippians, there are two women who are either divorced or separated from their husbands in the Philippines. One married recently and introduced her new husband, a Filipino, and their baby to the congregation.

Women in the church also express their opinions about men and traditional marriage practices in other direct ways. I was talking once with a group of middle-aged women after the lunch fellowship in the dining hall. There was good-natured banter and they were teasing me, trying to pair me off with one church member. I was enjoying the conversation because the joking was a sign that they had accepted me, two months after my fieldwork in the church. One of them, a woman in her late 50s, asked me: "*Ano ba ang type mo?*" (What type of women do you like? The shy type?). *Siya'y magluto, siya'y maglinis*" (She'll cook, she'll clean up). We all burst out laughing.

Her joke was a witty pun in Taglish, a play on the English word "shy" and the Tagalog pronoun and linking verb combination "*siya'y,*" which sounded phonetically similar to the English word. Such puns are common among Filipinos and are widely circulated. The joke was probably not original but was one that Filipino women repeated and circulated among themselves. What was important were the tone and the critical attitude that it expressed toward men and traditional Filipino expectations of women's role in marriage. The criticism was sharp but told as a witty pun, softening its sharpness but making its impact more effective as a result. The woman who told the joke then commented further in a mock serious tone after our laughter quieted down: "No, I don't advise you to get married. It's just enjoyable at night but after that, it's not much." The women sounded their assent by raunchy laughter. They probably felt free to voice their dissatisfaction with marriage and traditional gender roles to me who was not a member of the church and somewhat of a stranger to them.

Other issues related to gender views and practices in the church involve premarital sex and single motherhood. During the early part of 1998, I learned from Willie, the pastor's son, that a youth member had gotten pregnant and family members were discussing the case. Traditional ways of handling the situation would have been for the families of both parties involved to pressure the man, if single, to marry the young woman and support her and the child. The idea is to preserve the family's good name and maintain the cultural standards of premarital chastity for the woman. The young woman, however, refused to marry the man, though he offered marriage. According to Willie, "She thinks he's immature. He dropped out of school and he doesn't have a job. She has decided to have the child and raise her by herself. She knows him, so she has made a mature decision." The young woman was still in college and had a steady job. I expected the woman's family to send her away until she gave birth to reduce the social "stigma" on her and the family. To my surprise, she kept going to church and singing in the choir until late in her pregnancy. After she gave birth, she brought her baby to church, just as the other mothers do. During the church celebration of Mother's Day, she joined the other mothers with their babies to be honored at the altar. I asked Willie, who was her cousin, if her family supported her. He said, "They talked about it. It was good that she approached her relatives, so that they were not taken by surprise." It

seems that what the young woman did was to get the support of her immediate family and other close relatives to counter criticism arising from traditional notions of women and marriage.

Traditionally, Filipinos hold that the "dignity" of a Filipino woman rests on fulfilling her duties as wife and mother. In this context, marriage is a bond that cannot be dissolved, and the wife is primarily responsible for preserving the marriage. Women in Philippians Church, particularly young women, are resisting and changing these traditional gender practices. They are bringing to the practical agenda of the church and their families the issues of divorce, premarital sex, and single motherhood, issues that challenge the core values of the traditional family and the church. In this way, they are working out for themselves what it means to be a Filipina American.

Yet, it is important to see gender relations in a wider context. In real life, gender intersects with race/ethnicity and class. Filipino American women are forced to make the best choices within a field narrowed by overlapping categories of oppression. The family is an important source of support against the pressures of the workplace and a racialized society. Because of this, Filipino American women are choosing and holding on to aspects of the traditional Filipino family, especially its communal and nurturing characteristics, such as the value of the extended family and the orientation toward children. Yet they are also asserting their equality with men, their autonomy and independence, and in the process changing the traditional Filipino family while struggling to live as family in U.S. society.[25]

Notes

1. Agbayani-Siewert, Pauline and Linda Revilla. "Filipino Americans." Pp. 148–50 in *Asian*

Americans, edited by P. G. Min (Thousand Oaks, CA: Sage Publications, 1995).

2. Go, Stella P. *The Filipino Family in the Eighties* (Manila: Social Development Research Center De La Salle University, 1993), pp. 25–26.

3. Jocano, F. Landa. *Growing Up in a Philippine Barrio* (New York: Holt, Rinehart and Winston, 1969), pp. 56–57.

4. Jocano, F. Landa. *Slum as a Way of Life, A Study of Coping Behavior in an Urban Environment* (Quezon City: University of the Philippines Press, 1975), pp. 93–94.

5. Yu, Elena and William T. Liu. *Fertility and Kinship in the Philippines* (Notre Dame, IN: University of Notre Dame Press, 1980), p. 264.

6. For a comparison of the attitudes of young Christian and Muslim students in the southern Philippines regarding parents and their children's marriage partners, see Lacar, Luis, "Familism among Muslims and Christians in the Philppines," *Philippine Studies* 43(1, 1995):42–65.

7. Go (1993), p. 27; Vancio, J., "The Realities of Marriage of Urban Filipino Women," *Philippine Studies* 28(1, 1980):7.

8. Medina, Belen T. G. *The Filipino Family: A Text with Selected Readings* (Quezon City: University of the Philippines Press, 1991), pp. 124–31; Go (1993), p. 26: Jocano, *Slum as a Way of Life,* pp. 160–61.

9. Vancio (1980), pp. 13–15; Go (1993), p. 43.

10. Vancio (1980), pp. 12–13.

11. Vancio (1980), p. 17.

12. Go (1993), pp. 57–58; Yu and Liu (1980), p. 182.

13. Go (1993), pp. 54–56; Yu and Liu (1980), p. 179.

14. Yu and Liu (1980), pp. 179–80.

15. Di Leonardo, Micaela. "The Female World of Cards and Holidays: Women, Families, and the Work of Kinship." Pp. 246–61 in *Rethinking the Family,* edited by B. Thorne and M. Yalom. (Boston: Northeastern University Press, 1992); Di Leonardo, Micaela. *The Varieties of Ethnic Experience* (Ithaca, NY: Cornell University Press, 1984).

16. Carino, Benjamin, James T. Fawcett, Robert W. Gardner, and Fred Arnold. "The New Filipino Immigrants to the United States: Increasing Diversity and Change." (Honolulu, HI: East-West Center, 1990), p. 64.

17. Nee, Victor and Jimmy Sanders. "The Road to Parity: Determinants of the Socioeconomic Achievements of Asian Americans." *Ethnic and Racial Studies* 8(1, 1985):85, 89–90; Agbayani-Siewert and Revilla (1995), pp. 150–51; Barringer, Herbert R., Robert W. Gardner, and Michael J. Levin. *Asians and Pacific Islanders in the United States* (New York: Russell Sage Foundation, 1993), pp. 238–42.

18. U.S. Census Current Population Studies, 3-5, Table 4 (Washington, DC: U.S. Census Bureau, 1990); Barringer et al. (1993), pp. 136–44, 220–23; Agbayani-Siewert and Revilla (1995), pp. 150–51.

19. Ong, Paul and Tania Azores. "The Migration and Incorporation of Filipino Nurses." Pp. 164–95 in *The New Asian Immigration in Los Angeles and Global Restructuring,* edited by P. Ong, E. Bonacich, and L. Cheng (Philadelphia: Temple University Press, 1994).

20. Barringer et al. (1993), pp. 135–44, 220–23; Agbayani-Siewert and Revilla (1995), pp. 150–51.

21. For an account of a similar situation in a South Asian immigrant congregation, see George, Sheba, "Caroling with the Keralites: The Negotiation of Gendered Space in an Indian Immigrant Church." Pp. 265–94 in *Gatherings in Diaspora,* edited by R. S. Warner and J. G. Wittner (Philadelphia: Temple University Press, 1998).

22. Medina (1991), p. 123.

23. Barringer et al. (1993), pp. 136–44; U.S. Census Current Population Studies, 3-5, Table 1 (Washington DC, U.S. Census Bureau 1990).

24. U.S. Census Bureau (1990).

25. Feminist researchers are paying closer attention to the supportive side of families because of the evidence provided by the history of Latino, Asian American, and black families. They are seeking a more complex understanding of families as contradictory sites both of domination and cooperation, of nurturance and autonomy. See Thorne, Barrie, "Feminism and the Family: Two

Decades of Thought." Pp. 3–30 in *Rethinking the Family,* edited by B. Thorne and M. Yalom (Boston: Northeastern University Press, 1992); Rumbaut, R. G., "Ties That Bind: Immigration and Immigrant Families in the United States." Pp. 3–46 in *Immigration and the Family,* edited by A. Booth, A. C. Crouter, and N. Landale (Mahwah, NJ: Lawrence Erlbaum, 1997); Espiritu, Yen Le, *Asian American Women and Men* (Thousand Oaks, CA: Sage, 1997); Collins, Patricia H., *Black Feminist Thought* (New York: Routledge, 1991); Glen, Evelyn Nakano, *Issei, Nissei, War Bride* (Philadelphia: Temple University Press, 1986); Kibria, Nazli, *Family Tightrope* (Princeton, NJ: Princeton University Press, 1993).

Tizon:

1. How do changing gender roles affect the construction of Filipino American ethnicity?

2. In what ways do Filipinos in the United States differ from those in the Philippines with regard to gender relations?

30

Stanislaus Can't Polka: New Polish Immigrants in Established Polish American Communities

Mary Patrice Erdmans

In 1986, Janusz Matecki, an engineer working in the Lenin Shipyard, and his wife Dorota had a "giving away" party in Gdansk, Poland.[1] He was 47 at the time. They invited their closest friends to their small three-room apartment where they had lived for more than 20 years, and, amid the drinking and eating, they gave away most of their cherished possessions—the large collection of books printed on poor-quality paper, the heavy wooden cabinet that stood in the high-ceilinged main room, and the thick ornate crystal vases filled with dried rose petals from decades of name day celebrations. They left the dusty drapes, the cheap kitchen table and squat wooden stools, and a balcony full of empty vodka and wine bottles. Shortly thereafter, he and his wife took a train to Warsaw, walked into the American consulate, asked for political asylum because he feared persecution. Within a month, he was living in the United States.

Janusz feared persecution because of his involvement with *Solidarność* (Solidarity), a union/social movement formally organized in 1980. In December 1981, the communist government in Poland, with the blessing and

urging of the communist government in the Soviet Union, imposed martial law to quell the growing opposition and imprisoned thousands of activists. Martial law was lifted in July 1983, but in 1986 *Solidarność* was still outlawed, the opposition was still underground, and many activists still feared persecution. Janusz described his fear:

I go to jail just three weeks after martial law. After they released me from the jail I start to work underground. In 1986, I was very close to going to prison second time. Many of my colleagues go second time, and everybody of my colleagues tell me that the first time was much easier than second one because in this first time there was many political prisoners and everybody think about this, take care about family. But second time, there was only a small group of people who still fight and want to do something. But most of population don't believe in anything. They don't believe communists, they don't believe Solidarnosc, they just think about how they going day after day. It's very hard situation in Poland.

It was very difficult decision [to leave Poland]. I know that it's very hard to start new life in

Table 30.1

Polish Immigrants and Nonimmigrants Admitted into the United States, 1960–1996

Year	Total Number Polish Immigrants Admitted	Total Number Polish Nonimmigrants Admitted	Number (and Percentage) of Nonimmigrants as Visitors for Pleasure
1960–69	77,650	166,815	121,390 (73%)
1970–79	42,378	352,269	239,619 (68%)
1980–89	81,578	449,235	356,266 (79%)
1990–96	150,730	452,419	309,844 (68%)

Note: In addition to visitors for pleasure, nonimmigrants include temporary visitors for business, treaty traders and investors, intracompany transferees, returning resident aliens, transit aliens, parolees, students, temporary workers and trainees, exchange visitors, foreign government officials, international representatives, NATO officials, representatives of foreign information media, spouses and children of students, temporary workers, exchange visitors, and fiancées of U.S. citizens and their children.

Source: Annual Report of the Immigration and Naturalization Service, 1960–1976; Statistical Yearbook of the Immigration and Naturalization Service, 1977–1996, Tables: Immigrants admitted by selected class of admission and region and selected country of birth; nonimmigrants admitted by class of admission and region and selected country of birth.

America. The first year's gonna be very hard here. It was, especially for us. I am too old for America. I know this. But, it was not economic problem for me in Poland. There was only problem that I know secret police know everything about me, where I go, what I do this day, this day. Nobody like to be in prison, and for me it was very hard time. You know, if you got some good information—that everything is OK with your family or something happen, some demonstration or something like this—you think that you can stay in prison many years, no problem. Next day, when some bad information came, you are feel very bad. And you think about going to prison next time. If I go by car close to prison I every time think about this. I have many, during the night, dream—it was the same type of dream—that secret police come, want to catch you and take you to prison.

Janusz was resettled through Lutheran Family Services, one of the main refugee re-settling agencies in the United States. Between 1981 and 1990, 33,889 Polish refugees and asylees were granted permanent resident status in the United States. The number of Polish refugees dropped sharply in the 1990s after the collapse of the communist regime and the economic and political liberalization of Poland.[2]

New Polish Immigrants

In the 1990s, the decline in Polish refugees was offset by a rise in Polish immigrants. Although refugees need to prove that there is a fear of persecution if they return to their home country, immigrants do not—they just need a visa and usually a family member to sponsor them. The biggest obstacle for Polish immigrants has been getting an American visa, and so changes in U.S. policy rather than conditions in Poland have most contributed to the large number of new immigrants. Between 1990 and 1996, 150,730 Poles were admitted as immigrants, almost double the number admitted in the 1980s (see Table 30.1).

Changes in U.S. laws gave Polish immigrants more opportunities to get a permanent visa (a "green card," also known as permanent resident status). First, the Immigration and Refugee Control Act

Table 30.2

Number of Polish Immigrants Admitted into the United States, 1989–1996

Year	Total Number of Immigrants Admitted	Diversity Program	IRCA Legalization	Legalization Dependents	Refugee and Asylee Adjustments
1989	15,101	NA	5,497	—	2,467
1990	20,537	NA	7,123	—	2,294
1991	19,199	NA	2,561	—	2,609
1992	25,504	9,383	667	1,552	1,512
1993	27,846	14,806	117	477	731
1994	28,048	17,495	28	22	334
1995	13,824	4,916	20	—	245
1996	15,772	3,444	17	—	183
Total	165,831 (100%)	50,444 (30%)	16,030 (10%)	2,051 (1%)	10,375 (6%)

Note: IRCA = Immigration and Refugee Control Act of 1986.

Source: Statistical Yearbook of the Immigration and Naturalization Service, Table 8: Immigrants admitted by selected class of admission and region and selected country of birth, 1989–1996.

(IRCA) of 1986 gave amnesty to illegal immigrants who could prove they had been living in the United States continuously since 1982. Through IRCA, 16,030 Poles received permanent resident status. Second, the Immigration Act of 1990 raised the ceiling for all immigrants from 270,000 annually to a level of 700,000 for 1992 through 1994 and then 675,000 beginning in 1995. Included under that cap were slots for 55,000 "diversity immigrants," defined as aliens from countries adversely affected by the 1965 Immigration Act (i.e., immigrants not from Asia or Latin America, who make up 80 percent of all post-1965 immigrants). The Diversity Program was a transitional program from 1992 to 1995, and Poland and Ireland took the lion's share of the slots in the first two years. The program was made permanent in 1995, and since then an increasing number of diversity slots have gone to immigrants from African countries. Between 1992 and 1996, however, more than 50,000 Poles have been admitted through this program (see Table 30.2).

Anna, her husband Marek, and their daughter Grazyna represent new Polish immigrants. Anna's aunt sponsored them to the United States, to Chicago. Anna and Marek arrived first, leaving their 3-year-old daughter in Poland in the care of her grandmother. The young couple were unsure if they could "make it" in America, and they wanted to resettle first before disrupting Grazyna's life. Although refugees felt persecuted by the politically oppressive communist regime, Anna and Marek complained more about the problems of the communist economic system—the supply-driven economy meant that there were often shortages in Poland. People could not go out shopping when they needed something; instead, they had to buy when things were available. If rubber boots were sold that day, people bought rubber boots; if light bulbs were on the store shelf, they bought light bulbs. Of course, luxury items, such as stereos, imported fruits, and modern toys, were in short supply, but so were necessities like toilet paper, shoes for gym class, and nails.

One of the biggest problems was the housing shortage. Couples often registered their young infants for an apartment in hopes that when they reached age 21 the apartment would be ready. In the case of Anna and Marek, they were still living with her parents in their two-bedroom, four-room apartment. They wanted to live in America not because of abstract freedoms like the right to assemble or the right to free speech but for material freedoms like the ability to buy toilet paper, brown rice, and a house. They wanted to live in a system in which, as Anna said, "the harder you work the more money you make." They wanted the chance to "get ahead" in this world, and they assumed that in a capitalist world system, it would be easier to do that in a rich capitalist nation than in a poor communist nation.

Marek and Anna arrived in the early 1980s. Anna had worked as a pharmacist in Poland, and Marek was a medical doctor. When they arrived, neither of them spoke English well, and neither of their degrees transferred. In order for Marek to practice as a doctor, he first had to pass a medical exam for foreign students, and then he would have to repeat his residency program, even though in Poland he already had passed his medical exam, completed his residency, and had worked as a doctor for several years. Before he could begin to recertify his degree, he had to learn English; although he learned English, he needed to make some money. Within two weeks after arrival, he took a job in a nursing home changing bed pans on the third shift for $4.25 an hour. He worked almost 60 hours a week. Because of the long hours and the fact that many of his coworkers were also Polish immigrants, he did not learn English quickly; and because he was always tired at night, he could not focus well on his medical studies.

Anna took a bakery job in the Polish neighborhood known as *Jackowo*. The Polish American owners of the bakery paid their workers minimum wage. She rose at four o'clock every morning and worked until the early afternoon. She decided not to pursue her pharmacology career because it would require too much time—she would have to repeat almost three years of schooling. She con-

centrated instead on learning English, and she enrolled in free English as a Second Language courses at the local community college. Anna learned to speak English much quicker than Marek did. After they had been in Chicago for several years, Marek was eager to return home. He felt demoralized. Because of his problems with language, he never recovered from his drop in occupational status from doctor to nursing home attendant. Anna, however, liked living in Chicago. Because she decided not to become a pharmacist and her language skills improved quickly, she had an easier time emotionally adjusting to the United States.

Anna convinced Marek to stay, urging him to study harder and longer. They sent for their daughter from Poland; Grazyna's presence cheered up Marek. They also had managed to save enough in their first years working for minimum wage, working a lot of overtime, and spending very little on leisure activities, to make a down payment on a $195,000 two-story brownstone in Jefferson Park, a Polish neighborhood in northwestern Chicago. The transaction was done almost exclusively in Polish (although the documents were all in English). The realtor, lawyer, and banker spoke Polish, although none was an immigrant from Poland; they were Americans of Polish descent. Anna, Marek, and Grazyna moved into the top floor of the two-family house and rented out the first-floor apartment, which is how they paid their mortgage.

In the mid-1990s, almost 15 years after immigrating, Marek is still working in the same nursing home, but he is on the day shift and has moved up to a staff position. He makes $8.50 an hour. He still comes home in the evenings and tries to study for his medical exam, a dream that Anna will not relinquish. Anna worked a variety of part-time positions (as clerical or sales personnel), but has spent most of her time raising Grazyna (who is called Grace by her American friends). Grace is bilingual; she speaks Polish at home and

English outside her home. She goes back to Poland to visit in the summer but has no plans to live there permanently. Marek still wishes they could all move back "home" to Poland.

Anna and Marek have a life that is better than many other new Polish migrants in Chicago because they have a green card—permission to work and stay permanently. This has made it easier for them to improve their jobs, buy a house, and get medical insurance. More important, because they could stay, they began to adjust themselves psychologically to the idea of staying (Anna more so than Marek) and set about the tasks of assimilating into American life—learning English, developing American tastes for entertainment (e.g., learning to idolize Michael Jordan and the Chicago Bulls), and finding American friends.

Illegal Polish Immigrants

A large number of Polish immigrants overstay their temporary visas, work illegally, or both. This group is almost as large as that of the legal residents and maybe even larger—because of their illegal status, it is hard for social scientists and government officials to count them. Most enter the United States on tourist visas, which is why they are called *wakacjusze* (vacationer) in the Polish community. The tourist visa is valid for six months but not valid for employment, yet many *wakacjusze* come specifically to work and stay for several years.[3]

The *wakacjusze* are classified as "nonimmigrants," whereas permanent residents like Anna and Marek are classified as immigrants. Twice as many nonimmigrants come to the United States as do immigrants; between 1990 and 1996, 309,844 Poles arrived on tourist visas (see Table 30.1).

These temporary workers do not have the same chance to improve their jobs that permanent immigrants have; thus, they often remain in low-wage positions. Jobs for illegal immigrants in Chicago include babysitter, housekeeper, janitor, commercial maid, mechanic, and construction worker. Although they seldom work below minimum wage, they often work for less than the going rate for American workers. For example, in the early 1990s, certified home health care workers made roughly $15 and hour, whereas the Polish worker made $5; and unionized construction workers made close to $20 an hour, but the illegal Polish workers made $6.

Violeta came to the United States in 1987 on a B-2 tourist visa. She was 29 when she arrived, and she planned to stay for a few months. Most of the vacationers come to the United States for the same reason that permanent immigrants come—to make money. They often come during a transitional period in their life; in Violeta's case, it was a divorce that precipitated her departure; for others, it is summer vacation and the chance to earn "some green." Although many come intending to work, very few initially plan to stay for longer than six months. In one study of 35 illegal immigrants, none of them said they came intending to stay permanently, and at the time of the interview, only 20 percent were committed to staying in the United States.[4]

Violeta worked in the United States as a live-in caretaker for the elderly. In her two-year stay, she had three different live-in positions that she found through a Polish employment agency in Chicago. After the passage of the IRCA in 1986, it became harder for illegal immigrants to find work. The IRCA established sanctions prohibiting employers from hiring aliens unauthorized to work in the United States. As a result, illegal workers were more often asked to produce a social security card or other documents to prove they were legal. To get around this, Violeta, like most Poles working illegally, had an illegal social security card. In the late 1980s, these illegal cards—that were either forged or stolen—could be purchased for between $300 and $1,000 on the streets of Chicago.

These three types of newcomers—the refugee, immigrant, and temporary worker—have different experiences in the United States because they have access to different resources. The political refugee receives state resources, such as rent subsidies, monthly stipends, and food stamps for an initial period of time. The immigrant most often is sponsored by family members and, within a year of arrival, is eligible for almost the same state resources as are other U.S. citizens. The temporary migrant working illegally is not eligible for any state resources and often does not have family members here to help. Immigrants and refugees assimilate more quickly than do illegal temporary workers: Their legal status makes it easier to improve their job situation (structural assimilation), and their decision to stay permanently, or at least for a longer period of time, gives them more incentive to acculturate (e.g., learn the language). These three types of newcomers make up the population of new Poles in the United States. Despite the liberalization of Poland's economic and political system in the 1990s, Poles continue to immigrate to the United States and will continue to do so as long as the United States keeps open its borders.

Polish Newcomers in Established Polonia

Almost half of the people reporting Polish ancestry in the 1990 census lived in New York, Illinois, Michigan, Pennsylvania, and New Jersey. The new Polish immigrants are moving into those cities with established Polish American communities (e.g., Chicago, New York, Buffalo, Detroit, and Philadelphia). These communities, referred to as "Polonias," are composed of later-generation Polish American ethnics (from second to fifth generation). A fifth-generation Polish American

is someone whose great-great grandparents came from Poland around the 1860s, most likely from the western partition of Poland that was occupied by Prussia (thus, many of them spoke German as well as Polish).[5] These immigrants settled in developing industrial cities in the Northeast and Mid-Atlantic states as well as in farming communities in the Midwest. For example, a large tract of land in southwestern Michigan was bought by a German immigrant, who then went to Chicago and recruited German-speaking Poles to buy smaller 200-acre farms in the region. For the next three generations, this farming community, known as Wayland, was almost exclusively Polish.

A large number of Polish immigrants came during the great migration wave around the turn of this century. More than 1.5 million Poles arrived between 1891 and 1914.[6] One hundred years later, at the end of the twentieth century, the adult descendants of this migration cohort are mostly third and fourth generation (a *cohort* is a group of people who experience the same events at the same time in their life cycle). A large percentage of Polonia is composed of these later-generation Polish American ethnics (*ethnics* refer to people born in the United States who still identify with a foreign ancestry). According to the 1990 census, 9,366,106 people reported some Polish ancestry, and 94 percent of them were native-born Polish Americans as opposed to Polish immigrants.[7]

The second generation in Polonia is composed of the descendants of Polish émigrés who came around the time of World War II.[8] Most of the the World War II émigrés arrived as refugees under a program to resettle people displaced by the war (e.g., concentration and work camp victims, veterans who fought with the Allied Forces, farmers uprooted by changes in Poland's borders). More than 200,000 Poles arrived during and after the war, and 120,000 of them were admitted under the Displaced Persons Act of 1948.[9] The children of this migration cohort compose the majority of the adult second generation living in Polonia today.

When the new immigrants arrived in the 1980s, they came to these established Polish communities composed of World War II political émigrés and their children, as well as the descendants of the great migration from the turn of the century. Networks of family and friends attract immigrants, as do resources like jobs and language. Immigrants need and want to live in cities where they know people and where even strangers speak their language. A familiar language and cultural environment as well as strong networks help them find jobs, buy houses, and send materials back to Poland.

Although immigrants often settle in established Polish communities, and although the immigrant and ethnic may share the "Polish" adjective, the two identities—immigrant and ethnic—are distinct. As a result, it is difficult to define "who is a Pole" and "what is Polonia," a problem I encountered when I first tried to "find" the Polish community.

Finding the Polish Community

In spring 1986, I decided to study Polish refugees in Chicago. Because we often think of community as being located in a defined space, I started by asking local people "where" the Polish community was. They told me it was on Milwaukee Avenue in Chicago, south of Addison. I drove my old graduate school gas guzzler slowly down Milwaukee Avenue and stopped on a block where most of the store signs looked Polish (I did not speak Polish at the time, so I was sort of guessing—I knew the signs were not in Spanish). I walked up and down the street looking into storefronts, sat on a bench and smoked a cigarette watching people, then got bored and went home.

Having found the neighborhood, I now needed to find out how to get inside. I entered through those institutions opened to the public—churches, stores, bars, and restaurants. I started to learn Polish, and my first words were *"Ojcze nasz, ktory jest w niebie"* (Our Father, who art in heaven) and *"jeszcze jeden piwo"* (one more beer). Those first three months I made a lot of observations about churches and stores and men sitting in bars, but I made very few contacts with Polish immigrants because I did not speak Polish and, although they admitted outsiders, these institutions did not serve as convenient sites for making contacts.

I then looked in the phone book under "Polish" and found a list of Polish organizations. I phoned these organizations and talked with people who spoke English (without an accent), granted me two-hour interviews, and sent me organizational brochures and newsletters. They were all, however, Polish American organizations, not Polish immigrant organizations, and it became clearer to me that there were two Polish communities in Chicago, not just one. Access to the Polish American ethnic community did not necessarily give me access to the Polish immigrant community, and vice versa. I met few immigrants in the ethnic organizations, and few ethnics in the immigrant community.

Most Polish American organizations were not located on Milwaukee Avenue but were instead in the suburbs, as were the majority of Polish Americans. Compared to the immigrant neighborhood, it was easier to gain access to the Polish American ethnic organizations because they were formal, their documents were public, and their members spoke English. Because of time constraints (I had to complete my master's thesis), my first study was on Polish American fraternal organizations. Yet, in this process of trying to find the community, I learned that the immigrant community was distinct from the ethnic community.

A second important discovery was coming to understand that not all newcomers were the same. I wanted to meet political refugees because I was interested in the Solidarity movement in Poland. In the first year, I met no Polish refugees, but I met drunk old men who overstayed their visas and were not returning to Poland, a prosperous Polish businesswoman who started out cleaning houses and now owned a maid company, a mother and daughter team of janitors who worked 10 hours a day six days a week, and several Polish priests and mechanics. I met legal and illegal immigrants, but no refugees; and none of the immigrants I met was engaged in political activity directed back to the homeland—my topic of interest.

Finally, I ran into a new immigrant working for one of the Polish American organizations I studied, and she invited me to a political gathering of Polish refugees. It took me a long time to find them because their activities were private, their numbers were small, and their organizations were not established.

I stayed with this group of refugees for about five years, attending political demonstrations and marches, lectures and private parties, weddings and funerals. I started learning Polish, carried money to the Polish underground, and spent the summer in Poland so that I could better understand why they left. Not until well into the study did I begin to interview the new immigrants (I interviewed the Polish American leaders of organizations in the first year), and toward the end of the study I began to collect survey information about the new Polish community with the help of the Polish refugees who gave me access to a wide variety of venues.[10]

Immigrants and Ethnics: Structural and Symbolic Identities

Sociologists have argued that in late twentieth century America, the identity of white ethnics is largely symbolic.[11] Using data from the 1980 census, Stanley Lieberson and Mary Waters, in their book *From Many Strands* (1988), showed there was little difference among whites in this country. They found that the descendants of southern and eastern European groups looked similar to the white majority on indexes of education, income, and occupation. The structural assimilation of Polish Americans is evident in data from the 1990 census that shows, among people aged 25 years and older, 23 percent of Polish Americans (by definition, native-born) had received a bachelor's degree or higher, compared to 22 percent of the total white population.[12] It is their whiteness, not their ancestral identity of being Polish American, that influences their structural location and life choices. For the most part, European ancestry does not affect the choice of spouse, friends, residence, work, or education. Instead, this symbolic identity is more likely to influence the dishes placed on the table for Christmas and Easter or the few customs attached to rites of passage such as births, weddings, and funerals. For example, among the more distinctive features of Polish Americans are that they dance the polka and eat kielbasa (sausage).

Compared to white ethnics, immigrants, even if they are white and of European background, have a structural identity that influences things such as occupation and income. The structural identity of the immigrant is a result of bounded information networks and the loss of human and cultural capital; both are the result of migration. In the three cases presented previously, none of the newcomers was able to work in the same professions that they had in Poland because of their poor English language skills and because their degrees did not transfer completely. Janusz, who was an engineer in Poland, became a drafter; Marek, who was a doctor, became a nursing home attendant; and Krysia, who was a special education teacher, became an eldercare worker. All three Poles experienced a drop in status because they were migrants, not because they were Polish. It was because they did not speak English well, not that they spoke Polish, that was holding them back. The newness of the immigrant identity is what makes it a structural locator. The migrant loses cultural capital (e.g., language skills) when he or she moves from one society to another.

Newcomers also do not have the same networks in the United States that established members of society have. Polish immigrants have stronger and denser networks in Poland than in America because most of their family and friends still live in Poland. Most migrants arrive knowing few people. In addition, they are unfamiliar with American institutions (e.g., the education system), which makes it harder for them to negotiate their position in society.

Not sure how to access U.S. agencies and not speaking English well, the new immigrant often turns to Polish American organizations for help. Unfortunately, and by their nature, Polish American organizations are not set up to help new immigrants because they are ethnic organizations, not immigrant organizations. Ethnics do not have the same needs as immigrants. Because the basis of ethnic identity in America is at minimum a claim to some ancestral heritage, the goal of the ethnic is to maintain that attachment to ancestry. Ethnics do this by learning the history of the ancestral homeland, the literature, cuisine, customs, language, and arts. Third-generation Polish Americans maintain their cultural attachment, for example, by learning Polish, singing folk songs, and visiting Poland. Ethnic organizations help them do this by offering language classes, sponsoring choral groups, and organizing trips to the homeland.

In contrast, immigrants do not need to learn Polish, they need to learn English; they do not take tours to Poland but instead want packaged tours to Disneyland, the Grand Canyon, or the Wisconsin Dells. Immigrants need to get jobs, recertify their degrees or get

American diplomas, and find out how to access government agencies. The ethnic organization is not set up to provide for these immigrant needs. Polish American boy scouting troops or softball leagues do not have the resources or interest in sponsoring job retraining courses or English language classes. So, when Polish immigrants reach out to Polish American ethnic organizations because of the sentimental feeling that "we are all Poles," and Polish American organizations turn them away because of the practical fact that they cannot satisfy immigrant needs, the immigrants become critical of the established community for not helping. This conflict is a result of the different needs of immigrants and ethnics, differences related to the structural/symbolic nature of the identities.[13]

Differences between immigrants and ethnics were noticeable in the types of communities the two groups formed in Chicago. *Jackowo,* the immigrant community on Milwaukee Avenue, represents a dense concentration of stores and businesses that help immigrants get haircuts, hire lawyers, send packages to Poland, and get jobs (legally or illegally). Immigrants use the Polish neighborhood because the shop owners and workers speak Polish, because the community provides special services that immigrants need, and because the immigrants do not feel stigmatized by the fact that they do not speak English. In contrast, Polish Americans use the community to remind them of their cultural heritage, especially around the holidays. They go there to buy special foods. Immigrants are dependent on this service community; ethnics are optional consumers.

The ethnic community is more widely dispersed throughout the Chicago metropolitan area. It is represented more by an interlocking set of organizations, whose headquarters are mostly in the surrounding suburban communities. To be a member of this community does not require face-to-face contact. Ethnics can participate by reading Polish American newspapers, listening to a Polka Radio program, or buying insurance from a Polish American fraternal organization.[14]

The aspect of migration that makes the identity a structural identity is newness—and newness is a variable that by its very nature lessens over time so that in a few years (or, in some cases, decades) the immigrant begins to structurally assimilate. According to 1990 census data, immigrants who arrived prior to 1980 were more occupationally similar to native-born Polish Americans than post-1980 immigrants. Both pre-1980 immigrants and Polish Americans were more likely to be found in white-collar, middle-class, professional occupations than the newest immigrants.[15] In addition, family median income in 1990 for Polish American ethnics was almost $42,000 and near $40,000 for Polish immigrants who arrived before 1980, but only around $33,000 for immigrants who arrived after 1980.[16] The immigrant experience structurally locates the newcomer, but, over time (and influenced by other factors such as age, education, residence), the immigrant begins to assimilate.

Conclusion

The borders of the Polish community are contested and shifting, but the fault lines are within the community composed of various migration cohorts and generations. Comparative analyses often gloss over differences within community to compare it with other communities. In contrast, studies that focus on one group richly detail cultural, social, temporal, and biographical differences within communities. The understanding of ethnicity as a socially constructed identity necessitates that we look at how this identity is constructed both between communities and within community.

As a cultural identity, ethnicity represents a shared system of meaning. The historical forces that shape these identities in the United States are different from those that shaped the identities in the home country. An ethnic identity constructed in America will be different from a cultural identity constructed in Poland, or Israel, or Serbia. When new arrivals from these countries share space and community with ethnics, their symbols or meaning systems are as likely to be different as they are similar. Both groups may claim possession of a name (e.g., "Polish"), yet the meaning of this identity varies.

Defined too broadly, the ethnic community construct may include disparate and incompatible identities. For example, the boundaries of the Jewish community in America may be stretched to include recent Israeli immigrants, Russian Jewish refugees, Polish-Jewish survivors of the holocaust, and fifth-generation German-Jewish-Americans. Stretched this wide, Jewishness becomes useless as an explanatory construct.[17] The same is true for Polishness.

The political, economic, and geographic faces of Poland have changed dramatically in the last century. It moved from an agrarian region without statehood, to an independent industrializing state, to an industrial communist system. As a result, Polish, the character of Polish migrant cohorts, has changed over time. For example, because Poland was an agricultural society in the nineteenth century, most early immigrants came from rural backgrounds and were uneducated; as Poland industrialized, immigrants were more likely to come from urban areas with more schooling; and the communist system in Poland opened up the education system to a greater variety of people so that the most recent immigrants often have some post-secondary education.[18]

Historical events, such as World War II, industrialization, and the imposition of a communist system, have changed not only Poland's political and economic systems but also its culture. Thus, Polish Americans and Polish immigrants have different memories and different cultural expressions. These different interpretations of Polishness are expressed in language, musical and literary preferences, rituals and heroes, and social values and attitudes. Again, when we talk about Polish culture, the question becomes "which Poland?" and "which Polish culture?" For example, whereas the polka is associated with the Polish American community, most recent Polish immigrants do not know how to polka.

Generational differences refer to how far removed a cohort is from the immigrant generation. Although there are shades of difference between second- and third-generation ethnics, the most distinctive split occurs between the foreign-born immigrants and the subsequent generations of native-born ethnics. The third- and fourth-generation descendants of the early immigrants are working-class ethnics who have an emotional attachment to the folk culture of Poland as presented to them by their grandparents. In contrast to this sentimental attachment, the immigrant has an instrumental attachment to his or her homeland (e.g., they send money to family members still in Poland or help to sponsor family members to the United States). The ethnic and immigrant categories can overlap, and this occurs when an immigrant has lived for several decades in the host country. By the 1980s, those Polish émigrés who arrived after World War II possessed this hybrid immigrant-ethnic status, and, because of this, many became liaisons between the most recent immigrants and the Polish American ethnics. In addition to differences between migration cohorts and generations, there are also differences within the same cohort. Polish newcomers arrive in America as political refugees, permanent immigrants, and temporary visitors and workers. There is no one term useful for describing all these newcomers, except perhaps the term "newcomer." We often use the term immigrant, but in legal terms, the immigrant is different from a refugee and a temporary migrant; these differences are salient because they pro-

duce different experiences. Differences in why people left their homeland and the process through which they found themselves in the host country influence labor market participation, social mobility, and structural assimilation. Refugees, immigrants, and migrant workers have different agendas and act differently while in emigration. For example, refugees politically active in their home country are more likely to continue their political activities, and temporary migrant workers are less likely to join political organizations because they work long hours and have little free time.[19]

The Polish community, like all other ethnic communities, is heterogeneous. To understand how this community works—both its conflicts and its successes—and how it negotiates, constructs, and reconstructs the identity of Polishness in America, we need to pay attention to these internal group differences. The struggle over group identity or organizational ownership is a struggle that occurs within the community. When we fail to acknowledge the heterogeneity within groups, we ignore the complexity of the messy social world.

Notes

1. All of the names are pseudonyms. The data and quotations in this chapter come from interviews and participant observation conducted between 1986 and 1992 in Chicago. For a full description of the methods, see Appendix A in Erdmans (1998).

2. Numbers on refugees and asylees come from *Statistical Yearbook of the Immigration and Naturalization Service*, 1990 (table 34) and 1993 (table 33) (U.S. Department of Justice 1977–1996). In the 1990s, the few thousand Polish refugees given permanent resident status represented processing backlogs (Erdmans 1998:64). Both refugees and asylees are people who are seeking safe refuge in another country because they fear persecution if they return to their home country. Be-

cause they both fear "returning," they must be outside their home country; the difference between the two is where they apply—asylees are already in the United States, and refugees are in a third country. In the case of Janusz, the American consulate is figuratively on U.S. soil, and for this reason he applied for asylum. He was then sent to Germany where he waited in a refugee camp for two weeks before being sent to the United States as a refugee.

3. For a more complete discussion of Poles working illegally in the United States, see Erdmans (1996a, 1996b).

4. Erdmans (1998, Appendix A).

5. There are some excellent histories of Polish immigration, including Brozek (1985) and Pula (1995). The most famous and controversial history that documents the community only into the first two decades of this century is the sociological classic first published in 1918 by William Thomas and Florian Znaniecki ([1918] 1958).

6. For a discussion of the problems involved counting who was and was not a "Polish" immigrant, see Erdmans (1998:20–21), Brozek (1985:34–43), and Lopata (1976:34–42).

7. U.S. Census Bureau (1993a:59, 1993b:3).

8. The term emigrant (from which émigré derives) places the emphasis on leaving, whereas immigrant accents the process of arrival. The term émigré is used more synonymously with refugee to denote involuntary forced departure, in comparison to the perceived voluntary nature of the immigrant.

9. Erdmans (1998:43).

10. See Erdmans (1998, Appendix A).

11. See Alba (1990), Waters (1990), and Gans (1979, 1994).

12. U.S. Census Bureau (1993a:263; 1997, Table 243).

13. Erdmans (1998:84–123).

14. For a list of businesses in *Jackowo* in the late 1980s, see Erdmans (1995).

15. U.S. Census Bureau (1993a:36).

16. U.S. Census Bureau (1993a:467–68).

17. See the excellent study by Shokeid (1988).

18. For a more complete comparison of class differences between the various cohorts, see Blejwas (1981), Lopata (1976), Erdmans (1996a, 1998).

19. Erdmans (1998, Chapter 3).

References

Alba, Richard. 1990. *Ethnic Identity: The Transformation of White America*. New Haven, CT: Yale University Press.

Blejwas, Stanislaus. 1981. "Old and New Polonias: Tension within an Ethnic Community." *Polish American Studies* 38(2):55–83.

Brozek, Andrzej. 1985. *Polish Americans: 1854–1939*. Translated by W. Worsztynowicz. Warsaw, Poland: Interpress.

Erdmans, Mary. 1995. "Immigrants and Ethnics: Conflict and Identity in Polish Chicago." *Sociological Quarterly* 36:175–95.

———. 1996a. "Home Care Workers: Polish Immigrants Caring for American Elderly." Pp. 267–92 in *Current Research on Occupations and Professions*, Vol. 9, edited by Helena Znaniecka Lopata. Greenwich, CT: JAI Press.

———. 1996b. "Illegal Immigrant Home Care Workers: The Non-market Conditions of Job Satisfaction." *Przeglad Polonijny* 22(2):53–69. Krakow, Poland: Jagiellonian University.

———. 1998. *Opposite Poles: Immigrants and Ethnics in Polish Chicago, 1976–1990*. University Park: Pennsylvania State University Press.

Gans, Herbert. 1979. "Symbolic Ethnicity: The Future of Ethnic Groups and Cultures in America." *Ethnic and Racial Studies* 2(1):1–19.

———. 1994. "Symbolic Ethnicity and Symbolic Religiosity: Towards a Comparison of Ethnic and Religious Acculturation." *Ethnic and Racial Studies* 17:577–92.

Lieberson, Stanley and Mary Waters. 1988. *From Many Strands: Ethnic and Racial Groups in Contemporary America*. New York: Russell Sage Foundation.

Lopata, Helena. 1976. *Polish Americans: Status Competition in an Ethnic Community*. Englewood Cliffs, NJ: Prentice Hall.

Pula, James. 1995. *Polish Americans: An Ethnic Community*. New York: Twayne.

Shokeid, Moshe. 1988. *Children of Circumstance: Israeli Immigrants in New York*. Ithaca, NY: Cornell University Press.

Thomas, William and Florian Znaniecki. [1918] 1958. *The Polish Peasant in Europe and America*. Reprint, New York: Dover.

U.S. Census Bureau. 1993a. *Ancestry of the Population in the United States*. Washington, DC: Government Printing Office.

U.S. Census Bureau. 1993b. *Detailed Ancestry Groups for States*. Washington, DC: Government Printing Office.

U.S. Census Bureau. 1993c. *The Foreign-Born Population in the United States*. Washington, DC: Government Printing Office.

U.S. Census Bureau. 1997. *Statistical Abstracts of the United States*. Washington, DC: Government Printing Office.

U.S. Department of Justice. 1960–1976. *Annual Report of the Immigration and Naturalization Service*. Washington, DC: Government Printing Office.

U.S. Department of Justice. 1977–1996. *Statistical Yearbook of the Immigration and Naturalization Service*. Washington DC: Government Printing Office.

Waters, Mary. 1990. *Ethnic Options*. Berkeley: University of California Press.

Erdmans:

1. How are the experiences of refugees, migrants, and vacationers similar and different from one another?

2. How are Polish immigrants different from Polish Americans with regard to their cultural characteristics? Erdmans notes that "the two identities—immigrant and ethnic—are distinct." What does she mean?

Israeli Americans

Steven J. Gold

Israelis in the United States earn incomes that approach those of native-born whites, learn English easily, frequently marry U.S. citizens, and exhibit high rates of naturalization. Generally white, they encounter little racial discrimination. Moreover, they have easy access to the American Jewish community, within which they often live and work (Gold and Phillips 1996).

Despite these attainments, however, after residing in the United States for decades, Israelis almost never describe themselves as Americans, socialize almost exclusively with other Israelis, keep in touch with and visit Israel often, and frequently refer to their plans to return home (Shokeid 1988). Studies have shown that even the second generation continue to call themselves "Israelis" rather than Americans by a wide margin (Uriely 1995). Consequently, Israeli Americans are characterized by numerous opportunities to join the host society—especially the American Jewish community—yet retain strong feelings of attachment to and identification with their country of origin. This chapter discusses the experience of Israeli Americans and pays special attention to the ways they retain a home country-based identity while actively participating in the host society.

Methods

To understand the experience of Israeli migrants, three researchers (an American man, an American woman, and an Israeli woman) collected several forms of data between June 1991 and April 1996. A major source was 97 in-depth interviews (conducted in both Hebrew and English) with a socially diverse sample of Israeli immigrants and others knowledgeable about their community (44 women and 53 men, including both the wife and husband of nine couples). In addition to in-depth interviews, we also conducted participant observation research at a variety of religious and secular community activities and other Israeli settings (Gold 1992, 1994a, 1997).

I trace my personal interest in Israeli immigration to two issues. First, in contrast to many migrant groups who are driven to leave their homelands by political or economic tumult and crisis, Israelis make a conscious choice to emigrate and have the freedom to return. Having completed several years of research on refugee groups who were forced to go abroad to survive, I found the set of issues associated with a voluntary immigrant group—such as motives for exit, patterns of adjustment, and plans for returning home—intriguing (Gold 1992, 1995a). Second, as an American Jew, I am fascinated by the tension between my group's mixed and sometimes contradictory feelings of connection to the United States—home to the largest Jewish population in the world, albeit as a religious minority—and their emotions toward Israel, which came into existence as a homeland for all Jews.

The particulars of the relationship between American Jews and Israel are unique. However, because the United States is a nation of immigrants, most Americans have the potential to experience conflicting feelings of identification between the United States and the countries of their ancestors or co-religionists, be they China, Mexico, Holland, or Ghana.

Sources of Identity

Israelis in the United States have a complex ethnic identity. Although all are Jews, they vary greatly in their degree of religious involvement and the ways in which they practice their religion, which diverges considerably according to their denominational affiliation and philosophy of life. A small fraction of Israelis are devoutly orthodox and painstakingly conform to an extensive code of ritual requirements. The vast majority, however, are secular and follow a pattern of life typical of Western industrialized nations. As a nation of immigrants, Israel encompasses persons with various national origins, ranging from eastern and western Europe, to the Americas, North Africa, and the Middle East. All of these nationality groups are represented within the Israeli American population. Since its founding half a century ago in 1948, the nation of Israel has worked to develop a common culture, emphasizing the shared experiences as Israelis rather than as Jews, per se. Nevertheless, many of its citizens remain attached to the habits of their coun-

tries of origin—be they Morocco, Poland, Yemen, or Russia.

During the 1970s and 1980s, and in the 1990s to a lesser degree, Israeli immigrants have been viewed by American Jews and Israelis alike as violators of Zionist ideology and a potential threat to the survival of the Jewish state. As a consequence, they have been referred to as *Yordim*—a stigmatizing Hebrew term that describes those who "descend" from the "higher" place of Israel to the Diaspora, as opposed to immigrants, the *Olim,* who "ascend" from the Diaspora to Israel. However, in recent years, both Israel and the American Jewish community have taken a more conciliatory approach toward Israeli expatriates. American Jews provide Israelis with communal assistance, and Israel offers its overseas citizens a package of services and benefits, including outreach in the United States, and services and financial incentives to encourage their return home (Rosen 1993). Hence, the policies and actions of Israel and the American Jewish community have served both to facilitate and limit Israelis' merger into American Jewish life.

Motives for Migration

When asked why they came to the United States, most Israelis offered one of three overlapping responses—economic opportunities (including education), family factors, and a need for broader horizons (Gold 1997; Rosen 1993; Sobel 1986; Herman 1988). For example, Yossi, who now works as a building contractor, alludes to both "broadening his horizons" and increasing economic opportunities as he describes his desire to come to the United States.

I came here in February '78 as a student. Back in Israel, I see and hear so much about America and I figure America is somehow the final place in the progression of the world. Whatever happens in the world, somehow, America has a good hand in it. And so I decide that maybe it is the main source and I want to learn about America and open up my mind. And also, back home, there was not adequate opportunities.

A fairly large number, generally women and children, came to accompany their husbands and fathers who sought economic betterment and educational opportunity (Kimhi 1990; Lipner 1987). For example, in 1986, marriage to an American citizen accounted for a third of all Israelis who received immigrant status to the United States (Herman 1994:92). Furthermore, in fieldwork interviews, Israelis often mentioned coming to the United States to join relatives. Reflecting the other side of the same process, émigrés in the United States described bringing Israeli relatives and friends to join them.

Israelis who were self-employed prior to migration and who retain their entrepreneurial pursuits in the United States assert that the United States is a better location for capitalistic endeavors than Israel (Uriely 1994; Gold 1994b). This is reflected in the following exchange with an émigré in the garment business in Los Angeles:

For the people who were in business in Israel, you don't even have to ask why they came here. We just know that they came to do business. America is a better country for business. Less regulations, taxes and controls. They want you to do some business. Israel, it's too much socialism.

Like various groups in both previous and current migrant flows, Israelis are involved in chain migration. The presence of established coethnics in the host society is a valuable resource for later migrants. It lowers the social and economic costs associated with migration and plays a major role in organizing receiving communities. Israelis also ease their resettlement in the United States by residing in the Jewish neighborhoods in major cities (Herman and LaFontaine 1983).

Although most Israelis enter the United States with the specific goals of education, economic and career advancement, or family unification, another group arrives as part of a "Secular Pilgrimage" of world travel that is a common rite of passage among Israelis following their military service, which is compulsory for men and women alike (Ben-Ami 1992).

Israelis interviewed in Los Angeles and New York described how they had come to the United States as part of their travels, picked up a job to earn some cash, and then had "gotten stuck"—because of economic opportunities, relationships, or other factors—for a period longer than they had initially planned. Isaac described this:

Israel is a country that is not easy to live in. Everybody finishes the army after three or four years. After the army, you understand life differently. So you are ready to try something else. I came to Los Angeles, and then I met my wife and that's how I started. I got into the clothing business and I stayed. We had kids.

An additional explanation for Israeli emigration is the desire to be outside of the confines of the Jewish state. For supporters of Israel, direct criticism of the Jewish state by those living beyond its borders is seen as disloyal and, as such, is relatively infrequent among émigrés. However, in explaining why they left Israel, certain migrants described feelings of disillusionment or a general attitude of not being able to fit into the social order. Israelis who are from stigmatized ethnic backgrounds sometimes claim they left because of discrimination. Finally, Israelis occasionally describe their exit as an effort to escape military duty and the ever-present violence associated with life in the Middle East (Sobel 1986). According to an Israeli government estimate, about five percent of all permanent emigrants exit because of ideological reasons (Yisrael Shelanu 1995).

Demographic and Economic Characteristics

The number of Israelis in the United States has been a subject of intense controversy. In fact, given their broad array of national origins and their ongoing links to various nations and cultural forms, the very definition of an Israeli is problematic, making their enumeration difficult. However, estimates based on the 1990 U.S. census, the 1990 National Jewish Population Survey, and Israeli census data suggest that approximately 100,000 to 190,000 Jewish Israelis live in the United States, with about 30,000 in the greater New York area and approximately half that number living in Los Angeles (Gold and Phillips 1996).

Israelis in the United States tend to be young. For example, in 1990, 79 percent of Israel-born persons in New York and 70 percent of Israelis in Los Angeles were below age 44. In both communities, there were more males than females. The marriage rate of Israelis living in New York is quite high—about 80 percent in 1980. At the same time, New York-based Israelis' divorce rate—of between two percent and five percent—is lower than for other New York Jews, whose rate of divorce is 10 percent. Israelis also tend to have more children per family than American-born Jews.

According to the 1990 census, Israelis in the United States are relatively well educated. Fifty-four percent in New York and 58 percent in Los Angeles have at least some college, and less than 15 percent in either city are not high school graduates. In both New York and Los Angeles, almost half the population aged 24 to 65 are employed as managers, administrators, professionals, or technical specialists. Another quarter in both cities are employed in sales. According to the 1990 census, their rate of self-employment—22 percent—is the second-highest of all nationality groups in the United States, exceeded only by Koreans. This high rate of self-employment is achieved by extensive economic cooperation—involving coethnic hiring and subcontracting—and by the concentration of Israelis in a number of areas of economic specialization. Entrepreneurship long has been a viable economic strategy for Jewish immigrants to the United States who, as a group, are party to an extensive tradition of self-employment prior to their arrival in this country. Israelis are notably active in the real estate, construction, jewelry and diamond, retail sales, security, garment, engineering, and media industries (Gold and Phillips 1996).

As their generally lucrative occupations might indicate, the earnings of Israelis in the United States are considerable. In fact, persons tracing their ancestry to Israel rank fifth in family income out of 99 ancestry groups tabulated in the 1990 census (Yoon 1997). Employed Israeli men residing in New York City were making, on average, approximately $35,000 annually in 1989, and their counterparts in Los Angeles were making an average of almost $49,000. These figures exceed those of all foreign-born men in either city, and best the earnings of even native-born whites in Los Angeles. The greater earnings of Los Angeles Israeli men versus New Yorkers can be accounted for by their higher rates of self-employment and their concentration in construction, which was a lucrative occupation during much of the 1970s and 1980s in Southern California.

Employed Israeli women in New York and Los Angeles also earn more than the average for all foreign-born women but make less annually than native-born white women in these cities. As native speakers of Hebrew who are often trained as educators, Israeli women frequently find employment as instructors in American Jewish synagogues and schools. Others work as professionals, managers, and administrators and in clerical jobs.

Although men have very high rates of labor force participation, a surprisingly large fraction of Israeli women are not in the labor market. This can be considered an indicator of Israelis' economic advancement over their status in Israel because in the country of origin, a single income could not support the family, whereas it can in the United States. A survey of naturalized Israelis in New York found that only 4 percent of the women indicated "housewife" as their occupation in Israel, whereas 36 percent did so in the United States. This makes Israelis distinct from many other contemporary immigrant groups, which maintain higher labor force participation rates for women in the United States than in their countries of origin (Gold 1995b).

Communal Patterns

Most Jews who have entered the United States during the last 300 years have been de jure or de facto refugees, with few opportunities for returning to their countries of origin. By contrast, Israelis retain the real possibility of going back to Israel; indeed, American Jews, the Jewish state, and even the immigrants themselves generally agree that they should return. Consequently, this distinguishes Israelis from most other Jewish entrants in U.S. history.

Although most Jews immigrating to the United States have become staunchly nationalistic soon after their arrival, Israelis in the United States often discuss their desire to return home, and many make frequent trips back to the Jewish state, sometimes culminating in permanent repatriation, as seen in the words of a community leader in Los Angeles:

Israelis would always suffer a certain touch of nostalgia because they are missing the things that they grew up with. Psychologically, most Israelis did not come here to be Americans. They did not come here to swear to the flag, to sing the national anthem and to go to Dodgers games. They came here to have the house and the swimming pool and the two cars and the job and the money.

Despite their ambivalence about being here, Israelis have been active in building a life for themselves in the United States. In fact, Israeli immigrants in Los Angeles, New York, Chicago, and other cities have developed many activities and organizations to resolve their misgivings about being in the United States. Community activities include socializing with other Israelis; living near coethnics (and within Jewish communities); consuming Hebrew-language media (produced in both the United States and Israel); frequenting Israeli restaurants and nightclubs; attending coethnic social events and celebrations; joining Israeli associations; working with other Israelis; consuming goods and services provided by Israeli professionals and entrepreneurs; keeping funds in Israeli banks; sending kids to Israeli-oriented religious, language, recreational, day care, and cultural/national activities; raising money for Israeli causes; calling Israel on the phone; and hosting Israeli visitors.

In the course of fieldwork in Los Angeles, one research team identified some 27 Israeli organizations—ranging from synagogues, Hebrew schools, and political groups to scouting programs, sports teams, business associations, and even a recreational flying club (Gold 1994a). This number of organizations exceeds that created by other middle-class immigrant groups in Los Angeles, including Iranians and Soviet Jews. Such a multiplicity of organizations allows émigrés to maintain various Israeli practices and outlooks in the American setting.

Gender and Family Adaptation

In nearly every study of Israelis in the United States, we find that although migration was a "family decision" and the family as a whole enjoys economic benefits as a result of migration, the decision to migrate was made by the men for the expanded educational and occupational opportunities available in the

United States (Gold 1995b; Rosenthal and Auerbach 1992). For example, Irit described her move to the United States and eventual resettlement in Israel, as determined by her husband's attending graduate school:

For me changes are usually difficult. It affected our life at the beginning. It was kind of a crisis for me. But after a year, we had a good and peaceful life there. So also returning was difficult for me. I was stressed when we went there and when we returned. I was forced to leave, and to return.

Once in the United States, men often enjoy the benefits of such expanded opportunities and, accordingly, feel more comfortable with the new nation. Women, however, especially those with children and established careers, have more negative views of migration. Survey research revealed that Israeli women are less satisfied with America and retain a stronger sense of Israeli and Jewish identity than do men, who increasingly see themselves as American. Even when Israeli women work in the United States, they have less of a professional identity than men and would prefer to return home (Kimhi 1990:95).

Our own interviews as well as the literature indicate that a large fraction of Israeli women come to the United States not of their own volition but only to accompany their husbands, who seek economic and educational improvement, as seen in the words of Rachael:

For most of the people that came here, the men came and the women came after them. Like when I came, my husband came for a job. I had to leave my job and I had to find a new job and it was very painful. I think more and more now there are women coming on their own, but if you look at most cases, it is the men coming after jobs and it means that the women are the ones that have to take care of finding apartment, finding schools for kids and they get depressed, very badly depressed.

Once in the United States, through their immersion in education and work, men develop a social network and a positive sense of self. Women, however, often remain isolated in the home—saddled with the task of caring for children in a strange new country and lacking access to social networks. Furthermore, because they are responsible for child rearing and many of the family's domestic and social activities, Israeli women are the family members who most directly confront alien American social norms and cultural practices. Separated from the resources and knowledge to which they had access at home, Israeli immigrant women find their domestic and communal tasks—such as building social networks, finding appropriate schools and recreational activities, dealing with teachers and doctors, obtaining day care, and the like—to be quite difficult in the United States. This increase in difficulty in women's tasks is contrasted to the various advantages U.S. presence yields for husbands involved in the economic sphere, as described by Michal:

I am convinced from all my friends that the quality of life in Israel is better than the quality here and the problem for Israeli women, whether they have a career or they don't have a career, they have to tend to the children also and those worries here are tremendous. Where do you send your kids to school? You deal with the public system if you cannot afford to send to private school, all those things, and they fall on the woman. They don't fall on the man. And the man comes home and he hopefully brings the bread, that's all he does.

It is important to note that although many of the economic advantages of the U.S. stay can benefit Israeli women as well as men, due to the gender-based division of labor, they most commonly go to men alone. Lipner's (1987) research indicates that an Israeli woman's family status and involvement has much to do with her opinion of the United States. Younger women who had few social attachments prior to migration (i.e., no children or established careers) looked forward to migrating and enjoyed being in the States. However, women who had children and who were forced to give up good positions in Israel to come to the United States had a much harder time, experiencing their exit as "devastating" (Lipner 1987:144–45).

In reflecting on their experience in the United States, Israelis contrast the nation's positive economic and occupational environment to its communal and cultural liabilities: Immigrants almost universally regard Israel as a better place for kids. It is safer, has fewer social problems, and does not impose the manifold generational conflicts Israelis confront when raising children in the United States. Furthermore, in Israel, Jews are the culturally and religiously dominant group. The institutions of the larger society teach children Hebrew and instruct them in basic national, ethnic, and religious identity as well as in Jewish history. However, in coming to the United States, Israelis become a minority group and lose communal networks based on family, friendship, and neighborhood that provided a social life and assistance in raising children.

The presence of young or school-age children in Israeli immigrant families often heightens their ambivalence about being in the United States. Role changes sometimes occur between parents and children, with the younger generation gaining in power versus the older. This is because children generally become Americanized and learn English much faster than do their parents. For example, respondent Carmella reported that her teenage son would react to her advice by saying "What do you know about it? You're from Israel."

Another source of family conflict occurs when various family members disagree regarding their chosen country of residence. These problems are most dramatic when one spouse is American-born or has many American relatives, and the other's family resides in Israel. Similarly, children who have spent much of their lives in the United States often prefer to remain, whereas their parents wish to return to Israel. Finally, parents may wish to remain in the United States for career opportunities, whereas children wish to return to Israel.

In general, we found that Israeli families were relatively resilient in the United States and provided valuable assistance and support to their members. At the same time, Israeli families suffered from financial problems, separation from relatives, and generational conflicts in communication and identity. The presence of children appears to be a major incentive that motivates immigrant families to reevaluate their collective identity in the United States and often to take steps so that children will experience some form of Jewish and/or Israeli training.

Jewish Identity and Involvement in Jewish Life

Israeli and American Jewish notions of group membership contrast because the basic group identities associated with being Israeli, on the one hand, and American Jewish, on the other, are rooted in particular cultural and national contexts. For many Israelis, ethnic identity is secular and nationalistic. Although Israelis are knowledgeable about Jewish holidays and speak Hebrew, they connect these behaviors to "Israeliness" rather than Jewishness. The majority do not actively participate in organized religious activities—as is the case among many American Jews—and Israelis depend on the larger society and public institutions to socialize their children. The Western denominations of Reform and Conservative Judaism, with which the great majority of American Jews affiliate (denominations that permit American Jews to maintain their religious outlooks while incurring few conflicts with the larger Christian society), are all but unknown in the Jewish state—marriages performed by Reform rabbis in Israel have no legal standing. Finally, although American Jews are accustomed to life as a subcommunity in a religiously pluralistic society, Israelis grew up in an environment where religion and nationality were one and the same.

Because of Israelis' lack of familiarity with American forms of Jewish involvement, some pundits decry their assimilation into non-Jewish cultural patterns. They assert that Israelis' very exit from the Holy Land signifies a move away from the Jewish ideal and that their participation in and contribution to Jewish activities is limited and oriented toward secular pursuits with little religious content—meals, parties, Israeli folk dancing, and sports (Shokeid 1988).

In contrast, other observers argue that Israelis actively participate in American Jewish life and simultaneously maintain their links to Israel by noting that the Israelis speak Hebrew, live in Jewish neighborhoods, are involved in a variety of Jewish institutions, and visit Israel frequently. Although survey data on Israelis' Jewish behaviors are relatively scarce, those that exist indicate that established immigrants engage in many Jewish behaviors at higher rates than is the case among native-born Jews. For example, Israeli migrants' synagogue membership, at 27 percent, is above that of Americans. Furthermore, 80 percent of Israeli parents provide their children with some form of Jewish education—50 percent of Israeli children in Los Angeles and 35 percent in New York attend Jewish day schools. Their rate of intermarriage to non-Jews, at only 8 percent, is 40 percent less than the recent average for American Jews.

When comparing patterns in Israel with Israeli immigrants' observance of Jewish religious practices—lighting candles on Shabbat (the Jewish Sabbath) and Chanukah, attending Synagogue on the High Holy Days and Shabbat and fasting on Yom Kippur—we find that among naturalized Israelis in New York and Los Angeles, ritual behaviors have actually increased. Increased rates of ritual practice probably reflect the efforts of these Jewish migrants to retain their religious identity within a predominantly non-Jewish country (Gold and Phillips 1996).

Finally, a growing number of Israeli American parents are acting to reestablish connections with Israeli and/or Jewish behaviors through special family activities of their own creation or involvement in various Israeli American programs, such as after-school Israeli Hebrew courses and Hebrew language scouting activities.[1]

Transnational Israelis

Transnationalism, a new approach in the field of migration studies, has been created precisely to understand a growing number of international migrant communities, who, like Israeli Americans, maintain social, cultural, and economic links to multiple nation-states on a more or less permanent basis (Glick Schiller, Basch, and Blanc-Szanton 1992).

A central point of transnationalism is its view of migration as a multilevel process that involves various links between two or more settings rather than a discrete event constituted by a permanent move from one nation to another. The concept of transnationalism suggests that by retaining social, cultural, and economic ties with two or more countries, people can avoid the impediments traditionally associated with long distances and international boarders. At the same time, transnationalism reminds us that people often remain intensely involved in the life of their country of origin even though they no longer permanently reside there.

A whole series of factors surrounding Israelis makes their movement from the Jewish state to the United States relatively easy. They are well educated and often in the possession of occupational and cultural skills that are useful in both nation-states. They generally have access to networks in both countries that can provide a broad variety of resources, ranging from pretravel information to job opportunities, child care, housing, and a social life. Although some Israelis in the United States lack legal resident status, as a group, they are very likely to become naturalized and are among a select few allowed to have dual citizenship (Jasso and Rosenzweig 1990). Even prior to migration, Israelis often feel extremely familiar with American society from their exposure to popular culture, American visitors as and intergovernment relations. As Israeli social scientist Zvi Sobel (1986) put it, "America, it might be posited, has become the alter ego of Israel in political, economic and cultural terms" (pp. 192–93).

A great proportion of the Israeli population have resided within the Jewish state for fewer than two or perhaps three generations. Accordingly, their family lore and cultural baggage is rich with stories of—and techniques for coping with—life in other settings. Many émigrés we interviewed had lived in other nations, ranging from Japan and Hong Kong to Switzerland, England, South Africa, Italy, and Latin America, prior to their settlement in the United States. Although professionals and high-level entrepreneurs had lived overseas, so have less-skilled and less-educated migrants, such as carpenters and restaurant workers. Hence, many Israelis possessed a cultural orientation and life experience compatible with an existence beyond the borders of the Jewish state. William Petersen's classic migration typology accounts for the unique tendency of such groups to move:

The principal cause of migration may be prior migration. . . . In a framework where migration has been set as a social pattern, the individual motivations may be relatively trivial and the family and community structure more salient in mobility decision making. (As quoted in DeJong and Fawcett 1981:16)

Further facilitating Israel American transnationalism are the good political rela-

tions and extensive links shared by the United States and Israel. The U.S. government and American Jewish agencies have developed an active presence in the Jewish state. American firms have branches there, and American companies sometimes hire professional and skilled workers directly from Israel. At the same time, Israeli government agencies, banks, and industrial enterprises have offices in New York, Los Angeles, and other American cities. These not only give an Israeli flavor to the American environment but also provide employment for migrants (Sobel 1986). At the same time, we noted a variety of Israeli-oriented activities that allow migrants to maintain a semblance of the Israeli life in the United States.

Travel between the two nations is easily arranged. Israeli immigrants often report making frequent trips from the United States to Israel, and it is not uncommon for children to return to Israel to spend summer vacations with relatives. A Los Angeles obstetrician describes the great value he places on his trips back to Israel:

I was talking to my accountant two days ago—he is also an Israeli—he says "What is going on?" And I said "What can I tell you, we are in a concentration camp." Okay—this is the way you describe it, and it is so true. We are in a concentration camp and we get a relief once a year when we go to Israel for a vacation. This is the bottom line.

Sobel (1986), in his 1981–1982 pretravel survey of 117 Israel emigrants (most of whom planned to enter the United States), found clear evidence of a transnational outlook. About one half denied "that leaving Israel and moving to the United States was an act of emigration." Instead, they defined the travel as "temporary" or "commuting." Moreover, "almost all interviewees denied that their leaving meant a cessation of contributing to the development of Israel. . . . Almost all saw their departure as . . . to Israel's good" (Sobel 1986:196).

In all these ways, the Israeli context, history, and culture have prepared members of this group for transnationalism. It would appear that the whole notion of being an Israeli versus an American is not nearly as clear-cut a distinction as the literature on international migration would generally suggest. Instead, factors such as flexible notions of ethnic and national identity, access to and participation in social and occupational networks, and the ability of people to sustain cultural competence and legal status in more than a single society allow Israelis to maintain meaningful forms of involvement in multiple national settings at one time.

Despite these many factors that permit Israelis to maintain a transnational existence, many remain troubled by the distance—physical as well as cultural—between the two nations. As suggested in the following quotations, even those Israelis who have accomplished a great deal in the United States contrast America's favorable economic and career-related environment to its communal and cultural liabilities:

An Israeli is torn apart the minute he is leaving Israel [to come to the United States for an extended period]. It's not like people from other countries who come here and settle down, hoping for better life. An Israeli is torn apart the minute he leaves Israel and that's when he begins to wonder where is it better—here or there.

I think that the reason so many Israelis are here is the illusion of materialistic comfort they can find here, period. It has nothing to do with spiritual, cultural or emotional values they are looking for. The issue is materialism. And it doesn't fulfill all the needs a human being has. A person needs culture and some ideals to believe in. We Israelis continue to keep a close contact with Israel as if we left for a short time only. We come here and organize our lives as if we are going to stay for a short period and our life here is a make-believe. The reality is that we live here and at the same time we don't live here. We are torn apart and that leaves

the question for which I don't have an answer—what will happen and where are we?

Hence, for many Israelis, transnationalism is a reality. This does not mean, however, that it is an easy way of life. Although these migrants build communities and networks that help them cope with the social and cultural dimensions of ties to two nations, and although they enjoy economic benefits from migration, most are not quite comfortable with this status. In the words of a Los Angeles accountant, "Israel is my mother and America is my wife, so you can imagine the way I must feel."

Conclusions

Jews have been migrating to the United States since the 1600s, under a variety of circumstances and with different outlooks and resources. Israelis are among the most recent of these groups. American Jews' support of the state of Israel, along with Israel's own anti-emigration outlook, has sometimes resulted in a less-than-welcoming reception for these new arrivals. Furthermore, because Israelis and American Jews have distinct cultural and linguistic traditions and express their identities in different ways, Israelis have encountered some difficulties in joining the religious and communal activities of their American co-religionists. However, in terms of skills, education, and Jewish knowledge, Israelis have much to offer both to American society in general and the American Jewish community in particular. In recent years, the potential benefits provided by Israeli immigrants have become more apparent to American Jewish organizations, and efforts to facilitate either their merger into the American Jewish community or their return home have been undertaken with some success.

For many Israeli Americans, the best way to address their conflicting commitments to both the United States and Israel is by maintaining a transnational existence, which emphasizes the use of Hebrew and interaction within the Israeli immigrant community, coupled with frequent visits to the country of origin. Consequently, Israelis enjoy economic benefits from migration and build communities and networks to cope with the social and cultural contingencies of being attached to two homelands.

Note

1. Modern Israeli Hebrew is very different from the religious language typically studied as a part of an American Jewish education.

References

Ben-Ami, Ilan. 1992. "Schlepers and Car Washers: Young Israelis in the New York Labor Market." *Migration World* 20(1):18–20.

DeJong, Gordon F. and James T. Fawcett. 1981. "Motivations for Migration: An Assessment and Value-Expectancy Research Model." Pp. 13–58 in *Migration Decision Making: Multidisciplinary Approaches to Microlevel Studies in Developed and Developing Countries,* edited by G. F. De Jong and R. W. Gardner. New York: Pergamon.

Glick Schiller, Nina, Linda Basch, and Cristina Blanc-Szanton. 1992. "Transnationalism: A New Analytic Framework for Understanding Migration." Pp. 1–24 in *Towards a Transnational Perspective on Migration: Race, Class, Ethnicity and Nationalism Reconsidered,* edited by N. Glick Schiller, L. Basch, and C. Blanc-Szanton. New York: New York Academy of Sciences.

Gold, Steven. 1992. *Refugee Communities: A Comparative Field Study.* Newbury Park, CA: Sage.

———. 1994a. "Israeli Immigrants in the U.S.: The Question of Community." *Qualitative Sociology* 17:325–63.

———. 1994b. "Patterns of Economic Cooperation among Israeli Immigrants in Los Angeles." *International Migration Review* 28(105):114–35.

———. 1995a. *From the Workers' State to the Golden State: Jews from the Former Soviet Union in California.* Boston, MA: Allyn & Bacon.

———. 1995b. "Gender and Social Capital among Israeli Immigrants in Los Angeles." *Diaspora* 4:267–301.

———. 1997. "Transnationalism and Vocabularies of Motive in International Migration: The Case of Israelis in the U.S." *Sociological Perspectives* 40:409–26.

Gold, Steven J. and Bruce A. Phillips. 1996. "Israelis in the United States." Pp. 51–101 in *American Jewish Yearbook 1996,* edited by R. Seldin.

Herman, Pini. 1988. "Jewish-Israeli Migration to the United States since 1948." Presented at the annual meeting of the Association of Israel Studies, June 7, New York.

———. 1994. "A Technique for Estimating a Small Immigrant Population in Small Areas: The Case of Jewish Israelis in the United States." Pp. 81–99 in *Studies in Applied Demography,* edited by K. Vaninadha Rao and J. W. Wicks. Bowling Green, OH: Population and Society Research Center.

Herman, Pini and David LaFontaine. 1983. "In Our Footsteps: Israeli Migration to the U.S. and Los Angeles." Master's thesis, Hebrew Union College, Los Angeles, CA.

Jasso, Guillermina and Mark R. Rosenzweig. 1990. *The New Chosen People: Immigrants in the United States.* New York: Russell Sage Foundation.

Kimhi, Shaol. 1990. "Perceived Change of Self-Concept, Values, Well-Being and Intention to Return among Kibbutz People Who Migrated from Israel to America." Ph.D. dissertation, Pacific Graduate School of Psychology, Palo Alto, CA.

Lipner, Nira H. 1987. "The Subjective Experience of Israeli Immigrant Women: An Interpretive Approach." Ph.D. dissertation, George Washington University, Washington, DC.

Rosen, Sherry. 1993. "The Israeli Corner of the American Jewish Community" (Issue Series No. 3). New York: Institute on American Jewish-Israeli Relations, The American Jewish Committee.

Rosenthal, Mira and Charles Auerbach. 1992. "Cultural and Social Assimilation of Israeli Immigrants in the United States." *International Migration Review* 99:982–91.

Shokeid, Moshe. 1988. *Children of Circumstances: Israeli Immigrants in New York.* Ithaca, NY: Cornell University Press.

Sobel, Zvi. 1986. *Migrants from the Promised Land.* New Brunswick, NJ: Transaction Publishing.

Uriely, Natan. 1994. "Rhetorical Ethnicity of Permanent Sojourners: The Case of Israeli Immigrants in the Chicago Area." *International Sociology* 9:431–45.

———. 1995. "Patterns of Identification and Integration with Jewish Americans among Israeli Immigrants in Chicago: Variations Across Status and Generation." *Contemporary Jewry* 16:27–49.

Yisrael Shelanu. 1995. "For Those Returning Home" (in Hebrew). *Our Israel* (Supplement).

Yoon, In-Jin. 1997. *On My Own: Korean Businesses and Race Relations in America.* Chicago: University of Chicago Press.

Gold:

1. Discuss how the policies and actions of Israel and the American Jewish community have served both to facilitate and limit Israeli immigration to the United States.

2. What does Gold mean when he discusses "chain migration"? Discuss the benefits of such a type of migration.

32

Social Citizenship for Whom?
Young Turks in Germany and
Mexican Americans in the United States[1]

Thomas Faist

Why do different policy systems produce similar results in terms of integrating immigrants? Germany and the United States have evolved distinct systems for integrating young adults into labor markets and, ultimately, into social citizenship. Germany is characterized by a policy-based system in which the state, employers, and unions play a large role in directing and regulating a coherent system of job training, mainly through apprenticeship. The United States can be described as a market-based system, in which the transition from school to work is more diverse, less regulated, and more haphazard. Nevertheless, the results are similar. The two largest immigrant groups in Germany and the United States—Turks and Mexican Americans, respectively—end up in similarly disadvantaged positions relative to the majority groups—Germans and European Americans—and minority women more than men. There is even the possibility of long-term socioeconomic marginalization of these immigrant groups in both countries. School-work transition presents an ideal case through which to investigate the conditions

of social membership and citizenship in general and for immigrants in particular. The transition processes tell us about the worlds of both education and work. It is in school-work transitions that we can see the material foundations of social citizenship unfolding.

This article has three parts. The first part outlines the framework in which the empirical analysis of school-work transition proceeds, using the concept of social citizenship and placing this problem in the institutional context of welfare states and labor markets and offering a theoretical framework to synthesize "supply-side" explanations for school-work transitions—especially public policies and labor market segmentation—and the resources of the immigrants themselves, the "demand-side" explanations—educational qualifications, job networks, and training in immigrant businesses. In particular, it examines how public policies in Germany and the United States interact with the resources of competing immigrant groups in the experience of social citizenship. The third part presents the methods of research and some selected results of the empirical analysis of school-work transitions on a local level in a comparative cross-national perspective. It refers to a concrete analysis of the experience of social citizenship among immigrant and majority groups in two cities: Duisburg in Germany and Chicago in the United States. The third part then draws implications from school-work transitions concerning the condition of social citizenship among immigrant groups and the polities as a whole. In particular, the conclusion sketches a proposal that rights to a guaranteed minimum income for school-leavers could undergird public policies that promote the concept of citizenship as equality of opportunity and enable active participation in the polity.

Theoretical Concepts: Social Citizenship and Labor Market Theories

The major theorists of citizenship—Aristotle, Cicero, Macchiavelli, Burke, de Tocqueville, Mill, Arendt—all have argued that, to participate fully in public life and to achieve recognized social membership, one needs to be in a certain socioeconomic position. Citizenship carries an enabling aspect. In democratic states, the opportunity to earn has constituted an integral part of citizenship. Therefore, access to training and placement into jobs is of utmost importance if we want to understand the condition of citizenship in advanced Western welfare states. *Social citizenship* here refers to the material conditions of the existence of membership and recognition. Social citizenship is primarily constituted not by a right or duty to work but by the opportunities and constraints of participating in the working world. It depends largely on social status and recognition derived from participation in labor markets. Work is a condition of full participation in a polity in a way that social rights in the realms of health, housing, and education, as actually imple-

mented, are not. Paid work in particular enables participation in many of the social rights available over the life course of an individual—for example, unemployment benefits and old-age pensions. Therefore, this study does not merely examine the relation between work and social citizenship but also looks at how social citizenship is constituted through access to training and work.

In the United States, debates long have centered on the integration of immigrants. In western Europe, nearly all states hired immigrant labor during the boom cycles after World War II. Since then, all of these polities have restricted the importation of migrant labor. One of the essential questions is how the migrants hired in the 1960s and 1970s and their descendants have become integrated during the process of settlement. There is a puzzle to be explained: Overall, rates of job training of school-leavers in Germany are much higher than in the United States, and youth unemployment is lower. However, in both countries, we encounter similar differences between the majority and immigrant groups and between immigrant groups themselves with respect to enrollment in postsecondary institutions and unemployment.

The United States and Germany are of particular interest because they represent different types of welfare states. The German welfare state has been characterized by highly regulated labor markets, the U.S. welfare state by a lower degree of regulation (Figure 32.1). The institutions and policies of the vocational training politics and the labor market politics in Germany can be described as a policy-based or class-centered corporatism. First, the labor market is characterized by a close weave of regulations, such as certificates (policy-based). Second, the state grants the so-called social partners—unions and employer associations—a lot of autonomy with regard to the structure of vocational training politics (corporatism). Third, the German regulation system organizes interests along

Germany	Policy-based: Vocational education and on-the-job training linked institutionally
	Class-based: The main actors are organized along capital-labor divide
	Corporatism: Tripartite coordination of training policy (employers, unions, state)
United States	Market-based: Few institutional linkages between school and work; on-the-job training exclusively left to firms
	Ethnically segmented: Ethnicity and race are the most important dividing lines on the political level, above all locally
	Pluralism: Interest groups dominate defined territories of vocational education

Figure 32.1. Training and Employment Policies in Germany and the United States

the conflict lines of capital and labor, and it shows social-democratic elements in doing so (class-centered). The institutions and policies in the United States can be characterized as a market-based or ethnically segmented pluralism. Here, this means a system in which, first, the labor market shows less regulation than corporatist systems (market-based). Second, the existing ensemble of vocational training institutions and labor market institutions and policies is more fragmented (pluralism). Third, the conflict line capital-labor is strongly eclipsed by divisions along ethnic lines (ethnically segmented). Comparing these two distinctive models of school-work transition allows us to explain variations between the United States and the Federal Republic of Germany in terms of the uptake of job training by non-college- and non-university-bound school-leavers.

The expectation would be that the policy-based system in Germany and the market-based system in the United States reflect distinct institutionalized conceptions of social citizenship. Germany has a much more coherent system for dealing with the entry of school-leavers into the working world; therefore, one would expect Germany to integrate immigrant youth to a higher degree than does the United States: Turks would be better integrated into job training and work than

would Mexican Americans. The argument here is that Germany's policy-based, corporatist system represents a more political solution, whereas the United States' market-based, pluralist system is much less regulated and is a market solution. One would expect the political system in a democratic polity to favor the interests of citizens—voters—and disfavor noncitizens, such as Turkish immigrants, whereas one would expect a market-based system to be indifferent to civic status.[2] If this aspect of the system is more advantageous to immigrants, then this might compensate for its more haphazard nature, thus giving a similar result to Germany regarding the integration of immigrant school-leavers into training and work.

In the highly regulated German labor markets, public policies connect schooling and on-the-job training through the so-called apprenticeship or dual system. Germany also has an activist policy that rests on state mediation, intermediary organizations of capital and labor, and individual employers. The German system has been very inclusive in providing job training to school-leavers who do not go on to postsecondary education in universities. In Germany, more than two thirds of secondary school graduates enter formal postsecondary training, most of them in apprenticeships.

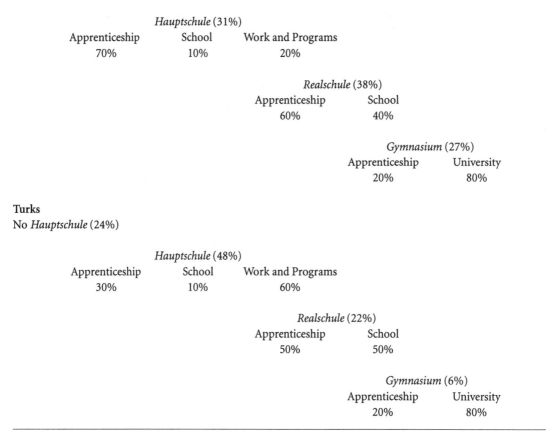

Germans
No *Hauptschule* (5%)

Hauptschule (31%)

Apprenticeship	School	Work and Programs
70%	10%	20%

Realschule (38%)

Apprenticeship	School
60%	40%

Gymnasium (27%)

Apprenticeship	University
20%	80%

Turks
No *Hauptschule* (24%)

Hauptschule (48%)

Apprenticeship	School	Work and Programs
30%	10%	60%

Realschule (22%)

Apprenticeship	School
50%	50%

Gymnasium (6%)

Apprenticeship	University
20%	80%

Figure 32.2. From School to Work in Germany: The First Year after Leaving School (Crude Estimates)

Note: The estimates apply to graduates of public high schools.

By contrast, in the United States, educational institutions and the labor markets are not linked institutionally to the same extent. There is a low degree of labor market regulation. Thus, the United States does not actively connect the states and markets through intermediary institutions. Non-college-bound school-leavers are left to their own devices to pass through a "moratorium" period. Non-college-bound school-leavers constitute about half of all high school graduates and dropouts. They are the "forgotten half." In general, non-college-bound high school-leavers enter low-wage jobs in nonregulated or secondary labor markets. Most non-college-bound school-leavers receive no formal training at all in their late teens and early twenties. Employers do not hire school-leavers for responsible jobs until they judge them to be mature enough, usually when young adults are in their early to mid-20s and have passed through the moratorium period. Moreover, practical job training and theoretical instruction in schools tend to be strictly separate. In

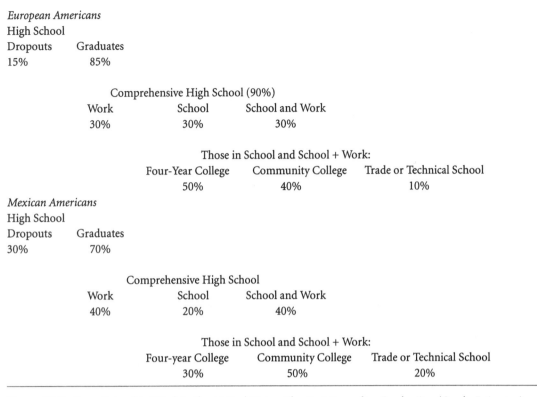

European Americans
High School

Dropouts	Graduates
15%	85%

Comprehensive High School (90%)

Work	School	School and Work
30%	30%	30%

Those in School and School + Work:

Four-Year College	Community College	Trade or Technical School
50%	40%	10%

Mexican Americans
High School

Dropouts	Graduates
30%	70%

Comprehensive High School

Work	School	School and Work
40%	20%	40%

Those in School and School + Work:

Four-year College	Community College	Trade or Technical School
30%	50%	20%

Figure 32.3. From School to Work in the United States: The First Year after Graduation (Crude Estimates)

short, the United States is characterized by a dichotomous framework of training: Public postsecondary institutions train school-leavers, and firms undertake on-the-job training for young adults (Figures 32.2 and 32.3).

The main difference between public policies in Germany and the United States is that German policies have ensured a higher rate of formal job training for school-leavers than have U.S. policies. In short, the German pattern has resulted in high rates of job training for school-leavers. About 85 percent of all youth either pass through systematic training, mostly in the apprenticeship or dual system, or are enrolled in a university. In total, about two thirds of all secondary school-leavers completed an apprenticeship in the 1970s and 1980s. The percentage of school-leavers undergoing formal training in Ger-

many compares very favorably with enrollments in training programs among U.S. youths who did not go on to four-year colleges after high school graduation or who dropped out before graduation.

Thus, at first sight, the German training system seems to be more favorable to school-leavers than the does U.S. system. In the Europe of the 1970s and 1980s, these high levels of job training for school-leavers were matched only by Sweden, Austria, and Switzerland. In addition to a high rate of job training for school-leavers in Germany, the ratio of youth unemployment to adult unemployment is much lower in Germany than in the United States and was consistently so throughout the 1980s. In comparison, youth unemployment as a percentage of total unemployment is lower in Germany. Thus, the

German system of training for non-university-goers has consistently resulted in one of the highest adult-youth unemployment ratios in the European Community and certainly a more favorable one than in the United States.

Nevertheless, it could be argued that the higher youth than adult unemployment rates in the United States are temporary phenomena, reflecting a selection process by employers in the absence of a formal, German-style apprenticeship system. We have to consider the fact that education and job training in the United States are less standardized and stratified than in the Federal Republic of Germany. With respect to inclusion, there are multiple pathways from school to work for non-college-bound school-leavers in the United States, compared to a single way for non-university-bound school-leavers in Germany. This argument is valid when we look at overall rates of unemployment: They significantly decrease after the moratorium period. Yet the experience of immigrant minorities differs from European American school-leavers in that a substantial minority among the immigrant group faces more serious obstacles than does the European American group. Immigrant youth, such as Mexican American school-leavers, tend to find it more difficult than European American youth to obtain long-term work in the youth labor market, and thus they become less attractive and even stigmatized in the eyes of potential employers. Therefore, the possibility that they will be relegated to long-term joblessness or low-skilled, poorly paid labor niches increases. Repeated unemployment during the moratorium period had disastrous consequences for minority and inner-city youth.

However, the results of integrating or excluding immigrant groups in the United States and Germany are quite similar. This becomes clear by comparing young second-generation immigrants to majority groups—that is, Turkish and German youth in Germany and Mexican Americans and Eu-

ropean Americans in the United States. The Turkish as well as the Mexican American youth have difficulties getting access to vocational training or jobs. Turkish youth in Germany are at the lowest ranks with regard to participation in the dual system. Although about two thirds of all Germans aged 16 to 19 complete apprenticeships, only about one third of the young Turks do; the share of Turkish women is even far below that (as of 1996). Mexican American youth lie far behind European American youth in attending secondary schools and in on-the-job training. We can even determine tendencies toward a lasting socioeconomic marginalization of these immigrant groups. Integration means that immigrants have access to formal or informal vocational training and therefore to qualified jobs. Exclusion, on the other hand, exists when, owing to missing vocational training, children of immigrants only get insecure jobs and therefore are exposed to the risk of being unemployed, which consequently pushes them into the fringe groups of the labor market.

We now have to bring out the crucial factors that decide success or failure when entering the labor market. We can distinguish between "supply-side" and "demand-side" factors. On the demand side, first, governmental policies and employers' recruitment have to be taken into account. Second, viewed from the supply side, young school-leavers are now not just objects of governmental politics who can be chosen by employers. The way they use educational degrees and contacts can have a decisive effect on their chances of training. The supply side includes human capital, job networks, and the ability of the immigrant groups to create jobs in enclaves and offer training vacancies.

Neither in the United States nor in Germany is there a right to education or work. In both systems, the reasons for the integration or exclusion of immigrants can be found on the supply side as well as on the demand side—that is, either with the immigrants

Demand Side	Supply Side
Policies and politics	Cultural capital
Policy-based dual system: Class-oriented corporatism (Germany)	Human capital
Market-based moratorium period: Ethnically segmented pluralism (United States)	
Labor markets	*Social capital*
Employment: Supply and demand	Job networks
Labor-market segmentation	Immigrant enclaves

Figure 32.4. Explanatory Approaches for the Integration and Exclusion of Immigrants in Vocational Training Systems and Labor Markets

themselves or with other participants in the labor market. Both these groups of explanatory approaches are explained shortly and examined with regard to their applicability to entering employment (Figure 32.4).

Factors such as politics or policies and the structures of the labor market (e.g., a dual labor market) that involve ethnic or other divisions of the employees are in the foreground of explanations that emphasize the demand side. Education and labor-market politics intensify integration and exclusion processes of immigrants in the labor market by changing selection processes in the labor market. As already mentioned, we can assume that politics and policies in the form of market- or policy-based systems may lead to similar results with regard to only partially integrating immigrants into the labor markets. They differ, however, in the mechanisms causing it. Theories of labor-market segmentation also emphasize the demand side. These theories, for example, see discrimination by employers and workers of the ethnic majority as the main cause for the problems of ethnic minorities in the labor market. The result is an ethnically segmented labor market, with the locals being employed in the primary labor market and the labor immigrants predominantly in the secondary labor market. This

approach is able to explain why it may be rational for employers and workers of the ethnic majority group to discriminate against the minority group for staff recruitment. Employers use the affiliation to an ethnic (e.g., immigrant) group as an indicator for the expected working productivity of applicants. Empirical analyses of the U.S. labor market repeatedly have shown that employers have their own hierarchy of preferences of ethnic groups for certain jobs. Therefore, surveys about staff recruitment repeatedly have shown that in the tertiary sector, European Americans are being preferred to Mexican American applicants. Even with equal qualifications, the expected individual productivity of the applicant is compared with the perception about the average productivity of each ethnic group. The weakness of these demand-side approaches is that they see the immigrants only as objects of labor-market processes and of the exclusion processes of the dominant groups in the labor market. The children of the first generation of immigrants, however, really do have resources when they enter the competition for jobs.

The second category of explanatory approaches emphasizes the supply side—the immigrants' own resources. We can distinguish between cultural capital (human capital) and social capital (job networks and immigrant enclaves). Human capital theorists put the immigrants' resources in the forefront. Accordingly, in Germany, this would be better school marks and higher education levels of the German youth compared with the Turkish, and in the United States, it would be the better reputation of the secondary schools the European Americans attend as opposed to those attended by Americans of Mexican descent, which explains the ethnic inequalities of access to apprenticeships or jobs in the youth labor market.

Overemphasizing human capital of individuals, however, neglects the fundamental importance of the social embeddedness of economic action—social capital. Therefore, human capital theorists fail to explain why, despite equal human capital, German youth in Germany or European American youth in the United States are preferentially employed in attractive apprenticeships. Here, theories about the role of networks go further. Network approaches more or less emphasize the contacts between applicants and employers. They start from the simple but empirically sound consideration that often personal relationships and contacts decide the allocation of jobs. Consequently, for example, children of employees usually have better chances of apprenticeships. The primary mechanism of this was called "social closure" by Max Weber. In this case, the closure of employment chances works in favor of employers' relations and against those without any contacts to the company. In view of the concentration of first-generation work immigrants in certain industries, their children mostly have chances of employment in these fields. Because second-generation immigrants' expectations about future careers closely correspond to those of the majority groups, these jobs, however, are less attractive for them.

Enclave theories, on the other hand, focus on the crucial role of immigrants' entrepreneurial activities in providing jobs and apprenticeship places for members of the same community. These are mostly small businesses that meet the needs of the immigrant community like grocers' shops or travel agencies. Enclave approaches see mutual trust and reciprocal norm control in business life as determining a successful allocation of resources—that is, the ability of immigrant groups to organize themselves economically, such as organizing personal loans to set up businesses. According to the enclave approach, those immigrant groups are successful who manage to both provide enough loans to set up businesses and insist on their repayment. The significance of the businesses in the immigrant enclaves now lies in the fact that they not only employ members of the immigrant community but also give them informal on-the-job training. Crucially important here is whether the immigrant group builds up an economically successful enclave and how apprenticeships are laid down by the policies of each country.

Empirical Research and Results

We make a twofold comparison: On the one hand, several systems of education and labor-market policies are compared. On the other hand, this comparative analysis refers to the differences between German and Turkish youth in Germany and European American and Mexican American youth in the United States. The empirical study used both analysis of aggregate statistical data on the nation-state and the community level and qualitative methods such as interviews and participant observations. Although the statistical analysis on the local level helped to establish patterns of general validity for each case, qualitative methods—such as face-to-face interviews, group discussion with students, and participant observation—probed into various paths from school to work. The case studies focused on two neighborhoods in Duisburg and Chicago. Hamborn in Duisburg and Pilsen/Little Village in Chicago have neighborhoods with high proportions of Turks and Mexican Americans, in both cases almost exclusively made up of first- and second-generation immigrants. Chicago also has third- and fourth-generation Mexican immigrants. It is easy to discern, however, that first- and second-generation migrants tend to live in areas different from third- or fourth-generation Mexican Americans, who are concentrated in south Chicago, near the steel mills and in selected suburban areas. Field research spanned about four months in each location (July–September 1990 and January–February 1991 in Duisburg, and September–December 1990 in Chicago). The local case studies, with their focus on specific and predominantly immigrant neighborhoods—Hamborn in Duisburg, and Pilsen/Little Village in Chicago—allow for a close analysis in the context of human ecology.

The local level was of great importance for the empirical analysis. Various studies have confirmed that geographical mobility of labor market entrants with noncollege degrees is not very high; their market is local. Local case studies also allow us to take account of the political economy of space in terms of schooling and work by examining the functional importance of these distributions. For example, it is no coincidence that school-employer linkages develop in distinct neighborhoods, reflecting the quality of the secondary school and the socioeconomic makeup of the neighborhood.

The empirical analysis provides two answers to the question of why different systems of vocational training, embedded in different types of welfare states and concepts of social citizenship, lead to similar results. First, the thesis that policy- and market-based systems integrate and exclude differently can be confirmed. Compared to German youth, Turkish immigrants' participation in the dual system is significantly less, not least because of their status. Turkish immigrants are not voters, and in a corporatist system decisions of vocational training politics are made in class-oriented institutions, such as the Federal Institute for Vocational Training. Therefore, ironically, the same factors that cause a comparably low unemployment rate and a high vocational training rate for German youth, in an international perspective, discriminate against Turkish youth. In this respect, the market-based system in the United States is more "immigrant-friendly," as it does not make political participation a prerequisite for successful integration.

Further results indicate that both policy- and market-based systems discriminate in their own way: Whereas employers in the highly regulated policy-based system put far more emphasis on formal degrees, in the market-based system the applicants are chosen by the selectiveness of their high school and their residential area. Because Turkish youth compared to German youth have less human capital, and Mexican American compared to European American youth are underrepresented in selective high schools, both immigrant groups have little chance to use their cultural capital. Moreover, each welfare state carries system-specific risks of exclusion. In the highly regulated German system, it is unemployment that Turkish youth face far more often than German youth, especially at the end of apprenticeships. This is so because policies channel school-leavers into apprenticeship and programs directly after high school. However, no such measures are available for those young adults who graduate from apprenticeship. In the less-regulated American system, Mexican Americans are far more often affected by income poverty than are European American youth and young adults. In the more deregulated labor market of the United States, it is comparatively easier to find jobs. Nonetheless, many jobs for first-time labor market entrants with no college degree are relatively low.

Second, supply- and demand-side factors act in combination. This can be seen from the contribution of immigrant enclaves to vocational training. In the past, employment of immigrants of the same group played an important part in career mobility in the United States. It becomes clear, however, that the low degree of Mexican Americans' social capital leads them to offer hardly any apprenticeship places in immigrant enclaves, although immigrants in the United States are less legally restricted, compared with those in Germany, with regard to setting up businesses and permission to instruct. In Germany, self-employed immigrants are not allowed to instruct if they have not themselves passed the German education system and got an instructor's certificate. Only a very small proportion of the self-employed Turks meet these requirements.

The combination of supply- and demand-side factors brings up some questions with regard to a permanent exclusion of certain groups from the labor market. If members of the second generation are discriminated against over long periods and barred from certain fields of activity by job ceilings, their motivations and expectations regarding training and work will decrease. Decreasing motivation goes with socioeconomic marginalization. This process can be observed among Mexican American men in inner-city ghettos. Decreasing expectations in vocational qualification due to combined discrimination and cultural roles already can be found among immigrant subgroups, especially among young Turkish women.

Discrimination on the part of employers and social closure through majority groups is especially detrimental to those migrant groups who are restricted by cultural roles in the immigrant communities. Among the eight groups analyzed and differentiated by ethnicity and gender, young Turkish women are those most severely affected. On the one hand, Turkish immigrant communities in western Europe have experienced a fundamentalist Islamic resurgence in the last two decades that restricts the social and occupational roles that women can take according to

religiously defined norms. On the other hand, parts of the majority group, in this case the German public, perceive the social position of Turkish women as one of the most striking symbols of the cultural differences between majority and minority groups. Religiously defined roles in certain families, together with the perception of head scarves as a symbol of not being qualified for high-quality occupations, restrict the opportunities and expectations of female Turkish school-leavers. Discriminatory employers and families and the decreasing expectations of young Turkish women reinforce one another.

If discriminatory job ceilings limit immigrants to inferior positions in the labor market in the long term, sometimes for several generations, the groups affected may change their attitudes and behavior toward schooling, training, and work. A belief may evolve that it does not pay to invest in human capital. Such processes can basically be observed among young Mexican American men who work in irregular employment in inner-city immigrant communities. In the course of recent changes in the labor markets, both Mexican American and Turkish youth face the risk of socioeconomic marginalization, through income poverty in the market-based system of the United States and through unemployment in the policy-based system of Germany.

Implications for Policy: A Training Compact and Basic Income for School-Leavers

This empirical study initially was inspired by a policy proposal. Various authors have claimed that a German-style apprenticeship system in the United States could help to improve employment prospects for non-college-bound school-leavers in general and for minority youth in particular. In an imaginative and provocative study, Stephen Hamilton concluded that crucial elements of the

German system of apprenticeship training should be adopted in the United States.[3] He claimed that the German system provides formal training for the majority of youth, whereas the U.S. system is characterized by a "floundering" period. Hamilton praised the integration of on-the-job training in companies and theoretical instruction in part-time vocational schools. Most relevant to this study, Hamilton favored the adoption of a modified version of the German system as "apprenticeship for adulthood," because it also would offer training opportunities to ethnic and racial minorities. For example, Hamilton proposed to link theoretical instruction in high schools and colleges with practical training in companies. Thus, recommendations for policy reform of school-work transitions have been based on comparisons between the United States and Germany—yet without a systematic comparative analysis of the experience of immigrants or ethnic minorities in both countries.

Although this policy proposal points toward important institutional prerequisites for successful school-work transitions, these policy recommendations are questionable for several reasons. Policy transfer implies institutional change. Current political opportunities for change are highly dependent on earlier political decisions and policy developments—they are "path-dependent." In general, because the United States is a market-based system, it would be exceedingly difficult to overcome entrenched ideological conceptions of a strict separation of the spheres of states and markets. Furthermore, because the United States is also characterized by a much higher level of ethnic conflict and diversity than is the Federal Republic of Germany, adoption of such policies could lead to immigrants and minorities being confined to the less prestigious fields in apprenticeships, as they are indeed in Germany. Doubts also arise when we consider that, in the late 1980s, about two thirds of all German youth went through apprenticeships, but

only one third of all Turkish youth did so, although the proportion of Turkish youth increased slowly throughout the 1980s. Moreover, although there are profound differences between the German system and the very much smaller U.S. apprenticeship system, the minority experience of apprenticeship in the United States is not encouraging. Immigrants and minorities remain severely underrepresented in registered apprenticeship systems, and although this is usually blamed on blatantly discriminatory construction trade unions, immigrants and minorities are equally if not more underrepresented in nonconstruction apprenticeships. Also, if a German-style apprenticeship system were introduced in the United States, employer recruitment patterns soon would adapt to increased levels of job qualifications. As in Germany, employers in the United States would probably increasingly tend to hire graduates from less prestigious apprenticeship programs for less skilled jobs that carry high risks of income poverty and unemployment.

Basically, my study found that adapting elements of the German apprenticeship system would have been no panacea for solving difficult school-work transitions in the labor markets of the 1990s that are increasingly characterized by uncertain career paths. In particular, it would not solve the problem of statistical discrimination by employers; social closure by majority workers in unions; and the extremely difficult task of giving incentives to immigrant groups, with relatively low cultural and social capital endowments, to build up their own resources.

Therefore, the results of my study call for other policy recommendations. Social citizenship should both enable participation in the labor force and create the means to partake in broader aspects of social life. To ensure participation in these spheres, education and job training are necessary prerequisites. We could start from the well-known concept of a "generational compact." This expression refers to the intertemporal transfer of funds from those working now to the retired, who, in turn, once supported the old-age pensions of the generation preceding them. One obvious connection to job training comes to mind: We could think of an obligation on those now in work to support job training for school-leavers because they once received such training themselves. Moreover, job training could help to contribute indirectly to financing old-age pensions for those now working, who will be dependent on pensions later. The question is: Who should be included in this "training compact"? In both polities, second-generation immigrants are members of the welfare state.

Public policies that contribute to the economic self-reliance of school-leavers could include a phased introduction of a right to a basic income for school-leavers, coupled with a requirement for job training or post-secondary education. This could help to integrate school-leavers who face difficult transitions. This policy proposal directly relates to the empirical findings of this study. Because only school-leavers with high amounts of social and cultural capital can take advantage of institutionalized job networks and establish informal channels, policies that aim to enable school-leavers, instead of those that channel them into programs for the disadvantaged, are of utmost importance.

We need to think about public policies that would provide incentives to employers to hire workers at high risk of being exposed to unemployment and income poverty and that would present both immigrant and majority youth with incentives to accumulate cultural and social capital. Such a strategy could tackle gross immigrant, namely minority/majority, inequalities regarding income poverty and unemployment and contribute to avoiding socioeconomic marginalization. In this way, job training policies could contribute to school-leavers' capacity to overcome uncertain labor market conditions and to design their own career paths. In short, the question addressed here is not about the transfer of public policies from one context to another and possible solutions to their adaptation. Instead, the more basic task at hand is to think of requirements for public policies to increase the autonomy of school-leavers in rapidly changing labor markets.

Active training and employment policies on the supply side can only constitute one element of social citizenship for all. German youth face the risk of unemployment to an even higher degree at the second than at the first threshold, and U.S. youth are exposed to income poverty. Traditionally, public policies have addressed difficulties at the entry into adult labor markets through active employment policies, such as retraining and further training. Immigrants in Germany have been underrepresented in these programs. However, we know that the gap between more highly skilled workers and employees and unskilled and semiskilled workers enrolling in further education increased during the 1970s and 1980s. Moreover, these instruments may not be sufficient to reach all those young adults who fail to find vacancies or who move back and forth from marginal jobs into spells of unemployment. In these cases, new instruments are necessary to increase employment opportunities. Also, previous employment strategies depended and focused on job growth, especially in the public sector. This was especially true in the United States during the 1970s. For some immigrants such as Mexican Americans and minorities such as African Americans in the United States, this avenue was of prime importance in the formation of a new middle class during the 1960s and 1970s. However, in an era of welfare state retrenchment, this option of expanding public sector employment is closed in both the United States and the Federal Republic of Germany.

The basic idea of public policies enabling social citizenship is to grant school-leavers a right to a basic income to help them cope with the structural changes in labor markets that force them to adapt to rapidly changing labor market demands regarding qualifications. The policy strategy proposed here is to grant all school-leavers and those in school beyond a certain age (e.g., 18 years old) a guaranteed basic income, tax-free and unconditionally. This policy is directed at overcoming the income poverty that results from low-paid work and nonparticipation in the labor force, such as unemployment. The basic income would be tied to membership in the polity and not to workforce participation, and all citizens and permanent residents would qualify for it. Therefore, means tests or work requirements would be absent. All school-leavers could receive this help, and it would substitute for college or university grants and other allowances. The basic income would be close to subsistence wages—*Sozialhilfe* in Germany and welfare payments in the United States. The main difference to means-tested payments lies in the fact that the basic income would be directed toward individuals: Family status would not matter, every school-leaver would be entitled to it. This strategy, coupled with job training and postsecondary education, could enhance fairness and autonomy and foster self-reliance in school-leavers.

With respect to fairness, two groups of school-leavers would benefit most from a guaranteed basic income: those not participating in the labor market and low-paid workers. Those not participating in the labor force mainly include those who stay at home to do family work—mostly women—and the unemployed.

The first group encompasses many young women of immigrant minorities who do unpaid care work at home. The basic income not only would give them monetary rewards but also would give them a social status, an essential element of social citizenship. Their work would be recognized as an important contribution on the same level as continuing education, job training, or paid work in the youth labor market. Indeed, this social status

even could act as an incentive and encourage young caregivers to return to school or start job training because they would have some financial means at their own disposal.

The basic income would be an entitlement for the second group: young, unemployed school-leavers. Generally, those young workers who have not yet worked are not eligible for unemployment benefits. Unemployment does not simply entail a reduction in income or no income at all but also a loss of social security and a deprivation of life chances more generally. The basic income would recognize this fact and give these young people a status without stigmatizing them as welfare recipients or giving them incentives to engage in irregular work activities. It would give unemployed youth basic security and incentives to look for alternatives, such as continuing education or job training. The basic income also could supplement the incomes of low-paid young workers. Income poverty despite being in full-time employment is a major problem in the United States. With respect to low-paid workers, the main idea of the basic income would be to supplement low wages so that those workers would have an opportunity to raise their income. At this point, a caveat must be added: In the case of low-paid workers, there is a danger that a guaranteed basic income—even more so, negative income tax schemes—could reinforce and institutionalize the immigrant/majority segmentation of youth labor markets. Employers could rely on the basic income scheme to enable them to pay lower wages to young workers. This would be a classic example of social policies giving employers opportunities to benefit from wage subsidies. In this way, it might reinforce the divergence in opportunities between school-leavers with a college degree and those without one in the United States, and in Germany, it might widen the differences between apprentices and unskilled young workers in the youth labor market. One way to minimize this adverse consequence would be to set a minimum wage, a threshold below which wages for young workers would not be allowed to fall.

The guaranteed basic income also would contribute to fairness in treating non-college- and university-bound school-leavers. It would have an added positive effect on non-college-bound school-leavers in the United States, even more so than in Germany. In the United States, on average, college students receive much more in subsidies than those who do not go to college. The guaranteed basic income would equalize opportunities. For example, non-college-bound school-leavers could use the basic income to cover reasonable tuition costs at community colleges.

The most important effect of the guaranteed basic income would be that it would increase the ability of school-leavers to act autonomously in the labor market. Although the basic income certainly would not be set above the subsistence level, this entitlement would give young people a basic sense of security and a social status. It could act as a catalyst to help young people cope with careers that are ever more precarious. Autonomous actors would be much better able to deal with increased demands to respond to new mixes and niches of employment. It even could contribute to giving young people a basic sense of income security, based on which they could be more enterprising in setting up small businesses, either individually or cooperatively. In this way, a basic income strategy, coupled with comprehensive training schemes for all school-leavers, could not only serve as an instrument for combating income poverty but also help to increase economic efficiency, because those school-leavers who receive the basic income would be able to make more creative contributions in rapidly changing labor markets.

A basic income strategy in which these specific policy proposals were embedded would have the advantage of tackling some severe problems associated with immigrant/majority inequality without overburdening affirmative action policies. It would not conflate policies designed to address the enabling aspect and the equal opportunity aspect of social citizenship. Policies to further equal opportunity and to overcome discrimination could be introduced once basic income guarantees had been established for all school-leavers, irrespective of ethnicity, race, and gender. In addition, unlike targeted policies including affirmative action, the basic income strategy would not promote thinking in ethnic and racial terms. The basic income strategy would not be ethnically or racially specific, as is the case with affirmative action policies or programs for the "disadvantaged." Public policies that specifically address the disadvantages of immigrants and ethnic minorities would be most successful if they took a radically egalitarian approach. Nevertheless, the basic income strategy, coupled with training schemes, would not eradicate all gross inequalities in access to training and jobs. On the whole, it could provide resources enabling school-leavers of all backgrounds to escape long-term marginalization and second-class social citizenship. Whether these common social citizenship rights and obligations are sufficient to address all the special needs of minority groups is a different question. The claim here is that common social citizenship rights are the foundation upon which a democratic consensus on school-work transition policies could develop.

All this is not to say that policies directed at removing discriminatory effects in the job recruitment process are not necessary to supplement universal policies regarding a guaranteed basic income. Yet, as both the theoretical considerations and the empirical analysis have indicated, the main causes of immigrant youth disadvantages are not to be found in discriminatory behavior by individual members of the majority group. Rather, groups such as Turks, Mexican Americans, and descendants of other working-class immigrant groups face major difficulties resulting from institutional discrimination, entry into labor markets at a time of major job retrenchment, deficits in general education, and weak job networks. Basic income measures could enable those most at risk to develop adequate coping strategies while providing them with a basic sense of economic security. After introducing universal coverage, it would remain to be seen which groups were still at risk.

The introduction of basic income schemes would not simply be a means to improve the condition of social citizenship among immigrants and ethnic minorities. Indeed, it would be difficult to legitimize a fundamental change in regulating entry into the working world if we expected it to be beneficial for only a minority among school-leavers. This empirical study also has shown that a substantial proportion of European Americans face precarious moratorium periods, and German school-leavers, to a lesser extent, lack opportunities to enroll in apprenticeships.

The question also arises whether a right to a basic income also would imply obligations and responsibilities on the part of school-leavers. Neoconservative critics of welfare-state policies have argued adamantly that citizens or denizens are individual actors who are rationally calculating. In this view, giving rights without imposing obligations would lead school-leavers to shirk job training or work. Other authors have argued that generous social and labor market policies undermine the competence of citizens because they are morally undemanding. These general objections to citizenship rights without obligations could be read as a criticism of an unconditional right to a basic income for school-leavers. Certainly, granting a basic income without asking for responsibilities in return could encourage school-leavers to become dependent on public income transfers. This danger does not necessarily lead us to argue for an obligation to undertake paid work. These arguments can easily be used to justify workfare regimes that tie income transfers to eventual

participation in paid work. However, basic income guarantees that were tied to training could open a variety of options to school-leavers. These options include paid work, on-the-job training, apprenticeship, and enrollment in academic or vocational post-secondary educational institutions. They also could encompass unpaid work in the community in which the members of a polity live.

Seen in this way, a guaranteed basic income for school-leavers would come very close to what T. H. Marshall called a "welfare right."[4] A welfare right is not a specific right to a job or a training place. It is, as Marshall argued with respect to education, a type of right that enables members of a community to partake in its life. As this analysis has argued, job training is a crucial juncture at which prospective citizens need a range of options from which to choose. A guaranteed and unconditional basic income for a limited period and for the specific purpose of training could enhance the ability of young adults to find their way in labor markets that require rapidly changing qualifications and continuous reorientation.

Designing and implementing public policies that address the material foundation for social citizenship is of prime importance at a time when social rights and the membership of immigrants in Western welfare states have become matters of intensive conflict and when distributional issues increasingly have come to be perceived in ethnic terms. In recent years, the political parameters of welfare state integration and immigrant integration have changed significantly. The social rights of immigrants are disputed, and immigration is increasingly seen in terms of the economic costs and benefits arising for the countries of settlement. Both high levels of immigration and welfare state retrenchment have opened political space for a debate over the effects of immigration on welfare state provision and social rights, including the regulation of immigration and the extent to which immigrants should be incorporated into the countries of settlement. These developments not only concern immigrant citizenship in advanced welfare states but also raise the question of whether a highly differentiated set of unequal opportunities for members of democratic polities can be maintained without endangering the rights and the quality of social citizenship, even for those currently included.

Notes

1. This article is a synopsis of selected parts of the study *Social Citizenship for All? Young Turks in Germany and Mexican Americans in the United States* (Aldershot, UK: Avebury, 1995).

2. Reforms of naturalization procedures will ease the access to citizenship among second-and-plus generation people of Turkish descent in Germany (1999).

3. Stephen Hamilton, *Apprenticeship for Adulthood: Preparing Youth for the Future* (New York: Free Press, 1990).

4. T. H. Marshall, *Citizenship and Social Class* (Cambridge, UK: Cambridge University Press, 1950).

Faist:

1. How are the systems for integrating immigrant groups into labor markets of Germany and the United States similar and different?

2. Why do different systems of vocational training, embedded in different types of welfare states, lead to similar results?

Drawing Conclusions—Part IV

The new immigrants are an extremely diverse group. Some are doing well economically; others are not. Some are adjusting to a new culture; others are not. Some prefer to move out of ethnic enclaves; others do not. Some have begun to take seriously the idea of citizenship by becoming engaged in politics; others have not. Based on the essays in this part and on any personal experience you may have had with new immigrants, how do you assess the current situation of this immigrant wave? How difficult is it to generalize about new immigrants? Why? What do you think will happen to immigrant groups in the future? Will they follow the path of earlier immigrants, or will they take different routes?

PART V

What Is Multicultural America?

It is increasingly commonplace for us to speak about America as a multicultural nation, yet it is by no means clear what people mean by this term, nor is there anything approaching consensus about whether "multiculturalism" offers an adequate description of contemporary intergroup relations. Likewise, considerable controversy can be found about whether multiculturalism is a worthwhile goal or a problem. In other words, there is considerable controversy about its definitional, descriptive, and prescriptive utility. This concluding part, far from attempting to provide definitive answers to these questions, is designed to provide insights into the phenomenon from rather differing perspectives, affording various critical angles of vision. Our intention is both to bring into somewhat new perspective many of the issues addressed in the preceding parts and to raise questions about possible futures.

One thing that should be noted at the outset is that multiculturalism stands in stark contrast to the prior dominant metaphor of ethnic group relations, which was designed to capture America's presumed capacity to absorb newcomers into the nation. Though similar notions could be found in the nineteenth century, the most powerful image was that expressed at the beginning of the twentieth century by the immigrant playwright Israel Zangwill: the melting pot. A melting pot was a cauldron that took various metals and heated them to boiling, with the result being that the original ingredients disappeared and a qualitatively new alloy was created. In ethnic terms, the melting pot suggested that over time the Germans, Irish, Italians, Poles, Swedes, Dutch, Hungarians, Finns, Jews, and so forth would disappear. Their children and grandchildren would "assimilate"—a term that can be seen as the theoretical articulation of the melting pot metaphor. Ethnics would lose their ancestral identities, but in the process they would acquire a new one: the American.

Two types of critics of the melting pot could be found earlier in the century. First, there were those who claimed that the melting pot only worked for some groups, but not for all. These were the nativists who were hostile to the new immigrants from southern and eastern Europe. In their view, some of these groups constituted base metals that simply could not be blended into the mixture, or, if they could, the result would be dross metal. Another group critical of the melting pot questioned the claim that the goal of assimilation was, in fact, desirable. These critics contended that it was appropriate and desirable for groups to seek to maintain their distinctive group identities over time. Their position became known as "cultural pluralism," a term used by their most articulate spokesperson, Horace Kallen, who went so far as to claim that democracy required cultural pluralism. Thus, assimilation was a threat to the nation's political system.

By the 1960s, assimilation as a goal was under attack. Many white ethnics claimed they were "unmeltable," and many sociologists thought they saw evidence of an ethnic revival among European origin groups. As a consequence, cultural pluralism was seen by many as an alternative to assimilation, both in terms of description and prescription. More recent scholarship has suggested that, when looking at European Americans, cultural pluralism proved to have a short lease on life. Assimilation does, indeed, seem—for better or worse—to characterize the situation for this sector of the American population.

However, for racial minorities, the situation was quite different. African Americans had not assimilated; they had been prevented from doing so. Moreover, the Black Power movement took hold in the late 1960s, and many blacks questioned the desirability of assimilating. Maintaining a distinctive group identity became integral to what Rhea earlier in this collection has termed "racial pride." A similar phenomenon could be seen among American Indians, Latinos, and Asians. It might appear reasonable to conclude that cultural pluralism is the operative term here, but in practice it has been largely discarded, in no small part because when Kallen used the term he seemed only to have in mind Europeans and not racial minorities from other parts of the globe.

Enter the term "multiculturalism." It has been embraced by non-Europeans intent on promoting racial pride, and it has been decried by critics who argue that it is leading to the disuniting of America. Thus, whatever its merits as a description of racial minorities who have not managed to enter the mainstream of the society, it is also a highly controversial prescriptive concept. Unfortunately, trying to make sense of the term is not made easy by the highly polemical character of much debate, which has tended to shed more heat than light on the subject. With this in mind, the four essays included here to round out this collection were selected because they do manage to shed light on the subject. Moreover, they do so by offering genuinely fresh and original perspectives.

Nathan Glazer contends that in the heated debates surrounding multiculturalism, participants both for and against have failed to appreciate that, as he provocatively writes, "We are all multiculturalists now." Glazer offers his sense of what he means by this claim, and he sketches out why he thinks such a state of affairs has arisen. He then discusses some of the implications of the multicultural future. One of the points Glazer seeks to make is that although multiculturalism has become well entrenched, it also has lost its edge as a threat to the status quo.

Such a message is repeated in Alan Wolfe's essay on what he calls "benign multiculturalism." Based on interviews conducted with white suburbanites in several cities around the country, he and his colleagues found a general acceptance of diversity and a widespread endorsement of notions of equality and social justice. However, as with the article by Jaynes and Williams at the beginning of the book, Wolfe notes some of the limits to this particular—in his view generally widespread—version of multiculturalism.

Orlando Patterson views multiculturalism from a different perspective. This Jamaican-born sociologist located at Harvard University is interested in examining the ways transnational cultures are emerging and, in so doing, are opening America up in novel ways. Patterson suggests that if one were to draw a map of the contemporary United States, the map would look rather different depending on whether you were to draw its political boundaries or its cultural boundaries. In the latter case, the focus of his attention, the boundaries transcend the political, encompassing a larger regional geoculture, or cosmos. He argues that there are four such geocultural regions that have developed: one encompassing the Caribbean; another the Tex-Mex border culture; and two on the West Coast, one located in southern California and the other in the Pacific Northwest. Patterson offers speculations about the potential implications of this transnational diffusion of cultures in the future, especially in terms of national identity.

These three essays, taken together, seem to suggest that those who have argued that we are in the midst of culture wars, in part due to the influence of multiculturalism, have proven to be alarmist. However, this does not necessarily imply that multiculturalism is no longer a significant political issue. The volume concludes with Ronald Takaki's diagnosis of the potential divisiveness of multiculturalism as a political agenda and also offers insights into the ways that multiculturalism's agenda might serve the nation well in coming to terms with diversity. Appropriately, although Takaki's own position is made clear, the conclusion of his essay is open-ended, reflecting the uncertain future of race relations in the twenty-first century.

33

We Are All Multiculturalists Now

Nathan Glazer

I have long been interested in the issue of how the various subgroups of American society, however defined, relate to the larger society, and as long ago as the 1950s pondered in various articles the prospects for the future, and the range of alternatives between what was then called "cultural pluralism" and assimilation. It seemed to me, as it seemed to most sociologists at the time, that assimilation was undoubtedly the greater force, and would work its effects on all American ethnic groups. But in time I began to think that I had not fully understood the special role that blacks, or Negroes, or African Americans, play in the American mind and in American society, and that I had erred in considering them just another "ethnic group" with some special historical characteristics. When I served in the 1990s on a committee to consider the social studies curriculum of New York State I found myself diverging from committee members to whom I felt close, and indeed from earlier positions I had myself taken, in that I found more justification and justice than they did in the demands for greater attention to a black perspective on American and indeed world history. In this chapter, I spell out my reasons why I think for some time we will see a strong multicultural thrust in American education. I do think in the end assimilation works. But it works much more slowly for some groups, in particular African Americans, than for Europeans or Asians or Latin Americans.

Multiculturalism is the price America is paying for its inability or unwillingness to incorporate into its society African Americans, in the same way and to the same degree it has incorporated so many groups.

Multiculturlism appears on the surface to encompass much more than that, and indeed it reflects and is responsive to a variety of other developments: the remarkable rise of the women's movement and women's studies, the change in sexual mores and morality which makes gays and lesbians a visible and open presence in culture, politics, and education, the impact of the new immigration, the declining self-confidence or arrogance of the United States as the best, as well as the richest and most powerful, country. All these play a role in how we conceive our past and our future, in how we educate our children, in how we speak to one another, and in how we conceive of the role of race and ethnicity in American society, government, and culture.

But the role of African Americans in multiculturalism is quite different from that of women, or gays and lesbians, or new immigrants, or Hispanics or Asians or Native Americans. No one has to argue the primacy of the fate and history of American blacks among the forces making for multiculturalism in America—or so it would appear. But even those most sensitive to this issue, such as Todd Gitlin, are nevertheless overwhelmed by the flux of identities, and see that as the danger to a better life based on common values: "American culture in the late twentieth century is a veritable stewpot of separate identities. Not only blacks and feminists and gays declare that their dignity rests on their distinctness, but so in various ways do white Southern Baptists, Florida Jews, Oregon skinheads, Louisiana Cajuns, Brooklyn Lubavitchers, California Sikhs, Wyoming ranchers."[1]

True enough. There is evidence for all of this. The changes that increase the visibility, size, and presence of so many of these groups are real, and we find their equivalents in many countries. But even the powerful women's movement pales in significance for the future of American society contrasted with the far greater separateness, the far greater weight of grievances, the far greater capacity to harm the common enterprise because of the distinctive condition and hurts, of American blacks.

We have changed sharply our ideas about the role of women in society, as they have moved into key professions in which they were once scarcely represented, as they have changed our language and our sense of the proper relations between the sexes. But the change that has taken place in our conception of how blacks would relate to the rest of American society is of quite a different order of magnitude. In the 1960s we—and in that "we" I include blacks and whites—thought that the future of American blacks would show a rapid increase in their income, their education, their participation as equals in American society, and their integration in our common society. Perhaps our ideas were not as clear as that, but no one expected the degree of separation in ways of life and thought that prevails [today]. "The Ameri-

can dilemma" continues to refer to only one thing. It is not what place women should play in our common life, though there are complicated and troubling issues enough under that rubric.

If we were to read today Disraeli's comment on the England of his day, "Two nations, between whom there is not intercourse and no sympathy . . . ignorant of each other's habits . . . ordered by different manners," we might perhaps think, as Disraeli intended, of the rich and the poor, and of the increasing economic inequality by some measures among Americans.[2] But in truth that does not seem to affect our politics or our lives much. When we say today in America that we are two nations, we mean what Andrew Hacker meant when he titled his book *Two Nations: Black and White, Separate, Hostile, Unequal.*[3]

The two nations for our America are the black and the white, and increasingly, as Hispanics and Asians become less different from whites from the point of view of residence, income, occupation, and political attitudes, the two nations become the black and the others. The change that has shaken our expectations for the future of American society is not the rise of women or of gays and lesbians. It is rather the change in our expectations as to how and when the full incorporation of African Americans into American life will take place. Only twenty years ago we could still believe that African Americans would become, in their ways of life, their degree of success, their connection to society, simply Americans of darker skin. I still believe that will happen eventually. But our progress in moving toward that goal, while evident in some respects, shows some serious backsliding, and more than that, a hard institutionalized difference, one example of which is multiculturalism in American education. It is not easy to see how these institutionalizations of differences will be overcome soon.

Those of us who were students of ethnicity and race in the 1960s, and held the perspective that assimilation—or, if one prefers the milder term, integration—was what happened to ethnic and racial groups in America, could look unconcernedly on many of the signs of continuing black separation and difference. Of course blacks clustered together. But isn't this what all new immigrant and migrant groups had done? Of course blacks on average earned less than other Americans—but weren't there differences among all racial and ethnic groups, depending on their specific histories? And wouldn't these differences decline as an age of prejudice and discrimination and enforced separation became ever more distant? Of course blacks organized politically around the issues that meant most to them, and were appealed to by politicians on the basis of their common race. But isn't that what had happened with all ethnic and racial groups even while the forces of assimilation were at work on them?

The middle years of this century saw the abolition of all limitations in law on grounds of race and ethnicity. In his history of naturalization in the United States, Reed Ueda writes of the McCarran-Walter Act of 1952, at the time execrated because of its maintenance of national quotas in immigration: "At one stroke the arbitrary category of 'aliens ineligible for citizenship,' which had consigned Asian nationalities to the inferior status of permanent-resident aliens for a century, was swept away." He concludes his authoritative account of the history of American naturalization optimistically: "By the mid-20th century the racial restrictions of naturalization [they had never affected blacks] seemed impolitic and impractical. Experience had shown that all ethnic groups, given time and encouragement, had the capacity to assimilate into the national civic culture, and so U.S. citizenship was opened to all . . . Fears that ethnocultural or racial background would inhibit the proper exercise of citizenship

rights were supplanted by a confidence that citizenship was a transcendent status obtainable by all individuals who shared a common membership in a democratic polity."[4]

In 1964 a wide-reaching Civil Rights Act banned discrimination on the basis of race or ethnicity or national origin in employment, public facilities, education, government programs; in 1965 a powerful Voting Rights Act ensured access to the ballot and more, and an Immigration Reform Act eliminated national quotas. Twenty years ago, few would have challenged the notion that the expansion of American citizenship and the rights that came with it had overcome all racial and ethnic limitations to become universal in its reach. That's what American history taught us, and no one dreamed there could be any regress from the high points of the Civil Rights Act of 1964 and the Immigration Act of 1965. That was law, common practice might still be different, and whites, Christians, Protestants might still be favored in many areas of life as they could not be favored in law. But how long would that last in the face of legal changes, and powerful agencies to enforce them? This was the period when, for example, anti-Semitism rapidly declined, and Jews were becoming for the first time presidents of major universities and CEOs of major corporations. This was also the period in which expressions of prejudice and practices of discrimination against blacks were rapidly declining. The anti-Japanese sentiments of World War II, indeed the anti-Asian sentiments epidemic in America since the mid-nineteenth century, were also in rapid decline. One could be optimistic that the last barriers to difference in treatment based on race, religion, nationality were being swept aside.

This was the point of view I expressed in a book of 1975, *Affirmative Discrimination*.[5] It was within that circle of change and expectation that the book criticized affirmative action in employment, then still in the first few years of its development, as well as busing for the racial integration of schools, and housing policies that imposed requirements to achieve a target racial mix in housing. All these, it seemed to me, were unnecessary in view of what was happening to American attitudes, and transgressed the spirit and specific provisions of the Civil Rights Act of 1964. The first chapter of the book laid out the basis of this criticism of the new race-conscious policies by arguing that the spirit of the American Revolution and our founding documents aimed at this ultimate color blindness, whatever the limitations that had hindered the fulfillment of this aim for two centuries.

We know that when Jefferson wrote "all men are created equal," slavery existed, there was legal discrimination against Jews and Catholics, American Indians were outside the polity, and if there had been any Asians or Hispanics around at the time there would undoubtedly have been discrimination against them, too. But, I asserted, with more boldness and self-confidence than I would today, the spirit of our culture and polity made all these anomalies that would in time be eliminated. The pattern of American history steadily moved us to a more expansive notion of the "American," to reach the final culmination of 1964 and 1965.

But what does one mean when one makes such claims for "the spirit of our culture," "the pattern of our history"? Who can pronounce on these with confidence? In *Affirmative Discrimination* I drew on some leading authorities on the development of American nationality and American national ideals: Seymour Martin Lipset, in his 1963 book, *The First New Nation;* Hans Kohn in his 1957 *American Nationalism: An Interpretation;* Yehoshua Arieli, in his 1964 *Individualism and Nationalism in American Ideology.* All three were quite confident that the pattern of American history showed this tendency toward greater inclusion or equality from its origins, and that the facts that indicated oth-

erwise were anomalies that would in time be swept aside, as indeed was happening.

These days, critics of this argument would probably note, if they were unkind enough, that my three chief authorities were a child of immigrants, a refugee, and an Israeli, all Jews, who understandably might take this generous view of the course and aims of American history (as I, the child of Jewish immigrants, would too). It was not long after the publication of *Affirmative Discrimination* that Ronald Takaki strongly attacked this optimistic view of the pattern and direction of American history in its treatment of the foreigner, the nonwhite, the Other, as it is now put. He had plenty of quotations from founding fathers to set against those that Lipset, Kohn, and Arieli (and I, following them) had recorded to defend our optimistic views on the inclusion of the nonwhite and non-European in American society and polity.[6]

It seemed there could be very wide divergence in how to interpret the pattern of American history. Originally this divergence was surprising to me, and possibly to the main body of interpreters of American history and society. Who could dispute in 1965, or in 1975, the viewpoint that the Civil Rights Act and Immigration Act of 1964 and 1965 marked a permanent advance to full inclusiveness? That challenge became easier to pose over time, and has climaxed in the dispute over multiculturalism.

The weight of that challenge came home to me at one point in the course of the discussions of the New York State committee on the social studies curriculum. While searching for an appropriately broad-based and general statement to help us introduce our recommendations, I came across a statement in a report by the Curriculum Task Force of the National Commission on Social Studies in the Schools, which was composed of leading historians and teachers of social studies and which seemed to me sound and unassailable. It read:

Classrooms today bring together young people of many backgrounds with a broad spectrum of life experience. We can expect an even more diverse student population in the twenty-first century. This diversity enriches our nation even as it presents a new challenge to develop the social studies education that integrates all students into our system of democratic government and helps them subscribe to the values from our past—especially our devotion to democratic values and procedures. The coexistence of increasing diversity and cherished tradition require social studies in our schools to cultivate participatory citizenship . . . The study of social involvement and often competing loyalties addresses basic questions: "Who am I?" "To what communities do I belong?" "What does citizenship in our nation require of me as an individual and as a member of the various groups to which I belong?"[7]

I will admit I was astonished when the co-chairman of our small committee of two which had been assigned the task of writing the introductory statement for our report, a Hispanic scholar, vigorously objected to the use of these, to me, unobjectionable and bland statements. To him, they suggested that "there is a fund of common values in the U.S. that should be imposed on all immigrants." He thought the contrast between "increasing diversity" and "cherished traditions" "uncharitable." He felt the use of the word "ours" was exclusionary. He saw in the statement the "xenophobic language of the nativists and the Americanization movement," of "the worst moments of U.S. chauvinism." He objected that the reference to "competing loyalties" depreciated the significance of group distinctiveness and group loyalty for minority groups. I interpret this objection to mean that he refused to place subgroup loyalty on the same level as a larger American loyalty. Subgroup loyalty rather trumped American loyalty. He feared the "retreat of the Euro-American minority [he is referring to the time when the Euro-Americans will become a mi-

nority] from the cherished guarantees found in the Constitution."

How broadly these sentiments would be held among Hispanic Americans, or Hispanic American scholars, I do not know. There is no necessary equivalence between a person's race or ethnicity and the views that person holds. It is one of the errors of the more extreme versions of multiculturalism to believe there is. But these suspicions are not simply personal, or isolated among intellectuals and academics. There is enough evidence that among one group in the American population they are widespread indeed, and lead to a radically different outlook on American history and society from the outlook commonly found not only among European Americans but, I would warrant, among Hispanic and Asian Americans, too. The group in which we find this radical divergence from the norm is American blacks, and it is matched by a radical difference, on the average, in living conditions from that found among most other Americans.

As we saw when we looked at the history of assimilation and discrimination, and at the distinctive residential patterns of blacks, maintained through decades when prejudice and discrimination declined and was banned in law, when we considered the unique black exception from the prevailing patterns of inter-group marriage, and the maintenance and perhaps exaggeration of dialectal variations which are given significant cultural and political meaning, the situation of African Americans is different. Of course all groups are different. There were significant differences in the ways European immigrant groups assimilated. But there are orders of magnitude in difference. The differences between the rate of assimilation of Irish and Germans, or Italians and Jews, become quite small when we contrast them with the differences over time between white European immigrants of any group and American blacks. These differences create different perspectives, on our historic past, on our present, on the shape of our culture.

Very likely, in view of all the other changes that have affected American society in the past twenty years, we would have seen multiculturalism of some form affecting American education, whatever the degree to which the common expectations regarding black assimilation were realized. After all, even homogeneous European countries, with no equivalent in their history of the deep division between majority and minority that characterizes the United States, have their various versions of multiculturalism, and make use of the same term.

But this term does not have, cannot have, the weight in Britain, France, Germany, or Sweden that it has in the United States. For these countries, multiculturalism means the more or less grudging acknowledgment that they will have to bring into line with their principles, which are the increasingly universal Western principles of the equal worth of all men and women, some of their common public and private practices, in the provision of social services, in schooling, in housing, in patterns of hiring and promotion. They will have to deal with and modify an often matter-of-fact discrimination based on the unquestioned reality that the people of these countries have been for centuries dominantly of one linguistic and cultural group, sharing some degree of suspicion of and distaste for outsiders. These countries have been reminded by their own scholars that they have in the past incorporated larger numbers of immigrants than they were aware of, and that in the world of the late twentieth century the pattern of incorporation of new immigrants will have to be somewhat different from what it was in the nineteenth and earlier twentieth centuries, the ages of European self-confidence and evident superiority. They will have to pay somewhat more attention to difference, will have to be more tolerant of the institutions created by new groups that maintain difference.

This is not to say there are no serious problems for this new European multiculturalism, in particular those raised by large resident Muslim communities. Islam, for complicated historical reasons, has chosen to emphasize its differences within Western liberalism. It therefore becomes a potentially rebellious element within Western societies, and in so becoming creates dilemmas for them in their commitment to liberal values. Separate schools for Jews, Catholics, Protestants, or atheists seem to pose no great problem for the dominantly liberal societies of Western Europe. Separate schools for Muslims do, primarily because, in their attitudes toward women and heterodoxy, they sharply challenge liberal values. So the acceptance of difference, in the case of Islam, poses a serious problem for liberal values, as is the case whenever a liberal society confronts a group that rejects the very values that undergird the support of difference. This is the central issue that a resurgent Islam raises for liberal Western societies. It is serious enough.

It is, however, quite different from the issues raised by African Americans, who have been closely bound up with white Americans since the time of the founding of the English colonies of the Atlantic coast. The only possible comparison with Europe would be if the Saxons of England, or the Gauls of France, had been held in a position of caste subservience for centuries. This kind of split, sunk deep in the history of societies, does not exist in Europe. We believed in the 1960s that our founding principles, elaborated as they had been over two centuries until they reached the all-embracing form of the civil rights and immigration legislation of the 1960s, would serve to overcome this deep fissure in our own society. Our history, after all, has been one of an increasingly expansive liberalism in our conception of who is legitimately American, an increasing effectiveness in bringing groups ever more distant from the founding stock into full membership in American polity and society.

We were in our origins dominantly of English stock, along with less numerous groups from Northwestern Europe, of various Protestant religions, and including a large minority of black slaves. There was, fortunately, no formal and binding recognition of these origins in our major founding legal documents. Because we were establishing our independence in revolt against a nation of the same stock, and because of our anxiety about favoring one Protestant church or sect over another, our founding documents are cast in general terms, appealing to universal principles. Whatever the practices of exclusion—and they were many—they were in time (and not without backsliding) steadily reduced. The eligibility of all the world to become Americans on an equal basis with all others was regularly asserted by American presidents, regardless of party and ideology.

Practice in all the spheres of American life was expected to follow, and in large measure it has. No one can ignore the remarkable transformation in the role of African Americans in the South, and the changes in their position in many sectors of American society.

But we also cannot ignore the remarkable and unique degree of separation between blacks and others. The caste characteristic still holds, and one evidence of it is that one is either black or not—partial degrees of blackness, despite the reality of a very mixed genetic inheritance, will not be recognized, not by our Census, not by our society. We do not recognize partial or loose affiliation with the group, or none at all, for blacks, as we do for all other ethnic and racial groups.

The racial categories the census uses to place each Asian group within its own special "race"—so that the Chinese, Japanese, Koreans, Asian Indians, and so on are each statistically a different "race"—is an anomaly and does not reflect the social reality that we recognize the children of white-Asian intermarriage as mixed, while we recognize the children of black-Asian intermarriage (or black-white intermarriage) as black. This is the reality that reflects the caste status of black in the American mind.

This is not to say that the caste is uniformly considered inferior. Even in the home of caste society, India, persons of lower castes rise to the highest positions, and caste somewhat weakens its hold over time, and this is true in the United States. This castelike character of American blacks will and must change, but it has not yet, and we do not know all the processes by which it will change, and what measures precisely will contribute to that change.

Insistence in our schools that we are all Americans and nothing less, that the changes that fully incorporate blacks have already occurred, that blacks are only Americans of darker skin, while true enough in law, is contradicted by reality. That contradiction has undermined the uniform education regarding our past and our culture [that so] many of us underwent and whose passing we lament. But it has passed, and we do not know, as our recent experiences with curricular change have shown, how it can be reconstructed. It seems we must pass through a period in which we recognize difference, we celebrate difference, we turn the spotlight on the inadequacies in the integration of our minorities in our past and present, and we raise up for special consideration the achievements of our minorities and their putative ancestors. All this is premised on our failure to integrate blacks. Others are included in this process; but it is the response to blacks, their different condition, their different perspective, that sets the model.

If I were writing in a normative mode—what is best, what do I prefer, what do I propose for America concerning its ethnic and racial diversity—I would say more or less what David Hollinger and others who respect the diversity of American origins but appreciate fully the power of the integrating values of our common society say: Let us have respect for identity in the context of a common culture, but let us avoid the fixing of lines of division on ethnic and racial bases. Let us accept the reality of exit from an ethnic-ra-cial-religious group, as well as the right of differential attachment, as a common American way, and let us agree that ethnic and racial affiliation should be as voluntary as religious affiliation, and of as little concern to the state and public authority. Let us understand that more and more Americans want to be Americans simply, and nothing more, and let us celebrate that choice, and agree it would be better for America if more of us accepted that identity as our central one, as against ethnic and racial identities.

Hollinger's "postethnic perspective" favors "voluntary over involuntary affiliations, balances an appreciation for communities of descent with a determination to make room for new communities, and promotes solidarities of wide scope that incorporate people with different ethnic and racial backgrounds . . . [It] resists the grounding of knowledge and moral values in blood and history, but works within the last generation's recognition that many of the ideas and values once taken to be universal are specific to certain cultures."[8] I agree. My own list of preferences would be slightly different, with somewhat different nuances, but Hollinger's is good enough for our common society. But his prescription does not take account of the African American condition, where affiliation is hardly voluntary, where the community of descent defines an inescapable community of fate, where knowledge and moral values are indeed grounded in blood and history; one wonders how, or when, it will be otherwise.

"We are all multiculturalists now." Of course we are not *all* multiculturalists, but one would be hard put, if one works in schools and with black schoolchildren, so many of whom attend schools in which they make up all or a good part of the enrollment, to find someone who is not. The expression "We are all multiculturalists now" harks back to others that have been pronounced wryly by persons who recognized that something unpleasant was nevertheless unavoidable; it is not employed to indicate a wholehearted embrace. "We are all socialists now," Sir William Harcourt, Chancellor of the Exchequer in one of Gladstone's cabinets, was reputed to have said in 1889.[9] His best-known achievement was to get Parliament to accept progressive taxation on estates at death, a modest progressive tax at the time but one which outraged owners of the great estates. One assumes that Sir William did not mean socialism was the right thing, or the best thing, but simply that, if one considered progressive taxation on estates at death socialism, it was the inevitable thing, and one had to accept it. One could still argue about the details, as one can still argue about the details of just what kind of multiculturalism we should have.

The problems of divisiveness that multiculturalism raises at the level of the curriculum, or the school, or the culture, cannot be settled within the curriculum, the school, or the larger culture. The "culture wars" reflect many things, but when it comes to the division of blacks and others, they reflect a hard reality that none of us wants, that all of us want to see disappear, but that none of us knows how to overcome. It is only change in that larger reality that will reduce multiculturalism to a passing phase in complex history of the making of an American nation from many strands.

Notes

1. Todd Gitlin, *The Twilight of Common Dreams* (New York: Metropolitan Books, 1995), p. 227. He is certainly aware that all these groups are of different weight consequence, and a page later writes: "Yet in many ways, the jargon of multiculturalism, whether as angel or bogey-man, evades the central wound in American history. America's national history . . . is thick with slaughter and misery, and none of the consequences are more biting, more disturbing, than today's conflicts between whites and blacks." But he hurries past this in his concern for his central point, the need to

construct a new alliance of the left transcending race, ethnicity, sex, and other bases for identity claims.

2. The "two nations" quotation is from Disraeli's *Sybil,* as quoted in Mark Gerson, *In the Classroom: Dispatches from an Inner-City School That Works* (New York: Free Press, 1996), p. 203.

3. Andrew Hacker, *Two Nations: Black and White, Separate, Hostile, Unequal* (New York: Scribner, 1992). For Gerson (*In the Classroom*) too the "two nations" are more the black and white than the rich and poor.

4. Reed Ueda, "Naturalization and Citizenship," *Harvard Encyclopedia of American Ethnic Groups* (Cambridge, MA: Harvard University Press, 1980), p. 748.

5. Nathan Glazer, *Affirmative Discrimination: Ethnic Inequality and Public Policy* (New York: Basic Books, 1975; Cambridge, MA: Harvard University Press, 1987).

6. Ronald Takaki, "Reflections on Racial Patterns in America," in Takaki, ed., *From Different Shores* (New York: Oxford University Press, 1987), pp. 26–37.

7. *Charting a Course: Social Studies for the 21st Century,* Report of the Curriculum Task Force of the National Commission on Social Studies in the Schools, 1989, p.1.

8. David Hollinger, *Postethnic America* (New York: Basic Books, 1995), p. 3.

9. It may be apocryphal. The source is Hubert Bland, in George Bernard Shaw, Sidney Webb, William Clark, Syndey Olivier, Annie Besant, Graham Wallas, and Hubert Bland, *Fabian Essays* (London: George Allen and Unwin, 1962; 1st ed., 1889), p. 244.

Glazer:

1. Why does Glazer argue for assimilation? Why does he say it will work better than "cultural pluralism"?

2. Discuss the reasons why Glazer says that the multiculturalism of African Americans is different from that of women, gays or lesbians, new immigrants, or Latino, Asian, or Native Americans.

34

Benign Multiculturalism

Alan Wolfe

An American born as the twentieth century ends will grow up to live in a society completely different from that into which an American was born as the twentieth century began. In 1900, few would have described this country as seriously divided by race. To be sure, black and white Americans lived in distinct worlds. In the South, slavery had been abolished, but officially sanctioned segregation maintained uncrossable bridges between the races. And in the North, informal but no less powerful customs and habits created patterns of living in which substantial racial inequality and injustice persisted. Yet most white Americans, who did not want to think about these injustices, kept questions of race safely at a distance, and many black Americans, deeply offended by such patterns of inequality, lacked an effective voice for making their concerns heard.

Despite these racial divisions, Americans in 1900 were united in other ways. For one thing, the country at that time was predominantly Christian; whatever differences existed between blacks and whites, both usually believed in the same God. They also shared the same language, a pattern that was not disturbed all that much by the arrival of large numbers of immigrants who came to the United States at that time. For these immigrants either, like the Irish, spoke English already or, like Italians and Poles, were determined to leave the old country and its customs behind in the hopes that their children would succeed in the new land. Nor were Americans spread across the entire continent; the West Coast in 1900 was still relatively underpopulated, and most Americans grew up and eventually died not all that far from where they were born. In short, most Americans in 1900 took something called America for granted. They had a strong sense of what America meant to them, they outdid each other in expressing their patriotism, and they believed that their country was especially blessed by God to do great things.

This sense of an America whose meaning was relatively uncontested is a far cry from the situation that exists today in the United States. For one thing, as divided by race as the United States was at century's beginning, its racial situation appears remarkably divisive at century's end. This is not to say that there has been no racial progress. The past two or three decades have witnessed a substantial growth in the black middle class in America. Most white Americans no longer expressed deeply prejudicial views toward black Americans, and although vestiges of segregation remain, particularly in housing and school attendance, there can be little doubt that race relations have improved in the years since the century began. Still, there does remain a gap between blacks and whites. In part, this is a gap of opportunity: The chances of an inner-city child succeeding in life are far lower than those of a suburban child. In part, it is a gap of attitude: Black Americans continue to believe that racism is omnipresent in American life, whereas white Americans do not.

If tensions remain between blacks and whites, they have been complicated by the fact that our racial landscape is no longer painted in just two colors. We were a land of immigrants in 1900, but the law gave a priority to people from countries in Europe whose populations were white. Those laws were revised in the 1960s and 1970s, however, with the consequence that immigrants these days often come from Asia, Latin America, and Africa. Our population is now officially divided into five races: whites, blacks, Asians, native Americans, and (in what is really an ethnic or linguistic category) Hispanics. And even those categories are anything but clear-cut. Is someone from Puerto Rico whose skin color is black properly classified as African American or as Hispanic? The answer is usually the latter, but what does such a person have in common racially or ethnically with a white person who emigrated as a political refugee from Cuba? Because race is not a hard-and-fast category, America's racial landscape is not only more complicated, it is also more fluid.

If we can no longer speak of an America divided by black and white, it makes even less sense to talk of America as a Christian country. There have been Jews in the United States since the earliest days, but the religious diversity brought about by America's immigration policies has been without precedent. It is true that in 1900 many immigrants to America, although white, were distinct from those Americans already here, for the latter tended to be Protestant and the former Catholic. The result was serious battles over public schools and suspicion on the part of each religious group of the intentions of the other. But despite these hostilities, both were Christian and in that sense worshiped the same God. Now, there are as many believers in Islam in the United States as there are Episcopalians. Religious diversity is as strong as racial diversity, and no one, least of all the U.S. Supreme Court, knows how to apply principles guiding the separation of church and state in such a context.

Religious diversity, like racial diversity, has important implications for what kind of society we are going to be. There are at least some Americans who believe that for a country to flourish, it has to have a common morality. And, they also believe, religion is the most important source of moral belief. If both of these propositions are true, it follows that a society that has no common religion—which is clearly the case in the United States now—can have no common morality. For those of this persuasion, a number of America's social problems—such as rising rates of divorce and crime—are due to this lack of a common morality. But that is untrue, others would reply. In fact, the most important moral virtue in America, what made it different from Europe from the start, is its appreciation for and tolerance of difference. For that reason, the fact that we are all no longer Christians is a sign of a more mature country, one in which people can live together despite believing in different conceptions of God.

What do Americans make of all this diversity in their midst? We know what those who write on the subject believe. Among academics and intellectuals, there has taken place a furious war about diversity. Some insist that principles of equality, toleration, and respect for difference lead to the conclusion that we should welcome the presence of many cultures in the United States and celebrate our racial, ethnic, and religious differences. Others believe just as strongly that all previous immigrants to this country assimilated to the United States by dropping their languages and cultures of origin and becoming American in the process. It is only fair that recent immigrants do the same, they argue. Indeed, they must if we are to remain one society capable of defending itself and passing on its legacy to the next generation.

Issues of multiculturalism and diversity tend to be subject to passionate argument in this country. If the subject is affirmative action, for example, those who believe that colleges and universities should take special steps to diversify their student bodies generally believe that those who feel otherwise are, to one degree or another, racist. And, to return the favor, those who believe that quotas and preferences violate American principles of liberalism and merit tend to argue that their opponents are engaged in an effort to lower standards and to politicize learning. The passions, if anything, intensify when students who are African American or Asian American ask for recognition in the form of programs that focus on their ethnic or racial heritage. Few issues stir the pot as much as those involving the question of who we are—and who we ought to be—as a people.

Although the intellectuals have spoken, however, most ordinary Americans have not. Polls give us a snapshot of the way Americans think about diversity, but, based on quickly asked and answered questions, they do not tell us enough. And referenda, such as those restricting affirmative action or immigration in California, are often worded ambiguously enough to make interpretation of their results difficult. In an effort to find out more, my research assistant and I conducted long conversations with a sample of middle-class Americans in four parts of the country: Brookline and Medford near Boston, Massachusetts; Cobb and Dekalb counties outside of Atlanta, Georgia; Broken Arrow and Sand Springs, Oklahoma; and Rancho Bernardo and Eastlake, two suburbs on either side of San Diego. We talked with them about their views on God, country, family, race, poverty, work, and civic life. Our findings were published in a book entitled *One Nation, After All*.[1] In what follows, I offer a summary of

what they told us about the subject of diversity, plus some reflections on what it all means.

One conclusion emerges in sharp clarity from these interviews: If support for multiculturalism means support for bilingualism, middle-class Americans are against it. Americans place great store on English as the language of the country: When given a series of statements about the obligations of citizenship—voting, keeping informed, serving in war—being able to speak and understand English placed second in importance, behind only reporting a crime that one has witnessed. That helps explain why, according to the 1994 General Social Survey, 62.9 percent of the American people favor making English the official language of the United States compared with 27.6 percent who do not. Groups such as U.S. English, which promote the notion of one official language for the United States, have had some political success: Although their efforts to pass a constitutional amendment requiring English as the official language of the country failed, state measures, such as California's Proposition 63 in 1986, generally have passed. Indeed, Proposition 63 passed by 73 percent of the vote and won a majority in every county in the state. English, it is clear, matters.

Middle-class Americans, it would seem, think about other languages the same way they think about homosexuality, a subject on which they are not especially tolerant, and not the way they think about minority religions, an area in which they are very tolerant. Our respondents were strongly opposed to bilingualism, no matter where in America they lived, and, overall, the percentage of those unsympathetic to the rationale behind bilingualism was four times greater than the proportion that was sympathetic. Survey researchers use the concept of a "bell curve" to describe responses in which the majority clusters in the middle with two extremes at each end. On the issue of bilingualism, as Table 34.1 shows, public opinion deviates substantially from that pattern.

Table 34.1

Table 34.1

"People Who Do Not Speak English Well Should Be Taught in the Schools in Their Native Language"

	Strongly Agree	Agree	No Opinion	Disagree	Strongly Disagree
Brookline	0	6	2	13	4
Medford	0	4	0	13	8
Broken Arrow	0	2	1	13	9
Sand Springs	0	5	2	11	7
DeKalb	0	4	0	19	2
Cobb	1	4	0	15	5
Eastlake	1	7	0	5	12
Rancho Bernardo	0	1	0	11	13
Total	2	33	5	100	60

What accounts for this opposition? Although many of those with whom we talked insisted that their opposition to bilingualism was meant to help immigrant children get along better in their new country, in fact, hostility to bilingualism is primarily symbolic in nature. Bilingualism is one of those issues that generates passionate research, each side claiming empirical support for how much such programs can work or how little they achieve. But even if they were persuaded that bilingual programs worked effectively, our respondents still would be likely to oppose them. For them, a willingness to learn English is one of the marks, if not the most important mark, of the good immigrant. It is a test: Pass it and you belong; refuse to take it and you do not. To a considerable degree, public policy has had to accommodate itself to such sentiments, as have the debates over bilingualism; increasingly, defenders of such programs emphasize not the political imperative of protecting minority languages, but how bilingualism, when done right, can help smooth the transition to English.

Because insistence on English is seen as a test, it is likely to be resented by those being tested. But middle-class America did not invent the symbolic dimension of bilingualism: It has been part of the arguments made for these programs. Some claim that bilingualism is a political challenge to a dominant culture, an argument likely to lead those who uphold the dominant culture to dig in their heels. Others suggest that all immigrants eventually will learn English anyway, so that we ought to allow bilingualism to show respect for those who came here under such trying conditions. Our respondents simply turn that symbolism around. We all know they are going to learn English anyway; therefore, the sooner they do, the better off they will be. Respect for immigrants is important, but respect for the country is more important. On this issue, for most of our respondents, the idea that we are one nation clearly takes precedence over the idea that difference should be celebrated.

Despite the large proportion of people who expressed hostility to bilingualism in our survey, it would not be correct to conclude that these attitudes represent an intolerance comparable to, or greater than, the way our respondents thought about homosexuality. For one thing, the intensity of the language they used when discussing bilingualism was not the same as the language they used when respect for homosexuality was the issue: People do not think of those who want to preserve Spanish as perverted or

Table 34.2

"There Are Times When Loyalty to an Ethnic Group or to a Race Should Be Valued over Loyalty to the Country as a Whole"

	Strongly Agree	Agree	No Opinion	Disagree	Strongly Disagree
Brookline	0	6	4	12	3
Medford	0	7	2	12	4
Broken Arrow	0	3	2	14	6
Sand Springs	0	4	2	14	5
DeKalb	0	11	4	9	1
Cobb	0	6	0	13	6
Eastlake	1	2	1	20	1
Rancho Bernardo	0	2	3	12	8
Total	1	41	18	106	34

immoral. For another, despite strong support for making English the official language of the United States, the General Social Survey also discovered that there are majorities in America behind both bilingualism in schools and multilingual ballots. As much as they like the idea of English as the official language of the country, it would seem Americans want those who speak other languages to preserve them: A 1987 poll taken just about the time that Proposition 63 in California passed discovered that a substantial majority of the state's residents thought it was "a good thing" for immigrants to keep their languages and traditions. Opposition to bilingualism and support for the preservation of original languages sound as if they are in contradiction to each other, but the more one listens to how people express themselves, it becomes clear that they are not. As most Americans grapple with these issues, they support the principle that groups within the United States ought to be allowed to retain their distinctiveness, but only so long as they do so within an official culture that insists on the priority of the national community over subnational ethnic groups.

This is certainly the way our respondents thought about the conflict between the larger nation as a whole and the specific nations that make it up. On the one hand, they had little doubt that group loyalties had to take second place to national ones; Table 34.2 presents data from our survey question dealing with this issue. Although one can detect some racial polarization in their responses—primarily, black respondents in DeKalb County were more sympathetic to the claims of ethnic and racial groups than those elsewhere—the overwhelming majority sentiment across the country, not surprisingly, puts the nation first.

Yet, there is also another side to the story, one that revealed itself to me in an unexpected way. As a college professor and writer, I have been deeply involved in debates over "multiculturalism," the idea that we have a strong obligation to emphasize the differences and special characteristics of the groups that compose the American mosaic; my position in those debates generally has been unsympathetic to multiculturalist claims, preferring instead an assimilationist position that I identify with my own familial and ethnic experiences. Because the middle-class Americans with whom I spoke were so hostile to bilingualism, I naturally assumed that they would share my personal distaste for multiculturalism. They did not. And therein lies a story that may have implications for the larger discussion of race and multiculturalism in our society.

Let us turn, then, to the question of multiculturalism specifically. When we asked people how they felt about taking special steps to recognize and celebrate specific cultures, most of those with whom we spoke put aside their opposition to bilingualism and indicated strong sympathy with multiculturalism. Often, there was some confusion in people's minds about the two. When we asked people whether they supported multiculturalism, a number of them responded by denouncing bilingualism. When we explained that we were not asking about language but culture, many said that was different: Of course, we ought to respect other cultures. Teaching children respect for the many cultures brought to this country was variously described by our respondents as "very good," "real good," "important," "fine," "great," "really great," "neat," "superb," "helpful," and "necessary"; only a few said it was "harmful" or an example of "political correctness run amok." Even when challenged—on this question, we tried to be very challenging—people rarely backed down from their enthusiastic support for the idea. "Spend a week on this and a week on that, that way the person is full-rounded," said J. W. Cotton of Broken Arrow, Oklahoma. "Well," my research assistant intervened, "some people say we need to stress the basics." "Like I said," he responded, "a week or two on each. I mean when you've got four or five months in school, I am sure you can sneak in a week or something. . . . There's room for fluffy stuff." Although survey researchers have demonstrated that support for multiculturalism is stronger in the Northeast than in the other regions of the country, we found strong support in each region, perhaps reflecting the fact that multiculturalism is also more popular among better-educated Americans.

The middle-class African Americans with whom we spoke were the most unabashedly enthusiastic about multiculturalism. "You should automatically respect someone when you first meet them," Gerald Stevens pointed out. "It's almost like unconditional, until maybe that person does something to make you lose respect." The same rule, he believes, applies to groups. Black people like him ought to have the benefit of the doubt for their culture unless or until that respect is lost. "As a young child," Vaughn Hyde added, "I knew far more about Europeans than they could ever possibly know about me. That's not fair." Over and over, African Americans brought up the example of Christopher Columbus, proving, in passing, how controversies over historical symbols have real cogency in the country at large. How could he have discovered America, they wanted to know, when people of color were already here? Latinos in California shared the same point of view. Their enthusiasm for multiculturalism ranged from the practical—"I would be out of a job" without it, as an educational training coordinator laughingly put it—to such idealistic reasons as the "need to expand ourselves."

White Americans, although sympathetic to multiculturalism, were not quite as enthusiastic. For one thing, even those who support multiculturalism have qualms about forcing it on people; they think about cultural diversity in the same laissez-faire way they think about religious diversity, as a good thing as long as no one tries to impose their views on others. Multiculturalism, William Fahy of Cobb County argued, should be "low key," which to him meant that "you don't take it to extremes." Searching for the right word to characterize his feelings, he finally found it: multicultural education is all right so long as it is not "political." Whether he knew it or not, and I think he probably did, Mr. Fahy was trying to support the idea of multiculturalism without supporting the agenda of the activists behind it. He would object to multiculturalism as its most passionate defenders understand it. They believe we should teach respect for all groups as a means to achieve equality among them, whereas he would teach respect for all groups because they exist here in the same country with us.

Multiculturalism usually is identified with particularism. To its supporters, the majority culture tends to overlook the accomplishments of particular cultures, requiring an emphasis on the singular achievements of special groups, whereas to its opponents, multiculturalism represents a splintering of society into its ethnic and racial fragments. One reason that multiculturalism can be so popular in middle-class America is that many of those who support it do so for universalistic rather than particularistic reasons. Just as they believe there is only one God, despite myriad ways of worshiping him, they also believe, as Samina Hoque, a Medford physicist from Bangladesh, put it, that "People are not very different. Deep down, they are all the same." They even look the same, according to Sand Spring's Diana Hamilton: "When was the last time you saw a kid in Egypt dressed in a linen thing wrapped around their waist?" she asked us.

They look just like the rest of us. . . . So if you could really have a multicultural curriculum that . . . explained people's differences and then showed how we're all the same, that would be good. But a lot of the ones I've observed don't do that at all. Like I said, it serves to point out all the differences, and say "Oh, isn't that weird."

Multiculturalism that is tailored to be compatible with the more universal values of America can be described as "benign." To do it right, as Eastlake's Jason Cooper put it,

You don't institutionalize the celebration of those differences. You let people celebrate those differences by association and by civic groups and by public interest organizations. You don't have to institutionalize that in society by saying that on this day we're going to celebrate Cinco de Mayo in public schools to recognize that there is a group among you that happens to be affiliated with that heritage.

Benign multiculturalism is informal rather than official, soft in its particularism rather than hard, and assimilationist in its objectives; it is, in short, an example of a modest virtue. The national culture, like middle-class morality, requires occasional revitalization, which particular identities can provide. But those particular identities can only do so by subsuming themselves under the broad umbrella of Americanism.

There is, along these lines, a generally unrecognized conservative set of arguments in favor of multiculturalism, ones that the more conservative among our respondents were quick to make. Brian Fischer, a conservative resident of Cobb County, dislikes multiculturalism vehemently: "To predicate an educational environment on stressing dissimilarities so people can understand where they came from, I think is the greatest load of crap," he said in no uncertain terms. But, he also noted, in the South, individuals "need to know who their people are." He would have all students sit down with a tape recorder and talk to their parents and grandparents, getting a sense of their struggles and hopes. In that way, he believes, multicultural education "gives a person a sense of worth and a sense of tradition." A number of our respondents thought that learning about your background gives you roots, anchoring you in the scheme of things in a way that strengthens your sense of place in the society. Taking pride in your group is a way of taking pride in yourself: "I mean, there's nothing wrong with heritage-type education, you know, like a background," said Alex Molinari. "For example, my heritage is Italian. Hey, there's nothing wrong with a little Italian in school. That's great." Everybody should learn something about their heritage, even if, as Jose Velasquez put it, "You should be American and then something else, not the other way around." Even African Americans, who supported multiculturalism more strongly than our other respondents, did so in essentially conservative ways. Kenneth Easterbrook sees nothing wrong with black students at university having their own dorms and congregating with each other. "That's not because I want to separate, that I don't want to deal with you," he added. "It just says that at times I just want to touch base with who I am."

Benign multiculturalism has one additional advantage: It is practical. If you really want to make money in mutual funds, you have to invest globally, said Jeremy Toole of Cobb County; for that reason alone, he would have his children learn more about the rest of the world. Cathy Ryan tells us that her husband would require that the president of the United States spend a year abroad, like an exchange student; if he is going to make decisions that involve other places, he ought at least have an appreciation for them. Even selling products here in the United States now requires familiarity with all the cultures and languages that live here: "I think that with the mixture of people that we have in America now too, we have to learn the languages of other people," as George Slade put it. In reality, both America and the world are changing, and multiculturalism can help with the transition.

The preponderance of conservative and practical arguments in favor of multiculturalism suggests an answer to how middle-class Americans would choose between the principle of pluralism and the principle of patriotism. By avoiding the extremes of parochialism on the one hand and particularism on the other, benign multiculturalism enables middle-class Americans to avoid making that choice. Herbert Gans once coined the term "symbolic ethnicity" to characterize the way earlier immigrant groups, among them Ital-

ians, Irish, Poles, and Jews, took pride in their group but always at somewhat of a distance from its tribalist claims on them. It is that experience with multiculturalism in the past that shapes how middle-class Americans view multiculturalism in the present. They want newer groups of immigrants, as well as African Americans, to be able to express their ethnic diversity, but they also want them to move quickly toward what the historian David Hollinger calls a "post-ethnic" perspective. "The national community's fate can be common," Hollinger wrote, "without its will being uniform, and the nation can constitute a common project without effacing all of the various projects that its citizens pursue through their voluntary affiliations."[2] If multiculturalism is organized in such a way that it serves American goals and values, it becomes possible to respect the diversity of the groups that belong to America and to respect America at the same time.

The story of Americans' attitudes toward their country over the past three decades is the story of one shock after another. Vietnam and Watergate in the 1960s and 1970s, immigration and the emergence of global capitalism in the 1980s, multiculturalism and culture wars in the 1990s. And as if that was not enough, Americans have experienced a questioning of their country's sense of purpose at the same time that their faith in God and family has undergone significant change. So much has happened so quickly, it is no wonder that serious students of American history have raised the question of whether the Union is falling apart. Yet, it is remarkable how few of their worries about the country's future have filtered down to most of the people who live here. In the opinion of the middle-class Americans with whom we talked, as Table 34.3 indicates, the idea of living in any other country in the world is barely conceivable.

These middle-class Americans have a message to deliver to those who worry that America might fall apart: Calm down. Yes, the country has changed, perhaps for the

Table 34.3

"Even Though It Has Its Problems, the United States Is Still the Best Place in the World to Live"

	Strongly Agree	Agree	No Opinion	Disagree	Strongly Disagree
Brookline	9	11	3	2	0
Medford	12	11	1	1	0
Broken Arrow	16	9	0	0	0
Sand Springs	18	4	2	1	0
DeKalb	11	11	3	0	0
Cobb	12	12	0	1	0
Eastlake	18	6	1	0	0
Rancho Bernardo	19	5	1	0	0
Total	115	69	11	5	0

better, perhaps not. But everything changes all the time. The trick is not to lament what has passed but to come to terms with what is emerging. We are not facing the disuniting of America but its reuniting. This being America, it cannot be bad.

The confidence that America will reemerge as a strengthened society draws on a number of sources. Religious Americans who believe that God has always taken a special interest in this country believe that, as Mrs. McLaughlin of Broken Arrow put it, "If we get down on our knees and pray to Him, He will change, you know, change our land and help us to heal our land." Others, such as Judy Vogel of Cobb County, think that disagreement and discord offer more of a secular test, and that when faced with political conflicts and different versions of the meaning of the country, "I think we need to listen with our hearts a little better and try somehow to find answers," for "this country has a strong foundation," one that enables it to struggle through until we find the right thing to do. Over and over again, people stressed two things about the country that, in their view, will never change. One is that the people here are too good for bad things to persist too long. The other is that the history of America is a history of generosity and caring; Americans are the kind of people

who help out when times are tough. If things get bad enough—they have not quite gotten to that point yet—the way in which Americans pull together when facing floods and earthquakes will help them move beyond their political disagreements and controversies.

The most significant source of national regeneration, however, stems from what many middle-class Americans see as an inevitable cycle: Our freedoms make us special; taken to extremes, they cause us problems; but when we experience those problems, our very freedoms will help us find a way out. This whole cycle of distinctiveness, decline, and possible rebirth was expressed in one sentence by Rancho Bernardo's Megan Graff:

I think the obvious freedom of speech that we have, I think when we compare ourselves to the other countries, we are definitely the best, that when you try to run a country of this size with all the ethnic diversity, you're going to have major, major blowups and problems, but we do try to sort them out and I don't think a lot of other countries put as much effort into keeping everything on a smooth keel.

As that cycle works itself out, the country will move toward what Elizabeth Tyler of Brookline called some sense of shared purpose and commitment to continuation of our culture, some sense of survival of the next generation, some sense of things living in a proper way . . . and some sense of living in a country that is free with free choice and some measure of leisure and some measure of economic freedom . . . fairness, and correct moral and ethical values in the way we treat one another and the world.

Statements such as these suggest that, for all the passion and turbulence with which intellectuals and academics discuss issues involving multiculturalism, most ordinary Americans do so in a much quieter voice. To indicate how remarkable that voice is, we ought to return, once again, to the beginning of this century. Then, as I argued at the start of this essay, America was less divided racially and in terms of religious diversity than it is now. Yet there was, if anything, more of a sense that the country was fighting a serious culture war then than there is now. Protestants and Catholics disagreed far more strongly, for example, with each other in those days than Christians do with non-Christians these days. And even though our racial landscape was simpler in the sense that there were only two major races in the country then compared to five now, there was also far more violence and hostility on the part of whites toward blacks than there is between any of our racial groups at the present time.

It also may be helpful, to understand the importance of benign multiculturalism, to compare the situation at century's end with the situation that existed right in the middle of the twentieth century. We now call that time the McCarthy period, and it was a time when questions about a changing national identity were also very much on the minds of the American people. In the 1950s, when charges of treason filled the air, American identity was not especially threatened; the economic and political power of the United States was unsurpassed; there was relatively little immigration; no significant domestic disputes upset a national consensus; women and children were not in rebellion; and rapid technological change was just around the corner. In the 1990s, by contrast, the power of America is weakening economically and politically, the country has become far more diverse, its ideals are challenged constantly, and new technologies seem to flower annually, yet Americans have not responded by accusing each other of lacking sufficient love for their country. Benign multiculturalism enables us to celebrate our differences and our similarities at the same time. That is not a bad accomplishment.

Notes

1. Alan Wolfe, *One Nation, After All* (New York: Viking, 1998).
2. David Hollinger, *Post-Ethnic America: Beyond Multiculturalism* (New York: Basic Books, 1995), p. 157.

Wolfe:

1. What are the reasons that Wolfe says that people living in the United States at the turn of the twentieth century would have been surprised at how divided our society is now?
2. What does Wolfe mean by "benign multiculturalism"?

35

Ecumenical America: Global Culture and the American Cosmos

Orlando Patterson

The modern process of global cultural interaction has repeatedly been subjected to two criticisms. The first is that it threatens the diversity and particularism of the world's cultures, resulting in a deadening homogenization of the human cultural experience. The other is that this growing global uniformity results from the dominance of America's culture—that, in effect, global culture is nothing more than American cultural imperialism. Hannah Arendt's lament that we have been brought to a "global present without a common past [which] threatens to render all traditions and all particular past histories irrelevant," is typical of the first. Theodor Adorno's famous diatribe against American popular music is the *locus classicus* of the second. Both objections are without foundation.

The argument that Americanization is resulting in the homogenization of the world ignores the increased vitality of local cultures and ethnicities in recent times and the complexity of global cultural diffusion, in particular the extent to which so-called peripheral regions are increasingly contributing to American popular culture and to the world music scene. Nor does it explain the emergence of a special kind of regional system,

what I shall call the regional cosmos, or the great cultural divisions in America itself. The American cosmos, as we shall see, is not a single cultural space, but is divided among three Americas: a traditional America, multicultural America, and ecumenical America.

The Diffusion of Global Culture

Industrialization and modernization both entailed the spread of common sets of behaviors and attitudes within the context of economic change. However, the globalization of culture also takes place independent of whatever economic changes are occurring in a particular region of society. Traditionally, the transmission of culture across societies was facilitated by two main media: migration and literacy. People learned about other cultures either through traveling themselves or from travelers, or by reading about other cultures and adopting or adapting what they learned. These traditional media could, under certain circumstances, be effective means for the transmission of cultures across the globe.

The distinctive feature of literary transmissions, and all diffusions through individuals except during mass migrations, is that they tend to be largely confined to elites, or, where not, to enclaves of non-elite persons cut off from the mass of their societies. This was true of the diffusion of Hellenism in the Mediterranean world and was largely true of the imperial influence on the societies of Asia and Africa. Until the end of the Second World War, Westernism was largely confined to a tiny minority of the populations of these continents, largely the educated native elites and urban workers. Since the fifties, however, this has changed radically. The globalization of culture, largely (although by no means solely, as the spread of Islam indicates) through the impact of, and *reaction to,* the diffusion of Western popular and elite culture, has not only greatly increased in terms of its spread over the surface of the world, but in terms of the depth to which it has influenced the populations of other societies.

Four factors account for this sudden change of pace. The first is the spread of mass literacy throughout the world, which resulted from the new nations of the post-colonial era investing vast sums and human energy in their educational systems, the structure and content of which were largely influenced by Western models. The second is the rise of mass communication. The third is the growth of global organizations, both private and public, such as the multinational corporation, the United Nations, the World Bank, the International Monetary Fund, and the large number of regional agencies, themselves often modeled on and directly influenced and promoted by the former. The fourth is the revolution in long-distance transportation, which has resulted in the emergence of an entirely new kind of global, or more properly, subglobal system, the regional cosmos. The most remarkable of these emerging regional cosmoses is the West Atlantic system, encompassed by the eastern seaboard of North America and the circum-Caribbean societies of Central America and the islands.

The Global Popular Music Culture

The emergence of the regional cosmoses provides perhaps the best evidence of the complexity of global cultural diffusion. But before turning to the subject of their development, let us consider one example of global cultural diffusion—namely, how mass communication has facilitated the diffusion and creation of global popular musical culture. I choose to focus on popular music because it is in this area of the globalization process that the strongest claims of homogenization have been made. Its classic statement was given by the musicologist Alan Lomax who, in 1968, lamented the presumed passing of the great local cultures of the world under the impact of American popular culture, which, he feared, would lead to global rootlessness and alienation as the peoples of the earth all sank into desolate gloom of the great, global "cultural grey-out."[1]

As someone who has studied this process in a Third World society that has perhaps been more exposed to the full glare of American culture than nearly any other—namely, Jamaica—I can say unequivocally that such charges are utter nonsense. It is simply not true that the diffusion of Western culture, especially at the popular level, leads to the homogenization of the culture of the world. Indeed, my research, and that of the best scholars working in this area, suggests that just the opposite is the case. Western-American cultural influence has generated enormous cultural production, in some cases amounting to near hypercreativity in the popular cultures of the world.

If what I say is correct, it must be wondered where the popular misconception of the homogenizing effect of the Western impact came from. One source is the propagandistic reaction of traditional cultural gatekeepers in Third World societies whose monopoly and influence has been threatened by the Western cultural impact. That impact, in generating new cultural forms, invariably stimulates the emergence of new and competing cultural agents and managers. To monopolize the cultural resources of a country is to exercise enormous power, not to mention to control economic resources. What usually upsets traditional cultural gatekeepers about the Western impact on their mass cultures is less the content of Western culture—because this is invariably transformed—and more the choice it immediately offers to the consumers of culture.

The second source of misconceptions about the impact of Westernism comes from important segments of the cultural gatekeepers in the West itself, on both the right and the left, who think and talk about this issue. The more abstract of these complaints about the influence of American global popular culture stem from elitist, postmodernist pessimism, of the sort that stimulates similar complaints about the stultifying effects of popular culture on the working class of the West. Cultural critic Paul Willis has recently taken issue with these pretentious criticisms. He notes that people never simply passively absorb cultural messages. There is always what Willis calls symbolic work at play: "The incandescence is not simply a surface market quality. It produces, is driven by, and reproduces further forms and varieties for everyday symbolic work and creativity, some of which remain in the everyday and in common culture far longer than they do on the market."[2]

There is a great deal of sloppy and ill-informed criticism of Americanization in what passes for serious, empirically based research. It is simply assumed that illiterate and semi-literate Third World peoples are powerless in their responses to Western popular culture. Experts on the subject have in mind a world of passive consumers, homogenized and manipulated into Marx's notorious sack of (Westernized) potatoes.[3] It is nothing of the sort. The semi- and non-literate masses of the Third World invariably react to Western

cultural influence in a nonpassive manner, reinterpreting what they receive in the light of their own cultures and experience. One of my favorite examples of this is the story about the British officer in a remote part of northern Greece following the general elections in Britain at the end of the Second World War. The officer asked a Greek peasant if he knew the results of the elections. "Oh yes," replied the peasant excitedly, "the Labour party has won the elections, the king has been assassinated, and Mr. Churchill and his party have fled to the mountains!"

Either the Western cultural form is reinterpreted in light of traditional meanings, or Western meanings are adapted to traditional patterns. In any case, something new, although still local, emerges. As the musicologist Peter Manuel points out, not only do local cultures "adapt foreign elements in distinctly idiosyncratic ways that substantially alter their function, context and meaning," but even what appears to Western ears and perception to be a major intrusion, may, in fact, be so shallow functionally to the native listener as to not even be perceived. This is true, for example, of the influence of American music on the thriving Indian pop-culture.[4]

In their comparative analysis of eight cultures, musicologists Deanna Robinson, Elizabeth Buck, and others have demonstrated, in my opinion conclusively, that "world musical homogenization is not occurring." As they put it, "even though information-age economic forces are building an international consumership for centrally produced and distributed popular music, other factors are pulling in the opposite direction. They are encouraging not only what we call 'indigenization' of popular music forms and production but also new, eclectic combinations of world musical elements, combinations that contradict the continuing constraints of national boundaries and global capitalism."[5]

Furthermore, the common notion that the globalization of culture, especially on the popular level, is a one-way process, from the Western metropolis to the passive and vulnerable periphery, is simply not the case, although it is certainly true that the major diffusionary source of this culture is a single Western country: the United States.

Not homogenization, then, but the revitalization and generation of new musical forms has been the effect of the global exchange process. Some of these forms remain local, providing greater choice and stimulus to the local culture. Examples of such revitalization include the modernization of the traditional Camerounian *makassi* style with the introduction of the acoustic rhythm guitar; the development of the *highlife* music of Ghana, which fused traditional forms with jazz, rock, and Trinidadian calypso rhythms; the vibrant local modernization of traditional Afro-Arab music in Kenya. Elsewhere, musical forms under Western impact have broken out of their provincial boundaries to become regional currency, as, for example, the Trinidadian and American pop influenced *kru-krio* music of Sierra Leone, which swept West Africa and beyond during the sixties and seventies; the Brazilian *samba,* the pan-American *salsa; merengue* (the latter of Dominican Republic origin); the originally Cuban *nueva trova,* which became a radical pan-Latin form, stimulating the even more radical and pan-Latin *nueva canción;* and the Colombian *cumbia,* which has become an important part of the music of the Tex-Mex regional cosmos. And there are those musical forms that experience their fifteen minutes of fame as the latest fad in the "world music" scene: the Argentinean *tango;* the Algerian *rai;* the Zairian *soukous;* the Brazilian *bossa nova.*

Out of Jamaica

One of the most globally successful cultural creations of a Third World people is the musical form known as *reggae.* Indeed, the development of reggae perhaps more than any other musical form illustrates the complexity of global cultural interaction. The creation of the Jamaican working classes and lumpen proletariat, reggae emerged in the late fifties from a variety of influences, especially American. Jamaica had always had a rich musical tradition, originating mainly in the music of West Africa brought over by the slaves, but also influenced in its lyrical and melodic lines by British, especially Celtic, popular music of the late eighteenth and nineteenth centuries. At the turn of the century, a popular secular form, *mento,* ideal for dancing, emerged. Similar to the Trinidad calypso in its topical and satirical lyrics and in its reliance on the guitar for a Latinate ostinato, *mento* soon established itself as *the* traditional popular music of the island.

By the late fifties, however, young working-class Jamaicans had grown weary of *mento.* What they did like were the rhythm-and-blues records being brought back by farm laborers returning from cutting cane in Florida and the "cowboy music" of bluegrass they picked up on short-wave early in the mornings. Aspiring young Jamaican singers—including the teenage Bob Marley, Peter Tosh, Bob Andy, and numerous others—began singing imitations of American soul songs at the many talent parades that preceded the weekend triple bills at the working-class cinemas. These imitations were, at first, ghastly renditions of the original. (I can still recall hearing a pimpled, short-haired Bob Marley singing an American soul song hopelessly out of tune.) At this point, Jamaica would seem to have had the worst of all possible worlds. A delightful native musical tradition had been abandoned, and in its place the island found its middle class swooning over syrupy white American ballads while its lower class sang imitations of African American music.

What happened next, however, demonstrates just how complex the dialectics between local and foreign influences that generate the global culture are. First of all, the imitations were so bad that they were unwittingly original. Furthermore, the Jamaicans instinctively brought their own local musical cadences and rhythms to bear on the tunes being imitated. This coincided with an infusion of the very African music of the Far-Jamaican cults, which was lifted straight from the "laboring" movements made by cult celebrants as they worked themselves up to the point of spirit possession. Both the movement and the accompanying rhythm were secularized (in a manner similar to the crossover from gospel to soul music among African Americans), and a wholly new musical form and accompanying dance, known as *ska*, was created.

At the time—the late fifties and early sixties—the vast majority of working-class Jamaicans were still too poor to buy record players or expensive imported records. This led to the formation of the *sound system,* a hi-fidelity system outfitted with enormous bass speakers which the owners rented out, along with their record collections and themselves in the role of disc jockey. The disc jockeys, partly out of boredom, partly out of increasing dissatisfaction with the rhythmic patters of the imported African American records but above all, out of a desire to give a "live" quality to the performance of their systems, started to deliberately play around with the records as they were being played. They voiced over the imported records with their own rhythmic commentary, improving their "riddim" as they understood it, either through grunts and screams, or through an accompanying screed that sometimes made sense, sometimes was mere nonsense lyrics, which mattered little since the voice was actually being used as an additional bass instrument. This was rapidly to become a distinctive feature of reggae. The disc jockey would also "play" the turntable, stopping and pushing the record as it turned on the platter in order to induce strange new sounds. This, too, was

later to become an essential part of the music, except that the strange noises were to be made through the manipulation of sophisticated studio electronics.

What emerged from these activities was another distinctive musical form, *dub.* When the disc jockeys were unable to match the love lyrics of the imported black American rhythm-and-blues songs, they resorted to what they knew best, local politics. Thus was born reggae dub, with its strong emphasis on the political, a clear departure from popular American music, black and white.

At about the same time that these developments were taking place, the Ras Tafari cult, a millenarian back-to-Africa movement that was the religious component of the reaction to Western influence, was taking hold among the Jamaican proletariat of the Kingston shanties. The spiritualism and radical racial ideology of the cult—a religious form of negritude, exemplifying Sartre's "anti-racist racism"—greatly appealed to the very people developing the music, and it was not long before the two merged, Rastafarian theology giving substance and ideological content to what were previously soppy imported lyrics or garbled political chatter.

The music swiftly went through several formal changes, first from ska to *rock-steady,* a more complex slow-tempo music, and finally, in response to the demands of the entrepreneurs who ran the weekend dance halls and who wanted music with a faster beat so their patrons would drink more of the Red Stripe beer on which they largely depended for their profits, to reggae.

Reggae swiftly caught on, not only among locals, but with the American tourists who were now visiting Jamaica in increasing numbers. Several major singers emerged in the late sixties and early seventies, the most successful of whom was Bob Marley, whose enormous showmanship and song-writing ability were important in internationalizing the music. However, one other factor was equally important in explaining the rapid spread of reggae and its eventual emergence as a global musical form. This was the mass movements of Jamaican working-class migrants. The first such movement was to Britain, where Jamaicans effectively transformed what was a previously all-white country into a multiracial society. By 1964, a thinly Anglicized version of ska known as *blue beat* was already in vogue.[6] Today, reggae has been completely embraced by white British youth, who now view it as an integral part of their culture.[7] From its British base, it was to spread rapidly throughout continental Europe and north and sub-Saharan Africa.

Similarly, reggae spread to the United States as a result of a second mass migration of the Jamaican working class, which began with the liberalization of American immigration laws in the early 1960s. A new kind of West Indian migrant now entered America, not the relatively well-educated, highly motivated petty-bourgeois migrants of previous generations, but the working-class and lumpen-proletarian people from the Kingston slums. Eventually, the reggae music these new migrants brought over with them, along with their disk jockeys and dance halls (as well as their gangs, the notorious posses), were to influence black American youth, but what is interesting is how long it took to do so. Black Americans, in fact, strongly resisted most versions of reggae. Reggae, however, rapidly caught on among the white college students of America, especially after the enormous success of the reggae movie, *The Harder They Come,* and soon broke out of the campus circuit with the success of Bob Marley and other international stars, such as Jimmy Cliff and Peter Tosh.[8]

Eventually, by the late 1970s and early 1980s, even the underclass African American young began to respond to reggae. They were simply unable to prevent themselves from listening to the version of reggae brought over to the ghettoes by the latest wave of underclass Kingston migrants: the dance-hall music. The fact that they also soon developed a healthy

respect for the violent Jamaican posses also explains their changed attitude.

The music had gone full circle, from its beginnings in the crude imitations of the 1950s' African American lower-class music, to the late 1970s' and early 1980s' imitations of dance-hall dub by the New York underclass. The American music that emerged from this extraordinary proletarian cross-fertilization was *rap*, the first popular American music to have an explicitly political lyrical content. The Jamaicans had repaid their debt.

The West Atlantic Regional Cosmos

The transmission of reggae to the American center from the Jamaican periphery not only illustrates the complexity of global cultural interaction, but was a forerunner of a much more complex process that has now integrated parts of the United States with other countries as deeply or more deeply than those parts are integrated with other regions of America. This aspect of the globalization of culture, which has resulted in the development of regional cosmoses, is entirely new. Indeed, it has emerged only over the past two decades or so, largely because it was dependent upon the revolution in cheap mass transportation.

The regional cosmos is best conceived of as a system of flows between a metropolitan center and a set of politically independent satellite countries within what the urban sociologist Saskia Sassen calls a "transnational space."[9] People, wealth, ideas, and cultural patterns move in both directions, influencing both the metropolitan center as well as the peripheral areas, although asymmetrically. Although they are similar in many respects to the other migratory systems, such as those of the Mediterranean, there are several unique features of the regional cosmoses that are of special importance to the problem of the globalization of culture.

In the West Atlantic regional cosmos, made up of eastern America and the circum-Caribbean societies, the peripheral areas are either contiguous with or within easy reach of the dominant metropolitan society.[10] The separate units are legally autonomous, but sovereignty becomes merely a resource to be used in the interaction between the main collective actors. In spite of legal restrictions on the movement of peoples, there is a vast flow in both directions—legal and illegal migrants from the periphery, tourists and investors from the center. There is no simple flow of cheap labor to capital in this system, as in the classic colonial regimes. Skilled and cheap labor flow in both directions. Legal and illegal capital also moves in both directions.

The Third World countries of the periphery are only too eager to attract such capital, but with capitalization their economies become dualized, as is true of the center, between an urban-modern sector and a traditional-rural sector. This disrupts traditional labor patterns at a much faster rate than it provides new job opportunities. The result is massive unemployment, the rise of the urban slums—marking the first state in the migration process—and from there the mass movement to the center. These migrants rarely compete directly with native workers in the center; instead, a wholly new sector—what sociologist Alejandro Portes calls the immigrant enclave—is created for them.[11] Thus, dualization at the center reinforces, and is reinforced by, dualization in the periphery.

An important aspect of the regional cosmos is the rise of the cosmopolis—a major urban center that shifts from being a major metropolis of the center to being the metropolis of the entire regional cosmos. This is precisely the role that Miami has come to play in the West Atlantic regional cosmos.[12] Miami is no longer an American city; it is a West Atlantic city, more vital to, and more dependent on, the needs of the circum-Caribbean societies and cultures than it is on the other sectors of the U.S. economy. It is the political,

cultural, social, and economic hub and heart of the Caribbean.

Culturally, the periphery is greatly influenced by the society of the center, but the reverse is also the case, as the example of reggae demonstrates. Another example of periphery-to-center cultural flows is the transmission of Spanish and Haitian creole, which has resulted not simply in the creation of a multilingual center where English once prevailed but, more broadly, in the Latinization of English and the Anglicization of Spanish. This process of creolization, in turn, has resulted in the creation of wholly new cultural forms in the transnational space, such as "Nuyorican" and Miami Spanish. The same process of cosmopolitan creolization can be found in other areas of culture: in the rapid spread of Spanish-American food, Franco-Haitian-American dishes, and the recent diffusion of the Jamaican "jerk" method of cooking in both Jamerican (Jamaican-American) and mainstream American cooking; in the Latin and West Indian carnivals that are now a standard part of the festivals of the cosmopolis; in the infusion and transformation of Afro-West Indian and Afro-Latin cults, whose animal sacrifices were recently offered constitutional protection by the Supreme Court after a major nativist challenge; in the ironic revival of the game of cricket, once an elite sport among the dominant Anglo-Americans, under the impact of the Afro-West Indian working-class immigrants; in the spread of the dreadlocks style of hair grooming among African Americans and, increasingly, among white Americans from the Jamaican Rastafarian immigrants. These are only some of the more visible expressions of this extraordinary process of periphery-induced creolization in the cosmopolis.

Afro-Caribbean Intellectualism

One of the most fascinating, and neglected, areas of cultural exchange between the cosmopolis and the West Atlantic periphery is in intellectual and professional life. The British, Spanish, and French academic and professional cultures have traditionally dominated the countries of the periphery, the result of their respective colonial experiences. The ruthlessly selective nature of these European traditions created intellectual cultures that were at once highly sophisticated and elitist. What emerged in the black Caribbean—a vibrant engagement with European intellectualism in which the culture of Europe was critically embraced, dissected, and reintegrated through the filter of a creolized neo-African sensibility and aesthetic—had no parallel on the American mainland. It was possible only because of the overwhelming demographic presence of blacks in the West Indies, in contrast with the minority status of blacks in the mainland cosmopolis. In the periphery, the neo-European culture of the elite was mediated through agents of the hegemonic powers, who were themselves black or light-skinned. Hence race, per se, was muted as a factor in the cultural conflict that accompanied the decolonization process.

The ironic effect was that the European experience could be adjudicated, and dialectically explored, in purely cultural terms, devoid of the confounding effects of racial segregation and rejection. In contrast with the black American condition, where any engagement with the dominant culture always ran the risk of the loss of racial identity and the fear of racial betrayal, resulting in an understandable rejection of all intellectualism, the West Indian intellectual developed a love-hate relationship with the culture of the "mother country" that was mediated through fellow blacks. The paradigmatic challenge in this situation became, not the rejection and suspicion of all intellectualism, but a desperate need to outdo the imperial culture at its own game. Intellectualism, however, went far beyond mere anti-imperial one-up-manship. For the ambitious black West Indian, it was, until recently, the only path to mobility, given

the paucity of resources and the monopolization of the limited commercial positions by whites and Asians.

The net result has been a virtual hotbed of intellectualism among Afro-Caribbean peoples. These small, poor islands have, arguably, the highest per capita concentration of scholars, professionals, and real, as well as would-be, intellectuals as any place in the world. It is not Germany, Switzerland, or the United States that has produced the greatest proportion of Nobel laureates per thousand, but the tiny, dirt-poor island nation of St. Lucia. With an at-home population of under 100,000, it has produced two Nobel laureates, the economist Sir A. W. Lewis and the poet Derek Walcott. And they are merely the tip of the iceberg: Trinidad's V. S. Naipaul is generally considered one of the two or three best novelists writing in English; its late scholar-statesman, Eric Williams, was a major historian; its late radical intellectual C. L. R. James one of the foremost Marxist theoreticians. The poet-novelists Edward Brathwaite and George Lamming are only the most recent in a long line of internationally acclaimed writers from Barbados; indeed, Barbados was used by the colonial British as the seedbed for black professionals and missionaries in its cultural penetration of Africa and Asia and still lives to a considerable degree on the remittances of its large number of professional emigrants. What is true of the English-speaking Caribbean islands holds true equally for the French-speaking islands where, to take the most noteworthy example, the poet-statesman Aimé Césaire has long been recognized by French critics as one of the best poets in their language.

This extraordinary intellectual and professional tradition is now being rapidly incorporated into the West Atlantic cosmopolis. American educational aid has been accompanied by American models of education, transforming the elitist nature of these systems. At the same time, there has been a massive redirection of the flow of talent from the region. All roads no longer lead to the old colonial metropoles of London and Paris but increasingly to the great East Coast cosmopolitan centers. Budding West Indian intellectuals now experience their required period of creative exile, not in Europe, but in America, where many take up permanent residence. What is more, a disproportionate number of American academic and other professionals are of West Indian ancestry. Paralleling the cross-fertilization of African American lower-class popular culture by West Indian immigrants is the interaction of Afro-Caribbean and African American traditions within the cosmopolitan academe, which has significant implications not only for the cultures of both traditions, but for the wider culture of the cosmopolis.

The special contribution of West Indian intellectualism in the cosmopolitan context will be a transference of its distinctive strategy of aggressive engagement with the dominant tradition of neo-European civilization—a strategy that, at its worst, generates enormous identity crises and self-destructive emotional and physical violence, but at the same time, and at its best, is the crucible for the explosively competitive syncretism that finds expression in Rastafarianism and *voudon,* reggae and merengue, and negritude, magical realism, *omeros,* and the self-loathing genius of V. S. Naipaul. Such engagement African Americans have independently achieved so far only in the universalizing vitalism of rock music and the jazz aesthetic. My prediction is that the West Indian presence in the cosmopolis will act as a catalyst for the promotion of this transcendent Afro-European contribution to the emerging global culture.

In structural terms, the mass migration of peoples from the periphery in this new context of cheap transportation and communication has produced a wholly different kind of social system. The migrant communities in the center are not ethnic groups in the traditional American sense. In the interaction between center and periphery, the societies of the periphery are radically changed, but so is the traditional immigrant community of the center. What has emerged is, from the viewpoint of the peripheral states, distinctive transnational societies in which there is no longer any meaningful identification of political and social boundaries. Thus, more than a half of the adult working populations of many of the smaller eastern Caribbean states now live outside of these societies, mainly in the immigrant enclaves of the United States. About 40 percent of all Jamaicans, and perhaps half of all Puerto Ricans, live outside of the political boundaries of these societies, mainly in America. The interesting thing about these communities is that their members feel as at home in the mainland segment as in the original politically bounded areas.

These communities are more like self-contained colonies—in this respect, they remind one of the *politeumata* of the Hellenistic cities—within the body politic of the United States, and it is a serious error to confuse them with the traditional ethnic communities, including native African Americans. They are what the Jamaican folk poet, Louise Bennett, calls "colonization in reverse." The former colonies now become the mother country; the imperial metropolis becomes the frontier of infinite resources, only now the resources consist not simply of unexploited land but of underutilized deindustrializing capital and the postindustrial service and professional sectors. There is no traumatic transfer of national loyalty from the home country to the host polity, since home is readily accessible and national loyalty is a waning sentiment in what is increasingly a postnational world. Jamaican, Puerto Rican, Dominican, and Barbadian societies are no longer principally defined by the political-geographical units of Jamaica, Puerto Rico, the Dominican Republic and Barbados but by *both* the populations and cultures of these units and their postnational colonies in the cos[mo]polis.

Other Regional Cosmoses

In addition to the West Atlantic system, there are at least three other emerging multinational spaces with the body politic of contemporary America: the Tex-Mex cosmos of the southwest, incorporating northern Mexican and Southwestern Euro-Indian cultures, peoples and economies; the Southern California cosmos, with its volatile, unblended mosaic of Latin, Asian, and Afro-European cultures; and the newly emerged Pacific Rim cosmos of the Northwest, which integrates the economies and bourgeois cultures of industrial Asia and traditional Euro-America.

While the processes of incorporation and creolization are broadly similar in all four regional cosmoses, they differ sharply in their degrees of integration in the volume and velocity of cultural, economic, and demographic flows, in the levels of asymmetry in the transfer of ideas, cultural products, and skills, in the patterns and stages of creolization, and in the nature and extent of the social and cultural conflicts that inevitably accompany the process of cosmopolitanization.

On all these indices, the West Atlantic cosmos is, in my view, the most advanced especially in the degree of integration and the extent to which the nation-state has been transcended as a major basis of collective commitment and constraint on livelihood. The major outlyers in this system are Haiti and Cuba, but in light of the already large contingent of Cubans and Haitians on the mainland, it is best to see their integration as a temporarily halted process, the one on ideological, the other on racist grounds. It is only a matter of time before both these restraints are eroded.

Next in level of integration is the Tex-Mex cosmos. Although it is the oldest of the four, the Tex-Mex cosmos is confined to a limited range of interactions and, in many respects, is the most asymmetric in its flows. The economic interaction consists largely of cheap, unskilled labor serving labor-intensive agricultural and light-industrial capital. Cultural flows are limited to popular music and the culinary arts. The hegemonic Anglo-American culture has remained strikingly oblivious to any significant Latinization. The architecture of the great cities of the region is aggressively Anglo-American, as is its professional and academic life, which takes account of the Latin presence in well-funded programs of Latin American and Latino studies.

The Southern California cosmos is the most heterogeneous and least integrated of the four and undoubtedly the most volatile. South and East Asian people of highly varied provenance meet Latin, Anglo-, and African Americans at all socioeconomic levels. Economic flows are complex, involving highly skilled, professional, and entrepreneurial Asians, professional and working-class Latinos, as well as blacks of all classes and hegemonic Anglo-Americans. There has, as yet, been surprisingly little cross-fertilization of cultures in the cosmos; the process of creolization remains mainly at the pidgin stage, in language as in other areas of culture. The cultural mix has been correctly described as a salad, and a thoroughly unappetizing one at that. That the nation's worst ethnic riot has recently taken place in this cosmos comes as no surprise. That the riot was not a traditional black-white conflict, as erroneously reported by the press, but a multiethnic conflagration engaging more Latinos than blacks, in spite of its origins in the police beating of a black man, Rodney King, is understandable in light of the extreme differences between the interacting cultures and classes.

The Pacific Rim cosmos is the newest, least complex, and potentially most integrated of the four systems. It is, in effect, the transnational space of the most advanced economic sectors of East Asia and the American mainland. Its boundaries in North America extend beyond the U.S. polity, incorporating the Canadian province of British Columbia. Unlike the other regional cosmoses, it is largely bourgeois in its demographic component, involving a large net flow of entrepreneurial capital and talent from industrial Asia. This asymmetric economic and occupational inflow is counterbalanced by a highly asymmetric cultural and social incorporation of the immigrant population. Nothing better demonstrates the globalization of bourgeois capitalist culture than the ease with which these immigrants have been integrated into the mainland cosmos; the cultural capital they bring with them was already highly Americanized.

The American Cosmos

What are the implications of all this for our understanding of contemporary America? I believe that it is best to conceive of not one, but three Americas, traditional America, multicultural America, and ecumenical America—a vast sociological cosmos bounded by a single, powerful polity. The three are obviously related, but it is important not to confuse them, especially in discussions of multiculturalism.

Multicultural America is made up of the mainland or metropolitan populations of the four "transnational spaces" or regional cosmoses discussed above. It has been called immigrant America by Portes and others, and while this term obviously captures an important dimension of this sector, it is likely to be misleading to the degree that it invites too close a comparison with the immigrant America of earlier years. As I have pointed out, there is something fundamentally different in the relationship between these immigrant communities with both their home societies (to which they remain strongly linked socially and culturally) and the broader American society, with which they are permanently intertwined. Multicultural America is a great socio-cultural concourse, a space where all the cultures from the center's several regional cosmoses meet, resist, embrace,

display their cultural wares at annual parades, gawk at, fight, riot, and learn to live with each other, sometimes even learn a little something from each other.

By traditional America, I mean the Euro-African world that emerged from the Puritan North, the industrial smokestacks, the prairie farms, and the slave South. It is the America of the Midwestern main street, of the old and new south, and the ethnic working classes. It is the America of Richard Nixon, J. Edgar Hoover, and Louis Farrakhan. But it is also the America of Jimmy Carter and the Congressional Black Caucus, of the land grant colleges and the United Negro Colleges. Socially, it is committed to enhanced opportunities and intergenerational mobility, but it is also historically racist, though changing in this regard, and profoundly separatist in its basic orientation. It embraces all races and classes, and today a great many African Americans are as committed to the separatist ideal as their Southern white counterparts. There has been some progress: instead of "separate and unequal," the ethic of this America, as a result of African American pressure, is now "separate but *truly* equal." There is profound disagreement about how such an America is to be achieved—witness the war over affirmative action—but all parties, except for the fringe extremists, are in agreement in their desire to live peacefully and separately.

Ironically, traditional America does have a common culture. At the elite level, it is largely the Anglo-American tradition modified by interactions with the older, more traditional ethnic groups, including mainstreaming African Americans, and by continental European influences. At the popular level, traditional America has been deeply influenced by the African American working class: in its language, music, art, and religion, and in many of its attitudes. For a long time, it simply refused to acknowledge this influence, but in recent decades it has come to do so. It does so even while remaining committed to a separatist society, though one less and less rationalized in racist terms. The persisting racial segregation among black and white traditional Americans is today as much a product of class as of race and is in many ways more voluntary than imposed.

Perhaps the stronger unifying cultural feature of traditional America is its Christian heritage. Originally and still largely Protestant, traditional America is rapidly losing its hostility toward Catholicism, as an overriding convergence of conservative religious values becomes more important: the belief in a Christian God and regular churchgoing; the commitment to patriarchy; the demonization of abortion rights; the preference for punitive law-and-order forms of childrearing and justice; the neo-Puritan fear of sex; uncritical patriotism; reverence for, and for many, dependence on, the military; and the parochial suspicion of the foreign. Even while firmly settled in their separate communities, the many different white ethnic groups and the large core of working- and middle-class blacks who make up traditional America are fully committed to this still thriving system of values.

The Mapping of Race

In one important area, traditional America is under strong pressure from the multicultural sector to change one of its central values, namely, the meaning and conception, though not the significance, of race. Traditionally, race has been defined among both black and white Americans in binary terms: the so-called one-drop rule sociologically excluded any intermediary racial groups on a continuum between blacks and whites. While the binary rule was originally constructed and rigidly imposed by whites out of their commitment to notions of racial purity and exclusion, it is one that traditional African Americans have come to embrace for political and cultural reasons. The rule operated with

extraordinary tenacity not only because both the traditional "races" came to accept it, but because later immigrant groups quickly conformed. Jews, dark-skinned southern Europeans, and Caucasoid Hispanics, once rejected as "true whites," eagerly struggled for, and eventually won, acceptance within the Caucasian chalk circle of white people—in contrast with the excluded blacks, whose presence is required for the extraordinary valorization of whiteness. (The point is best made by noting that for the average Irishman in non-black Ireland, whiteness has no social meaning; Ireland is, in fact, one of the least racist of European societies, as any well-traveled African American or West Indian tourist will attest; however, whiteness is instantly embraced as a valued social, cultural, and economic asset by the marginal, socially insecure Irish immigrant in America, as the well-documented historical negrophobia of working-class Irish Americans, their liberal politics notwithstanding, will also readily attest.)

The rise of the multicultural sector strongly undermines the binary rule in two important respects, one demographic, the other cultural. One reason why the binary rule worked so well was that African Americans were, by and large, the only significant "other" in the American population for most of the nation's history. Until recently, Asians and dark-skinned Latin and South Asian immigrants were an insignificant demographic presence; and Native Americans—who up to the end of the eighteenth century constituted the second significant racial "other"—were removed from consideration through decimation and confinement on reservations.

All this has changed dramatically with the rise of the regional cosmos and the multicultural sector. Visibly nonwhite Asians and Latin Americans, who by no stretch of the imagination can be socially redefined and incorporated within the social category of "white people," now exist in significant numbers in society; indeed, they will outnumber blacks by the turn of the century. Since these groups are clearly neither whites nor blacks, a serious crisis of racial definition now confronts those clinging to the binary conception of race.

Quite apart from the purely demographic factor, however, is the cultural refusal of most of the new immigrants to play by the binary rule, as early streams of immigrants have done. On the one hand, most of the new Asian immigrants have a strong sense of their own racial identity, are proud of the way they look, and do not wish to be redefined racially as anything else. And this sense of racial pride is further reinforced by the multicultural celebration of ethno-racial differences. On the other hand, most immigrants from Latin America bring with them, in addition to their racial heterogeneity, their own highly developed nonbinary or "interval-type" notions of race. That is, socially significant distinctions are made among persons on a continuum between obviously black and obviously white persons. A visibly nonwhite, but light- or brown-skinned Puerto Rican, Dominican, Jamaican, or Brazilian does not consider himself "black." One only has to observe the elaborate shade gradations and mating and marriage patterns of Cuban, Puerto Rican, and other Latin immigrants to recognize that a wholly different principle of racial classification is at play. A similar nonbinary pattern prevails among South Asians between black-skinned "Dravidian" types and fair-skinned "Aryan" types. And the same holds for East Asians. Indeed, nonbinary racial classification is the norm among the vast majority of non-European peoples.

Added to these two factors is a third challenge to the binary rule: the pre-eminence of Japan as a major economic power. The coincidence of the advanced industrial world with the white world strongly reinforced notions of racial purity and superiority. The challenge to American and European economic hegemony from a clearly nonwhite power, one that until as late as the sixties was

castigated as the "yellow peril," its immigrants unashamedly herded into concentration camps during the Second World War, has created confusion for traditional Americans holding fast to their binary notion of race. When one adds to this the out-performance of whites in the educational system by the former "yellow devils"—especially on I.Q. tests, which have functioned so prominently as a "scientific" justification for the binary, purist dogma—it is easy to understand why the binary rule is now in crisis.

Ecumenical America

Ecumenical America is not merely cosmopolitan, for it goes beyond the simple embrace of many cultures maintaining their separate identities. It is, rather, the universal culture that emerged and continues to develop in the great cities and university towns of the nation. This culture is a genuinely ecumenical one: it draws from everywhere, not just from the local cultures of the traditional ethnic and immigrant sectors and the traditional Euro-American culture at its doorstep. The image of the melting pot fails to describe the process by which it emerges, for it does not indiscriminately absorb all and everything into some common stew. There is a complex process of selection and universalization of particular cultural forms and styles generating its great cultural innovations for itself and for the world: in science, technology, literature, dance, painting, music, and cuisine.

Like traditional America, it has both a formal or elite and a popular or vernacular level. English, both of the streets and the academy, is its common language. Its shared art thrives in the works of a Jasper Johns or an Andy Warhol (with their ironic ecumenization of traditional America's most beloved icons) but, perhaps most quintessentially, in the musical form of jazz. On the popular level, the shared art of ecumenical America is also strongly influenced by African Americans. Increasingly, the products of the regional cosmoses are selected out for universalization, as in the ecumenization of Chinese and Mexican cuisine, the poetry of Derek Walcott, the fiction of Saul Bellow and Maxine Hong Kingston, and the drama of Eugene O'Neill. Ecumenical America also draws directly from the wider world in meeting the needs of its art and its technology. The culture it produces, in turn, has become the koine, or common currency, of the world, the first genuinely global culture on the face of the earth.

Ecumenical America is based primarily in the postindustrial economy, with its advanced technological plants, complex services, and multinational corporations. It is no utopia, as the legion of previously secure unemployed workers and managers of smokestack industrial regions and rapidly obsolescent high-tech sectors can attest. It is almost as class-ridden as traditional America. It is politically mainly liberal, but it includes the politically very conservative elites and middle managers of the multinational corporations and silicon suburbs. It also includes the elite managers, scientists, and intellectuals from all over the world—Indian engineers, Japanese and Hong Kong businessmen, Argentinean doctors, European managers and artists, and Caribbean intellectuals—who enter this sector at the top and are not to be confused with the working-class or sweatshop entrepreneurs of the immigrant enclave economy.

A New Cultural Policy

Let me conclude with a few reflections on the kind of cultural policy that this interpretation of the American cosmos implies. In the first place, it seems to me that any attempt at a single policy for all America is a nonstarter. Any cultural policymaker must begin by recognizing the fundamentally tripartite nature of America. It is a waste of time trying to persuade a traditional American to embrace a

Robert Mapplethorpe; it might even be unreasonable. The most we can reasonably expect is that he or she respect the right of ecumenical Americans to publicly view Mapplethorpe's photographs.

Second, it should now be clear that the multicultural social philosophy and approach to the arts and culture is wholly inadequate for the American cosmos. It very inadequately addresses the needs of immigrant or multicultural America but is inappropriate as a strategy for the other two cultural systems that embrace the vast majority of Americans.

Indeed, it is questionable whether there can be a single policy even for the multicultural sector itself. In the first place, as we have seen, the American, cosmopolitan parts of the four regional cosmoses that together constitute the social bases of multicultural America are at different stages of development, especially in their degrees of integration. What holds true for the highly integrated West Atlantic cosmos, with its harmonizing processes of creolization, simply does not apply to the fissiparous Southern California cosmos.

But there is a more profound problem with regard to any attempt at a single multicultural policy. This is the inherent self-contradiction of all programs that adhere to the dogma of relativism. If all ideals, all values, and all art in all cultures and subcultures are of equal worth, there is no basis for the view that relativism—the basic value of the multicultural theorists and policy advocates—is of any greater worth than the basic values of any of the celebrated subcultures that deny the worth of others—including that of the relativists—in absolutist terms. Relativism requires the acceptance of its condemnation by the very antirelativists it embraces. This is no academic abstraction, as Americans have already learned in the course of their current bitter culture wars. A multicultural relativist is in no position to condemn the traditionalist fundamentalist's insistence that not only is the Christian God the only true God, but that no one has the right to prevent his children from attending public schools where the day begins and ends with Christian prayers. Similarly, a black nationalist has no moral basis for condemning a white supremacist. Indeed, partly out of recognition of the contradiction, there has been an astonishing recent convergence of interests between several white and black racist nationalists. The present volatile debate over speech codes, and more generally, over the First Amendment, is disturbing testimony to the potentially catastrophic social and cultural implications of an unthinking commitment to the self-contradictions of the relativistic dogma that is basic for multiculturalist theorists.

Traditional America is inherently hostile to such a strategy and rightly complains of its disregard for a common center. In its extreme commitment to relativism, multiculturalism well serves the needs of immigrant peoples and cultures thrown upon each other and who must learn basic principles—often contrary to their own traditions—of tolerance for others. But discrimination is the essence of cultural creation, and this same relativism, when applied to the other two areas of the American cosmos, could be deadening in its impact.

The multicultural ideology, then, is certainly needed, but its limits must be understood. Making it the American creed would be a serious mistake. In general, art within the immigrant sector should be encouraged preferably by private foundations rather than the government, but only where it looks toward, and strives to become, a part of the shared art of the ecumene. However, where the immigrant artist is atavistic, looking only back at his or her original culture, he or she should be tolerated, respected, and accepted in good faith, but not actively supported. It is not the business of the ecumenical to promote the atavistic.

Ecumenical America is no utopia. Nonetheless, it seems clear to me that this is the fu-ture of America, for better or for worse. There is no basis for the commonly heard criticism that associates the ecumenical with a grey, homogenized world. Nor is there any justification for the view that the ecumenical is dominated by a global financial elite having no responsibility to any local community. The ultimate thrust of the ecumenical is indeed transnational and, in many respects, postnational. But this is the way of the world in the twenty-first century, and such postnational orientation is by no means confined to the financial elite. Indeed, as I have shown, it is the migrant peasants, working classes, and intellectuals from the periphery of the world's transnational spaces who are most postnational in their attitudes and behavior. The typical Jamaican resident of Brooklyn or Mexican resident of Texas has already gone far beyond any transnational capitalist of New York in his or her attitudes, migratory movements, and life-style.

We have no choice but to accept the inevitable; but we do have choices in what we make of it. Ecumenical America and its advocates, among whom I count myself, should recognize its special place, not only as the most advanced part of the American cosmos, but as the vital source of the world's first truly global culture. It should support artists, scientists, and other cultural creators in and out of America whose work resonates and who are dialectically engaged with the emerging shared art and shared ways of the global ecumene, at both the advanced and vernacular levels of social and cultural life.

Notes

1. Alan Lomax, *Folks Song Style and Culture* (Washington, DC: American Association for the Advancement of Science, 1968).

2. Paul E. Willis, *Common Culture* (Boulder CO: Westview, 1990), p. 26.

3. For the standard Frankfurt School criticisms, see Theodor W. Adorno, *Introduction to the*

Sociology of Music (New York: Continuum, 1988); and Herber Marcuse, *One-Dimensional Man* (Boston: Beacon, 1964).

4. Peter Manuel, *Popular Music of the Non-Western World* (New York: Oxford University Press, 1988), p. 20.

5. Deanna Robinson, Elizabeth Buck, et al., *Music at the Margins: Popular Music and Global Cultural Diversity* (Newbury Park, CA: Sage, 1991), p. 4.

6. Orlando Patterson, "The Dance Invasion of Britain: On the Cultural Diffusion of Jamaican Popular Arts," *New Society*, no. 207 (September 1966).

7. See Simon Jones, *Black Culture, White Youth* (Basingstoke: Macmillan Education, 1988).

8. See Stephen Davis and Peter Simon, *Reggae Bloodlines* (New York: Da Capo, 1979).

9. See Saskia Sassen, *The Mobility of Labor and Capital* (New York: Cambridge University Press, 1988).

10. For a detailed analysis of this cosmos, see my essay, "The Emerging West Atlantic System: Migration, Culture and Underdevelopment in the U.S. and Caribbean," in *Population in an Interacting World*, ed. William Alonso (New York: Cambridge University Press, 1987).

11. Alejandro Portes and Rubén G. Rumbout, *Immigrant America* (Berkeley: University of California Press, 1990).

12. For a spirited journalistic tour of this regional cosmos and Miami's central role in it, see Joel Garreau, *The Nine Nations of North America* (Boston: Houghton Mifflin, 1981), pp. 167–206.

Patterson:

1. What is a regional cosmos?
2. Distinguish between traditional America, multicultural America, and ecumenical America.

Multiculturalism:
Battleground or Meeting Ground?

Ronald Takaki

"It is very natural that the history written by the victim does
not altogether chime with the story of the victor."

José Fernández of California, 1874[1]

In 1979, I experienced the truth of this statement when I found myself attacked by C. Vann Woodward in the *New York Review of Books.* I had recently published a broad and comparative study of blacks, Chinese, Indians, Irish, and Mexicans, from the American Revolution to the U.S. war against Spain. But, for Woodward, my *Iron Cages: Race and Culture in Nineteenth-Century America* was too narrow in focus. My analysis, he stridently complained, should have compared ethnic conflicts in the United States to those in Brazil, South Africa, Germany, and Russia. Such an encompassing view would have shown that America was not so "bad" after all.

The author of scholarship that focused exclusively on the American South, Woodward was arguing that mine should have been cross-national in order to be "balanced." But how, I wondered, was balance to be measured? Surely, any examination of the "worse instances" of racial oppression in other countries should not diminish the importance of what happened here. Balance should also insist that we steer away from denial or a tendency to be dismissive. Woodward's contrast of the "millions of corpses" and the "horrors of genocide" in Nazi Germany to racial violence in the United States seemed both heartless and beside the point. Enslaved Africans in the American South would have felt little comfort to have been told that conditions for their counterparts in Latin America were "worse." They would have responded that it mattered little that the black population in Brazil was "17.5 million" rather than "127.6 million" by 1850, or whether slavery beyond what Woodward called the "three-mile limit" was more terrible and deadly.

What had provoked such a scolding from this dean of American history? One might have expected a more supportive reading from the author of *The Strange Career of Jim Crow,* a book that had helped stir our society's moral conscience during the civil rights era. My colleague Michael Rogin tried to explain Woodward's curious reaction by saying that the elderly historian perceived me as a bad son. History had traditionally been written by members of the majority population; now some younger scholars of color like me had received our Ph.D.'s and were trying to "re-vision" America's past. But our critical scholarship did not chime with the traditional version of history. Noting my nonwhiteness, Woodward charged that I was guilty of reverse discrimination: my characterization of whites in terms of rapacity, greed, and brutality constituted a "practice" that could be described as "racism." Like a father, Woodward chastised me for catering to the "current mood of self-denigration and self-flagellation." "If and when the mood passes," he lamented, "one would hope a more balanced perspective on American history will prevail."[2]

Looking back at Woodward's review today, we can see that it constituted one of the opening skirmishes of what has come to be called the culture war. Some of the battles of this conflict have erupted in the political arena. Speaking before the 1992 Republican National Convention, Patrick Buchanan urged his fellow conservatives to take back their cities, their culture, and their country, block by block. This last phrase was a reference to the National Guard's show of force during the 1992 Los Angeles riot. On the other hand, in his first speech as President-elect, Bill Clinton recognized our ethnic and cultural diversity as a source of America's strength.

But many of the fiercest battles over how we define America are being waged within the academy. There minority students and scholars are struggling to diversify the curriculum, while conservative pundits like Charles J. Sykes and Dinesh D'Souza are fighting to recapture the campus.[3]

The stakes in this conflict are high, for we are being asked to define education and determine what an educated person should know about the world in general and America in particular. This is the issue Allan Bloom raises in his polemic, *The Closing of the American Mind.* A leader of the intellectual backlash against cultural diversity, he articulates a conservative view of the university curriculum. According to Bloom, entering students are "uncivilized," and faculty have the responsibility to "civilize" them. As a teacher, he claims to know what their "hungers" are and "what they can digest." Eating is one of his favorite metaphors. Noting the "large black presence" at major universities, he regrets the "one failure" in race relations—black students have proven to be "indigestible." They do not "melt as have *all* other groups." The problem, he contends, is that "blacks have become blacks": they have become "ethnic." This separatism has been reinforced by an academic permissiveness that has befouled the curriculum with "Black Studies" along with "Learn Another Culture." The only solution, Bloom insists, is "the good old Great Books approach."[4]

Behind Bloom's approach is a political agenda. What does it mean to be an American? he asks. The "old view" was that "by recognizing and accepting man's natural rights," people in this society found a fundamental basis of unity. The immigrant came here and became assimilated. But the "recent education of openness," with its celebration of diversity, is threatening the social contract that had defined the members of American society as individuals. During the civil rights movement of the 1960s, Black Power militants had aggressively affirmed a group identity. Invading college campuses, they demanded "respect for blacks as blacks, not as human beings simply," and began to "propagandize acceptance of different ways." This emphasis on ethnicity separated Americans from each other, shrouding their "essential humankindness." The black conception of a group identity provided the theoretical basis for a new policy, affirmative action, which opened the doors to the admission of unqualified students. Once on campus, many black students agitated for the establishment of black studies programs, which in turn contributed to academic incoherence, lack of synopsis, and the "decomposition of the university."[5]

Bloom's is a closed mind, unwilling to allow the curriculum to become more inclusive. Fortunately, many other educators have been acknowledging the need to teach students about the cultural diversity of American society. "Every student needs to know," former University of Wisconsin chancellor Donna Shalala has explained, "much more about the origins and history of the particular cultures which, as Americans, we will encounter during our lives."[6]

This need for cross-cultural understanding has been grimly highlighted by recent racial tensions and conflicts such as the black boycott of Korean stores, Jewish-black antagonism in Crown Heights, and especially the 1992 Los Angeles racial explosion. During the days of rage, Rodney King pleaded for calm: "Please, we can get along here. We all can get along. I mean, we're all stuck here for a while. Let's try to work it out." But how should "we" be defined?[7]

Earlier, the Watts riot had reflected a conflict between whites and blacks, but the fire this time in 1992 Los Angeles highlighted the multiracial reality of American society. Race includes Hispanics and Asian Americans. The old binary language of race relations between whites and blacks, *Newsweek* observed, is no longer descriptive of who we are as Americans. Our future will increasingly be multiethnic as the twenty-first century rushes toward us: the western edge of the continent called California constitutes the thin end of an entering new wedge, a brave new multicultural world of Calibans of many different races and ethnicities.[8]

If "we" must be more inclusive, how do we "work it out"? One crucial way would be for us to learn more about each other—not only whites about peoples of color, but also blacks

about Koreans, and Hispanics about blacks. Our very diversity offers an intellectual invitation to teachers and scholars to reach for a more comprehensive understanding of American society. Here the debate over multiculturalism has gone beyond whether or not to be inclusive. The question has become, How do we develop and teach a more culturally diverse curriculum?

What has emerged are two perspectives, what Diane Ravitch has usefully described as "particularism" versus "pluralism." But, by regarding each as exclusive, even antagonistic, Ravitch fails to appreciate the validity of both viewpoints and the ways they complement each other.[9]

Actually, we need not be forced into an either-or situation. Currently, many universities offer courses that study a particular group, such as African Americans or Asian Americans. This focus enables students of a specific minority to learn about their history and community. These students are not necessarily seeking what has been slandered as self-esteem courses. Rather, they simply believe that they are entitled to learn how their communities fit into American history and society. My grandparents were Japanese immigrant laborers, and even after I finished college with a major in American history and completed a Ph.D. in this field, I had learned virtually nothing about why they had come to America and what had happened to them as well as other Japanese immigrants in this country. This history should have been available to me.

The particularistic perspective led me to write *Strangers from a Different Shore: A History of Asian Americans*. This focus on a specific group can also be found in Irving Howe's *World of Our Fathers: The Journey of the East European Jews to America,* Mario Garcia's *Desert Immigrants: The Mexicans of El Paso, 1880–1920,* Lawrence Levine's *Black Culture and Black Consciousness,* and Kerby Miller's *Emigrants and Exiles: Ireland and the Irish Exodus to North America.*[10]

Increasingly, educators and scholars are recognizing the need for us to step back from particularistic portraits in order to discern the rich and complex mosaic of our national pluralism. While group-specific courses have been in the curriculum for many years, courses offering a comparative and integrative approach have been introduced recently. In fact, the University of California at Berkeley has instituted an American cultures requirement for graduation. The purpose of this course is to give students an understanding of American society in terms of African Americans, Asian Americans, Latinos, Native Americans, and European Americans, especially the immigrant groups from places like Ireland, Italy, Greece, and Russia.

What such curricular innovations promise is not only the introduction of intellectually dynamic courses that study the crisscrossed paths of America's different groups but also the fostering of comparative multicultural scholarship. This pluralistic approach is illustrated by works like my *Different Mirror: A History of Multicultural America* as well as Gary Nash's *Red, White, and Black: The Peoples of Early America*, Ivan Light's *Ethnic Enterprise in America: Business and Welfare among Chinese, Japanese, and Blacks*, Reginald Horsman's *Race and Manifest Destiny: The Origins of American Racial Anglo-Saxonism*, and Benjamin Ringer's *"We the People" and Others: Duality and America's Treatment of Its Racial Minorities.*[11]

Even here, however, a battle is being fought over how America's diversity should be conceptualized. For example, Diane Ravitch avidly supports the pluralistic perspective, but she fears national division. Stressing the importance of national unity, Ravitch promotes the development of multiculturalism based on a strategy of adding on: to keep mainstream Anglo-American history and expand it by simply including information on racism as well as minority contributions to America's music, art, literature, food, clothing, sports, and holidays. The purpose behind this pluralism, for Ravitch, is to encourage students of "all racial and ethnic groups to believe that they are part of this society and that they should develop their talents and minds to the fullest." By "fullest," she means for students to be inspired by learning about "men and women from diverse backgrounds who overcame poverty, discrimination, physical handicaps, and other obstacles to achieve success in a variety of fields." Ravitch is driven by a desire for universalism: she wants to affirm our common humanity by discouraging our specific group identities, especially those based on racial experiences. Ironically, Ravitch, a self-avowed proponent of pluralism, actually wants us to abandon our group ties and become individuals.[12]

This privileging of the "unum" over the "pluribus" has been advanced more aggressively by Arthur Schlesinger in *The Disuniting of America*.

In this jeremiad, Schlesinger denounces what he calls "the cult of ethnicity"—the shift from assimilation to group identity, from integration to separatism. The issue at stake, he argues, is the teaching of *"bad* history under whatever ethnic banner." After acknowledging that American history has long been written in the "interests of white Anglo-Saxon Protestant males," he describes the enslavement of Africans, the seizure of Indian lands, and the exploitation of Chinese railroad workers. But his discussion on racial oppression is perfunctory and parsimonious, and he devotes most of his attention to a defense of traditional history. "Anglocentric domination of schoolbooks was based in part on unassailable facts," Schlesinger declares. "For better or worse, American history has been shaped more than anything else by British tradition and culture." Like Bloom, Schlesinger utilizes the metaphor of eating. "To deny the essentially European origins of American culture is to falsify history," he explains. "Belief in one's own culture does not require disdain for other cultures. But one step at a time: no culture can hope to ingest other cultures all at once, certainly not before it ingests its own." Defensively claiming to be an inclusionist historian, Schlesinger presents his own credentials: "As for me, I was for a time a member of the executive council of the *Journal of Negro History*. . . . I have been a lifelong advocate of civil rights."[13]

But what happens when minority peoples try to define their civil rights in terms of cultural pluralism and group identities? They become targets of Schlesinger's scorn. This "exaggeration" of ethnic differences, he warns, only "drives ever deeper the awful wedges between races," leading to an "endgame" of self-pity and self-ghettoization. The culprits responsible for this divisiveness are the "multicultural zealots," especially the Afrocentrists. Schlesinger castigates them as campus bullies, distorting history and creating myths about the contributions of Africans.[14]

What Schlesinger refuses to admit or is unable to see clearly is how he himself is culpable of historical distortion: his own omissions in *The Age of Jackson* have erased what James Madison had described then as "'the black race within our bosom'" and "'the red on our borders.'" Both groups have been entirely left out of Schlesinger's study: they do not even have entries in the index. Moreover, there is not even a mention of two marker events, the Nat Turner insurrection and Indian Removal, which Andrew Jackson himself would have been surprised to find omitted from a history of his era. Unfortunately, Schlesinger fails to meet even his own standards of scholarship: "The historian's goals are accuracy, analysis, and objectivity in the reconstruction of the past."[15]

Behind Schlesinger's cant against multiculturalism is fear. What will happen to our national ideal of *"e pluribus unum"?"* he worries. Will the center hold, or will the melting pot yield to the Tower of Babel? For answers, he looks abroad. "Today," he observes, "the nationalist fever encircles the globe." Angry and violent "tribalism" is exploding in India,

the former Soviet Union, Indonesia, Guyana, and other countries around the world. "The ethnic upsurge in America, far from being unique, partakes of the global fever." Like Bloom and Ravitch, Schlesinger prescribes individualism as the cure. "Most Americans," he argues, "continue to see themselves primarily as individuals and only secondarily and trivially as adherents of a group." The dividing of society into "fixed ethnicities nourishes a culture of victimization and a contagion of inflammable sensitivities." This danger threatens the "brittle bonds of national identity that hold this diverse and fractious society together." The Balkan present, Schlesinger warns, may be America's prologue.[16]

Are we limited to a choice between a "disuniting" multiculturalism and a common American culture, or can we transform the "culture war" into a meeting ground? The intellectual combats of this conflict, Gerald Graff suggests, have the potential to enrich American education. As universities become contested terrains of different points of view, gray and monotonous cloisters of Eurocentric knowledge can become brave new worlds, dynamic and multicultural. On these academic battlegrounds, scholars and students can engage each other in dialogue and debate, informed by the heat and light generated by the examination of opposing texts such as Joseph Conrad's *Heart of Darkness* and Chinua Achebe's *Things Fall Apart.* "Teaching the conflicts has nothing to do with relativism or denying the existence of truth," Graff contends. "The best way to make relativists of students is to expose them to an endless series of different positions which are *not* debated before their eyes." Graff turns the guns of the great books against Bloom. By viewing culture as a debate and by entering a process of intellectual clashes, students can search for truth, as did Socrates "when he taught the conflicts two millennia ago."[17]

Like Graff, I welcome such debates in my teaching. One of my courses, "Racial Inequality in America: A Comparative Historical Perspective," studies the character of American society in relationship to our racial and ethnic diversity. My approach is captured in the phrase "from different shores." By "shores," I intend a double meaning. One is the shores from which the migrants departed, places such as Europe, Africa, and Asia. The second is the various and often conflicting perspectives or shores from which scholars have viewed the experiences of racial and ethnic groups.

By critically examining these different shores, students address complex comparative questions. How have the experiences of racial minorities such as African Americans been similar to and different from those of ethnic groups such as Irish Americans? Is race the same as ethnicity? For example, is the African American experience qualitatively or quantitatively different from the Jewish American experience? How have race relations been shaped by economic developments as well as by culture—moral values about how people think and behave as well as beliefs about human nature and society? To wrestle with these questions, students read Nathan Glazer's analysis of assimilationist patterns as well as Robert Blauner's theory of internal colonialism, Charles Murray on black welfare dependency as well as William Julius Wilson on the economic structures creating the black underclass, and Thomas Sowell's explanation of Asian American success as well as my critique of the "myth of the Asian-American model minority."[18]

The need to open American minds to greater cultural diversity will not go away. Faculty can resist this imperative by ignoring the changing racial composition of student bodies and the larger society, or they can embrace this timely and exciting intellectual opportunity to revitalize the social sciences and humanities. "The study of the humanities," Henry Louis Gates observes, "is the study of the possibilities of human life in culture. It thrives on diversity.... The new [ethnic studies] scholarship has invigorated the tradi-

tional disciplines." What distinguishes the university from other battlegrounds, such as the media and politics, is that the university has a special commitment to the search for knowledge, one based on a process of intellectual openness and inquiry. Multiculturalism can stoke this critical spirit by transforming the university into a crucial meeting ground for different viewpoints. In the process, perhaps we will be able to discover what makes us an American people.[19]

Whether the university can realize this intellectual pursuit for collective self-knowledge is uncertain, especially during difficult economic times. As institutions of higher learning face budget cuts, calls for an expansion of the curriculum often encounter hostility from faculty in traditional departments determined to protect dwindling resources. Furthermore, the economic crisis has been fanning the fires of racism in society: Asian Americans have been bashed for the seeming invasion of Japanese cars, Hispanics accused of taking jobs away from Americans, and blacks attacked for their dependency on welfare and the special privileges of affirmative action.

This context of rising racial tensions has conditioned the culture war. Both the advocates and the critics of multiculturalism know that the conflict is not wholly academic; the debate over how America should be defined is related to power and privilege. Both sides agree that history is power. Society's collective memory determines the future. The battle is over what should be remembered and who should do the remembering.

Traditionally excluded from the curriculum, minorities are insisting that America does not belong to one group and neither does America's history. They are making their claim to the knowledge offered by the university, reminding us that Americans originated from many lands and that everyone here is entitled to dignity. "I hope this survey do a lot of good for Chinese people," an immigrant told an interviewer from Stanford in the 1920s. "Make American people realize that Chinese people are humans. I think very few American people really know anything about Chinese." As different groups find their voices, they tell and retell stories that liberate. By writing about the people on Mango Street, Sandra Cisneros explained, "the ghost does not ache so much." The place no longer holds her with "both arms. She sets [her] free." Indeed, stories may not be as innocent or simple as they might seem. They "aren't just entertainment," observed Native American novelist Leslie Marmon Silko.[20]

On the other side, the interests seeking to maintain the status quo also recognize that the contested terrain of ideas is related to social reality. No wonder conservative foundations like Coors and Olin have been financing projects to promote their own political agenda on campuses across the country, and the National Association of Scholars has been attacking multiculturalism by smearing it with a brush called "political correctness." Conservative critics like Bloom are the real campus bullies: they are the ones unwilling to open the debate and introduce students to different viewpoints. Under the banner of intellectual freedom and excellence, these naysayers have been imposing their own intellectual orthodoxy by denouncing those who disagree with them as "the new barbarians," saluting Lynne Cheney, the former head of the National Endowment for the Humanities for defending traditional American culture, and employing McCarthyite tactics to brand ethnic studies as "un-American."[21]

How can the university become a meeting ground when the encounter of oppositional ideas is disparaged? What Susan Faludi has observed about the academic backlash against women's liberation can be applied to the reaction to multiculturalism. "The donnish robes of many of these backlash thinkers cloaked impulses that were less than scholarly," she wrote. "Some of them were academics who believed that feminists had cost them

in advancement, tenure, and honors; they found the creation of women's studies not just professionally but personally disturbing and invasive, a trespasser trampling across *their* campus." Her observation applies to multiculturalism: all we need to do is to substitute "minority scholars" for "feminists," and "ethnic studies" for "women's studies." The intellectual backlashers are defending "their" campuses against the "other."[22]

The campaign against multiculturalism reflects a larger social nervousness, a perplexity over the changing racial composition of American society. Here Faludi's insights may again be transferrable. The war against women, she notes, manifests an identity crisis for men: what does it mean to be a man? One response has been to reclaim masculinity through violence, to "kick ass," the expression George Bush used to describe his combat with Geraldine Ferraro in the 1984 vice-presidential debate. Eight years later, during the Persian Gulf war against Saddam Hussein, Bush as President demonstrated masculine power in Desert Storm. In a parallel way, it can be argued, the expanding multicultural reality of America is creating a racial identity crisis: what does it mean to be white?[23]

Demographic studies project that whites will become a minority of the total U.S. population some time during the twenty-first century. Already in major cities across the country, whites no longer predominate numerically. This expanding multicultural reality is challenging the traditional notion of America as white. What will it mean for American society to have a nonwhite majority? The significance of this future, *Time* observed, is related to our identity—our sense of individual self and nationhood, or what it means to be American. This demographic transformation has prompted E.D. Hirsch to worry that America is becoming a "Tower of Babel," and that this multiplicity of cultures is threatening to tear the country's social fabric. Nostalgic for a more cohesive culture and a more homogeneous America, he contends,

"If we *had* to make a choice between the *one* and the *many,* most Americans would choose the principle of unity, since we cannot function as a nation without it." The way to correct this fragmentization, Hirsch argues, is to promote the teaching of "shared symbols." In *Cultural Literacy: What Every American Needs to Know,* Hirsch offers an appendix of terms designed to create a sense of national identity and unity—a list that leaves out much of the histories and cultures of minorities.[24]

The escalating war against multiculturalism is being fueled by a fear of loss. "'Backlash politics may be defined as the reaction by groups which are declining in a felt sense of importance, influence, and power,'" observed Seymour Martin Lipset and Earl Raab. Similarly, historian Richard Hofstadter described the impulses of progressive politics in the early twentieth century in terms of a "status revolution"—a widely shared frustration among middle-class professionals who had been displaced by a new class of elite businessmen. Hofstadter also detected a "paranoid style in American politics" practiced by certain groups such as nativists who suffered from lost prestige and felt besieged by complex new realities. Grieving for an America that had been taken away from them, they desperately fought to repossess their country and "prevent the final destructive act of subversion."[25]

A similar anxiety is growing in America today. One of the factors behind the backlash against multiculturalism is race, what Lawrence Auster calls "the forbidden topic." In an essay published in the *National Review,* he advocates the restriction of immigration for nonwhites. Auster condemns the white liberals for wanting to have it both ways—to have a common culture and also to promote racial diversity. They naively refuse to recognize the danger: when a "critical number" of people in this country are no longer from the West, then we will no longer be able to employ traditional reference points such as "our West-

ern heritage" or speak of "our Founding Fathers." American culture as it has been known, Auster warns, is disappearing as "more and more minorities complain that they can't identify with American history because they 'don't see people who look like themselves' in that history." To preserve America as a Western society, Auster argues, America must continue to be composed mostly of people of European ancestry.[26]

What Auster presents is an extreme but logical extension of a view shared by both conservatives like Bloom and liberals like Schlesinger: they have bifurcated American society into "us" versus "them." This division locates whites at the center and minorities at the margins of our national identity. "American," observed Toni Morrison, has been defined as "white." Such a dichotomization denies our wholeness as one people. "'Everybody remembers,'" she explained, "'the first time they were taught that part of the human race was Other. That's a trauma. It's as though I told you that your left hand is not part of your body.'"[27]

In their war against the denied parts of American society, the backlashers are our modern Captain Ahabs. In their pursuit of their version of the white whale, they are in command; like Ahab directing his chase from the deck of the *Pequod,* they steer the course of the university curriculum. Their exclusive definition of knowledge has rendered invisible and silent the swirling and rich diversity below deck. The workers of the *Pequod* represent a multicultural society—whites like Ishmael, Pacific Islanders like Queequeg, Africans like Daggoo, Asians like Fedallah, and American Indians like Tashtego. In Melville's powerful story, Ishmael and Queequeg find themselves strangers to each other at first. As they labor together, they are united by their need of mutual survival and cooperation. This connectedness is graphically illustrated by the monkey-rope. Lowered into the shark-infested water to secure the blubber hook into the dead whale, Queequeg is held by a rope tied to Ishmael. The process is perilous for both men. "We two, for the time," Ishmael tells us, "were wedded; and should poor Queequeg sink to rise no more, then both usage and honor demanded that, instead of cutting the cord, it should drag me down in his wake." Though originally from different shores, the members of the crew share a noble class unity. Ahab, however, is able to charm them, his charisma drawing them into the delirium of his hunt. Driven by a monomanic mission, Ahab charts a course that ends in the destruction of everyone except Ishmael.[28]

On college campuses today, the voices of many students and faculty from below deck are challenging such hierarchical power. In their search for cross-cultural understandings, they are trying to re-vision America. But will we as Americans continue to perceive our past and peer into our future as through a glass darkly? In the telling and retelling of our particular stories, will we create communities of separate memories, or will we be able to connect our diverse selves to a larger national narrative? As we approach a new century dominated by ethnic and racial conflicts at home and throughout the world, we realize that the answers to such questions will depend largely on whether the university will be able to become both a battleground and a meeting ground of varied viewpoints.

Notes

1. David J. Weber, ed., *Foreigners in Their Native Land: Historical Roots of the Mexican Americans* (Albuquerque: University of New Mexico Press, 1973), p. vi.

2. C. Van Woodward, "America the Bad?" *New York Review of Books*, 22 Nov. 1979; Ronald Takaki, *Iron Cages: Race and Culture in Nineteenth-Century America* (New York: Knopf, 1979).

3. Charles J. Sykes, *The Hollow Men: Politics and Corruption in Higher Education* (Washington, DC: Regnery Gateway, 1990); Dinesh D'Souza, *Il-liberal Education: The Politics of Race and Sex on Campus* (New York: Free Press, 1991).

4. Allan Bloom, *The Closing of the American Mind: How Higher Education Has Failed Democracy and Impoverished the Souls of Today's Students* (New York: Simon & Schuster, 1987), pp. 19, 91–93, 340–41, 344.

5. Ibid., pp. 27, 29, 33, 35, 89, 90, 347.

6. *University of Wisconsin–Madison: The Madison Plan* (Madison: University of Wisconsin, 1988).

7. Rodney King's statement to the press; see *New York Times*, 2 May 1992, p. 6.

8. "Beyond Black and White," *Newsweek*, 18 May 1992, p. 28.

9. Diane Ravitch, "Multiculturalism: E Pluribus Plures," *American Scholar*, 59(3):337–54 (Summer 1990).

10. Ronald Takaki, *Strangers from a Different Shore: A History of Asian Americans* (Boston: Little, Brown, 1989); Irving Howe, *World of Our Fathers: The Journey of the East European Jews to America and the Life They Found and Made* (New York: Simon & Schuster, 1976); Lawrence W. Levine, *Black Culture and Black Consciousness: Afro-American Folk Thought from Slavery to Freedom* (New York: Oxford University Press, 1977); Mario T. Garcia, *Desert Immigrants: The Mexicans of El Paso, 1880–1920* (New Haven, CT: Yale University Press, 1981); Kerby A. Miller, *Emigrants and Exiles: Ireland and the Irish Exodus to North America* (New York: Oxford University Press, 1985).

11. Ronald Takaki, *A Different Mirror: A History of Multicultural America* (New York: Little, Brown, 1993); Gary Nash, *Red, White, and Black: The Peoples of Early America* (Englewood Cliffs, NJ: Prentice Hall, 1974); Ivan Light, *Ethnic Enterprise in America: Business and Welfare among Chinese, Japanese, and Blacks* (Berkeley: University of California Press, 1972); Reginald Horsman, *Race and Manifest Destiny: The Origins of American Racial Anglo-Saxonism* (Cambridge, MA: Harvard University Press, 1981); Benjamin Ringer, *"We the People" and Others: Duality and America's Treatment of Its Racial Minorities* (New York: Tavistock, 1983).

12. Ravitch, "Multiculturalism," pp. 341, 354.

13. Arthur M. Schlesinger, Jr., *The Disuniting of America: Reflections on a Multicultural Society* (Knoxville, TN: Whittle Communications, 1991), pp. 2, 24, 14, 81–82.

14. Ibid., pp. 58, 66.

15. James Madison, quoted in Takaki, *Iron Cages,* p. 80; Arthur M. Schlesinger, Jr., *The Age of Jackson* (Boston: Little, Brown, 1945); idem, *Disuniting of America,* p. 20.

16. Schlesinger, *Disuniting of America,* pp. 2, 21, 64.

17. Gerald Graff, *Beyond the Culture Wars: How Teaching the Conflicts Can Revitalize American Education* (New York: Norton, 1992), p. 15.

18. Nathan Glazer, *Affirmative Discrimination: Ethnic Inequality and Public Policy* (New York: Basic Books, 1975); Robert Blauner, *Racial Oppression in America* (New York: Harper & Row, 1972); Charles Murray, *Losing Ground: American Social Policy, 1950–1980* (New York: Basic Books, 1984); William Julius Wilson, *The Truly Disadvantaged: The Inner City, the Underclass, and Public Policy* (Chicago: University of Chicago Press, 1987); Thomas Sowell, *Ethnic America: A History* (New York: Basic Books, 1981); Takaki, *Strangers from a Different Shore.* For an example of the debate format, see Ronald Takaki, *From Different Shores: Perspectives on Race and Ethnicity in America* (New York: Oxford University Press, 1987).

19. Henry Louis Gates, Jr., *Loose Canons: Notes on the Culture Wars* (New York: Oxford University Press, 1992), p. 114.

20. Pany Lowe, interview, 1924, Survey of Race Relations, Hoover Institution Archives, Stanford, CA; Sandra Cisneros, *The House on Mango Street* (New York: Vintage, 1991), pp. 109–10; Leslie Marmon Silko, *Ceremony* (New York: New American Library, 1978), p. 2.

21. Dinesh D'Souza, "The Visigoths in Tweed," in *Beyond PC: Towards a Politics of Understanding,* ed. Patricia Aufderheide (St. Paul, MN: Graywolf Press, 1992), p. 11; George Will, "Literary Politics," *Newsweek,* 22 Apr. 1991, p. 72; Arthur Schlesinger, Jr., "When Ethnic Studies Are Un-American," *Wall Street Journal,* 23 Apr. 1990.

22. Susan Faludi, *Backlash: The Undeclared War against American Women* (New York: Doubleday, 1992), p. 282.

23. Ibid., p. 65.

24. William A. Henry III, "Beyond the Melting Pot," *Time,* 9 Apr. 1990, pp. 28–31; E. D. Hirsch, Jr., *Cultural Literacy: What Every American Needs to Know* (Boston: Houghton, Mifflin, 1987), pp. xiii, xvii, 2, 18, 96, 152–215.

25. Lipset and Raab quoted in Faludi, *Backlash,* p. 231; Richard Hofstadter, *The Age of Reform: From Bryan to F.D.R.* (New York: Random House, 1955), pp. 131–73.

26. Lawrence Auster, "The Forbidden Topic," *National Review,* 27 Apr. 1992, pp. 42–44.

27. Toni Morrison, *Playing in the Dark: Whiteness in the Literary Imagination* (Cambridge, MA: Harvard University Press, 1992), p. 47; Bonnie Angelo, "The Pain of Being Black," *Time,* 22 May 1989, p. 121. Copyright © 1989 Time Inc. Reprinted by permission.

28. Herman Melville, *Moby Dick* (Boston: Houghton Mifflin, 1956), pp. 182, 253, 322–23.

Takaki:

1. What does Takaki mean when he discusses "defining America"? What is involved in that definition, and what is at stake?

2. Why does Takaki say that the debate over how America should be defined is about power and privilege?

Drawing Conclusions—Part V

Multiculturalism means different things to different people. Compare and contrast the meaning of the idea for Glazer, Wolfe, Patterson, and Takaki. In what ways are their perspectives similar, and how do they differ? How do you understand this term? Does it signal a greater sensitivity to diversity or does it spell an increased amount of divisiveness in the nation? Does it promote good citizenship or is it a threat to citizenship? Parallel to the ways each of these four authors speculates about possible futures, offer your own informed speculations, making use of any of the other readings in this collection that have proven especially helpful to you in coming to terms with the post-civil rights era.

Sources and Permissions

Collins, Sharon M. "Black Mobility in White Corporations: Up the Corporate Ladder But Out on a Limb" from *Social Problems*, Vol. 44, No. 1, February 1997, pp. 55-67. Used by permission of the author and University of California Press Journals.

Feagin, Joe and Hernán Vera. White Racism: A Case Study from the Heartland" from *White Racism*, 1994, pp. 20-34. Copyright © 1994. Reproduced by permission of Routledge, Inc.

Ferber, Abby L. "Mongrel Monstrosities" from *White Man Falling: Race, Gender, and White Supremacy*, 1998, pp. 111-129. Used by permission of Roman & Littlefield.

Fong, Timothy P. "The First Suburban Chinatown: The Remaking of Monterey Park, California" from "Introduction: A New and Dynamic Community" and excerpt from Chapter 3, "I Don't Feel at Home Anymore" in *The First Suburban Chinatown: The Remaking of Monterey Park, California*, 1994, pp. 3-6 and 58-67. Reprinted by permission of Temple University Press. © 1994 by Temple University. All Rights Reserved.

Glazer, Nathan. "We Are All Multiculturalists Now" from *We Are All Multiculturalists Now*, 1997, pp.147-161. Copyright © 1997 by the President and Fellows of Harvard College. Reprinted by permission of Harvard University Press.

Hacker, Andrew. "The Racial Income Gap: How Much Is Due to Bias?" from *Two Nations: Black and White, Separate, Hostile, Unequal*, 1992, pp. 93-106. Reprinted with permission of Scribner, a Division of Simon & Schuster. Copyright © 1992 by Andrew Hacker.

Hochschild, Jennifer L. "Rich and Poor African Americans" from *Facing Up to the American Dream: Race, Class, and the Soul of the Nation*, 1995, pp. 39-51. Copyright © 1995 by Princeton University Press. Reprinted by permission of Princeton University Press.

Jaynes, Gerald David and Robin M. Williams, Jr. "Changes in White Racial Attitudes" from "Racial Attitudes and Behavior" in *A Common Destiny; Blacks and American Society*, 1989, pp. 116-129. Reprinted by permission of the National Academy of Sciences. Courtesy of the National Academy Press, Washington, D.C.

Lincoln, C. Eric and Lawrence H. Mamiya. "The Black Church and the Twenty-First Century," from *The Black Church in the African American Experience*, 1990, pp. 383-394. Copyright 1990, Duke University Press. Reprinted by permission. All rights reserved.

Mahler, Sarah J. "Immigrant Life on the Margins: Descent into Disappointment" excerpted from "Expectations, Disillusionments" in *American Dreaming: Immigrant Life on the Margins*, 1995, pp. 89-104. Copyright 1995 by Princeton University Press. Reprinted by permission of Princeton University Press.

Min, Pyong Gap. "Caught in the Middle: Korean-African American Conflicts" from "Korean-African American Conflicts" in *Caught in the Middle: Korean Merchants in America's Multiethnic Cities*, 1996, pp. 146-162. Used by permission of the Regents of the University of California and the University of California Press.

Moore, Joan and James Diego Vigil. "Barrios in Transition" from *In the Barrios: Latinos and the Underclass Debate*, edited by Joan Moore and Raquel Pinderhughes, 1993, pp. 27-41. Copyright © 1993 Russell Sage Foundation. Used with permission of Russell Sage Foundation.

Patterson, Orlando. "Ecumenical America: Global Culture and the American Cosmos" from *World Policy Journal*, 1994, X1:2 Summer, pp. 103-117. Used by permission of the author and *World Policy Journal*.

Portes, Alejandro and Min Zhou. "Should Immigrants Assimilate?" from *The Public Interest*, No. 116, Summer 1994, pp. 18-33. © 1994 by National Affairs, Inc. Reprinted by permission of the authors.

Sears, David O. "Urban Rioting in Los Angeles: A Comparison of 1965 with 1992" from *The Los Angeles Riots: Lessons for the Urban Future*, edited by Mark Baldassare, 1994, pp. 237-253. Copyright © 1994 by Westview Press, a member of Perseus L.L.C. Reprinted by permission of Westview Press, a member of Perseus Books, L.L.C.

Takaki, Ronald. "Multiculturalism: Battleground or Meeting Ground?" from *Annals of the American Academy*, AAPSS, 530, Nov. 1993, pp. 109-121. © 1993 by Ronald Takaki. Reprinted by permission of Sage Publications, Inc.

Waldinger, Roger. "Who Gets the 'Lousy' Jobs" from *Still The Promised City? African Americans and New Immigrants in Postindustrial New York*, 1996, pp.1154-173. Copyright © 1996 by the President and Fellows of Harvard College. Reprinted by permission of Harvard University Press.

Wilson, William Julius. "When Work Disappears: Societal Changes and Vulnerable Neighborhoods" from *When Work Disappears*. ©1995 by William Julius Wilson. Reprinted by permission of Alfred A. Knopf, Inc.

Winant, Howard. "Racism Today: Continuity and Change in the Post-Civil Rights" from *Ethnic and Racial Studies*, Vol. 21, No. 4, 1998. Reprinted by permission of Taylor & Francis, Ltd.

Index

anti-Semitism, 63-66
Dubuque case study, 5, 44-46, 51
ideological analysis, 5. *See also*
Racism, conceptual/
theoretical analysis
major publications information,
67-69
racial mixing discourse, 58-60
See also specific groups, publications
Williams, Eric, 472
Williams, Robin M., Jr., 3-4, 7-17
Williams, Walter F., 36-37, 199
Williamson, Joel, 101
Willis, Paul, 467
Wilmington, Michael, 236
Wilson, Midge, 60
Wilson, Ron, 131
Wilson, William Julius, xxxiii, 19, 150,
190, 219-228, 291, 486
Winant, Howard, xxxii, 4, 19-26, 58
Wolfe, Alan, 443, 455-464
Women's affirmative action, 280-281
Women's issues. *See* Feminism; Gender
issues
Women's studies, 487

Wood, Tom, 36
Woods, Tiger, 106
Woodward, C. Vann, 481
Work ethic, immigrants versus African
Americans, 336
Working class blacks, 214
World Union of National Socialists, 68
Wu, Frances, 377-378

X, Malcolm, 263-264

Yacub, 25
Yamasees, 120
Yorty, Sam, 86
Young, Mary, 120
Young, Whitney, 274

Zangwill, Israel, 441
Zhou, Min, 314, 317-327
Zionist ideology, 410
Zydeco music, 99, 176-178
Cajun interactions, 179-182